MARINE INSURANCE
AND GENERAL AVERAGE IN THE
UNITED STATES

MARINE INSURANCE AND GENERAL AVERAGE IN THE UNITED STATES

An Average Adjuster's Viewpoint

LESLIE J. BUGLASS

*Member of the Association of Average Adjusters
of the United States*

THIRD EDITION

CORNELL MARITIME PRESS
Centreville, Maryland

Library of Congress Cataloging–in–Publication Data

Buglass, Leslie J.
    Marine insurance and general average in the United States :   an
average adjuster's viewpoint / Leslie J. Buglass. — 3rd ed.
        p.   cm.
    Includes   index.
    ISBN   0-87033-415-8 :
    1. Insurance, Marine—United States. 2. Average (Maritime law)–
–United States.   I. Title.
KF1135.B8   1991
346.73'08622—dc20
[347.3068622]   90–55450
                                                                        CIP

Manufactured in the United States of America
First edition, 1973. Second edition, 1981. Third edition, 1991

To my grandchildren,
David and Elizabeth, may their ships come home
without recourse to salvage, general average,
or even sue and labor

Contents

Chapter 4

Total Losses : 101

Chapter 5

Particular Average : 130

Chapter 6

General Average : 194

Chapter 7

Salvage Expenses and Sue and Labor Charges : 329

Chapter 8

Liabilities to Third Parties : 363

Chapter 9

Subrogation and Double Insurance : 441

Chapter 10

Miscellaneous Insurances of a Special Nature : 460

Chapter 11

Marine Insurance Claims on the Great Lakes : 488

Chapter 12

Marine Insurance on the Rivers, Harbors, and Coastal and Inland Waterways of the United States : 498

Chapter 13

Punitive Damages : 510

Appendix A

Marine Insurance Clauses : 515

Foreword

In 1967, when he was chairman of the Association of Average Adjusters of the United States, Leslie Buglass enlightened the marine insurance world by explaining with astonishing clarity and simplicity why he believed that a commercial doctrine established almost nine centuries before the birth of Christ deserved to be observed and practised not only in 1967 but well into the era of Sputnik, Challenger, and Star Wars. What was amazing to some was not only that he truly believed everything he said in his speech, "General Average in the Space Age," but that, once delivered, his speech converted almost everyone in the room to his cause; and for those who didn't instantly see the logic of his thesis—the most militant of the general average abolitionists—his remarks gave them serious cause to pause in their crusade, a crusade which, incidentally, never really made much progress subsequent to that day.

The above illustrates the genius of Leslie Buglass—his ability to discuss and write about the most technical of subjects in such a way that even the novice can easily understand it and then quickly wonder why others thought it was so complicated. During his distinguished career in both England and the United States he has written several books and countless articles on marine insurance claims and general average, and in each case he has approached the subjects from the American point of view. By so doing, he has made an invaluable contribution to the international marine insurance industry. Prior to the publication of his books there was never as complete a treatise on these highly technical subjects in such a readable and understandable form. While he has been generous in his recognition of and gratitude to those American textbook writers who preceded him, none of them dared attempt a work as ambitious as his first edition of *Marine Insurance and General Average in the United States* and none of them produced a text which, on the one hand, is easily understood by the student and, on the other hand, considered an invaluable research tool by the professional.

I have been a student and a friend of Leslie Buglass' for almost four decades and have no hesitation in saying that I speak for all of us in the marine insurance industry when I say that his thoughtful opinion on any of the many subjects covered in this, his latest labor of love, brings instant respect and credibility to the individual quoting him.

When read carefully and thoughtfully, the contents of this book, the third edition of *Marine Insurance and General Average in the United States*, will more than adequately reward you whether you are embarking on a career in marine insurance or refining the skills you have already developed in this great profession.

> JOHN H. CASSEDY
>
> *Chairman,* Shipowners Claims Bureau, Inc.
>
> *Manager*, The American Steamship Owners Mutual Protection & Indemnity Association Inc. (The American Club)
>
> *Full Member,* Association of Average Adjusters of the United States

Preface to the Third Edition

When in 1981 I wrote the preface to the second edition of this work it never occurred to me that I would be called upon to preside over an updated third edition some nine years later. Much has happened in those nine years. A new convention on salvage was introduced in 1989 to replace the convention of 1910. The convention's possible effect on marine insurance and general average is considered herein and the full text of the International Convention on Salvage, 1989 (as it is to be known) is included as Appendix H.

Perennial subjects such as proximate cause, limitation of liability, the carriage of goods by sea, and the international laws relating to oil pollution —all of which affect marine insurance—have continued to make news and the writer has tried to keep abreast of developments in these as well as in other areas.

Litigation has continued unabated, sometimes producing unexpected results for both plaintiffs and defendants. For example, there has been new law on both sides of the Atlantic regarding disclosures and representations during the negotiations culminating in the insurance of a marine risk. Similarly it has been made more difficult in England for hull underwriters to deny a claim when an assured is *suspected* of having scuttled the subject-matter insured. These and other changing nuances of the law of marine insurance (such as developments in the continuing debate as to whether, as a practical matter, the implied, modified warranty of seaworthiness in an American time hull policy differs to any great degree from English law on the same subject) are reported in this edition.

Subjects dealt with for the first time include mortgagee's interest insurance (which has prospered—perhaps an indication of the hard times which shipowners have been enduring), maritime service contractors' liabilities, other insurance (or escape) clauses, certificates of insurance, held covered clauses, the insurance of containers, bills of lading insurance, the insurance of yachts, etc. I have at last had the temerity to include a new chapter (appropriately Chapter 13) on punitive damages—a new form of torture for insurers! Even general average has moved with the times: a new

American practice bringing time charterers' bunker fuel into contribution is unveiled in this edition, as is a new general average absorption clause. All in all, this third edition includes over 100 pages of new material.

As before, I have attempted to interpret all these subjects, and others, from the viewpoint of those engaged in and involved with the profession of marine insurance. This includes vessel owners, cargo owners, insurance brokers, admiralty lawyers, average adjusters, company claims adjusters, students, and of course underwriters insuring hulls, cargoes, and all the liabilities arising from maritime adventures, not forgetting their assureds who, as I once said, pay for it all.

I am sometimes asked why I do not write a separate textbook dealing solely with cargo insurance. My answer is that the same basic principles and practices of marine insurance apply equally to cargo insurance and whenever these principles and practices are discussed in this book, reference is always made to their application to the insurance of cargo. If a reader wishes *only* to study cargo insurance (which I do not recommend) he or she simply has to look up "cargo" in the index and refer to the various entries listed under that heading. By so doing they will have their cargo textbook—two for the price of one!

It only remains for me to acknowledge the help I have received throughout my career in marine insurance. For over fifty years in the average adjusting profession it has been my good fortune to work with many experts in the various fields of endeavor mentioned earlier. All have been generous with their expertise. It is not possible to mention them by name but I must admit that without their wisdom and assistance through the years none of the three editions of this book would have been possible.

In conclusion, a special word to students entering marine insurance for the first time. I envy you; may you all enjoy your profession as much as I have.

Preface to the First Edition

The reception given my earlier efforts to produce a modern American textbook on marine insurance matters has encouraged me to embark on a third attempt. This time I have been rather more adventurous, trying to encompass the entire field of marine insurance and general average within the covers of one book. Of necessity, some of the material has appeared in my previous books but has now been greatly expanded. This current work is not confined to claims only and among the many additional subjects I have attempted to cover are: insurable interest, insurable value, disclosure and representations, warranties, war risk insurance, establishment of date of loss, removal of wreck, deductible average clauses, liner negligence clause, oil pollution liabilities and expenses, American protection and indemnity policies and claims, ship-repairers' liability insurance, tower's liabilities, recoveries, shipbuilding insurances, loss of earnings insurance, insurance of oil rigs, and reinsurance. While, as before, I have adopted an American viewpoint, on this occasion I did not, indeed could not, ignore the basic English legal decisions on which much of the American law of marine insurance has been founded. Marine insurance is truly international and it is hoped that this American textbook will stand the test of time and be of assistance to students and practitioners of marine insurance of all nationalities.

Writing a textbook of any kind is largely a matter of editing, analyzing and building on the earlier basic works in the particular field involved. I must therefore express my debt to the marine insurance textbook writers on both sides of the Atlantic commencing with the nineteenth century works of Phillips, Arnould and Lowndes, continuing with the early twentieth century texts of Congdon, Coe, Winter and Rudolf and culminating with the more recent books of Templeman, Mullins and Dover. Without the durable foundation laid by these men (and many others) the marine insurance profession would be indescribably poorer.

Finally, I must express my appreciation to all those of my own generation in the average adjusting, marine insurance and legal professions who have assisted me in many ways. I will not attempt to name them individually but must acknowledge that without their assistance this labor of love would never have been completed.

List of Cases Cited

MARINE INSURANCE
AND GENERAL AVERAGE IN THE
UNITED STATES

Chapter 1

Introduction to Marine Insurance

Probably the earliest record of marine insurance in America is a notice by a Mr. John Copson, in the *American Weekly Mercury* of May 25, 1721, announcing that he had opened at his house in High Street, Philadelphia, "an Office of Publik Insurances on Vessels, Goods and Merchandizes" because "the Merchants of this City of Philadelphia and other parts have been obliged to send to London for such Assurance, which has not only been tedious and troublesome, but even very precarious."

The first marine insurance company in the United States (the Insurance Company of North America) was established in 1792 and by 1845 there were probably 75 or more American marine companies. Sparked by the superb American clipper ships—the "jets" of that era—the marine insurance profession in America expanded enormously between 1845 and 1860, during which time American tonnage increased threefold. However, heavy losses were sustained during the Civil War and this, coupled with other reverses, resulted in the virtual demise of hull underwriting in the United States by the dawn of the twentieth century. At the time of the outbreak of World War I, 65-75 percent of American marine insurance was placed abroad. After the war, in 1920, the American Hull Insurance Syndicate (as it is now known) was founded. The fascinating story of the growth of the syndicate during its first 50 years is told in *Touching the Adventures and Perils* (New York, 1970). Today the American Hull Insurance Syndicate has over 50 subscribing insurance companies including many major foreign companies. While the syndicate was originally formed to insure domestic tonnage, today it is international in outlook and is indeed one of the major hull insurance markets of the world.

Willard Phillips, one of the earliest American authorities on marine insurance and certainly one of the best, defined marine insurance in 1840 in the following terms:

> Marine insurance is a contract whereby, for a consideration stipulated to be paid by one interested in a ship, freight or cargo subject to ma-

rine risks, another undertakes to indemnify him against some or all of those risks during a certain period or voyage.

In England, the traditional home of marine insurance, an act was passed by Parliament in 1906 to codify the law relating to marine insurance. Section I of that act defines a contract of marine insurance as a contract whereby the insurer undertakes to indemnify the assured, in manner and to the extent thereby agreed against marine losses; that is to say, the losses incident to marine adventure.

The similarity in these two basic definitions of marine insurance cannot be attributed to the long arm of coincidence. Rather it is another example of how the English-speaking peoples have drawn upon a common heritage. Indeed, it is safe to say that there is no better example of Anglo-American cooperation than the profession of marine insurance.

In the early days of commerce in the United States the words "marine" and "transportation" were synonymous. Thus the term "ocean marine insurance" was coined to differentiate it from "inland marine insurance." (In point of fact, inland marine insurance is a misnomer, for it is primarily the insurance of transportation by rail or truck, and as such will not be referred to again.)

These uniquely American colloquial expressions, "ocean marine" (wet) and "inland marine" (dry), persist to this day because the real marine insurance (wet) is dealt with by one department of an insurance company and the misnamed inland marine insurance (dry) by another—but only in America!

Prior to the passage of the Marine Insurance Act, the law of marine insurance in England rested almost entirely on common law or recognized commercial usage. In the United States, where there is no statute codifying the law relating to marine insurance, this still remains the position.

English companies have been writing marine insurance in the United States since colonial times and it was inevitable that English common law and usage should be reflected in the law of the United States.

In the *Eliza Lines* (199 U. S. 119), Justice Holmes said:

Of course it is desirable, if there is no injustice, that the maritime law of this country and of England should agree.

And again in *Queen Ins. Co.* v. *Globe & Rutgers Fire Ins. Co.* (263 U. S. 487), the court felt constrained to say:

There are special reasons for keeping in harmony with the marine insurance laws of England, the great field of this business.

Yet it must be said that on occasions American law does deviate from the English law and for that reason, while the English Marine Insurance Act will always be a valuable source of reference to all concerned in the profession in America, it is to the case law, practices, and usages of the United States that we must principally apply ourselves. Indeed, when an American broker places hull insurance in the English market on behalf of an American assured, an American suable clause is invariably included in the policies issued in England. Such a clause (known as a New York Suable clause) reads as follows:

> The place of physical and actual issue and delivery of this policy is the City of London. Nevertheless, at the option of the Assured, as between the Assured and the Assurers, the place of issue and delivery of the policy shall be considered the City of New York and all matters arising hereunder shall be determined in accordance with American Law and practice. Any suit hereon may be brought against these Assurers in any court in the State of New York. The summons and other legal processes may be served on this Company by and in behalf of the Assured by mailing a copy thereof by United States registered mail addressed to . . . .
> . . . . each of whom this Company authorizes to accept by and in its behalf such summons and other legal processes against this Company in any Court in the State of New York. The mailing, as herein provided, of such summons or other legal processes shall be deemed personal service and accepted by this Company as such, and shall be legal and binding upon this Company for all the purposes of the suit. Final judgment against this Company in any such suit shall be conclusive; and it may be enforced in any other jurisdictions, including Great Britain, by suit on the judgment, a certified or exemplified copy of which shall be conclusive evidence of the fact and of the amount of this indebtedness. The right of the Assured to bring suit as provided herein shall be limited to a suit brought in its own name and for its own account. For the purposes of suit as herein provided, the word "Assured" includes any mortgagee under a ship mortgage and any person succeeding to the rights of any such mortgagee.

It would appear that this clause enables the assured to take advantage of either American law and practice or English law and practice, whichever might prove to be the more advantageous to him. The clause was considered by the English courts in *Armadora Occidental* v. *Horace Mann Ins. Co.* (1977 L. L. R. 2, Pt. 1); the issue was, however, affected by the inclusion of a "follow London" clause which provided:

Assurers herein shall follow Lloyd's underwriters and/or British insurance companies in regard to amounts, terms, conditions, alterations, additions . . . and settlement of claims hereunder and all matters pertaining to this insurance with or without prior notice. Notice to Lloyd's Underwriters and/or British insurance companies of any matter requiring notice shall be deemed notice to American Underwriters and/or American insurance companies interested in these insurances.

The lower court found that:

(1) The "follow London" clause was of paramount importance; and the scheme of the insurance cover as a whole was that the English and American policies should contain the same provisions and that settlements should be dealt with on a uniform basis to be determined by the London market; and it must have been an overriding consideration in the minds of all the parties that all the policies should be governed by one system of law and that this should be the law of the London policies and therefore English law.

(2) Only the first sentence of the New York Suable clause should be disregarded, and since the option under the clause was not exercised, English law was the proper law of the policies and the court had jurisdiction to exercise its discretion . . . to allow service of the writ on the defendants in the United States.

In upholding the lower court, the court of appeals held:

(1) The object of the "follow London" clause was that any negotiations in regard to any claims and the settlement of them should be undertaken in the first instance by Lloyd's underwriters or a British insurance company and, once a settlement was made, the American underwriters were to follow the lead of the Lloyd's underwriters or British insurance company.

(2) The learned judge was right in holding that the underlying inference and understanding of the clause must be that the insurance with regard to the American policies would be governed by English law.

(3) The purpose of the New York Suable clause was simply to enable the assured at their option to sue in the United States; the first sentence of the clause was inapplicable to the American policies and could be ignored, but the remainder of the clause could be applied, and as the option had not been exercised the clause was not applicable.

(4) The New York Suable clause did not alter in any way the effect of the "follow London" clause; the learned judge was right in holding that the "follow London" clause was of paramount importance and indicated that the contract was to be construed, interpreted, and applied according to English law; and that the contract was therefore governed by English law.

It has been held by an American court that the inclusion of a "London following" clause in an American marine insurance policy issued in New York does not necessarily mean that English substantive law applies

(*Navegacion Goya* v. *Mutual Boiler & Machinery Ins. Co., et al.*, 1977 AMC 175).

The federal courts of the United States are divided geographically into thirteen circuits. In each of the circuits there is at least one federal district court for each state included in the circuit and a court of appeals to which appeals are taken from the district courts in that circuit. The circuit court of appeals is not bound to follow the decision of other circuits, which sometimes results in a lack of uniformity in case law. While application can be made to the Supreme Court for a writ of certiorari to review any such conflict, very often, because of pressure of more important work, this is not granted in admiralty cases.

Admiralty libels are of two kinds, *in personam* and *in rem*. The *in personam* suit is against a named individual; the *in rem* suit is peculiar to admiralty law and gives the person suing the right to obtain the property proceeded against as security for his claim, pending the obtaining of judgment. Thus the claimant is entitled to arrest the ship or other property and to have it detained until his claim has been decided or acceptable security has been given in lieu.

The federal district courts are given "exclusive original cognizance of all civil causes of Admiralty and Maritime jurisdiction" but in certain circumstances maritime law cases not involving *in rem* procedure may be tried by state common law courts.

As to usages and practices in the United States, these inevitably differ from place to place in a country so large. In some instances East Coast and West Coast practices differ, while on the Great Lakes, as we shall see, long-established customs are recognized and accepted by the parties concerned. The Supreme Court of New York once said that the true test of usage is its having existed a sufficient length of time to have been generally known. Phillips enlarged on this, saying:

So the place where the insurance is made . . . affects its construction, since every contract must be construed in reference to the customs and usages of the country, and even the port where it is entered into, as well as by the subject-matter to which it relates, and the surrounding circumstances. Such customs and usages are in effect included in the contract and . . . have a material bearing in respect to the character and extent of the risks and perils included in the insurance. (Subsect. 36)

Examples of usages and practices are to be found in the Rules of Practice of the Association of Average Adjusters of the United States (Appendix B).

While the main purpose of this book is to deal with marine insurance and general average according to American law and practice, the author has drawn freely from the English Marine Insurance Act where there is no record of any discrepancies between the law of the two countries. In doing so, he is fortified by the attitude of the Supreme Court as evidenced by the cases already quoted. Although the act has no legal force in the United States, its influence is not inconsiderable.

BASIC MARINE INSURANCE TERMS

For the uninitiated, Phillips writes:

The party undertaking to make the indemnity is called the insurer or underwriter; the party to be indemnified, the assured or insured. The agreed consideration is called a premium; the instrument by which the contract is made, a policy; the events and causes of loss insured against, risks or perils; and the property or rights of the assured, in respect to which he is liable to loss, the subject or insurable interest. (Subsect. 2)

Every lawful marine adventure may be the subject of a contract of marine insurance. The Marine Insurance Act states that there is a marine adventure where:

(a) Any ship, goods or other moveables are exposed to maritime perils. Such property is in this Act referred to as "insurable property";

(b) The earning or acquisition of any freight, passage money, commission, profit, or other pecuniary benefit, or the security for any advances, loan, or disbursements, is endangered by the exposure of insurable property to maritime perils;

(c) Any liability to a third party may be incurred by the owner of, or other person interested in or responsible for, insurable property, by reason of maritime perils. (Sect. 3)

The principal, but by no means the only, subjects of marine insurance—namely, ship, freight, and cargo—are defined by the Marine Insurance Act (Rules for Construction of Policy, Nos. 15/17), as follows:

The term "ship" includes the hull, materials and outfit, stores and provisions for the officers and crew, and, in the case of vessels engaged in a special trade, the ordinary fittings requisite for the trade, and also, in the case of a steamship, the machinery, boilers, and coals and engine stores, if owned by the assured.

The term "freight" includes the profit derivable by a shipowner from the employment of his ship to carry his own goods or movables, as well as freight payable by a third party, but does not include passage money.

The term "goods" means goods in the nature of merchandise, and does not include personal effects or provisions and stores for use on board.

THE POLICY

A contract of marine insurance is embodied in a policy which specifies:

(1) The name of the assured, or of some person who effects the insurance on his behalf.

(2) The subject-matter insured and the risk insured against.

(3) The voyage, or period of time, or both, as the case may be, covered by the insurance.

(4) The sum or sums insured.

(5) The names of the insurers. (Marine Ins. Act., Sect. 23)

Most marine insurance contracts are effected through brokers acting on behalf of the assured and in many instances the policies are issued in the broker's name "and/or as agent." It is well established in England that insurance brokers are agents of the assured (and not the insurers) for purposes of the negotiating and placing of the insurance (*Anglo-African Merchants Ltd.* v. *Bayley*, 1970 1 Q. B. 311, 322). Thus the broker, in drawing up a policy, is not the insurer's agent or responsible to him for any want of care (*Chalmer's Marine Ins. Act,* 1906, 4th ed., p. 68). The same holds true in the United States (*Pyne* v. *Trans-Atlantic Marine*, 1972 AMC 274; *Welded Tube* v. *Hartford Fire*, 1973 AMC 555); *Edinburgh Assurance Co.* v. *R. L. Burns Corp.*, 1980 AMC 1261, *aff'd.* 1982 AMC 2532). Nevertheless, the broker performs various functions which are in the interest of both the assured and the underwriter. It is the broker's duty to do his best to see that the assured's obligations of disclosure and representation are fulfilled. The broker's skill and expertise extend beyond merely giving his client advice and complying with his client's instructions. He must make use of his knowledge of the market and use appropriate skill. He must approach suitable leaders. He must negotiate realistic premium levels and terms of insurance with those leaders. If he fails to do this he will fail to find sufficient following underwriters willing to subscribe to the risk and therefore fail to obtain for his client the cover he requires. In all these duties the broker is expected to exercise his professional function with reasonable skill and diligence as a professional man. In London, the broker has been described as the servant of the market who owes a duty of care to underwriters as well as to his client (*General Accident Fire and Life Assurance Corp.* v. *Peter William Tanter,* 1984 L.L.R. Vol. 1 p. 58).

American cargo policies usually contain a Brokerage clause reading as follows:

> It is a condition of this policy, and it is hereby agreed that the Assured's brokers or any substituted brokers, shall be deemed to be exclusively the agents of the assured and not of this company in any and all matters relating to, connected with or affecting this insurance. Any notice given or mailed by or on behalf of this company to the said brokers in connection with or affecting this insurance, or its cancellation, shall be deemed to have been delivered to the Assured.

In the United States agents are often appointed and licensed by cargo underwriters. If such an agency agreement is in effect between an insurance company and an insurance broker or agency there can be no question but that the insurance broker is the agent of the insurance company. An independent insurance broker is in a different category; he is the agent of the assured. The distinction is important because a notice given to an assured's broker is binding on the assured, but this is not necessarily the case if the notice is merely given to an *agent* of the cargo underwriters. The position is further complicated by the practice in some parts of the United States to refer to insurance brokers as *insurance agents,* which is a misnomer.

Sometimes an Affiliated Companies clause is added to the policy. This clause states that the policy covers the named assured and affiliated companies of the assured. It is also agreed that the insurers waive any right of subrogation against any affiliated company of the assured excepting to the extent that any such company is insured against the liability asserted. The whole point of the Affiliated Companies clause is to avoid the clerical chore of listing, in some cases, many affiliated companies as additional assureds. The object of listing affiliated companies as additional assureds is to prevent an insurer, after accepting a premium and paying a claim to one member of the assured's corporate family, from recouping his loss from another member of the same family by way of subrogation. However, the clause is not meant to help another insurer avoid a liability which he insured for an affiliate, hence the proviso included in the Affiliated Companies clause limiting the waiving of subrogation against affiliated companies to those cases where the affiliated company is not insured against the liability asserted.

In the United Kingdom, the policy is a negotiable document and no claim can be collected thereunder without production of the original policy on which the amount paid is endorsed. This is not the case in the United

States where the policy is merely the evidence of the contract of marine insurance. However, as we shall see, American policies include a Loss Payee clause, and losses are payable in accordance with that clause without it being necessary to produce the original policy.

There are many varieties of marine policies: voyage policies, time policies (*see* Marine Ins. Act, Sect. 25), valued policies and unvalued policies (*see* Marine Ins. Act, Sect. 27/28), floating policies (*see* Marine Ins. Act, Sect. 29), policies on mixed sea and land risks (*see* Marine Ins. Act, Sect. 2), policies on vessels under construction (*see* Marine Ins. Act, Sect. 2), legal liability policies, loss of earnings (or hire) policies, and policies against special risks, such as oil rigs, and control of oil well policies. All these different types of marine policies (many of which will be discussed later) have two things in common: the subject-matter insured must be designated with reasonable certainty (*see* Marine Ins. Act, Sect. 26), and before the contract can be negotiated and the policy issued the assured must have an insurable interest.

While most marine insurance on vessels is written under time policies (usually of twelve months' duration), most insurance on cargo in the United States is written under open policies or open covers. These are not quite the same as floating policies which are defined by Sect. 29 of the Marine Ins. Act. Floating policies describe the insurance in general terms, leaving the particulars to be defined by subsequent declarations; they differ from open policies in that they are effected for a specific amount which is drawn upon until it is exhausted. Such policies were used in the United Kingdom because of the Stamp Act; this act required a fixed sum to be stated on which the correct stamp duty could be assessed. The Stamp Act was repealed in 1970. Marine insurance was never subject to a stamp tax in the United States, where open policies are widely used. Such open policies, unlike floating policies, are usually stated for a specific period of time and, indeed, may remain in force indefinitely until cancelled. Individual successive shipments are reported or declared, the assured having automatic coverage (within the terms, conditions, and limitations stated in the open policy). All shipments must be declared as soon as practicable, but unintentional failure to report does not void the insurance, the goods being held covered subject to policy conditions. Open cargo policies are tailored to the assured's particular business and include a schedule of premium rates which are based on the assured's experience and record.

Certificates of insurance (sometimes called Memoranda of insurance) will be prepared, signed, and issued by the insurers on open cargo policies when requested by the assured. Such certificates are often required by assureds to provide satisfactory evidence of insurance where the financing of shipments is being handled through a bank or lending institution.

This obviates making copies of voluminous open policies. The certificate should contain all the principal clauses from the open policy having a bearing on the particular shipments involved and usually makes reference to the open policy as background information. When the assured under the policy is the party concerned at the time of any loss, the reference to the open policy has the effect of incorporating all the terms of the policy, including those not specifically mentioned in the certificate. However, if the certificate is issued to a third party, that party is entitled to rely on the description of the insurance in the certificate itself. When issued by the insurer, such certificates constitute a policy in miniature and for the holder become an actual policy of insurance (there having been no individual policies issued under the open policy). Such certificates of insurance are therefore binding on the insurer.

There is a market (but not an Institute) clause which is sometimes included in open policies to regulate the conditions under which the assured (for example, a freight forwarder) can issue certificates of insurance. This "Issuance of Certificates clause" reads as follows:

> Authority is hereby granted the Assured to issue and countersign certificates of insurance of the Company for any or all shipments in respect of which insurance is provided hereunder, and in consideration thereof the Assured warrants that no certificate will be issued with terms thereon varying from the conditions of this Policy and/or any written instruction that are or may be given by the Company from time to time.

Insurance brokers frequently issue documents which are also described as certificates of insurance. These are misnamed and are really only confirmations of insurance. They are issued to satisfy banks and lending institutions of the existence of insurance and often confirm that the party who has requested the certificate has been named as an additional assured and/or loss payee. Certificates of this nature are used, for example, to satisfy lessors of equipment (such as containers) that the shipowner (lessee) has insured such equipment, as is invariably required in the lease. Such certificates issued by brokers in no way supersede or vary the terms of the insurance as described in the open policy. However, if the broker issuing such certificates describes the coverage erroneously, presumably he would be responsible for any adverse consequences resulting from such negligence. Often the broker issuing this type of certificate seeks to protect himself by stating on the certificate that reference should be made to the open policy for full details of the insurance.

In the following chapters of this book we shall explore the various facets of marine insurance in greater detail. However, before embarking on this project it is appropriate to emphasize that a contract of marine insurance is a contract based on the utmost good faith.

Phillips states:

> The assured must not make any material misrepresentation, either written or oral, relative to the risk, importing that it is less than it really is.
>
> The assured must state to the insurer every fact known to him that is material to the risk, and which is not known to the insurer, or presumed to be so.

The standard of ethics laid down by Phillips over 100 years ago prevails today.

The importance of making a full disclosure of the material facts when negotiating a marine insurance policy was shown in the case of *Fireman's Fund Insurance* v. *Wilburn Boat Co., et al.* (1962 AMC 1593). In that case, the court pointed out that it was a firmly established principle of marine insurance that "a mistake or commission material to a marine risk, whether it be wilful or contractual, or result from mistake, negligence or voluntary ignorance, avoids the policy."

This principle of good faith is the foundation stone of marine insurance, as we shall see.

Chapter 2

The Contract of Marine Insurance

INSURABLE INTEREST

It is essential to every contract of insurance that the assured should have an interest at risk; otherwise he is not exposed to any loss and there is nothing against which the insurer can agree to indemnify him (Phillips, Subsect. 172). The mere holding of a policy on an adventure is not, in itself, evidence of a valid interest.

The Marine Insurance Act defines insurable interest as follows:

(1) Subject to the provisions of this Act, every person has an insurable interest who is interested in a marine adventure.

(2) In particular a person is interested in a marine adventure where he stands in any legal or equitable relation to the adventure or to any insurable property at risk therein, in consequence of which he may benefit by the safety or due arrival of insurable property, or may be prejudiced by its loss, or by damage thereto, or by the detention thereof, or may incur liability in respect thereof (Sect. 5)

Gilmore & Black (p. 55) express the view that this definition is probably as good a summary as any of the American cases on the point. If the assured does not have an insurable interest, the insurance is a gambling policy and has no legal status. The Marine Insurance Act has this to say on wagering or gaming contracts:

(1) Every contract of marine insurance by way of gaming or wagering is void.

(2) A contract of marine insurance is deemed to be a gaming or wagering contract—

(a) Where the assured has not an insurable interest as defined by this Act, and the contract is entered into with no expectation of acquiring such an interest; or

(b) Where the policy is made "interest or no interest," or "without further proof of interest than the policy itself," or

14

"without benefit of salvage to the insurer," or subject to any other like term:

Provided that, where there is no possibility of salvage, a policy may be effected without benefit of salvage to the insurer. (Sect. 4)

A subsequent act in England declared all contracts coming within Sect. 4, Subsect. 2 of the Marine Insurance Act not merely void but also illegal. Such policies continue to be effected in cases where, although the assured has an insurable interest, it is difficult or impracticable to submit actual proof. These policies are honor policies, that is, binding in honor only. In England no action at law can be brought in regard to them. In the United States suit may be brought under a policy which waives proof of interest, but the assured must prove that he has an insurable interest, and is permitted to recover only to that extent. In other words, in the United States the policy is not rendered void if the assured in fact has an insurable interest (*Republic of China, China Merchants Steam Navigation Co., Ltd. and U. S. A.* v. *National Union Fire Ins. Co.,* 1958 AMC 1529). The assured must be interested in the subject-matter insured at the time of the loss, though he need not be interested when the insurance is effected (Marine Insurance Act, Sect. 6).

There are many different types of insurable interests, some of which are listed by the Marine Insurance Act as follows:

(1) Defeasible and contingent interests are insurable (Sect. 7).

(2) Partial interests of any nature are insurable (Sect. 8).

(3) The insurer under a contract of marine insurance has an insurable interest in his risk and may reinsure in respect of it (but the original assured has no right or interest in respect of such reinsurance) (Sect. 9).

(4) The lender of money on bottomry or respondentia has an insurable interest in respect of the loan (Sect. 10).

(5) The master or any member of the crew of a ship has an insurable interest in respect of his wages (Sect. 11).

(6) In the case of advance freight, the person advancing the freight has an insurable interest, insofar as such freight is not repayable in case of loss (Sect. 12).

(7) The assured has an insurable interest in the charges of any insurance which he may effect (Sect. 13). [As Phillips (Subsect. 1221) points out, this demonstrates that the amount of insurable interest is not precisely the current market value of the subject-matter insured.]

(8) Where the subject-matter insured is mortgaged, the mortgagor has an insurable interest in the full value thereof, and the mort-

gagee has an insurable interest in respect of any sum due or to become due under the mortgage (Sect. 14 (1)).

(9) A mortgagee, consignee, or other person having an interest in the subject-matter insured may insure on behalf of and for the benefit of other persons interested as well as for his own benefit (Sect. 14 (2)).

(10) The owner of insurable property has an insurable interest in respect of the full value thereof, notwithstanding that some third person may have agreed, or be liable to indemnify him in case of loss (Sect. 14 (3)).

The leading American case on the subject of insurable interest is *Hooper* v. *Robinson* (98 U. S. 528) which states:

A right of property in a thing is not always indispensable to an insurable interest. Injury from its loss or benefit from its preservation to accrue to the assured may be sufficient, and a contingent interest thus arising may be made the subject of a policy. In the law of marine insurance, insurable interests are multiform and very numerous. The agent, factor, bailee, carrier, trustee, consignee, mortgagee, and every other lien-holder, may insure to the extent of his own interest in that to which such interest relates; and by the clause, "on account of whom it may concern," for all others to the extent of their respective interests, where there is previous authority or subsequent ratification. Numerous as are the parties of the classes named, they are but a small portion of those who have the right to insure.

It is apparent that several persons may be so situated with regard to the same subject-matter as each to have an insurable interest therein, separate and distinct. Where the assured assigns or otherwise parts with his interest in the subject-matter insured, he does not thereby transfer to the assignee his rights under the contract of insurance, unless there be an express or implied agreement with the assignee to that effect (Marine Insurance Act, Sect. 15). Phillips points out that reinsurance is an illustration of the distinction between an insurable interest and ownership. An underwriter, by subscribing to a policy, acquires no part of the subject insured yet he acquires an insurable interest and may reinsure. His interest, however, exists only in relation to the perils against which he has insured in the original policy (Subsect. 377).

The "for account of whom it may concern" clause in an open marine insurance cargo policy has been liberally construed by the U. S. Supreme Court. In *Hagen* v. *Scottish Ins. Co.* (186 U. S. 423) the Court stated:

We concur in the view that by virtue of the language contained in the policy "on account of whom it may concern" it is not necessary that the person who takes out such a policy should have at that time any specific individual in mind. If he intended the policy should cover the interest of any person to whom he might sell the entire or any part of the interest insured, that would be enough. In *Hooper* v. *Robinson*, 98 U. S. 528, it was said that a policy upon a cargo in the name of A, on account of whom it may concern, will insure to the interest of the party for whom it was intended by A, provided he at the time of effecting the insurance had the requisite authority from such party or the latter subsequently adopted it. The facts in that case differ materially from those presented by this record, but the meaning of the language "on account of whom it may concern" is stated in the opinion of the court, and authorities are therein cited which show that it is not necessary that at the time of effecting the insurance the person taking it out should intend it for the benefit of some then known and particular individual, but that it would cover the case of one having an insurable interest at the time of the happening of the loss, and who was intended to be protected at the time the party took out the insurance.

It is usual in the United States for mortgagees to be named as joint assureds. However an "innocent" mortgagee can have no better rights under the policy than the other assured (the mortgagor) (*Padre Island*, 1970 AMC 600). This decision led to a re-assessment of the "innocent" mortgagee's need for specific mortgagee's interest coverage; the reader is directed to Chapter 10 for a full discussion of this type of insurance.

While policies which forego proof of insurable interest have no legal standing in England and are only valid at law in the United States if an insurable interest can be proven, it has always been the practice of underwriters in both countries to accept risks on such terms. Such policies are known as P.P.I. (policy proof of interest) or F.I.A. (full interest admitted) policies; they have no legal standing and are binding in honor only. Such policies are used to insure nebulous interests such as "disbursements" of vessel owners, a term covering many interests including total loss insurances on a vessel additional to the agreed or insured value (sometimes described as "increased value" insurances), commissions, profits, etc. In short, P.P.I. policies are used as a commercial convenience in situations where, although the assured may have an insurable interest, it would be difficult and time-consuming to substantiate that interest. The American Institute Hull Clauses (in common with all hull forms) contain a Disbursements clause reading as follows:

It is a condition of this Policy that no additional insurance against the risk of Total Loss of the Vessel shall be effected to operate during the currency of this Policy by or for account of the Assured, Owners, Managers, Operators or Mortgagees except on the interests and up to the amounts enumerated in the following Sections (a) to (g), inclusive, and no such insurance shall be subject to P. P. I., F. I. A. or other like term on any interests whatever excepting those enumerated in Section (a); provided always and notwithstanding the limitation on recovery in the Assured clause a breach of this condition shall not afford the Underwriters any defense to a claim by a Mortgagee who has accepted this Policy without knowledge of such breach:

(a) DISBURSEMENTS, MANAGERS' COMMISSIONS, PROFITS OR EXCESS OR INCREASED VALUE OF HULL AND MACHINERY, AND/OR SIMILAR INTERESTS HOWEVER DESCRIBED, AND FREIGHT (INCLUDING CHARTERED FREIGHT OR ANTICIPATED FREIGHT) INSURED FOR TIME. An amount not exceeding in the aggregate 25% of the Agreed Value.

(b) FREIGHT OR HIRE, UNDER CONTRACTS FOR VOYAGE. An amount not exceeding the gross freight or hire for the current cargo passage and next succeeding cargo passage (such insurance to include, if required, a preliminary and an intermediate ballast passage) plus the charges of insurance. In the case of a voyage charter where payment is made on a time basis, the amount shall be calculated on the estimated duration of the voyage, subject to the limitation of two cargo passages as laid down herein. Any amount permitted under this Section shall be reduced, as the freight or hire is earned, by the gross amount so earned. Any freight or hire to be earned under the form of Charters described in (d) below shall not be permitted under this Section (b) if any part thereof is insured as permitted under said Section (d).

(c) ANTICIPATED FREIGHT IF THE VESSEL SAILS IN BALLAST AND NOT UNDER CHARTER. An amount not exceeding the anticipated gross freight on next cargo passage, such amount to be reasonably estimated on the basis of the current rate of freight at time of insurance, plus the charges of insurance. Provided, however, that no insurance shall be permitted by this Section if any insurance is effected as permitted under Section (b).

(d) TIME CHARTER HIRE OR CHARTER HIRE FOR SERIES OF VOYAGES. An amount not exceeding 50% of the gross hire which is to be earned under the charter in a period not exceeding 18 months. Any amount permitted under this Section shall be reduced as the hire is earned under the charter by 50% of the gross amount so earned but, where the charter is for a period exceeding 18 months, the amount insured need not be reduced while it does not exceed 50% of the gross hire still to be earned under the charter. An insurance permitted by this Section may begin on the signing of the charter.

(e) PREMIUMS. An amount not exceeding the actual premiums of all interest insured for a period not exceeding 12 months (excluding premiums insured as permitted under the foregoing Sections but including, if required, the premium or estimated calls on any Protection and Indemnity or War Risks and Strikes insurance) reducing pro rata monthly.

(f) RETURNS OF PREMIUM. An amount not exceeding the actual returns which are recoverable subject to "and arrival" or equivalent provision under any policy of insurance.

(g) INSURANCE IRRESPECTIVE OF AMOUNT AGAINST. Risks excluded by the War, Strikes and Related Exclusions clause; risks enumerated in the American Institute War Risks and Strikes clauses; and General Average and Salvage Disbursements.

This clause prohibits additional insurances against the risk of total loss of the vessel except on those interests and to the extent enumerated in Sects. (a) to (g) of the clause. In Sect. (a), "total loss only" insurances effected without proof of interest are limited to 25 percent of the agreed (or insured) value. Thus Sect. (a) limits the insurances which may be effected on P.P.I. or F.I.A. terms. The other additional insurances permitted under Sects. (b) through (g) are all subject to proof of interest. However, they may be effected (subject to the limitation in each individual section) in addition to the 25 percent total loss insurances permitted on P.P.I. or F.I.A. terms under Sect. (a). The object of the clause is to prevent vessel owners insuring under the hull policy for a low valuation and then effecting other total loss insurances on P.P.I. terms for disproportionate amounts in relation to the agreed valuation in the hull policies. It is not the intention to limit other insurances on freight, etc., for which the assured can prove an interest. It is only the nebulous total loss insurances on disbursements, etc., where the assured may not be able to prove an interest, which are controlled in relation to the agreed valuation in the basic hull policy.

Open cargo policies contain a clause dealing with insurable interest reading as follows:

To cover all shipments consigned to, or shipped by the Assured, or consigned to or shipped by others for the account or control of the Assured and in which the Assured may have an insurable interest, but excluding shipments sold by the Assured on f.o.b.; f.a.s.; cost and freight or similar terms whereby the Assured is not obligated to furnish Ocean Marine Insurance and excluding shipments purchased by the Assured on terms which include insurance to final destination; also to cover all shipments which the Assured may be instructed to insure provided such instructions are given in writing prior to sailing of vessel and before any known or reported loss or accident.

It is important, therefore, to understand the various types of contracts covering the sale of goods:

F. O. B. (*FREE ON BOARD*). Under this term, the seller quotes a price covering all expenses up to, and including, delivery of the goods upon the overseas vessel provided by, or for, the buyer at the named port of shipment. Thus the shipper's interest ceases when the goods are lifted over the side of the vessel and he is only liable for damage, insurance and freight charges to port of loading.

F. A. S. (*FREE ALONGSIDE*). Under this term, the seller quotes a price including delivery of the goods alongside the overseas vessel and within reach of its loading tackle.

Thus the shipper's interest ceases when the goods are delivered to the dock where the vessel is or will be docked.

C. & F. (*COST AND FREIGHT*). Under this term, the seller quotes a price including the cost of transportation to the named point of destination.

Under c.&f. sales contracts, the seller is not required to furnish the buyer with a policy of marine insurance. The seller is required to give "such notice to the buyer as may enable him to insure . . . during . . . sea transit" and the onus is on the buyer to arrange insurance for his own interest. In such circumstances, the seller may be without insurance coverage during the period from the commencement of the risk until the acceptance of the documents of title by the buyer (that is from the time the shipment leaves seller's plant, or warehouse, until delivered on board the overseas vessel, or until title passes to the buyer). To overcome this situation, the shipper may effect "seller's interest" insurance in respect of goods sold on c.&f. terms. This is in the nature of a contingency insurance which becomes effective only when ownership in the goods remains with the seller. When a manufacturer, supplier or merchant sells goods either on a c.&f. basis or on an f.o.b. basis, and when the buyer arranges to cover the marine insurance under his own policy with a Warehouse-to-Warehouse clause, if the seller is not included as an assured under the buyer's insurance then, despite the Warehouse-to-Warehouse clause, coverage under the policy does not attach until title passes to the buyer. In other words, it is up to the manufacturer, supplier, exporter, or merchant to see that he is fully covered for insurance from the time the goods leave the factory or warehouse for the period he retains title, or he must take the risk of loss until title passes to the buyer.

C. I. F. (*COST, INSURANCE, FREIGHT*) Under this term, the seller quotes a price including the cost of the goods, the marine insurance, and all transportation charges to the named point of destination.

A seller under a c.i.f. contract must provide the buyer with a policy that protects the shipment from the time the buyer has an insurable interest until the buyer's interest ceases. The seller should cover his own risk of loss, therefore, until the buyer has an insurable interest. A buyer under a c.i.f. contract receives a policy which has been effected by the seller. The policy may be made out in the specific name of the buyer, or may show the seller as the assured. The seller, in the latter instance, transfers the policy by endorsing the policy "in blank."

The open cargo policy is therefore only concerned with shipments which are purchased on terms whereby the assured is either obliged or instructed to insure.

It will be evident that, in insurances on cargo, the question as to when title to the goods passes is of paramount importance both to the assured and the underwriter in determining whether an insurable interest exists. Nevertheless, it is not only the actual owner of the goods who possesses an insurable interest. When goods are sold c.i.f., the seller (having arranged the insurance) is covered throughout the transit of the goods (although the risk passes to the buyer on shipment, the title usually passes when shipping documents are tendered and the purchase price paid; thus if the contract is not consummated, the risk remains with the seller who is covered by the insurance he has effected). If the goods are lost or damaged, the resultant claim under the insurance effected is usually assigned to the buyer of the goods. When goods are sold c.&f., the goods are at the risk of the buyer during the transit. Thus, if title (which passes as in a c.i.f. contract) is never taken by the buyer, the seller has no insurance coverage. If goods are shipped f.o.b, in theory both risk and title pass to the buyer on loading; however, the transfer of risk and property cannot always be arranged simultaneously because the tendering of documents of title may be delayed. Thus if the goods are rejected by the buyer, the risk reverts to the seller and, because of the terms of the sale, he has no insurance coverage. The contingent interest of the seller in c.&f. and f.o.b. sales can, however, be protected by contingency insurance. Under such an insurance, if a sale is repudiated by the buyer during the transit, the coverage attaches from the commencement of the risk and any loss or damage caused by insured perils is recoverable by the seller. It should be mentioned that as regards contingency interests, the main difficulty is to determine, not whether there is an interest, but whether the interest has attached at the time of the loss (Chalmers, MacKenzie, ed., *Marine Insurance Act*, 1906, 4th ed.).

In summary, as the court put it in *Sidney J. Groban et al.* v. *American Casualty Co.* (1972 AMC 460):

> Whether or not he holds legal title, a person has an insurable interest if he has any economic advantage from the continued existence, or pecuniary loss from the destruction or damage, of the insured property.

INSURABLE VALUE

It is usual for policies of marine insurance to be valued, but unvalued policies are written from time to time—and the Marine Insurance Act lays down the rules to be followed in computing the insurable value as follows:

> Subject to any express provision or valuation in the policy, the insurable value of the subject-matter insured must be ascertained as follows—
>
> (1) In insurance on ship, the insurable value is the value, at the commencement of the risk, of the ship, including her outfit, provisions and stores for the officers and crew, money advanced for seamen's wages, and other disbursements (if any) incurred to make the ship fit for the voyage or adventure contemplated by the policy, plus the charges of insurance upon the whole:
>
> The insurable value, in the case of a steamship, includes also the machinery, boilers, and coals and engine stores if owned by the assured, and, in the case of a ship engaged in special trade, the ordinary fittings requisite for that trade:
>
> (2) In insurance on freight, whether paid in advance or otherwise, the insurable value is the gross amount of the freight at the risk of the assured, plus the charges of insurance:
>
> (3) In insurance on goods or merchandise, the insurable value is the prime cost of the property insured, plus the expenses of and incidental to shipping and the charges of insurance upon the whole:
>
> (4) In insurance on any other subject-matter, the insurable value is the amount at the risk of the assured when the policy attaches, plus the charges of insurance. (Sect. 16)

The value of the subject-matter insured given in the policy is, in the absence of fraud, conclusive as between the insurer and the assured (*N. Y.*

& *Cuba Mail S. S. Co.* v. *Royal Exchange Assn.*, 154 Fed. Rep. 315; *cf.* Marine Ins. Act, Sect. 27 (3)). The value placed on a vessel for insurance purposes is of great significance in connection with claims under the policy, as will be seen later.

The valuation clause in the American Institute Hull Clauses reads as follows:

> The Subject Matter of this insurance is the Vessel called the . . . . or by whatsoever name or names the said Vessel is or shall be called, which for purposes of this insurance shall consist of and be limited to her hull, launches, lifeboats, rafts, furniture, bunkers, stores, supplies, tackle, fittings, equipment, apparatus, machinery, boilers, refrigerating machinery, insulation, motor generators and other electrical machinery.
>
> In the event any equipment or apparatus not owned by the Assured is installed for use on board the Vessel and the Assured has assumed responsibility therefor, it shall also be considered part of the Subject Matter and the aggregate value thereof shall be included in the Agreed Value.
>
> Notwithstanding the foregoing, cargo containers, barges and lighters shall not be considered a part of the Subject Matter of this insurance.

This clause makes it clear that all leased equipment is to be considered part of the subject-matter insured and included in the agreed value. Conversely it is stipulated that cargo containers, barges, and lighters shall not be considered as part of the subject-matter of the insurance.

Generally speaking, the insurable value is the value of the vessel at the commencement of the risk, including fuel, provisions, and stores. In the case of a vessel engaged in a special trade, the value of any equipment required for that trade should also be included. There are many reasons why shipowners often maintain their hull valuations at a level which is much higher than the current market value of their vessels. In times of rising freights, vessel valuations respond very quickly and it is not desirable for an annual policy to be altered frequently to reflect such changes.

Conversely in a failing freight market, advances or loans on the security of a vessel might still be outstanding and therefore insurance for the original sum would still be required by the mortgagee. A valuer's estimate of the value of a vessel is based chiefly on comparison of prices obtained in the market for similar vessels and is, therefore, in the nature of a second-hand price. This does not necessarily represent the value of a particular vessel to her owner. In fact, it is extremely difficult to say what the true value of any vessel is to her owner. Even a new vessel may have been built for a special trade and neither her contract price nor the cost to build a similar vessel may fully represent the value she possesses to her owner as a potential freight earner. Nor does the value in the owner's books necessarily represent the true value, for this must depend on what he has been able to write off for depreciation—a factor which may vary with the profits the vessel has been able to earn in good times and the basis adopted for writing down.

In the *Medina Princess* case (1965 1 L. L. R. 361) the English court confirmed that there was no legal objection to a vessel with a low market value being insured for a high agreed value, where such an agreement accorded with the wishes of both parties to the transaction. This is a situation that often arises because from the shipowner's point of view it is better to have a relatively high valuation and correspondingly lower rate percent of premium than a lower value and a high rate percent. Underwriters also often prefer a high insured value which enables their premium income to be maintained without the necessity for an increase in the actual rate percent of premium. Furthermore, as will be easily seen, the chances of the assured being able to demonstrate a constructive total loss becomes more remote. It is usual for the underwriter to accept the owner's assessment of the value of the vessel to him. Sometimes the problem of arriving at a mutually acceptable insured value is solved by the inclusion of a Dual Valuation clause in the policies. This clause is often resorted to when insuring older vessels, in order to provide one value for total loss purposes and a higher value for other purposes. The lower value is the one on which all questions of total loss depend and usually represents the approximate market value of the vessel. The higher value (fixed by negotiation at a sum above the market value) applies to all other claims, namely particular average, general average, sue and labor, and collision claims, etc. Thus, if the insured vessel is damaged to the extent that the cost of repairs exceeds the value fixed for total loss purposes, the assured has two choices. First, he can abandon the vessel to underwriters as a constructive total loss and receive the lower valuation in the Dual Valuation clause. Such a course would carry with it the right to collect under any other total loss insurances, such as increased value, disbursements, etc. The assured's second choice would be to effect repairs, the cost of which he could collect up to the higher value named in the Dual Valuation clause. However, as we shall see, if the assured does not effect repairs but prefers to claim on an unrepaired damage basis, the Dual Valuation clause usually restricts the amount he can recover to the amount which he would recover for a total loss under the clause. Indeed, it has been suggested that where dual valuations are used, claims for unrepaired damage based on depreciation should be calculated by applying the percentage depreciation to the lower total loss valuation and not to the higher valuation. However, since claims for unrepaired damage are partial losses it would seem difficult, on the literal wording of the clause, to justify applying the percentage of depreciation to the total loss valuation. Sometimes the amount of additional total loss insurances permitted under the disbursements warranty in the policy is stipulated in the Dual Valuation clause. That calculation may be based on either the higher value or the lower value according to the wishes of the respective parties. The effect of the Dual Valuation clause can be summarized thus: when values fall but repair costs remain high, the clause gives the vessel owner indemnity both for total loss and for average claims, while enabling the underwriter to estimate a premium commensurate with his liabilities for both risks. It is submitted that the Dual Valuation clause is a somewhat contrived clause and should only be used when absolutely necessary to meet the requirements of the assured and/or underwriters in specific situations.

In insurances on cargo there are many types of valuation clauses, but the type most frequently used requires that the insured value be made up of the invoice value of the goods plus all charges thereon plus prepaid or guaranteed freight (if any) plus 10 percent to cover the importer's profit. Sometimes, by agreement, the mark-up for profit may exceed 10 percent. The valuation clause is doubly important as, in the case of an open policy, it is also applicable to shipments which have inadvertently not been declared.

American open cargo policies contain a Limits of Insurance clause which limits the amount covered on any one vessel or in any one place. The clause is specifically limited to incidents which occurred at one place and one time, or on one vessel or conveyance. It cannot be invoked in bankruptcy situations involving many claims arising in various places, at various times, and on various vessels or conveyances (*Interpool Ltd. v. U.S. Fire Insurance Co.,* 553 F. Supp. 385 (1983)). There are also limitations in respect to shipments stowed on deck on any one vessel. When the value of the goods shipped exceeds the amount stipulated in the policy, the principle of co-insurance applies.

The Accumulation clause also limits the amount recoverable under the policy and reads as follows:

Should there be an accumulation of interests beyond the limits expressed in this policy by reason of an interruption of transit or occurrence beyond the control of the Assured, or by reason of any casualty or at a transshipping point or on a connecting conveyance, this Company shall, provided notice be given as soon as known to the Assured, hold covered such excess interest and shall be liable for the full amount at risk, but in no event to exceed twice the policy limit.

Under this clause, provided the accumulation results from causes beyond the control of the assured, the policy attaches for the full amount at risk subject to a maximum of twice the policy limit.

Often the value of a bulk cargo will fluctuate during the course of a voyage and a buyer who has purchased the cargo on c.i.f. terms can cover any anticipated increase in value by effecting an additional insurance on the increased value of the cargo. Such insurances increase the c.i.f. valuation in the primary insurance of the cargo to the amount required, although two separate contacts of insurance are involved. The respective underwriters pay any claims for loss or damage pro rata, the primary underwriter usually bearing the major part of the loss. It has to be remembered that the original insurer will have full subrogation rights and the increased value underwriter will only share in any recovery if any excess remains after the original underwriter has been made whole. Nor does the increased value underwriter respond for sue and labor expenses which fall on the primary underwriter. All the increased value policy does is to increase the insured value beyond what is insured under the primary insurance (*Armada Supply Inc.* v. *Philip Gaybell Wright* (the *Agios Nikolas*), U.S. District Court, Southern District of New York 1987).

DISCLOSURE AND REPRESENTATIONS

As has already been pointed out, a contract of marine insurance is a contract based upon the utmost good faith, and, if the utmost good faith is not observed by either party, the contract may be avoided by the other party (Marine Ins. Act, Sect. 17).

Before the contract is concluded, the assured must disclose every material circumstance known to him and he is deemed to know every circumstance which in the ordinary course of business ought to be known to him. Failure to make such disclosure entitles the insurer to avoid the contract (Marine Ins. Act, Sect. 18). Whether every material circumstance has been disclosed is a question of fact (*Alexander* v. *National Union Fire Ins. Co.*, 1939 AMC 923). Similarly, all representations made during the negotiations of the contract of insurance (whether by the assured or his broker) must be true (that is to say, substantially correct) *if they are material to the risk*. Otherwise the underwriters may avoid the contract (Marine Ins. Act, Sect. 20).

Phillips defines misrepresentation and concealment as follows:

⚓ A misrepresentation is a false representation of a material fact, by one of the parties to the other, tending directly to induce the other to enter into the contract, or to do so on terms less favorable to himself when

Misrepresentation
concealment

he otherwise might not do so, or might demand terms more favorable to himself. (Sect. 529) and

A material misstatement by the assured through misconstruction of his information, is a misrepresentation; and the unwitting omitting to state a material fact is a concealment. (Sect. 546)

In dealing with the effect of misrepresentation or concealment, Phillips has this to say:

> One of the implied stipulations by the assured, on which the underwriter subscribes, is, that he is informed by the assured of all material circumstances known to the latter, and not known, or presumed to be so, to himself, and that no misrepresentation has been made by, or is imputable to, the assured; and if this stipulation is not substantially complied with, he is wholly or partially exonerated from the liabilities to which he would otherwise have been subject. (Sect. 675) and
> The non-communication or misrepresentation of material facts, though it be through mistake or forgetfulness, and without any fraudulent purpose, has nevertheless the effect to defeat the contract. (Sect. 682)

In short, non-disclosure or misrepresentation, whether fraudulent or completely innocent, strikes at the very basis of the contract, for the risk which the insurer has accepted is not that which he contemplated. Under English law whether or not the non-disclosure or misrepresentation has a causal connection with the loss is immaterial; if it materially affected the risk, the underwriter may avoid the policy. In the United States the effect of a material misrepresentation having no connection with the loss may depend upon state statutes (see *Wilburn Boat Co.* v. *Fireman's Fund Ins. Co.,* 348 U. S. 310).

The Marine Insurance Act states that every circumstance is material which would influence the judgment of a prudent insurer in fixing the premium, or determining whether he will take the risk (Sect. 18 (2)). The act gives an identical definition regarding materiality in dealing with representations (Sect. 20 (2)). These words ("which would influence the judgment or a prudent insurer") were considered by the English courts in the case of *Container Transport International* v. *Oceanus Mutual Underwriting Association (Bermuda) Ltd.* (1982 2 L.R. 178 and 1984 L.R. 476, C.A.) The lower court held that in order to be able to void the contract, the insurer must establish that, if the undisclosed circumstance had been disclosed to him, a prudent insurer would, not might, either have declined the risk altogether or in the alternative have accepted it only at a higher premium. However, the court of appeals decided that, to void the policy, underwriters need only show that, before the contract was concluded, there had been a non-disclosure of any circumstance which a prudent insurer *would take into account* when reaching his decision to take the risk or in deciding what premium to charge. The yardstick was any prudent insurer and not the particular insurer actually involved (as the lower court had held). The court of appeals' decision thus makes it easier for insurers to void a policy since they do not need to establish that a prudent insurer, if the undisclosed circumstance had been disclosed to him, would either have declined the risk or would have accepted it only at a higher premium than he would otherwise have done. Insurers now only need to show that the non-disclosure is one which any prudent insurer *would take into account*—a reduced test of materiality.

This question of materiality also came before the American courts recently. The district court held that in spite of inaccurate and/or incomplete loss records having been submitted during the negotiations preceding the acceptance of the risk, the insurers had failed to prove that they would not have issued the policy had all the material facts been accurately disclosed. In accepting the risk they had apparently relied on the judgment of the leading underwriters rather than on the information presented in the as-sured's application. In a 2-1 decision the U.S. Court of Appeals for the Second Circuit affirmed the lower court, commenting that while the parties to a marine insurance contract are held to the highest degree of good faith (*uberrimai fidei*) this does not require the voiding of the contract unless the undisclosed facts were material and relied upon. A fact is not material unless it is "something which would have controlled the underwriter's decision" (quoting *Btesh* v. *Royal Insurance Co.*, 49 F.2d 721). A marine insurance policy "cannot be voided for misrepresentation when the alleged misrepresentation was not relied upon and did not in any way mislead the insurer" (quoting *Rose and Lucy Inc.* v. *Resolute Insurance Co.*, 249 F. Supp. 991). An assured complies with the rule of materiality if he discloses sufficient information to call the attention of the insurer in such a way that if the latter desires further information he can ask for it. The insurers had failed to carry their burden of proving that the non-disclosures were material and that they relied on them (*Puritan Insurance Co.* v. *Eagle Steamship Co.*, 1986 AMC 1240). This American decision appears to be at variance with the English court of appeals' decision referred to earlier, although the dissenting judge commented that the majority of the court appeared to have indirectly reduced the effect of *uberrimae fidei* which was intended to relieve insurers from many usual duties of investigation. No doubt the quest for the true meaning of the words in the Marine Insurance Act ("which would influence the judgment of a prudent insurer") will continue to exercise both judicial and commercial minds on both sides of the Atlantic.

would be waived by underwriters where they received information which would put a careful insurer on inquiry and nevertheless failed to inquire, description of goods in this policy would not have put a prudent underwriter on inquiry as to precise nature of goods;
and that, therefore, plaintiffs' claim failed.

However, as we have seen, non-disclosure or misrepresentation differs from non-compliance with a warranty in two important respects: first, the test of *materiality* must be applied to non-disclosure and misrepresentation and secondly, while a warranty must be exactly complied with, whether material or not, it is sufficient that a representation be merely substantially correct.

A contract of marine insurance is deemed to be concluded when the proposal of the assured is accepted by the insurer whether or not a policy is immediately issued (*see* Marine Ins. Act, Sect. 21). In the United States reference may be made to the application for insurance (or "binder" as it is often called) which, when signed by the insurer, signifies the acceptance of the risk. It is of the utmost importance, therefore, that this document should be carefully and accurately drawn to reflect the understanding reached between the underwriter and the assured (or as is usually the case, the assured's broker). Such "binders" are usually claused "subject to all terms, etc., of the policy to be issued, which when delivered, replaces the binder."

The obligation to disclose all material facts is applicable:

(a) From the commencement of negotiations until the completion of the contract, viz., by acceptance of the proposal;

(b) At renewal of the policy, as this is equivalent to the making of a new contract;

(c) When alterations to the contract during its currency are required.

In deciding whether to accept a risk or to renew an existing policy, underwriters have a valuable guide in the assured's loss record. This document, usually prepared by the insurance broker's claims (or average adjusting) department, customarily lists all losses paid or pending during the previous five years (the last four years plus the current year). Pending claims are estimated on the basis of whatever surveys have been held on the insured vessels either afloat or on dry dock. The net premium paid to underwriters during the same period is also shown on the loss record and the loss ratio percentage is calculated for each of the past four completed years. Thus underwriters can readily see whether the particular account has been profitable or not and base their quotations for acceptance or renewal of the account accordingly. To some degree loss records reflect the ownership or management of a vessel or a fleet of vessels. They provide, in effect, some indication as to the quality of management, a factor of great importance to underwriters. In the preparation of loss records, a cut-off date is agreed for the current year (usually two or three months prior to the expiration of the current policy). The importance of accurate loss records was shown in *Container Transport International* v. *Oceanus* (1982 2 L.R. 178 and 1984 1 L.R. 476), an English court of appeals case. The assured had put forward an inaccurate and misleading claims record; consequently there were both misrepresentation and concealment of material facts. The insurer was entitled to avoid the contract under Sect. 18 (1) of the Marine Insurance Act as the misrepresentation was a circumstance which any prudent insurer would take into account when reaching his decision whether or not to accept that risk or when deciding what premium to charge. The effect of inaccurate and/or incomplete loss records in the United States was considered in *Puritan Insurance Co.* v. *Eagle Steamship Co.* (1986 AMC 1240). Both the lower court and the court of appeals reached the conclusion that on the facts in that particular case, the misrepresentation was not relied upon by the insurers for, in accepting the risk, they had apparently relied on the judgment of the leading underwriters rather than on the information presented in the assured's loss record.

It should be pointed out that loss records not infrequently prove in the final analysis to be inaccurate, being based to some extent on estimates of pending claims. Often, for example, when a vessel is dry-docked concealed bottom damage is found which had not been anticipated and therefore the cost of anticipated repairs included in the loss record had been inadvertently understated. This of itself would not entitle an underwriter to void the policy. Only if the assured knowingly falsified the loss record by either deliberately understating losses or omitting to report same would there have been a breach of good faith. Furthermore, as we have seen the burden of proof in the United States is on the complaining underwriters to show that any non-disclosure or misrepresentation was material and if known would have caused them not to take the risk or would have affected the rate of the premium charged.

An example of the importance underwriters place on being kept informed of any change in the risk they have underwritten is to be found in the Change of Ownership clause in the American Institute Hull form of policy. This reads as follows:

> In the event of any change, voluntary or otherwise, in the ownership or flag of the Vessel, or if the Vessel be placed under new management, or be chartered on a bareboat basis or requisitioned on that basis, or if the Classification Society of the Vessel or her class therein

be changed, cancelled or withdrawn, then, unless the underwriters agree thereto in writing, this Policy shall automatically terminate at the time of such change of ownership, flag, management, charter, requisition or classification; provided, however, that:

(a) if the Vessel has cargo on board and has already sailed from her loading port, or is at sea in ballast, such automatic termination shall, if required, be deferred until arrival at final port of discharge if with cargo, or at port of destination if in ballast;

(b) in the event of an involuntary temporary transfer by requisition or otherwise, without the prior execution of a written agreement by the Assured, such automatic termination shall occur fifteen days after such transfer.

This insurance shall not inure to the benefit of any transferee or charterer of the Vessel and, if a loss payable hereunder should occur between the time of change or transfer and any deferred automatic termination, the Underwriters shall be subrogated to all of the rights of the Assured against the transferee or charterer in respect of all or part of such loss as is recoverable from the transferee or charterer, and in the proportion which the amount insured hereunder bears to the Agreed Value.

The term "new management" as used above refers only to the transfer of the management of the vessel from one firm or corporation to another, and it shall not apply to any internal changes within the offices of the Assured.

The clause speaks for itself and is indicative of the importance underwriters place on the quality of management of the vessel insured.

Similar clauses are often included in Protection and Indemnity policies. Whether there has been a "change of management" under such clauses depends on the identity of the individuals exercising actual direction and control of the insured vessel. Thus the sale of all of the stock in a closely held tug-owning corporation and the election of new directors and officers voided the policy (*Hilton J. Parfait* v. *Central Towing Inc. et al.*, 1982 AMC 698).

Before leaving this subject it must be said that good faith in marine insurance is a two-way street and there is a reciprocal duty on the part of the insurer to deal fairly with the assured. As one court put it: Insurance obligations must not be construed so as to render the coverage mere gossamer.

WARRANTIES

There are two types of warranties:

first, a promissory warranty, "that is to say, a warranty by which the assured undertakes that some particular thing shall or shall not be done, or that some condition shall be fulfilled, or whereby he affirms or negatives the existence of a particular state of facts" (Marine Ins. Act, Sect. 33 (1));

second, the term is used to denote a mere limitation on, or exception from, the general words of the policy.

In the case of a promissory warranty, the warranty must be exactly complied with, whether it is material to the risk or not. If not complied with, the insurer is discharged from liability as from the date of the breach of warranty but without prejudice to any liability incurred by him before that date (Marine Ins. Act, Sect. 33 (3)).

It was thought that the effect of a breach of warranty was similar under U.S. law in that under the general maritime law there must be literal absolute compliance with all promissory warranties. However, in *Wilburn Boat Co.* v. *Fireman's Fund Ins. Co.* (348 U. S. 310) the Supreme Court found that there was no federal rule dealing with the consequences of a breach of warranty in marine policies and did not choose to establish one. In that case the assured had breached a warranty that the insured vessel should be used solely for private pleasure and had carried passengers for hire. The U.S. Court of Appeals for the Fifth Circuit, following the orthodox views of general maritime law, held that this breach of warranty voided the policy from the date of the breach. The appeals court regarded as inapplicable certain Texas statutes which would have made the breach of warranty relevant only if the breach had contributed to the loss. The Supreme Court decided otherwise and the case was remanded to give effect to the Texas statutes. The circuit court of appeals subsequently dutifully gave effect to those statutes, which provide that a claim shall not be barred unless the concealment or misinterpretation relates to a material fact or a fact which contributes to bring about the loss (1962 AMC 1593).

This decision of the Supreme Court has been widely criticized. Indeed, Justice Frankfurter, although concurring with the result reached by the majority of the Court, in a separate opinion noted:

Is it to be assumed that were the *Queen Mary* on a world pleasure cruise, to touch at New York City, New Orleans and Galveston, a Lloyd's policy covering the voyage would be subjected to the varying insurance laws of New York, Louisiana and Texas? Such an assumption, I am confident, would not prevail were decision necessary. The business of marine insurance often may be so related to the success of many manifestations of commercial maritime endeavor as to demand application of a uniform rule of law designed to eliminate the vagaries of state law and to keep harmony with the marine insurance laws of other great maritime powers.

Justice Douglas, in a separate dissent, said:

> Adherence to British precedents in this field was early admonished, *Queen Ins. Co.* v. *Globe & Rutgers Fire Ins. Co.*, 263 U. S. 487. The rule of the foregoing English cases is for me the most authentic standard for interpreting the present contract.

In the dissenting opinion of Justices Reed and Burton, the following appeared:

> Our admiralty laws, like our common law, came from England. As a matter of American judicial policy, we tend to keep our marine insurance laws in harmony with those of England. *Queen Ins. Co.* v. *Globe Ins. Co.,* 263 U. S. 487; *Calmar Steamship Corp.* v. *Scott,* 345 U. S. 427. Before our Revolution, the rule of strict compliance with maritime insurance warranties had been established as the law of England. That rule persists. While no case of this Court has been cited or found that says specifically that the rule of strict compliance is to be applied in admiralty and maritime cases, that presupposition has been consistently adopted as the basis of reasoning from our earliest days. Other courts have been more specific. No case holds to the contrary.

The effect of the Supreme Court's decision is discussed by Gilmore & Black (pp. 61-63) who conclude:

> It is utterly impossible to guess at this time [1957], how the Court will resolve these perplexities and contradictions. *Wilburn* may mean merely that the States are to have a limited competency to regulate certain terms of marine policies. It could as a matter of cold logic be read to mean that there is no federal maritime law at all. It may very well turn out to mean anything between these extremes.

Alex L. Parks, in his text *Law of Tug, Tow and Pilotage,* finds that the tendency is to restrict *Wilburn* to cases involving policy warranties, while Herbert R. Baer in his *Admiralty Law of the Supreme Court* (2d ed., p. 280) ventures the prediction that this controversial decision will in time be "whittled away by future decisions of the court so as to become barely recognizable." In a subsequent comment Parks writes:

> What have the courts done in the light of *Wilburn Boat?* Maritime law was never intended as an all-inclusive and definitive system. The interplay between state law and federal law has always recognized that the former could supplement the maritime law where not otherwise

inconsistent and antagonistic to its characteristic features. If a trend after *Wilburn* can be discerned, it is that its reasoning will be restricted to marine insurance cases, and moreover, the tendency appears to be to limit the holding to cases involving policy warranties. Notwithstanding the language in the majority opinion, American courts continue to stress that guidance should be sought from the English decisions on maritime insurance. Needless to say, the areas of similarity are infinitely greater than the areas of difference. On more than one occasion, the United States Supreme Court has stated that there are special reasons for maintaining continuity with the marine insurance laws of England and to "accord respect to established doctrines of English maritime law." The lower courts almost universally applied this concept prior to *Wilburn Boat*, and there appears to be little tendency to depart from the principle in the wake of the Court's decision. (*Maritime Lawyer*, Vol. III, No. 2, October 1978, pp. 131-32).

In a recent case one lower court circumvented *Wilburn* by holding that, because federal maritime law strictly construes geographical warranties in marine insurance policies and Georgia state law was not to the contrary, the court was not mandated to apply the Georgia doctrine requiring a causal relationship between the breach of warranty and the loss. The insured vessel had breached the warranty in the hull policy restricting the vessel's navigation to within 100 miles offshore and had subsequently sunk during a hurricane. The insurer was therefore not liable for the loss, the policy having been void from the time of the breach of warranty (*Lexington Ins. Co.* v. *Cooke's Seafood et al.*, 1988 AMC 574).

After over thirty years of dissatisfaction with *Wilburn* there is a current move afoot by the Maritime Law Association of the United States to attempt to nullify that decision. A proposed statute is being drafted to that end with a view to having it inserted into Title 46 of the U.S. Code. It remains to be seen whether this statutory attempt to reverse *Wilburn* will have the necessary political support to achieve passage and thereby restore international uniformity on the subject of warranties.

An example of how the enforcement of the strict literal compliance with a warranty may operate harshly against the assured is to be found in a subsequent case, *Continental Sea Foods Inc.* v. *New Hampshire Fire Ins. Co.* (1964 AMC 196). In that case the policy, covering a consignment of frozen shrimp from Pakistan to New York, contained a warranty requiring that the shipment be inspected by "proper Government authorities" in country of origin prior to loading and a certificate be issued certifying as to the soundness of the shipment. At the material time there was no government organization in Pakistan authorized to issue such a certificate and the shipper had to rely on a surveyor appointed by Lloyd's agent, who issued the required certificate. The shrimps arrived decomposed and were rejected. The case was unique in that performance of the warranty was impossible, yet the court felt constrained to enforce the rule regarding strict literal compliance of a warranty, and in consequence the assured was unable to recover from his insurers. The court reached its decision in spite of the fact that a New York State insurance law provided that no breach of warranty shall avoid an insurance contract or defeat recovery thereunder unless such breach materially increased the risk of loss, damage, or injury within the coverage of the contract.

The word "warranties" is frequently used in marine insurance clauses though not all such references are true promissory warranties but, as stated previously, merely limit the scope of a policy. Thus the warranty "free from capture and seizure" does not require the assured to undertake that the ship or cargo shall not be captured; it is merely a stipulation that the policy shall not apply to such a loss. It follows that the provisions of Sect. 33 of the Marine Insurance Act are inapplicable. Similarly, any breach of the Institute Trading Warranties, which are customarily attached to the policy to limit the areas in which the insured vessel is permitted to trade, would not result in the automatic termination of the policy but would merely call for an additional premium to cover the breach. On the other hand, a promissory warranty stipulating that the insured vessel must be kept classed in a specific classification society if breached would presumably void the policy as from the time of the breach.

The importance of classification societies to underwriters cannot be overemphasized. Such societies have rules regarding the survey and maintenance of vessels and require periodic dry-dockings. An underwriter contemplating the insuring of a particular vessel will first look it up in the classification society's register. He will base his premium, at least in part, on the fact that it is fully classed ("A 1 at Lloyd's"). As we have seen, the basic American hull policy's Change of Ownership clause provides that if the classification society of the vessel or her class therein be changed, the policy is automatically cancelled unless underwriters agree otherwise. Indeed, in the case of older vessels it is often warranted that a vessel must remain "in class" and that if for any reason the classification society withdraws her classification, the policy is void. When such a warranty is included in the policy, underwriters insist that the average adjuster obtain a statement from the classification society that the vessel has remained in class from the inception of the policy to the date of the casualty before settling any claim arising from such casualty.

The classification of ships is even more important to cargo underwriters. When effecting an open cover on cargo, an underwriter does not know which vessels will be carrying the goods he is insuring. Since, among other things, the type, class, and age of the carrying vessels affect the premium to be charged, open cargo policies contain a Classification clause. Such a clause describes vessels which are not subject to additional cargo premiums (such as cargo liners, or other vessels not over 20 years of age and classed A 1 with the American Bureau of Shipping or 100 A1 with Lloyd's Register of Shipping). For other vessels the clause goes on to list minimum additional premiums based on the age of the vessel. Indeed, in recent years, sometimes even cargo liners over 15 years old have carried an additional premium. The result is that assureds under open cargo policies are reluctant to ship their cargo in vessels which require cargo underwriters to levy an additional premium on the cargo being shipped. This reaction is, of course, the cargo underwriters' objective.

It has been held in the United States that an underwriter, by actions inconsistent with non-liability, can be estopped from denying liability for a loss which occurred while the insured vessel was being operated in violation of a warranty. In *Reliance Ins. Co.* v. *Yacht Escapade* (1961 AMC 2410), an insurer was estopped from asserting forfeiture of a marine policy upon a yacht because of breach of the private pleasure warranty, when, with full knowledge of the breach and without denying liability, it demanded that the assured incur liability for salvage by a salvor of its choice, for preservation at a repair yard, and for cleaning up in order to permit a survey; by such action the policy was revived.

A breach of warranty is excused when, by reason of a change of circumstances, the warranty ceases to be applicable to the circumstances of the contract, or when compliance with the warranty is rendered unlawful by a subsequent law; a breach of warranty may also be waived by the insurer. It is no excuse that a breach of warranty was repaired and the warranty complied with before loss (Marine Ins. Act, Sect. 34).

Express warranties appear in the policy or are incorporated therein by reference (Marine Ins. Act, Sect. 35). The warranty regarding the shrimps discussed above is an example of an express warranty. The most important express warranties in hull insurances are the Disbursements Warranty and the Institute Warranties (which will be dealt with later). Other examples of warranties are to be found in the Adventure clause in the American Institute Hull Clauses which reads:

> Beginning the adventure upon the Vessel, as above, and so shall continue and endure during the period aforesaid, as employment may offer, in port or at sea, in docks and graving docks, and on ways,

gridirons and pontoons, at all times, in all places, and on all occasions, services and trades; with leave to sail or navigate with or without pilots, to go on trial trips and to assist and tow vessels or craft in distress, but the Vessel may not be towed, except as is customary or when in need of assistance, nor shall the Vessel render assistance or undertake towage or salvage services under contract previously arranged by the Assured, the Owners, the Managers or the Charterers of the Vessel, nor shall the Vessel, in the course of trading operations, engage in loading or discharging cargo at sea, from or into another vessel other than a barge, lighter, or similar craft used principally in harbors or inland waters. The phrase "engage in loading or discharging cargo at sea" shall include while approaching, leaving or alongside, or while another vessel is approaching, leaving or alongside the Vessel.

The Vessel is held covered in case of any breach of conditions as to cargo, trade, locality, towage or salvage activities, or date of sailing, or loading or discharging cargo at sea, provided (a) notice is given to the Underwriters immediately following receipt of knowledge thereof by the Assured, and (b) any amended terms of cover and any additional premium required by the Underwriters are agreed to by the Assured.

It will be noted that the vessel may not be towed, except as is customary or when in need of assistance; she may not render assistance or undertake towage or salvage services *under a contract previously arranged*. Nor shall the vessel, in the ordinary course, engage in loading or discharging cargo at sea other than to or from a barge, lighter, or similar craft used principally in harbors or inland waters. In other words, the clause warrants that the insured vessel shall not, in the ordinary course, engage in activities for which she is not equipped or of a nature which would expose her to perils not contemplated in the insurance contract. However, breach of any of these warranties is held covered, subject to notice being given to underwriters immediately when the breach is known to the assured, and subject to the payment of an additional premium.

In similar strain, London Institute Trading Warranties are customarily inserted in standard hull policy forms issued by British marine underwriters to restrict the trading limits for ships which are not engaged in regular services. These trading warranties are inserted to enable underwriters to assess the risk more closely, and shipowners who wish to trade with ports in the prohibited areas (where there is a greater risk of damage) or to carry prohibited dangerous cargoes are free to do so on payment of additional premiums. These trading warranties (or navigational limits) permit worldwide trading, subject to the specific exclusions in the clause. An equivalent worldwide trading warranty in the United States is the American Institute Trade Warranties (7/1/72). Another form of trading warranty often used in the United States is the AGWI Extended Trade Warranties (7/1/72). The acronym AGWI abbreviates Atlantic, Gulf, and West Indies and permits trading in an area encompassing the east coast of the United States, the Gulf of Mexico, the Caribbean, the West Indies, and the east coast of Central America. It also includes part of the east coast of South America, etc. This clause, in common with most trading warranties limited to a specific area, holds the insured vessel covered in the event it operates outside the AGWI trade area subject to prompt notice being given to underwriters, who have the right to require an additional premium should they consider it to be appropriate. Under such a "held covered" clause the assured does not necessarily have to give notice to underwriters before the original trading warranties are broken. Prompt notice simply means reasonable notice. Policies intended for use by coastwise or small craft operating on inland waterways in the United States usually contain trading warranties which, if violated, cause the *suspension* of the policy until such time as the insured vessel, in a *seaworthy condition*, re-enters the trading area specified in the policy.

Generally speaking, in most hull policies there is usually a Breach of Warranty clause expressly extending the coverage to continue where there has been a breach of warranty, subject to the payment of an additional premium. In the American Institute Hull Clauses the Breach of Warranty clause is included in the Adventure clause quoted above.

Held covered clauses in general were discussed in principle in *Liberian Insurance Agency* v. *Mosse* (1977 L. L. R. Vol. 2 566). That case involved an insurance on a cargo of enamelware. The policy included a "held covered" clause in case of change of voyage or of any omission or error in the description of the interest, vessel, or voyage. J. Donaldson, reached the conclusion that the underwriter was not agreeing in any circumstances to hold the assured covered on terms which differed from those of the policy, other than as to premium. He considered that there were various limitations on such clauses; they only applied if the assured could have obtained a quotation in the market at a premium which could properly be described as "a reasonable commercial rate." In short, if the nature of the risk was changed materially from that originally accepted, the assured was not entitled to the protection of the held covered clause. It should be noted that in this case the assured had made an "error" in the description of the interest which materially altered the nature of the risk.

Implied warranties do not appear in the policy, but in England are part of the statutory law and in the United States are part of the general maritime law. They cover the seaworthiness of the vessel and the legality of the adventure (Marine Ins. Act, Sects. 39 and 41). Cargo policies usually contain an Illicit Trade warranty such as:

Warranted free from any charge, damage or loss, which may arise in consequence of a seizure or detention, for or on account of any illicit or prohibited trade, or any trade in articles contraband of war, or the violation of any port regulation.

Before leaving the subjects of disclosures, representations and warranties, it might be useful to sum up the general position:

1) Any *misrepresentation* or *non-disclosure* must be material (i.e., in influencing the underwriter to accept or reject the risk, or in fixing the premium) before it affects the validity of the policy.

(2) If any *misrepresentation* or *non-disclosure* is material, the underwriter may *avoid the policy from inception* regardless of whether or not the *misrepresentation* or *non-disclosure* has a causal connection with the loss.

(3) *Warranties* must be exactly complied with whether material to the risk or not.

(4) If a warranty is not complied with, the underwriter is discharged from liability *as from the time of the breach*.

However, it should be noted that *in the United States*, because of the *Wilburn Boat* decision (*supra*), any material misrepresentation, or any material non-disclosure, or any failure to comply with a warranty, may be subject to state laws and therefore possibly subject to some connection with the loss before the underwriter may avoid the policy.

DOCTRINE OF WARRANTY OF SEAWORTHINESS

Dealing with the implied warranty of seaworthiness in marine insurance policies, Phillips writes:

In a marine insurance, whether it be on the ship, freight or cargo, or the commissions or profits to accrue upon the cargo, the assured is understood impliedly to warrant, by the mere fact of effecting the insurance, independently of the particular terms used, that the ship is at the commencement of the voyage seaworthy; namely, that the materials of which the ship is made, its construction, the qualifications of the captain, the number and description of the crew, the tackle, sails, and rigging, stores, equipment, and outfit, generally, are such as to render it in every respect fit for the proposed voyage or service. A similar warranty is implied in river, lake, and canal navigation. (Subsect. 695)

According to the Marine Insurance Act, in a voyage policy there is an implied warranty that at the commencement of the voyage the ship shall be seaworthy for the purpose of the particular adventure insured (Sect. 39).

The law of the United States gives a wide extent to the implied warranty of seaworthiness. In the case of voyage policies, it has been held that the assured is bound not only to have his vessel seaworthy at the commencement of the voyage but also to keep her so, as far as it depends on himself and his agents, throughout the voyage.

In time policies, the assured's obligation is more limited. Although there is an implied warranty of seaworthiness at the time of attachment of the insurance (*Papoose*, 1966 AMC 385; 1969 AMC 781), the courts have said that there is not the usual warranty of seaworthiness but only the implied condition "that the vessel is in existence as such at the commencement of the risk, capable of navigation, and safe, whether at sea or in port, and seaworthy when she first sails, or, if at sea, had sailed seaworthy, and is safe" (Phillips, Subsect. 727).

In England, in a time policy, there is no implied warranty that the ship shall be seaworthy at any stage of the adventure, but where, with the privity of the assured, the ship is sent to sea in an unseaworthy state, the insurer is not liable for any loss attributable to unseaworthiness (Marine Ins. Act, Sect. 39). However, the insurer must show that the loss was attributable to unseaworthiness of which the assured was aware. This was considered by the English courts in the case of the *Eurysthenes* (L. L. R. 1976, Vol. 2, p. 171). It was held that "privity" meant that the assured personally knew beforehand of the ship being sent to sea in an unseaworthy condition and concurred in it being done. (In the case of a corporation, "personally" refers to its directors or head men—such as managing director, or head of the traffic department, or whoever might be the right person to be considered as *alter ego*—but not to its servants.) The breach did not need to amount to wilful misconduct (although that would be conclusive). In his judgment Lord Denning said:

> If the ship is sent to sea in an unseaworthy state, with the knowledge and concurrence of the assured personally, the insurer is not liable for any loss attributable to unseaworthiness, that is, to unseaworthiness of which he knew and in which he concurred. To disentitle the shipowner, he must, I think, have knowledge not only of the facts constituting the unseaworthiness but also knowledge that those facts rendered the ship unseaworthy, that is, not reasonably fit to encounter the ordinary perils of the sea.

In other words, only if the vessel is lost partly or wholly through unseaworthiness within the reasonable knowledge of the owner is coverage denied.

where, with the privity of the assured, the ship was sent to sea in an unseaworthy state, the insurer was not liable for any loss attributable to unseaworthiness. Yancey commented that practitioners of marine insurance had reached the conclusion that this distinction between English and American law might be more apparent than real. After reviewing the origins of the theory that there was, in American law, a warranty of seaworthiness at the time the insurance becomes effective, Yancey reached the conclusion that, although there has been a great deal of talk in terms of a "warranty," there was no single instance where, in spite of such an implied warranty of seaworthiness, a loss by an insured peril wholly unconnected with the unseaworthiness was held to be not recoverable from underwriters. If the situation was one of true warranty, and the true warranty was violated, then there would be no effective insurance at all. In short none of Yancey's research supported the notion that violation of the so-called warranty so far voided the policy that a loss wholly unconnected with the warranty was not covered. Nevertheless, Yancey felt it was a truism on which all should be able to agree that any loss solely attributable to unseaworthiness is not a loss by an insured peril. Yancey referred to several cases decided in 1957 which went a considerable way towards closing any gap which might exist between American law and the English Marine Insurance Act on the subject of seaworthiness in a time hull policy. He reached the conclusion that the American rule as stated by the Fifth Circuit (*Saskatchewan Govt. Office v. Spot Pak Inc.,* 1957 AMC 655, and *Sea Pak Tropical Marine Products Inc. v. Birmingham Fire Insurance Co.,* 1957 AMC 1946) was now "very substantially similar" to the rule as stated in the English Marine Insurance Act.

After reviewing the above cases a similar conclusion was reached by the U.S. District Court, District of Alaska (*Richard Gregoire v. Underwriters at Lloyd's,* 1982 AMC 2045). The court commented:

> Since the great majority of the decided cases in this country are consistent with the English rule, it should be applied in this case. I therefore hold that in a time hull policy of marine insurance there is no implied warranty that a vessel will not break ground in an unseaworthy condition. Where, however, the owner of the vessel or those in privity with him send their vessel to sea knowing it to be unseaworthy, the insurer is not liable for damages proximately caused by the unseaworthiness.

However, it should be noted that the Eighth Circuit Court of Appeals diverged from the English maritime law requirements that an assured must be privy to any unseaworthiness before being denied coverage for an insured peril under the policy. In the case before the court the insured barge overturned at sea and was beached. On being surveyed, the barge's hull was found to be seriously deteriorated. The insurer denied a claim for total loss based on an exclusion in the policy "for any loss, damage or expense arising out of the failure of the assured to exercise due diligence to maintain the vessel in a seaworthy condition." The district court had found for the insurer. The appeals court affirmed the lower court, saying that the divergence from English law was justified by the clear and plain language in the policy exclusion, (*L. & L. Marine Services* v. *Insurance Co. of North America*, 1987 AMC 2283).

It would appear that some American courts still consider that there is a difference (albeit slight) between English and American law as to whether or not there is an implied warranty of seaworthiness in a time policy. Of course the law in both countries is quite clear that any loss or damage attributable to unseaworthiness is not recoverable.

It should be mentioned that a charterer's liability policy is not subject to an implied warranty of seaworthiness and therefore covers the liability of the charterer for loss of cargo due to unseaworthiness of the vessel with (or without) owner's privity *(Martin &Robertson Ltd.* v. *Orion Ins. Co. Ltd.,* 1971 AMC 515).

Nothing written above overrides the requirement that, to be claimable from underwriters, a loss must be proximately caused by an insured peril.

Nevertheless, although it is the tendency of the courts to construe insurance policies strictly against the insurer, the insured cannot, by their own wilful misconduct, enlarge the insurer's risk to include the ordinary and inevitable action of the sea with respect to an unseaworthy vessel *(N. Y., N. H. & Hartford R. R. Co.* v. *W. S. Gray* [one of Lloyd's underwriters] *and Orion Ins. Co. Ltd.,* 1956 AMC 1396).

As to the effect of the warranty of seaworthiness in policies on cargo and freight, Phillips states:

> Under a policy upon cargo and freight, the warranty of seaworthiness is not complied with, if the cargo is put on board for the voyage when the ship is in so defective a state that the cargo must be relanded in order to make necessary repairs, and the policy, therefore, does not attach on the cargo if the risk is to commence at the time of loading. (Subsect. 723)

In these days a cargo owner has no control over the seaworthiness of the vessel on which his cargo is being shipped and it is customary for insurances on cargo to contain a stipulation that the seaworthiness of the vessel is admitted as between the cargo insurer and an innocent insured. This appears in the so-called Bill of Lading, etc., clause which reads in part as follows:

> The seaworthiness of the vessel as between the Assured and these Assurers is hereby admitted and the wrongful act or misconduct of the shipowner or his servants causing a loss is not to defeat the recovery by an innocent Assured if the loss in the absence of such wrongful act or misconduct would have been a loss recoverable on the policy.

The reference to *innocent* assureds arose as a result of the *Grigorios* case (*P. Samuel & Co.* v. *Dumas*, 18 L. L. R. No. 7, p. 211) in which it was held that a loss of a ship by scuttling was not a loss by "perils of the sea." It was realized that in such circumstances cargo owners would not be able to recover from their underwriters even though in most cases they were innocent of the fraudulent act of the shipowner. It was to correct this inequity that the word "innocent" was introduced into the Bill of Lading, etc., clause. Thus the words "innocent assured" apply to participation in the "wrongful act or misconduct of the shipowner or his servants"—not to the seaworthiness of the vessel. Furthermore, an assured's (cargo owner's) duty of disclosure under a "seaworthiness admitted" clause does not apply to unseaworthiness developing after the policy has been issued (*Escambia Trading Co.* v. *Aetna Casualty & Surety Co.*, 1977 AMC 1285). The "innocent cargo owner" clause enables innocent cargo interests to recover under a cargo policy even when the cargo is lost by the intentional act of the shipowners or their servants in scuttling the vessel. However, according to English law, the clause only relates to losses caused by scuttling and was framed to remedy an obvious injustice. The clause achieves its objective by treating the loss of cargo by scuttling as a loss by perils of the sea, excluding from consideration the privity of the shipowner to the scuttling. However, the clause does not extend to loss of cargo due to a dishonest taking of the vessel and its cargo by a shipowner (the *Salem*, 2 A.C. (1983) 375).

DURATION OF RISK

When the subject-matter is insured by a voyage policy "at and from" or "from" a particular place, its voyage, by implication, is to be commenced within a *reasonable* period of time. If it is not, the underwriter may avoid the contract unless it can be shown that he was aware of the possibility of delay or waived the implied condition (*see* Marine Ins. Act, Sect. 42). If the place of departure is changed and if the port of destination is changed before the vessel sails, the risk does not attach (Marine Ins. Act, Sect. 44). Furthermore, if after the commencement of the risk the destination of the vessel is voluntarily changed, the underwriter is discharged from liability as from the time of the decision to make the change of voyage, even though

the vessel may not, in fact, have left the course of the voyage contemplated by the policy when a loss occurs (Marine Ins. Act, Sect. 45).

When a vessel, without lawful excuse, deviates from the voyage contemplated by the policy, the insurer is discharged from any liability as from the time of deviation even though the vessel may have regained her route before the loss occurs. The intention to deviate is immaterial; there must have been an actual deviation before the underwriter is discharged from liability under the policy (Marine Ins. Act, Sect. 46). Any delay in prosecuting the voyage with reasonable dispatch discharges the underwriter from liability as from the time when the delay became unreasonable (Marine Ins. Act, Sect. 48).

The position is the same in the United States, where one court stated:

> If an insured shipowner fails to pursue that course of navigation which experience and usage have prescribed as the safest and most expeditious mode of proceeding from one voyage terminus to the other, he violates a tacit but universally implied condition of the contract between himself and his underwriter, who is therefore freed from liability for loss subsequent to deviation because the assured has enhanced or varied the risks insured against. (The *Citta de Messina*, 169 Fed. Rep. 472)

Most policies on vessels are now written for a period of time, consequently the doctrine of deviation is no longer the important factor it once was. However, it was invoked in a recent case involving a vessel insured under a port risk policy. In that case the removal of the insured vessel from the prescribed port area at Hirohata to Osaka, some 40 miles distant, without notice to underwriters was held by the court to be a material deviation which discharged underwriters from liability for a loss occurring at Osaka three weeks after her arrival there. The port risk policy (in common with voyage policies) included a "held covered at premium to be arranged" clause, but this was held to be inapplicable absent proof that the parties agreed upon a premium for coverage at a port other than the one named in the policy (*Bristol Steamship Corp.* v. *The London Assurance and H. O. Linard*, 1976 AMC 448).

Deviation or delay is excused in the following circumstances:

(a) Where authorized by any special term in the policy; or

(b) Where caused by circumstances beyond the control of the master and his employer; or

(c) Where reasonably necessary in order to comply with an express or implied warranty; or

(d) Where reasonably necessary for the safety of the ship or subject-matter insured; or

(e) For the purpose of saving human life, or aiding a ship in distress where human life may be in danger; or

(f) Where reasonably necessary for the purpose of obtaining medical or surgical aid for any person on board the ship; or

(g) Where caused by the barratrous conduct of the master or crew, if barratry be one of the perils insured against. (Marine Ins. Act, Sect. 49)

Once the "lawful excuse" ceases to operate, the vessel must regain her course "in reasonable dispatch" (Marine Ins. Act, Sect. 49).

In insurances on cargo, if the policy does not contain a clause extending the period of the coverage (such as the Warehouse to Warehouse clause) and if the policy is claused "from the loading thereof aboard the said ship," the risk does not attach until such cargo is actually on board, and the insurer is not on risk while the goods are in transit from the shore to the ship.

As cargo owners have no control over their goods once the vessel has sailed, insurances on cargo invariably contain a deviation clause reading as follows:

> This insurance shall not be vitiated by any unintentional error in description of vessel, voyage or interest, or by deviation, overcarriage, change of voyage, transhipment or any other interruption of the ordinary course of transit, from causes beyond the control of the Assured. It is agreed, however, that any such error, deviation or other occurrence mentioned above shall be reported to this Company as soon as known to the Assured, and additional premium paid if required.

It is important to note that it is necessary for the assured to give prompt notice to underwriters when he becomes aware of any event for which he is "held covered." However, under this clause, failure to report a deviation does not affect the coverage since such notice is not made a condition precedent nor is any forfeiture of coverage provided for. Some cargo policies expressly note that it is necessary that the assured give prompt notice to underwriters when he becomes aware of an event for which he is "held covered" and that the right to such cover is dependent on compliance with this obligation.

In practice, it is difficult for cargo owners to comply with the "held covered" provisions of the Deviation clause; consequently the Marine Extension clauses (*q.v.*) were added to the cargo policy. Basically, these clauses provide the same coverage as is provided by the Deviation clause and the Warehouse to Warehouse clause but remove the need for prompt notice to underwriters and additional premium payments. In other words, under the Marine Extension clauses notice to underwriters is not a condition precedent to coverage.

(Deviation is a much more important issue under contracts of carriage, and this aspect was the subject of the address of the chairman of the Association of Average Adjusters in 1976, H. B. Chassen.)

The Warehouse to Warehouse clause is an example of mixed sea and land risks referred to in the English Marine Insurance Act (Sect. 2). The clause in the basic cargo policy reads as follows:

> This insurance attaches from the time the goods leave the Warehouse and/or Store at the place named in the policy for the commencement of the transit and continues during the ordinary course of transit, including customary transhipment, if any, until the goods are discharged overside from the overseas vessel at the final port. Thereafter the insurance continues whilst the goods are in transit and/or awaiting transit until delivered to final warehouse at the destination named in the policy or until the expiry of 15 days (or 30 days if the destination to which the goods are insured is outside the limits of the port) whichever shall first occur. The time limits referred to above to be reckoned from midnight of the day on which the discharge overside of the goods hereby insured from the overseas vessel is completed. Held covered at a premium to be arranged in the event of transhipment, if any, other than as above and/or in the event of delay in excess of the above time limits arising from circumstances beyond the control of the Assured.

It will be noted that the insurance attaches from the time the goods leave the warehouse ". . . for the commencement of the transit and continues during the ordinary course of transit"—which implies that any deviation from the ordinary course of transit would terminate the policy. The intent of the clause is to extend the coverage for the entire period the assured is at risk, and if the risk extends from warehouse to warehouse, the policy covers. However, the controlling factor is the assured's insurable interest which is governed by the terms of sale. If a New York importer purchases goods f.o.b. Hamburg, his policy will not cover warehouse to warehouse but only port to warehouse. If, however, his purchase is c.i.f. ex seller's warehouse, then his policy does not come into play at all since the seller has the obligation to insure the goods warehouse to warehouse. If the purchase is c.&f. ex seller's warehouse, then the importer assumes the obligation to insure the goods, which are automatically insured under his open cargo policy from warehouse to warehouse. The clause continues to provide coverage after discharge until delivered to final warehouse at the destination named in the policy, or until the expiry of 15 days after discharge from the overseas vessel if the destination is within the port, or 30 days if outside the limits of the port. This only defines the maximum time period, and the insurance will terminate sooner if the goods are delivered to the final warehouse prior to this time period or if ordinary course of transit is interrupted. There is a "held covered" provision at additional premium in the event of delay in excess of the 15-day or 30-day period, if arising out of circumstances "beyond the control of the assured" and "prompt notice" is given to the underwriters when the assured becomes aware of such an event. Sometimes the policy stipulates that it is necessary for the assured to give prompt notice when they become aware of an event for which they are "held covered" under the policy, and the right to such cover is dependent on compliance with this obligation.

Cargo owners often had difficulty in complying with this requirement since they seldom have control over their goods once they are in the carrier's possession. To deal with this problem, the Marine Extension clauses were introduced into the policy by endorsement. These clauses read as follows:

> Notwithstanding anything to the contrary contained in or endorsed on this policy it is understood and agreed that in consideration of premium as agreed the following terms and conditions shall apply to all shipments which become at risk hereunder:
>
> (1) This insurance attaches from the time the goods leave the warehouse at the place named in the policy, certificate or declaration for the commencement of the transit and continues until the goods are delivered to the final warehouse at the destination named in the policy, certificate or declaration, or a substituted destination as provided in Clause 3 hereunder.
>
> (2) This insurance specially to cover the goods during,
>
> (i) deviation, delay, forced discharge, re-shipment and transhipment.
>
> (ii) any other variation of the adventure arising from the exercise of a liberty granted to the shipowner or charterer under the contract of affreightment.
>
> (3) In the event of the exercise of any liberty granted to the shipowner or charterer under the contract of affreightment whereby such contract is terminated at a port or place other than the original insured destination, the insurance continues until the goods are sold and delivered at such port or place; or, if the goods be not sold but are forwarded to the original insured destination or to any other destination this insurance continues until the goods have arrived at final warehouse as provided in Clause 1.
>
> (4) If while this insurance is still in force and before the expiry of 15 days from midnight of the day on which the dis-

charge overside of the goods hereby insured from the overseas vessel at the final port of discharge is completed, the goods are re-sold (not being a sale within the terms of Clause 3) and are to be forwarded to a destination other than that covered by this insurance, the goods are covered hereunder while deposited at such port of discharge until again in transit or until the expiry of the aforementioned 15 days whichever shall first occur. If a sale is effected after the expiry of the aforementioned 15 days while this insurance is still in force the protection afforded hereunder shall cease as from the time of the sale.

(5) Held covered at a premium to be arranged in case of change of voyage or of any omission or error in the description of the interest, vessel or voyage.

(6) This insurance shall in no case be deemed to extend to cover loss damage or expense proximately caused by delay or inherent vice or nature of the subject matter insured.

(7) It is a condition of this insurance that there shall be no interruption or suspension of transit unless due to circumstances beyond the control of the Assured.

All other terms and conditions of the policy not in conflict with the foregoing remain unchanged, it being particularly understood and agreed that the F.C.&S. clause remains in full force and effect, and that nothing in the foregoing shall be construed as extending this insurance to cover any risks of war or consequences of hostilities.

These clauses, in effect, override the Warehouse to Warehouse clause and the Deviation clause in the basic policy, thus ensuring coverage from warehouse to warehouse provided the goods are in due course of transit; that is, if there be no interruption or suspension of transit unless due to circumstances beyond the control of the assured. The limits of 15 or 30 days in the Warehouse to Warehouse clause (with the proviso that the delay was not within the control of the assured) and the requirement for prompt notice to underwriters and additional premium payment are dispensed with by the inclusion of the Marine Extension clauses endorsement.

Insofar as cargo consigned to South America is concerned, both the Warehouse to Warehouse and Marine Extension clauses are overridden by the South American endorsement, which reads as follows:

It is hereby mutually understood and agreed that the following clause will apply to all shipments insured in U. S. currency and shipped to South America:

Notwithstanding anything contained elsewhere herein to the contrary, (particularly the Warehouse to Warehouse and Marine

     I   \ the insurance provided hereunder shall con-
     t   xty (60) days (ninety (90) days on shipments
     '   River) after completion of discharge of the
                 rt of destination or until the goods are de-
                 arehouse at destination, whichever may
                 en terminate.
                 'o above to be reckoned from midnight
of the   discharge of the overseas vessel is completed.

This endorsement affords continuous coverage for 60 days (90 days on shipments via the Magdalena River) after completion of discharge of the overseas vessel at the port of destination or until the goods are delivered to the final warehouse at destination. Any loss, therefore, that is discovered within 60 days from the date of discharge from the overseas vessel will be recoverable (subject to terms of average). If cargo arrives at destination prior to expiration of the 60 days, then the coverage ceases on arrival. If a consignee uses a warehouse in the port of discharge as the termination of the venture, the insurance ceases immediately when the goods are placed in the warehouse. While the coverage provided under this endorsement is not limited to delay beyond the control of the assured, it does stipulate a maximum time period of 60 days.

With regard to shipments to the Philippines (and in a similar strain), the Philippine Islands endorsement overrides the Warehouse to Warehouse and Marine Extension clauses by limiting the assured to 7 days after landing goods at the final port in the Philippine Islands. The clause reads as follows:

> With respect to shipments of goods and/or merchandise to the Philippine Islands (excluding all mail shipments), and notwithstanding anything contained elsewhere in this policy to the contrary, particularly the Warehouse to Warehouse and Marine Extension Clauses, the insurance provided hereunder shall cease upon delivery to consignee or not later than seven days after landing of the goods and/or merchandise at the final port in the Philippine Islands, whichever may first occur.
>
> Survey for loss or damage must be held within seven days after landing of the goods and/or merchandise at the final port in the Philippine Islands.
>
> The time limits referred to above to be reckoned from midnight of the day on which the landing of the insured goods and/or merchandise at the final port in the Philippine Islands is completed.
>
> With regard to shipments to the Philippines, this policy may be cancelled by either party giving to the other party five days' written

or telegraphic notice to that effect, but such notice shall be withc
udice to any shipments which have already attached under this p

This endorsement is not often used by American underwriters si
congestion and general conditions in the Philippine Islands which g
to its introduction have improved to a point where the strict provi
longer necessary.

ASSIGNMENT OF POLICY

A marine insurance policy is assignable either before or after the loss unless such assignment is expressly prohibited in the policy itself (Marine
Ins. Act, Sect. 50); that is to say, an assured may transfer his beneficial
rights under the policy. This assignment or transfer of beneficial rights
under the policy should not be confused with the assignment of *interest*.
Where the assured transfers his *interest* in the subject-matter insured he
does not automatically transfer his rights under the contract of insurance
unless there is an agreement to that effect (Marine Ins. Act, Sect. 15). Furthermore, once the assured has parted with or lost his interest in the subject-matter insured he cannot assign his interest in the policy (Marine Ins.
Act, Sect. 51). This does not prevent an assured assigning a policy after a
loss provided he had an insurable interest at the time of the loss. Once a
loss has occurred, the right to indemnity accrues and this right can be assigned. Thus it is possible for an assured to sell the insured vessel in damaged condition and assign all claims for unrepaired damage existing at the
time of the sale to the buyer. What cannot be assigned, once the assured has
parted with or lost his interest, is the policy coverage applying to events
occurring after he is no longer interested in the property insured.

The quality of a vessel's ownership and/or management is all-important to the underwriter, affecting as it does both his decision to accept or
reject the risk, and, if accepted, the rate of premium to be charged. However, as a marine insurance policy is freely assignable, the policy could
follow the sale of the vessel and continue to cover it, however inferior the
new ownership might be. To control such situations, hull policies invariably contain a change of ownership clause along the lines previously discussed. In the context of a marine insurance policy, "change in
management" does not refer to any change in crew but rather to a surrender
of control over the vessel and her employment (*S. C. Loveland* v. *East West
Towing et al.*, 1978 AMC 2293).

In American cargo policies it is usually warranted by the assured that
the assignment of the policy or of any insurable interest therein without the
consent of the underwriter shall render the insurance void.

LOSS PAYEE CLAUSE

American marine insurance policies are unique in that they contain a Loss Payee clause. In the American Institute Hull Clauses this reads as follows:

> Loss, if any, payable to . . . . or order. Provided, however, Underwriters shall pay claims to others as set forth in the Collision Liability clause and may make direct payment to persons providing security for the release of the Vessel in Salvage cases.

Under this clause, losses are only payable to the party or parties stipulated and no deviation whatever is permissible unless the payees named voluntarily waive payment in favor of other parties. The only exception to this is the provision in the clause that underwriters may pay claims to others "as set forth in the Collision Liability clause" (that is to say, they may pay the surety if the surety has paid damages to any other person in respect of the collision). The clause also specifically authorizes underwriters to make direct payments to anyone providing security for the release of the vessel in salvage cases. This proviso was added to the Loss Payee clause in the most recent (1977) version of the American Institute Hull Clauses.

As a practical matter, the Loss Payee clause, in effect, makes the policy negotiable, although the policy does not pass.

The position is different in the United Kingdom: British marine insurance policies contain no Loss Payee clause; the assured or assureds named in the policy have complete title to the policy; and (in the absence of specific instructions from them) losses can only be paid to the named assureds. Furthermore, in the London market, losses cannot be paid unless the policy is actually produced and the claim paid is endorsed thereon. This difference in practice between the American and British marine insurance markets has sometimes caused difficulties, particularly in settling claims in London under the American hull form of policy containing a Loss Payee clause. Before the London insurance broker can collect, he has to present payment orders signed by the loss payees. Indeed, in the case of major losses, British underwriters have, on occasions, required payment orders signed also by the named assureds if they differ from the loss payees. The difference in practice stems from the fact that British policies are documents of title and after they have been issued, the named assured can assign the right of collection thereunder without the knowledge of the underwriters, who are bound to rely on the document itself for evidence of the right of the party to collect the claim.

The effect of a loss payee executing payment orders authorizing underwriters to pay a repairer for repairs effected to the insured vessel was considered by the American courts in *Reliable Maritime Boiler Repair Inc.*

v. *Frank B. Hall Inc., et al.* (1971 AMC 1941). In that case, the loss payee was estopped from subsequently revoking these instructions to the prejudice of the unpaid repairer who had effected repairs in reliance upon the assignment of the insurance proceeds.

THE PREMIUM

The premium is due on the completion of the contract and delivery of the policy. In the United Kingdom, when the insurance is effected through a broker, the broker is directly responsible to the insurer for the premium but the insurer is directly responsible to the assured for losses, return of premium, etc. (Marine Ins. Act, Sect. 53 (1)). This is not the case in the United States where the assured is responsible for payment of the premium. ("In the United States an insurance broker is not distinguished from other brokers and agents; not being himself a party in respect of the premium any more than in respect of any other liability or claim arising on the contract negotiated by him for his principal, unless he becomes so by special agreement." (Phillips, Sect. 508))

The American Institute Hull Clauses include the following clauses relating to premiums:

PREMIUM. The Underwriters to be paid in consideration of this insurance . . . . Dollars being at the annual rate of . . . . per cent., which premium shall be due on attachment. If the Vessel is insured under this Policy for a period of less than one year at pro rata of the annual rate, full annual premium shall be considered earned and immediately due and payable in the event of Total Loss of the Vessel.

RETURNS OF PREMIUM. Premium returnable as follows:

Pro rata daily net in the event of termination under the Change of Ownership clause;

Pro rata monthly net for each uncommenced month if it be mutually agreed to cancel this Policy;

For each period of 30 consecutive days the Vessel may be laid up in port for account of the Assured,

. . . . . . cents per cent. net not under repair, or

. . . . . . cents per cent. net under repair;

provided always that:

(a) a Total Loss of the Vessel has not occurred during the currency of this Policy;

(b) in no case shall a return for lay-up be allowed when the Vessel is lying in exposed or unprotected waters or in any location not approved by the Underwriters;

(c) in the event of any amendment of the annual rate, the above rates of return shall be adjusted accordingly;

(d) in no case shall a return be allowed when the Vessel is used as a storage ship or for lightening purposes.

If the Vessel is laid up for a period of 30 consecutive days, a part only of which attaches under this Policy, the Underwriters shall pay such proportion of the return due in respect of a full period of 30 days as the number of days attaching hereto bear to 30. Should the lay-up period exceed 30 consecutive days, the Assured shall have the option to elect the period of 30 consecutive days for which a return is recoverable.

NON-PAYMENT OF PREMIUM. In event of non-payment of premium 30 days after attachment, or of any additional premium when due, this Policy may be cancelled by the Underwriters upon 10 days written or telegraphic notice sent to the Assured at his last known address or in care of the broker who negotiated this Policy. Such proportion of the premium, however, as shall have been earned up to the time of cancellation shall be payable. In the event of Total Loss of the Vessel occurring prior to any cancellation or termination of this Policy full annual premium shall be considered earned.

It should be noted that:

(a) the premium is due on attachment;

(b) if the policy is for a period of less than one year at pro rata of the annual rate, the full annual premium is payable in the event of a total loss; and

(c) the policy may be cancelled by the under-writers in the event of non-payment of premium upon 10 days, written notice to the assured.

Sometimes, as an accommodation to the assured, special arrangements are made for the premiums to be paid in installments, usually quarterly. In such cases the policy is endorsed accordingly and a schedule of payments included. A specific cancellation clause is often included which takes effect in the event of non-payment of premium when due. Such clauses stipulate that a certain period of written notice must be given by underwriters before any cancellation becomes effective.

Chapter 3

Risks Covered by a Policy of Marine Insurance

THE PERILS INSURED AGAINST

In a standard American policy of marine insurance, the basic maritime perils insured against are described in venerable terms having as their origin the Perils clause in the ancient Lloyd's form of policy which dates back to the early eighteenth century. The Perils clause in the American Institute Hull Clauses reads as follows:

> Touching the Adventures and Perils which the Underwriters are contented to bear and take upon themselves, they are of the Seas, Men-of-War, Fire, Lightning, Earthquake, Enemies, Pirates, Rovers, Assailing Thieves, Jettisons, Letters of Mart and Counter-Mart, Surprisals, Takings at Sea, Arrests, Restraints and Detainments of all Kings, Princes and People, of what nation, condition or quality soever, Barratry of the Master and Mariners and of all other like Perils, Losses and Misfortunes that have or shall come to the Hurt, Detriment or Damage of the Vessel, or any part thereof, excepting, however, such of the foregoing Perils as may be excluded by provisions elsewhere in the Policy or by endorsement thereon.

At first blush it might seem that the coverage afforded by this clause in general, and by the words "all other like perils" in particular, is all-embracing. This is not so, as was demonstrated by the court in the case of *Dwyer* v. *Providence Washington Ins. Co.* (1958 AMC 1488). That case concerned the loss of a vessel while on an inland lake. The packing nut on the packing box of the driving shaft became disengaged, permitting water to flow into the vessel. With regard to the term "perils of the sea," the court remarked that it did not embrace all losses happening on the seas and that a policy insuring against perils of the sea covered only extraordinary risks. Reference was made to an earlier decision in which the court had adopted the view that perils of the sea included losses caused by extraordinary risks, wind and waves, injury from without as opposed to loss from ordinary wear and tear, or unseaworthiness or weakness from within the vessel existing at the outset of the voyage. Thus, the mere fact that a vessel develops a leak in ordinary weather and seas does not establish causation by a peril of the sea (*Tropical Marine Products Co. v. Birmingham Fire Ins. Co.*, 1956 AMC 567).

Phillips states:

> Whatever risks are assumed by the underwriter, his liability is subject to two limitations; he is not liable for the consequences of the perils assumed, except when they operate in an extraordinary degree, and he is liable only for loss and damage of an extraordinary kind. (Subsect. 1086)

The term "perils of the sea" is defined in the Marine Insurance Act as the fortuitous accidents or casualties of the seas and not the ordinary action of the winds and waves (Rules for Construction of Policy, No. 7). This part of the act is based on the old English case of *Thomas Wilson v. The Xantho* (12 App. Cas. 503) in which the court stated that

> it is clear that the term "perils of the sea" does not cover every accident or casualty which may happen to the subject-matter of the insurance on the sea. It must be a peril "of," the sea. Again, it is well settled that it is not every loss or damage of which the sea is the immediate cause that is covered by these words. *They do not protect, for example, against that natural and inevitable action of the winds and waves, which results in what may be described as wear and tear. There must be some casualty, something which could not be foreseen as one of the necessary incidents of the adventure.* The purpose of the policy is to secure an indemnity against accidents which may happen, not against events which must happen. It was contended that those losses only were losses by perils of the sea, which were occasioned by extraordinary violence of the winds or waves. I think this is too narrow a construction of the words, and it is certainly not supported by the authorities, or by common understanding. It is beyond question, that if a vessel strikes upon a sunken rock in fair weather and sinks, this is a loss by perils of the sea.

This definition was followed in an affreightment case (*Freedman & Slater v. M. V. Tofevo*, 1963 AMC 1525) when the court quoted the following from the *Giulia* (218 Fed. 744):

> Perils of the sea are understood to mean those perils which are peculiar to the sea and which are of an extraordinary nature, or arise from irresistible force or overwhelming power, and which cannot be guarded against by the ordinary exertions of known skill and prudence

and stated that an important factor in determining if the weather experienced is a sea peril, is the extent of the damage sustained by the vessel. In another case the court, discussing the standard Perils clause in the policy, said:

> "Perils of the seas" insures against wave action, wind action and obstructions which are "fortuitous," as differentiated from ordinary or expected action of the waves or wind. The essence of the concept of "perils of the seas" is that the cause of the danger is outside the vessel, as differentiated from an internal weakness of the vessel. (*Pacific Dredging Co., Inc.* v. *James Hurley*, 1965 AMC 836)

However, the degree of the accidental or unexpected may be very slight, as is indicated in *Whittle* v. *Mountain* (A. C. 1921): when a powerful tug caused waves so high that it forced water into defective seams above the waterline of the houseboat it was towing, the court held that the resultant loss was due to a peril of the sea. In an American decision it was held that where a crane barge, engaged in delicate salvage operations, collapsed due to swells caused by a passing vessel, the swell from the passing vessel was a peril of the sea (*Allen N. Spooner & Son Inc.* v. *Connecticut Fire Ins. Co.*, 1963 AMC 859). In a similar vein, an English court has commented that in interpreting the phrase "perils of the seas" it was immaterial that the weather conditions which caused the damage were not exceptionally bad (the *Miss Jay Jay*, 1985 1 L. R. 264, and 1987 1 L. R. 32).

It has been suggested that the mere incursion of seawater, howsoever brought about, is a loss by a peril of the sea. This may be the law in England, where in *Canada Rice Mills* v. *Union Marine & General Ins. Co. Ltd.* (67 L. L. R. 549) the court stated that where there is an accidental incursion of water at a part of the vessel and in a manner where seawater is not expected, there is prima facie a loss by perils of the sea. However, as the House of Lords pointed out, the burden of proving on a balance of probabilities that a ship is lost by perils of the sea is on the shipowner. If a seaworthy ship sank in unexplained circumstances in good weather and calm seas, the idea that there was a rebuttable presumption that she was lost by perils of the sea was applicable only if it was accepted that the vessel was in a seaworthy condition at the time of the loss (the *Popi M.*, 1985 2 L.R. 1). There is some support in the United States for the theory that the mere incursion of seawater is a loss by perils of the sea. The court in the case of *New York, N. H. & H. R. R.* v. *Gray* (240 F2d 460) stated:

> The loss resulted from a "peril of the seas." It is enough that damage be done by the fortuitous action of the sea. For instance, where cargo was damaged by the incursion of sea-water through a hole in a pipe

gnawed by rats, the House of Lords held this to be a peril of the seas. That the sea is calm makes no difference.

The same court repeated this prior interpretation of perils of the sea with approval in *Allen N. Spooner & Son* v. *Connecticut Fire Ins. Co., supra.*

A similar verdict was reached in *Carter Tug Service* v. *Home Ins. Co.* (1972 AMC 498). In that case a towboat foundered and sank when water entered her engine room through the hull opening, lines, hose, and pump of her port discharge system. This was found to constitute a peril of the waters of the Illinois River, insured against under the perils clause of the tug's hull policy.

The Fifth Circuit Court of Appeals required underwriters to prove affirmatively unseaworthiness as a cause of any sinking in order to defend successfully a suit under the American hull form of policy when the loss being claimed was caused by sinking (*Tropical Marine Prod.* v. *Birmingham Fire Ins. Co.*, 247 F2d 116). More recently the Fifth Circuit reiterated that a seaworthy boat's unexplained sinking was fortuitous and thus presumably caused by an insured peril of the sea (*Darien Bank* v. *The Travelers Indemnity*, 1985 AMC 1813).

These American decisions appear to endorse the English concept of the entry of seawater per se being a peril of the sea. Yet in other cases involving unexplained sinkings, American courts have firmly stated:

> Where a ship sinks in fair weather and calm seas, it is presumed that the loss was due to unseaworthiness (*Federazione Italiana Dei Corsorzi Agrari* v. *Mandas, Compania de Vapores, S.A.*, 1968 AMC 315).
>
> The vessel having sunk for reasons and causes unknown, its unseaworthiness is presumed. (*Martin & Robertson* v. *S. S. Barcelona*, 1968 AMC 331).
>
> When a vessel sinks at a dock in clear weather, a presumption of unseaworthiness arises (*Charles Rosenburg* v. *Maritime Ins. Co. Ltd.*, 1968 AMC 1609).
>
> Sinking in calm water raises a presumption that a vessel was unseaworthy, and the burden is on the assured to prove her seaworthy, or that the cause of the sinking was within the Inchmaree clause (*Capital Coastal Corp. et al.* v. *Hartford Fire Ins. Co.*, 1974 AMC 2039).

For an interesting and erudite discussion of perils of the sea and unexplained sinkings, the reader is directed to *Tulane Law Review*, Vol. XLI, No. 2. The writer therein contends (p. 266) that "the law of England is broader than that of the United States insofar as concerns the obligation of underwriters to respond for a sinking of a vessel insured under a policy containing the customary perils clause without any applicable exclusions." This may well be true and since many American policies give the assured the right to apply either American or English law, it is a theory which may one day be tested. In the meantime it can be concluded that it is probable most American courts would presume unseaworthiness when a vessel sinks in smooth water without apparent cause. On the other hand, if the assured can prove that the vessel was seaworthy immediately before the loss, some American courts have accepted the corollary that the loss must therefore have arisen from a peril of the sea. Against this, other American courts have held that proof of seaworthiness before the loss does not discharge the assured from the obligation of demonstrating a loss by an insured peril (*Tulane Law Review*, p. 269).

In a very early U. S. Supreme Court decision (*Hazard's Admir. v. New England Marine Ins. Co.*, 33 U. S. (8 Pet.) 557), it was asserted that perils of the seas means extraordinary occurrences only, a loss through ordinary circumstances not being insured against. It is submitted that the unexpected and unexplained sinking of a vessel which was seaworthy prior to the loss is surely an "extraordinary occurrence" rather than "a loss through ordinary circumstances."

In 1982 the chairman of the Association of Average Adjusters of the United States, Benjamin W. Yancey, a former President of the Maritime Law Association of the United States dealt with the problem of unexplained sinkings in his address to the Association of Average Adjusters. After examining several cases, Yancey reached the conclusion that the presumption is in favor of seaworthiness but, where a ship springs a leak without having met any peril, this raises a presumption that she was unseaworthy when she sailed. This presumption may in turn be rebutted by proof of actual seaworthiness at the time of sailing. In such a case a jury might reasonably infer that the loss was a fortuitous event of the kind covered by the policy even if it was not possible to ascertain from the evidence the exact and specific cause of the loss. Nevertheless, Yancey emphasized that unseaworthiness per se was not an insured peril and that if a court, after considering all the evidence, became convinced that the sole cause was unseaworthiness, the underwriters would prevail.

In 1984 the Eleventh Circuit Court of Appeals reached a similar conclusion in a case involving the disappearance of a vessel in good weather conditions, the circumstances being such that no proof could be adduced as to the cause of her loss. The court referred to a line of authority known as the "unexplained sinking" cases. In those cases it was decided that, where a vessel sank in calm seas, it would be assumed that the proximate cause of the loss was unseaworthiness. However, where proof was presented that the vessel was in fact in a seaworthy condition when she sailed, a presumption would arise in favor of the insured that the loss was due to a peril of the sea. The court held that similar presumptions to those arising in the "unexplained sinking" cases should be applied in situations of "mysterious sinkings." As the insurers in the case before the court had failed to prove that the vessel was unseaworthy when she sailed and had failed to bring any evidence in rebuttal of the presumption that the loss was due to a peril insured against, the vessel owner was entitled to recover the loss as being due to a peril of the sea (*Insurance Co. of North America* v. *Lanasa Shrimp Co.*, 1984 AMC 2915).

Examples of loss by sea perils are heavy weather, stranding, collision, strikings on rocks or on bottom, contacts with floating objects, and ice damage. It will be noted that fire is specifically mentioned in the policy as a peril insured against. Even if it were not, Phillips is of the opinion that fire would be construed in the policy as a peril of the sea.

Many of the perils enumerated in the Perils clause in the basic marine insurance policy are either obsolete or else are seldom encountered in the enlightened days in which we now live. For the most part these perils are of a warlike nature, and in the American Institute Hull Clauses, as we have seen, they are described in ancient language as follows: "Men-of-War . . . Enemies . . . Letters of Mart and Counter-Mart, Surprisals, Takings at Sea, Arrests, Restraints and Detainments of all Kings, Princes and Peoples, of what nation, condition or quality soever . . . " As Charles McArthur commented:

> The common feature of this group of perils is violence at the hands of man. The underwriter takes upon himself the burden of all loss or damage caused by such acts of violence, whether it consists of injury to the vessel's hull or materials, or of the loss of the property insured. (2d ed., 1890)

In other words, this group of perils is associated with the seizure of the insured vessel by external force or threat thereof in the context of "Arrests, Restraints and Detainment of all Kings, Princes and Peoples." Surprisals and Takings at Sea" are merely another way of expressing seizure or capture; however, the peril does not extend to a dishonest taking by a shipowner (the *Salem*, 2 A.C. (1983) 375).

The peril "Restraints and Detainments of all Kings, Princes and Peoples" was considered in an arbitration in London before Mr. Justice Staughton. The vessel in question (the *Bamburi*) had been trapped in the Persian Gulf following the outbreak of war between Iraq and Iran in 1980. The authorities in Iraq informed the master that all movements of merchant shipping had been prohibited and the owners of the *Bamburi* had tendered notice of abandonment to underwriters. In his award, Mr. Justice Staughton declared that the *Bamburi* was a constructive total loss by the peril "Restraints and Detainments of all Kings, Princes and Peoples" at the time notice of abandonment was given (the *Bamburi, 1982* 1 L. R. 312).

However, the War, Strikes, and Related Exclusions clause (formerly the Free of Capture and Seizure (F.C.&S.) clause) in the policy excludes such coverage from the marine policy. This clause reads as follows:

WAR, STRIKES AND RELATED EXCLUSIONS

The following conditions shall be paramount and shall supersede and nullify any contrary provisions of the Policy. This Policy does not cover any loss, damage or expense caused by, resulting from, or incurred as a consequence of:

(a) Capture, seizure, arrest, restraint or detainment, or any attempt thereat; or

(b) Any taking of the Vessel, by requisition or otherwise, whether in time of peace or war and whether lawful or otherwise; or

(c) Any mine, bomb or torpedo not carried as cargo on board the Vessel; or

(d) Any weapon of war employing atomic or nuclear fission and/or fusion or other like reaction or radioactive force or matter; or

(e) Civil war, revolution, rebellion, insurrection, or civil strife resulting therefrom, or piracy; or

(f) Strikes, lockouts, political or labor disturbances, civil commotions, riots, martial law, military or usurped power; or

(g) Malicious acts or vandalism, unless committed by the Master or Mariners and not excluded elsewhere under this War Strikes and Related Exclusions clause; or

(h) Hostilities or warlike operations (whether there be a declaration of war or not) but this subparagraph (h) not to exclude collision or contact with aircraft, rockets or similar missiles, or with any fixed or floating object, or stranding, heavy weather, fire or explosion unless caused directly by a hostile act by or against a belligerent power which act is independent of the nature of the voyage or service which the Vessel concerned or, in the case of a collision, any other vessel involved therein, is performing. As used herein, "power" includes any authority maintaining, naval, military or air forces in association with a power.

If war risks or other risks excluded by this clause are hereafter insured by endorsement on this Policy, such endorsement shall supersede the above conditions only to the extent that the terms of such endorsement are inconsistent therewith and only while such endorsement remains in force.

To ensure a comprehensive exclusion of war-related risks, additional exclusions of other types of war risks are enumerated such as "any mine, bomb or torpedo not carried as cargo on board the vessel" and "malicious acts or vandalism." It will be noted that in this latest (1977) version of the American Institute Hull Clauses it is made clear that barratry, even of a malicious nature, continues to be covered by the marine policy. This is achieved by qualifying the exclusion of "malicious acts or vandalism" by the words "unless committed by the Master or Mariners."

One of the objects of the War, Strikes, and Related Exclusions clause is to exclude from the marine coverage all damage which is intentionally done. Thus the marine policy is only to provide coverage against accidental or fortuitous risks.

It should be mentioned that in the United Kingdom, the F.C.&S. clause does not apply to liabilities assumed by an underwriter under the Collision clause. The Collision clause is deemed to be a separate contract and its interpretation is not affected by the F.C.&S. clause even in cases where the collision itself is deemed to be a war casualty.

In the United States, the reverse was held to be true in the case of the *John Worthington* (1949 AMC 254). However, this decision was appealed and on a question of fact unrelated to the Collision clause, the decision of the district court was reversed by the court of appeals and the latter court was upheld by the Supreme Court (1951 AMC 1). The circumstances of this case were such that it is difficult to be categorical as to whether or not, under American law, the F.C.&S. clause (or its successor) excludes the Collision clause when the collision is a consequence of warlike operations. It seems that, since underwriters' liability under the Collision clause in a hull policy can only arise because of negligent navigation, there is no apparent reason why the Collision clause should be affected by the F.C.&S. clause or, to give it its new name, the War, Strikes, and Related Exclusions clause.

There can be little doubt that enhanced marine risks due to a state of war were originally intended to be covered by the war policy, but the English courts have never taken this view. They have said that to increase marine risks is not to convert them into war risks. Thus, enhanced marine risks, due to sailing in convoy, blackout of lights, zigzagging to avoid submarines, extinction or dimming of lighthouses, and removal of buoys, were not converted into war risks. The courts did, however, find that if a merchant ship was carrying war stores to or from a war base, she must be regarded as if she were a warship, and if that vessel was in collision with a peaceful merchant ship, the resultant loss would be due to a war risk unless solely caused by the fault of the peaceful merchant ship. (The term used to describe a merchant-warship was "quasi-warship.") In the spate of litigation which followed World War I there was a tendency to consider doubtful casualties as being due to war risks. When World War II broke out, this trend culminated in the *Coxwold* decision (A. C. 691, 73 L. L. R. 1 (1942)). In that case a government-requisitioned merchant vessel (quasi-warship) stranded while she was engaged in warlike service. To the consternation of the marine insurance market, the courts ultimately held that the stranding damage was recoverable as a war risk because of the nature of the service in which the vessel was engaged ("a warlike operation"). As a result of this decision, the British marine insurance market amended the F.C.&S. clause drastically, eliminating completely the doctrine of the quasi-warship and switching back to the marine policy those risks which would have been covered thereunder had the vessel not been engaged on a so-called warlike operation. The British F.C.&S. clause introduced during World War II differs very little from the clause presently in use, although the amendment was not adopted in the United States until after the war. In fact, the new F.C.&S. clause adopted by the British was more in keeping with American opinion, which was to attempt to draw a realistic line between war-occasioned perils and losses which would have been equally probable under peacetime conditions. Even without the amendment, the American courts, in fact, held losses to be war risks only when resulting from traditional war perils and have not followed the English cases in treating even collision with a warship as necessarily being a consequence of hostilities or warlike operations. While there can be no doubt that the wording of the current F.C.&S. clause makes the division between war and marine perils less nebulous, causation will always require careful consideration. A yardstick which is often quoted with approval is the case of a vessel entering a port with two channels, one of which has been mined by the enemy and the other left free. If she entered by the one and was blown up by a mine, the loss is due to a war risk; but if, in order to avoid that channel, she used the other and by unskillful navigation ran ashore, it would be a marine loss. The difficulties often encountered in wartime in determining whether a loss falls on the marine policy or on the war risks policy were dealt with by the chairman of the American Association of Average Adjusters, John A. Hickey, in his illuminating address to the association in 1988. This address gives the history of the division of coverage between the marine and war risk policies and of the development of the F.C.&S. clause since it was first introduced in 1889.

The American Institute Hull War Risks and Strikes clauses (*see* Appendix A) which are drawn up for attachment to the American Institute Hull Clauses are used to insure the war and other risks excluded from the marine policy by the War, Strikes, and Related Exclusions clause. The War Risks and Strikes clauses state that the risks covered are those which the

American Institute Hull Clauses would cover but for the operation of the War, Strikes, and Related Exclusions clauses. The War Risks clauses then detail some (but not all) of the war risks covered. Thus the war risk policy automatically covers "capture," "seizure," "arrest," "restraint," "detainment," and any taking of the vessel even though these perils are not individually repeated as insured perils. Actually the War Risks clauses incorporate additional risks to those excluded from the marine policy, as will be seen from the following extract:

(1) Any mine, bomb or torpedo not carried on board the Vessel;

(2) Any weapon of war employing atomic or nuclear fission and/or fusion or other like reaction or radioactive force or matter;

(3) Civil war, revolution, rebellion, insurrection, or civil strife arising therefrom;

(4) Strikes, lockouts, political or labor disturbances, civil commotions, riots, martial law, military or usurped power;

(5) Malicious acts or vandalism to the extent only that such risks are not covered by the attached Policy;

(6) Hostilities or warlike operations (whether there be a declaration of war or not) but this paragraph (6) shall not include collision or contact with aircraft, rockets or similar missiles, or with any fixed or floating object, or stranding, heavy weather, fire or explosion unless caused directly by a hostile act by or against a belligerent power which act is independent of the nature of the voyage or service which the Vessel concerned or, in the case of a collision, any other vessel involved therein, is performing. As used herein, "power" includes any authority maintaining naval, military or air forces in association with a power.

To conform with the marine form to which the war clauses are designed to be attached, the coverage of "malicious acts or vandalism" is qualified by the words "to the extent only that such risks are not covered by the attached policy." Thus barratry, even if malicious in intent, continues to be covered by the marine policy. In fact, the English courts have said that the peril of persons acting maliciously was obviously intended to deal with damage sustained in the course of some civil disturbance (the *Salem*, 2 A.C. (1983) 375).

However, there are certain general limitations which *exclude* any loss, damage or expense caused by, resulting from, or incurred as a consequence of:

(a) Any hostile detonation of any weapon of war described above in paragraph (2);

(b) Outbreak of war (whether there be a declaration of war or not) between any of the following countries: United States of America, United Kingdom, France, the Union of Soviet Socialist Republics, or the People's Republic of China;

(c) Delay or demurrage;

(d) Requisition or preemption;

(e) Arrest, restraint or detainment under customs or quarantine regulations and similar arrests, restraints, or detainments not arising from actual or impending hostilities;

(f) Capture, seizure, arrest, restraint, detainment, or confiscation by the government of the United States or of the country in which the vessel is owned or registered.

One of the exclusions, "requisition," has been defined as the formal taking of a vessel by a government against whom the owner would have a claim for payment (*Santo Domingo*, 1970 AMC 1678). However, any requisition by a power other than the government of the United States or of the country in which the insured vessel is owned or registered would more properly fall into the category of "seizure" which is, of course, one of the perils excluded from the marine policy by the War, Strikes, and Related Exclusions clause and therefore automatically covered under the war risk policy.

The exclusion of delay or demurrage is not intended to apply to detention of a general average nature.

The automatic termination clause which is included in all commercial war risk coverage stipulates that the insurance is to be terminated on (1) the occurrence of any hostile detonation of any nuclear weapon of war, or (2) the outbreak of war between any of the five Great Powers: Great Britain plus the British Commonwealth of Nations), the United States of America, the U.S.S.R., France, and Communist China. The word "between" is important in that it implies that the war risk policies remain in force in the event any one of the aforementioned nations becomes involved in hostilities without being opposed by any of the other four. War risk insurance is provided by the U.S. government to cover American shipowners and shipbuilders from the time commercial war risk insurance ceases to provide adequate coverage, until 30 days after the outbreak of war involving the major powers. War risk binders attach automatically and simultaneously with the time the commercial war risk insurance terminates.

The War Risks clauses also require condemnation before the vessel can be abandoned after capture, seizure, or detention. This is intended to prevent abandonment as a constructive total loss unless there is condemnation, presumably as a prize of war. Under modern conditions many countries have no prize courts and, consequently, it is doubtful whether such countries would ever issue any formal decree of condemnation. It would thus appear that under this warranty underwriters are not liable for a constructive total loss until it is apparent that there is no likelihood of the assured recovering his vessel in the foreseeable future. Indeed, the opinion has been expressed that while efforts to obtain the return of seized property are continuing, the assured cannot claim for a constructive total loss because of the aforementioned warranty. In short, according to this opinion, a vessel either becomes an actual total loss (by never being returned) or else the owner receives it back (see *Tulane Law Review*, Feb. 1967, p. 312). No doubt the object of the warranty is to prevent an assured claiming a constructive total loss immediately when the insured vessel is seized. On the other hand, if the assured is deprived of his vessel for a considerable time, it is doubtful whether underwriters would seek to take advantage of the fact that the property had not been formally condemned and thus deny liability for the loss.

The term "arrests, etc. of kings, princes and people" refers to political or executive acts and does not include a loss caused by riot or by ordinary judicial processes (Marine Ins. Act, Rules for Construction of Policy, No. 10).

A similar method of excluding war risks coverage from the marine policy is followed in cargo insurance. A typical clause in an open cargo policy would read as follows:

The following Warranties shall be paramount and shall not be modified or superseded by any other provision included herein or stamped or endorsed hereon unless such other provision refers specifically to the risks excluded by these Warranties and expressly assumes the said risks:—

(a) Notwithstanding anything herein contained to the contrary, this insurance is warranted free from capture, seizure, arrest, restraint, detainment, confiscation, preemption, requisition or nationalization, and the consequences thereof or any attempt thereat, whether in time of peace or war and whether lawful or otherwise; also warranted free, whether in time of peace or war, from all loss, damage or expense caused by any weapon of war employing atomic or nuclear fission and/or fusion or other reaction or radioactive force or matter or by any mine or torpedo, also warranted free from all consequences of hostilities or warlike operations (whether there be a declaration of war or not), but this warranty shall not exclude collision or contact with aircraft, rockets or similar missiles or with any fixed or floating object (other than a mine or torpedo), stranding, heavy weather, fire or explosion unless caused directly (and independently of the nature of the voyage or service which the vessel concerned or, in the case of a collision, any other vessel involved therein, is performing) by a hostile act by or against a belligerent power; and for the purposes of this warranty "power" includes any authority maintaining naval, military or air forces in association with a power.

Further warranted free from the consequences of civil war, revolution, rebellion, insurrection, or civil strife arising therefrom, or piracy.

(b) Warranted free of loss or damage caused by or resulting from union strikes, lockouts, labor disturbances, riots, civil commotions or the acts of any person or persons taking part in any such occurrence or disorder.

If strike risk cover is required, it is provided by attaching an S.R.&C.C. (Strikes, Riots, and Civil Commotions) endorsement which might read as follows:

This insurance also covers damage, theft, pilferage, breakage or destruction of the property insured directly caused by strikers, locked-out workmen, or persons taking part in labor disturbances or riots or civil commotions and destruction of or damage to the property directly caused by persons acting maliciously.

While the property insured is at risk under the terms and conditions of this insurance *within the United States of America, the Commonwealth of Puerto Rico, the Canal Zone, the Virgin Islands and Canada*, this insurance is extended to cover damage, theft, pilferage, breakage or destruction of the property insured directly caused by "Vandalism," "Sabotage" and "Malicious Mischief," and as so extended shall include such losses directly caused by acts committed by an agent of any government, party or faction engaged in war, hostilities or other warlike operations, provided such agent is acting secretly and not in connection with any operation of military or naval armed forces in the country where the described property is situated.

Nothing in this endorsement shall be construed to include or cover any loss, damage, deterioration or expense caused by or resulting from:

(a) change in temperature or humidity

(b) the absence, shortage, or withholding of power, fuel, or labor of any description whatsoever during any strike, lockout, labor disturbance, riot or civil commotion

(c) delay or loss of market

(d) hostilities, warlike operations, civil war, revolution, rebellion or insurrection, or civil strife arising therefrom, excepting only the acts of certain agents expressly covered above

(e) any weapon of war employing atomic or nuclear fission and/or fusion or other reaction or radioactive force or matter.

The Assured agrees to report all shipments attaching under this cover and to pay premiums therefor at the rates established by the Company from time to time.

This endorsement may be cancelled by either party upon forty-eight hours written or telegraphic notice to the other party, but such cancellation; shall not affect any risks which have already attached hereunder.

If full war risks coverage is required in insurances on cargo, a separate policy is issued, the Perils clause of which would read:

This insurance is only against the risks of capture, seizure, destruction or damage by men-of-war, piracy, takings at sea, arrests, restraints, detainments and other warlike operations and acts of kings, princes and peoples in prosecution of hostilities or in the application of sanctions under international agreements, whether before or after declaration of war and whether by a belligerent or otherwise, including factions engaged in civil war, revolution, rebellion or insurrection, or civil strife arising therefrom; and including the risks of aerial bombardment, floating or stationary mines and stray or derelict torpedoes, and weapons of war employing atomic or nuclear fission and/or fusion or other reaction or radioactive force or matter but excluding loss, damage or expense arising out of the hostile use of any such weapon; and warranted not to abandon (on any ground other than physical damage to ship or cargo) until after condemnation of the property insured.

Generally speaking, the war risks policy on cargo follows the marine open cargo policy in the description of the cargo, etc. Apart from the fact that the policy covers war risks and not marine risks, an important difference is that the war risks policy basically covers cargo during the sea passage; there is no warehouse to warehouse type of coverage. It also includes a "frustration" clause warranting that the policy is free from any claim based solely upon loss of, or frustration of, the insured voyage or adventure caused by arrests, restraints, or detainments. In other words, there must be physical loss or damage to the the cargo to justify a claim under the policy. The policy does not cover loss caused by "commandeering, preemption, requisition or nationalization by the government (defacto or otherwise) of the country to or from which the goods are insured."

The term "pirates" or "piracy" included in the Perils clause presents some difficulty in our modern times. Article 15 of the Geneva Convention on the High Seas (1958) defines piracy as:

> Any illegal acts of violence, detention or any act of depredation, committed for private ends by the crew or the passengers of a private ship . . . and directed:
>
>   (a) On the high seas, against another ship . . . or against persons or property on board such ship . . .
>
>   (b) Against a ship . . . persons or property in a place outside the jurisdiction of any State.

Under this definition acts committed on board a ship by the crew or passengers and directed against the ship itself, or against persons or property on the ship, cannot be regarded as acts of piracy. Even where the mutineers' purpose is to seize the ship, their acts under this definition do not constitute acts of piracy. However, piracy under a marine insurance policy may also be governed by the municipal laws of a particular state. Thus, for marine insurance purposes, the term "pirates" or "piracy" included in the Perils clause includes passengers who mutiny and rioters who attack the ship from the shore (Marine Ins. Act, Rules for Construction of Policy, No. 8). In terms of marine insurance, piracy is usually restricted to acts committed on the high seas which are limited to the open waters of the sea as distinguished from the waters of ports, harbors, and bays. However, in a recent case an English court saw no reason to limit piracy to acts outside territorial waters. For the purposes of an insurance policy, it was sufficient if a ship could be said to be "at sea" or if the attack upon her could be said to be a "maritime offence." In any event, theft without force was not piracy under a policy of marine insurance (the *Andreas Lemos,* 1982 2 L.R. 483).

The definition of piracy is important because it will have been seen that the risk of piracy is removed from the marine policy by the War, Strikes, and Related Exclusions clause and therefore has become a war peril. The difference, therefore, between pirates and assailing thieves (*q.v.*) can be crucial in cases involving the hijacking of small craft. The subject is dealt with exhaustively by Lawrence C. Delay in the *Maritime Lawyer,* Vol. IV, No. 2 (1979). It should be noted that when the London market introduced new Institute War Risks clauses in 1983 specifically detailing all the war perils covered, the risk of piracy was switched back to the marine policy although at the time of writing it remains a war risk in the United States (absent any specific endorsement to the contrary). This is a rare example of divergence from the uniformity which generally exists between the American and British marine insurance markets.

Another of the perils which is seldom encountered these days is that of barratry. This is defined by Phillips as:

> Unlawful, fraudulent, or dishonest act of the master, mariners, or other carriers, or of gross misconduct, or very gross and culpable negligence, contrary in either case, to their duty to the owner, and that might be prejudicial to him or to others interested in the voyage or adventure. (Subsect. 1062)

According to the Marine Insurance Act, barratry includes every wrongful act wilfully committed by the master or crew, to the prejudice of the owner, or, as the case may be, the charterers (Rules for Construction of Policy, No. 11). This definition is accepted in the United States. Thus, as the House of Lords has reminded us, where the shipowner is privy to what would otherwise have been the barratrous acts of the master and crew there can be no loss by barratry; barratry can only be committed against an innocent shipowner (the *Salem,* 2 A.C. (1983) 375).

To constitute barratry, the act has to be more than mere negligence—it must be an action of criminal intent. All the definitions and cases up to 1870 are reviewed in *Atkinson* v. *Great Western Ins. Co.* (Asp. Mar. Cas. N. S. 382). A much more recent case involving barratry was that of *National Union Fire Ins. Co.* v. *The Republic of China, et al.* (1958 AMC 751). In that case, several vessels were lost by the defection of their crew. The court rejected the contention that masters and mariners who change sides in a civil war and take their ships with them cannot be considered to have committed barratry. The court endorsed the definition of barratry given in the English Marine Insurance Act, adding that the characterization of an act as barratrous is independent of the motives which provoked the act, and quoting *Earle* v. *Rowcroft,* 8 East 126:

> It can make no difference . . . whether the prejudice (the owner) suffers be owing to an act of the master, induced by motives of advantage to himself, malice to the owner, or a disregard to those laws which it was the master's duty to obey, and which (or it would not be barratry) his owners relied upon his observing.

In an even more recent case, a vessel was deliberately scuttled by a crew member. The English court held that since this was done without any consent or foreknowledge on the part of the assured, the claim for a loss by barratry succeeded *(Permay Shipping Co.* v. *Chester,* 1979 L. L. R., Vol. 1, Pt. 1). Similarly, a master's deliberate act in sailing his vessel beyond the hull policy's navigational limits, contrary to shipowner's orders, constitutes barratry (*Daniel Whorton* v. *Home Insurance Co.,* 1984 AMC 937). In the same vein the Eleventh Circuit Court of Appeals decided that barratry includes deliberate and wilful disobedience by a vessel's master or seamen of the shipowner's oral or written instructions. Where the insured vessel stranded and burned after her master had taken her beyond the 150-mile offshore geographic limit included in the hull policy without her owner's knowledge or consent, the insurer is liable for the loss since barratry, grounding, and fire were all perils covered by the policy. However there was a dissent in this case on the grounds that the stranding (not the barratry) was the proximate cause of the vessel's loss and the policy specifically did not cover losses occurring beyond the geographic limits expressly warranted by the assured shipowner (*U.S. Fire Insurance Co.* v. *Cavanaugh,* 1985 AMC 1001). A few years earlier it had been decided by the Fourth Circuit Court of Appeals that barratry had been committed when a crew member (in charge of the insured vessel) took the vessel beyond the navigational limit imposed in the policy. The vessel was under charter and the court expressed the view that, even if the charterer had participated in the wrongful act, as long as the real owner was not a party to the barratrous act, there was barratry (*Nautilus Virgin Charters* v. *Edinburgh Ins. Co.,* 1981 AMC 2082, *aff'd.* 1982 AMC 696). In that case, however, it was held that where crew members' conduct resulted in the yacht being seized by a foreign government the loss of the vessel was proximately caused by the yacht's seizure and not by the prior barratrous acts, so owners were not entitled to recover under a policy excluding loss by seizure. It will not have escaped the reader's attention that the difficult principle of proximate cause played an important role in the decisions reached in these cases. Proximate cause is dealt with hereinafter.

As stated earlier, under the latest (1977) wording of the American Institute Hull Clauses it is made plain that barratry remains a marine peril in spite of the exclusion of "malicious acts or vandalism" from the marine policy. This is achieved by qualifying the exclusion with the words "unless committed by the Master or mariners."

The term "assailing thieves" in the Perils clause implies theft accompanied by violence and does not include clandestine theft. If coverage of pilferage is required, it must be expressly mentioned in the policy. But for the use of the adjective "assailing," the word "thieves" under American law would cover larceny or theft committed by passengers or members of the crew. Actually the adjective "assailing" was added to American policies following the decision in the case of *Atlantic Ins. Co.* v. *Storrow* (5 Paige 285, N. Y. Ch. 1835), which held that "furtive theft not accompanied by violence was a covered peril." The holding in *Storrow* broke with existing precedents emanating from early English decisions which had held, under policies insuring against "all fortuitous events," that theft accompanied by violence from without the vessel was a fortuitous event, while furtive theft was a matter within the control of the vessel owner. The term "assailing" was added to American policies following the *Storrow* decision in order to re-establish the element of fortuitousness to the theft peril.

In *Felicione & Sons* v. *Citizens Cas. Co. of N. Y.* (430 F2d 136, 1970) the court reached the surprising conclusion that the peril of "assailing thieves" was limited to theft of property or equipment on vessels taken by force and did not contemplate theft of the entire vessel. The decision was based on the "paucity of authority" involving the theft of an entire vessel. But surely this paucity of authority merely demonstrates that it is so generally understood that the term contemplates theft of entire vessels that it has been unnecessary to litigate the point. This court's proposition is entirely contrary to the understanding and practice of the marine insurance profession. Indeed, it is illogical that one peril (assailing thieves) should be singled out as being limited to partial losses only. Certainly no sophisticated marine underwriter would seek to limit the peril of assailing thieves to property on board the insured vessel and deny that it also applied to the vessel itself. It is true that insurances on small craft often emphasize the coverage by specifying "theft of the entire yacht" per se as an insured peril. However, this is only because such vessels (for example, motorboats) can often be stolen without any force or violence at all. The Supreme Court of New York subsequently found that the peril of assailing thieves did cover the theft of an entire vessel when there was evidence of a forcible taking (*Aqua Craft* v. *Boston Old Colony Insurance Co.,* 1987 AMC 1943). The court specifically disagreed with *Felicione* (*supra*) on the subject of assailing thieves referring to that court's remarks as a "gratuitous dictum."

An arbitration in New York arising out of the theft of a moored carfloat is of interest and was reprinted in the *Bulletin of the Association of Average Adjusters of the United States* (No. 4, 1987). The arbitrator, R. M. Hicks, Jr. (a former chairman of the association) also criticized the *Felcione* case (*supra*). He found that a carfloat moored alongside a pier and subsequently found to be missing (her mooring lines having been forcibly removed) must be assumed to have been taken by assailing thieves (a peril covered by the policy). Simply put, the mysterious disappearance of an insured vessel is covered by the peril of assailing thieves when the circumstances are such that a theft can reasonably be assumed.

The precise meaning and scope of the words "all other like Perils, Losses and Misfortunes" in the Perils clause is difficult to define, but Rule for Construction of Policy, No. 12, states that the term "all other perils" includes only perils similar in kind to the perils specifically mentioned in the policy. In a recent English case (*Nashima Trading Co. Ltd.* v. *Chiyoda Fire & Marine Ins. Co. Ltd.,* L. L. R. 1968, Vol. 2, p. 52), the court quoted an amusing passage from an older case (*Cory* v. *Burr*) in which it was recalled that the bat in the fable had said: "I am not a bird, look at my ears; I am not a beast, look at my wings." It had then been suggested that a loss by bats would be covered under a policy which insured against loss by birds, beasts, and all other perils, losses, and misfortunes. In an American case (*Feinberg* v. *Ins. Co. of North America*, 260 F2d 52), the court commented:

> We see no difficulty in giving some meaning to the "all other like perils" clause quoted above. It does not, of course, cover perils unlike those enumerated. But it does cover similar perils, or else it means nothing. We think the clause must have been included in the policy to serve a purpose and that its obvious purpose was to include in the coverage all losses which, although perhaps not technically or strictly speaking covered in the specific perils enumerated, are losses very similar to or very much like the enumerated perils. (See *Tulane Law Review*, Vol. XLI, pp. 270-273 for an interesting discussion of this matter.)

It seems clear that the phrase "all other perils" was included in the policy to cover losses similar to those specifically enumerated. As Mullins succinctly comments: "It permits the specified perils to be taken in a broad sense but does not add any new causes of loss" (*Marine Insurance Digest*, 1959, p. 11).

While many of the perils enumerated in the traditional Perils clause quoted above may be no longer operative, the basic coverage originally afforded vessel owners has been greatly extended by the addition to the policy of the Latent Defect, Negligence, and Additional Perils clause. This clause is more widely known as the Inchmaree clause, so named after a famous case that gave rise to the necessity for certain of its provisions. The clause reads as follows:

ADDITIONAL PERILS (INCHMAREE)
Subject to the conditions of this Policy, this insurance also covers loss of or damage to the Vessel directly caused by the following:
Accidents in loading, discharging or handling cargo, or in bunkering;
    Accidents in going on or off, or while on drydocks, graving docks, ways, gridirons or pontoons;
Explosions on shipboard or elsewhere;
Breakdown of motor generators or other electrical machinery and electrical connections thereto, bursting of boilers, breakage of shafts, or any latent defect in the machinery or hull (excluding the cost and expense of replacing or repairing the defective part);
Breakdown of or accidents to nuclear installations or reactors not on board the insured Vessel;
Contact with aircraft, rockets or similar missiles, or with any land conveyance;

> Negligence of Charterers and/or Repairers, provided such Charterers
> and/or Repairers are not an Assured hereunder;
> Negligence of Masters, Officers, Crew or Pilots;
>
> provided such loss or damage has not resulted from want of due dili-
> gence by the Assured, the Owners or Managers of the Vessel, or any
> of them. Masters, Officers, Crew or Pilots are not to be considered
> Owners within the meaning of this clause should they hold shares in
> the Vessel.

It will be seen that the Inchmaree clause introduces several additional
perils into the policy, one of the most important being negligence of crew.
The interpretation of this clause in stating claims under the policy is dealt
with in Chapter 5.

The Perils clause in cargo policies follows that of the hull policy and
reads as follows:

> Touching the adventures and perils which this Company is contented
> to bear, and take upon itself, they are of the seas, fires, assailing
> thieves, jettisons, barratry of the Master and Mariners, and all other
> like perils, losses and misfortunes that have or shall come to the hurt,
> detriment or damage of the said goods and merchandise, or any part
> thereof except as may be otherwise provided for herein or endorsed
> hereon.

These basic insured perils are augmented by the Inchmaree, Shore,
and Explosion clauses.

The abbreviated Inchmaree clause included in American cargo policies reads:

> This insurance is also specially to cover any loss of or damage to the
> interest insured hereunder, through the bursting of boilers, breakage
> of shafts or through any latent defect in the machinery, hull or appur-
> tenances, or from faults or errors in the navigation and/or manage-
> ment of the vessel by the master, mariners, mates, engineers or pilots.

This inclusion of the Inchmaree (or additional perils) clause in a cargo
policy is unique to the American market. The intent is, of course, to provide
additional coverage. In practice, it is questionable whether the additional
perils named in what is essentially a hull clause add any coverage to cargo.
If any of the Inchmaree perils operated, any resultant loss of or damage to
cargo would probably be of a type which would be already covered by the
other insured perils enumerated in the cargo policy. Furthermore, while the
standard hull policy Inchmaree clause insures against negligence of the
crew without limitation, the Inchmaree clause used in cargo insurances

limits such coverage to loss resulting from acts of negligence for which recovery from the carrier cannot be had under the Harter Act or the Carriage of Goods by Sea Act and as to which the shipper otherwise would be without indemnity. Thus, the phrase "navigation or management of the vessel" excludes acts of negligence in the care of cargo (*Larsen* v. *In. Co. of North America*, 1965 AMC 2576). In short, the Inchmaree clause in a cargo policy only covers losses attributable to causes for which the carrier is exempt from liability under the terms of the contract of affreightment (*Shaver Transportation Co. and Weyerhauser Co.* v. *Travelers Indemnity*, 1980 AMC 393). As a matter of interest, the standard cargo clauses issued by the British market do not contain an Inchmaree clause.

The Explosion clause in cargo policies reads as follows:

> Including the risk of explosion, howsoever or wheresoever occurring during the currency of this insurance, unless excluded by the F.C.&S. Warranty or the S.R.&C.C. Warranty set forth herein.

This clause is also unique to American cargo policies and was introduced to provide cover against the risk of explosion wheresoever and howsoever caused other than by a war peril. It has no counterpart in the British market, presumably because it is considered that explosion damage would usually fall on the war policy or that any consequential damage to cargo resulting from an explosion would be already covered by the basic perils named in the policy under the *ejusdem generis* rule. However, to put the coverage for explosion beyond doubt the London Institute F.P.A. and W.A. cargo clauses were amended in 1944 to specifically include any loss of or damage to the interest insured which could reasonably be attributed to (but which might not necessarily have been directly caused by) explosion. In other words, proximate cause is ignored and all damage attributable to explosion is covered. The coverage is thus similar to that achieved in American cargo policies by the Explosion clause.

The Shore clause in cargo policies reads as follows:

> Where this insurance by its terms covers while on docks, wharves or elsewhere on shore, and/or during land transportation, it shall include the risks of collision, derailment, overturning or other accident to the conveyance, fire, lightning, sprinkler leakage, cyclones, hurricanes, earthquakes, floods (meaning the rising of navigable waters), and/or collapse or subsidence of docks or wharves; even though the insurance be otherwise F.P.A.

This clause was added to the policy to set forth the risks which are covered while goods are on shore or during land transportation; in other words, the clause provides coverage for the basic perils of shore transportation and storage during the extra period covered by the Warehouse to Warehouse clause.

In insurances on cargo, the perils covered are often augmented. Hazards often specifically provided for include theft, pilferage, non-delivery, freshwater damage, oil damage, sweat damage, contact with other cargo, breakage, leakage, hook hole damage, and damage to refrigerated cargo resulting from the breakdown of refrigerating machinery. Very often coverage is provided for on the so-called "all risks" basis. This type of clause reads:

> To cover against all risks of physical loss or damage from any external cause irrespective of percentage, but excluding, nevertheless, the risks of war, strikes, riots, seizure, detention, and other risks excluded by the F.C.&S. Warranty and the S.R.&C.C. (Strikes, Riots and Civil Commotion)Warranty in this policy, excepting to the extent that such risks are specifically covered by endorsement.

The "all risks" coverage is not so comprehensive as it might appear to be. The emphasis is placed on the word "risk" and underwriters are not liable unless there is some fortuitous accident or casualty resulting in damage attributable to any external cause. However, under "all risks" coverage, it is not necessary to prove the exact nature of the accident. The assured is merely required to show that the shipment, at the time the insurance attached, was in good order and condition and on outturn was damaged. This is a prima facie case. The burden then shifts to the underwriter to come forward with evidence to prove a condition excluded by the insurance (*Welded Tube Co.* v. *Hartford Fire Ins. Co.*, 1973 AMC 555). Needless to say, claims for loss, damage, or expense proximately caused by delay or inherent vice are not recoverable even under an "all risks" policy. It is the intention only to cover fortuitous happenings.

Theft and pilferage of cargo are covered by an "all risks" policy on the grounds that such losses are fortuitous as far as the assured is concerned. Similarly, a loss occasioned by unlawful detention or conversion of goods by a person who has no contractual relationship with the assured (cargo owner) is a fortuitous loss and within the coverage of an "all risks" policy. Indeed in England the conversion of goods by the ship's master (acting on behalf of the shipowner) was held to be covered by the peril "takings at sea" in a named perils policy. (*Nishima Trading Co. Ltd.* v. *Chiyoda Fire & Marine Insurance Co. Ltd.* [the *Mandarin Star*], C.A. 1969 1 L.R. 293). However, this decision was overruled by the House of Lords in 1983 when considering another case involving the theft (or conversion) of a bulk cargo as a result of a shipowner wrongfully misappropriating the cargo. Their lordships said that prior to the decision of the court of appeals in the *Mandarin Star* it had been the established law of England that the peril "takings at sea" was synonomous with "seizure" or "capture" and that the decision in the *Mandarin Star* to the effect that it included the risk of a shipowner wrongly misappropriating the goods (that is, conversion or theft) was wrong. Their lordships ruled that the basic Perils clause in Lloyd's S.G. policy did not cover wrongful misappropriation of a cargo by a shipowner nor could such a loss be attributable to either "takings at sea" (the *Mandarin Star* not followed) or barratry. The cargo owner could have taken out an "all risks" policy (which would have covered conversion or theft) or insisted on a specific extension to cover theft but did not (*Shell International Petroleum Co. Ltd.* v. *Gibbs* [the *Salem*], 2 A.C. (1983) 375).

In an "all risks" insurance on containers it has been held that an insurer is liable for the loss of the insured containers due to "mysterious disappearance," a cause not exempted under the policy (an "all risks" marine insurance policy protects against risks which are not expressly excluded) (*Northwestern National Insurance Co.* v. *Chandler Leasing Corp.*, 1982 AMC 1631). In a previous case in another circuit, the court of appeals had reached a similar conclusion, saying that the court could not believe that the average assured would not equate a mysterious disappearance with a fortuitous loss and would not believe that this was not a risk or hazard against which he has insured when he purchased "all risks" insurance (*Atlantic Lines* v. *American Motorists Insurance Co.*, 1976 AMC 2522).

PROXIMATE CAUSE

Under a policy of marine insurance, the risk undertaken by an underwriter is that if the subject-matter insured is lost or damaged as a result of the operation of an insured peril, he will be responsible. The fact that the loss or damage is remotely caused by an uninsured peril is irrelevant, as the English courts established in two very old cases:

> It is only necessary to see whether the loss comes within the terms of the contract and is caused by perils of the sea; the fact that the loss is partly caused by things not distinctly perils of the sea does not prevent it from coming within the contract. (*Grill* v. *General Iron Screw Collier Co.*, L. R. 1 C.P. 600) and
>
> We must look only to the immediate and proximate cause; it seems to me impracticable to go back ultimately to the birth of a person, for if he had never been born, the accident would not have happened. (*Lawrence* v. *Accidental Insurance Co., Ltd.*, 1881)

Thus, before the introduction of the Inchmaree clause, the hull policy responded for loss or damage caused by stranding, fire, or collision, even though the operation of those perils may have been brought about by negligence on the part of the crew. At that time the basic policy did not, of course, insure against negligence of the crew per se.

Many years ago a distinguished American attorney (D. Roger Englar) expressed the view that much of the discussion of proximate cause was misleading. The marine insurance policy insured not against causes, but against results. When one of the results insured against occurred, the cause of it was immaterial unless expressly excepted in the policy. The ordinary cargo policy did not insure against the negligence of the crew but it did insure against the accepted marine perils such as stranding, fire, collision, and jettison. When one of those events had occurred, the underwriters were liable for the damage, even if caused by the negligence of the crew; they were not liable because of any doctrine of proximate cause peculiar to marine insurance, but because the policy insured against the particular thing which had happened, and the cause of it was, thus, immaterial.

Thus, in the case of *Howard Fire In. Co.* v. *New York Transportation Co.* (79 U. S. (12 Wall) 194) the vessel was insured against fire only—and was damaged by a fire following and resulting from a collision. The U.S. Supreme Court said:

> In the case before us, there is no exception of collisions or fires caused by collisions. It must therefore be understood that the insurers took the risk of all fires not expressly excepted.

In the case of *St. John* v. *American Mutual Ins. Co.* (11 N. Y. (1 Kern) 516) a fire policy contained an exception of any loss occasioned by the explosion of a steam boiler. Fire having resulted from such an explosion, the insurance company was held not liable.

In the *Howard Fire Ins. Co.* case, the court said of the *St. John* case:

> It exhibits the difference, in effect, between an express exception from a risk undertaken, and silence in regard to a peril not insured against.

As Englar pointed out, this is an important distinction to be borne in mind in connection with proximate cause. More recently, the U.S. Supreme Court defined proximate cause as being "that cause which is most nearly and essentially connected with the loss as its efficient cause." (*Standard Oil Co.* v. *U.S.*, 340 U.S. 54 (1950)).

The Marine Insurance Act states that the insurer is liable for any loss proximately caused by a peril insured against and conversely that he is not liable for any loss which is not proximately caused by a peril insured against (Sect. 55). Sometimes, however, event follows event with such rapidity that it is difficult to determine which is the predominant cause. The law has expressed its conclusion in the phrase *causa proxima non remota spectator* (looking to the immediate cause and not the remote cause).

One English judge commented that "direct cause" would be a better expression than "proximate cause." Another judge thought that the cause need not be exclusive to be proximate and, indeed, rarely was. There can be no rule of thumb, and in each case it remains to be determined what cause is proximate in efficiency. The true proximate cause is that which is dominant or predominant; effective or immediate; actual or real—in short, the overriding or common sense cause.

Phillips comments:

> In case of the concurrence of different causes, to one of which it is necessary to attribute the loss, it is to be attributed to the efficient predominating peril, whether it is or is not in activity at the consummation of the disaster. (Subsect. 1132)

If two causes exist, one must look to the cause which rendered the loss inevitable: that which was the proximate cause and that which was the remote cause. Was there an interval in time in which the loss could have been prevented? Regard must be paid to the proximate cause and not the remote cause, even though the proximate cause might not have caused the loss but for the remote cause or causes. Thus, one factor may be the instrument but not the cause of the loss. This is illustrated in the case of the yacht *Duet* (1967 AMC 1144) which had a small hole in her starboard side 12 or 14 inches above the waterline. Subsequently, her mooring was moved into shallow water nearer the shore and she grounded and leaned over to starboard with every low tide. Consequently water entered the hole in her hull and she sank at her moorings. It was held that the sinking was caused by a peril of the sea and that the hull underwriters were liable under their policy. Water had entered through the hole in the hull, but the sinking was not inevitable merely because of the existence of the hole.

The question of proximate cause most frequently comes before the courts in determining whether a loss falls on war risk or marine policies of insurance. The reader's attention is drawn to the case of *Muller* v. *Globe & Rutgers Fire Ins. Co.* (246 Fed. Rep. 759). In that case, the following rules were laid down:

> (1) That cause is proximate which sets the other causes in motion; only when causes are independent is the nearest in time looked to.
>
> (2) If there is an unbroken connection between act and injury, the act causes the injury; an intervening act is not the proximate cause of the injury, unless it is efficient to break the causal connection.

In a more recent case, the court expressed the view that in interpreting the notion of proximate cause, admiralty courts have applied a stringent canon of construction and look no further than "the first cause from which the event flows in a natural, almost mechanical and inevitable manner; what has been called 'the real efficient cause of the loss' . . . yet, ultimately the courts must employ the fallible judgments of common sense in deciding which strand in the net of causation is the proximate cause of the accident" (*Flota Mercante Dominicana* v. *American Manufacturers Mutual Ins. Co.*, 1970 AMC 1678).

The interesting case of *Nautilus Virgin Charterers* v. *Edinburgh Insurance Co.*, referred to earlier in discussing barratry, also involved the principle of proximate cause. Barratry is a marine peril and was covered by the relevant policy. Seizure is a war peril and was not covered by the policy. The master of the insured vessel (a yacht) made an unauthorized deviation to Colombia for the purpose of engaging in smuggling (which in the circumstances of the case constituted barratry). The vessel was subsequently seized by the Colombian government for carrying marijuana. It was held that the proximate cause of the loss of the yacht was the governmental seizure and not the earlier barratry. The court quoted with approval from an earlier case (*Republic of China* v. *National Union Fire Insurance Co.*, 1958 AMC 1529) in which the court had concluded that, where barratry was one of the causes of the loss, recovery might be had if the ultimate cause were not excluded from coverage by an exclusion clause but that "where the ultimate cause of the loss is excluded from coverage by a warranty or an exclusion clause, recovery may not be had on the grounds of barratry" (*Nautilus Virgin Charters* v. *Edinburgh Insurance Co. Ltd.*, 1981 AMC 2082, *aff'd*. 1982 AMC 696).

Yet another illustration of the vagaries of proximate cause is the case of the *Morning Star* which came before the South African courts. The facts were that a trawler was arrested for illegal fishing and was confiscated when the resultant fine was not paid within the required fifteen days. The South African Supreme Court held that the confiscation did not result from the arrest of the vessel but rather from the failure to pay the fine. The failure to pay was the proximate cause of the confiscation, and non-payment of the fine was not a peril covered by the (war risk) policy (the *Morning Star*, 1987 1 L.R. 401).

In short, causation will always require careful consideration; it is often a matter of degree, with the conclusion depending on the facts in each individual case. Thus the questions as to whether there has been an intervening cause or whether an intervening act of negligence has merely resulted in a failure to overcome the effect of the original cause are often difficult to answer. As the House of Lords put it, "questions of causations are mixed questions of fact and law and opinions may and often do differ upon them" (the *Salem,* 1983 2 A.C. 392).

Under English law, if there are two concurrent and equally effective causes of a marine loss (that is to say, two proximate causes) and one comes within the terms of the policy and the other does not, the insurers must pay (*J. J. Lloyd Instruments Ltd.* v. *Northern Star Insurance Co.,* [the *Miss Jay Jay*], 1987 1 L.R. 32).

ESTABLISHMENT OF DATE OF LOSS

This question arises most frequently when, under the Inchmaree clause, an act or acts of negligence cause damage, not at the time of the operation of the insured peril (the negligence), but at a later date when there has been a change in policies between the act of negligence and the resultant damage. Which is the material time for the purpose of determining on which policies the claim falls: the time the damage was sustained, or the time of the act of negligence?

One rather narrow view which used to be held was that there was no liability under a policy of marine insurance for damage caused by an act of negligence which took place *before the policy came into force* even though the actual damage did not arise until after the policy attached; in short, the *act of negligence* was the peril insured against. A more popular view was that the insurance is against the *results of negligence* happening during the currency of the policy and that, therefore, the policy on which the *damage* occurred was liable and not the policy on which the *negligence* occurred. A third view was that if it was inevitable that the negligence occurring on a previous policy would cause damage on the subsequent policy, the underwriter on the subsequent policy had unwittingly covered a certainty and not a risk, consequently the damage was not recoverable from him; but if it was uncertain whether loss or damage would result from the negligence occurring before the policy was entered into, then. on such damage happening the underwriter was liable because he had in fact taken a proper risk.

In this connection it is interesting to note that under the Norwegian Plan, 1964 (the most recent Marine Insurance Statute issued by a leading maritime nation), the *primary damage* always falls on the policy in force "when the peril struck" (that is, when the insured peril operated) even if such damage were unknown at the expiry of that policy. This assumes, of course, that some damage took place at the time of the operation of the insured peril. The Norwegian Plan goes on to say that the *consequential damage* (that is to say, any damage eventually resulting from the operation of the insured peril), even if it did not occur until a later policy period was in effect, falls on the original insurers but *only if some damage originated on the prior policy and that such damage was known to exist on expiry of the original policy.* However, if damage originating at the time of the operation of the insured peril was *unknown on the expiry of that policy,* the new *consequential damage* would fall on the new insurer (that is to say, the policy in effect at the time of the new casualty). (*See* Norwegian Plan, 1964, Sect. 18.)

In practice, in most cases where damage to a vessel resulting from the operation of an insured peril on a prior policy culminates in a breakdown in operation, it is customary to show the resultant claim on the policies covering the date of the breakdown. On the other hand, if damage to a vessel (such as a fractured tailshaft caused by a peril insured against or the damage to bottom shell plating caused by heavy weather) is merely discovered at a routine examination, the claim is usually apportioned on a "damage date unknown" basis. In other words, the damage is apportioned over the policies in existence from the time the damage was last known not to exist to the date of the discovery of the damage.

Difficulties arise in cases where the operation of an insured peril on a prior policy does not result either in an actual breakdown in operation or in the complete fracture or condemnation of a part. An example of such a case would be where the damage discovered during a routine examination is really a "condition" such as a corroded part (caused, say, by a peril insured against, such as repairers' negligence). In such cases it would not be correct to charge the underwriters on risk at the time the corrosion was discovered. Nor would it be proper to apportion the damage on a "damage date unknown" basis because it did not take place at one time; there was no death blow. Furthermore, while the damage was cumulative, it was not cumulative in the sense that it was caused by the continuing operation of a peril. If the insured peril operated *on one specific occasion* and resulted in some immediate damage, and subsequent cumulative damage was unavoidable, it seems reasonable that the claim should fall on the policy during which both the insured peril operated and *during which the damage was originated.* The subsequent operations merely affect the measure of the loss. To put it another way, it is submitted that once the *damage* has been *originated* and the final result is inevitable, the underwriters on risk at the time the damage originated are liable (always assuming the assured cannot be faulted in not arresting the damage). It is sometimes suggested that such claims should be apportioned on a cumulative or progressive damage basis and this would be so *if the damage did not actually originate at the time of the operation of the insured peril.*

The *Natalie* arbitration (1959 AMC 2379) is often cited as authority for the theory that, in all cases, the policies during which the damage was actually sustained should respond regardless of when the operation of the insured peril occurred. Actually the *Natalie* case has no force at law and was not even followed in its entirety by the underwriters in whose favor the arbitrator decided. In reaching his decision the arbitrator leaned heavily on a legal liability case involving cumulative damage to cargo (*Export S. S. Corporation* v. *American Ins. Co.—the Exmoor*, 1939 AMC 1095). In that case there was a continuing "peril" of improper stowage which continued day after day and could have been arrested at any time by the exercise of due diligence. Thus there can be little quarrel with the arbitrator's decision in that particular case to apportion the liability on a daily basis because there was a continuing peril.

On the other hand, the chairman of the British Association of Average Adjusters, E. W. Reading, in his address to the association in 1942 expressed the view that an underwriter can be liable for a loss which *culminates* after the expiry of the policy. As Reading put it, in claims for particular average (as opposed to general average), "the peril which *has* operated is the deciding factor." He rejected the theory that an underwriter's liability is limited to the damage existing at the time the policy expires. The implication from this is quite clear: Mr. Reading was referring to cases where not only has the insured peril *operated* during the currency of the policy but by "operating" he meant operating to the extent that part of the resultant damage had also been sustained during that policy. The fact that the *extent* of the damage is not ascertainable until after the expiry of the policy is not material.

> An injury to a ship may fairly be said to cause its loss, if, before that injury is or can with reasonable diligence be repaired, the vessel is lost by reason of the existence of that injury; i.e., under circumstances which, but for that injury, would not have affected her safety. (*Reischer* v. *Berwick,* 7 Asp. M. C. 493) and
>
> . . . it cannot be predicated of the subject-matter insured that no loss has happened to it when it has been so affected by perils insured against that nothing can save it from ultimate destruction. *The element of uncertainty as to the effect of subsequent events may go to the measure of the loss* . . . but it cannot prevent an operative peril which has already taken charge of the ship from being its cause of loss when its complete operation cannot be arrested. (*Clan Mathieson,* 1929 L. L. R. 1)

In interpreting an insurance on containers, the English court of appeals gave some support to this approach. In that case the plaintiff carried on the business of leasing containers which were insured with the defendant underwriters. The insurance was to indemnify the assured in the event of their being unable to recover from any lessees or others for all risks of loss or damage to the containers. The lessees ultimately were adjudged bankrupt and the plaintiff took steps to recover the containers which were scattered throughout the world. The defendant admitted that as far as the lost and damaged containers were concerned, that claim would be admitted in principle; however, the claim for recovery costs (sue and labor expenses) would be denied, since there was no question of an insured peril having operated to cause the loss. Quite apart from this defense, the defendant argued during the course of the hearing that it had not been established that the envisaged loss of containers would have taken place within the year of the policy coverage (at the time of the bankruptcy the policy still had six months to run). In the judgment Lord Justice Everleigh commented (*Integrated Container Service* v. *British Traders Ins. Co.*, 1984 1 L.R. 154):

> The embracing picture which covered all of the containers was that until they were recovered they were lost and at the mercy of whatever should befall them. That loss was an insured risk for which the assured could claim. As the policy was an all risks policy it would not matter how any ensuing loss or damage occurred, for the insurers would be liable to indemnify the assured in respect of it as well as the original loss (partial loss). Moreover, it did not matter if further loss might occur after the expiration of the policy, for the containers had already been the victims of an insured peril within the policy period. They had received a potential death blow. There was consequently a duty upon the assured to avert such a further deterioration in the situation. They were entitled to act under the sue and labor clause and to recover their expenses. The cost of discharging a lien is properly included in these expenses, for if that had not been done the charges would have mounted to the extent where a partial loss became a constructive total loss (Marine Ins. Act, Sect. 60 (2)).

In most cases, there is no question but that the underwriter on risk at the time the damage is sustained is liable; this for the reason that in most cases the operation of the insured peril and the resultant damage are simultaneous. A different situation exists when an act of negligence (or other insured peril) takes place and then a period of time elapses before the resultant damage occurs. In the latter case there is no certainty as to when or indeed whether there will be any resultant damage; thus a new underwriter coming on risk before the damage occurs has not underwritten a certain loss. However, in those cases where the negligent act (or other insured peril) is not completely separated from the inception of the damage, and the insured peril so operates that its complete operation cannot with due diligence be arrested, a strong case can be made for the proposition that the liability attaches to the underwriter on risk at the time of the operation of the insured peril *and the inception of the inevitable damage*. It might even happen that the vessel is lost before the damage can with due diligence be repaired; and it does not matter how long the death agony if the vessel eventually would have been lost by reason of the existence of the injury. The question to be asked is "was the loss *inevitable* at the time of the operation of the insured peril?" That is to say, was the damage itself originated before the expiry of the policy?

Claims falling under the additional perils or Inchmaree clause are more likely to require apportionment on a daily basis than claims directly attributable to the basic perils covered by a marine insurance policy. This for the reason that, once a basic marine peril has operated (such as striking a submerged object), damage has probably been initiated even though it may not culminate until a later date. On the other hand, some of the additional perils introduced by the Inchmaree clause (such as negligence of crew or negligence of repairers) might not immediately result in damage. In most such cases, damages subsequently found are clearly of a progressive nature and therefore an apportionment over the policies covering the period involved may be reasonable.

However, this problem of determining which policy period should respond often occurs even when a peril of the sea operates on some specific occasion and immediately originates damage (as opposed to claims under the Inchmaree clause involving negligence over a period of time or the results of negligence continuing over a period of time). For example, a vessel may strike a submerged object on one policy without apparently sustaining damage and some months later on the succeeding policy a propeller blade may fall off; apparently the striking cracked the propeller and set up a progressive damage which culminated in the loss of a blade. Such cases involve two accidents: the first caused by an insured peril occurring on one policy, and the second occurring during a new policy period (being the culmination of the damage initiated at the time of the first accident) with no new cause intervening. Consequently, it is not surprising that there are several methods which might be adopted in adjusting the resultant claim.

One method would be to charge the whole cost of repairs to the original accident which, on the face of it, was the sole and proximate cause of the damage. When the initial damage is such that it could not have been repaired (even if there had not been a second accident), it would appear that such treatment is beyond doubt. (In the old case of *Coit* v. *Smith*, 3 Johns. 16 (1802), a horse was insured until safely landed. During the voyage the horse sustained injuries during heavy weather but did not die until a few days after landing; it was accepted that the horse could not have recovered from its initial injuries.)

On the other hand, when a partial loss becomes merged with a total loss at a later date, it is an accepted principle that the total loss falls on the policies current at the time of the total loss. Thus if, in the case described above of striking a submerged object, a liner negligence clause is included in the policies during which the damage culminates in a new accident, the entire claim might well be stated on the second policy period as an accident occurring during those policies.

A third method would be to apportion the damage over both policies, either on a daily basis from the time of the first accident to the time of the second or, if possible, by a more accurate and factual division of the damage.

The principle which forms the background to consideration of this topic is the underlying rule, applicable to all insurance, and expressed by eminent judges in various phrases to the same effect—namely, that a policy of insurance "covers a risk, not a certainty." It would seem, therefore, that the first method discussed above is the more correct and that (in the case of striking a submerged object) the underwriters on risk at the time the first accident occurred and the damage originated should respond.

While every case must be treated on its own merits, the practice in establishing the date of loss may be summarized very generally as follows:

(1) The date of the negligent act (if any) is not *necessarily* controlling in determining the policies on which the claim falls.

(2) In the vast majority of cases, the date on which the *damage* is known to have been sustained is controlling in determining the policies on which the claim falls.

(3) When the *damage* is known to have been originated by an insured peril under one policy but culminates in a breakdown under a subsequent policy, the resultant claim is shown under the first policy provided there was no lack of diligence on the part of the insured in not effecting repairs immediately. (This is particularly true in those cases where one of the basic insured perils has operated, as opposed to the additional perils covered by the Inchmaree clause.)

(4) However, when, without any prior warning or known history, an insured peril results in a breakdown in operation, the claim falls on the policies operative *at the time of the breakdown* or culmination of the *damage*. (In these cases the breakdown and the damage are assumed to have been simultaneous.)

(5) In cases where an insured peril results in progressive or cumulative damage but does not result in a breakdown in operation, it is usually (but not always) necessary to apportion the claim over the various policies during which the *damage* was progressing. (This method is chiefly resorted to in connection with claims arising out of the Inchmaree clause.)

It must be stressed that even in cases where an apportionment of the damage over several policies is mandatory, questions regarding franchise or deductible average requirements should not arise (always assuming the *total* claim is in excess of the franchise or deductible in the policy, if any). In such cases, the damage resulting from the insured peril is merely apportioned over one or more sets of policies because the damage itself was sustained during the currency of those policies. Nevertheless, the entire damage resulted from the operation of an insured peril on one occasion only and consequently it is the total cost of repairs, regardless of apportionment, which qualifies for franchise purposes. If, for example, a deductible average was applicable, only one deductible would be applied, the entire claim having resulted from one accident or occurrence. It would be otherwise, of course, if it was the peril itself which continued over a period of time.

SUPERIMPOSED DAMAGE

It might be appropriate here to consider also the question of superimposed damage. Let us suppose a vessel sustains contact damage to her shell plating which it is estimated would cost $900 to repair. Repairs are deferred and the vessel subsequently sustains additional damage in the same area which also occasions repair (not renewal); the cost of repairs is now $3,000. In such circumstances, it is the practice to charge the first accident with $900 and the second with $2,100. The test is whether there is anything included in the ultimate repair cost for repairing the first damage. A like practice is followed when a vessel sustains damage to plates which requires them to be renewed. If repairs are deferred and the vessel sustains further damage in the same area, absorbing all previous damage, the estimated cost of the prior plate renewals are chargeable to the first accident out of the total repair cost.

When damage to plating is sustained requiring repair (not renewal) and repairs are deferred, and further damage is sustained in the same area requiring the same plating to be renewed, the question as to whether the first accident bears any part of the cost of renewal requires careful consideration. If the second accident is of such severity that it is probable the plating would have required renewing even had there been no prior damage in the same area, it seems that the second and more severe accident should bear the entire cost of renewal. However, if the second accident was of a minor nature, being merely "the straw which broke the camel's back," it would be reasonable to charge the first accident with the estimated cost of effecting repairs to the damage existing at the time they were deferred. This on the theory that the greater repair, as a result of the second accident, might not have reached such a magnitude had the earlier damage not been in existence.

The position is different if a vessel with damage necessitating repair receives further damage in the same area resulting in a total loss of the part. For example, a vessel's rudder has been damaged in an accident but, before being repaired, the rudder falls off in heavy weather (a new accident) and is lost. In such a case there would be no claim in respect of the first accident (applying the test, it will be seen that nothing is included in the cost of replacing the rudder for repairing the first damage).

INSUFFICIENT OR IMPROPER REPAIRS

It is well established that underwriters are responsible for restoring the vessel to the condition she was in before the operation of an insured peril. Thus, if in effecting average repairs the repairers are guilty of improper workmanship, or inefficient or insufficient repairs, the assured is entitled to recover the cost of any repairs which have had to be done over again, and the entire cost goes back to the original accident. As Gow put it:

> The shipowner is entitled to recover the cost of repairs which have to be done over again in consequence of the work being done badly, or the repairs being effected in a manner which does not leave the ship as fit to sail or to sell as she was before the accident. (Gow, 1913, p. 214)

A more recent text writer also expressed the view that in such cases insurers are liable for the actual cost of effecting complete repairs, that is to say, including the cost of replacing inefficient repairs (Dover, 1957, p. 550).

In assessing the measure of damages in a collision case, it has been stated that a second set of repairs made necessary because of defective work in the first instance was part of the cost of repairing the original damage because the two sets were connected and the direct result of the collision (*see* Hurd, p. 65). Such reasoning would appear to be equally relevant to the cost of effecting complete repairs to damage caused by a peril insured against under a policy of marine insurance.

It has already been pointed out that the mere fact that repairers' negligence is covered in the Inchmaree clause does not mean that the assured is obliged to claim as repairers' negligence the cost of further repairs to damage attributable to a prior accident simply because the additional repairs were made necessary because of repairers' negligence in effecting the original repairs. On the other hand, if repairers' negligence has caused an entirely new, separate, and unconnected damage, there has been a new accident and the new damage is a separate claim, subject to whatever Franchise clause or Deductible Average clause is applicable.

DAMAGE DATE UNKNOWN

Damage is sometimes discovered on dry dock, the nature of which clearly indicates that it has been caused by an insured peril; nevertheless, the date of the loss is unknown.

Bottom damage caused by heavy weather falls into this category and the practice is to examine, in conjunction with underwriters' surveyors, the vessel's logbooks back to the date of previous dry-docking (when the damage was last known not to exist) and extract therefrom the number of days (or watches) on which heavy weather was encountered. The heavy weather repair account is then apportioned on the basis of the number of days (or watches) on which heavy weather occurred. Although this method is somewhat arbitrary, it is accepted by underwriters as a reasonable and equitable manner in which to allocate heavy weather damage. Common repair expenses (such as dry-docking) are divided on a common user basis when the number of periods of heavy weather in respect of which a claim under the policies can be substantiated is ascertained, bearing in mind the policy conditions (that is to say, voyage Franchise clause or Deductible Average clause, as the case may be).

Very often damage to shell plating is discovered on dry dock which is clearly due to a striking on one occasion, although the vessel owner has no knowledge as to when the damage was actually sustained. Here again, it is the practice to apportion the damage on a "damage date unknown" basis; that is to say, commencing from the time the damage was known not to exist (usually the last dry-docking), the number of days up to the time the damage was discovered are totalled and the damage is allocated over the various policies in force during that period on a pro rata basis. If a voyage franchise is applicable, the entire cost of repairs (regardless of the apportionment over policies) is used in testing for franchise. If a Deductible Average clause is in effect, only one deductible is applied. If there is an apportionment over various policies and the deductible average changes, the applicable deductible averages are themselves apportioned on the same basis as the "damage date unknown." Thus, whatever proportion of the total claim is allocated to a particular policy period, the same proportion of that policy's deductible average is applied.

CONTINUATION CLAUSE

As we have seen, an underwriter can be liable for a loss which culminates after the expiry of the policy. For example, the insured vessel may be so badly damaged by the operation of a peril insured against shortly before the termination of the policy that she cannot even with due diligence be saved before the new policy attaches. Such situations tend to result in disputes as to whether the old or the new policy would respond. Such circumstances, though rare, are anticipated by and provided for by the Continuation clause. The Continuation clause in the American Institute Hull Clauses reads as follows:

> Should the Vessel at the expiration of this Policy be at sea, or in distress, or at a port of refuge or of call, she shall, provided previous notice be given to the Underwriters, be held covered at a pro rata monthly premium to her port of destination.

This clause was originally intended to operate in cases where, because the vessel was at sea, or in distress, or at a port of refuge, on the termination of the previous policy, difficulty might be experienced in renewing the insurance. Under the Continuation clause the policy may be extended until the vessel arrives at her port of destination, but the assured must:

(1) Give due notice to underwriters.

(2) Pay an additional premium at the rate of 1/12th the annual premium each month or part thereof that the insurance is extended.

Nowadays, shipowners usually arrange for the renewal of time policies well in advance of expiry of the old policies, with attachment to take place at the expiry of the previous policies. Nevertheless, the Continuation clause remains a useful clause because it is possible that a situation could arise in which, at the close of the current policy, the vessel may be at sea in a damaged condition, a condition so perilous that she may be lost within a few hours of the attachment of the new policies. In such a situation, there might be some dispute as to whether the entire claim fell on the old or the new policies, and to forestall any such dispute it would be wise for the assured to invoke the Continuation clause in the old policies and cancel the attachment of the new policies.

Another example of the use of the Continuation clause would be where the original policies expire almost directly after the accident and before it is possible to determine whether the vessel is a constructive total loss. Under the Continuation clause, the policies can be automatically continued. The opinion has been expressed that if an additional premium is charged in such a case for the coverage under the Continuation clause, the amount paid is recoverable from underwriters should the vessel subsequently prove to be a constructive total loss.

It is interesting to note that it has been held that in potential constructive total loss cases, where underwriters decline notice of abandonment (which they invariably do), the interest in the vessel survives to the owner and his notice to invoke the Continuation clause is binding on underwriters.

EXCEPTED PERILS

Underwriters are not liable for losses not proximately caused by a peril insured against. In particular, in the words of the Marine Insurance Act:

(a) The insurer is not liable for any loss attributable to the wilful misconduct of the assured, but, unless the policy otherwise provides, he is liable for any loss proximately caused by a peril insured against, even though the loss would not have happened but for the misconduct or negligence of the master or crew;

(b) Unless the policy otherwise provides, the insurer on ship or goods is not liable for any loss proximately caused by delay, although the delay be caused by a peril insured against;

(c) Unless the policy otherwise provides, the insurer is not liable for ordinary wear and tear, ordinary leakage and breakage, inherent vice or nature of the subject-matter insured, or for any loss proximately caused by rats or vermin, or for any injury to machinery not proximately caused by maritime perils. (Sect. 55 (2))

In general, this section of the act reflects the position under American law, except for the much-criticized decision in the case of the *Smaragd* (302 U. S. 556). This decision, which is discussed later, was not acceptable to the market and resulted in the inclusion of a clause in cargo policies which has the effect of nullifying the position taken by the court.

In 1924 a majority of the English House of Lords found that scuttling was not a peril of the sea. When a vessel is scuttled it is the scuttling—not the inrush of water—which is the cause of the loss; the entrance of the water cannot be divorced from the act which occasioned it. ("The possibility of scuttling is not a peril of the sea; it is a peril of the wickedness of man and would have to be mentioned expressly in the policy, like barratry or pirates, in order that the assured should recover from the underwriter in respect of it") (*P. Samuel & Co.* v. *Dumas* [the *Gregorios*], A.C. 1924 431). In those rare cases where underwriters have reason to believe that the insured vessel has been scuttled or otherwise cast away rather than lost due to the operation of an insured peril, it is on Sect. 55 (2) (a) that they rely. Indeed, for more than fifty years it had been accepted by the courts in the United Kingdom that, in rejecting a claim for total loss on the grounds of scuttling, underwriters need only assert that "the loss of the vessel was caused by the wilful misconduct of the assured in procuring or conniving at the casting away of the vessel" without giving any specific particulars other than by inference. It was then up to the assured to bring action against the underwriters and prove to the satisfaction of the court that the loss was caused by an insured peril (such as a peril of the sea or a latent defect in the hull). In short, if underwriters allege that a ship was scuttled with the con-nivance of the assured, they were not obliged to give any further particulars of such allegation (*Coulouras* v. *British General Ins. Co.*, L. L. R. 1922, Vol. XI, p. 100). However, in the *Gold Sky* (L. L. R. 1972, Vol. 1, p. 331), the court of appeals condemned this long-standing practice as being wrong and, but for the application in that case having been made "far too late," would presumably have ordered that the particulars of the alleged "scut-tling with the connivance of the assured" be disclosed prior to trial. In fact this was ordered by the court of appeals in a subsequent case (the *Dias*, L. L. R. 1972, Vol. 2, p. 60). In the words of the court:

> The defendants (underwriters) should be required in effect to give the best particulars they are able of all acts and omissions which are al-leged to have caused or resulted in the sinking of the vessel, of the acts or conduct alleged to constitute the procuring, of the acts or con-duct alleged to constitute the conniving, and of all facts relied upon in support of the allegation that the plaintiff company's conduct in alleg-edly procuring or conniving at the casting away of the vessel was wilful. (p. 75).

Nor is it sufficient for underwiters to advance suspicions and/or circum-stantial evidence in support of their contention that a vessel has been wil-fully cast away; a high standard of proof is required in such cases (the *Zinova*, 1984 2 L.R. 264). In an American case, it was held that although the evidence submitted by insurers was sufficient to rebut a presumption that the loss was by an insured peril, it was not sufficient for the court to find that the vessel was scuttled. However, the assured had failed to dis-charge the burden that the loss fell within the policy (*Northwestern Mutual Life Ins. Co.* v. *Linard et al.*, 1974 AMC 877).

Cargo underwriters are not responsible, for claims for *inter alia,* loss of market, trade losses, or inherent vice, and for loss, damage, or deteriora-tion arising out of delay. The latter exclusion was thought to be implied in every marine insurance policy, but the decision of the court in the case of the *Smaragd (Lanasa Fruit* v. *Universal Ins. Co.*, 302 U. S. 556) made it necessary to specify the exclusion in the policy. In that case, the *Smaragd*, carrying a cargo of bananas, stranded and, before she could be refloated, the entire cargo became overripe and was a total loss. The court found that "the spoiling of a perishable cargo of bananas, which would have been merchantable at the end of the voyage had it not been for the delay due to the stranding of the vessel, is proximately caused by the stranding and is therefore within the coverage of insurance against loss caused by perils of the sea." It was further stated that "a loss is within the coverage of a marine insurance policy although within the network of causation there may be found the operation of natural forces to which the disaster within the coverage of the policy has been given play."

The *Smaragd* decision is entirely contrary to Sect. 55 (2) (b) of the Marine Insurance Act quoted earlier and provides a good example of how the English law of marine insurance is not always followed by American courts. As noted above, the effect of this decision is nullified by the Delay clause in most cargo policies.

Cargo underwriters are also not responsible for inherent vice which has been defined as "anything which by reason of its own inherent qualities is lost without negligence by anyone" (*Greenshields* v. *Stephens,* 1908 1 K. B. 51). Other definitions include "the natural behavior of the subject matter being what it is, in the circumstances in which it is carried" and "inability to withstand the incidents of a normal voyage." Many cargoes are subject to inherent vice but it is the onus of the insurer to prove that inherent vice was the proximate cause of loss or damage if he seeks to decline liability. On the other hand, the assured may be called upon to produce evidence to demonstrate that the damage did not arise solely from natural causes and perhaps point to some external cause or unusual circumstances (usually involving negligence on the part of the carrier) which would refute the insurer's plea of inherent vice. Thus, to sum up, inherent vice can be assumed to be the proximate cause of loss or damage if the facts indicate that no fortuity or casualty had occurred. In the words of an American court of appeals, the insurer, under an "all risks" policy, has the burden of proving the existence of inherent vice before attachment of the cover if he wishes to avoid the claim (*Morrison Grain Co.* v. *Utica Mutual Insurance Co.,* 1982 AMC 658). Nevertheless, where a cargo of soya beans was specifically insured to cover "against the risks of heat, sweat and spontaneous combustion," the English House of Lords commented that both sweat and spontaneous combustion were clearly descriptive of particular kinds of inherent vice. Thus, by its wording, the policy displaced the rule laid down in Sect. 55 (2) (c) of the Marine Insurance Act that the insurer is not liable for "inherent vice or nature of the subject matter insured" (*Soya G.m.b.H. Mainz Komm* v. *White,* 1983 1 L.R. 122).

Turning to the subject of wear and tear, Phillips states:

> The underwriters are not liable to make indemnity for the mere deterioration of the subject by age or wear and tear, where no extraordinary peril intervenes. (Subsect. 1088)

In recent years the importance of fatigue of metal in causing, or initiating, failures in the structure of a ship have often been debated without any definite conclusion being reached. Briefly, fatigue of material results from the many, intermittent applications of a load resulting in the structure's final failure under a load that it was quite capable of bearing when new. The use of the word "fatigue" is unfortunate, for it tends to suggest wear and tear, which is not necessarily the case. The relation between fatigue and heavy weather damage is a case in point. For instance, a crack at a hatch corner, noted after heavy weather, might be put down to fatigue stresses acting for a long time, and not to a few cycles of violent stresses experienced immediately before the crack was noticed. The opinion has been expressed by experts that such fatigue cracks might be classed as heavy weather damage, because the normal alternating stresses imposed on a ship in her lifetime are probably not sufficiently severe to result in fatigue failure proper. If it is reasonable to assume that the material would have lasted indefinitely but for the heavy weather, the underwriters would seem to be liable for the damage.

Phillips supports this conclusion, saying that, while the underwriter is not answerable for wear and tear and decay from ordinary causes, he is answerable for the risks insured against, though they may have been enhanced by the ordinary effects of the elements (Subsect. 1546). This is sometimes called the "death blow" theory (see *Integrated Container Service* v. *British Traders Insurance Co., supra*) but it is really a question of proximate cause; the question to be asked is "would this damage have occurred but for the operation of an insured peril?" Thus, if a vessel is classed with a reputable classification society and has been properly maintained in accordance with the requirements of that society and her plating fails in heavy weather, there is a prima facie claim under the policy even though her plating may have been subject to thinning or "aging" and even though it might have been necessary to effect maintenance repairs very soon. In arriving at the reasonable cost of repairs, no deduction is made for any enhanced cost arising out of the vessel's age and condition, for the policies will invariably contain a clause stipulating that there shall be no deduction for the substitution of new material for used or old material. In one English case, the court was satisfied that as the loss was proximately caused by a peril of the sea (heavy weather), it was recoverable, although it might not have occurred but for the concurrent action of some other cause not within the policy, namely, unseaworthiness (*Frangos* v. *Sun Ins. Co. Ltd.*, L. L. R., Vol. 49, p. 354; *see also* yacht *Duet* discussed earlier). In another American case (*Moran Towing Corp.* v. *M. A. Garmino Construction Co.*, 1966 AMC 2262), wear and tear was defined as normal depreciation arising from the practices in the service for which the vessel is intended. In the same case it was also stated that the effects of negligence do not become wear and tear merely because they may be anticipated (the case concerned damage due to the negligent dumping of cargo [boulders], the vessel being in the riprap trade).

The exclusion of "any loss proximately caused by rats or vermin" (Sect. 55 (2) (c)) has been the subject of some amusing comments. One English court, no doubt with tongue in cheek, decided that a rat gnawing a cheese in the hold of a ship was not a peril of the sea and the shipowner was liable for the damage, although he had proved that he had two cats on board! The House of Lords in *Hamilton* v. *Pandorf* (12 App. Cas. 518) conceded that this decision was good law but found that even though the damage caused by a rat gnawing a hole in a pipe might not in itself be a peril of the sea, the shipowner was nonetheless responsible for damage (to cargo) caused by the resultant ingress of seawater. In other words, the entry of seawater was the proximate cause of the loss, not the action of the rat. As we have seen in discussing perils of the sea, some American courts have declined to follow this particular interpretation of proximate cause. If we were to accept Englar's theory on the subject of proximate cause (discussed earlier), the fact that there is a specific exclusion of damage by rats (as there is in English law) should be conclusive. However, the English courts (and as we have seen, some American courts) do not look at it in this light. Thus, even considering the traditional excluded losses, the principle of proximate cause has to be faced and a conclusion reached on the facts in each individual case.

In essence, all the exclusions in Section 55 of the Marine Insurance Act refer to losses which are inevitable and therefore not fortuitous in nature.

Most insurances on freight contain a clause relieving underwriters of any claim consequent on loss of time, whether arising from an insured peril or not.

CONSTRUCTION OF POLICIES

In interpreting policies of marine insurance, it is the general rule that any ambiguity must be construed against the underwriter; that is to say, most favorably to the assured. There is authority for the doctrine that, since the policy is written by the underwriter, all cases of ambiguity are to be construed against him (see *America S. S. Co.* v. *Indemnity Mut. Ins. Co.*, 108 Fed. Rep. 421 and *Hagen* v. *Scottish Ins. Co.*, 186 U. S. 423). The predominant intention of the parties in a contract of marine insurance is indemnity, and this intention is kept in view and favored in putting a construction on the policy (*see Dixon on Marine Insurance*, p. 33).

An old English case (*Robertson* v. *French*, 4 East 130) lays down the rule that the policy shall be construed "according to the sense and meaning as collected in the first place from the terms used, which terms are to be understood in their plain, ordinary and popular sense." Over 170 years later, an American court echoed this sentiment, saying that, in construing the language of a contract, such as a policy of insurance, the standard is what a normally constituted person would have understood it to mean in its actual setting (*Atlantic Lines* v. *American Motorists Insurance Co.,* 1976 AMC 2522). Anything written on the face of the policy or any printed or written clause attached thereto (for example, the F.C.&S. clause), overrides any printed matter in the policy itself.

As the court said in *Bluewaters Inc.* v. *Boag* (1964 AMC 71), "the policy and attachments are to be considered as a single document and type-written provisions prevail over printed clauses if there is a conflict." Thus it was held that a typewritten navigational limits warranty describing an insured yacht as "laid up and out of commission" superseded the printed "privilege" giving leave "to go on trial trips," and recovery for the yacht's sinking during a voyage in the Pacific Ocean was denied (*Linton Harris* v. *Glen Falls Ins. Co.,* 1972 AMC 138). Furthermore, an insurer must make policy exclusions clear and unmistakable; otherwise there is coverage (*Mayronne Mud & Chemical Corp.* v. *T-W Drilling Co.,* 1959 AMC 403). Another court commented that the fine print in a policy must be construed more strictly against the insurer and more liberally in favor of the insured (*Soil Mechanics Corp.* v. *Empire Mutual Ins. Co.,* 1968 AMC 491). Yet another judicial comment was that an underwriter seeking to avoid liability under an exclusion in its policy has the burden of proof of non-coverage, and ambiguous language will be strongly construed against it (*Gulf Oil Corp.* v. *the Margaret,* 1978 AMC 868).

On the other hand, it has sometimes been suggested that since many insurance clauses are prepared and submitted to the underwriter by the insurance broker as agent for the assured, any ambiguity in the clauses introduced by the broker should be construed against the assured. However, American courts generally have been on the side of the assured in such matters and appear to have accepted the doctrine that, regardless of its authorship, once the policy has been signed by the underwriter, it becomes his words.

This general proposition that, in the case of ambiguity, an insurance policy is construed against the insurer is not always followed. In *Eagle Leasing Corp.* v. *Hartford Fire Ins. Co.* (1978 AMC 604), the court drew a distinction in those cases where "the insured is not an innocent but a corpo-ration of immense size ... managed by sophisticated businessmen and rep-resented by counsel on the same professional level as the counsel for insurers." Refusing to apply the general rule, the court construed the policy provisions "to give a reasonable meaning that most closely reflects the probable intentions of the parties and is most reasonable from a business point of view."

The courts have often criticized the parties to a marine insurance contract for not making their intention clear; great care should therefore be taken in drawing up policy conditions.

Certain rules for the construction of the policy are incorporated in the Marine Insurance Act (see Appendix E).

It should be remembered that most marine insurance policies (especially those effected on vessels) are "named perils" policies and an assured has the burden of showing that both the loss and the peril which caused it fall within the meaning of the policy terms (*Northwestern Mutual Life Insurance Co.* v. *Linard,* 1974 AMC 877). However, as we have already seen, this is not the case with "all risks" policies where the assured is only required to make a prima facie case that a loss has in fact occurred. The burden of proof then shifts to the insurer to show that the loss resulted from a cause excluded by the language of the policy (*Goodman* v. *Firemen's Fund Insurance Co.,* 1978 AMC 846).

Chapter 4

Total Losses

The main object of marine insurance is to protect the individual person or corporation against a catastrophic loss. An Elizabethan statute of 1601 read:

> By means of a Policy of Insurance it cometh to pass that upon the loss or perishing of any ship there followeth not the undoing of any man but the loss lighteth rather easily upon many than heavily upon few.

It would be difficult to improve upon that early justification of marine insurance, and today the protection afforded against total loss is all-important in the financing of shipping and trade.

A total loss may be either an actual total loss or a constructive total loss and unless a different intention appears from the terms of the policy, an insurance against total loss includes a constructive as well as an actual total loss (Marine Ins. Act, Sect. 56).

In a total loss, the assured is entitled to recover from the underwriter the whole amount insured by the policy on the subject so lost (Phillips, Subsect. 1486).

ACTUAL TOTAL LOSS

Phillips defines an actual total loss as follows:

> A total loss of a subject of an insurance is where, by the perils insured against, it is destroyed, or so injured as to be of trifling or no value to the assured for the purposes and uses for which it was intended, or is taken out of the possession and control of the assured, whereby he is deprived of it; or where the voyage or adventure for which the insurance is made is otherwise broken up by the perils insured against. (Subsect. 1485)

The definition given in the Marine Insurance Act is:

> Where the subject-matter insured is destroyed, or so damaged as to cease to be a thing of the kind insured, or where the assured is irretrievably deprived thereof, there is an actual total loss. (Sect. 57)

An actual total loss may take any of three forms:

(1) Physical destruction (for example, foundering, loss by fire, missing ship).

(2) Loss of specie. This has been defined as cargo which no longer answers the description of the interest insured or which cannot be regarded from a mercantile and business viewpoint as being saleable as a thing of the kind originally shipped (for example, foodstuffs so badly damaged by seawater as to be unfit for human consumption).

(3) Irretrievable deprivement (for example, capture).

The meaning of the term "actual total loss" came before an American court in *Edinburgh Assurance* v. *R. L. Burns Corp.* (1980 AMC 1261, *aff'd.* 1982 AMC 2532). Underwriters had declined a claim under a policy against "actual total loss only" on the grounds that term entailed catastrophic physical destruction or loss, without regard to considerations of value or cost of repair. In other words, the subject-matter insured must be *destroyed* as stated in the Marine Insurance Act. As to the second test under the act (whether the thing is "so damaged as to cease to be a thing of the kind insured"), underwriters maintained that it was only applicable to instances where, for example, a chemical change occurs, causing a cargo to decompose; such a test could only apply to a vessel if, for example, there were an explosion, fire, or similar catastrophe. The third test ("where the assured was irretrievably deprived thereof") fell in the same category as the first test (destruction) and the underwriters maintained that, in applying both these tests, if an object is physically capable of being retrieved and repaired without regard to cost, then the object is not destroyed or irretrievably lost. Since the subject-matter insured, an oil rig (the *Gatto*), could be salvaged and repaired, although at considerable cost, it was not an actual total loss. This was the underwriters' case for declining the claim. On the other hand, the assured argued that the second test under the Act was concerned with whether, as a practical business matter, the subject-matter insured was still "a thing of the kind" insured: if it has become a "wreck," then it is an actual total loss.

The court, interpreting English law, found that the oil rig was not an actual total loss under the "irretrievably deprived" test, since its location was known and accessible; in other words, the assured had not been irretrievably deprived thereof. Turning to the other statutory tests, destruction and loss of specie, the court found clear authority for the assured's position that English law considers commercial reality in determining whether the thing insured is an actual total loss. In *Berger and Light Diffusers Ply. Ltd.* v. *Pollock* (2 L. L. R. 442, 1973), that court found a group of corroded steel injection molds an actual total loss, for the only way to overcome the damage was by recutting the mold, which was "commercially impossible," and the molds therefore had only a scrap value. While the court in *Edinburgh* v. *Burns* quoted this decision with approval, it felt constrained to point out that the entire question could not be reduced to whether as a practical business matter the thing was no longer what was insured or had been destroyed. A distinction must be retained between actual total loss and constructive total loss, and complete dependence upon commercial reality or practicability creates the danger of obliterating the difference between the two concepts. There were cases clearly recognizing an intermediate position between the argument that a thing is an actual total loss when, as a practical business matter, it is not worthwhile recovering and rebuilding the thing insured, and the argument that a thing is only an actual total loss when it is not within the scope of present technology to recover and repair it. In the court's view, case law recognized such an intermediate position: where situations give rise to an actual total loss while significant, accessible physical remains still exist. Cases referred to a ship being an actual total loss because it was a "wreck" (*Sailing Ship Blairmore Co.* v. *Macredie (1898)*, A. C. 593, House of Lords).

The court concluded that, under English law,

> the subject matter of insurance may cease to be a thing of the kind insured, or be destroyed, and hence be an actual total loss, even though there are accessible physical remains of the vessel or like entity. This court also concludes that the question whether those remains may be utilized in the reconstructing of a thing of the same kind as that insured is not dispositive of the determination whether the thing is an actual total loss. It is a matter of degree. and

> it is proper generally to apply the same standards to the test, "where the subject-matter is destroyed" and to the test ("where the subject-matter is) so damaged as to cease to be a thing of the kind insured," reserving the right under the facts to come to different conclusions on the two tests.

The court felt that both concepts had meaning under several standards:

> If the effort required to either recover or refurbish the thing insured is too disproportionate an effort for the resulting operational entity, then the thing insured is an actual total loss.

> A second standard is whether the refurbishing effort is so extensive as not reasonably to be characterized as repair. If not so extensive, then the thing insured is not an actual total loss. If the refurbishing effort is so extensive as not reasonably to be character-

ized as repair, but rather must be considered rebuilding, then the thing insured is an actual total loss.

A third standard is whether the cost of recovering and refurbishing the thing insured is so out of proportion to the value of the resulting operational entity that the thing must reasonably be considered an actual total loss.

Under all three above standards, this court's findings of fact compel the conclusion that, under English law, the *Gatto* was an actual total loss within the term of the insurance at issue; in that the *Gatto* ceased to be an offshore exploratory platform and was destroyed.

While the court was interpreting an actual total loss according to English law, it appears that American law is similar. In interpreting an actual total loss, American courts have accepted not only physical annihilation or destruction of the subject-matter insured but also loss of specie or of value to the assured. Many early cases found actual total losses when the estimated cost of repairs exceeded the sound value of the subject-matter insured. The reason for this is, no doubt, that, under American law (*Bradlie* v. *Maryland Ins. Co.,* 37 U. S. 378), there is a constructive total loss when the cost of repairing the vessel exceeds *one-half* of her repaired value.

In *Soelburg* v. *Western Assn. Co.,* 119 F. 23, 1902, the court said:

> There is an actual total loss when the subject-matter of the insurance is wholly destroyed or lost to the insured, or where there remains nothing of value to be abandoned to the insurer.

In short, even though something may remain of the subject-matter insured, if there is nothing of value to abandon to underwriters an actual total loss has occurred.

There is no question, of course, that a vessel or its cargo is an actual total loss if it is completely destroyed, but the test of an actual total loss also includes the factor of the value remaining in the subject-matter insured in other words, loss of specie. This is perhaps more easily documented in cargo cases. In *Berger* v. *Pollock, supra,* four large steel injection molds were delivered damaged by rust due to the incursion of seawater. The English court found that there was an actual total loss of the goods because the rust had left them incapable of use as molds, with no more value than scrap metal. Although on their arrival it was thought that they could be restored by an expenditure of between £4,000 and £5,000, that amount was, in fact, spent to no avail.

American cases follow a similar course. As long ago as 1873 the U.S. Supreme Court considered a policy insuring a sugar packing machine. The carrying vessel and its cargo were lost, but a large number of the pieces comprising the machine were recovered. However, that which was saved was entirely useless as machinery and had only a minimum scrap value. The Supreme Court affirmed the lower court's view that, in the circumstances, there was a total loss of the subject-matter insured although some of the material itself, albeit not in specie, existed. The Court said that the destruction suffered was a destruction as to specie and not a mere physical extinction (*Great Western Ins. Co.* v. *Fogarty,* 86 U. S. 640).

It is therefore well established that loss of specie must be regarded from a mercantile and business point of view. If, as a result of the action of an insured peril, cargo arrives at destination in a condition which no longer answers to the commercial denomination in which it was shipped, it is no longer "a thing of the kind insured" (Marine Ins. Act, Sect. 57). The fact that it may still have considerable value is irrelevant; it has lost specie and on that basis is an actual total loss under the policy. On payment of a total loss, underwriters are of course entitled to receive credit for the value remaining in the insured cargo.

Where the ship concerned in the adventure is missing and when a reasonable time has elapsed with no news of her, an *actual total loss* may be presumed (Marine Ins. Act, Sect. 58). In such cases, the vessel is presumed to be lost by a marine peril unless circumstances indicate that the vessel may have been lost due to war perils (as when a vessel "disappears" in a combat zone in wartime). Should an underwriter wish to raise the defense of unseaworthiness in the case of a "missing" ship, he would have to sustain the burden of proof. To avoid possible disputes between marine and war risk underwriters as to which policies respond when a vessel is reported "missing," a Missing Vessels clause is sometimes included in one or other of the policies. This clause reads as follows:

> This insurance also covers loss of the subject matter of this insurance by reason of the vessel within named being missing from any cause during the currency of this policy. If such vessel be recorded at Lloyd's as "untraced" or "posted as missing," she shall be deemed missing for the purpose of this insurance. No claim shall attach under this clause where the specific cause of the loss of the within named vessel is proved by Underwriters.

There are other versions of Missing Vessels clauses. One such clause in use on the West Coast of the United States is sometimes added to the war risk policies and reads:

> In the event of the vessel insured hereunder being posted as missing at Lloyd's or is announced by the Admiralty as missing it is specially agreed that such vessel is to be treated as a War Loss for the purpose

of this insurance and this policy will pay claims hereunder accordingly within 30 days of presentation of proper documents. In consideration of such payment Underwriters are to have subrogation to any claim which the assured may have against the Marine Underwriters with whom the vessel is insured, but this insurance is not to operate as a double insurance.

In the event of this clause becoming operative it is understood that Underwriters hereon will in no circumstances pay more than the sums insured hereunder for War Risks, either for Hull and/or Increased Value of Hull or Protection and Indemnity Risks.

It is further understood that the sum payable hereunder on Hull and/or Increased Value of Hull shall not exceed the total amount insured on Hull and Disbursements for Marine Risks and that the sum payable hereunder for War Protection and Indemnity Risks shall not exceed the amounts recoverable under the Marine Protection and Indemnity placings unless and until such time as arbitration decides the vessel is a War Loss.

All such Missing Vessels clauses are merely intended as "quick payment" provisions designed to help the assured, leaving the respective marine and war risks underwriters to resolve liability later. However, the wording used should be carefully scrutinized by underwriters to prevent any possibility of the clause being erroneously construed as putting the burden of proof on the underwriters (whose policy includes the clause) to show the cause of the loss (marine or war risks) rather than their being able to rely on the normal assumptions as to cause referred to previously. Missing Vessels clauses are the progeny of the London marine insurance market and, while everyone in that market understands what is intended, difficulties can arise when the marine risks and war risks are insured in different markets.

In the event of an actual total loss, no notice of abandonment is necessary (Marine Ins. Act, Sect. 57), but to support a claim for a total loss of a vessel in the United States, it is necessary to provide the following documents:

(1) Note of protest or affidavit of witnesses setting forth the circumstances attending the accident.

(2) Affidavit of insurance (a sworn statement by the assured detailing all the insurances in effect at the time of the total loss).

(3) The policies of insurance.

(4) Certified copy of registry certificate. (This is a document issued by the United States government describing the vessel in detail and recording any mortgages.)

The purpose of the affidavit of insurance is to satisfy the hull underwriters that the Disbursements Warranty in the hull policy has been complied with. In other words, that the total loss insurances permitted, for example, under *para.* (a) in the Additional Insurances section of the American Institute Hull Clauses, 1977 (Lines 210/238), do not exceed 25 percent (in aggregate) of the insured value of the vessel. If the insurances permitted under *para.* (a) did exceed 25 percent of the vessel's insured value, the policy would be void and no total loss recoverable. The affidavit of insurance is sometimes known as a "disbursements letter."

To support a claim for a total loss of cargo, the documents required are:

(1) Evidence of loss.

(2) Invoices confirming the value of the cargo.

(3) Insurance policy or insurance certificates.

(4) A full set of the original bills of lading evidencing the shipment of the cargo, duly endorsed.

(5) In most cases, a letter of subrogation from the assured authorizing the underwriter to use the assured's name in any proceedings with a view to effecting recovery from other parties responsible for the loss.

These documents are retained by the underwriter and serve as proof of his interest in any salvage or recovery from third parties without committing him to assume any liabilities arising therefrom.

There is a total loss in the case of freight insured for a period of time when the vessel itself is an actual total loss by insured perils. Freight on any particular voyage may be a total loss without a corresponding loss of the vessel but this does not necessarily constitute a claim for total loss under a time insurance on freight.

CONSTRUCTIVE TOTAL LOSS

Phillips defines a constructive total loss of a vessel as follows:

It is a general rule in the United States, that, if the ship or goods insured are *damaged to more than half of the value*, by any peril insured against, or more than half of the freight is lost, the assured may abandon and recover for a total loss. The same rate of damage has also been mentioned by early writers and in foreign jurisprudence as one criterion of total loss. (Subsect. 1535)

The requirements for a constructive total loss in England are more exacting, for the Marine Insurance Act states:

Subject to any express provision in the policy there is a constructive total loss where the subject-matter insured is reasonably abandoned on account of its actual total loss appearing to be unavoidable, or because it could not be preserved from actual total loss *without an expenditure which would exceed its value when the expenditure had been incurred.*

In particular there is a constructive total loss—

(i) Where the assured is deprived of the possession of his ship or goods by a peril insured against, and

(a) it is unlikely that he can recover the ship or goods, as the case may be, or

(b) the cost of recovering the ship or goods, as the case may be, *would exceed their value when recovered;* or

(ii) In the case of damage to a ship, where she is so damaged by a peril insured against that the cost of repairing the damage *would exceed the value of the ship when repaired.*

In estimating the cost of repairs, no deduction is to be made in respect of general average contributions to those repairs payable by other interests, but account is to be taken of the expense of future salvage operations and of any future general average contributions to which the ship would be liable if repaired; or

(iii) In the case of damage to goods, where the cost of repairing the damage and forwarding the goods to their destination *would exceed their value on arrival.* (Sect. 60)

In the *Bamburi* arbitration mentioned in connection with the Perils clause in Chapter 3, Mr. Justice Staughton concluded that the word "possession" in Sect. 60 (2) (i) of the Act should be given the meaning of "free use and disposal." In the circumstances of that case (the vessel was "trapped" in the Persian Gulf) the owner had therefore been deprived of the possession of his ship (even though it remained intact). As to the interpretation of the requirement of Sect. 60 (2) (i) (a), namely that it is unlikely that the owner can recover his ship, Mr. Justice Staughton concluded that twelve months from the notice of abandonment was a reasonable time frame to put on this requirement. Thus, if at the time abandonment was tendered it was unlikely that the shipowner would recover possession within twelve months, this met the requirements of the act and the vessel was a constructive total loss (the *Bamburi*, 1982 1 L.R. 312).

In any event, the legal formula applicable in the United States (namely that, if the insured property is damaged to more than half its value, the assured may abandon the property to underwriters and recover for a constructive total loss) is not acceptable to underwriters, and policies on hull and machinery invariably stipulate that there will be no recovery for a constructive total loss unless the expense of recovering and repairing the vessel *exceeds the insured value*. Thus, the American Institute Hull Clauses state:

> There shall be no recovery for a Constructive Total Loss hereunder unless the expense of recovering and repairing the Vessel would exceed the Agreed Value . . .
> In ascertaining whether the Vessel is a Constructive Total Loss the Agreed Value shall be taken as the repaired value, and nothing in respect of the damaged or break-up value of the Vessel or wreck shall be taken into account.

In the case of the *Armar* (1954 AMC 1674), the court held:

> In the calculation of repair and recovery costs it is proper to include expenditure necessary to deliver the ship from its peril to a port of safety and thereafter to make it a seaworthy vessel. Accordingly, in addition to repair costs, the expenses of salvage, drydock and surveys, pilotage and towage and superintendence are allowable.
> Not to be included, however, in determining the existence of a constructive total loss is the allowance provided for by the "tender clause" of the policy, whereby the assured is awarded 30 per cent per annum of the insured value from the time of completion of the survey to the acceptance of the tender for repair "in cases where a tender is accepted with the approval of underwriters" for here there was no such acceptance.

The items to be included, in computing constructive total loss costs were also discussed in *Lenfest et al. Extrs.* v. *Coldwell* (1975 AMC 2489).

It is also, perhaps, worth repeating that in ascertaining whether a vessel is a constructive total loss, only the *vessel's share* of any salvage or general average charges can be included in the calculation.

During the course of a somewhat controversial address to the British Association of Average Adjusters in 1982, the chairman (none other than Lord Justice Donaldson, as he then was) took issue with this long-established practice of average adjusters. He expressed the view that the entire cost of any salvage operations must be included as part of the cost of repairs (or, as the American policy puts it, "the cost of recovering and repairing the vessel") and that general average contributions from cargo interests towards that expense are to be disregarded in computations made to determine whether a vessel is a constructive total loss. Lord Justice Donaldson was of course speaking as an individual and indeed during his address reserved the right to disagree with his address if he ever had to consider the problems of constructive total losses in a judicial capacity. In spite of his views it is doubtful whether average adjusters or underwriters will abandon long-established market practices without law being developed showing the existing practices to be wrong.

The dry dock expenses referred to by the court in the *Armar* are the dry dock dues that would be incurred if the vessel were to be repaired. Any expenses incurred merely to prove a constructive total loss (including any dry dock dues) cannot be brought into consideration. Here again, Lord Justice Donaldson, in the address previously referred to, questioned this long-accepted practice of average adjusters. He expressed the view that in those cases where it is not immediately certain that the vessel is a constructive total loss and has to be dry-docked for examination, the expense of such a dry-docking was recoverable under the Sue and Labor clause in the policy. The fact that the dry-docking and survey were necessary to prove the claim for constructive total loss did not mean that the cost was not recoverable as a sue and labor expense. However, in 1985 a subsequent chairman of the British Association of Average Adjusters (G. S. Hughes, an average adjuster) took issue with Lord Justice Donaldson. He thought that up to the point of getting the vessel into dry dock the expenses may sometimes be sue and labor (if it was immediately necessary to dry-dock in order to preserve the vessel). However, once the vessel was dry-docked, it had been "defended, safeguarded and recovered." If the vessel was found to be a constructive total loss as a result of the survey on dry dock, the assured would recover for a total loss but underwriters would not be liable for the cost of dry-docking and opening up for survey in addition to the insured value. This cost would be a charge against the proceeds of the sale of the vessel and in most cases the assured would recoup this outlay in that manner. Indeed, it is difficult to see how the cost of dry-docking solely to ascertain whether a vessel is a constructive total loss can be said to have been incurred for the purpose of averting or minimizing the loss to underwriters and therefore recoverable under the Sue and Labor clause.

It has always been a matter of controversy as to whether the assured can add several partial losses together and by so doing claim a constructive total loss. The question was raised by the chairman of the British Association of Average Adjusters, W. T. Wood, in 1957 and the consensus was that successive losses cannot be added together to prove a constructive total loss, especially if the successive losses occurred on different voyages. However, when the policy franchise unit is an Institute voyage, it is submitted that the total damages sustained during the voyage (even if incurred on separate occasions) can be added together to establish a constructive total loss. The point was discussed in the *Medina Princess* (L. L. R. 1965, Vol. 1, p. 361) when the court observed:

Nor do I propose to deal with the question when a vessel during the currency of the policy suffers partial losses by perils insured against *on separate occasions*, neither of which partial losses of itself creates a constructive total loss, the assured may, when the figures justify his so doing, aggregate those successive partial losses and claim for a constructive total loss under his policy . . . If underwriters in the future wish to ensure that an assured will not seek to aggregate separate partial losses in order to create a constructive total loss it would not be difficult to secure that result by making an appropriate provision in the Institute Time Clauses to make clear that he is not entitled to do so.

The drafters of the latest version of the American hull form of policy have accepted the court's advice and included the following clause:

There shall be no recovery for a Constructive Total Loss hereunder unless the expense of recovering and repairing the Vessel shall exceed the Agreed Value. In making this determination, only expenses incurred by reason of a single accident or a sequence of damages arising from the same accident shall be taken into account.

The matter is thus now put beyond doubt insofar as claims under the American hull form of policy are concerned.

When a vessel is incapable of recovery or repairs within a foreseeable time, the assured is justified in abandoning her to his underwriters as a constructive total loss *Calmar Steamship Corp. v. Sydney Scott, et al.,* (the *Portmar,* 1954 AMC 558).

In cases of constructive total loss the assured must give notice of abandonment to his underwriters within a reasonable time after receipt of reliable information of the loss. However, even in cases where no formal notice of abandonment has been given, it has been held by American courts that any actions of the assured specifically implying the intention to abandon will be deemed to be sufficient notice (see *Patapsco Ins. Co. v. Southgate,* 30 U. S. 604 (1831)). In *Rock Transport Properties Corp. v. Hartford Fire Ins. Co.* (1970 AMC 590, 597, 2185), the court held that failure to give notice of abandonment did not defeat a claim for constructive total loss when the insurer disclaims liability from the outset; by such disclaimer the insurer makes tender of abandonment futile and, in effect, waives it. Nevertheless, it is desirable that notice of abandonment be given at the earliest possible moment should the facts warrant such a course.

The Marine Insurance Act has this to say about notice of abandonment:

(1) Subject to the provisions of this section, where the assured elects to abandon the subject-matter insured to the insurer, he must

give notice of abandonment. If he fails to do so the loss can only be treated as a partial loss.

(2) Notice of abandonment may be given in writing or by word of mouth, or partly in writing and partly by word of mouth, and may be given in any terms which indicate the intention of the assured to abandon his insured interest in the subject-matter insured unconditionally to the insurer.

(3) Notice of abandonment must be given with reasonable diligence after the receipt of reliable information of the loss, but where the information is of a doubtful character the assured is entitled to a reasonable time to make inquiry.

(4) Where notice of abandonment is properly given, the rights of the assured are not prejudiced by the fact that the insurer refuses to accept the abandonment.

(5) The acceptance of an abandonment may be either express or implied from the conduct of the insurer. The mere silence of the insurer after notice is not an acceptance.

(6) Where notice of abandonment is accepted the abandonment is irrevocable. The acceptance of the notice conclusively admits liability for the loss and the sufficiency of the notice.

(7) Notice of abandonment is unnecessary where, at the time when the assured receives information of the loss, there would be no possibility of benefit to the insurer if notice were given to him.

(8) Notice of abandonment may be waived by the insurer.

(9) Where an insurer has re-insured his risk, no notice of abandonment need be given by him. (Sect. 62)

It is customary for underwriters to decline to accept abandonment when it is tendered to them. In the United States the validity of the abandonment is subsequently tested by the circumstances existing at the time of abandonment, not at the time of bringing suit, as is the case in England. In that country, when an assured tenders notice of abandonment to underwriters and it is declined, under English law the assured must then enforce his claim by the issue of a writ (that is, the instituting of a suit). To avoid unnecessary litigation, it is usual for the underwriters to agree to place the assured in the same position as if a writ had been issued. There is no specific wording of such a "writ" clause, but a typical wording would be as follows:

Underwriters decline to accept abandonment but agree to place the assured in the same position as if a writ had been issued this day.

It is the state of facts prevailing at the time a writ is issued (or the assured is placed in the same position as if a writ had been issued) which determines whether the vessel is a constructive total loss. The effect of the so-called "writ" clause is to bring English law into line with the law in the United States.

The fact that an assured tenders notice of abandonment, which is in turn declined by his underwriter, does not excuse the assured from continuing to exercise his best efforts to recover, save, or preserve the property insured. In most policies of marine insurance, it is expressly declared and agreed that no act of the underwriter or assured in recovering, saving, or preserving the property insured will be considered as a waiver or acceptance of abandonment.

There may be a difference in law and practice between the United States and England on the question as to what items may be used to prove a constructive total loss. In England it is generally accepted that only the expenses to be incurred subsequent to tendering notice of abandonment (or for which liability is pending at that time as, for example, a salvage award to which the assured is committed but which has not yet been determined or paid) can be taken into account in determining whether or not a vessel is a constructive total loss (*see* Sect. 60, Marine Ins. Act). However, it should be noted that Arnould casts some doubt on this general proposition (Sect. 1118). In any event, this is not the case in the United States. In *Northern Barge Line Co.* v. *Royal Ins. Co. Ltd.* (1974 AMC 136), it was confirmed that where a marine policy precluded recovery for constructive total loss "unless the expense of recovering and repairing the vessel shall exceed the insured value," the assured may defer tendering abandonment of the vessel to underwriters until she has been raised and the repair costs can be determined. Furthermore, the assured was entitled to include the recovery expenses (cost of raising) incurred *prior* to tender of abandonment in determining whether there was a constructive total loss under the policy and, on proof of such a loss, to recover the Sue and Labor expenses incurred (cost of raising) in addition to the stipulated policy valuation of the vessel. As another court had previously said in the *Armar* case (*supra*) at p. 1683, "if we are to give the word 'recovering' any meaning, these items (incurred prior to the date of notice of abandonment) must be included" (that is, taken into consideration in computing a constructive total loss). Thus, under American law and practice, the timing of the notice of abandonment should not prejudice the assured's rights under the policy.

As a result of the *Northern Barge Line* decision, underwriters felt it necessary to amend the constructive total loss clause in the standard American hull policy to read (in part):

There shall be no recovery for a constructive Total Loss hereunder unless the expense of recovering and repairing the Vessel would exceed the Agreed Value. In making this determination, only expenses incurred or to be incurred by reason of a single accident or a sequence of damages arising from the same accident shall be taken into account, but expenses incurred prior to tender of abandonment shall not be considered if such are to be claimed separately under the Sue and Labor clause.

As a practical matter, the change in wording, which is in effect an attempt to contract out of the law, achieves little because an assured, by tendering a reasonable but early notice of abandonment when faced with a major casualty involving Sue and Labor expense (or, indeed, recovery expenses of any type), puts himself back in the same position he was in before the amendment: namely, he has the right to include all recovery expenses in determining whether the vessel is a constructive total loss and to recover expenses of a Sue and Labor nature in addition to a total loss payment even though he may have used such expenses in the constructive total loss computation. It cannot, therefore, be too strongly emphasized that prompt notice of abandonment should be tendered to underwriters *before* any substantial recovery expenses are incurred (other than salvage services on a "no cure—no pay" basis).

As long ago as 1862, Dixon stated that the effect of abandonment was as follows:

> Immediately, therefore, that the emergency arises, and before notice of abandonment has been given, the master is bound to take every necessary measure for the defence, safeguard and recovery of the thing insured; in so doing he acts as the agent for both parties, or, more accurately speaking, as agent of the party who may eventually turn out to be interested in the salvage, and, as such, derive benefit from his exertions.
>
> If no abandonment be made, that party is, of course, the assured himself; it is as agent for the assured that the master will turn out to have acted, and it is to the assured himself he must look for making good all expenses *bona fide* incurred by him in his endeavors to save the property insured. If, however, an abandonment be made, which is either accepted, or ultimately proves effectual, the effect of such abandonment is, as we have seen, to constitute the underwriter owner of the property, from the moment of the casualty, and, therefore, to make the master, by operation of law, the agent of the underwriters in all that he has done *bona fide* for the recovery of the property from that time. *(Dixon on Marine Insurance*, p. 215)

In *Gilchrist* v. *Chicago Ins. Co.* (104 Fed. Rep. 566), the court held that the services of a wrecker (salvor) employed by the master before abandonment of the ship were chargeable to the underwriters. The court pointed out that the liability of the underwriters arose "from the rule of law which, in the case of a valid abandonment, makes the insurer the owner of the vessel from the time of the original disaster."

A more contemporary view is that where there is a valid abandonment of a vessel, the insurer is merely *entitled* to take over the interest of the assured in whatever may remain of the subject-matter insured and all proprietary rights incidental thereto (*The Republic of China, China Merchants Steam Navigation Co., Ltd. and the United States of America v. National Union Fire Ins. Co.*, 1958 AMC 1529). This is in accord with Section 63 of the Marine Insurance Act. Thus it is now generally accepted that a tender of abandonment, even if justified, does not automatically vest the property in the underwriter as from the date of the loss, where the tender is declined or not otherwise accepted. This is based on the thesis that although an underwriter is *entitled* to take over the property, he is not obliged to do so. In *Rhinelander* v. *Ins. Co.* (4 Cranch (2 U. S.) 29) the court stated that:

> The act of abandonment vests the *right* to the thing abandoned in the underwriters, and the amount of insurance in the assured.

However, unless the underwriter waives interest in the property or otherwise declines to exercise ownership (sometimes by mere silence), it becomes his property on a valid tender of abandonment, together with all the privileges and liabilities of ownership. As between the underwriter and his assured, the practice of declining abandonment protects the rights of the underwriter as to his liability or non-liability for a total loss. It also leaves open the question as to whether or not he will ultimately decide to exercise rights of ownership in the event the notice of abandonment proves to have been justifiable and the insured vessel is, in fact, a constructive total loss. It must be emphasized that even if the underwriter, while admitting and paying a constructive total loss, decides not to exercise rights of ownership of the wreck, he retains any rights he might have against third parties under subrogation.

If, in spite of the assured's efforts under the Sue and Labor clause, the vessel becomes a constructive total loss and is accepted as such by underwriters, it is generally agreed that any expenses incurred *after* notice of abandonment are recoverable under the Sue and Labor clause in addition to the constructive total loss payment on the broad grounds that the owner has been put to these expenses as a result of the underwriter's refusal to accept abandonment on notice being given. Absent any instructions from the underwriter, the assured was obliged to do what he thought best. The underwriter had been put on notice and if he continued to "sit on the fence" he must expect to foot the bill; he could not have it both ways (*see* discussion following the chairman's address to the British Association of Average Adjusters in 1951). Underwriters usually counter this argument by asserting that assured is bound under the terms of the Sue and Labor clause "to take such measures as may be reasonable for the purpose of averting or minimizing a loss." If the expenses incurred after notice of and declination of abandonment fell under this category, they were recoverable as sue and labor expenses. If they did not, they were charges on the proceeds of sale of the vessel (assuming the vessel ultimately was shown to be a constructive total loss). In a case before an American court involving an actual total loss, underwriters argued that if expenditures are made after the alleged loss has occurred, then those expenses cannot possibly have been incurred in an effort to prevent that loss. They asserted that one cannot prevent what has already happened and, therefore, there can be no sue and labor charges after a loss is sustained. The court rejected this argument, commenting that although it may ultimately be decided that the subject-matter insured is a total loss, it may not be clear at the moment of the casualty that such an extreme loss has occurred. Expenditures made by the insured with a view to ascertaining whether in fact a total loss existed were properly recoverable under the Sue and Labor clause (*Edinburgh Assurance Co.* v. *R. L. Burns Corp.,* 1980 AMC 1261, *aff'd.* 1982 AMC 2532). This decision anticipated Lord Justice Donaldson's remarks regarding expenses of drydocking, etc., incurred to prove a claim for a constructive total loss and dealt with earlier in this chapter. On the other hand, it has been argued that expenses incurred *before* notice of abandonment cannot be recovered in addition to a constructive total loss if those expenses were used by the assured to prove the constructive total loss. Underwriters have also on occasion insisted that any expenses incurred before notice of abandonment and which are being claimed in addition to a constructive total loss must come within the strict terms of the Sue and Labor clause; in particular they have suggested that a "no cure-no pay" salvage contract *for a fixed amount* does not come within the Sue and Labor clause since it constitutes salvage services and therefore a charge on the wreck (that is to say, a charge on the proceeds of sale of the wreck). If the agreed payment to salvors exceeds the value of the wreck, the difficulties resulting are apparent. The better opinion is that if a constructive total loss is proven, underwriters, in addition to the constructive total loss payment, are liable for all expenses incurred for the recovery and preservation of the vessel from the date of the accident, the master or owner having acted throughout in good faith as the agent of the underwriters, as indicated in the passage from Dixon quoted earlier (*see also* British Association of Average Adjusters Reports, 1951, p. 18, and 1959, p. 17). If it were otherwise, the assured would not be receiving a true indemnity. In short, the Sue and Labor clause, as a supplementary contract, applies to the situation both before and after abandonment by the assured. That clause is followed by the Waiver clause, which would be meaningless if the Sue and Labor clause itself did not apply after, as well as before, abandonment. The whole purpose of the Sue and Labor clause is to encourage the assured to take all reasonable steps to reduce the loss falling on underwriters; it is in accordance with the purpose of the clause that it should apply to expenses incurred after, as well as before, abandonment, irrespective of whether or not the prior expenses were required to prove a constructive total loss. In considering expenses incurred after notice of abandonment has been declined, it must be remembered that underwriters have a right to the subject-matter insured and are therefore interested in its further preservation as a means of reducing the loss falling on them under the policy.

The "death blow" theory discussed in Chapter 3 sometimes comes into play in determining whether an insured vessel is a constructive total loss under the terms of the policy. For example, take the case of a vessel which, while very old and decayed, is nonetheless seaworthy and capable of fulfilling its assigned tasks. If, as a result of the operation of an insured peril, the vessel is damaged to such an extent that the cost of repairing it would exceed the insured value, there is, of course, a constructive total loss. The fact that the vessel was particularly old and decayed would not defeat the claim if she was serviceable before the encounter with the insured peril. The insurer must either restore the vessel to its previous serviceable condition under the "death blow" theory or pay a constructive total loss if the facts support such a settlement. Furthermore, in estimating the cost of repairs of damage caused by the insured peril, no deduction is to be made for any increased cost arising from her age or state of decay (*Hyde v. Louisiana State Insurance Co.*, (1824) 2 Martin (N.S.) 410) (*See also* Arnould, 13th Ed., Sect. 1130/32).

REMOVAL OF WRECK

Since there is usually a wreck involved in cases of constructive total loss, it may be profitable to discuss the vexed question of removal of wreck.

When a vessel is sunk in the navigable waters of the United States in such a manner as to interfere with navigation, the U.S. government has the right to remove such a wreck (the Rivers and Harbors Act of 1899, also referred to as the Wreck Statute, 33 U.S. Code Sect. 401 *et seq.*). Until 1967 the courts had held that the U.S. government only had the benefit of a right of recovery *in rem* against the wreck and its cargo and had no further remedy against the owners of the sunken vessel *in personam*. Thus, the expense of removal was a charge against the wreck and its cargo (if any) which could be sold to defray the removal costs incurred (*Union Reliance*, 1963 AMC 1439).

In the United Kingdom the position was and is a little different: there the various harbor authorities are usually empowered to remove obstructions interfering with traffic. They are entitled to sell vessel and cargo to defray the expense of the removal but they are also entitled to look to the owner of the wreck for the balance. Furthermore, this right of proceeding against the owners of the wreck is not dependent on the vessel owner having been negligent in the first instance. Nor is the vessel owner entitled to limit his liability for removing the obstruction if the right to proceed against him arose out of the authority's statutory powers as opposed to negligent navigation. Incidentally, since the duty of removing a wreck under statutory powers is not voluntary, it has been held by the English courts that public authorities are not entitled to claim salvage remuneration for removing a vessel as an obstruction (*Bostonion* v. *Gregerso*, L. L. R. 1971, Vol. 1, p. 220).

In 1967 the law regarding wreck removal in the United States was brought more in line with the law in the United Kingdom as a result of the U.S. Supreme Court's decision in *Wyandotte Trans. Co.* v. *U.S.* (1967 AMC 2553). In that case, it was held that where, as a result of negligence, a vessel is wrecked in navigable waters of the United States, the government may obtain *personal relief* directly against all those responsible for the negligent sinking of the vessel. Thus, if the sinking is due to the negligence of the vessel owner, the wreck cannot be legally abandoned to the United States and its owner remains personally liable for the cost of removal. Prior to the decision in the *Wyandotte* case, it had been the practice of vessel owners to abandon wrecked vessels to the U.S. government through the U.S. Army Corps of Engineers. As we have seen, the courts had generally held that if the Corps of Engineers removed the wreck following such abandonment, the U.S. government could only recover the costs of removal up to the value of the wreck and its cargo (if any) and beyond that had no right to recover *in personam* from the owner of the wreck, even if he had been negligent.

The decision in the *Wyandotte* case is limited to vessels which were sunk due to negligence. Thus, *if no negligence is involved*, it appears that the earlier decisions would still apply and a non-negligent owner would have no *in personam* liability for wreck removal. Consequently, a non-negligent owner can still legally abandon the wreck to the authorities without further liability for the cost of removal or subsequent third party claims. Under the terms of the Wreck Statute, when a vessel sinks in a navigable channel, it is the duty of the owners to mark it immediately with a buoy or beacon during the day and a lighted lantern at night and to maintain such marking until the sunken craft is either removed or abandoned. However, it seems that a non-negligent owner has no further duty to mark the wreck after legal abandonment. Under the act, the owners of the wrecked vessel are required to commence the immediate removal of the wreck; failure to do so subjects the vessel to removal by the U.S. government. Furthermore, if negligence were involved in the sinking, the owners of the wrecked vessel would be liable for any third party claims which might arise prior to removal.

In view of all of the foregoing, it is advisable that non-negligent vessel owners (after taking immediate steps to mark the wreck) give prompt formal notification of the abandonment to the government authorities and to any state or local authorities which may be concerned. Assuming there was, in fact, no negligence on the part of the vessel owner, such a formal abandonment terminates the requirement to maintain the marking of the wreck and presumably terminates possible liability for a vessel subsequently colliding with the wreck. Should the U.S. Army Corps of Engineers decline the abandonment (as will probably be the case), the Corps should be asked to maintain the marking of the wreck and to proceed with its removal for account of whom concerned. Of course, if the vessel owner is obviously negligent in connection with the sinking and is obliged to admit such negligence, he must, in conjunction with his underwriters covering wreck removal, make his own arrangements (either through the Corps of Engineers or privately) for the marking and eventual removal of the wreck. The mere fact that the U.S. government assumes the obligation to mark the wreck does not relieve a negligent owner of the responsibility for removing the wreck (*Humble Oil & Refining Co. v. tug Crochet, et al.*, 1972 AMC 1843).

The position was summed up in a recent case wherein the court found:

(1) When an innocent or non-negligent sinking occurs, the owner is not liable for the U. S. government's expenses of removal of the wreck, including disposal of dangerous cargo.

(2) The owner's duty to locate and mark a wreck exists whether the vessel is sunk carelessly, voluntarily or accidentally. Hence the United States may recover from the owner the costs of locating a wreck not marked by reason of the violence of a hurricane (*Petition of Marine Leasing Services and Pittsburgh Plate Glass Company of Limitation of Liability*, 1971 AMC 1329).

The U.S. Court of Appeals (Fourth Circuit) had anticipated the difficulties subsequently created by the *Wyandotte* decision when it said:

... since in almost every foundering there will be some basis for a claim of negligence on the part of the owner or operator, extension of an *in personam* liability for a negligently created obstruction would result in great uncertainty and extensive litigation before the obligations of the owners and operators can be ascertained. The old rule, the one which logically derives from the statute, at least has the virtue of clarity and certainty in application. (*United States* v. *Moran Towing & Transportation Co.,* 1967 AMC 1733)

Unfortunately for vessel owners and their underwriters, the Supreme Court apparently rejected such a viewpoint.

It is under Sect. 409 of the Rivers and Harbors Act that the U.S. government must prove negligence on the part of the wrecked vessel to recover wreck removal costs. However, Sect. 408 of the act should not be overlooked. This section prohibits any person from injuring, obstructing, or impairing the usefulness of a structure built by the United States for the abatement of navigable waters or flood prevention. More importantly, it imposes strict liability (that is, liability without fault). The interpretation of this section was considered in *United States* v. *Federal Barge Lines (*1978 AMC 2308), and the court ruled that Sect. 408 applies only to those rare situations where a wreck may not damage a government structure but may affect its operation. In all other wreck removal cases, the court observed, the government must still proceed under Sect. 409 and prove negligence.

Wreck removal expenses are not normally covered by hull underwriters. In fact, the Collision clause in the American Institute Hull Clauses specifically excludes any sum for which the assured may become liable in respect of "removal or disposal of obstructions, wrecks or their cargoes under statutory powers or otherwise pursuant to law"; this, of course, refers to wreck removal following a collision.

Protection and Indemnity underwriters do cover wreck removal expenses but it must be emphasized that, absent any specific agreement to the contrary, underwriters insuring wreck removal expenses are only liable if their assured is *legally liable* for removing the wreck. The U.S. Third Circuit Court of Appeals has stated that in order to impose liability on Protection and Indemnity underwriters for the cost of wreck removal, the legal compulsion to remove must arise within a reasonable time after the loss or the expiration of the policy (*East Coast Tender Service* v. *Robt. T. Winzinger Inc.,* 1986 AMC 114). However, under such Protection and Indemnity coverage, the assured usually remains protected and indemnified for as long as he has a possible liability. Thus, if the insured vessel sinks as a result of the original accident and the wreck cannot be located but resurfaces at a later date, any *legal liability* falling on the assured to remove the wreck is covered by the original insurance.

From the foregoing it will be seen why (in constructive total loss cases) hull underwriters decline abandonment and take no positive steps to exercise rights of ownership. In most cases, the fear of potential liabilities attaching to the vessel greatly outweighs any potential monetary value remaining in the wreck or hulk. If underwriters are consulted regarding the sale of the wreck (as they should be) they usually take the position that the disposal of the wreck is a matter for owners and qualify their agreement to any sale with "so far as concerned"; they are anxious lest any action of theirs could be construed as exercising rights of ownership. Ultimately, if there are any net proceeds resulting from the sale of the wreck, underwriters may decide to avail themselves of their right to accept such proceeds. By doing so they would be exercising their rights of ownership under abandonment but at their option. Somewhat naturally, they would not accept the proceeds if there was any possibility of their becoming involved in liabilities in excess thereof. If the circumstances or potential liabilities are such that underwriters decide immediately following a major casualty to waive interest in the wreck by categorically stating that they do not intend to exercise rights of ownership, it follows that any net proceeds resulting from the subsequent sale of the wreck or hulk would accrue to the vessel owner. Even if equipment is subsequently recovered from the wreck, it would belong to the vessel owner. Indeed, in such circumstances underwriters would decline to accept ownership of such equipment in case there should be some unknown and perhaps greater liability attaching to ownership of the vessel or any part thereof. In short, underwriters, by accepting the proceeds, would in effect have accepted the abandonment of the insured vessel (and with it any liens or other liabilities attaching thereto). Here it should be stressed that the tendering of notice of abandonment is conclusive only as between the shipowner and his underwriters. Thus, a shipowner may abandon to his underwriters and be paid a total loss, yet, because underwriters declined that abandonment, retain his rights and liabilities of ownership.

If, in fact, the removal of the wreck costs less than the value of the wreck, the costs of such removal may be general average, special charges, or Sue and Labor. To determine the category in which the expenses of removal fall, it is necessary to look to the intention in the minds of those raising the vessel. This is so even when at the time of the salvage operation it is not known whether or not the cost of raising or refloating a vessel and her cargo will exceed the salved value of the property. In *Seaboard Shipping Corp.* v. *Jocharanne Tugboat Corp.* v. *G. L Sibring and other under-*

writers at Lloyd's (1972 AMC 1358), the cost of refloating a leaking barge containing a cargo of gasoline did, in fact, exceed the salved value, the barge being a constructive total loss. The court somewhat arbitrarily ruled that the cost of the "salvage expenses" should be borne equally by the barge owner's Hull, Protection and Indemnity, and cargo liability underwriters; this on the grounds that the owner had "sued and labored" on behalf of all interests in seeking to recover the barge (for the benefit of hull underwriters), to prevent a possible disaster by explosion (thereby avoiding liabilities which would fall on the Protection and Indemnity underwriters), and to save the remainder of the cargo (which would reduce the claim on the barge owner's legal liability underwriters). The decision appears to have been based on evidence given by the underwriters' surveyor that he thought he was representing all three classes of underwriters during the salvage operation. The court of appeals subsequently reversed the lower court, holding that the Protection and Indemnity underwriters were not liable to contribute to Sue and Labor expenses recoverable under the hull policy even though such efforts may have avoided possible liabilities covered by the Protection and Indemnity policy. The court quite properly pointed out that none of the expenses were incurred solely to avoid losses covered by the Protection and Indemnity policy; indeed, at the time the expenses were incurred, it was in the hope of saving the vessel. In short, they were not removal of wreck expenses compulsorily incurred (1972 AMC 2151). In considering such claims, it is necessary to know the exact reason for the removal at the time the task is undertaken. Where, for example, the expenditure is incurred in the hope of saving the ship and its cargo, it falls under the principle of general average; the vessel's share of such expenditure is, therefore, recoverable either under the hull policy or as a special charge against the property saved. The fact that removal would have been compelled in any event under the Wreck Statute does not automatically make the cost payable by Protection and Indemnity underwriters. For wreck removal expenses to be recoverable from those underwriters, the vessel must have been known to be a wreck, and the removal must have been compulsory. Simply stated, the question of compulsory removal does not turn upon whether hypothetically there would eventually have been a compulsory removal of the vessel, but rather upon the actual motivating factor for its removal at that time.

In all cases involving removal of wreck, the vessel owners' hull and Protection and Indemnity underwriters and any other underwriters concerned in wreck removal should be kept fully informed. If the cost of removing the wreck is likely to exceed the value of the wreck, it is possible that underwriters will require a limitation of liability application to be filed as a safeguard (thus hopefully limiting the wreck owners' liability to the value of the wreck). Whether limitation of liability is available to the vessel owner is conditioned on whether or not he was privy to the negligence (if any) which resulted in the vessel becoming a wreck. Indeed, it is a moot point whether it is possible for a negligent shipowner to limit his liability against a claim of the U. S. government for reimbursement of wreck removal costs. It appears that the U. S. government will take the position that such removal costs are a statutory liability and not "loss or damage" or "debt or liability" within the meaning of the Limitation of Liability Act. In one case which was litigated, the court found that even though the owners of a vessel which was wrecked as the result of a mutual fault situation may otherwise be entitled to limit their liability, their statutory obligation to remove the wreck was not subject to limitation since the non-compliance was within their privity and knowledge (*Esso Seattle—Guam Bear*, 1970 AMC 1592). In another case (*Complaint of Chinese Maritime Trust Ltd.*, 1972 AMC 1478), the court held that once a shipowner became aware that his wrecked vessel was obstructing navigation in the Panama Canal, the shipowner had privity and knowledge of regulations making him liable for the Canal Company's expenses in removing the wreck, and he was therefore not entitled to limit liability against such a claim. Whether these views will be supported by other courts remain to be seen.

Returning to the general subject of constructive total loss, the position may be summarized as follows:

(1) Notice of abandonment should be given to underwriters at the earliest possible moment; certainly *before* incurring any substantial expense. This is because, under English law, expenses incurred *before* notice of abandonment cannot be included in calculations purporting to show a constructive total loss. In particular, no salvage contract should be entered into for a *fixed sum* even on a "no cure—no pay" basis *unless notice of abandonment has previously been tendered*. If possible no salvage agreement should be entered into on any other terms than the standard "no cure—no pay" contract *with the amount of the salvage award to be determined later and to be based on the salved value*. (This would ensure that the cost of salvage services would not exceed the salved value of the property.)

(2) It is customary for underwriters to decline to accept abandonment when it is tendered to them. Thereafter, the assured should keep underwriters informed of any and all steps taken, or financial liabilities incurred, to preserve the property (thus precluding underwriters from later suggesting that the steps taken were unreasonable).

(3) If the policies expire shortly after the accident and before it is possible to determine whether or not the vessel is a constructive total loss, care should be taken to ensure that under the Continuation clause the poli-

cies are automatically extended (any additional premium paid by the assured would be recoverable from underwriters if a constructive total loss is subsequently proven).

(4) On *payment* of a constructive total loss, underwriters have the *right* to assume ownership of whatever remains of the vessel, and underwriters' instructions should be requested with particular reference as to whether they wish to waive all interest in the wreck. Underwriters usually take the position that it is premature to ask them to waive interest in the wreck until such time as the proceeds of sale (if any) and removal costs (if any) are known. A decision becomes particularly important in cases where the vessel is sunk in navigable waters; in such cases if the wreck has no value or the potential liabilities outweigh the wreck's potential value, underwriters' approval to abandon the wreck to the appropriate authorities should be immediately requested. Their instructions should be promptly complied with; in such a situation, if no instructions are received from underwriters, the assured should abandon the wreck as soon as possible to the appropriate authorities. (In the United States, the appropriate authority would be the government of the United States as represented by the U.S. Army Corps of Engineers.) Assuming hull underwriters have not by their actions assumed ownership of the wreck and the vessel owner has not been able successfully to abandon the wreck, he (as owner at the time of the accident) may be responsible for its removal. The vessel's Protection and Indemnity underwriters (or any other underwriters covering wreck removal) would respond for such expenses. For this reason the Protection and Indemnity underwriters, etc., should be kept advised of all steps taken subsequent to the notice of abandonment.

It must be stressed that, under the terms of the U.S. Wreck Act, when a vessel sinks in navigable waters of the United States it is the duty of the owners to mark the wreck and maintain such marking until the sunken craft is removed or abandoned.

(5) If the wreck (or hulk) is still in specie and has value, it should be sold by the assured for account of whom concerned. Usually hull underwriters will approve such a course but only "so far as concerned." It goes without saying that such sales are always subject to the purchaser being willing to assume all future liabilities and responsibilities attaching to the wreck. If a salvor or local authority has a lien on the wreck for services rendered, their approval to the sale should also be obtained. Usually the Salvage Association, London, will be willing to cooperate in the sale of the wreck. Whether or not underwriters are willing to give instructions regarding the disposal of the wreck, they should be advised of all steps before they are taken, so that they at least have the opportunity to object to the proposed course of action.

(6) If the wreck has not been sold or otherwise disposed of at the time underwriters pay a constructive total loss and the hull policies are cancelled, it is advisable to effect an insurance on the wreck (assuming it has value) on full Port Risk conditions. This is necessary because the original Protection and Indemnity underwriters may take the position that their coverage ceases once the vessel is established to be a constructive total loss (that is, on *payment* of a constructive total loss by hull underwriters). Such an insurance would be placed for account of whom it may concern and the premium would be a charge against the proceeds. However, even if it is accepted that Protection and Indemnity coverage ceases on payment of a constructive total loss by hull underwriters, it must be stressed that any liabilities or expenses directly arising out of the original accident continue to be covered. What are not covered are increased risks which follow a major casualty but which do not flow directly from that casualty. For example, an extended dangerous salvage operation may be mounted, resulting in increased exposure to liabilities not envisaged in the original contract of Protection and Indemnity insurance. In other words, although the wreck or hulk may remain in the control of the assured while being disposed of, it has, in fact, ceased to be the vessel originally covered; hence the need for special insurance as above. However, if the wreck has no value and the assured successfully abandons her to the appropriate local authorities after complying with all local requirements (such as marking the wreck), it would appear that there is no need for continuing Protection and Indemnity coverage. If the wreck has to be removed, such removal expenses would of course flow from the original accident and would be recoverable under the Protection and Indemnity insurance in effect at the time of the accident. The position would be the same regarding any legal liability of the assured which was the direct consequence of the original accident. In brief, the original Protection and Indemnity coverage continues for as long as the assured has a possible liability arising directly from the original accident.

In the past there has been much discussion as to whether, on payment of a constructive total loss under the hull policy, the entire policy is cancelled, thereby depriving the assured of protection under the Collision clause in the hull policy. In the latest American hull form of policy, it is put beyond doubt that, in the event of payment by underwriters of a total loss under the policy, the policy is automatically terminated— hence the desirability of attempting to obtain some form of insurance including the collision liability of the assured in such circumstances (always assuming that the wreck or hulk remains in specie).

(7) Even if the underwriters waive interest in the wreck, they would still retain their rights of subrogation. Thus, if the assured had any remedies against third parties for the loss, underwriters would be entitled to partici-

pate in any recovery obtained from such third parties. In short, the right of the assured to recover damages from a third party is not one of the rights which are incidental to the subject-matter insured.

(8) Finally, the assured, under the terms of the Sue and Labor clause, is required to take all reasonable steps to reduce the loss falling on underwriters. Furthermore, the Sue and Labor clause applies to the situation both before and after notice of abandonment.

When a constructive total loss is proven, all expenses actually incurred for the preservation of the vessel by the Master are recoverable from underwriters in addition to the constructive total loss. Furthermore, it is submitted that if underwriters do exercise rights of ownership on payment of a constructive total loss (by, for instance, accepting proceeds of sale), the rights and liabilities attaching to ownership would be retrospective.

To sum up, if a constructive total loss is claimed and proven, underwriters may take possession of the vessel and dispose of same for their account, the shipowners receiving the full amount of the insurances on hull and machinery and any other total loss insurances (such as Increased Value, Disbursements, Freight, etc., dealt with below). As already indicated, the underwriters are liable for any general average or salvage attaching to the wreck as well as any expense incurred within the terms of the Sue and Labor clause.

On the other hand, if the shipowner preferred not to claim a constructive total loss because he wished to keep and repair the vessel, the claim would be adjusted on a partial loss basis, and underwriters' maximum liability in respect of any and all claims for salvage, general average, and particular average would be for the total amount of the insured value on the hull and machinery policies only. The shipowner would have to bear any excess amount over the insured value and could not collect anything under his other total loss insurances.

At this point, it must again be mentioned that the American Hull form of policy permits certain additional insurances on Increased Value of Hull and Machinery, Freight, etc., and in the event of an actual or constructive total loss of the insured vessel, such total loss insurances are payable. The aggregate of such additional total loss insurances must not exceed 25 percent of the insured value of the vessel in the hull and machinery policies. As stated above, these additional total loss insurances are not recoverable in cases where the assured prefers to keep his vessel and claim on a partial loss basis. To support a claim for a constructive total loss of a vessel, underwriters usually require evidence that the cost of saving and repairing the vessel will exceed her insured value, in addition to the following documents:

(1) Note of protest or affidavit of witnesses setting forth the circumstances attending the accident.

(2) Affidavit of insurance.

(3) The policies.

(4) Certified copy of registry certificate.

The American hull form of policy provides that in the event of an actual total loss or a constructive total loss, no claim is to be made by underwriters for any freight earned by the vessel.

Sometimes the assured's claim for a constructive total loss is compromised—usually by the assured accepting a settlement which is less than the face value of the policy and retaining his vessel. Such agreements are known as compromised or arranged total losses and are resorted to when there is some doubt as to whether the vessel is or is not a constructive total loss. Very often the assured wishes to keep his vessel, and this fact influences him in compromising his claim with underwriters. Generally speaking, before underwriters will consider a compromised total loss they have to be convinced of the possibility that the ultimate cost of repairs might reach the insured value. Furthermore, in negotiating a compromised total loss with underwriters, it is necessary for an assured to demonstrate some savings to underwriters in order to obtain a compromised figure acceptable to both parties. On the other hand, in such cases underwriters have to bear in mind that if repairs are effected they might well have to pay up to the insured value; whereas, if they negotiate a compromised total loss, the compromised figure would not only be less than the insured value but would also reflect credit for the value remaining in the hulk or wreck. A further factor to be considered by underwriters is that, as a consequence of negotiating a compromised total loss, the policies are cancelled with full premium earned; underwriters thereby receive full premium without further risk. When a claim for constructive total loss is compromised for, say, 90 percent of the agreed or insured value in the basic hull policy, any other total loss underwriters must respond similarly (that is to say, any underwriters insuring Increased Value, Disbursements, or Freight must also respond for 90 percent of the sums which they insure). In other words, any compromised settlement reached by the assured and his basic hull underwriters carries with it the other total loss insurances. It should be emphasized that where an insured shipowner abandons his claim for a constructive total loss and the claim is settled as a particular average loss—even to the extent of one hundred percent of the insured value—this does not constitute a compromised total loss (see *Aronsen* v. *Compton*, 1974 AMC 480).

There is a constructive total loss of cargo in the United States when the goods are damaged to more than half of their value (Phillips, Subsect. 1608; see also *Washburn Manufacturing Co.* v. *Reliance Marine Ins. Co.*, 179 U. S. 1). This legal definition of a constructive total loss of cargo is always modified by express policy conditions, just as the definition anent the vessel is modified by insurances on hull and machinery. A typical Constructive Total Loss clause in an American cargo policy would read as follows:

> No recovery for a constructive total loss shall be had hereunder unless the property insured is reasonably abandoned on account of its actual total loss appearing to be unavoidable, or because it cannot be preserved from actual total loss without an expenditure which would exceed its value when the expenditure had been incurred.

This follows the principles enunciated in Sect. 60 (1) and 60 (2) (iii) of the English Marine Insurance Act. It will be noted, however, that unlike the Constructive Total Loss clause in hull policies, the insured value plays no part in determining a constructive total loss under a cargo policy. A constructive total loss exists when the expense of recovering and repairing the goods would exceed their value after the expenditure has been incurred. Of course, once a constructive total loss on cargo has been established, the insured value would be payable to the assured.

The rules regarding abandonment under a cargo policy are the same as in the case of a constructive total loss under a hull policy, and the clause quoted above is intended to indicate that an assured cannot abandon his property to underwriters without just cause. There is also a constructive total loss when the insured goods are necessarily sold short of destination due to the intervention of an insured peril. This is known as a *salvage loss*, the term given to a settlement under a cargo policy whereby the assured receives the insured value of the goods, less the proceeds of sale of the damaged goods sold short of the original destination. It is really a form of total loss settlement. However, the mere fact that cargo is sold short of destination for reasons of commercial expedience does not automatically entitle the assured to claim on a salvage loss basis. Only in circumstances where the cargo is impossible to forward, or where forwarded cargo is unlikely to arrive in specie, can a total loss payment—less the salvage (or proceeds)—be obtained. Alternatively, as provided by the Constructive Total Loss clause, only if the cost of recovering, reconditioning, and forwarding would exceed the anticipated arrived value of the goods is a salvage loss settlement applicable. In short, if an actual or constructive total loss cannot be demonstrated, the claim is adjusted on a particular average basis (*q.v.*).

It is not easy to define a constructive total loss of freight and, indeed, in considering freight policies, it is difficult to differentiate between an actual total loss and a constructive total loss. Phillips states that if more than half the freight is lost, the assured may abandon and recover for a total loss (Subsect. 1535, *supra*). He also states:

> A constructive total loss of the cargo by capture, arrest, or detention is a constructive total loss of freight. (Subsect. 1645)

In practice, there is a constructive total loss of freight where, as a result of the vessel having been damaged or lost due to an insured peril, the cargo may have been discharged at an intermediate port and forwarded. If the cost of forwarding exceeds the freight at risk, there is a constructive total loss of freight.

If the vessel is what has been termed a *commercial loss*, there is a claim under most freight insurances for the gross freight as a total loss, but not for the insured value. There is a *commercial loss* of the vessel when ship's proportion of salvage and general average expenses plus temporary repairs sufficient to enable the cargo to be delivered exceed the vessel's market value in damaged condition at the completion of the adventure. There is also a *commercial loss* of the vessel entitling the owner to a total loss of the actual freight at risk, where the vessel is a constructive total loss by comparison with her permanently repaired market value.

The above remarks relate to a total loss of gross freight actually at risk on the voyage concerned. Usually before the insured value of the freight can be claimed, the above comparisons must be made with the insured value in the ship's policies.

Chapter 5

Particular Average

If the main object of marine insurance is to afford protection against total loss of ship, cargo, and freight, there is no gainsaying the fact that the most numerous claims under marine insurance policies are those for partial losses of the subject-matter insured.

Here we enter the domain of the average adjuster. The Oxford English Dictionary defines *average* as the "apportionment of loss of ship, cargo or freight, through unavoidable accident (*particular average*) or through intentional damage to ship or sacrifice of cargo (*general average*) among the owners or insurers." The dictionary—wisely perhaps—does not attempt to define an average adjuster.

In the United States, the average adjuster is a man of many parts. He is employed by the shipowner and paid by the underwriter. His findings are issued in the form of an average statement which has no legal force, yet is but rarely questioned in a court of law. The Association of Average Adjusters of the United States (whose *Rules of Practice* comprise Appendix B of this book) was established in 1879 to:

(1) Maintain the honor and dignity of the profession of average adjusting.

(2) To promote correct principles in the adjustments of averages.

(3) To promote uniformity in practice among average adjusters.

The average adjusting profession in the United States was the subject of the address of the chairman of the Association of Average Adjusters in 1983, L. O. Haefner, and provides a wealth of information and commentary on the role of the modern American average adjuster.

The profession of average adjusting had existed long before the formation of the Association of Average Adjusters. In 1907 the then chairman of the British Association of Average Adjusters was so bold as to say:

For 3,000 years at least the necessities of commerce have needed the services of men like ourselves. Our calling is therefore both ancient and honourable, and one in which a little professional pride is pardonable.

Some eighty years later the chairman in 1986, K. Wood, said:

One of the delights [of average adjusting] lies in the satisfaction to be gained from finding acceptable solutions to all the various problems raised, in a spirit of businesslike practicality, common sense and fairmindedness.

To sum up: An average adjuster, unlike a lawyer, is not an advocate. He must, like an arbitrator, strive to be impartial and his adjustment, whether of particular average or of general average, should be drawn up (stated) without fear or favor in accordance with the principles and practices which have been developed by average adjusters throughout the world during the last 115 years. The first formal Association of Average Adjusters was founded in Britain in 1873, closely followed by the formation of the U.S. association in 1879.

Particular average claims constitute the bulk of the average adjuster's work and are the subject of this chapter.

Phillips's definition of particular average reads:

A Particular Average is a loss borne wholly by the party upon whose property it takes place, and is so called in distinction from a general average for which divers parties contribute. (Subsect. 1422)

A later and universally accepted definition is that used in the Marine Insurance Act:

A particular average loss is a partial loss of the subject-matter insured, caused by a peril insured against, and which is not a general average loss. (Sect. 64)

A more precise definition is probably that given by Gow:

Particular average is the liability attaching to a Marine Insurance policy in respect of damage or partial loss accidentally and immediately caused by some of the perils insured against, to some particular interest (as the ship alone or the cargo alone).

Common examples of particular average on a vessel are heavy weather damage, damage caused by stranding, collision damage, and fire damage. Cargo may be damaged by seawater entering the vessel in heavy weather. Particular average can arise under a freight policy when there is a partial loss of the freight brought about by failure to deliver part of the cargo as, for example, when part of a cargo of sugar is dissolved by seawater.

PARTICULAR AVERAGE ON VESSEL

Franchise Clause

Since particular average is a partial loss caused by a peril insured against, underwriters are liable for the claim subject to any restrictive clause in the policy. Prior to the revision of the hull clauses in 1970, the American Institute Time (Hulls) form of policy contained a Franchise clause which read as follows:

> Notwithstanding anything herein contained to the contrary, this Policy is warranted free from Particular Average under 3 per cent, or unless amounting to $4,850, but nevertheless when the Vessel shall have been stranded, sunk, on fire, or in collision with any other Ship or Vessel, Underwriters shall pay the damage occasioned thereby, and the expense of sighting the bottom after stranding shall be paid, if reasonably incurred, even if no damage be found.
>
> Grounding in the Panama Canal, Suez Canal or in the Manchester Ship Canal or its connections, or in the River Mersey above Rock Ferry Slip, or in the River Plate (above a line drawn from the North Basin, Buenos Aires, to the mouth of the San Pedro River) or its tributaries or in the Danube or Demerara Rivers or on the Yenikale Bar, shall not be deemed to be a stranding.

Under such a clause it will be seen that if a particular average claim reaches 3 percent of the hull and/or machinery valuation or amounts to $4,850, it is recoverable from underwriters. Furthermore, the policy pays damage caused by stranding, sinking, fire, or collision with any other ship or vessel whether or not the franchise is reached. The definition of these four categories is, therefore, of some importance.

A *stranding* is a grounding attended by unusual and accidental features, and the vessel must remain fast on the ground for an appreciable period of time. In this connection, Lowndes wrote:

> Grounding, whether arising from stress of weather, ignorance of the locality, blunder or stupidity . . . in short, for any reason out of the ordinary course of things on the voyage, is considered one of the perils of the seas. But when a ship is in the ordinary course put on the ground in a place where she is intended to lie, as, to load cargo alongside a quay, or to dredge up a tidal river, and sustains damage merely through not being fit to take the ground, this is not a peril for which underwriters are liable.

It has been much discussed as to whether the fact that a vessel takes the ground at low tide in the ordinary course of a voyage constitutes a *stranding.* The doctrine accepted on this subject is that where there is nothing extraordinary in the grounding, it is not a *stranding* within the meaning of the Franchise clause (*see* Phillips, Subsect. 1758). On the other hand, even when a vessel which expects to take the ground in the normal course of her voyage when the tide ebbs is damaged in doing so because of a heavy swell at the time, underwriters are liable.

In other words, it is accepted that damage sustained through grounding in an unexpected manner, as where there is some unknown danger in the berth, is a loss by a peril of the sea, and, depending on the length of time the vessel is aground, may also be considered to be a *stranding* for franchise purposes.

The American Institute Time (Hulls) form of policy listed a number of localities where groundings are not to be construed as *strandings* within the meaning of the Franchise clause. This does not preclude claims for damage arising out of groundings in these areas. It only means that any damage is subject to the franchise requirements.

The Franchise clause also included a provision stipulating that the expense of sighting the bottom after stranding will be paid, if reasonably incurred, even if no damage is found. This is to encourage the shipowner, if in doubt, to dry-dock the vessel to examine her bottom following a stranding. It must be stressed that to qualify for this concession, the vessel must be dry-docked specifically for an inspection of the bottom after the grounding.

Sinking (due to a peril insured against) is the second occurrence which "breaks the franchise" (i.e., is recoverable from underwriters whether or not the franchise is reached). A vessel has sunk within the meaning of the term when she has sunk as far as is physically possible.

The third peril which "breaks the franchise" is *collision with any other ship or vessel.* This implies forcible contact with another ship or vessel. The statutory definition of a vessel in the United States is:

> The word "vessel" includes every description of water craft or other artificial contrivance used, or capable of being used as a means of transportation on water.

Thus, the striking of a dock wall or floating wreckage is not a collision within the meaning of the Franchise clause, nor is striking a buoy or pontoon. In *Burnham* v. *China Mutual Ins. Co.* (1889 Mass. R. 200), the Supreme Court of Massachusetts held that striking a sunken vessel, the cost of repairing which would have exceeded her repaired value, was not "a collision with another vessel" but with a wreck. A floating dry dock in service, permanently moored to the shore, has been held not to be a vessel because it was not capable of being used as a means of transportation on water but was permanently moored to land and thus became part of the shore (*Cope* v. *Vallette Drydock Co.*, 119 U.S. 625; *Chahoc* v. *Hunt Shipyard and Ins. Co. of North America*, 1971 AMC 2452). On the other hand, a floating dry dock which was being towed to sea for sinking was held to be a vessel because "it was capable of use as a means of transportation on water as other specialized craft which have been held to be vessels" (*U.S.A.* v. *Moran Transportation Co.*, 1969 AMC 1209). In the same case, the court commented that several strange craft had been held to be vessels: a floating derrick engaged in pouring concrete for a bridge; a barge moored behind pilings on a river bank and serving as a platform for coal cleaning machinery; a floating pile driver. A flying boat has been held not to be a vessel even whilst on the water (*Polpen Shipping Co.* v. *Commercial Union*, 74 L. L. R. 157). A leading Protection & Indemnity club has expressed the view that a hovercraft must be considered to be a vessel. A tubular section destined to become a part of a tunnel for vehicular traffic beneath a river has been held not to be a vessel even though it was being towed at the time of the accident (*Rudolph E. Hill* v. *B. F. Diamond*, 1963 AMC 591).

The relatively recent advent of oil rigs has resulted in questions as to whether the submersible rig or the elevated hull are vessels within the meaning of the Franchise clause, that is to say, those rigs which are moved from location to location and sunk or elevated for the drilling of a well. In this connection, it has been held that a submersible oil drilling rig is a vessel (*Earl J. Guilbeau* v. *Falcon Seaboard Drilling Co. and Standard Ins. Co.*, 1965 AMC 346; *Wilton Cheramie* v. *Liberty Mutual Ins. Co.*, 1965 AMC 2063; and *Producers' Drilling Co. and Liberty Mutual Ins. Co.* v. *Luther Gray*, 1966 AMC 1260). However, a fixed, unmanned platform supporting an oil tank has been held not to be a vessel (*Ocean Drilling & Exploration Co.* v. *Berry Bros. Oilfield Service*). A recent decision which caused some consternation in marine insurance circles was that in the case of *Dressler Industries* v. *Fidelity and Casualty Co. of New York* (580 F2d 806, 5th Cir., 1978). The court concluded that a jack-up drilling rig, when jacked up with its legs resting on the floor of the ocean, is not a vessel but rather a fixed object. It was a vessel only when navigating. This surprising decision is contrary to the marine insurance profession's conception of mobile drilling rigs, for these rigs are written on hull conditions complete with *Collision clause*. The decision, if followed in other circuits, illustrates how litigation can upset settled practices and procedures. The notion that an oil rig capable of navigating is not a vessel but rather a chameleon—a vessel when navigating and a fixed object when drilling—will necessarily affect the right to limit liability; moreover, it throws into question whether a collision with this strange animal would fall under the offending vessel's hull or Protection and Indemnity coverage. A recent decision is more in keeping with the marine insurance profession's concept. In *Drilling Unit "Sedco 135" Limitation Proceeding* (1982 AMC 1461), the court held that a semisubmersible drilling rig is a vessel for the purposes of the Limitation of Liability Act. The craft was operating under registry; was subject to a preferred ship mortgage, Coast Guard inspection, and annual A.B.S. surveys; was intended to be used as a means of transport exposed to sea perils; and was not permanently attached to the shore or seabed.

On the Pacific Coast of the United States, large timber rafts made up of a number of sections, each carrying navigation lights and moved about by tugs, are recognized as coming within the category of "ship or vessel" but probably only because such a mode of transportation is a recognized custom of the timber trade.

In general, the test as to whether a floating structure comes within the term "ship or vessel" seems to be whether it can be said that the structure was designed to navigate (though not necessarily under its own power) from one place to another to convey cargo or passengers, and that such movement is not exceptional. In other words, the structure must have been built to perform its work of transportation on the seas or other waters. However, the vessels must not have deteriorated to the point where they are no longer capable of use as vessels. The moment when a sunken vessel becomes a wreck and not a vessel depends to a large extent on whether there was any reasonable expectation of raising her. If there were such expectation and another vessel collides with her, the collision is with another "ship or vessel"; if there were no salvage possibilities, the contact was with a wreck.

In considering this difficult question, it is perhaps wise to recall the old English case of *Merchants Marine Ins. Co.* v. *North of England P. &. I. Assoc.* (26 L. L. R. 201) in which the court commented:

> . . . there may be an infinite degree of variety in the facts to which the definition is applied. It may depend on the use being made for the time, and for how long a time, of the particular object: it may have been a ship which ceased to become a ship by its use: it may depend upon the degree of stationariness and mobility—the extent to which the object remains stationary and the extent to which it moves, and it may depend upon the purposes for which the object is used: it may depend upon its adaptability and navigability, and further than that I do not feel able to go. One can only deal with the objects as they turn up, to see whether they are or are not ships or vessels.

While there must be a striking together of two vessels before a collision can be said to have taken place, it is not essential that the hulls should come into contact. If one vessel strikes another with any part of her fabric, whether hull or materials, she collides with her. However, the collision must be with a part of a vessel's basic construction, including her anchor and chains. For example, collision with the suction pipeline of a dredger or the net of a trawler has been held not to break the Voyage Franchise clause.

As most (if not all) current hull forms no longer include a Voyage Franchise clause, the question as to whether the insured vessel has collided with another vessel has become somewhat less important. Nevertheless, it is still an important factor in considering the Collision clause in the policy and in the area of limitation of liability, because the right to limit liability is one which is only given to the owner of a "vessel." The issue is also important in determining eligibility for a salvage award.

Finally, the Franchise clause committed underwriters to pay the damage occasioned by the insured vessel being *on fire*, whether or not the franchise is reached.

In *Thames & Mersey Marine Ins. Co.* v. *Pacific Creosoting Co.* (223 Fed. Rep. 561), the meaning of the words *on fire* was considered. The court reached the conclusion that the words *on fire* were not to be construed as meaning the same as *burnt*, which was formerly used in their place, but as having reference to a present state or condition regardless of any definite fixed result. It was decided that the effect of their use is to open the warranty if some structural part of the vessel was actually on fire, without regard to its extent. The meaning of the more restrictive expression *burnt* is discussed in *London Assurance* v. *Companhia, etc.* (167 U. S. 149).

Voyage Clause

When the Franchise clause was in general use, it was invariably qualified by a Voyage clause. In an American Institute Time (Hulls) form of policy, the Voyage clause read as follows:

> The warranty and conditions as to Average under 3 per cent or unless amounting to $4,850 to be applicable to each voyage as if separately insured, and a voyage shall commence at the Assured's election when the vessel either begins to load cargo or sails in ballast to a loading port. Such voyage shall continue until the Vessel has made not more than three passages or not more than two passages with cargo (whichever first occurs) and extend further until the Vessel thereafter begins to load cargo or sails (whichever first occurs), but such extension shall not exceed 30 days in port. A passage shall be deemed to be from the commencement of loading at the first port or place of loading until completion of discharge at the last port or place of discharge, or, if the Vessel sails in ballast, from the port or place of departure until arrival at the first port or place thereafter other than a port or

place of refuge or a port or place for bunkering only. Each period in port of 30 days in excess of 30 days between passages shall itself constitute a passage for the purposes of this clause. When the Vessel sails in ballast to effect damage repairs such sailing or passage shall be considered part of the previous passage. In calculating whether the 3 per cent or $4,850 is reached, Particular Average occurring outside the period covered by this Policy may be added to Particular Average occurring within such period, providing it occur on the same voyage as above defined, but only that portion of the claim arising within the period covered by this Policy shall be recoverable hereon. A voyage shall not be so fixed that it overlaps another voyage on which a claim is made on this or the preceding or succeeding Policy. Particular Average which would be excluded by the terms of this Policy shall not be included in determining whether the 3 per cent or $4,850 is reached.

The object of the Voyage clause was to define the duration of a "voyage" during which claims could be added together for franchise purposes.

The assured had the option of choosing when the voyage commenced. These options were when the vessel: (a) began to load cargo, or (b) sailed in ballast to a loading port.

The voyage could be continued until the vessel had made not more than three passages or not more than two passages with cargo (whichever first occurred) and could be extended thereafter until the vessel began to load cargo or sailed (whichever first occurred), but such extensions were not to exceed 30 days in port.

A passage was defined as:

(1) From the commencement of loading at the first port or place of loading until completion of discharge at the last port or place of discharge, or

(2) If the vessel sailed in ballast from the port or place of departure until arrival at the first port or place thereafter other than a port or place of refuge or a port or place for bunkering only, or

(3) Each period in port of 30 days in excess of 30 days between passages.

When the vessel sailed in ballast to effect damage repairs, such passage was considered part of the previous passage.

Any voyage as defined in the Voyage clause in the policy was a "franchise unit" and the claims resulting from all accidents occurring during the voyage chosen by the assured could be added together for franchise purposes. If the total reached or was in excess of $4,850, underwriters responded.

Deductible Average Clauses

Since World War II, there has been an increasing tendency to incorporate in hull policies a Deductible Franchise or Deductible Average clause in lieu of the Voyage Franchise clause. Indeed, since 1970, it has been almost impossible to obtain full form coverage (that is to say, coverage on a voyage franchise basis). The basic American Institute Hull Clauses now contain a Deductible Average clause which reads as follows:

> Notwithstanding anything in this Policy to the contrary, there shall be deducted from the aggregate of all claims (including claims under the Sue and Labor clause and claims under the Collision Liability clause) arising out of each separate accident, the sum of $ . . . . , unless the accident results in a Total Loss of the Vessel in which case this clause shall not apply. A recovery from other interests, however, shall not operate to exclude claims under this Policy provided the aggregate of such claims arising out of one separate accident if unreduced by such recovery exceeds that sum. For the purpose of this clause each accident shall be treated separately, but it is agreed that (a) a sequence of damages arising from the same accident shall be treated as due to that accident and (b) all heavy weather damage, or damage caused by contact with floating ice, which occurs during a single sea passage between two successive ports shall be treated as though due to one accident.

It will be noted that the deductible average applies to the aggregate of all claims "arising out of each separate accident" and, furthermore, that "a sequence of damages arising from the same accident shall be treated as due to that accident." The deductible is applied to all claims other than total loss claims. Heavy weather damage and ice damage occurring during a single sea passage between two successive ports are to be treated as though due to one accident. This is a concession and is strictly construed. In other words, the "single sea passage between two successive ports" may be a very short passage of a few hours. Conversely, it may be of a few months' duration. Furthermore, one of the ports may be a bunkering port or a port of refuge; the "two successive ports" are not limited to ports of loading or discharge. Insofar as ice damage is concerned, this concession was only introduced in the 1977 version of the American Institute Hull Clauses.

Sometimes policy conditions stipulate that the deductible average is to be applied to "each separate accident or occurrence" (as, for example, the English Institute Time Clauses, Hulls). Whether the inclusion of the word "occurrence" extends the scope of the clause is a moot point. The word "occurrence" has been defined as an event or continuous or repeated exposure to conditions which unexpectedly cause injury during the policy period. It has also been suggested that "occurrence" includes voluntary and intentional acts and that the element of fortuity, as required for "accident," is absent. However, in a non-marine case it was held that there were two occurrences when two separate acts of negligence occurred (*Forney* v. *Dominion Ins. Co., Ltd.*, 1969 1 L. L. R. 502). A special committee set up by the British Association of Average Adjusters to consider the interpretation of the expression "each separate accident or occurrence" expressed the view that "accident or occurrence" required a wider interpretation than "accident" alone, and that the word "separate" suggested that in some instances involving more than one accident or occurrence, only one deductible might be applicable when those accidents or occurrences formed a connected set of events.

In the field of product liability, U.S. courts have been loath to construe "occurrence" (in the context of deductibles) to the detriment of assureds. In *Champion International* v. *Continental Cas. Corp.* (546 F2d 502, 2d. Cir., 1976) the insured sold defective material to various manufacturers who in turn installed it in their vehicles and boats. As the material failed, 1,400 individual claims for damages were asserted by the vehicle and boat owners. The dispute centered on the number of occurrences for the application of the per occurrence deductible. The insured argued that the damage to all vehicles and boats arose out of a single occurrence, and that the policy only required the application of one deductible. The court agreed on the grounds that the sales of the material even to 26 different manufacturers was one occurrence, since the eventual property damage arose "out of continuous or repeated exposure to substantially the same general conditions." (see *Insurance Coverage Disputes in the United States by Arthur J. Liederman—Lloyd's Maritime and Commercial Law*). Another American court has stated, "There is only one 'occurrence or accident' when damage to a variety of persons or objects arises immediately from a single cause" (*McKeithen* v. *Prosta*, 1978 AMC 31). Similarly, under a Protection and Indemnity policy providing a limit of $100,000 for "any one occurrence" and stating that a "series of claims hereunder arising from the same occurrence shall be treated as due to the occurrence," five deaths resulting from the insured vessel's capsizing were held to constitute a single occurrence (*Albany Ins. Co.* v. *Blain*, 1987 AMC 1469).

The question as to whether a series of incidents giving rise to a series of damages to the subject-matter insured constitute one accident, casualty, or occurrence within the meaning of a Deductible Average clause is one of fact and depends not on the lapse of time between the various incidents but whether:

(a) they are the result of the same act of negligence (if negligence was involved), or

(b) there is an *unbroken* connection between each incident which caused damage; that is to say, were the subsequent incidents *inevitable* (or at the very least something which might be expected to happen) once the first incident took place.

It is usually considered that if there is an intervening act of unconnected negligence between the various incidents, or the sequence of cause and effect is broken by the intervention of a new, unconnected, and unexpected incident, then the various incidents cannot be said to constitute one accident, casualty, or occurrence. Thus, when a vessel first grounded her bow on an uncharted obstacle while entering her berth and later grounded her stern on the same ledge as a result of negligent efforts to maneuver out of the berth, the court held that the second grounding was separate and distinct from the first because the negligent factors were not present at the time of the first grounding (*Newark Ins. Co.* v. *Continental Cas. Co.*, 1975 AMC 307). Yet in a case involving collision damages, it was held that negligence subsequent to a casualty does not necessarily break the chain of causation (the *Calliope*, 1970 1 L. L. R. 84). Needless to say, where there is no break in the chain of causation, the original accident and any consequential damages would usually constitute one accident, casualty, or occurrence. No two cases are alike and the question has to be considered and answered on the facts prevailing in each individual case. However, in applying the number of deductible averages, an American practice has been established in the following situations:

Ice Damage: Prior to the concession introduced in the 1977 version of the American Institute Hull Clauses and discussed earlier, a deductible was applied to the damage sustained as a result of entering *each* separate ice field.

If, when approaching a port, a vessel sustained ice damage while entering that port, while at the port, and when leaving the port, two deductibles were applied: one for the damage sustained entering and while at the port, and the other for the damage leaving.

The ice damage sustained was separated on the basis of the time spent in the ice under each category.

Contacts with Locks: A deductible is to be applied to the damage sustained as a result of each striking unless it can be demonstrated that the vessel was out of control due to the operation of an insured peril (say, heavy weather) and before control could be regained she struck the lock wall on several occasions. If during the same weather conditions the vessel proceeded through several locks, one deductible is applied to each separate lock.

The Chairman of the British Association of Average Adjusters in 1970, David L. Towers, expressed the view that the following circumstances should call for the application of only one deductible:

> Multiple accidents where, for example, a vessel goes out of control upon striking some object and then proceeds to strike other objects or, perhaps, runs aground. Similar events may arise from damage to machinery and result from the fact that the damaged machinery is not operating properly, thereby extending the sequence of damages either to hull or machinery.
>
> Ranging damage in a port, at least to the extent that such ranging stems from any one period of heavy swells encountered in that port.
>
> Progressively developing damages emanating from a single cause, even although the damage becomes steadily greater over a protracted period, until the cause is traced and effectively dealt with. There may, however, be difficulty where, in relation to complex modern ship's machinery, it is some considerable time before the basic cause is eventually identified (for example where some parts are slightly out of alignment), even though partial repairs have been effected in the meantime without curing the originating trouble.
>
> A slowly developing cause (provided it is of the same nature throughout) such as that where an engineer negligently omits to perform certain actions which ought to have been performed at regular intervals, but which have not been so performed.

On the other hand, Towers felt that the following series of incidents could not be regarded as separate accidents:

> A series of groundings when proceeding through shallow waters where each grounding is not directly contingent upon the preceding grounding. A similar situation exists where a series of contacts occur when proceeding through a canal system.
>
> Negligence damage to more than one part of the machinery, etc., where, even although the negligence may be by the same man and during the same period of time, each damage in fact exists independently of and bears no relation to, the other damage.
>
> Unrecorded damages, except to the extent that it can be demonstrated, by the nature of the damage itself, that it must have arisen from one single incident.

The Special Committee of the British Association of Average Adjusters, referred to previously, expressed the opinion that none of the following factors were relevant in determining how many deductibles should be applied:

(a) The fact that there were different heads of claim, e.g. particular average, general average contribution and 3/4ths collision liability, arising out of the accident or occurrence.

(b) The fact that certain items of claim might be recoverable under different principles if the policy conditions were varied by the attachment of other clauses, i.e. the "Liner" Negligence and Additional Perils Clause.

(c) The fact that in certain instances of progressive damage the claim might be divisible over more than one policy period.

(d) The fact that a repair of part of the damage may have been effected prior to the ascertainment of other damage arising out of the same accident or occurrence.

The committee further suggested that:

(a) One deductible is to be applied when either:—

(i) there is only one accident or occurrence from which the claims arise, or

(ii) even though there is more than one accident or occurrence, these accidents or occurrences are not separate but form a connected set of events from which the claims arise.

(b) On the other hand, if one or more of the events from which the claims arise are the result of a new cause, not directly connected with the previous events, i.e. that which would be considered in law a novus actus interveniens, then more than one deductible is to be applied to the claims.

These suggestions would appear to represent a reasonable and practical approach to what can be a difficult problem although it is not easy to generalize and the particular circumstances in each case must be carefully considered. Sometimes the policy expresses the deductible as being applicable to each "event" and defines an event as a single accident or occurrence or a series of accidents or occurrences arising from the same cause. This is where we came in, as used to be said at the movies when there were continuous performances of "talking pictures." A dog can only chase its tail for so long and we must conclude by repeating that the particular circumstances and probable intention of the parties in each case should be scrutinized closely and, as in determining questions of proximate cause, a commonsense view should be taken.

The last twenty years have seen the introduction of Annual Aggregate Fleet deductibles. As the name implies, such deductibles are not related to one loss but to an accumulation of losses over a stated period of time, usually one year. By the use of such deductibles, the shipowner is becoming substantially self-insured with what is, in effect, re-insurance on an "aggregate basis." Such plans often incorporate an "accident or occurrence" deductible applicable to each claim before the net claim is applied against the annual aggregate deductible.

Clauses of this kind reduce the number of claims under the policy, but it is essential that proper adjustment procedures are followed and accurate records of claims kept, even before the aggregate deductible is exceeded.

Latent Defect, Negligence, and Additional Perils Clause

The Latent Defect, Negligence, and Additional Perils clause is more widely known as the Inchmaree clause, so named after a famous case that gave rise to the necessity for certain of its provisions. The text of the clause has already been given in Chapter 3, to which the reader is referred.

The words "loss of or damage to the subject-matter insured *directly caused* by the following," in the first paragraph of the clause, are very important as they are construed as limiting claims arising from "bursting of boilers, breakage of shafts" to consequential damage only, i.e., excluding the cost of replacing the boilers or shafts. In other words, the bursting of boilers and breakage of shafts are perils insured against and the damage done to the vessel by the operation of these perils is recoverable from underwriters (subject to any franchise or deductible average requirements). Underwriters are only liable for broken shafts or burst boilers *simpliciter* when proximately caused by perils insured against. This is similar to the treatment accorded claims arising out of "any latent defect in the machinery or hull."

What constitutes a latent defect within the meaning of the Inchmaree clause has always presented some difficulty. A defect has been said to be latent when it cannot be discovered by a person of competent skill using ordinary care. Other definitions include:

A flaw in welding existing at the commencement of the voyage and not discoverable with the exercise of care (the *Rover*, 33 Fed. Rep. 515).

The words "latent defect" as ordinarily understood apply to something existing at the time the vessel or other vehicle was constructed, and such as was not discovered and might not be discovered by ordinary methods of examination (the *Carib Prince*, 63 Fed. Rep. 267).

If it [the defect] was not discoverable prior to departure for sea by all known and customary tests, it was latent and covered under the policy (*Tropical Marine Products, Inc.* v. *Birmingham Fire Ins. Co.*, 1956 AMC 567).

A true latent defect is a flaw in the metal (*Waterman Steamship Corp.* v. *U. S. Smelting*, 155 F2d 687).

If a defect is discoverable by any of the tests which a careful and competent owner would use in examining the part in question, it cannot be said to be latent (*Dimitrios N. Rallios*, 13 L. L. R. 363).

The Chairman of the British Association of Average Adjusters in 1956, D. V. Moore, during the course of his address on the Inchmaree clause, expressed the view that the expression "latent defect" conveyed the idea that, *through some manufacturing accident*, the defective part is not as it was designed to be, not that the design itself was wrong. This is in accord with the old English case of *Jackson* v. *Mumford* (8 Com. Cas. 61) which decided that the term "latent defect" did not include weakness in design. However, in a recent affreightment case in the United States it was held otherwise. In that case, water entered a new vessel through a suction valve which, on being dismantled, was found to be improperly designed. The court found that the defect was not discoverable by due diligence and the shipowner was not therefore liable for damage to cargo as a result of the ingress of water (*Natural Sugar Refining Co.* v. *M. V. Las Villas*, 1964 AMC 1445). As a leading admiralty attorney has commented, it is difficult in principle to distinguish defects in design from other latent defects, or to understand why underwriters should pay for the consequential damage resulting from a manufacturer's concealed mistake (see *Ellaline, infra*) but not the naval architect's mistake, even though the latter is no more patent to the assured than the former (*Tulane Law Review*, Vol. XLI, p. 330).

The classic example of a latent defect is a flaw or defect in the material of a part which existed at the time of manufacture but which is not discoverable by any means which a shipowner can reasonably be expected to employ. This obvious definition of a latent defect was referred to in the case of *Alf Larsen* v. *Insurance Company of North America* (1956 AMC 2576) when the court commented:

> These decisions have confined the term to a defect inherent in the metal itself or in the original basic material of which the part concerned is defective and latent in the sense that the defect is not one which could be discovered by any feasible test, even with the exercise of due diligence. An example, of course, could be such a basic weakness in a portion of the steel of the hull; or presumably, in a wooden vessel, in the lumber of the hull, as distinguished from material from which the vessel or part

was constructed, but which became weakened by chemical and/or electrolytic action or other wear and tear. Although the distinction is a fine one, it seems to the court that the authorities have laid down sufficient guides to enable this court to determine as a matter of law whether, in this case, the weakness of the suction pipe which broke off was, or was not, caused by a latent defect.

There is no evidence available or offered which would show that the breaking off of the suction pipe was due to any sudden action of wind and/or wave which caused it suddenly to collapse from any unusual strain imposed on a part weak from any inherent or other defect in the metal, but rather the only evidence expected to be adduced would indicate that the weakness in the pipe was caused by gradual action of the sea water, electrolysis, galvanic action or corrosion over a substantial period of time—from several months to several years—similar to other processes of wear and tear.

While there is no doubt whatever that any part which fails solely due to wear and tear cannot be said to have contained a latent defect, it is doubtful whether it can be successfully maintained that a defect cannot be truly latent unless it is a defect arising in the manufacture of the material itself. It has also been suggested that if a defect was discernible by the manufacturer it cannot be a "latent defect" even if it were truly latent insofar as the assured is concerned (as, for example, in the case of a sealed unit defectively manufactured but which unit the assured is never required to open). It is surely self-evident that the due diligence required under the Inchmaree clause is confined to "the assured, the owners or managers of the vessel." Thus, the better opinion appears to be that, in determining whether a defect is latent within the meaning of the Inchmaree clause, the test is whether it is discernible *by a diligent assured* using all the proper, reasonable tests available to him.

Nor can the thesis be supported that a latent defect is confined to those unexceptionable cases where no one, not even the manufacturer of the faulty material, is aware of the defect. In one of the earliest of the latent defect cases (*Ellaline—Hutchins Bros.* v. *Royal Exchange Assur. Corp.*, 16 Com. Cas. 132, 242), the manufacturers were not only aware of a cooling crack in the stern frame but they deliberately concealed the crack. Thus, although the defect was certainly not latent insofar as the manufacturer was concerned, it was truly latent to the assured, and the court so found.

It has sometimes been maintained by purists that if negligence is involved on the part of the manufacturer or builder, the defect could not be truly latent. Both the *Carib Prince, supra,* and the *Ellaline* dispose of this hypothesis. In the *Carib Prince,* the cause of the accident was a defect in a rivet arising from the fact that the quality of the iron had been injured by too much hammering at the time it was annealing, so that it became brittle and weak. This defect could not be discovered by the exercise of due diligence and the court held that there was a latent defect in the rivet which gave way.

In summation, it is submitted that a latent defect within the meaning of the Inchmaree clause is any defect which has not resulted from wear and tear and which cannot be discovered *by a diligent assured* by the use of any of the methods available to him; in particular, latent defects are not limited to defects in metal. (See *Tulane Law Review*, Vol. XLI, p. 337.) A similar conclusion was reached by the Chairman of the British Association of Average Adjusters in 1968, G. R. Heselton, in his address to the Association (p. 9):

> If the defect was not discernable by the shipowner or his servants using reasonable care the defect can be classed as latent.

A similar conclusion was reached by an American court in a case in which the insured vessel sank as a result of a defective bilge pump. The court held that the proper test was whether the defect could have been discovered through the exercise of due diligence; as it could not, the sinking was the result of a latent defect of the pump (*William F. Weber, Jr.,* v. *New Hampshire Ins. Co.,* 1986 AMC 2378).

The measure of indemnity in latent defect cases was considered in the case of the *Rensselaer* (1925 AMC 1116). The court pointed out that:

> The Inchmaree Clause in a marine insurance policy covers loss of or damage to the hull and/or machinery caused by an accident due to a latent defect, but does not cover the cost of replacement of a part which is condemned because of such defect, and
>
> an underwriter under the Inchmaree Clause does not become a guarantor of the fitness of the hull and/or machinery of the vessel nor does the underwriter guarantee that the hull and/or machinery of the vessel is free from latent defects as such an interpretation of the clause would mean that all latent defects would be repairable at the expense of the underwriter; the word "insurance" negatives any such interpretation. This judgment is reflected in the current version of the Inchmaree clause which specifically excludes the cost and expense of replacing or repairing the defective part (see also *El Mundo*, 1926 AMC 1449).

One of the most important and recent of the risks added to the American hull form of policy is that part of the Inchmaree clause which reads "breakdown of motor generators or other electrical machinery and electrical connections thereto." This covers accidental damage resulting from an electrical breakdown. It does not cover the correcting of a condition that might lead to a breakdown if not corrected. There must be an accident during operation to have a claim under the clause. The mere discovery of a faulty condition is not the basis of a proper claim. This part of the clause merely means that underwriters accept the breakdown of electrical machinery as a peril and the consequences would be paid for, even if the cause of the breakdown could not be established. The breakdown is the new peril, and "breakdown" means the stoppage of the machinery while in operation. This part of the clause is also subject to a deduction for the cost of replacing or repairing an identifiable defective part, but in most electrical failures, the part in which the defect existed is no longer identifiable as such.

The Inchmaree clause also permits claims arising out of negligence of crew. Negligence has been defined as "doing something which ought either to be done in a different way or not at all, or omitting to do something which ought to be done." When, as a result of negligence of crew, a breakdown of machinery takes place, it is the practice to assume that the whole loss is sustained on the date of the breakdown and the date of the negligence is, therefore, of no moment. However, when negligence has taken place over a prolonged period of time and the damage is not discovered until the vessel undergoes a routine survey, it is sometimes necessary to apportion the cost of repairs over the period during which the negligence and cumulative damage occurred.

Machinery claims arising out of negligence of crew have increased in the past decade at an alarming rate, and in 1972 the London market introduced a Machinery Damage Co-insurance clause for use with the American Institute Hull Clauses. (The British had included such a clause in their standard forms, but American underwriters had been unwilling to follow suit on the grounds that American shipowners had no control over the allocation of crew members by unions and consequently had little control over the quality of personnel.) The Machinery Damage Co-insurance clause reads as follows:

> In the event of a claim for loss of or damage to any boiler, shaft, machinery or associated equipment, arising from any of the causes enumerated in the Additional Perils (Inchmaree) Clause (except contact with aircraft, rockets or similar missiles, or with any land conveyance, drydocks, graving docks, ways, gridirons or pontoons) attributable in part or in whole to negligence of Masters, Officers or Crew and recoverable under this insurance only by reason of the Additional Perils (Inchmaree) Clause, then the Assured shall, in addition to the deductible, also bear in respect of each accident or occurrence an amount equal to 10 percent of the balance of such claim. This clause shall not apply to a claim for total or constructive total loss of the Vessel.

The object is to penalize assureds in crew negligence cases by requiring them to be co-insurers to the extent of 10 percent of such claims. The inclusion of the clause is not always mandatory and there is no equivalent American clause.

The protection accorded by the Inchmaree clause against negligence of repairers covers negligence of repairers while effecting repairs of any description, including owner's repairs as well as average repairs. However, this additional peril is intended to cover repairers' negligence which has resulted in an entirely new and separate damage. The presence of this coverage in the policy in no way reduces underwriters' responsibility for completely repairing damage caused by the operation of an insured peril.

The coverage against accidents in loading, discharging, and handling cargo, or in bunkering is widely construed: if the particular damage could have been avoided by the exercise of greater care it cannot be said to have been inevitable, and therefore conversely, it must have been accidental. In short, the assured has protection against any accident occurring during the activities enumerated in this part of the clause.

The coverage against explosions on shipboard or elsewhere was considered by the American courts in the case of the *Vainqueur*. That vessel sank as a result of an internal explosion and the circumstances were such that underwriters declined the claim on the grounds that the vessel had been intentionally cast away. It was argued by the assured that since the Inchmaree clause specifically covered loss by explosion, this altered the burden of proof, so that it was no longer necessary for the assured to prove that the loss was covered by insured perils, but that it was for the underwriter, in the case of loss by explosion, to rebut the claim. The court rejected this argument, pointing out that the Inchmaree clause was intended to provide additional coverage and not intended to shift the burden of persuasion. Although underwriters had failed to prove their "casting away" defense and although the shipowner had established that the insured vessel sank because of an explosion, the shipowner must still prove that the explosion was a fortuitous event rather than the result of wilful misconduct or design (*Northwestern Mutual Life Ins. Co.* v. *Harry Oliver Linard*, 1974 AMC 877).

In other words, the coverage under the Inchmaree clause against explosions refers to *accidental* explosions. Any damage or loss caused by an explosion arising from a malicious act or vandalism (other than barratry of the master or crew) or as a result of "any mine, bomb or torpedo not carried as cargo on board the vessel" would be excluded by the War, Strikes, and Related Exclusions clause. Such coverage would be provided by the war risk insurance (if any).

The Inchmaree clause concludes with a general proviso reading as follows:

> Provided such loss or damage has not resulted from want of due diligence by the Assured, the Owners or Managers of the Vessel, or any of them. Masters, Officers, Crew or Pilots are not to be considered Owners within the meaning of this clause should they hold shares in the Vessel.

In this context, the exercise of due diligence by the owners or managers refers to the provision of a seaworthy vessel, it not being the intention on the part of underwriters to respond for the renewal of defective parts. However, the term "due diligence" is not to be construed as being the equivalent of the duty to exercise due diligence imposed on a carrier under a contract of affreightment governed by the Carriage of Goods by Sea Act. While the courts have usually interpreted very strictly this requirement in affreightment cases, the shipowner is in a better position when the meaning of due diligence is being considered in the context of the Inchmaree clause. For one thing, in considering this aspect of the clause, the burden of proof of lack of due diligence is on the underwriter if he wishes to defeat coverage on that score. He must also prove that the assured's lack of diligence occurred at the managerial level.

Under the Inchmaree clause, underwriters, among other things, do assume liability in respect of damage to the subject matter insured directly caused by "negligence of master, officers, crew or pilots." To prove such a loss it must be shown that the loss was caused by one of the persons named, who, although being conversant with his duties, fails to carry them out correctly or efficiently, or at all. If the loss or damage was caused by the negligence of the persons named in the clause, it is recoverable in its own right. In *Allen M. Spooner & Son, Inc.* v. *The Connecticut Fire Insurance Co.* (1963 AMC 859) the court expressed the view that the language of the Inchmaree clause as a whole reflected a recognition of the different treatment to be accorded *seagoing* and *preparational* carelessness. There was no other explanation for the use of the term "negligence" in referring to the master, and the phrase "want of due diligence" in referring to the owner. Clearly the draftsman had quite different operations in mind. The court reached the conclusion that:

> The Inchmaree Clause was designed to insure against seagoing or operational negligence of the master (whether or not he is also the charterer or owner) and to exclude from coverage damage due to the shoreside failure of the shipowner's managerial staff properly to prepare or equip the vessel or the voyage or service she is about to perform.

The Chairman of the British Association of Average Adjusters, D. V. Moore, reached a similar conclusion in his address in 1956, stating that the provision in the Inchmaree clause insuring against negligence of the master, etc., provided coverage against negligence by the persons named in the discharge of their duties as such, that is, the navigation and day-to-day running of the ship. The exception, excluding liability for damage due to want of due diligence by the assured, owners and managers, applied to negligent failures in the discharge of duties that fell within their executive province. Thus, the provision of proper officers and crew or sufficient bunkers for the voyage is a matter falling within the general province of the owner or manager. Failure to exercise due diligence in that respect would be a failure of the owners or managers and would excuse the underwriters of liability for damage resulting therefrom.

It is well settled in marine insurance law that negligence of agents or servants below the level of management cannot be imputed to the assured so as to constitute a "want of due diligence by the assured, the owners or managers of the vessel, or any of them" (*Russell Mining Co.* v. *Northwestern Fire and Marine Ins. Co.*, 1963 AMC 130). Furthermore, the proviso regarding due diligence refers only to acts of which the owners have privity or knowledge (*Saskatchewan Government Office* v. *Spot Pak Inc.*, 1957 AMC 655). In *Founders Ins. Co.* v. *H. J. Rogers and R. G. Rogers* (1963 AMC 116), a yacht sank when a slight change in the yacht's trim while laid up at her winter moorings caused water to enter holes that must have existed for some time. It was held that the loss was the result of negligence of the master in the performance of his duties in connection with the lay-up of the boat. The court held that the owners had exercised due diligence within the meaning of the Inchmaree clause as they had not known that repairs were required; they were entitled to rely on the competence of the master they employed.

In a recent case involving an unmanned barge, it was held that a construction superintendent who was on the barge every day and made seagoing decisions for its protection was its master within the meaning of the Inchmaree clause. Therefore his imprudent failure to alter mooring lines to provide better protection against a storm did not bar recovery from underwriters after the barge capsized (*Continental Ins. Co.* v. *Hersent Offshore*, 1978 AMC 234).

Thus it is well established that the exercise of due diligence is confined to the owners of the vessel or the managers and does not extend to the acts or omissions of their agents. Furthermore, there must be a causal connection between the damage or loss and the lack of due diligence (*see also* address of the Chairman of the British Association of Average Adjusters, G. R. Heselton, 1968, p. 12).

In considering the effect of the proviso in the Inchmaree clause regarding due diligence, regard, must be given as always, to the circumstances of the particular claim under review. As the court put it in *Founders Ins. Co. v. H. J. Rogers and R. G. Rogers, supra*:

Due diligence is always a relative term and what constitutes due diligence must be measured in the light of the facts and circumstances of the particular case which brings the term into question.

The due diligence requirement is included in the Inchmaree clause to protect insurers in those cases where the vessel has been flagrantly mismanaged to such an extent as to render the vessel grossly unseaworthy and thereby to result in a claim for loss or damage under the Inchmaree clause. Generally speaking, courts are reluctant to deprive an assured of coverage under a policy of insurance unless the facts indicating such a course are irrefutable. Consequently, underwriters seldom rely on this aspect of the clause as a defense to a claim.

Liner Negligence Clause

A much broader Additional Perils clause is the Liner Negligence clause, which is often incorporated in hull policies in lieu of the basic Inchmaree clause. The American Hull Insurance Syndicate Liner Negligence clause (May 1, 1964) reads as follows:

The so-called Inchmaree clause of the attached Policy is deleted and in place thereof the following inserted:
"This insurance also specially to cover, subject to the Average Warranty:
a. Breakdown of motor generators or other electrical machinery and electrical connections thereto; bursting of boilers; breakage of shafts; or any latent defect in the machinery or hull;
b. Loss of or damage to the subject matter insured directly caused by:
1. Accidents on shipboard or elsewhere, other than breakdown of or accidents to nuclear installations or reactors on board the insured Vessel;
2. Negligence, error of judgment or incompetence of any person; excluding under both a and b above only the cost of repairing, replacing or renewing any part condemned solely as a result of a latent defect, wear and tear, gradual deterioration or fault or error in design or construction;
provided such loss or damage (either as described in said a or b or both) has not resulted from want of due diligence by the Assured(s),

the Owner(s) or Manager(s) of the Vessel, or any of them. Masters, mates, engineers, pilots or crew not to be considered as part owners within the meaning of this clause should they hold shares in the Vessel."

The Liner Negligence clause is a variation or extension of the standard Inchmaree clause and was officially introduced in the London market as long ago as 1931. At that time, as its name implies, the clause was confined to vessels engaged in a liner or berth service. Even before 1931 many liner owners had their own particular forms of Additional Perils clauses which varied from fleet to fleet. All these so-called Liner clauses had this in common: they were a form of "all risks" insurance and provided a much wider coverage than did the standard Inchmaree clause. Under such "all risks" clauses, the burden is on the *insurer* to show that the cause of the loss is a cause excluded by the language of the policy (*Goodman* v. *Fireman's Fund Ins. Co.*, 1978 AMC 846). The assured need not prove that the loss was fortuitous—only that it occurred; he must, however, furnish the insurer with such information as is known as to the cause of the loss (*Atlantic Lines* v. *American Motorists Ins. Co.*, 1976 AMC 2522). Nevertheless, an "all risks" comprehensive hull insurance policy covers only physical loss or damage from external causes; it does not, for example, encompass defects in title (*Robert M. Nevers* v. *Aetna Ins. Co.*, 1977 AMC 2017). Nor does it cover normal wear and tear or internal deterioration or decomposition (*Contractors Realty Co.* v. *Insurance Company of North America*, 1979 AMC 1864).

It was not until 1964 that the American marine insurance market first offered an official Liner Negligence clause of its own. When introducing the clause, the American Hull Insurance Syndicate made it plain that it was intended to apply to liner and berth service fleets only, but in practice the clause is in more universal use than was originally contemplated. The clause was also to be subject to an additional premium. This is not to be wondered at because the American Hull Insurance Syndicate Liner Negligence clause (to give it its full name) provides an "all risks" coverage, something frequently seen in cargo insurances but seldom in hull insurances. Under this clause, as long as there has been an accident and damage has resulted, it is not necessary for the assured to point to a specific peril. If the claim is to be avoided, the underwriters must rely on the exclusions part of the clause. This reads:

> excluding . . . only the cost of repairing, replacing or renewing any part condemned *solely* as a result of a latent defect, wear and tear, gradual deterioration or fault or error in design or construction.

This part of the clause appears to have caused some difficulty to the uninitiated but it means only that the mere discovery of a latent defect, a wear and tear condition, or a fault or error in design or construction during a routine examination in port does not provide grounds for a claim under the clause. The exclusion would also apply even if, at a routine examination, the defect had manifested itself. This for the reason that, in those circumstances, there has been no accident, no actual failure in operation, but merely the condemnation of a part owing to the presence of a latent defect, wear and tear, gradual deterioration, or fault or error in design or construction. Thus underwriters do not respond when a part is merely condemned on inspection or survey and has not been damaged due to a previous accident in operation. Conversely, underwriters are liable if the defective part failed in operation; in those circumstances the defective part has reached the breaking point and there has been an accident within the meaning of the clause.

A somewhat similar exclusion was interpreted recently by the English courts. The exclusion read as follows:

> no claim shall be allowed in respect of . . . any loss or expenditure incurred solely in remedying a fault in design . . . or for the cost and expense of replacing or repairing any part condemned solely in consequence of a latent defect or fault or error in design or construction.

The decision reached was that the exclusion applied only where a part was condemned solely in consequence of a latent defect or error in design or construction. The word "solely" meant "without the intervention of any peril" (the [*Miss Jay Jay*] *J. J. Lloyd Instruments* v. *Northern Star Insurance Co.*, 1985 1 L.R. 264, 1987 1 L.R. 32). The thrust of this decision is that, if an insured peril intervenes between the original flaw and the resultant damage, the insurers are not entitled to rely on the exclusion.

In summary, in determining whether the exclusion in the liner negligence clause is applicable in any particular case, the questions to be asked are:

(a) has there been an accident in operation—that is to say, a failure in service? (an accident is an insured peril); or

(b) has any other insured peril operated in conjunction with any of the defects (latent defect, wear and tear, gradual deterioration, or fault or error in design or construction) enumerated in the exclusion and, if so, was it this combination which resulted in the defective part in question being condemned?

If the answer to either of these questions is in the affirmative, the exclusion does not operate, because there has been no part condemned *solely* as a result of a latent defect, etc. However, the exclusion is not restricted to the condemnation of an apparently sound part whose defects have not yet been manifested. For example, if on opening up machinery at a routine survey it is found that a latent defect has become patent (as when cracks are discovered in a part formerly thought to be sound) and there has been no intervention of an insured peril, the exclusion is still applicable. In particular it cannot be argued that the exclusion does not apply because there has been an accident in operation resulting in the cracks discovered on opening up. The clause requires that damage be caused by an external accidental event. If the sole cause of the damage giving rise to the condemnation of the defective part was an inherent defect (that is, latent defects, wear and tear, and design defects, etc.), any claim for repairing or replacing the part is caught by the exclusion in the clause. To suggest otherwise would be to construe the clause as providing a permanent guarantee or the shipbuilder's or designer's work and entitle an assured to improve his vessel at underwriters' expense. This is certainly not the intent of the clause.

Before leaving the subject of the exclusions, it should be pointed out that this part of the clause simply restates the position under common law; the exclusions are precautionary and operate when no accident has occurred. Furthermore, as is the case in every "all risks" insurance, once a prima facie claim has been presented to underwriters, the onus of proof lies with them should they wish to reject the claim.

Turning from the exclusion in the Liner Negligence clause to the coverage given by the clause, paragraph a covers the breakdown of motor generators, electrical machinery, bursting of boilers, breakage of shafts, and any latent defect, all *without any qualification*. That is to say, the words *"directly caused by"* are omitted, with the result that, providing there has been an accident, not only does the assured recover the consequential damage, as is the case under the standard Inchmaree clause, but he also recovers the cost of replacing the boiler or shaft or part containing the latent defect.

On the other hand, the risks or perils enumerated under paragraph b of the clause are still preceded by the words *"directly caused by."* This is the wording used in the standard Inchmaree clause and results in the recovery only of the *consequential damage* caused by the perils enumerated in paragraph b. Paragraph b covers loss or damage directly caused by *accidents* on shipboard or elsewhere, and negligence, error of judgment, or incompetence of any person. For example, if there has been an *accident* resulting from wear and tear, gradual deterioration, or fault or error in design or construction, the *consequential damage* would still be recoverable from underwriters. Therefore, even though the accident be due initially to wear and tear or any of the other exclusions, providing every endeavor has been made by the assured to ensure that the vessel was properly maintained and in class, the breakdown was an accident within the meaning of the Liner Negligence clause because it was sudden and unexpected insofar as the assured was concerned. However, it must be clearly understood that the cost of repairing or replacing the worn out part or correcting the error in design or construction would not itself be recoverable, if clearly identifiable; it is only the consequential damage which is recoverable.

To sum up, only the perils mentioned under paragraph a are not restricted by the words "*directly caused by.*" It is the omission of these words which indicates that it is the perils mentioned in paragraph a, and those perils only, which are covered absolutely or without limitation. On the other hand, only the *consequences* of the perils mentioned in paragraph b are covered.

Broadly speaking, the American Hull Insurance Syndicate Liner Negligence clause covers damage resulting from any *accident*. In interpreting liner negligence clauses, a wide interpretation is given to the word "accident." It is construed to cover "something fortuitous, sudden, and unexpected," a "casualty," a "happening," "something unforeseen, unusual, extraordinary"; in short, something unlooked for and out of the usual course of things.

The Liner Negligence clause also covers the negligence, error of judgment, or incompetence of *any person* whereas the standard Inchmaree clause only covers the negligence of certain enumerated persons. For example, negligence of builders or designers is covered under the Liner Negligence clause but not under the Inchmaree clause.

In short, the following *additional coverage* is provided by the American Hull Insurance Syndicate Liner Negligence clause:

Boilers bursting in operation from any cause (including the cost of replacing the boiler),

Shafts breaking in operation from any cause (including the cost of replacing the shaft),

Latent defects becoming patent in operation (including the cost of replacing the part containing the latent defect),

Any *accidental* damage (and a wide application is given to the word "accident"),

Damage due to negligence of builders or designers (in fact, the clause says "negligence of any person").

The Liner Negligence clause has one factor in common with the standard Inchmaree clause, that is, the proviso regarding the exercise of due diligence by the assured, the owner, or the managers of the insured vessel.

MEASURE OF INDEMNITY FOR PARTICULAR AVERAGE ON VESSEL

The English courts, in a very famous old non-marine case, describe indemnity as being the basis of insurance law:

The very foundation, in my opinion, of every rule which has been applied to insurance law is this, namely that the contract of insurance contained in a marine or fire policy is a contract of indemnity, and of indemnity only, and that this contract means that the assured, in case of a loss against which the policy has been made, shall be fully indemnified, but shall never be more than fully indemnified. That is the fundamental principle of insurance, and if ever a proposition is brought forward which is at variance with it—that is to say, which either will prevent the assured from obtaining a full indemnity, or which will give to the assured more than a full indemnity—that propostion must certainly be wrong (*Castellain* v. *Preston,* All E. R. Rep. 493).

Certainly the intention of a marine policy is to place the assured as nearly as possible in the same position after the accident as before (subject, of course, to specific policy conditions). However, a valued policy (and in practice almost all marine policies are valued) may well violate the principle of indemnity insofar as claims for total loss are concerned. The reason for this is the fact that the agreed insured value is binding between the parties regardless of whether or not it represents the actual value of the insured vessel. This does not affect particular average claims under a policy of marine insurance on ship since such claims are not based on the insured value in the policy, and the cost of repairs is paid by underwriters regardless of whether or not the vessel is fully insured for her market value (*International Nav. Co.* v. *Atlantic Mutual Ins. Co.,* 100 Fed. Rep. 323).

Under English law, underwriters' liability arises when the insured vessel is damaged by an insured peril and insurers, if they wish, can reject claims not presented within the statutory period of six years (English Limitation Act, 1939). Generally speaking, underwriters do not avail themselves of this legal right. However, this question of time limitation was raised in *Chandris* v. *Argo,* (1963 2 L.R. 65). The court held that underwriters' obligation under a policy of insurance and the assured's cause of action accruing therefrom arise as soon as the damage occurs, not when the repairs are effected. In the case of collision claims, the court held that the six-year time-bar runs from the date when damages are paid. There is no such statutory time-bar in the United States insofar as claims under marine insurance policies are concerned.

Underwriters' liability is usually quantified at a later date by the incurring of repair expenses. In this connection the Chairman of the British Association of Average Adjusters in 1954, G. E. Towers, commented:

If a vessel is damaged by an insured peril, then, under the insurance contract, the underwriter is from the moment under an obligation to restore her to sound condition and there is no reason in law why the owner must wait to have the restoration carried out . . . if the required repairs are immediately necessary or not, provided he does them at such time and under such conditions . . . as a reasonable owner might be expected to do them. (1954 Report, p. 12)

The measure of indemnity for particular average to ship is the reasonable cost of repairs, a cost which must not exceed the insured value in respect of any one accident (Marine Ins. Act., Sect. 69). In Phillips's words:

The underwriter is responsible for the repair or restoration of the damaged or destroyed part of the ship or article belonging to it with materials, workmanship, style, and finish corresponding to its original character (Subsect. 1428).

To determine the reasonable cost of repairs, each particular case must be evaluated in all its circumstances. Some years ago an eminent King's Counsel in a well-known opinion made a brave attempt to define "reasonable cost of repairs." In part, he said:

In many matters arising under the hull policy, it is the judgement of a prudent owner, arrived at irrespectively of all insurance conditions, which is determinative. The standpoint should be that of a fairminded business man considering what was reasonable in such circumstances. The question is what a man of average prudence would do in similar circumstances. A crucial criterion as to reasonableness is that, by the contract of insurance, both parties contemplate that the ship is being insured, not merely as a piece of valuable property, but as a freight-earning instrument. The indemnity intended by the contract of insurance is the making good to the assured the loss which he sustains by sea damage. Whether the assured will ultimately be a gainer or a loser by the transaction is a matter beyond the scope of the contract and one with which the underwriter has no concern. The business sense of the matter is that the damaged ship should be brought back into service as soon as practicable and I think the Courts will say that this must have been in the contemplation of the underwriters when they wrote the risk. There is something fantastic in the concept that, under a contract of insurance, it is contemplated that a ship . . . should remain immobilized for weeks . . . the contention that the underwriters receive no benefit from the extra expense and the consequent saving of time does not counter these considerations. The policy is not designed to confer benefits on the underwriters (except premiums). The suggestion that the owner should be paid less because he benefits from the quicker repairs is, in my opinion, irrelevant, and indeed based on a fallacy. The question is not whether he benefits, but whether the cost of repairs is reasonable. The actual outlay on the repairs, if bona fide made, would be strong evidence what the reasonable cost was.

While underwriters might consider some of counsel's views to be rather severe, text writers in general support the view that reasonable cost of repairs does not necessarily mean the lowest cost of repairs. McArthur stated that:

> The general policy of the law of insurance sanctions and requires only that method of procedure which a prudent uninsured owner might be expected to adopt.

In short, what constitutes the reasonable cost of repairs must be carefully considered in each individual case and, always assuming the assured adopts a reasonable method of effecting repairs, the expenditure actually incurred is very persuasive in determining the measure of indemnity. By way of illustration, if a unit (such as a turbine or generator) is supplied to a repairer by the assured out of his own stock and installed in the vessel to replace a unit damaged by an insured peril, and if the damaged turbine or generator taken from the vessel is subsequently repaired to replace the spare unit used ex stock, then the measure of indemnity would be the cost of installing the spare unit plus the cost of repairing the damaged unit. On the other hand, if for some valid reason the damaged unit was not repaired, the measure of indemnity would be the value of the spare generator or turbine which was installed plus the cost of installation, less credit for the damaged unit. The facts in each case determine what is, in that particular case, the reasonable cost of repairs or the true measure of indemnity.

The real issue is whether the incurring of extra expense to avoid serious loss of a vessel's time is "reasonable" and hence a part of the underwriters' obligation to indemnify and make the assured whole. In his treatise on marine insurance, Lowndes said:

> The shipowner is entitled to repair his vessel in that manner which a prudent man would employ if uninsured; and, therefore, if the extra payment for despatch is no more than he would reasonably incur for his own sake apart from insurance, the underwriter would be liable for it.

This question of reasonableness in the cost of repairs must be examined from the standpoint of both vessel owner and underwriters. Thus, when a part required to effect repairs is not available except at an unreasonable cost (as, for instance, when a new engine would have to be especially built for an obsolete type ship), an adequate used or reconditioned part is all underwriters can be expected to provide. Furthermore, in spite of the "new for old" clause in the policy, there would be no claim for depreciation in addition to the claim for the secondhand part. The foregoing is based on the assumption that the repair provided proved satisfactory. This type of problem came before the courts in *Salvatore Ferrante, et al.,* v. *Detroit Fire & Marine Ins. Co., et al.,* (1954 AMC 2026). In that case it was held that the cost of a replacement shaft was recoverable, and also the cost of removing the shaft and putting in the replacement shaft, but not the difference in cost between a used shaft, which was actually installed as the replacement, and a new one—the used shaft being an adequate replacement.

Similarly, "the adjuster must not allow the underwriter to be charged with an extravagant or unnecessary expenditure in repairs or permit an addition to be made to the ship's fabric, or any substitution of superior materials for what was taken away, unless in some places where the former are the only materials available" (Dixon on Marine Insurance, p. 165).

Nor is an underwriter liable for any increased damage or any increased cost of repairs brought about because a shipowner *deliberately* defers making repairs to his vessel for his own convenience. In applying the yardstick of reasonableness to deferred repairs, one very important principle must be adhered to: if a shipowner postpones damage repairs solely for the purpose of earning freights, he must not expect underwriters to pay any increased cost due to such postponement. However, determining whether there has in fact been any increased cost by reason of deferment of repairs often presents great difficulties. One must start at the beginning, and the beginning in this instance depends on establishing *when* the shipowner should be expected to effect his repairs. Underwriters have never in any of their clauses tried to stipulate *when* a vessel must be repaired. A special committee set up by the British Association of Average Adjusters many years ago was of the opinion that underwriters' liability for damage to a vessel is *limited* to the reasonable cost of repairs as if effected at *the first reasonable time and place* after the occurrence of the accident. The difficulty is, of course, in deciding what is the "first reasonable time and place" after the accident. The committee referred to felt that the first reasonable time was immediately on completion of the voyage on which the vessel was engaged at the time of the accident causing the damage. While there are few shipowners who would not complain if underwriters insisted that damage repairs be effected after each accident, nevertheless this has come to be accepted as the *maximum* liability of the underwriter. In practice, unless the repairs are immediately necessary to the vessel's seaworthiness, the shipowner invariably defers repairs until the next regular dry-docking of the vessel and such deferments are usually in the best interests of underwriters. Deferring repairs until the vessel is due for dry-docking usually results in a saving to underwriters by reason of owners and the effects of other accidents participating in the common charges of dry-docking, pilotage, and towage, etc. It is for this reason that any aggravation of the damage due to continued operation is usually recoverable from underwriters as long as the shipowner has acted "reasonably" in deferring repairs (which would always be the case if the deferment was merely to the vessel's next regular dry-docking—always assuming he had a certificate of seaworthiness permitting him to do so). However, when the assured (having acted reasonably in deferring to the next regular dry-docking) effects only *partial repairs* at that dry-docking and, *for his own benefit*, does not effect complete repairs, then, in the absence of some compelling reason, there has been a deliberate deferment and underwriters should not be expected to contribute to any duplication of common charges when the final repairs are carried out. In such circumstances, any additional dry dock dues or other common charges would clearly be an enhanced cost by reason of a deliberate deferment from the first dry-docking. This is true even though the total amount charged to that one damage at both dry-dockings might be less than the cost of effecting complete repairs immediately following the accident. By voluntarily deferring some of the repairs from a normal dry-docking when all the repairs could have been effected, the assured has forfeited his right to use the "immediately after the accident" yardstick. In effect, that dry-docking has become the first reasonable time and place after the accident. His action of deferring part of the repairs has enhanced the "reasonable cost of repairs." Thus, when partial repairs are effected at one dry-docking and the remainder deferred to a subsequent dry-docking for owner's convenience, that accident should not be charged with any part of the duplicated common charges when the final repairs are effected.

To sum up, a shipowner can either repair immediately following an accident or can defer repairs until a convenient time (usually but not necessarily the vessel's next regular dry-docking) and still be acting reasonably. What he cannot do is to enjoy the best of both methods. Naturally, if the shipowner has a good reason for again deferring part of the repairs (such as unavailability of materials or lack of dry dock facilities, etc.), the underwriter is liable for any increased cost by reason of such deferment. Determining whether there has been any increased cost of repairs by reason of deferment can prove to be a difficult question, and each case must be treated on its merits.

Sometimes clauses are included in hull policies stipulating that repairs must be effected within a certain period, the object being to protect underwriters from the effect of inflation. Such a clause is the Cameron Webb Cut Off clause used in the British market. This provides for claims based on the repairs effected to be payable by underwriters only if the repairs have been effected within 18 months of the expiry of the policy, or effected within 24 months of the expiry of the policy provided that a properly and correctly adjusted claim based on such repairs is presented to underwriters within the same period. Under this clause, any claim for depreciation in respect of unrepaired damage must be presented within 24 months of the expiry of the policy.

In spite of what has been written earlier about the incurring of extra expense to avoid loss of a vessel's time, it has long been accepted that overtime worked to *expedite repairs* is not recoverable from underwriters unless it results in some saving to underwriters (such as the reduction of dry dock dues). Yet, as we have seen, in determining whether the cost of repairs is reasonable or not, the traditional view that underwriters are not concerned in the *expedition* of repairs does not necessarily hold good in dealing with other forms of increased expenditure. Benjamin Franklin's advice to young tradesmen in 1748—"remember that time is money"—is even more appropriate today. The subject-matter of the insurance is the ship as a living instrument for commerce. An example of this is the acceptance by underwriters of the cost of transporting parts by air freight as part of the reasonable cost of repairs in certain circumstances. Whether the cost of such air transportation is allowable in full as part of the cost of repairs seems to hinge on whether it was good or prudent management to use air freight instead of other, and cheaper, modes of transportation. Rule XXI of the Association of Average Adjusters of the United States deals with "Air Freight" and reads, in part, as follows:

> The cost of air freight on repair parts shall be allowed as part of the reasonable cost of repairs when the shipment of such parts by water and/or land conveyance would result in unreasonable delay.

Here again the yardstick of reasonableness has to be resorted to and each case examined carefully. If a particular assured habitually transports spare parts by air whether they be necessary for average repairs or owner's maintenance, such a practice would be quite persuasive in considering the allowance of air freight as a proper charge against underwriters. Another factor would be the length of time saved to the assured by using air freight and what this represented to the shipowner in earnings vis-à-vis the cost of the air freight. However, such considerations as goodwill, loss of future contracts, etc., would probably be considered too remote to be factors in concluding whether the extra cost of air freight was or was not part of the reasonable cost of repairs.

Temporary repairs are allowable in particular average as part of the reasonable cost of repairs if they save expense to underwriters, or if it is not possible to effect permanent repairs, or if it is not possible to effect repairs without unreasonable delay. The Association of Average Adjusters has a rule of practice in this connection, reading:

XI. TEMPORARY REPAIRS—PARTICULAR AVERAGE. The cost of reasonable temporary repairs shall be allowed:

When made in order to effect a saving in the cost of permanent repairs;

When complete repairs cannot be made at the port where the vessel is;

When the material or parts necessary for permanent repairs are unobtainable at the port where the vessel is, except after unreasonable delay.

The Adjuster shall insert a note in the average statement in explanation of the allowances made.

What constitutes "unreasonable delay" can be as difficult a question as what constitutes "reasonable cost of repairs." What is an unreasonable delay to the owner of a large vessel operating under a remunerative charter might not seem so unreasonable to an underwriter viewing it from the point of view of indemnity under a marine insurance policy. Nevertheless, all the facts must be taken into consideration, including the earning capacity of the vessel. However, it would be difficult to argue categorically that merely because a vessel would lose money by waiting for spare parts, whereas by effecting temporary repairs she would not be delayed, the cost of temporary repairs is therefore recoverable from underwriters as part of the reasonable cost of repairs. To come within the rule, the loss and/or the delay avoided would have to be fairly considerable. It would perhaps be unreasonable to expect a large vessel to wait, say, seven days or more for repair parts but not unreasonable for her to wait two or three days, whatever the amount of the vessel's earning capacity. In other words, the test of reasonableness must be applied to underwriters as well as to shipowners. The mere fact that it is economically desirable for a shipowner to pursue a certain course does not necessarily mean that the underwriter should bear the increased cost of that course as part of the reasonable cost of repairs. The greater the earnings a shipowner saves by avoiding an unreasonable delay, the firmer ground he is on in claiming the cost of temporary repairs (which have avoided that delay) as part of the reasonable cost of repairs. Conversely, if the saving in earnings is very little more than the cost of the temporary repairs, then it would appear difficult to support claiming the temporary repairs on the grounds of having avoided an unreasonable delay.

While the Association of Average Adjusters' rule of practice summarizes admirably the chief tests to be applied in considering whether temporary repairs are properly allowable as part of the reasonable cost of repairs, the rule is not necessarily all-embracing. For example, many American shipowners make a practice of repairing in the United States except in cases of necessity; thus, if such owners effect temporary repairs abroad merely to enable a vessel eventually to effect permanent repairs in the United States, it would appear that (by virtue of the assured's established practice) such temporary repairs are part of the reasonable cost of repairs even though they do not come specifically within the above rule of practice. It seems appropriate here to make the point that rules of practice are designed as aids and should not be worn as a straitjacket.

It should be mentioned that, in the case of liners, there is a difference in practice between the American and British marine insurance markets in dealing with the extra cost of overtime on repairs and in the allowance of temporary repairs to avoid unreasonable delay. Perhaps this difference stems from the difference in the meaning of the term "liner" in the two insurance markets. A liner in the United States is a passenger liner sailing on an advertised schedule. In the British market, a cargo vessel, "maintaining a regular schedule in accordance with advertised sailing dates to which they strictly adhere or are committed" is also considered a liner. In the United Kingdom, reasonable overtime and temporary repairs incurred to enable such vessels (either passenger or cargo) to maintain their advertised schedules is considered part of the reasonable cost of repairs. In the United States, such generous treatment is confined to passenger liners. However, on payment of an additional premium an endorsement to American policies can be obtained, giving cargo "liners" the same treatment as passenger liners. The position of American underwriters on the question of the reasonable cost of repairs was admirably stated by the chairman of the Association of Average Adjusters of the United States, R. M. Hicks, Jr., in his 1978 address.

When American flag vessels repair abroad, they are subject to duty on the repair account when the vessel returns to the United States. To avoid payment of such duty it must be shown that the repairs were of an emergency nature. Unfortunately, the U.S. government's interpretation of "emergency nature" is limited to the basic perils of the sea—such as heavy weather, collision, stranding, etc.—and does not embrace repairs made necessary by the operation of other insured perils—such as the additional perils enumerated in the Inchmaree or Liner Negligence clauses. As a result, although repairs may result from an insured peril, the assured is obliged to pay duty. Such duty is meant to bring the cost of repairs into line with repair costs in the United States. In such circumstances, it is submitted that the duty paid forms part of the reasonable cost of repairs and is, therefore, recoverable from underwriters. In short, underwriters who insure American flag vessels must expect to respond for repairs as if they were effected in the United States.

Any extra repair expenses incurred for ecological reasons may form part of the reasonable cost of repairs. For example, a vessel leaking oil may not be allowed into a repair port or into a repair yard unless expensive anti-pollution measures are provided. If the vessel is under general average, the cost of such measures will be allowable in either general average or particular average, according to the facts. Any such measures at the repair yard itself will follow the nature of the repairs being effected.

The concept of reasonable cost of repairs changes with changing times, and the reader will profit from the remarks of the chairman of the British Association of Average Adjusters in 1976, A. B. Dann, who made this the subject of his address.

One of the duties of average adjusters is to endeavor to ascertain that repair accounts have been paid. Before the age of computers and electronic transfers of funds, average adjusters were required by underwriters to insert a note in average adjustments confirming that receipted accounts were in their possession. Because of modern methods of transferring funds, receipted accounts seldom, if ever, exist. Recognizing these changes in accounting practices, the London marine insurance market has agreed that if the average adjuster has made every effort to obtain the necessary evidence of payment, underwriters will accept a statement in the average adjustment that all customary vouchers for disbursements included in the adjustment have been sighted and that the adjusters have either seen documentary evidence indicating payment or have received, in response to their specific enquiry, advice from the assured that payment has been made by the assured. A similar practice is followed by average adjusters in the United States.

Removal Expenses

If reasonably and prudently incurred, removal expenses—that is to say, the cost of removing a damaged vessel to a repair port—are recoverable from underwriters as part of the reasonable cost of repairs. The assured has a valid claim for removal expenses if he interrupts the vessel's trading to effect repairs and if, in doing so, he is acting as an ordinary prudent shipowner would. This is true even though the damage repair is not immediately necessary for seaworthiness; the test is again that of the prudent, uninsured shipowner.

The cost of the removal—usually the outward port charges from the original port and the inward port charges at the repair port plus the wages and maintenance of crew, cost of fuel and stores, etc., on the voyage—are allowed as part of the cost of repairs. Sometimes, if the facts warrant, both the inward and outward port charges at the repair port are allowed as removal costs. However, if the inward and outward port charges at the repair port are allowed, then normally the outward port charges from the port from which the vessel was removed would not be allowable. The only circumstances which would justify the allowance of two outward port charges would be those in which a vessel had been removed from one port to another for repairs and then returned immediately after completion of repairs to the original port.

All repairs *for which the vessel may be said to have been removed* (whether they be general average, particular average, or owner's repairs) must bear their proportionate share of the removal expenses. Furthermore, any of the removal expenses allowed as part of the cost of particular average repairs would rank for franchise purposes. When a vessel is removed for various classes of repairs, the allocation of the removal expenses has to be carefully considered; the reason for the removal has to be ascertained. If a vessel is removed from a port where repairs cannot be effected (either because of lack of repair facilities or because the facilities, though adequate, would not be available except after an unreasonable delay), it has been argued that as the shipowner has really no choice in the matter, the removal expenses ought to be allocated on a "common-user" basis; that is to say, on the same basis that dry dock dues are allocated. At first sight this appears to be a reasonable approach, but further inspection reveals obvious objections, such as the fact that one class of repairs might be relatively minor compared to another and yet on a common-user basis might have to bear a large part of the removal expenses—a share out of all proportion to the cost of that particular class of repairs. Consequently, it is the usual practice to apportion removal costs pro rata to the individual cost of each class of repairs for which the removal was made.

When the vessel is removed from a port where repairs can be effected to another port merely to effect a saving in the cost of repairs, it is logical that the removal expenses should be apportioned on the basis of the actual savings effected on each class of repairs. As a practical matter, however, the removal expenses are usually apportioned over the actual cost of each class of repairs effected at the repair port, on the assumption that the percentage saving in cost on each class of repairs would be substantially the same. The cost of the various classes of repairs should include any extra repairs found to be necessary at the actual repair port because, of course, such extras would have been equally necessary at the first port. In apportioning the removal expenses, care should be taken to exclude from the repair cost any major repair parts such as propeller, rudder, stern frame, etc., supplied by a manufacturer other than the repairer because the cost of such parts would have been no different even if the vessel had not been removed for repairs. In other words, where the removal did not effect any savings with regard to a particular repair part, the cost of that part should not be reflected in the apportionment of the removal expenses.

Another point to be considered is the effect of owner's repairs on the treatment of removal expenses. Generally speaking, only owner's repairs immediately necessary to the vessel's seaworthiness are expected to bear a proportion of removal expenses. However, if owner's repairs were contemplated or if the vessel was due for dry-docking, it is customary to allocate part of the removal expenses to those repairs. Owner's repairs not immediately necessary for seaworthiness and which were not contemplated are never brought into the apportionment of removal expenses on the grounds that the owner is entitled to the incidental advantage.

The British Association of Average Adjusters has a Rule of Practice (D1) which deals with removal expenses. This rule stipulates that if the removal results in a new freight being earned or any normal voyage expenses being saved, the net earnings or savings are to be credited to the cost of the removal. This practice is also followed in the United States. The British rule also stipulates that the cost of any temporary repairs necessary to enable the vessel to be moved to the repair port is part of the cost of the removal. This is also the American practice except in such cases where the necessity for the temporary repairs has arisen because of one particular accident. In such cases, if repairs attributable to other accidents are bearing part of the removal expenses, such temporary repairs are charged to the particular accident which necessitated them and not to the general removal expenses. In 1988 the British association appointed a special committee to reconsider their Rule of Practice D1 (which had been in existence since 1896) in light of modern conditions. In particular it was thought that the expenses of removing a vessel should be calculated more precisely so that the assured shipowner would obtain a true indemnity. In addition the rule should establish the basis on which removal expenses should be apportioned between the assured and underwriters. In 1989 a new and more detailed Rule D1 was introduced to replace the former rule. The new rule and especially the report of the special committee will provide useful general guidance to all practitioners of marine insurance, although it must be remembered that American marine insurance practice has never been quite as generous to assureds in the allowance of removal expenses (particularly in the allowance of wages of crew) as has been the practice in the London market. See, for example, lines 107/10 of the American Institute Hull Clauses, 6/2/77, and the writer's remarks in connection therewith (*infra*).

The Claims (General Provisions) clause in the American Institute Hull Clauses deals in part with removal expenses (when such expenses are incurred at the express request of underwriters). The clause reads, in part, as follows:

In the event of any accident or occurrence which could give rise to a claim under this Policy, prompt notice thereof shall be given to the Underwriters, and:

(a) where practicable, the Underwriters shall be advised prior to survey, so that they may appoint their own surveyor, if they so desire;

(b) the Underwriters shall be entitled to decide where the Vessel shall proceed for docking and/or repair (allowance to be made to the Assured for the actual additional expense of the voyage arising from compliance with the Underwriters' requirement);

(c) the Underwriters shall have the right to veto in connection with any repair firm proposed;

(d) the Underwriters may take tenders, or may require in writing that tenders be taken for the repair of the Vessel, in which event, upon acceptance of a tender with the approval of the Underwriters, an allowance shall be made at the rate of 30 per cent per annum on the amount insured, for each day or pro rata for part of a day, for time lost between the issuance of invitations to tender and the acceptance of a tender, to the extent that such time is lost solely as the result of tenders having been taken and provided the tender is accepted without delay after receipt of the Underwriters' approval.

Due credit shall be given against the allowances in (b) and (d) above for any amount recovered:

(1) in respect of fuel, stores, and wages and maintenance of the Master, Officers or Crew allowed in General or Particular Average;

(2) from third parties in respect of damages for detention and/or loss of profit and/or running expenses;

for the period covered by the allowances or any part thereof.

By virtue of the above clause, underwriters can exercise control over repairs to the vessel and the selection of the repair port, although they seldom avail themselves of this right. They may also require the assured to take tenders for repairs, but where a tender is accepted with the approval of underwriters, an allowance is made at the rate of 30 percent per annum on the insured value for the time lost in taking tenders. Thus, on the one hand underwriters receive the benefit of a competitive price for the repairs, and on the other hand the assured receives a specific allowance for the time occupied in fulfilling underwriters' requirements. It must be stressed that when *underwriters* exercise their rights under the Tender clause, no part of the removal expenses can be charged to the owner regardless of the nature of the owner's repairs. It should also be noted that the mere fact that the assured himself decides to take tenders does not qualify him for an allowance under the Tender clause. Underwriters take the position that it is the assured's *duty* to take tenders if the circumstances indicate that course of action is desirable. Nor does the approval of underwriters' surveyor to the taking of tenders automatically open the door to an allowance under the Tender clause. To qualify for such an allowance, tenders must have been taken at the express request of the *underwriters themselves in writing* (through the vessel's insurance brokers). This happens so infrequently as to make the provisions regarding allowances under the Tender clause almost of academic interest only.

It will be seen, however, that underwriters have no right of veto as to the *time* of repairs. If repairs are deferred, removal expenses are not properly allowable if the repairs might have been effected at cheaper or equivalent priced ports during the period of deferment.

The Chairman of the British Association of Average Adjusters in 1954, G. E. Towers, dealt authoritatively with the entire subject of removal expenses in his address, and the reader will gain much by referring to same.

Dry-docking expenses also form part of the reasonable cost of repairs, but in certain instances these expenses are divided between owner and underwriters. There is no American law on this subject, but *Rule of Practice IX* of the Association of Average Adjusters of the United States stipulates:

IX. DRY-DOCKING AND EXPENSES INCIDENTAL TO DRY-DOCKING—PARTICULAR AVERAGE. When a vessel is dry-docked:

(1) For owners' account and repairs are found necessary for which underwriters are liable and which can only be effected in dry dock; or

(2) For survey and/or repairs for which underwriters are liable and repairs for owners' account are made which are immediately necessary for her seaworthiness, or she is due for ordinary dry-docking (in accordance with the owners' custom), the cost of removing the vessel to and from the dry dock, of docking and undocking, and as much of the dock dues as is common to both classes of work, shall be divided equally between the owners and underwriters.

When the vessel is dry-docked for underwriters' account and the owners avail of her being in dry dock to scrape and paint or to do other work for their own account which is not immediately necessary for seaworthiness, all the expense incidental to the dry-docking of the vessel shall be charged to the underwriters.

The Adjuster shall insert a note in the average statement in explanation of the allowances made.

The object of the rule is to give recognition to the facts prevailing, i.e., the purpose or purposes for which the vessel was dry-docked. Where work necessitating dry-docking was contemplated, the cost of which falls on both underwriters and owners, the dry-docking charges in the terms of the rule are divided accordingly.

Sometimes even at a regular scheduled dry-docking a vessel contains cargo. Because of the presence of cargo, an extra dry-docking charge is entailed. In such cases, the extra cost of dry-docking with cargo on board is customarily borne by the shipowner, since the cargo was left on board for his convenience.

However, with the advent of container vessels it has been suggested that, since such vessels are seldom without cargo, the resultant extra cost of dry-docking is in a sense unavoidable and therefore part of the reasonable cost of repairs. The argument in favor of this proposition follows the reasoning used in favor of allowing (in the case of liners) overtime on repairs and temporary repairs to avoid unreasonable delay. Not surprisingly, therefore, the extra cost of dry-docking with cargo on board is allowed in the case of container liners in the United Kingdom as part of the reasonable cost of repairs but is not allowed in the United States where such an extra expense is considered the consequence of the shipowner's method of operating. However, on payment of an additional premium, American policies can be endorsed so that the extra cost of dry-docking with cargo is recoverable as part of the reasonable cost of repairs in particular average situations.

The principle applied to dry-docking expenses is followed in dealing with the cost of drawing a vessel's tailshaft. If the drawing of the shaft is required as a result of the operation of an insured peril, the cost becomes part of the reasonable cost of repairs. However, if the shaft would have been drawn at that time in any event, either to comply with classification requirements or for owner's purposes, the cost of drawing is treated as a common charge and is borne equally by underwriters and owner.

Any amount charged to the vessel owner in accordance with the above dry-docking rule (plus the amount of any other common charges which are similarly treated) can be taken into consideration in testing for franchise under the Voyage Franchise clause. In other words, the entire cost of dry-docking and any other common charges necessary to effect average repairs are used in determining whether or not the voyage franchise has been reached. This differs from the British practice whereby only the amount actually charged to average repairs is considered for franchise purposes, although any subdivision of dry-docking, etc., *among other accidents* (thereby bringing the individual claims below the franchise) does not defeat the claims. The American practice is predicated on the assumption that the assured is entitled to effect repairs after each accident; if at that time the cost of repairs would have reached the voyage franchise, he should never be in a worse position by reason of deferring repairs. This does not hold true when unknown damage is discovered on dry dock; in such cases the assured was already committed to the dry-docking before he was aware of the damage and, consequently, in testing for franchise, only the proportion actually chargeable to the damage discovered on dry dock can be considered. In view of the demise of the Voyage Franchise clause, much of the foregoing is now academic.

Other expenses necessarily incurred in carrying out average repairs—such as the port charges incurred in entering and leaving the repair port, cost of gas-freeing (steaming and cleaning of tanks), pilotage and towage to and from the repair yard, watchmen during repairs, etc.,—are claimable from underwriters. In considering these expenses, the principle of contemplation reflected in the dry-docking rule is followed. In other words, if a vessel owner *contemplates* effecting repairs for his own account, he must share those expenses which are common to both average and owner's repairs. On the other hand, if a vessel owner merely takes advantage of the vessel being at a repair yard to effect repairs for his own account which are not immediately necessary for seaworthiness or to meet immediate classification requirements, he is not required to contribute to any of the expenses of proceeding to and from the yard. Needless to say, the carrying out of owner's repairs must not have resulted in any enhancement of the cost of average repairs.

One type of common charge which is increasing with the size of oil tankers is the cost of tank cleaning or gas-freeing. The treatment of the cost of steaming and cleaning tanks depends on the reason for which the gas-freeing is performed. Thus it may be that only a preliminary or rough cleaning is necessary for certain repairs (perhaps to permit the vessel to safely enter a repair yard), but if hot work is to be carried out after the vessel arrives at the yard, then a more thorough or fine cleaning may be necessary. As already indicated, the cost of either or both such gas-freeing operations is treated on a common-user basis with the necessity for the type of cleaning and the contemplation of the various types of repairs both playing their part in determining the division among the various classes of repairs on a common-user basis. The British Association of Average Adjusters has a Rule of Practice (D6) dealing with tank cleaning and/or gas-freeing which reads as follows:

TANKERS—TREATMENT OF THE COST OF TANK CLEANING AND/OR GAS-FREEING.

1. That, in practice, where repairs, for the cost of which underwriters are liable, require the tanks to be rough cleaned and/or gas-freed as an immediate consequence of the casualty, or the vessel is taken out of service especially to effect such repairs, the cost of such rough cleaning and/or gas-freeing shall be chargeable in full to the underwriters, notwithstanding that the shipowner may have taken advantage of the vessel being rough cleaned and/or gas-freed to carry out survey for classification purposes or to effect repairs on his account which are not immediately necessary to make the vessel seaworthy.

2. (a) Where repairs on Owner's account which are immediately necessary to make the vessel seaworthy and which require the tanks being rough cleaned and/or gas-freed are executed concurrently with other repairs, for the cost of which underwriters are liable, and which also require the tanks being rough cleaned and/or gas-freed,

(b) Where the repairs, for the cost of which underwriters are liable, are deferred until a routine drydocking or repair period, at which time repairs on Owners' account which also require the tanks being rough cleaned and/or gas-freed are effected, whether or not such Owners' repairs affect the seaworthiness of the vessel, the cost of such rough cleaning and/or gas-freeing as is common to both repairs shall be divided equally between the shipowners and the underwriters, irrespective of the fact that the repairs for which underwriters are liable may relate to more than one voyage or accident or may be payable by more than one set of underwriters.

3. The cost of fine cleaning specifically for a particular repair or particular repairs shall be divided in accordance with the principles set forth above.

4. Sub-division between underwriters of the proportion of rough tank cleaning and/or gas-freeing and/or fine cleaning chargeable to them shall be made on the basis of voyages, and/or such other franchise units as are specified in the policies.

5. In determining whether the franchise is reached the whole cost of rough cleaning and/or gas-freeing and/or fine cleaning necessary for the repair of the damage, less the proportion (if any) chargeable to Owners when Section (a) of paragraph 2 applies, shall be taken into consideration, notwithstanding that there are other damages to which a portion of the cost of rough tank cleaning and/or

gas-freeing and/or fine cleaning has to be apportioned in ascertaining the amount actually recoverable.

Survey fees and superintendence expenses also form a constituent of the reasonable cost of repairs. The Association of Average Adjusters of the United States has the following rules on this subject:

XV. CLASSIFICATION SURVEYORS' FEES—PARTICULAR AVERAGE. Fees of Classification Societies for surveys of particular average damages shall be allowed (notwithstanding that a survey of such damages would have been required for classification purposes) in addition to a fee paid an independent surveyor.

XVI. COMPENSATION AND EXPENSES OF OWNERS' SUPERINTENDENT. In cases where a superintendent, or other shore employee, in the permanent employ of the owner of a vessel, superintends the repair of average damage, compensation for such service and incidental expenses shall be allowed in average:

First— When an independent surveyor, or outside man, has not been employed for this purpose, and the vessel is repaired at a port other than where the superintendent, or other employee, makes his headquarters; or

Second—When the owner has incurred extra expense by employing, temporarily, another man to do the work of the superintendent, or other shore employee, while either of the latter is engaged in superintending repair of average damage.

Strictly speaking, a shipowner is probably only entitled to recover the cost of the services of a local surveyor (at the repair port) to survey and superintend the average repairs. Indeed, there is an English decision to that effect (*Agenoria Steamship Co.* v. *Merchants Marine Ins. Co.*, 8 Com. Cas. 212). However in practice shipowners prefer, if possible, to send their own superintendent to perform these duties, and underwriters gladly accept such fees and expenses provided they are reasonable.

The association also has a rule dealing with credit for old material; viz.,

VI. CREDITS FOR OLD MATERIAL. Where old material is replaced by new, credit shall be given in the average statement for the value of proceeds of the old material, or, if there is no credit, the Adjuster shall insert a note in explanation.

From time to time the question has been raised as to whether, when the discharge of cargo is necessary in order to effect repairs, the cost is recoverable as part of the cost of repairing the vessel. The question arises most frequently when cargo is damaged so badly as to lose its character as cargo—where it, in fact, ceases to be the commodity originally shipped. Such cargo (or debris which was once cargo) cannot be delivered to the consignees, and the vessel owner is faced with what is often the very considerable expense of discharging it from the vessel before repairs can be effected and the vessel returned to service.

While there is no American law on the subject, the practice is to follow the principle laid down in the old English case of *Field* v. *Burr* (8 Asp. 529). This case came before the English courts in 1899 and concerned a vessel, carrying a cargo of cottonseed, which was in collision and had her bottom holed. As a result, her cargo was so badly damaged by seawater and mud that it became rotten and worthless; and neither the consignees nor their underwriters would pay the freight or take delivery. The shipowner incurred charges in removing the cargo from the vessel and brought suit to recover these charges from the hull underwriters of the vessel. The hull underwriters paid all claims in respect of damage to the vessel but declined liability for the charges of dealing with and removing the cargo prior to effecting repairs. In holding that the shipowner was not entitled to recover the cost of removing the cargo under the policy on the vessel, the court commented that if cargo is sound, or partially damaged, or putrid, it has to be discharged at the port of destination by the shipowner, if it is to be got out of the vessel at all. This cost formed no part of any deterioration of the subject-matter insured (the vessel). Many hypothetical cases were suggested during the argument, among which was that of a cargo of bagged cement powder becoming consolidated into a hard mass by the action of the seawater passing through a hole in the vessel's bottom. In such a case as that, the court considered underwriters might be liable for the charge of clearing *the inside of the vessel of the cement adhering to it,* for that adherence might be reasonably regarded as a damage to the structure of the vessel. But any consideration of the charge of clearing away the rest of the cement at the port of destination would merely present the question before the court in another form.

The question of the treatment of such discharging expenses was the subject of an arbitration at San Francisco. The arbitrator (a former chairman of the Association of Average Adjusters, Martin P. Detels) held that where a cargo of asphalt solidified in a barge and could only be removed at enormous expense—by cutting accesses in the main deck and installing portable heating units, because the heating coil system was rendered inoperative as the result of an accident during loading—only the cost of repairing the damage to the heating coils and to the main deck plus the cost of removing material adhering to the tanks after all sound product had been discharged was payable under the policy as particular average. The remaining expenses were merely the cost of discharging cargo and, as such, not recoverable under a hull policy, aggravated and abnormal though they might be. The arbitrator quoted *Field* v. *Burr* with approval (barge *J. Whitney*, 1968 AMC 995).

In practice if, for example, the damaged cargo has solidified and has adhered to the structure of the vessel so that in effect the vessel has sustained damage, the cost of removing that part which has adhered to the vessel is recoverable from hull underwriters as part of the reasonable cost of repairs. This is necessarily an arbitrary division, but usually a percentage is allowed, depending on the width of the solidified mass. Similarly, if the cargo debris has entered places where cargo would not normally be (such as the engine room, pump room, or double-bottom tanks), the cost of cleaning and removing such cargo is considered "damage" and therefore part of the reasonable cost of repairs. In all other circumstances, the cost of removing cargo debris from a vessel (whether or not such removal is necessary to effect repairs) is not considered to be part of the cost of repairs but rather a consequential loss or enhanced voyage expense. Such extra expenses may be recoverable from freight underwriters or Protection and Indemnity underwriters, depending on the circumstances in each individual case.

In 1982 this long-established practice was challenged in the American courts as a result of an American average adjuster inexplicably departing from established practice by allowing in particular average the cost of removing a cargo of acrylic acid which had exploded and solidified inside a cargo tank, causing structural damage to the vessel. To enable the structural damage to be repaired, it was necessary to remove the cargo debris by hand, ultimately using jackhammers. The process took thirty days, was very expensive, and, as already stated, the cost was claimed from the hull underwriters as part of the reasonable cost of repairs. Relying on the established practice of over eighty years based on *Field* v. *Burr* (*supra*), the American hull underwriters refused to accept the claim as drawn up by the average adjuster. Underwriters acknowledged liability under the hull policy for actual damage to the insured vessel caused by the explosion, the cost of removing the cargo debris from the cofferdam (where cargo would normally be), and the removal of the residue of the cargo adhering to the bulkheads of the cargo tanks. What was objected to was liability for the cost of removing the bulk of the hardened mass from the cargo tanks, which was in excess of $350,000. The lower court found for the assured on the grounds that the added expense of removing solidified chemical cargo from the vessel's tanks constituted part of the "damage to the vessel" resulting from the explosion (an insured peril). On appeal, the lower court's decision was reversed. The appeals court stated in part:

We conclude that the cargo debris in a cargo tank at the port of destination does not constitute "damage to the vessel" within the parties' intended meaning of the "Inchmaree Clause," and that the lower court's finding on this issue was clearly erroneous. Every merchant vessel requires repair work at some time or other and often cargo must be discharged to do that work. Once a voyage is completed, hull underwriters are not concerned with the cost of cargo discharged, no matter what its form. This view on the coverage of blue water hull policies has been prevalent in marine insurance law for 85 years. We think it must be well understood by now.

An interesting side issue was dealt with in this case. The American Hull Insurance Syndicate insured only 70 percent of the vessel, the remaining 30 percent being insured in the London market. Those underwriters had paid the claim as adjusted. The plaintiff pointed this out to the court and argued that this payment undercut defendant's argument that the law, especially English law, required rejection of the plaintiff's claim. The syndicate suggested that since the average adjuster had erroneously categorized the disputed expense as "cleaning required solely in connection with damage repairs" this might have motivated the underwriters in London to pay their 30 percent of the claim. The appellate court commented that, whatever the reason for the English underwriters' payment, such a payment had little or no probative value as to the liability of American underwriters under the same policy terms.

To sum up: The appellate court endorsed the principle, based on *Field* v. *Burr* (*supra*), that once a voyage is completed hull underwriters are not concerned with cargo discharging costs. This is true even though such a discharge is necessary to effect repairs to damage which falls within the coverage afforded by the hull policy (*Antilles Steamship Co.* v. *American Hull Ins. Syndicate*, 1982 AMC 1100, AMC 2444).

Needless to say, the foregoing remarks do not apply to the removal of cargo or cargo debris before effecting repairs at a port of refuge when a vessel is under general average. In such circumstances the cost of cargo removal is usually allowable as a general average expense but not, it should be added, as part of the cost of repairs.

Marine insurance policies often incorporate restrictive clauses which must be rigidly complied with in stating claims. The American Institute Hull Clauses, for example, include the following clause:

No claim shall in any case be allowed in respect of scraping or painting the Vessel's bottom.

This clause vetoing any allowance for scraping or painting the vessel's bottom is strictly enforced and means that in no circumstances is the cost of scraping and painting the vessel's bottom recoverable—irrespective of whether or not the paint was destroyed by a peril insured against or whether or not any bottom plating was damaged. At this point it should be stated that the underwater bodies of most vessels are coated first with a bare metal primer, followed by an anticorrosive paint and finally by an antifouling composition. The last two coats are renewed every time a vessel dry-docks. This regular treatment of a vessel's bottom is part of a shipowner's maintenance program, and the object of the clause is to relieve underwriters of liability for such maintenance costs even when the vessel's bottom has been damaged by an insured peril. However, the clause does not preclude the allowance in particular average of the cost of a prime coating of paint to new plates when the replacement of bottom plating is a claim under the policy. It is only the normal cost of bottom painting which is excluded. For the purpose of interpreting the clause, the boot topping— that is, the portion of the side plating between light and loaded draft lines needing a special protective covering of anticorrosive paint—is not construed as part of the vessel's bottom.

It will be seen that when average repairs include the replacement of bottom plating, the clause does not result in a true measure of indemnity. Nevertheless, as the Historic Records Working Party of the Insurance Institute of London has pointed out, it ensures a uniform method of dealing with a controversial subject.

In recent years there have been dramatic advances in the qualities and expected life of modern bottom coatings and also in changes in the surface preparation required. Some modern bottom coatings can be expected to last up to eight years; thus it has been suggested that since there is now a real financial loss to shipowners when the bottom painting is damaged or destroyed by an insured peril, the traditional bottom painting exclusion should be reconsidered. Accordingly, in 1978 a committee of British average adjusters and underwriters considered the matter. The result was that underwriters in the British market agreed that the following costs would not be excluded by the bottom painting clause when the bottom had been damaged by an insured peril:

(1) The cost of sand-blasting new plates and supplying and applying "shop" primer ashore.

(2) Sand-blasting:

(a) the butts or areas of plating immediately adjacent to any renewed or re-fitted plating which were damaged during the course of welding and/or repairs.

(b) areas of plating damaged during the course of fairing, either in place or ashore.

(3) Supplying and applying the first coat of anti-corrosive applied to the particular areas mentioned in (1) and (2) above since the purpose of such a coat was different from subsequent coating and really served the purpose of the conventional primer.

However, underwriters were adamant in rejecting liability for the cost of sandblasting or coating any other plates from which the paint had been scored and/or removed by the insured peril.

Another restrictive clause in hull policies deals with wages of crew and reads:

No claim shall be allowed in Particular Average for wages and maintenance of the Master, Officers or Crew, except when incurred solely for the necessary removal of the Vessel from one port to another for average repairs or for trial trips to test average repairs, in which cases wages and maintenance will be allowed only while the Vessel is under way. This exclusion shall not apply to overtime or similar extraordinary payments to the Master, Officers or crew incurred in shifting the Vessel for tank cleaning or repairs or while specifically engaged in these activities, either in port or at sea (lines 107/10, American Institute Hull Clauses, 6/2/77).

Prior to the introduction of this new clause in the American Institute Hull Clauses in 1970, it had been the practice to allow the wages of crew when the crew carried out work connected with repairs which were recoverable from underwriters. Examples of this are the assistance of crew in gas-freeing a vessel for repairs and wages, and overtime of the insured vessel's engineers in effecting machinery repairs. In the United Kingdom the practice went even further, and wages of crew were allowed in lieu of shore personnel while the vessel was undergoing average repairs; for example, allowances were made in lieu of watchmen and in lieu of riggers moving a ship during repairs. The 1970 clause vetoed all such allowances (in practice, whether wages or overtime), the theory being that a shipowner is obligated to pay the crew in any event and is therefore not out-of-pocket insofar as the specific services rendered are concerned; only if commercial firms are employed is the cost of such services recoverable from underwriters. The veto did not apply to crew's wages during a removal voyage for the purpose of effecting average repairs. Nevertheless, it should be noted that to qualify for the allowance of wages and maintenance of crew, the removal of the vessel must have been necessary *solely* for average repairs. If the removal was for both average and owner's repairs no removal expenses are chargeable to underwriters because in such cases the shipowner was already committed to incurring the removal costs to effect the owner's repairs. However, if at the time of the removal the *sole* reason was to effect average repairs, the shipowner is permitted to effect owner's repairs at the repair port without losing the allowance of wages of crew, etc., during the removal. This holds true even if the owner's repairs are to damage discovered at the repair port after the removal and are immediately necessary for seaworthiness. In short, to justify the allowance of removal expenses the *sole* purpose *at the time of the removal* must have been to effect average repairs. However, in the 1977 version of the hull clauses it was conceded that the general exclusion was not to apply to overtime or similar extraordinary payments to the master, officers, or crew incurred in shifting the vessel for tank cleaning or repairs or while specifically engaged in these activities, either in port or at sea.

A committee set up by the British Association of Average Adjusters to consider the meaning of "wages and maintenance" of crew as used in a similar clause in the English Institute Time Clauses, reported in 1972 as follows:

(a) *Wages.* The term "wages" comprises the gross amount of all those payments made by the Shipowners to the members of the crew on a monthly, weekly or other periodic basis including leave pay, overseas allowance, etc. and the employers' contribution to State and other Insurance and/or Pension Schemes which relate to those payments, and also payments of overtime to the crew in pursuance of their normal watchkeeping and/or other duties which may loosely be termed regular overtime.

However, when a vessel is in need of repair, whether at sea or in port, and the members of the crew are called upon to assist in those repairs, any payment for such services additional to wages as described above does not fall within the definition of the word because it is not earned on a regular periodic basis. This applies whether the payment is due under the terms of the contract of employment or whether it is a special payment made to the crew for additional services, the quantum of which is determined without reference to the crew basis wage of overtime structure.

(b) *Maintenance.* The term "maintenance" comprises the cost of provisions, laundry, etc. for the crew, together with the cost of providing accommodation on shore in certain circumstances.

If the foregoing view is accepted, it would seem that the policy exclusion of wages and maintenance of crew is not interpreted as strictly by the British market as is the case in the United States.

In its strictest form, the principle of indemnity does not permit an assured to be placed in a better position, following an accident, than he was in before the accident. Thus, it was the custom when settling claims for repairs to wooden vessels to make a deduction of one-third "new for old," unless the accident happened on the vessel's maiden voyage. With the advent of iron vessels, the deductions "new for old" were greatly modified but were rather complicated, the greater deductions being applied to those parts of a vessel which tended to depreciate more rapidly. Today most policies of marine insurance on vessels include a clause stipulating that no deductions are to be made from the cost of repairs when new material is used to replace old material. In theory, the assured is thus better off than he was before the accident, but in actual fact the gain (if any) is negligible. However, if the repairs do result in any specific betterment in kind as, for example, when a more powerful and more expensive machinery unit is installed, the claim on underwriters is confined to the cost of replacing like with like—in other words, the cost of replacing the damaged unit with a similar one.

Claims for Unrepaired Damage

In cases where damage remains unrepaired on the expiration of the policy, the assured is entitled to recover from underwriters for the depreciation in value of the vessel arising from the existence of the damage. The allowance for depreciation must not exceed the reasonable cost of repairing such damage. (*See* Marine Insurance Act, Sect. 69.)

The question as to the measure of indemnity in such cases came before the court in the case of the *Armar* (1954 AMC 1674). The court said:

> Federal Courts look to the laws of England for guidance in matters of marine insurance and follow them unless, as a matter of policy, a different rule has been adopted . . .
>
> In the circumstances of this case, Sect. 69 (3) of the English Marine Insurance Act of 1906 applies. It provides: . . . the assured is entitled to be indemnified for the reasonable depreciation arising from the unrepaired damage, but not exceeding the reasonable cost of repairing such damage . . .
>
> Applying the formula to the instant case the evidence shows the value of the vessel in her present condition to be $218,000. Her sound value undamaged was $675,000. The depreciation therefore was 67.7 per cent. An equal percentage of the insured value would be $812,400 (67.7% of $1,200,000) which would be the maximum plaintiffs could recover for repairs. Since I have found the cost of repairs to be $736,315 it is within the bounds of the limitation imposed by the formula and thus recoverable.

This method of arriving at the reasonable depreciation, namely that the percentage of depreciation determined by comparison of the sound and damaged values must be applied to the insured value, was first enunciated by the English courts in *Elcock* v. *Thomson* (82 L. L. R. 892). The same formula was endorsed in *Irvin* v. *Hine* (83 L. L. R. 162). The chairman of the British Association of Average Adjusters, M. H. Downes, commented on these developments in his address in 1959 and, while deploring that it had been found necessary to complicate the calculation of the "reasonable depreciation" referred to in the Marine Insurance Act, he accepted the fact that the law had been decided on the point. Prior to the *Armar* case, unrepaired damage claims in the United States had been settled on the basis of the reasonable cost of repairs (but not exceeding the estimated depreciation) and less one-half of any "common charges" included in the estimated cost of repairs (such as dry dock dues, gas-freeing, towage and pilotage, etc.). This practice has been replaced by the formula set forth not only in the *Armar* case but also in the case of *Delta Supply Co.* v. *Liberty Mutual Ins. Co.* (1963 AMC 1540). In England it had long been the practice to negotiate unrepaired damage claims. However, the law cases enumerated above (and which reflected English law) created a new situation and in 1966 the chairman of the British Association of Average Adjusters, N. M. Gordon, dealt exhaustively with the situation in his address. He also reached the conclusion that the insured value of the vessel must now be brought into consideration in calculating claims for depreciation; in his view, the only question remaining was whether the percentage or depreciation was to be applied to the insured value (as in the *Armar* case) or whether the damaged value of the vessel should be deducted from the insured value to arrive at the depreciation. Practical difficulties remain in applying either of these legal formulae because it is sometimes difficult to prove with certainty either the sound or damaged values of a vessel. Nevertheless, in those cases where these values are readily and accurately ascertainable, the law and practice is now well established in the United States and the *Armar* formula is followed. The question has also been asked as to the time at which the various values are to be assessed. However, the generally accepted position is that, because claims for unrepaired damage do not crystallize until the termination of the policy, the value of the vessel in sound and damaged condition and the estimated cost of repairs prevailing at that time are controlling. (In the *Medina Princess* case, 1965 1 L. L. R. 361, it was held that the material time for quantifying the partial loss was the date of expiry of the policy.)

American underwriters were never very happy with certain aspects of the *Armar* formula, and in the latest (1977) version of the American Institute Hull Clauses the following clause was introduced:

No claim for unrepaired damages shall be allowed, except to the extent that the aggregate damage caused by perils insured against during the period of the policy and left unrepaired at the expiration of the policy shall be demonstrated by the Assured to have diminished the actual market value of the Vessel on that date if undamaged by such perils.

The effect of this clause is to contract out of the *Armar* formula in those cases where the vessel is damaged, to such an extent that she is reduced to a scrap value. In such cases, the clause limits the recovery to the difference between the scrap value and the sound value. But for this clause, the *Armar* formula would require the percentage of depreciation to be applied to the insured value. The resultant figure would be recoverable (limited, of course, to the estimated cost of repairs). In the type of case postulated, if the insured value was greater than the sound value, a greater recovery from underwriters might result than that permitted under the above clause.

All claims for unrepaired damage are limited to the estimated cost of repairs—and this in itself can be a matter of controversy. As we have seen, the former American practice in arriving at unrepaired damage claims embraced a "discount" of one-half the common charges (if any) included in the estimated cost of repairs. It is submitted that, as a result of the *Armar* and *Delta Supply Co.* v. *Liberty Mutual Ins. Co.* decisions, this former practice is no longer valid. In this connection, it is interesting to note that as long ago as 1926 no less a person than G. R. Rudolf, the distinguished British average adjuster, stated that the estimated cost of repairs in unrepaired damage cases should reflect the cost of dry-docking necessary to effect the repairs: "the whole cost, not lessened by the fact that at a later date the owner would have had to dry-dock his vessel for several accidents" (*see* British Association's 1926 report, pp. 14, 15). The expression "estimated cost of repairs" must surely be given its everyday meaning, which obviously includes the entire cost of dry-docking, gas-freeing, and any other charges necessary to effect the repairs. Indeed, in the *Medina Princess* case, the court said: "The question is, what would the cost of repairs have been on that date?' " (that is, the expiration of the policy); and again, "What would have been expended to put the ship right?" The court reached the conclusion that "reasonable cost of repairs" was in all cases a question of fact and, following *Irvin* v. *Hine*, that it should be interpreted broadly to include those expenses which the shipowner would in fact have had to incur to make his ship seaworthy again.

The measure of indemnity for unrepaired damage claims can be affected by the inclusion of a *Dual Valuation clause* in the policy. A usual requirement of that clause is that underwriters' liability in respect of claims for unrepaired damage shall in no case exceed the value agreed for total loss purposes (which value is usually lower than the value stipulated in the clause for other types of claims).

In cases where a vessel is sold with unrepaired damage *during the currency of the policy*, the position is not so clearly established. There is some authority in England to the effect that there is a claim on underwriters for the depreciation arising from the existence of the damage. Such a case came before the American courts, and the court followed the English law. The depreciation was assessed by deducting, from the sound value of the vessel prior to the accident, the price for which it was sold in damaged condition, the remainder being the depreciation in value as a result of the accident. The proportion of depreciation was then applied to the insured value of the vessel in accordance with the *Armar* formula described above (*Delta Supply Co.* v. *Liberty Mutual Insurance Co.*, 211 F. Supp. 429).

In adjusting claims for unrepaired damage, average adjusters need to establish the value of the insured vessel both in sound and in damaged condition as of the termination of the policy. To obtain such figures a ship valuer has to be consulted. Unfortunately, ship valuing, like average adjusting, is not an exact science and ship values can vary from valuer to valuer. A distinguished ship valuer, ship surveyor, and long-time advisor to the average adjusting profession, Harry J. Ottaway served as chairman of the Association of Average Adjusters of the United States in 1985. He chose as the subject of his address to the association "Ship Appraisals" (with particular reference to unrepaired damage claims). The address is of much interest to all connected with the marine insurance profession and covers the subject in depth.

Claims in Excess of the Insured Value

The potential liability of an underwriter on hull and machinery *arising out of one accident* is usually stated to be 100 percent of the insured value in respect of the total loss of or repairs to the vessel, a further 100 percent of the insured value under the Collision clause, all legal expense properly incurred under the Collision clause, and any expenses reasonably incurred under the Sue and Labor clause (the latter also being limited to the insured value of the vessel).

Successive Losses

Where there are successive losses arising from several accidents during the currency of the policy, the underwriter is liable for the successive losses even though the total amount may exceed the sum insured (see *Matheson* v. *Equitable Marine Ins. Co.*, 118 Mass. 209). This is on the assumption that the assured elected to effect repairs to the vessel. The potential liability of the underwriter accrues when each accident occurs even though it is not quantified until repairs are effected and the repair accounts paid.

It must be pointed out, however, that if the vessel remains unrepaired and, before the expiry of the policy, is totally lost as a result of another accident, the assured can only recover in respect of the total loss. The American Institute Hull Clauses specifically state:

> In no case shall the Underwriters be liable for unrepaired damage in addition to a subsequent Total Loss sustained during the period covered by this Policy.

All the foregoing is in accord with the Marine Insurance Act (Sect. 77).

PARTICULAR AVERAGE FOR CONSIDERATION

Generally speaking, and subject to the remarks made in Chapter 3 regarding construction of policies, the onus of proof is on the party making a claim under a policy of marine insurance—the assured. It is the duty of the average adjuster, before stating a claim on underwriters, to satisfy himself that the claim is proper. Occasionally a case arises where there is doubt as to the cause of the damage, yet there is as much to be said in favor of the claim as there is to be said against it. In such cases, if the adjuster considers the facts warrant it, he can put the claim forward "for consideration" of underwriters, giving his reasons for so doing. "Claims for Consideration" are seldom resorted to.

DUTIES OF SURVEYORS

When an insured vessel is involved in an accident, it is the duty of the assured to notify underwriters through his insurance brokers. Underwriters can then appoint a surveyor to represent them at the survey on the vessel.

The chief functions of the underwriters' surveyors are to establish the cause and time of origin of the damage and to agree with the owner's representative on the extent and cost of repairs. The Association of Average Adjusters has a rule in connection with the approval of repair accounts which reads:

> VII. APPROVAL OF REPAIR ACCOUNTS. All repair accounts shall be examined, when practicable, by the owners' surveyor and a surveyor for underwriters before the statement is issued.
>
> The Adjuster shall insert a note in the average statement that this has been done and the result of same.

Any approval of repair accounts given by underwriters' surveyor is invariably claused "without prejudice and subject to adjustment"; it must be stressed that such approval does not relieve the average adjuster of his responsibilities in stating the claim on underwriters.

The ideal survey report contains all the technical information necessary to assist the adjuster in preparing the average adjustment. In particular, where applicable, the survey report should indicate the following:

(1) The number of days required on dry dock for damage repairs (separating each accident) and owner's work.

(2) The extra cost of any overtime work with advices as to any savings effected by working such overtime.

(3) If temporary repairs are effected, the cost of and reason for such temporary repairs.

(4) When temporary repairs previously effected are removed, the cost of such removal.

(5) If any repairs are deferred, the reason for such deferment.

(6) If repairs are effected which require tank cleaning, the surveyor should indicate the various classes of work requiring such tank cleaning.

(7) If the cause of damage was a latent defect, the report should give the cost of replacing or repairing the defective part, also the cost of any incidental work common to both the defective part and the consequential damage.

PARTICULAR AVERAGE ON CARGO

Whether or not particular average is recoverable under a cargo policy depends on the terms of the insurance. This may seem a rather obvious statement, but the types of cargo insurance available are many and varied and are often tailored to special requirements. While total losses from any of the perils enumerated in the policy are recoverable up to the policy limits (insured value), partial losses resulting from these same perils (that is, particular average claims) are recoverable only as specified by the average clause.

The average terms and conditions are specified in the policy and are applicable to under-deck shipments only. The average clause is therefore one of the most important clauses in a cargo policy. The assured selects the average clause most suited to his circumstances; and the principal clauses available are as follows:

"Free of Particular Average" (F. P. A.) coverage, as its name implies, provides only limited protection. Under the Institute of London Underwriters Cargo (F. P. A.) Clauses, in addition to total losses, partial losses resulting from perils of the sea are recoverable, but only when the carrying vessel has been stranded, sunk, or burnt, or the damage has been caused by fire, explosion, collision, or by contact of the vessel or craft with some substance other than water. There need not be any connection between the damage and the stranding, sinking, or burning of the vessel, although the damage itself must, of course, have resulted from a peril of the sea. The mere fact that the vessel strands, sinks, or is burnt during the voyage breaks the F. P. A. warranty, insofar as the cargo on board the vessel at the time of the stranding, etc., is concerned, and in effect the policy then becomes a "With Average" policy. Somewhat similar coverage is provided by the American Institute Cargo Clauses (April 1, 1966). In that form, the F. P. A. clause reads:

> Warranted free from Particular Average unless the vessel or craft be stranded, sunk, or burnt, but notwithstanding this Warranty these Assurers are to pay any loss of or damage to the interest insured which may reasonably be attributed to fire, collision or contact of the vessel and/or craft and/or conveyance with any external substance (ice included) other than water, or to discharge of cargo at port of distress . . .

It is stipulated, however, that the foregoing warranty does not apply "where broader terms of average" are provided for in the certificate, declaration, or special policy to which the clauses are attached.

Also in the United States a slight modification of the above conditions is to be found in the F. P. A. English Conditions clause (F. P. A.—E. C.). Under this clause, particular average is recoverable provided the vessel has been stranded, sunk, burnt, *or in collision*, even though there be no connection between the claim and the stranding, etc. This variation introduces collision (with another vessel) as a fourth type of accident which breaks the F. P. A. warranty.

Another type of F. P. A. coverage is the F. P. A. American Conditions clause (F. P. A.—A. C.). Under this clause, particular average is only recoverable when the loss or damage is actually *caused* by the stranding, sinking, burning, or collision of the vessel with another vessel.

When coverage of partial losses is on a limited F. P. A. basis, the Craft, Etc., clause included in most cargo policies becomes important. This clause reads:

> Including transit by craft and/or lighter to and from the vessel. Each craft and/or lighter to be deemed a separate insurance. The Assured are not to be prejudiced by any agreement exempting lightermen from liability.

The coverage is extended by this clause to include transit by craft and/or lighter to and from the ocean vessel. While the goods are on such craft, the insurance of the cargo thereon is deemed to be a separate insurance. Thus even if, say, only 10 percent of the insured shipment is on board a craft or lighter and that portion of the entire shipment is totally lost in transit to the ocean vessel due to an insured peril, the loss would be recoverable as a total loss even though the entire shipment was insured on F. P. A. conditions. Normally, under such conditions a total loss of a part is not recoverable, but the Craft, Etc., clause negates this by specifically stating that each lighter load is to be deemed a separate insurance.

The "With Average" (W. A.) form of coverage provides a more comprehensive type of protection. The average clause in such a policy might read:

> Subject to particular average if amounting to 3 percent, unless general or the vessel and/or craft is stranded, sunk, burnt, on fire, and/or in collision, each package separately insured or on the whole.

Such coverage gives the assured protection for particular average by sea perils, if the particular average amounts to 3 percent (or other percentage as specified) or more of the value of the whole shipment or of a shipping package. If the vessel has stranded, sunk, been on fire, or in collision, the percentage requirement is waived and losses from sea perils are recoverable in full. A series of losses occurring at different times during an insured voyage may be added together to reach the franchise percentage.

The essential difference in cover between the W. A. and F. P. A. conditions occurs when a partial loss is caused by heavy weather, and the vessel has not been stranded, sunk, burnt, or in collision during the voyage. Under the W. A. conditions the loss is recoverable subject to the franchise, but under the F. P. A. conditions it is not recoverable at all.

Additional perils may be added to the W. A. clause. Theft, pilferage, non-delivery, freshwater damage, sweat damage, breakage, and leakage are commonly covered.

As we have seen earlier, cargo can also be insured with All Risks conditions. There are many variations in the wording of such clauses besides that given in Chapter 3. For example, the wording used may be any one of the following:

> Against all risks of whatsoever nature, irrespective of percentage,
> Against all and every risk, irrespective of percentage,
> To pay physical loss or damage from any external cause, irrespective of percentage.

This type of very wide coverage, however worded, is given the designation of "all risks." Such clauses cover "all risks" of physical loss or damage *from any external cause*. They cover risks, not certainties: something which happens to the subject-matter from without, not the natural behavior of that subject-matter, being what it is in the circumstances under which it is being carried (*Gaunt* v. *British & Foreign Marine Insurance Co.*, 1921, 8 L. L. R. 15). Thus, the following types of loss are not covered even by the "all risks" form:

(1) Loss of market, or loss, damage, or deterioration arising from delay.

(2) Loss arising from inherent vice of goods.

(3) Loss or damage arising from strikes, riots, or civil commotions. (This coverage may be and usually is added by endorsement.)

(4) Loss or damage arising from acts of war. (This is usually covered under a companion war risk policy.)

Special trade clauses also exist for certain types of commodities. For example, special clauses have been adopted for the corn, flour, rubber, sugar, timber, jute, and frozen meat trades.

Cargo shipped on deck is only insured free of particular average but damage caused by the vessel being stranded, sunk, burnt, on fire, or in collision is covered, as is jettison and/or washing overboard irrespective of percentage. However, cargo shipped on deck, under an underdeck bill of lading, without the knowledge and consent of the shipper, is treated as underdeck cargo and is fully covered in accordance with the average clause in the policy. With the advent of containerized cargoes, bills of lading often give the carrier the right to stow on deck or underdeck. In such cases, the cargo owner has no control over the stowage of his cargo and, notwithstanding the wording of the bill of lading (with which the assured is cognizant), the assured is customarily given the benefit of the underdeck average conditions even though the shipment is carried on deck.

American cargo policies usually include a Warehouse and Forwarding clause which, notwithstanding the average clause, agrees to pay any landing, warehousing, forwarding, and special charges made necessary as a result of an accident caused by an insured peril. This is really an extension to the average clause—a concession to the assured. Such expenses are payable even if the insured goods are undamaged. Thus, for example, if the carrying vessel strands and is so badly damaged that the voyage has to be abandoned, the cost of discharging and forwarding the insured cargo will be recoverable under the cargo policy.

The same clause also agrees to pay the insured value of any package or packages which may be totally lost in loading, transshipment, or discharge. Such claims do not depend on the other perils insured against and frequently arise from the loss of packages from cargo slings. It is, in effect, the introduction of a new peril into the policy by making the loss of a package in such circumstances an insured peril in itself. One American court took a different view in finding that the clause does not add additional risks to the policy but rather refers to liability in the case of a loss resulting from risks covered elsewhere in the policy (*J. A. Jones Construction Co.* v. *Niagara Fire Ins. Co.*, 170 F2d 667). However, this is not the intent of the policy nor is it so construed in practice in either the United States or the United Kingdom.

Another clause which provides additional coverage is the Fumigation clause, which reads:

> In the event of the vessel being fumigated and direct loss or damage to Assured's merchandise results therefrom, this Company agrees to indemnify the Assured for such loss or damage, and the Assured agrees to subrogate to this Company any recourse that they may have for the recovery of such loss or damage from others.

Most insurances on cargo are effected under open policies. This type of policy automatically covers all shipments which come within its scope and it usually warrants that all shipments be reported as soon as possible and the insured amounts declared as soon as they are ascertained. However, unintentional failure by the assured to report shipments is excused and such shipments are usually held covered subject to policy conditions.

Measure of Indemnity for Particular
Average on Cargo

Claims for particular average on cargo may be either for a total loss of part of the interest insured or for a depreciation in value by reason of damage caused by a peril insured against. In the case of a total loss of part, the measure of indemnity is, in the case of a valued policy, such proportion of the sum insured as the insurable value of the part lost bears to the insurable value of the whole (Marine Ins. Act, Sect. 71).

Two examples of the adjustment of claims for a total loss of part of the goods are as follows:

(1)	Insured Value	$ 1,200.
	Less Invoice Value	1,000.
	Insured Advance = 20% or	$ 200.
	Loss:	
	Invoice Value Items Lost	$ 100.
	Advance = 20% or	20.
	Claim	$ 120.

(2) If the cargo is homogeneous or fungible, i.e. capable of mutual substitution, a typical adjustment would be as follows:

100,000 lbs. rice insures for $12,000. or $0.12 per lb.

Loss:
1,000 lbs. short at $.12 per lb. $ 120.

As we have seen, this is quite different from the position with regard to particular average claims under a policy of insurance on a vessel where the insured value has no bearing on claims for particular average beyond limiting the total amount recoverable in respect of any one accident.

Where the whole or any part of the goods or merchandise has been delivered damaged at its destination, the measure of indemnity is such proportion of the sum fixed by the policy as the difference between the gross sound and damaged values at the place of arrival bears to the gross sound value. *Gross value* means the wholesale price or, if there be no such price, the estimated value, with, in either case, freight, landing charges, and duty paid beforehand; provided that, in the case of goods or merchandise customarily sold in bond, the bonded price is deemed to be the gross value. *Gross proceeds* means the actual price obtained at a sale where all charges on sale are paid by the sellers (Marine Ins. Act, Sect. 71). For example:

200 yards of piece goods invoiced at $.60 per yd. are damaged.
Agreed depreciation 50%
Adjustment:

Insured Value	$1,200.
Less Invoice	1,000.
Insured Advance = 20% or	$ 200.

Loss:
200 yds. at $.60 per yd. = $120 x 50% depreciation = $60.
Insured Advance = 20% or   12.
    Claim $72.

When the percentage of depreciation cannot be mutually agreed upon, the damaged goods must be sold promptly in order to arrive at the extent of the loss. When this method is used, the calculation is based upon a comparison of the sound value of the goods and the damaged value on the date of sale. This percentage is then applied to the insured value of the damaged articles. Auction charges and other costs of sale are added to determine the total amount recoverable. By comparing the gross sound and damaged values, the element of market fluctuation is eliminated. Thus, there is no opportunity for the claim to be either increased or decreased by a change in the market value of the goods during the time they have been in transit.

Thus:

Damaged goods: 50 pairs of shoes (invoice value $5.00 pair)
Sound Market Value on date of sale $7.00 pair
Damaged Market Value   <u>3.50</u> pair

    Depreciation 50% or   <u>$3.50</u> pair

Sales expenses of $30.00 are incurred in disposing of the damaged shoes.

Adjustment:

Insured Value	$1,200.
Less Invoice Value	<u>1,000.</u>
Insured Advance = 20% or	<u>$ 200.</u>
Loss:	
50 pairs of shoes invoiced at $5.00	$ 250.
Advance = 20% or	<u> 50.</u>
Insured Value	<u>$ 300.</u>
$300. at 50% depreciation	150.
Sales expenses	<u> 30.</u>
Claim	<u>$ 180.</u>

Note: The net proceeds of sale are paid directly to the cargo owner by the party selling the damaged goods.

American cargo policies usually contain a Partial Loss clause spelling out the procedure to be followed:

In case of partial loss by perils insured against, the proportion of loss shall be determined by a separation of the damaged portion of the insured property from the sound and by an agreed estimate (by survey) of the percentage of damage on such portion; or if such agreement is not practicable, then by public sale of such damaged portion for the account of the owner of the property and by comparison of the amount so realized with the sound market value.

In other words, a particular average loss is quantified by ascertaining the percentage of depreciation by comparing the gross sound and damaged values at destination and applying that percentage of depreciation to the insured value. This long-established method of calculating a particular average loss of cargo was endorsed by the court in *M. W. Zack Metal Co. v. Federal Ins. Co.* (1967 AMC 125, 1968 AMC 1384).

When goods are sold short of destination to minimize the loss, and neither an actual total loss nor a constructive total loss can be proved, American underwriters are sometimes willing, as a concession to an assured, to settle on a salvage loss basis (that is, to pay the difference between the insured value of the goods and the net proceeds of sale). As stated previously, if an actual or constructive total loss cannot be demonstrated, such claims should be adjusted on a particular average basis. However, even minor claims are sometimes adjusted on a salvage loss basis simply to avoid obtaining sound and damaged market values and computing the percentage of depreciation for application to the insured value. Settlement of claims on this basis is merely a simple, convenient way of disposing of small claims with a minimum of technicality and should not be construed as replacing the legal method of calculating particular average claims.

Cargo policies often include clauses which restrict or affect the measure of indemnity under the policy. The Labels and Machinery clauses are examples of this. The Labels clause limits claims for damage to labels, capsules, or wrappers to an amount sufficient to pay for the cost of new labels, capsules, or wrappers plus the cost of reconditioning the goods. The Machinery clause limits claims on shipments of machinery or manufactured products to the insured value of the part or parts lost or damaged or, at the assured's option, the cost and expense of replacing or duplicating the lost or damaged part or parts, and/or repairing the machine or product. The intention of both clauses is to prevent the abandonment of an entire shipment or an entire machine merely because the labels, etc., or some part or parts of a machine are lost or damaged.

Most American cargo policies contain a clause requiring that all claims for loss of or damage to the goods insured be promptly reported to the insurers or their agents. In the case of import shipments, the following claim documents are required:

(1) Insurance coverage: Original and/or duplicate insurance certificate—or copy of the "Declaration" covering the shipment.

(2) Invoice: True copy of the shipper's invoice *plus* packing list or weight note.

(3) Bill of lading: issued by the carriers involved, i.e., ocean, inland (truck or rail), air waybill, or post office receipt.

(4) Copy of the Customs document showing import tax (duty) imposed—if specifically insured.

(5) Claim against carrier: Copy of claim letter and reply, if received.

(6) Proof of Loss:

(a) Inspection (survey) report by claim agent shown on insurance certificate or Lloyd's or American Institute representative.

(b) Copy of "exception" given to the pier or truckman showing shortage or damage.

(c) Truckman's affidavit of "exception" signed in the pier tally book.

(d) Carrier's written confirmation of non-delivery—if claim is for non-delivery.

PARTICULAR AVERAGE ON FREIGHT

Insurance of freight covers the risk of loss of the subject-matter insured by reason of a loss of either the ship by perils insured against, whereby it is prevented from transporting the cargo, or a loss of the goods by the perils insured against, whereby the earning of freight by the transportation of them is prevented (see Phillips, Sect. 1142).

Phillips further defines particular average on freight in the following terms:

> A particular average or partial loss on freight is occasioned by the loss of the ship after a part of the voyage is performed, which makes it necessary to hire another ship to carry on the cargo to the port of destination in order to earn the freight (Subsect. 1438).

and

> A loss of part of the cargo, whereby the ship is prevented from earning a part of its freight, is a particular average on freight; and it does not appear to make any difference in this respect that the loss is on an article of a perishable nature and of more than ordinary liability to damage; as in case of tobacco being damaged by sea-water (Subsect. 1439).

Measure of Indemnity for Particular Average on Freight

In practice, the measure of indemnity for loss under a freight insurance is governed by specific provisions incorporated in the policy. Subject to any express provision in the policy, the measure of indemnity in the case of a partial loss of freight is such proportion of the insured value as the proportion of freight lost by the assured bears to the whole freight at the risk of the assured under the policy (Marine Ins. Act, Sect. 70). However, most policies of insurance on freight limit the recovery, in the case of partial losses, to the gross freight lost by the assured, and he is not permitted to make a profit because the insured value may exceed the gross freight at risk.

RATES OF EXCHANGE APPLICABLE TO CLAIMS UNDER MARINE INSURANCE POLICIES

Fluctuations in rates of exchange and devaluation of currencies between the time repair invoices are paid and the time the resultant claim is presented to underwriters often cause difficulties. This is particularly true when the repair expenses are incurred in one currency and the assured is out of pocket in that currency while the vessel is insured in another currency.

Underwriters on a policy of marine insurance are liable to indemnify the assured in the currency of the policy. Thus, if disbursements for which underwriters are liable have been incurred in a currency other than that of the policy, it is necessary to exchange the disbursements into the currency of the policy. In effecting this exchange, it is the practice to use the rate of exchange prevailing on the date or dates on which the disbursements were paid. At that time the loss was quantified, and by adopting this method, underwriters' liability is unaffected by any subsequent fluctuations in rates of exchange. There must, of course, have been no unreasonable delay in settling the repair accounts after the completion of repairs. If there were such unreasonable delay, and during that delay there was some movement in exchange rates which increased the amount of the claim, the average adjuster, in stating the claim, would have to consider whether underwriters' position had been unreasonably prejudiced. By way of illustration, some ship repairers offer three year credit facilities, and if currency rates fluctuated wildly during such a period it would not be reasonable to expect underwriters to bear the resultant loss on exchange.

As a result of volatile currency movements, the established practice described above was challenged by underwriters in the British market in 1979. On the grounds of equity it was suggested that if an assured incurred disbursements in sterling and was, in fact, out of pocket in sterling, he should be reimbursed in sterling regardless of the fact that the policy might be written in another currency. This argument referred to partial losses, it being admitted that total losses must be paid in the currency of the policy. Such a method of settling partial losses would inevitably give rise to other difficulties, such as applying the deductible average which would, of course, be in the currency of the policy. Very occasionally the deductible average is expressed in a currency different from that of the insured value. This problem was referred to by the chairman of the British Association of Average Adjusters, K. Wood, in his address to the association in 1986. His solution was to use the rate of exchange prevailing when the major items making up the claim were paid. The fact of the matter is that whenever rates of exchange are unstable, one of the parties to a contract of marine insurance will suffer. The best solution appears to be to include a Currency clause in the policy so that all concerned are aware of the procedure to be followed.

Chapter 6

General Average

General average is as old as the oldest commercial sea voyages and is a natural law of the sea founded on equity. A general average arises when a sacrifice or expenditure is intentionally made or incurred in time of peril by one of the parties to the adventure (usually the shipowner)—not for his own benefit alone, but for the benefit of all concerned in the enterprise, i.e., ship, cargo, and freight. For example, it might become necessary, consequent to an accident, for a vessel to put into a port of refuge not on her scheduled voyage in order to effect repairs which the master deems are necessary to enable the voyage to be safely prosecuted. If the repairs prove to be extensive, the shipowner is faced with a considerable incidental expenditure, including the wages and maintenance of the crew during the delay. As this expenditure has been incurred, not only to ensure the safety of the ship but also to ensure the safe delivery of the cargo, it is only fair that the cargo interests should pay their share of such extra expenses which, it must be borne in mind, were not envisaged when the shipowner contracted to carry the cargo. To cite another example of general average, a situation might arise in which the master considers it necessary, for the general safety, to jettison part of the cargo. Probably the cargo which is jettisoned is that which is most accessible, and it would be a travesty of justice if the unfortunate owners of the cargo so jettisoned were left to foot the bill themselves.

The international maritime law of general average has for centuries recognized such inequities, and the law of general average as it exists today has been evolved on the simple basis that, in such circumstances, all the parties engaged in a maritime adventure must contribute in proportion to the value of their property safely delivered. As Phillips put it, "Where expenses are incurred, or sacrifices made, on account of ship, freight, and cargo, by the owner of either, the owners of the others are bound to make contribution in the proportion of the value of the several interests." As long ago as 900 B.C., the principles of general average were practiced by the maritime community of Rhodes—a Mediterranean empire of that era—and centuries later the Romans incorporated the Rhodian Law in their own civil law. In spite of the many vicissitudes which the world has experienced since those early seafaring days, this law of the sea (for that we may call it) has survived and is today not only accepted by all the maritime countries of the world but is part of their common law. Inevitably, general average developed differently in different parts of the world but, although the practice varies from country to country, nevertheless, the fundamental principle of the sharing of misfortune has remained unaltered. As an eminent American jurist remarked in the nineteenth century, "The principle on which this contribution is founded is not the result of a contract but has its origin in the plain dictates of natural law." More recently, Lord Denning remarked, "A claim by shipowners against a cargo owner for general average contribution does not arise 'out of' the contract. It arises 'in the course of it.' It arises in the course of the voyage. It arises out of the perils encountered in carrying out the contract and not out of the contract itself" (the *Evje*, 1973 1 L. L. R. 509).

It must be emphasized that general average exists quite independently of marine insurance. It is a liability which faces every shipper who sends his merchandise by sea, or every consignee who receives such merchandise, whether the shipment has been insured or not. By this international law of the sea, a shipowner has a lien or legal right to retain any shipment until the shipper or consignee has paid that shipment's contribution to any general average which has arisen on the voyage. Not only has the shipowner the right to withhold delivery of cargo pending receipt of general average security, as it is called, but it is also his duty to do so in those cases where cargo interests are entitled to receive allowances in general average (as, for example, when part of the cargo is jettisoned for the common safety). This duty, therefore, holds true even though the shipowner may on balance be a debtor in general average (*American Tobacco Co., et al. v. Basil Goulandris, et al.*, 1959 AMC 1462).

It must also be repeated that general average is not dependent upon contract, although any provisions in the contract of affreightment regarding the adjustment of general average might limit, qualify, exclude, extend, or control such a claim. For example, the contract of affreightment (bills of lading in the case of a general cargo or a charter party in the case of a bulk cargo) invariably contains a general average clause, of which a typical example in the United States would be as follows:

> General Average shall be adjusted, stated and settled according to York/Antwerp Rules 1974 at the port of New York or last port of discharge at Carrier's option and as to matters not provided for in these Rules, according to the laws and usage at the port of New York or any other place at the option of the carrier.

The effect of such standard general average clauses is to write the York/ Antwerp Rules into the contract of affreightment; and, in fact, an English court has said the rules are incorporated as a matter of contract (*Alma Shipping Corp.* v. *Union of India*, 1971 2 L. L. R. 494). The contract of carriage is also an important factor in determining whether the shipowner can enforce his contribution. An unfortunate result flowing from the court's finding in the above case is that in the event of any dispute concerning the general average, such dispute would arise under the charter party and therefore would be subject to any arbitration clause which might be included therein. However, in a subsequent case (the *Evje*, 1972 2 L. L. R. 129) it was held that the arbitration clause did not apply to a letter of undertaking to pay any general average contribution "which may be legally due" from the cargo owners. Such a letter of undertaking coupled with the release of cargo placed the party giving the undertaking under a new contractual obligation to shipowners, viz., to pay them "any general average contribution which may be legally due" from the cargo owners, as distinct from the liability which might have fallen upon them had they not given the letter of undertaking. The court implied that the position would be the same if an average bond had been signed. In short, the arbitration clause in the contract of affreightment was held not applicable to a claim for general average contribution brought under a letter of undertaking or an average bond. This decision was appealed, but the court of appeals confirmed that an undertaking to pay any general average contribution which may be legally due is a new independent agreement, the consideration for which is the shipowner's agreement not to exercise his lien against cargo. Consequently, the arbitration clause in the charter party was inapplicable (the *Evje*, 1973 1 L. L. R. 509).

The contract of affreightment is, therefore, an important document in the adjustment of general average. Where there is a charter party governing the voyage in question, any bill of lading also issued in connection with the same contract of carriage merely operates as a receipt for the goods and does not vary the contract between the charterer and the shipowner (the *Marine Sulphur Queen*, 1972 1 L. L. R. 1122).

To sum up, although the York/Antwerp Rules have no legal effect in themselves, they are invariably included in the contract of affreightment, thereby becoming part of that contract. The use of these rules is universal, and it is therefore important to examine their development.

THE DEVELOPMENT OF THE YORK/ANTWERP RULES

The many differences in the practice of general average from country to country had long been a source of irritation and some confusion among the maritime communities of the world, with the result that international conferences were held from time to time to draw up common rules of practice acceptable to all maritime nations. It speaks volumes for the shipping, insurance, and mercantile communities that these conferences have met with such a large measure of success.

It was in the middle of the nineteenth century that real efforts were first made to achieve international uniformity in the adjustment of general average. These first attempts were concentrated on effecting uniformity by means of common legislation by the various maritime nations. The obstacles were almost insuperable and, as little or no progress was being made along these lines, shipowners, merchants, and underwriters took matters into their own hands and formulated twelve rules covering the adjustment of general average. These rules became known as the York/Antwerp Rules, 1877. At that time, no attempt was made to define general average and the rules dealt only with specific situations—probably because general average had already developed along two different lines. One school of thought (English) insisted that the general average act must have been performed or the expenses incurred "for the preservation of ship and cargo." Another school of thought (French) maintained that steps taken "for the common good" qualified as general average.

In 1890, the rules were revised and extended to eighteen in number and were known as the York/Antwerp Rules, 1890. Again, no attempt was made to grasp the nettle and endeavor to define the general principles of general average. In fact, one of the rules stipulated that cases not specifically covered by the rules (of which there were necessarily many) should be dealt with in accordance with the law and practice that would have governed the adjustment had the contract of affreightment not contained a clause to pay general average according to the York/Antwerp Rules.

Consequently, general average continued to develop in accordance with the two different schools of thought, with the result that the international uniformity achieved was confined to the specific situations dealt with by the rules.

It was inevitable that sooner or later this question of general principles would have to be tackled, but the York/Antwerp Rules worked so well in practice that it was not until 1924 that they were again revised. The York/Antwerp Rules, 1924, represented an enormous step forward, for they included for the first time lettered Rules A, B, C, D, E, and F which dealt with general principles. Rule A defined a general average act and, as we shall see later when we deal with the principles of general average, represented a victory for the "preservation of ship and cargo" school of thought. The definition adopted was, in fact, almost identical with the English statutory definition of general average. For this and other reasons, the

1924 Rules were the subject of considerable criticism in the United States, where they were adopted reluctantly, and with a number of important reservations, including the omission of all lettered rules except Rule F which dealt with substituted expenses.

In particular, American interests feared that Rule A was not broad enough to include the theory of "common benefit" and was therefore inconsistent with some of the numbered rules.

The principal objective of the revision of the York/Antwerp Rules in 1924 was to achieve a greater degree of uniformity in the adjusting of general average, but the common benefit theory traditionally incorporated in certain of the numbered rules was also extended. Specifically, Rules X (b) and XI (b) were amended to permit port of refuge expenses, handling of cargo, and wages of crew, etc., to be allowed in general average in cases where damage necessitating repairs for the safe prosecution of the voyage was merely *discovered* after loading cargo at a port of loading or call (that is to say, without any *accident* having taken place subsequent to the loading of cargo). In such cases it was, of course, open to cargo interests to exercise any rights they might have to avoid contribution to such general averages. This addition to the York/Antwerp Rules was an extension to what has been described as an "artificial" general average, or general average by agreement. The change also had the effect of affording shipowners additional coverage under their hull policies for vessel's share of such artificial general averages. Furthermore, if cargo interests considered that the facts in any particular case showed that the carrier had not exercised due diligence to provide a seaworthy vessel, they could always decline to contribute, and if such refusal was upheld, the shipowner's Protection and Indemnity insurers would respond for the proportion of the general average not recoverable from cargo interests.

It was not long before the American fear proved to be well founded: the new Rule A proved inconsistent with some of the numbered rules (including the two mentioned above).

Just such a situation arose in England as a result of the apparent discrepancy between the lettered rules and the numbered rules, some of which provided for certain situations to be treated as general average and were at variance with the principles now laid down in the lettered rules. In drawing up the lettered rules, the framers had not intended to disturb or interfere in any way with the numbered rules. The lettered rules were simply intended to provide common principles for dealing with any situation not expressly covered by the numbered rules. Unfortunately, the English courts in the *Makis* case (31 L. L. R. 313) decided that the numbered rules were not absolute but were qualified by the lettered rules. This decision was not acceptable to the British marine insurance market; as a result, British shipowners and underwriters arrived at an understanding by which it was agreed that effect should be given to the intention of the framers of the York/Antwerp Rules, 1924, and that the numbered rules were not to be restricted by the principles set out in the lettered rules. This agreement came to be known as the *Makis Agreement*. Unfortunately, it had obvious limitations and, when the rules were next revised in 1950, a Rule of Interpretation was incorporated, stating beyond question the relationship between the lettered and numbered rules. This Rule of Interpretation reads as follows:

> RULE OF INTERPRETATION. In the adjustment of general average the following lettered and numbered Rules shall apply to the exclusion of any Law and Practice inconsistent therewith.
>
> Except as provided by the numbered rules, general average shall be adjusted according to the lettered Rules.

In short, the numbered rules are paramount to the lettered rules. Only if the numbered rules do not cover a specific situation are the lettered rules to be referred to. However, this is not to say that if a numbered rule only deals partially with a specific subject or situation, recourse cannot be made to the lettered rules. As Selmer, a Norwegian authority, has put it, the lettered rules can be applied as a supplement to the numbered rules (but not as a limitation).

It will thus be seen that the York/Antwerp Rules, 1950, are a combination of the English and Continental (including American) schools of thought. The lettered rules cover the whole field of general average, thereby reducing the necessity of constant reference to the many existing codes and laws to determine whether the loss is general average or not. The numbered rules consist largely of examples of or exceptions to the principles contained in the lettered rules. The exceptions are deemed to be general average by agreement.

The British courts were not alone in having difficulty with the relationship between the numbered and lettered rules, as was shown in the decision of the Fifth Circuit Court of Appeals in *The Orient Transporter* (1974 AMC 2593). In that case, the court misread Rules X and XI, ignored the Rule of Interpretation, and confused the term "common safety" used in Rule A (which, as the court correctly pointed out, is "a phrase closely related to removal from peril") with the phrase "safe prolongation of the voyage" used in Rules X and XI. In brief, the court took the same line as the British courts had done in the *Makis* case, namely, that the numbered rules were qualified by the lettered rules, and, therefore, absent peril, Rules X and XI dealing with expenses at a port of refuge were not applicable. The Rule of Interpretation, however, disposes of this theory and renders the

Fifth Circuit's decision inexplicable. The decision has been charitably referred to as "judicial innocence" as far as the subject of general average is concerned. For a complete analysis of this "temporary aberration in the continuing and otherwise orderly application and development" of the York/Antwerp Rules, *see* Allen, "Peril in the Fifth Circuit," 7 *J. Mar. L. & Com.* 409 (1976). It cannot be too strongly emphasized that any adoption of the Fifth Circuit's interpretation of the York/Antwerp Rules by other circuits would to a great extent nullify one of the main objects of the York/Antwerp Rules, that is, to achieve uniformity in the adjustment of general average. In no other maritime country are the rules so construed, nor was it the intent of the drafters that Rules X and XI should be subject to the requirements of Rule A. Bad law is sometimes contagious and such proved to be the case in this instance. In 1980, to the consternation of average adjusters, the U.S. District Court in the Southern District of New York followed the lead of the Fifth Circuit in ruling that before Rules X and XI of the York/Antwerp rules could be applied, the requirements of Rule A regarding the presence of peril had to be met. The decision was appealed and the Association of Average Adjusters of the United States entered the fray in the role of *amicus curiae,* being represented by Nicholas Healy, a former chairman of the association. Fortunately for international uniformity the U.S. Court of Appeals for the Second Circuit reversed the lower court, concluding that the district court had erred in relying solely on Rule A to the exclusion of Rules X and XI. The Rule of Interpretation required that the lettered rules be given precedence. The appeals court observed that "although the York/Antwerp Rules lack the force of law because they are not formally sanctioned by governments, they reflect an important consensus of the international shipping industry and should be judicially recognized except where they conflict with equally important statutory or other policies" (*Eagle Terminal Tankers* v. *Ins. Co. of U.S.S.R.,* 1980 AMC 2083, 1981 AMC 137). The court could also have pointed out that, where the contract of affreightment between the shipowner and the concerned in cargo stipulates that any general average is to be adjusted in accordance with the York/Antwerp Rules, those rules become part of the contract. In Canada, the federal court of appeals also endorsed what to average adjusters is obvious: that the provisions of the numbered rules of the York/Antwerp Rules (specifically Rules X and XI) are to be applied even though the requirements of Rule A regarding the presence of peril are not met. To argue otherwise is to ignore the Rule of Interpretation (see *Ellerman Lines* v. *Gibbs, Nathanial (Canada) Ltd.,* 1986 AMC 2217). These cases graphically illustrate the difficulties courts of law face in interpreting the abstruse, esoteric subject of general average.

Perhaps the most important result of the revision of the York/Antwerp Rules in 1950 was the recommendation of the Maritime Law Association of the United States that the 1950 Rules be adopted *in toto* by American shipping interests. Most American shipowners, having dropped their objections to the lettered rules, included the 1950 Rules in their contracts of affreightment without any mutilation, although a few shipowners still excluded Rule XXII dealing with the treatment of cash deposits on the grounds that the provisions of that rule were unwieldy.

It is said that history repeats itself, and this is certainly true in the case of the York/Antwerp Rules. Although the 1950 Rules worked extremely well in practice, after the passage of some twenty years, hull and cargo interests once again clamored for further simplification and/or modernization of general average, and many of the leaders of the worldwide marine insurance community turned their efforts in that desirable direction.

Under the auspices of the Comité Maritime International, delegates from the various maritime nations set to work to draft yet another version of the York/Antwerp Rules. The result of their efforts was endorsed by the Comité Maritime International in 1974 and designated as the York/Antwerp Rules, 1974. As we shall see when the individual rules are discussed, a degree of simplification was achieved chiefly by sanctioning the use of invoice values as a basis in arriving at contributory values of cargo and allowances to cargo in general average (Rules XVI and XVII). Deductions from the cost of repairs when old material is replaced by new material were also greatly curtailed (Rule XIII). Perhaps an even more important change took place in the amendments to Rules X (b) and XI (b), the effect of which was to take certain expenses out of the realm of general average entirely. Among the items of expenditure no longer recoverable under the 1974 Rules are the cost of discharging and reloading cargo and detention expenses at a port of loading or call when the damage to the vessel (necessitating such handling of cargo and detention expenses) has been merely "discovered" at such ports without any "accident" having taken place subsequent to the loading of cargo. This amendment, in effect, eliminated the extension of general average which had been introduced into the 1924 Rules and to which reference has been made previously.

Other changes of varying significance were made and these will be dealt with when the rules in question are discussed.

However, as certain matters are not covered by the rules, the contracts of affreightment of American carriers usually stipulate that the rules shall be supplemented by American law and practice in respect of matters not covered by the rules. Under such a clause, the rules are all-controlling and American law and practice is only applicable when the rules do not deal with the situation, as, for example, the application of collecting commission.

Furthermore, the American law of general average remains of much more than academic interest for the following reason: when an insured vessel is proceeding in ballast and under charter, American practice does not recognize the general average clause in the contract of affreightment as governing the adjustment of general average; it follows that all general averages occurring when the vessel is in ballast are adjusted according to American law and practice as provided for in American policies on vessels. This is true whether the vessel is under charter or not.

This chapter will, therefore, deal with both the American law and practice of general average and general average in accordance with the York/Antwerp Rules as interpreted in the United States, for it is inevitable that there are minor differences in the interpretation of the rules by the various maritime nations.

Unless otherwise stated, all future references to the York/ Antwerp Rules in this book appertain to the 1974 Rules. In those instances where changes have been made in the new rules, the new wording is shown in italics.

DEFINITION OF A GENERAL AVERAGE ACT

General average has been defined by the U.S. courts on many occasions, and the following interpretations are representative:

> The object is to incur a partial loss and to risk a minor or contingent danger to avoid the more certain loss of all. (*Caze* v. *Reilly,* Fed. Cas. 2538)

In *Columbian Ins. Co.* v. *Ashby* (13 Pet. 331), the requirements for contribution were stated to be:

> First: That the ship and cargo should be placed in a common imminent peril.
> Secondly: That there should be a voluntary sacrifice of property to avert that peril.
> Thirdly: That by sacrifice the safety of the other property should be presently and successfully attained.

In the case of the *Star of Hope* (76 U. S. 203), it was stated:

> General Average contribution is defined to be a contribution by all the parties in a sea adventure to make good the loss sustained by one of their number on account of sacrifices voluntarily made of part of the ship or cargo to save the residue and the lives of those on board from an impending peril, or for extraordinary expenses necessarily incurred by one or more of the parties for the general benefit of all the

interests embarked in the enterprise. Losses which give a claim to general average are usually divided into two great classes: (1) those which arise from sacrifices of part of the ship or part of the cargo, purposely made in order to save the whole adventure from perishing, (2) those which arise out of extraordinary expenses incurred for the joint benefit of ship and cargo.

The last definition is particularly important because it embraces as general average "extraordinary expenses incurred for the joint benefit of ship and cargo."

Thus it will be seen that, while peril is a necessary element in a general average act, the U.S. courts have extended the consequences of the general average act to include certain expenses incurred after safety has been attained. For example, expenses incurred for the mutual benefit of ship and cargo to enable the voyage to be completed, such as temporary repairs at a port of refuge, are made good as general average. Indeed, general average embraces all expenses incurred in a port of refuge (save permanent repairs to accidental damage) on the view that they are all part of one continuous operation attached to and consequent on the original act of deviation or sacrifice (*Bowring* v. *Thebaud*, 42 Fed. Rep. 799). However, as the distinguished arbitrator, Martin P. Detels, commented in the barge *J. Whitney* arbitration proceedings (1968 AMC 995):

> The "mutual benefit" theory, which is the principal distinguishing hallmark between the British law of general average and the law of most of the other maritime nations, including the United States, deals with the question when the right to contribution in general average *ceases*. In no sense does it relieve the claimant to contribution of the necessity of establishing that, initially, the common venture was in "apparently imminent peril" (*Star of Hope*, 76 U. S. 203).

To sum up, when any voluntary and successful sacrifice is made of part of the property involved in a common maritime adventure *for the common benefit* of the adventure *at a time of peril*, or when, occasioned by a voluntary act *at a time of peril*, a reasonable extraordinary expenditure is incurred *for the common benefit* of the whole adventure, there exists a general average act under American law. However, the objective is not merely the attainment of safety but also the safe completion of the adventure. It is in this respect that American law and practice places greater emphasis on the "mutual benefit" principle and so extends the consequences of the general average act beyond the mere attainment of physical safety.

Turning to the York/Antwerp Rules, a general average act is defined by Rule A, which reads:

RULE A. There is a general average act when, and only when, any extraordinary sacrifice or expenditure is intentionally and reasonably made or incurred for the common safety for the purpose of preserving from peril the property involved in a common maritime adventure.

This definition is almost identical with the English statutory definition and restricts the general average to sacrifices or expenditure made or incurred for the common safety. This English conception of general average limits general average allowances to the attainment of safety, whereas American law and practice incorporates also the common benefit and the preservation of the adventure. It is submitted that this variance is not so much a disagreement in the definition of general average but rather a difference in putting the definition into practice. As Rudolf so aptly put it, "The difference lies in the extent to which the consequences of a general average act are regarded as forming part of the original act" (Lowndes and Rudolf, 7th ed., p. 391).

Although expenses incurred solely for the benefit of the adventure, such as are construed as general average under American law, do not come within the strict terms of Rule A of the York/Antwerp Rules, certain of the numbered rules specifically provide for allowances of that very nature. By virtue of the Rule of Interpretation, these numbered rules must be construed without regard to the limitations of the lettered rules, which only lay down the principles to be followed in cases not covered by the numbered rules. In this way, the York/Antwerp Rules are a combination of both American and English law and practice.

Rule B of the York/Antwerp Rules is complementary to Rule A and reads as follows:

RULE B. General average sacrifices and expenses shall be borne by the different contributing interests on the basis hereinafter provided.

This rule calls for no special comment.

VESSEL AND CARGO OWNED BY SAME PERSON

As against an insurer, a general average act is not affected by the consideration as to whether there will be a contribution or not. Therefore, it is no defense to a claim on underwriters that the vessel and cargo belong to the same person. Section 66 (7) of the Marine Insurance Act states that where ship and cargo are owned by the same assured, the liability of the insurers in respect of general average losses or contributions is to be determined as if those interests were owned by different persons. This is based on *Montgomery* v. *Indemnity Mutual Marine Ins. Co.* (1901 1 K. B. 147, 1902 1 K. B. 734).

THE DEGREE OF PERIL NECESSARY TO CREATE
A GENERAL AVERAGE SITUATION

The degree of peril necessary to create a general average situation has often presented difficulties. As Congdon has stated (2nd ed., pp. 10, 11) the degree of peril has been defined by the courts as follows:

Imminent peril *(Columbian Ins. Co.* v. *Ashby,* 38 U. S. 331);

Danger imminent and apparently inevitable *(Barnard* v. *Adams,* 51 U.S. 270; *The Star of Hope,* 76 U. S. 203);

Impending peril *(McAndrews* v. *Thatcher,* 70 U. S. 347);

Imminent peril and impending danger *(Fowler* v. *Rathbones,* 79 U. S. 102);

Imminent danger *(The Alcona,* 9 Fed. Rep. 172);

Impending danger of physical injury *(Bowring* v. *Thebaud,* 42 Fed. Rep. 794);

Imminent peril impending over the whole *(Ralli* v. *Troop,* 157 U. S. 386).

Indeed, whatever definition of general average we turn to, we find that *peril* is a necessary component or integral part of the general average act. As we have seen, American definitions refer to a "common imminent peril," "an impending peril," and a "danger imminent and apparently inevitable"; the York/Antwerp Rules state that the object of a general average act is "to preserve from peril the property involved in a common maritime adventure" and frequently include the phrase "for the common safety" which means the same thing and refers to the physical safety of the property and not to the successful conclusion of the voyage. There can be no doubt, therefore, that some degree of peril must be present before there can be a bona fide general average act. The question to be asked is: "How imminent need the peril be?" Congdon refers to an imminent or impending physical peril common to vessel and cargo. Lowndes (8th ed., pp. 28, 29) says that although the peril must be real it is not necessary that the vessel should be actually in the grip—or even nearly in the grip—of the disaster that may arise from the danger; that a liberal construction must be given to the words "time of peril"; that the time of peril has come when the danger is real and so near that it would be imprudent to delay the sacrifice. The English court on which Lowndes based his remarks added that "peril" is the same thing as "danger" and need not be immediate; that "it must be real and not imaginary—It must be substantial and not slight; it must be a danger and that is a matter of fact." Rudolf (p. 383) comments that the definition of general average in Rule A of the York/Antwerp Rules was intended to imply that although the danger was to be such as to threaten the common safety, it is not necessary that it be immediately pending. Berlingieri, an Italian authority, states (pp. 51, 52) that, except in some rare instances, jurisprudence has never been in the sense of asking that the peril be imminent. A shipmaster, faced by a peril threatening the properties entrusted to him, cannot and must not hesitate to undertake such acts as he may deem necessary to avert such peril, even if it does not press with a character of a true and real imminence. He alone is to judge as to the right moment when to make a sacrifice: it is sufficient if he has a reasonable fear that, without that sacrifice, he would meet with a common disaster. As will be seen later, the York/Antwerp Rules adopted and legalized the so-called "artificial general average" or "general average by agreement" in the numbered rules by admitting as general average port of refuge expenses incurred not only consequent on putting into port "for the common safety," but also while detained at a port of loading or call undergoing repairs necessary for the safe prosecution of the voyage. Selmer, a Norwegian authority, rationalizes this by reasoning that it is not the *actual* danger but rather the *eventual* danger that might arise during the subsequent part of the voyage which gives rise to the claim for general average contribution. In short, the principles laid down by Rule A are greatly modified; it is sufficient that a situation has arisen in which the further prosecution of the voyage might entail actual danger for vessel and cargo. Thus, for example, when a cargo of fishmeal overheats and is discharged at a port of call, the discharge is usually treated as being necessary "for the common safety" within the meaning of the York/Antwerp Rules, even though fire has not actually broken out. It is sufficient that the condition of things is such that there is an actual state of peril of fire and not merely a fear of fire. If the danger is such that, if nothing were done, spontaneous combustion and fire were sure to follow, then a general average situation exists (*Aktieselskobet Fido* v. *Lloyd Brazileiro*, 283 Fed. Rep. 62). To borrow Selmer's yardstick, it is sufficient that in the opinion of the master a situation has arisen in which the further prosecution of the voyage might entail actual danger to vessel and cargo were the fishmeal not discharged. As the court said in *Bowring* v. *Thebaud* (42 Fed. Rep. 797), "the question of common danger necessary to justify a general average act . . . is not nicely scrutinized . . . the determination of the amount of danger that requires it is left to the judgment of the master, to be exercised reasonably, and in good faith."

It seems clear from the foregoing that under the York/Antwerp Rules, as long as a peril does exist, not only need it not be imminent, it is permissible that it be merely anticipated; and presumably, as in other general average matters, the opinion of the master will not be lightly challenged. In practice, a situation of reasonable apprehension, although not of actual danger, is sufficient. Very often the average adjuster determines whether or not a vessel is in peril within the meaning of Rule A of the York/Antwerp Rules.

WHO HAS AUTHORITY TO ORDER
A GENERAL AVERAGE ACT?

Having examined the definition of a general average act, the next question to be asked is, "Who has the authority to order a general average act?" The York/Antwerp Rules are silent on this point and we have, therefore, to fall back on American law and practice. The first and unassailable answer to the question is "the master," for he alone is agent for both ship and cargo. In this connection, American courts are reluctant to question the judgment of the master. However, in the past, difficulties have arisen when prima facie general average acts have been ordered by third parties having no connection with the common adventure. In *Ralli* v. *Troop* (157 U. S. 386), port authorities ordered that a vessel, on fire, be scuttled and the resultant damage and expenses were held not to be general average. This decision is sometimes given a wider construction than is warranted because, in the case cited, the master was opposed to the scuttling and the controlling reason behind the port authorities' action was not to save the ship and cargo but rather to safeguard the facilities of the port and other shipping in the vicinity. A better exposition of the law on the subject is to be found in the case of the *Beatrice* (1924 AMC 914). In that case, it was held that where the master, or other member of the crew in authority at the time, orders the action taken for the common safety or where the master subsequently endorses the action taken, the resultant loss and/or expenditure is of a general average nature. Thus, actions taken by a shore fire department in extinguishing a fire come within general average if instigated by the master (or his deputy) or if subsequently endorsed by him.

WHEN A GENERAL AVERAGE ACT
IS ORDERED ERRONEOUSLY

We now turn to cases where a general average act is made in good faith at what is thought to be a time of peril but where subsequent events prove that, in fact, no peril existed.

There are two principal American cases bearing on this situation—the *Wordsworth* (88 Fed. Rep. 313) and the *West Imboden* (1936 AMC 696). In the former case, the master, erroneously thinking that a flooded forepeak was due to a hole in the ship, considered it essential for the common safety that the forepeak be emptied to stop the hole. He accordingly opened the sluices to drain the forepeak, thereby damaging the cargo. It was then found that the leak was in the port hawsepipe, which could have been repaired without opening the sluices. The court ruled that, as a peril apparently existed, the action taken was of a general average nature. The decision is open to some criticism and, fortunately, the *West Imboden* case establishes the legal position in such cases more clearly. In the *West Imboden* case, steam and water were forced into a vessel's hold in the mistaken belief that the cargo was on fire, and thereby damaged the cargo. The court held that as, in fact, there was no fire, and, therefore, no peril, the damage done to cargo was not recoverable in general average. The court distinguished the *Wordsworth* case on the grounds that in that case there was an actual peril to cargo, the master merely being mistaken as to the true source of the peril and the best means of combating it. The *West Imboden* case establishes the thesis that a sacrifice made in the mistaken belief that a peril exists does not constitute a general average act. On the other hand, the peril, if real, need not be just what the master supposed it to be (the *Wordsworth*).

CONSEQUENTIAL LOSS OR DAMAGE

Rule C of the York/Antwerp Rules reads as follows:

RULE C. Only such losses, damages or expenses which are the direct consequence of the general average act shall be allowed as general average.

Loss or damage sustained by the ship or cargo through delay, whether on the voyage or subsequently, such as demurrage, and any indirect loss whatsoever, such as loss of market, shall not be admitted as general average.

This rule is in accordance with American law and practice. In 1912, William R. Coe, a distinguished American average adjuster, wrote:

All the necessary consequences of a sacrifice must be regarded as the sacrifice itself (*Columbian Ins. Co. v. Ashby,* 38 U. S. 331).

and

All the immediate and direct consequences of a sacrifice, although these consequences were neither intended nor beneficial, are taken as entering into and forming a part of the sacrifice (the *Wordsworth,* 88 Fed. Rep. 313).

The noted American text writer, Gourlie, says (p. 13):

It may suffice to say, however, that not only all the necessary, but many of the unnecessary, consequences of the act may be regarded as the act itself. In regard to sacrifices not only the known, but the conjectural, and in some cases the accidental results of the original sacrifice are considered to follow as a logical consequence or extension of the intentional act.

Congdon writes (1st ed., pp. 16, 17):

Allowances in general average are not confined to the part of the vessel or cargo which was first selected to bear the voluntary sacrifice, but extend also to such other losses as are the direct consequence of the general average act, which in nearly all cases carries with it a first and a secondary loss. It is very difficult sometimes to distinguish between a direct and an indirect consequence but, generally speaking, all losses and damages which may reasonably be considered as fairly within the contemplation of the master at the time of the general average act, or are its natural and immediate result, are treated as direct consequences of the original act, and irrespective of whether the losses or damages exceeded his intention or expectation.

In practice, difficulty often arises in deciding what limitation is to be put on the phrase, "the direct consequence of the general average act." In each case it is, of course, a question of fact and must be decided in the light of the circumstances prevailing in that particular instance. A general average act carries with it all its natural, immediate, reasonable, and necessary consequences. If a specific loss was contemplated by the master as a possible result of the general average act, such contemplation would be conclusive. However, the fact that the master did not foresee all the consequences of the general average act does not in itself bar these consequences from being treated as general average. In such cases, it should then be considered whether the loss might reasonably have been anticipated. If so, the loss is directly consequential on the general average act and is recoverable in general average. On the other hand, where the sequence of cause and effect is broken by the intervention of a new, unconnected, and unexpected peril, the loss cannot be said to be a direct consequence of the general average act. In *McCall* v. *Houlder Bros.* (8 Asp. M. C. 252), when a hold containing a cargo of ice was opened to effect a general average repair, part of the cargo melted. The loss of cargo was held to be recoverable in general average, being consequent on the general average repairs (although not contemplated, it was incidental thereto).

It has been suggested by some text writers that if there has been no intervening act of negligence between the general average act and the secondary loss, the secondary loss is recoverable in general average. Selmer expresses the view that the criterion is that the secondary loss must be reasonably foreseeable. If a vessel, to get into a port of refuge, must pass through a particularly shallow or rocky fairway, the damage which may be caused during the entry must be allowed. Damage due to other incidental causes should not be allowed even if the damage would not have occurred had the vessel continued on her original course. In a Canadian case (the *Oak Hill*, 1970 AMC 227), two shipments of varying types of pig iron ore were discharged as a general average act at a port of refuge. Unfortunately, in the words of the court, "there was a serious neglect in the reloading of the cargo" which caused the two types to be mixed, with resultant loss in value. The court held that the loss was not a direct consequence of the general average act (and, therefore, not recoverable in general average), but rather that it resulted from the joint fault and negligent acts of the general average surveyor and the master. The court concluded that the carrier held no immunity for such negligent acts and was liable to the concerned in cargo under the contract of affreightment.

Damage done to the property of a third party may be recoverable in general average if the requirements of consequential damage (as discussed above) are met. In *Austin Friars Steamship Co.* v. *Spiller & Bakers Ltd.* (1 K. B. 833, *affirmed* 3 K. B. 586), a vessel was intentionally brought into collision with a pier "in order to take the reach off her" as she was being grounded in a sinking condition. The lower court, holding that the damages paid by the vessel owner to the pier owner were properly the subject of general average, said that "the collision with the pier was a foreseen result, and not the result of a subsequential accident." In affirming, the court of appeals observed that it was known to the master and the pilot that, in the conditions prevailing, it was practically certain that the ship and/or the pier would be damaged. Thus the damage and loss were clearly contemplated. In another case (the *Seapool*, 47 L. L. R. 331), the master of a vessel dragging her anchor in a gale brought the vessel broadside against a pier, using the pier as a lever to get her head into such a position that he could proceed to sea and safety. The damage to the pier and the ship was held to be recoverable in general average. In the words of the court:

> Was there then in this case any extraordinary sacrifice? I think there was. I think that the master did "intentionally"—that is also one of the words of Rule A—"intentionally" sacrifice a portion of his ship. I think he made his conscious act of putting his ship against the pier, and I think that by doing so he intended to, and did in effect, succeed in transferring to the ship alone what was a peril to the entire adventure. If he did this, and did it with his eyes open to what he was doing, that seems to me to comply with the real underlying meaning of Rule A. He was confronted, as it seems to me, with the alternative of certain damage to his ship and probably damage to the pier, as against a

problematical worse damage to the whole adventure, and he elected to take the first of the two alternatives.

These decisions were quoted with approval in *Australian Coastal Shipping Commission* v. *Green*, 1970 1 L. L. R. 209. A vessel had been carried away from her moorings and her owner engaged a tug at a fixed rate to remoor her. The towage contract incorporated the United Kingdom Standard Towage conditions, which conditions included a very wide indemnity in favor of the tug owner, even against the consequences of negligence by the crew of the tug. While the towage operation was under way, the towrope parted and fouled and jammed the propeller of the tug; as a result the tug ran aground and became a total loss. The tug's claim against the shipowner for indemnity under the terms of the United Kingdom Standard Towage contract failed but only because the tug was found to be unseaworthy. However, the costs incurred in defending the claim were not recovered and these costs were claimed as being recoverable in general average. In the same case, another tug had been employed to refloat a stranded vessel also under the United Kingdom Standard Towage contract. Here also the towrope parted and fouled the propeller of the assisting tug, resulting in the tug sustaining damage and having to accept salvage services from third parties. Under the terms of the towage contract, the shipowner was obliged to pay the salvors of the tug as well as the tug's damages. These payments were claimed as general average. The court, in holding that the expenses incurred in both accidents were recoverable in general average, stated that there was no law or authority to the effect that liabilities arising under the terms of a contract could not result in expenses which would be recoverable in general average. The court held in all the circumstances the expenses claimed in both instances were the direct consequence of the general average acts, because shipowners' servants brought to mind, or ought reasonably to have brought to mind, the possible liability to the tug owners consequent on the breaking of the towrope. Further, the actuality was so connected with the general average act of engaging the tugs as not to break the chain of causation. The decision was confirmed by the court of appeals (1971 1 L. L. R. 16) who found that, in each case, the general average act was the engagement of tugs on the towage conditions; that at the time of the act it was reasonably foreseeable that there was a distinct possibility that the towline might break and foul the propeller; and that the expenditure under the indemnity clause was reasonable. Accordingly, it was a direct consequence of the general average act and was therefore allowable in general average.

In a similar vein, when a vessel was in danger of stranding due to a defective steering system, the master ordered the starboard anchor dropped and the engines reversed full astern. As a result of these maneuvers the vessel did not strand. However, there were several electric cables in the area; two of these cables were damaged by the vessel's anchor and the vessel owner was held liable for the damage. The Norwegian arbitrator held that the dropping of the anchor was a general average act (an "act of salvage") and, even if the master did not realize that this could involve damage to the cables (which were marked on the chart), the damage was a foreseeable consequence of the measure adopted (Scandinavian Maritime Reports 1983, p. 329, reported in the British Association of Average Adjusters' Annual Report, 1984, p. 37).

Another example of the operation of Rule C is the occasional allowance in general average of oil pollution expenses when such pollution is the direct consequence of a general average act. Thus, when a vessel is obliged to enter a port of refuge for the common safety, following an accident which has resulted in the vessel leaking oil, any expenditure incurred to avoid or minimize such pollution or any liabilities arising from such pollution would be allowable in general average; such expenditure or liability would be the direct consequence of the general average act of entering the port of refuge. Similarly, any pollution directly resulting from the jettison of oil (whether cargo or bunkers) for the common safety would also be allowable in general average. The usual rules of consequential damage would, of course, be applicable and, if the pollution did not occur for some time following the general average act and/or was remote geographically, the pollution might be too remote to be considered a direct consequence of the general average act and therefore might not meet the requirements of Rule C.

If a vessel leaking oil was able to proceed directly to her next scheduled port, and the leakage was not the result of a general average act, any expenditure or liability resulting from the leakage would not concern general average. Such expenses would be the inevitable result of the accident giving rise to the leakage and not the result of a general average act or the direct consequence of a general average act; such leakage would, in fact, be of a purely accidental nature.

The problems involved in allowing oil pollution expenses in general average were the subject of the address of the chairman of the British Association of Average Adjusters in 1980, W. P. F. Bennett.

In summation, there are no problems more difficult to solve, nor any situations in which drawing a dividing line is more difficult, than those involving causation or remoteness. Each individual case must be carefully considered by the average adjuster, but the following guidelines will help in arriving at a decision:

(1) If the loss or damage was reasonably foreseeable and was anticipated by the master as being an unavoidable consequence of the general average act, there can be no doubt that the consequential damage is recoverable in general average.

(2) Even if the loss or damage was not actually contemplated by the master, if it was reasonably foreseeable and should have been contemplated, the consequential damage is recoverable in general average.

(3) Even if the loss or damage was neither foreseen nor foreseeable, nevertheless if it was, in fact, connected with the general average act decided on by the master so as to be the *necessary* consequence of the course embarked upon (that is, the general average act), then it forms part of the sacrifice or expenditure decided on by the master.

As will have been seen from the foregoing, it is well established that expenditure incurred in making good damage to the property of a third party (such as damage done to a pier) is allowable in general average, providing it was the natural consequence of a general average act as defined above.

The second paragraph of Rule C of the York/Antwerp Rules specifically stipulates that any loss or damage sustained by the ship or cargo through delay (such as demurrage of vessel or loss of cargo due to inherent vice) and any indirect loss (such as loss of market) are not made good in general average. Such losses are considered to be the *indirect or remote* consequences of the general average act. This is in agreement with American law and practice. As Congdon put it (1913, p. 22):

> Demurrage and loss of interest or market are not subjects of contribution, being considered as remote and not as direct consequences of a general average act; and, similarly, deterioration of or loss on cargo by *delay* at a port of refuge or through climatic conditions because of such delay are not allowed for. No allowance is made for loss of freight under a time charter, because such loss is the result of the contractual relation between the shipowner and the time charterer, with which the cargo owner is not concerned.

ONUS OF PROOF

Rule E of the York/Antwerp Rules provides a general directive on the question of onus of proof and reads as follows:

> RULE E. The onus of proof is upon the party claiming in general average to show that the loss or expense claimed is properly allowable as general average.

The rule is self-explanatory and is in accord with normal legal procedure. That is to say, he who alleges must establish that which he alleges on a balance of probabilities. In short, the party claiming an allowance in general average must prove his right to that allowance, and any doubt is resolved against the claimant.

In the absence of an agreement to the contrary, a statement of general average is without legal effect and is not conclusive on cargo's liability to contribute (*Great Eastern Associates and Farrell Lines* v. *Republic of India*, 1978 AMC 1288). However, a statement of general average prepared by an average adjuster is prima facie proof of:

(1) The losses, damages, and expenses which as factual matters are the direct consequence of a general average act,

(2) The values attaching to such losses, damages, and expenses, and

(3) The computations proportioning these losses, damages, and expenses between the parties to the venture, that is, ship and cargo.

However, in those rare cases where there is a dispute as to whether a general average situation existed, the onus is on the party which claims general average contribution to prove that a general average act in fact occurred (the *Clydewater*, 1967 AMC 1474).

Rule E must be read in conjunction with Rule D (to be discussed later).

BALLAST VOYAGES

When a vessel is insured commercially, the U.S. courts have held that the principles of general average are applicable even though the vessel may be in ballast and therefore the sole contributing interest.

In the case of *Potter* v. *Ocean Ins. Co.* (3 Sumner 27) the court said:

As I understand it, the phrase "general average" as found in our policies of insurance, is used in contradistinction to particular average. It means a voluntary sacrifice for the benefit of the voyage; and not merely an involuntary encounter of a loss, without action or design . . .

It looks to the consideration, whether the act is intended for the benefit of all concerned in the voyage; and not in particular to the consideration, who are to contribute to the indemnity. To be sure, if the owner stands as his own insurer throughout, the question degenerates into a mere distinction; for it is (then) a purely speculative enquiry. Not so, when there is insurance, for in such a case the underwriters are *pro tanto* benefited by the sacrifice or other act done; and they are in a just sense bound to contribute to it . . .

Suppose an empty ship, which is insured, is dismantled in a storm and is compelled to put away into a port of necessity, in order to repair; or otherwise she must be abandoned at sea; are not the expenses of the voyage, in such a case, to the port of necessity of the nature of a general average? Are they not as much for the benefit of the *underwriters* as for the shipowner? ... And it seems to me, it would be an entire novelty, in case of insurance, not to hold that under such circumstances the underwriters were liable for the charges, as in the nature of general average.

In the case of *Dollar* v. *La Foncière Compagnie* (162 Fed. Rep. 563), the court referred to *Potter* v. *Ocean*, saying:

This case is authority for the propositions; First, That it is not essential to a general average charge that there was cargo upon the vessel liable to make contribution on account of the expenditure claimed as a general average charge; that, if only the owner and the insurer are benefited by the expense incurred in taking the injured vessel to a port of necessity for repairs, the latter, upon the principles of general average, is bound to contribute his proportionate share of such expense. Second, That, although a vessel may be in a port and in no immediate danger of loss, yet if she is unseaworthy, and it is necessary, for her to seek another port for the purpose of necessary repairs, required in order to put her in a seaworthy condition, the expense incurred by the vessel in going to the port of necessity constitutes a general average charge.

The foregoing is contrary to English law, which requires more than one interest to be involved in a common adventure before a general average situation can exist. The American viewpoint is founded on the somewhat doubtful proposition that the liability of underwriters is an interest at risk and that the general average sacrifice or expenditure is incurred as much for the benefit of the underwriters as for the shipowner. However, whatever one may think about the merits of the reasoning, the law and practice is firmly established. Thus general average under American law does not depend on the number of interests involved but looks only to the nature of the act.

In the United States there is no law or practice which requires the chartered freight to contribute to general average when the vessel is in ballast and under charter; the general average clause in the charter party has, consequently, no bearing on the adjustment of any general average arising while the vessel is in ballast. In accordance with the general average clause invariably included in insurances on American vessels, such general averages may be adjusted according to American law and practice (at the option of the assured).

One important result of the American practice of not recognizing chartered voyages as a unit for general average purposes and therefore not bringing in chartered freight as a contributor to general average is that a ballast voyage ends when the vessel arrives at her port of destination (usually a loading port). Consequently, it is not possible to have a general average detention *at the end* of a ballast voyage before the vessel commences to load cargo. In other words, the ballast voyage is a separate voyage for general average purposes, and once it has been successfully completed there can be no claim in general average for detention expenses. Needless to say, it is still possible to have a general average at the end of a ballast voyage if, while a vessel is waiting for a loading berth, an accident occurs (such as a fire) which places the vessel in peril. In such a situation, if any part of the vessel is the subject of a general average sacrifice or if general average expenses are incurred, a general average situation would exist; it is only a general average detention which is barred.

The question might now be asked as to what yardstick is to be used for determining the duration of the voyage in ballast cases—a very important matter, for it must be remembered that, generally speaking, any allowance for wages and maintenance of crew, etc., in general average is only permissible when a vessel deviates from the course of her voyage to a port of refuge or is detained at a port of call in the general interest. The important point is that the delay must occur on a specific voyage, which must afterwards be resumed. If the voyage is abandoned, all allowances in general average cease. This was established in the *Joseph Farwell* (31 Fed. Rep. 844) when the court stated:

> But these expenses of the delay are general average only up to the time the continuation of the voyage remains in expectancy. When there is no longer any fair expectation of a continuation of the voyage, it is considered as broken up, and there are no longer any general average expenses.

In ballast cases, the voyage on which the vessel is proceeding is established by reference to contracts of affreightment (if any), operating schedules, orders to the master, log entries, etc. Having established the voyage, in practice it is sometimes difficult to determine if and when the voyage is terminated for general average purposes. A broad view is taken in this regard and even if a charter under which the vessel was proceeding in ballast is cancelled while the vessel is in a port of refuge, assuming the vessel proceeds to the same geographical destination within a reasonable time, it is considered that there has been no termination of the adventure in a geographical sense. In such circumstances, the general average continues until the vessel is ready to proceed from the port of refuge. On the other hand, if a change of geographical voyage occurs, the original adventure is terminated from the time the decision was taken or from the time events occurred to change it. Furthermore if, for example, a vessel is proceeding in ballast from A to B to load cargo but decides, en route, to put into port C for routine repairs for owner's account merely as a matter of convenience and without any accident having taken place, the voyage to B has been abandoned and the voyage is now from A to C for repairs. Even if, after completion of the repairs, the vessel proceeds from C to B, this is a new and separate voyage. In other words, the ultimate geographical area yardstick is not to be construed as a blank check for measuring general average ballast voyages. Needless to say, in all general average ballast cases, the reasonableness of the period of delay at a port of refuge must be considered. In this connection, the rules regarding abandonment of the original voyage which apply to loaded vessels apply equally to vessels under general average when in ballast. If the period of detention at the port of refuge is such that it would be considered unreasonable to retain cargo for that length of time, a detention of similar duration in a ballast general average situation would also be considered unreasonable, and the allowance of general average expenses would have to be limited accordingly. In general average ballast situations, the average adjuster has the responsibility to determine whether the period claimed in general average is reasonable.

It has to be said that occasionally, in ballast cases, some average adjusters overlook the importance of not giving preferential treatment to shipowners in considering when the voyage on which the general average situation arose, should be considered to be frustrated and therefore the general average terminated. Reasonableness and equity are fundamental prerequisites in all cases of general average. None of the legal cases on which the American concept of general average in ballast is founded even discuss the continuance of port of refuge expenses—the concept is based solely on the attainment of safety. If average adjusters do not strictly apply the same principles to ballast general averages which they would apply to cases involving cargo, hull underwriters may be obliged to limit their liability for port of refuge expenses in ballast general averages to the time when safety has been attained.

GENERAL AVERAGE SACRIFICES

As we have seen, general average can be divided into two categories—sacrifices and expenditure.

In considering general average sacrifices, it must always be remembered that the following requirements must be met:

(1) The property must be imperiled.
(2) The sacrifice must be a deliberate act.
(3) The purpose of the sacrifice must be the achievement of safety.
(4) The sacrifice must be reasonable.
(5) The sacrifice must be made not only under unusual circumstances but in an unusual and abnormal manner.

Sacrifices of Ship

DAMAGE SUSTAINED IN REFLOATING A STRANDED VESSEL. The most common type of sacrifice of ship is the working of a ship's machinery while aground and in a position of peril in order to refloat. It will be seen that all five requirements listed above are met, always assuming that the vessel is in a position of peril while aground. Whether or not peril exists is, of course, a question of fact. In practice, it is generally considered that a vessel is usually in peril when aground. This practice is supported by the courts, as in *Willcox, Peck & Hughes* v. *American Smelting & Refining Co.* (210 Fed. Rep. 89). In that case, the vessel ran aground in a comparatively sheltered part of New York Harbor. The court, in pointing out the broad discretion which must be allowed the master of the vessel in deciding the steps he thinks should be taken, made the following remarks:

> If he finds danger in a land-locked harbor, in shallows, at anchor, or moored to a wharf it should be no answer to register a landsman's opinion as to the necessary absence of danger at such a place.

There is also the *Mincio* case (1937 AMC 1506), where the court decided the question of peril to a vessel stranded in the Parana River. In that case, the vessel stranded in the channel on a muddy, sandy bottom of the river. The place where the strand occurred was in the zone of South American hurricanes. The master testified that there was danger of seams opening in the plating of the steamer, though, he said, the vessel was resting on an even keel with a slight list to starboard. The second officer testified that the ship was resting on the bottom at the bow and at the stern but not in the center; that, as the cargo was in the center, the ship would be strained and, if the wind increased in velocity, she might be pushed further into the bank of the channel. The master thought that the danger to the vessel was not immediate, but the second officer stated that it was imminent. The court held that the vessel was in peril and that the cargo was liable for its share of the general average. In their decision, the circuit court quoted from the *Willcox, Peck & Hughes* case referred to above and said that "when a vessel is stranded, she and her cargo are practically always in a substantial peril. Such a vessel is helpless because she cannot pursue her intended voyage or deal effectively with any emergency" and "if she should sink deeper into the mud and come to rest on some hidden submerged rock or other obstruction, that also would subject her to a further strain."

A case which casts some doubt on this general proposition that when a ship is stranded she is "practically always in a substantial peril," is that of the *Edward Rutledge* (1954 AMC 2070). In that case, the vessel was twice stuck in soft mud when attempting to sail and each time was released on the next tide by securing her lines to a nearby pier and using her engines. It was held that there was no peril and no general average.

Nevertheless, it is generally accepted that a vessel which is lying aground is usually in some degree of peril, whether it be imminent or ultimate. As the court put it in the *National Defender* (1969 AMC 1219):

> While every stranding may not give rise to a substantial peril in the factual sense, it is nonetheless undeniably true that a stranded ship which cannot refloat itself unaided is earning no money for its owner, is performing no function for which it was built and is deteriorating generally in monetary worth, in usefulness, and in reputation. The cases are clear—and the Court so holds—that such a situation as matter of law is peril enough to support an award of salvage

(and, it follows, general average).

Rule VI of the 1950 Rules dealt with a sacrifice of this nature and provided for the allowance in general average of the extraordinary use or abuse of sails in refloating a stranded vessel. The rule was eliminated from the 1974 Rules on the grounds that it was now obsolete. The principle, of course, holds good and if, in fact, a sailing vessel is involved in general average it would still be in order to make the allowance envisaged by Rule VI of the 1950 Rules, under Rule A of the 1974 Rules.

Rule VII of the York/Antwerp Rules reads as follows:

RULE VII. DAMAGE TO MACHINERY AND BOILERS. Damage caused to *any* machinery and boilers of a ship which is ashore and in a position of peril, in endeavoring to refloat, shall be allowed in general average when shown to have arisen from an actual intention to float the ship for the common safety at the risk of such damage; but where a ship is afloat no loss or damage caused by working the *propelling* machinery and boilers shall in any circumstances be made good as general average.

This rule deals with a common form of general average sacrifice already discussed above. The principle underlying the rule is that the ordi-

220 MARINE INSURANCE AND GENERAL AVERAGE

nary use of machinery and boilers is part of the shipowner's obligation to the cargo and only the extraordinary use or abuse of machinery and boilers is allowable in general average.

The exclusion of damage to machinery sustained while a ship is afloat was intended to cover only the main engines and the propelling machinery, not auxiliary machinery or pumps; even if such auxiliary machinery or pumps form part of the main engine, they are not considered part of the "machinery and boilers" referred to in the rule. Thus, if auxiliary machinery or pumps are damaged as a result of a general average act while the vessel is afloat, an allowance in general average is not prohibited by this rule. The addition of the word *propelling* in the 1974 rule is intended to make this clear.

However, any damage caused by working the *propelling* machinery when the vessel is afloat is categorically excluded from general average, even if such damage would otherwise have been recoverable under Rule A (because the Rule of Interpretation makes the numbered rules paramount). To this extent, the rule is more restrictive than the position under American law and practice which (in the absence of the York/Antwerp Rules) permits loss or damage to machinery while afloat to be made good, providing the facts come within the American definition of general average. It must, however, be emphasized that it is only damage caused by *working* the machinery when afloat which is excluded by the rule. The allowance of damage to the machinery sustained when afloat and caused by other general average acts is not prohibited.

Although the York/Antwerp Rules do not specifically deal with the point, it is the practice to allow in general average the *extra* fuel and engines stores consumed while working the engines in the efforts to refloat the vessel (always assuming the vessel was in peril while aground). The ordinary consumption while aground, i.e., the amounts used by such auxiliaries as would have been required if the vessel were lying at her dock completely idle, is not allowable.

So far, we have only contemplated the possibility of damage being sustained to machinery in the efforts to refloat a stranded ship. However, it is possible that damage could be done to the bottom of a vessel in forcing her off the ground.

There is nothing to prevent an allowance in general average for hull damage sustained by a vessel in efforts to refloat, but the onus of proof is on the party claiming and it is usually difficult to prove that the damage was due solely to the efforts to refloat and not to the stranding or pounding on the bottom while aground.

Thus, Templeman says that where it can be clearly shown that certain *specific* damage was done to the vessel's bottom in the operation of refloating, it is allowed in general average. The American text writers Coe and Congdon have this to say on the subject:

> Damage to vessel's bottom, as being attributable to the efforts to float her, is very rarely allowed in general average in this country, for the lack of clear proof that the damage was due solely to the efforts to float and not to the stranding and pounding on the bottom by the action of wind and sea. (Coe, quoted in Lowndes, 8th ed., pp. 295, 296.)
>
> In respect of damages to the hull *below* the water line the legal presumption is, except in cases of voluntary stranding, that they were *accidentally* caused, and it is only upon evidence removing this presumption that consideration can be had as to whether they were sustained as a *natural consequence* of the measures taken to float the vessel. (Congdon, p. 74)

When a vessel is ashore and in a position of peril, the test as to whether damage to the hull in endeavoring to refloat is allowable in general average is whether any *extraordinary* sacrifice has *intentionally* and *reasonably* been made for the common safety. It therefore follows that if the circumstances under which a vessel stranded were such that the mere operation of refloating her would *inevitably* cause some damage to the hull, such damage is not allowable in general average.

On the other hand, *if the master has a choice of action* and considers that the best course to adopt is a course which would probably result in *additional damage* to the vessel's bottom, such damage would be allowable in general average.

The question really is, "Was the damage already to all intents and purposes suffered by the vessel, so that the only reasonable conclusion is that it would have been present although the vessel had not been forced off but had been refloated in some other way such as by rising water level or lightening of cargo?"

It is true to say that there is nothing in principle against such claims, and the evidence in each case must be judged on its merits, bearing in mind that the onus of proof is on the claimant.

VOLUNTARY STRANDING. Voluntary stranding is a form of general average sacrifice about which much has been written. The subject is specifically dealt with by Rule V of the York/Antwerp Rules, which reads as follows:

> RULE V. VOLUNTARY STRANDING. When a ship is intentionally run on shore for the common safety, whether or not she might have been driven on shore, the consequent loss or damage shall be allowed in general average.

This rule should be read in conjunction with Rule A; in other words, the vessel must be reasonably as well as intentionally run on shore. Furthermore, it has been held that an intentional beaching constitutes a voluntary stranding notwithstanding that the vessel grounded sooner than was anticipated (*Anglo-Grecian Steam Trading Co. Ltd.* v. *T. Beynon & Co.*, 24 L. L. R. 122).

The former version of Rule V incorporated in the 1950 Rules had excluded claims for voluntary stranding in cases where the vessel would have gone ashore in any event. The distinction was thought to be rather nebulous and therefore unsatisfactory; the new rule removes the practical difficulties involved in deciding whether the vessel would have run aground eventually if she had not been voluntarily beached earlier.

American law and practice is now not quite as generous as the York/Antwerp Rules in cases of voluntary stranding. While the American courts have frequently held that damage sustained as a result of voluntary stranding is recoverable in general average whether or not the vessel would have run aground in any case, there is a proviso that the master must have exercised some control over the place in which the vessel grounded *(Barnard* v. *Adams*, 51 U. S. 270, 10 How. 270). The reasoning behind this is that, by choosing the best position to run aground, the master could minimize the resultant damage. On the other hand, if the vessel is voluntarily stranded in substantially the same position as that in which she would have stranded in any event, the damage is not made good in general average (the *Major William H. Tantum*, 49 Fed. Rep. 252).

The law is admirably stated by Phillips (5th ed., Vol. 2, p. 88) as follows:

> On the whole, then, if the intentional stranding is, under the particular circumstances, the direct result of voluntary agency rather than of the action of the elements, and the actual stranding is another than the one impending, and not merely an incidental and inconsiderable modification of it, the case is one for general average.

When the general average is being adjusted according to American practice, the wages and maintenance of crew while the vessel is aground following a voluntary stranding are allowed in general average. It is a moot point whether such an allowance can be made under Rule V in cases where the York/Antwerp Rules govern the general average, unless it can be successfully maintained that the place where a vessel is voluntarily stranded is in a "port or place of refuge" within the meaning of Rule XI. That is to say, whether the place of stranding is within the confines of a port or has some of the characteristics of a port (see *Humber Conservancy Board* v. *Federal Coal & Shipping Co.*, 29 L. L. R. 177).

SACRIFICE OF ANCHORS AND CHAINS. The loss of anchors and chains is recoverable in general average, provided the five requirements enumerated in "General Average Sacrifices" (*supra*) are met. In particular, the loss must have occurred under unusual circumstances and in an unusual and abnormal manner. For example, if an anchor is suddenly let go, without the usual preparations, to avoid a collision or to prevent the vessel running aground, and the anchor and chain are thereby lost, the loss is recoverable in general average. Similarly, damage to anchors and chains used in the efforts to refloat a stranded vessel is allowed in general average (always provided the vessel is in a position of peril while aground). Another example of a general average sacrifice of anchors and chains would be any damage sustained during a general average towage operation. On the other hand, if the anchor becomes foul of an obstruction on the bottom during the course of an ordinary anchoring and it cannot be raised, the consequent slipping of the anchor and chain is not recoverable in general average, even at a time of peril. This is because the anchor and chain were irretrievably lost while being used for the purpose for which they were intended and involved no general average sacrifice.

The entirely unobjectionable principle that there cannot be a sacrifice of a thing which has already been destroyed is also exemplified by Rule IV of the York/Antwerp Rules, which reads as follows:

> RULE IV. CUTTING AWAY WRECK. Loss or damage *sustained* by cutting away wreck *or parts of the ship* which have been previously carried away *or are effectively lost by accident* shall not be made good as general average.

This rule has been reworded in the 1974 Rules, the change being shown in italics. However, the meaning was not changed.

By laying down this hard and fast rule, any inquiry into nebulous damaged values becomes unnecessary.

This rule is not as liberal as American law and practice which permits the allowance in general average of the loss or damage due to cutting away wreck if the remains endanger the common safety (the *Magarethe Blanca*, 4 Fed. Rep. 59). This is on the hypothetical assumption that, if the storm subsided, the wreckage might have been saved. The allowance is based on the value the material would have had, had it been recovered.

SHIP'S MATERIALS AND STORES BURNT FOR FUEL. Rule IX of the York/Antwerp Rules reads as follows:

> RULE IX. SHIP'S MATERIALS AND STORES BURNT FOR FUEL. Ship's materials and stores, or any of them, necessarily burnt for fuel for the common safety at a time of peril, shall be admitted as

general average, when and only when an ample supply of fuel had been provided; but the estimated quantity of fuel that would have been consumed, calculated at the price current at the ship's last port of departure at the date of her leaving, shall be credited to the general average.

This rule indirectly raises the whole question of the validity of claims for general average and/or salvage arising solely as a result of a vessel running short of fuel. Gourlie (p. 241) states the position in American practice to be as follows:

When the expenses arise through want of provisions or fuel, they are only considered as general average, when it is shown that the vessel was fully and properly supplied before sailing, and that their loss occurred through no fault or neglect of the vessel, but by a peril of the sea.

In any discussion of this subject, it must be remembered that failure to ship an adequate supply of fuel to carry the vessel to her destination or her next bunkering port is unseaworthiness, and the shipowner would have to face the consequences.

Thus, in all cases of alleged general average, where a vessel merely puts into an unscheduled bunkering port to replenish her fuel, it must be shown that the vessel was fully and properly supplied before sailing. In this connection, the British Association of Average Adjusters has a Rule of Practice (B9) stipulating that the facts on which the general average is based are to be set forth in the adjustment, including the material dates and distances, particulars of fuel supplies and consumption. A sufficient supply would be a supply which reflects a margin of safety. What constitutes an adequate supply is in each case a question of fact, but American courts have held that a vessel should have onboard on sailing sufficient fuel to complete the voyage or the next stage of the voyage, under conditions which might reasonably be anticipated, with an excess safety margin of 20 to 25 percent. (See *Hurlbut* v. *Turnure*, 81 Fed. Rep. 208, and the *Abbazzia*, 127 Fed. Rep. 495.)

In the event that an insufficient supply of fuel to reach the vessel's destination, or the intended bunkering port for that stage of the voyage, had been provided, it would obviously not be possible to enforce contribution in general average from cargo. Furthermore, if the alleged general average expenses were confined to putting into an unscheduled bunkering port, such expenses were, in fact, not general average expenses at all but merely normal fueling expenses. Thus, the vessel's share of the alleged general average expenses would likewise not be recoverable from hull underwriters.

Difficulties arise in those cases where a vessel runs short of fuel at sea and has to accept salvage services. Where an adequate supply of fuel (i.e., reflecting a safety margin) had been originally shipped, no difficulty would arise; but what of such cases where an adequate supply had not been shipped? Obviously, cargo's share of the salvage services would not be recoverable from cargo and would presumably fall on the vessel's Protection and Indemnity club; similarly, if cargo interests had responded directly to the salvors for their share of the salvage award, they would be entitled to recover such payment from the vessel owner (*Cyprinia* arbitration, 1969 AMC 2193). In such circumstances it might well be asked whether there is a valid claim on hull underwriters for the vessel's share of the salvage award. It has been suggested that if the master is entrusted by the owner with the task of obtaining sufficient bunkers and he fails to do so, his action falls within the peril "negligence of masters, etc." in the Inchmaree clause of the hull policies. The better opinion seems to be that the provision insuring against negligence of masters, etc., provides cover against negligence by the persons named in the discharge of their duties as such (that is, the navigation and routine running of the vessel). Furthermore, the due diligence clause in the Inchmaree clause applies to negligent failure by the assured, owner and managers, in the discharge of duties that *fall within their province* as such. If there is such a failure, then this is "want of due diligence"; even if the performance of the duties has been entrusted to the master and ship's officers, the actual failure is that of the assured, owner and managers. Accepting this view, the supplying of sufficient bunkers for the voyage is a matter falling within the personal province of the shipowner. Failure to exercise due diligence in this respect would be failure of owner and managers and would excuse hull underwriters of claims *resulting therefrom*. Indeed, there is law to the effect that general average expenses such as port of refuge charges, etc., when occasioned solely and directly by unseaworthiness of the vessel and not by perils of the sea or negligence of master or crew, are not covered by the general marine insurance policy. However, this would only seem to support the conclusion already reached, that port of refuge expenses arising solely because an insufficient supply of fuel had been shipped are not recoverable as general average from either hull underwriters or cargo interests.

The problem remains of salvage services rendered where a vessel runs short of fuel at sea because an insufficient *safety margin* has been shipped; it is probable that in such cases the courts would take the view that the vessel was necessarily endangered by sea perils and that any salvage or general average expenses incurred to preserve her are recoverable under the hull policy. In short, according to this view, where a vessel is endangered by a peril insured against, the fact that the vessel was unseaworthy on sailing does not in itself afford any defense to underwriters under a time policy. This for the reason that, to avoid the claim, the underwriter has the burden of showing that the vessel was unseaworthy *with the privity of the assured* and that the loss was attributable thereto. In other words, hull underwriters must prove that the shipowner had deliberately allowed the ship to become unseaworthy. This burden is almost impossible to sustain.

Stated another way, in the case where a vessel runs short of fuel at sea and requires salvage assistance, the shipowner can recover his own contribution to the general average from his hull underwriters provided the peril is one for the consequences of which underwriters would be liable. On the other hand, it seems that if it was inevitable on sailing that the vessel would run short of fuel (that is, where the fuel could not possibly take the vessel to her next scheduled port), there might be no recovery from hull underwriters. An exception would be where a genuine miscalculation had been made, for in those circumstances it could not be said that the assured had deliberately allowed the vessel to become unseaworthy.

From the foregoing, the following basic principles emerge in shortage of fuel cases:

(1) Unless an adequate supply of fuel reflecting a safety margin is shipped, it is not possible to enforce cargo's contribution to general average.

(2) Unless an adequate supply of fuel reflecting a safety margin is shipped, any so-called port of refuge expenses are merely bunkering expenses and no general average situation exists at all.

(3) When a vessel runs short of fuel at sea and requires salvage or towage assistance, a general average situation does exist. Cargo's share would not be recoverable from cargo interests unless an adequate supply of fuel reflecting a safety margin had been shipped and would therefore be claimable against Protection and Indemnity insurers. However, vessel's share would be recoverable from hull underwriters unless the vessel owner was privy to the shortage of fuel, i.e., had deliberately allowed the vessel to proceed to sea with an inadequate supply.

Before leaving Rule IX of the York/Antwerp Rules, it should be mentioned that the burning of cargo in similar circumstances is not dealt with by the rule; such claims can, however, be dealt with under Rule A and, of course, are not conditioned upon an adequate supply of fuel having been provided. Were it otherwise, the innocent cargo owner would be penalized for the shipowner's guilt.

AMOUNT TO BE ALLOWED IN GENERAL AVERAGE FOR DAMAGE OR LOSS TO SHIP. Rule XVIII of the York/Antwerp Rules deals with this subject as follows:

RULE XVIII. DAMAGE OF SHIP. The amount to be allowed as general average for damage or loss to the ship, her machinery and/or gear *caused by a general average act shall be as follows:*

(a) When repaired or replaced, the actual reasonable cost of repairing or replacing such damage or loss, subject to deductions in accordance with Rule XIII.

(b) When not repaired or replaced, the reasonable depreciation arising from such damage or loss, but not exceeding the estimated cost of repairs. But where the ship is an actual total loss or when the cost of repairs of the damage would exceed the value of the ship when repaired, the amount to be allowed as general average shall be the difference between the estimated sound value of the ship after deducting therefrom the estimated cost of repairing damage which is not general average and the value of the ship in her damaged state which may be measured by the net proceeds of sale, if any.

This rule has been entirely redrafted primarily with a view to clarification. In particular, it has been put beyond doubt that even when a vessel is a commercial constructive total loss, should the shipowner elect to carry out repairs to the vessel which include repairs to damage resulting from a general average act, the cost of such general average repairs is recoverable in general average. In short, a shipowner under general average is not obliged to treat his vessel as a constructive total loss if it is in his best interest to effect repairs; on the contrary, he may elect to treat his loss as partial. By effecting repairs, he quantifies the general average sacrifice; his property has been sacrificed and he can point to repair accounts proving exactly how much that sacrifice cost him. Such a claim falls within paragraph (a) of the rule. Indeed, if repairs are actually effected, the vessel cannot be said to have been a constructive total loss at the termination of the general average voyage.

Paragraph (b) of the rule deals with the basis for allowances in general average when the vessel is not repaired. It specifically sets forth the formula to be followed in arriving at the amount to be allowed in general average when the ship is an actual total loss or a commercial constructive total loss.

The rule, in general, agrees with American practice, for "the amount to be allowed is usually the value of such property at the moment of sacrifice, considering its condition or state of service at the time" (Gourlie, pp. 462-464).

When there is an actual or commercial constructive total loss of the ship and the York/Antwerp Rules do not apply, some American adjusters arrive at the amount to be made good in a different manner from that provided for in Rule XVIII. Their method is to ascertain the difference between the sound value of the vessel and the proceeds and to allow such proportion of that sum as the amount of the general average repairs bears to the amount of the entire repairs. The formula provided in the York/ Antwerp Rules can result in a minus quantity and, therefore, no allowance in general average, while the American practice described above can never have such an effect.

Sometimes temporary repairs are effected to damage caused by a general average sacrifice after the completion of the voyage on which the sacrifice took place. Such temporary repairs do not fall under Rule XIV, but if the temporary repairs form part of the reasonable cost of repairing the damage caused by the sacrifice, they are allowable under Rule XVIII. Whether the temporary repairs do form part of the reasonable cost of repairs is a question of fact to be determined in each case. The standard required to justify claiming temporary repairs as particular average under a marine insurance policy would appear to be equally applicable in justifying the allowance of temporary repairs in general average under Rule XVIII.

DEDUCTIONS FROM COST OF REPAIRS ALLOWED IN GENERAL AVERAGE. In assessing the amount to be made good for damage to a vessel consequent on a general average sacrifice, it is universally accepted that the shipowner should not benefit by any betterment as a result of new materials used in effecting repairs. This principle was enunciated in Rule XIII of the York/Antwerp Rules, 1950. The rule embodied a complicated list of deductions and was susceptible to varying interpretations. As part of the move to simplify general average, it was originally intended to abolish all deductions from the cost of repairs when old material was replaced by new. It was felt that the advantage gained by the shipowner (if any) was of relative unimportance compared to the savings in time and effort which would be gained by abolishing the deductions. In the final analysis, by a narrow majority, the convention which adopted the 1974 Rules felt that there should still be a scale of deductions "new for old" applicable to vessels over fifteen years old. This was in the nature of a compromise; under the new rule, deductions "new for old" are abolished in the case of vessels less than fifteen years old while those vessels over fifteen years old are subject to a simplified scale of deductions.

The new Rule XIII reads as follows:

RULE XIII. DEDUCTIONS FROM COST OF REPAIRS. *Repairs to be allowed in general average shall not be subject to deductions in respect of "new for old" where old material or parts are replaced by new unless the ship is over fifteen years old in which case there shall be a deduction of one-third. The deductions shall be regulated by the age of the ship from the 31st of December of the year of completion of construction to the date of the general average act, except for insula-*

*tion, life-and similar boats, communications and navigational appa-
ratus and equipment, machinery and boilers for which deductions
shall be regulated by the age of the particular parts to which they
apply.*

*The deductions shall be made only from the cost of the new,
material or parts when finished and ready to be installed in the ship.*

*No deduction shall be made in respect of provisions, stores,
anchors and chain cables.*

*Drydock and slipway dues and costs of shifting the ship shall be
allowed in full.*

*The costs of cleaning, painting or coating of bottom shall not be
allowed in general average unless the bottom has been painted or
coated within the twelve months preceding the date of the general
average act in which case one-half of such costs shall be allowed.*

When the York/Antwerp Rules, 1974, are not applicable and a general average is stated in accordance with American law and practice, the
principle of deductions "new for old" must also be followed. Rule XIII of
the Association of Average Adjusters of the United States (Appendix B) is
identical to Rule XIII of the York/Antwerp Rules, 1974.

Prior to the adoption of the York/Antwerp Rules, 1950, there had
been differences in the manner in which the deductions "new for old" were
made. In some cases, the deduction was made from the cost of material
only, in the strictest sense. In other cases, it was made from the cost of
material and from the cost of labor incurred in making a particular part. A
third method was to make the deduction from the cost of material, including the labor in making the part, and also from the cost of installing that
part in the vessel.

Rule XIII of the York/Antwerp Rules, 1950, specifically stated that
"the deductions shall be made from the cost of new materials or parts,
including labor and establishment charges, but excluding the cost of opening up."

Unfortunately, even those who were present at the conference which
adopted the 1950 Rules were not clear as to the intention of the conference
in adopting this new wording. Was the deduction to be from the entire cost
of the new part, including the cost of installing the part onboard ship, or
was the deduction to be only from the new part itself, including the labor to
manufacture the new part?

Considerable controversy ensued in London on the subject and it was
not until some years after the adoption of the York/Antwerp Rules, 1950,
that British average adjusters finally agreed among themselves that the rule
should be interpreted as follows: The deductions were to be confined to:

(1) the cost of new material, (2) the cost of the manufacture of the new article from the material, and (3) the cost of such final preparation of the new material or the new article as may be necessary for fitting or otherwise. All other costs, including the actual fitting costs, were to be allowed in full, together with the cost of preparing any old material for the fitting of the new article and the cost of removal of the old article.

With regard to the transport charges, the costs of transport of new material or new parts were to be allowed in full, except in the case of local transporting costs as may occur on the repairers' or manufacturers' premises, or in the dry dock or yard. These are treated as part of the cost of manufacture or as part of the cost of preparation for fitting.

A solitary exception to the foregoing treatment is made in the case of scraping and painting the vessel's bottom. Here the deduction was to be made from the whole cost of the operation, both labor and material, because the advantage gained by the application of the new paint is measured by the actual cost of the paint itself and the cost of applying it.

The above practice was adopted by most (if not all) American average adjusters; the more limited deductions "new for old" called for under Rule XIII of the York/Antwerp Rules, 1974, will be applied similarly.

The deductions "new for old" under Rule XIII of the York/Antwerp Rules, 1950, can be summarized as follows:

Up to 1 year old.
No deductions except from scraping and painting vessel's bottom from which one-third to be deducted.

Between 1 and 3 years old.
One-third off:
Scraping and painting bottom
Ropes and hawsers (other than wire and chain)
Painting
Provisions and stores
One-sixth off:
Woodwork of hull
Wire ropes
Chain cables and chains
Insulation
Auxiliary machinery
Electrical machinery

Between 3 and 6 years old.
Similar deductions to those applying to between 1 and 3 years old except as follows:
One-third off:

Woodwork of hull

One-sixth off:

All machinery (including boilers)

Between 6 and 10 years old.

Similar deductions to those applying to between 3 and 6 years old except as follows:

One third off:

All ropes and hawsers

Insulation

All machinery (including boilers)

Between 10 and 15 years old.

One-third off all renewals except ironwork of hull and cementing and chain cables from which one-sixth to be deducted and anchors which are allowed in full.

Over 15 years old.

One-third off all renewals, except chain cables from which one-sixth to be deducted and anchors which are allowed in full.

From a scrutiny of the above, the following major divisions emerge:

(1) Ropes and hawsers (other than wire and chain), painting, provisions, and stores are subject to deduction of one-third when vessel or equipment is one year old.

(2) Woodwork of hull, wire ropes, chain cables and chains, insulation, and auxiliary and electrical machinery subject to deduction of one-sixth when vessel or equipment is one year old.

(3) Woodwork of hull subject to deduction of one-third when vessel is three years old.

(4) All machinery (including boilers) subject to deduction of one-sixth when machinery is three years old.

(5) All ropes and hawsers, insulation, and all machinery (including boilers) subject to deduction of one-third when equipment or machinery is six years old.

(6) When vessel or equipment is ten years old, one-third to be deducted from all renewals other than:

Ironwork of hull, cementing, and chain cables, which are subject to deduction of one-sixth;

Anchors which are allowed in full.

(7) When vessel or equipment is fifteen years old, one-third to be deducted from all renewals other than:

Chain cables which are subject to deduction of one-sixth;

Anchors which are allowed in full.

It will be seen that the deductions run the entire gamut from scraping and painting the vessel's bottom, which is subject to an immediate deduction of one-third even on the vessel's maiden voyage, to chain cables which are only subject to a deduction of one-sixth after they are fifteen years old and anchors which are never subject to any deduction. As already indicated, these complicated deductions will now only be applicable in those cases where the general average is being stated in accordance with the York/Antwerp Rules, 1950. It should always be remembered that the deductions should only be made from the amount by which the vessel can be regarded as having been enhanced by reason of the use of new materials or new parts. In the final analysis, each case must be dealt with on its merits.

In applying the much simpler deductions "new for old" called for under Rule XIII of the York/Antwerp Rules, 1974, similar considerations should be borne in mind.

Rule II (Damage by Jettison and Sacrifice for the Common Safety) and Rule III (Extinguishing Fire on Shipboard) of the York/Antwerp Rules also deal in part with sacrifices of ship but, as they also deal with sacrifices of cargo and are more important in that respect, they are dealt with in the following section.

Sacrifices of Cargo

JETTISON OF CARGO. Jettison of cargo was one of the earliest forms of general average sacrifice and is specifically dealt with by Rule I of the York/Antwerp Rules, which reads as follows:

> RULE I. JETTISON OF CARGO. No jettison of cargo shall be made good as general average, unless such cargo is carried in accordance with the recognized custom of the trade.

The rule is similar to Rule III of the Association of Average Adjusters of the United States, which reads:

> RULE III. DECK LOAD JETTISON. Where cargo consisting of one kind of goods is in accordance with a custom of trade, carried on and under deck, that portion of the cargo loaded on deck shall be subject to the same rules of adjustment in cases of jettison and expenses incurred, as if the same were laden under deck.

The object of both these rules is to emphasize that jettison of cargo is only to be made good in general average if it is being carried in accordance with the recognized custom of the trade. Earlier versions of the York/Antwerp Rules stipulated that no jettison of deck cargo should be made good in general average. This was because it was felt that deck cargo lent itself too easily to being jettisoned by reason of its accessibility. Later it was agreed that cargo habitually carried on deck (such as lumber) should not be arbitrarily deprived of an allowance in general average.

The question as to whether cargo is or is not being carried in accordance with the recognized custom of the trade is a question of fact to be decided in each individual case. The advent of containers has caused some difficulties in this respect but the tendency of the courts seems to be to accept the reasonableness of on-deck stowage of containerized cargo onboard container ships even when the bill of lading bears no reference to such stowage (*Mormacvega*, 1972 AMC 2366).

Neither of the aforementioned rules deals with jettison per se which must, of course, have been made "for the common safety for the purpose of preserving from peril the property involved in a common maritime adventure" (see Rule A of the York/Antwerp Rules) before the loss can be made good in general average. Thus, cargo jettisoned solely because of its physical condition and not for the common safety would not receive any allowance in general average.

In a case which came before the courts, a cargo of lumber being carried on deck in accordance with the custom of the trade was jettisoned for the common safety. It was held that although the bills of lading contained the clause "all lumber loaded on deck at shipper's risk," this did not preclude the cargo owner from recovery in general average. The court held that it was well settled that the shipowner's obligation to contribute to general average sacrifices was not affected by exceptions in the contract of carriage so stipulated in express terms (the *William G. Osment*, 1954 AMC 658).

It is convenient to deal with Rule II of the York/Antwerp Rules at this point. The rule reads as follows:

RULE II. DAMAGE BY JETTISON AND SACRIFICE FOR THE COMMON SAFETY. Damage done to a ship and cargo, or either of them, by or in consequence of a sacrifice made for the common safety, and by water which goes down a ship's hatches opened or other opening made for the purpose of making a jettison for the common safety, shall be made good as general average.

This rule restates the principle dealt with in Rule C, namely, that any loss sustained as a direct consequence of a general average act will be allowed in general average. The rule then gives a specific example.

It will be seen that the rule also deals with damage to a ship, and an interesting case involving such damage consequent on a jettison of cargo is that of the *Felix* (1927 AMC 844). In that case, it was held that the consequential damage done to a vessel's propeller by lumber jettisoned from on deck for the common safety was allowable in general average, even though the jettison itself could not be made good in general average because the York/Antwerp Rules, 1890, applied and specifically excluded such an allowance.

FIRE ON SHIPBOARD. Fire on shipboard has long been one of the major causes of loss of and damage to property at sea and, while modern fire prevention methods and improved fire-fighting techniques have greatly reduced the danger and consequences of fire, it continues to give rise to many general average claims.

Rule III of the York/Antwerp Rules deals with fire on shipboard and reads as follows:

> RULE III. EXTINGUISHING FIRE ON SHIPBOARD. Damage done to a ship and cargo, or either of them, by water or otherwise, including damage by beaching or scuttling a burning ship, in extinguishing a fire on board the ship, shall be made good as general average; *except that no compensation shall be made for damage by smoke or heat however caused.*

The rule deals with damage to ship as well as to cargo but, as damage to cargo is usually more widespread than damage to the ship, it was thought to be more convenient to deal with the rule in the section on "Sacrifices of Cargo."

This important rule has been amended to permit the allowance of *all* extinguishing damage, subject to the veto against any allowance for smoke or heat damage however caused. Under the previous version of the rule no allowance was made in general average for damage by water or other means used to extinguish the fire if the particular part of the ship or portion of a bulk cargo or separate package of a general cargo had been touched by the fire. This was based on the theory that the damage done in extinguishing the fire could not be said to have damaged any portion or package of cargo which was already on fire and therefore potentially lost. The trouble with this theory is that if carried to a logical conclusion, once any part of the ship or cargo is on fire the *whole* could be said to be potentially lost and hence no damage to the ship or cargo caused by the extinguishing operation could be said to have had an adverse effect. Be that as it may, the new rule stipulates that all damage caused by the extinguishing operations is now to be made good in general average. The new rule also specifically excludes any allowance in general average for smoke or heat damage however caused. The reason for this is that it is almost impossible to calculate with any certainty how much (if at all) damage by smoke or heat has been enhanced by the efforts to extinguish the fire.

Even before the introduction of this new veto of smoke and heat damage however caused, it was not the general American practice to allow such extra damage in general average. The objection to such an allowance arises with the difficulty of determining what part of the damage was due to the ordinary action of smoke and what part to the operation of steam and smoke. In the case of *Reliance Marine Insurance Co., Ltd.* v. *New York & Cuba Steamship Co.* (165 U. S. 720), this objection was upheld and the claim for the allowance in general average of increased smoke damage was rejected. In recent years it has been suggested that, with the universal use of CO_2 gas to attack fires, it might be possible to identify additional smoke damage caused by the extinguishing operations. CO_2 gas, unlike water, has no effect on cargo with which it comes in contact—not even on foodstuffs. In fighting a fire, the CO_2 gas displaces the atmosphere, thus reducing the oxygen in the air and in this way controlling the fire, often extinguishing it. However, to be effective, the hatches must be battened down and the ventilators closed while the gas is being injected. This also applies when steam is used instead of CO_2 gas. In both cases the smoke hovers about in the affected hold and does not escape until the hold is opened up. Thus, it is difficult to determine with reasonable certainty the extent of the *extra* smoke damage; most cargo surveyors seem to think that there will seldom, if ever, be clear evidence to support an allowance for *extra* smoke damage in a hold where a fire *had actually occurred*. However, this may not be true insofar as smoke damage to cargo in *adjacent holds* is concerned. Let us assume that a fire occurs in fish meal in one hold or compartment, and CO_2 gas is used to attack the fire. The holds are battened down and as a result the smoke and fumes are forced from the hold or compartment where the fire actually occurred into adjoining compartments where, say, green coffee was stowed; contamination by odor would result. On the other hand, if water had been used to attack the fire instead of CO_2 gas, presumably some of the smoke and fumes from the fire in the fish meal could also be expected to be forced into adjoining compartments through a common ventilating system (it having no other outlet). Hence, there would have to be *some* odor contamination in any event. However, it is probable that the CO_2 gas (or steam) would force more smoke and fumes into the adjoining compartments, with the result that more bags of coffee would be contaminated to an increased degree, resulting in an increased depreciation in the value of the coffee. In such a case, the adjuster would have to rely on the cargo surveyor to estimate the allowance to be made for *extra* smoke damage due to the use of the CO_2 gas. It is important to remember that before making allowances to cargo for *extra* smoke damage, the extra smoke damage must have resulted in a monetary loss to the cargo owners. To sum up, it may be possible to justify the allowance of *extra* smoke damage due to a general average act but only if the facts support such an allowance and only when there is a monetary loss as a result of the *extra* smoke. The latter point is very important because in the case of some commodities the degree of smokiness in taste or odor would have little effect on their damaged value; in other words, once initially tainted by smoke they would be depreciated in value as much as they ever would be, regardless of any further contamination. Adjusters must always look into the circumstances prevailing in each particular case because no two fires are alike; the type of vessel, type of compartments, method of stowage, and the nature of the commodities involved all vary. Any allowances for extra smoke damage must be supported by the particular conditions, the prevailing circumstances, and the type of cargo involved, and must be equitable to all interests. Of course, when the York/Antwerp Rules, 1974, are applicable, the problem does not arise since all such allowances are vetoed.

General average allowances to cargo in fire cases can be very considerable, and it is essential in such cases to appoint an expert cargo surveyor to act in the general interest and provide the average adjusters with a separation of cargo damage under the following headings:

(a) Damage by water and/or other means to extinguish the fire.
(b) Damage by fire, smoke and heat.

When the York/Antwerp Rules, 1974, are applicable it is not necessary for surveyors to further break down fire, smoke, and heat damage and this greatly simplifies their work and avoids difficult questions of fact.

However, if the contract of affreightment stipulates that general average is to be stated in accordance with American law and practice (that is, without any reference to the York/Antwerp Rules, 1974), the treatment of extinguishing damage will remain as it was under Rule III of the York/Antwerp Rules, 1950. That rule reads as follows:

RULE III. EXTINGUISHING FIRE ON SHIPBOARD. Damage done to a ship and cargo, or either of them, by water or otherwise, including damage by beaching or scuttling a burning ship, in extinguishing a fire on board the ship, shall be made good as general average; except that no compensation shall be made for damage to such portions of the ship and bulk cargo, or to such separate packages of cargo, as have been on fire.

Under the 1950 Rule, no allowance is made in general average for damage by water or other means used to extinguish the fire if the portion of the ship or bulk cargo or separate package of a general cargo has been touched by the fire. This is based on the theory (discarded in the 1974 Rules) that the damage done in extinguishing the fire cannot be said to have done any damage if the portion or package was already on fire and potentially lost.

It has been held in the English courts that the reference to "such portions of . . . bulk cargo" simply means so much of the cargo as had actually been on fire (*Greenshields Cowie & Co.* v. *Stephens & Sons*, 1908 1 K. B. 51). Separate packages of a general cargo means separate units; with the advent of container ships the question arose as to whether each container (in many cases containing several shipments) was in itself a "package of cargo" within the meaning of this rule. The better opinion seems to be that a container is not a package. Indeed the American courts (in interpreting "package" within the meaning of the Carriage of Goods by Sea Act) have declined to treat a container as a package: "it is illogical to assert that the container is one of the 'packages' in which goods are shipped" (*Mormaclynx*, 1970 AMC 1310). This was affirmed by a U.S. court of appeals: "A shipper-packed and sealed container said to contain 99 bales of leather is not a package" (1971 AMC 2383). In another case, it was pointed out that the proposed amendments to the rules relating to the carriage of goods by sea adopted at the Brussels Convention in 1968 stipulated that each package or unit enumerated in the bill of lading is deemed a "package" even though delivered to the ocean carrier in a sealed container (*Inter-American Foods Inc.* v. *Coordinated Caribbean Transport Inc.*, 1970 AMC 1303). Under the 1974 Rules, this problem has also been eliminated.

However, under the 1950 Rules (and when American law and practice governs the general average to the complete exclusion of the 1974 Rules), it will still be necessary to provide the average adjuster with a separation of cargo damage under the following headings:

(a) Damage by water and/or other means to extinguish the fire.

(b) Damage by fire.

(c) Damage by smoke and fire and water, etc.

(d) Damage by smoke.

(e) Damage by smoke and water, etc. (percentage of smoke damage to be given separately).

(f) Damage by heat and water, etc. (percentage of heat damage to be stated separately).

Apart from the actual physical damage to cargo, considerable extra expenses in connection with extra handling of cargo are often incurred in fire cases. The admissibility of such expenses in general average will be dealt with later under the heading of "General Average Expenditure."

Sometimes the fire is caused by the inherent vice of the cargo itself, such as the spontaneous combustion to which certain commodities are susceptible. In such cases, the cargo owner is not precluded from claiming contribution in general average unless he knowingly shipped the cargo in a dangerous condition (*Greenshields* v. *Stephens, supra*; see also *William J. Quinlan*, 168 Fed. Rep. 407, 175 Fed. Rep. 207, and 180 Fed. Rep. 681).

However, cargo which has overheated, thereby giving rise to a general average, has the burden of proving that the shipment was free from inherent vice at the time of loading, before any allowance can be justified in general average for damage sustained to that cargo in the extinguishing operations.

The treatment of damage sustained to the ship as a result of the efforts to extinguish the fire is also simplified by the amendment to Rule III in the 1974 Rules. Thus, any part of the hull or machinery which is damaged by the efforts to extinguish the fire now qualifies for an allowance in general average regardless of the fact that that part may also have been actually on fire. Under Rule III of the York/Antwerp Rules, 1950, difficulty arose in regard to the exclusion of "such portions of the ship . . . as have been on fire." Damage to machinery is sometimes attributed partly to water used in extinguishing the fire and partly to fire. The question arises as to whether machinery can ever be said to be on fire when it is only the oil and grease with which it is lubricated that are combustible. The better opinion seems to be that when any separate part of the hull or machinery has been touched by fire, the additional damage caused by water or other means used to extinguish the fire is not allowable in general average. Under the 1974 Rules the question will not arise, as stated earlier.

The Association of Average Adjusters of the United States has a rule regarding the allowance in general average of fire extinguishers used in putting out the fire. This is as follows:

> RULE XIX. FIRE EXTINGUISHERS. The cost of replacing gas or any commodity used in efforts to extinguish a fire on board a vessel shall be allowed in general average even though the gas or commodity was on board the vessel at the time the fire was discovered.

The rule is self-explanatory and merely makes the point that even though the gas or commodity is being used for the purpose for which it was intended (to extinguish a fire), it is a proper general average sacrifice.

DAMAGE TO CARGO IN HANDLING. Rule XII of the York/Antwerp Rules reads as follows:

> RULE XII. DAMAGE TO CARGO IN DISCHARGING, ETC. Damage to or loss of cargo, fuel or stores caused in the act of handling, discharging, storing, reloading and stowing shall be made good as general average, when and only when the cost of those measures respectively is admitted as general average.

This rule is self-explanatory and is a practical example of the principle established in Rule C. In practice, it is broadly construed, and damage sustained as a result of inadequate storage facilities at a port of refuge is admitted as general average. Similarly, if refrigerated cargo has to be discharged as a general average act and no refrigerated cargo storage accommodation is available, the resultant damage or loss is allowable in general average. On the other hand, damage to or loss of perishable cargo at a port of refuge due solely to the general average detention cannot be allowed, as it results entirely from delay and does not come within the terms of Rule XII. Furthermore, Rule C expressly prohibits such an allowance (see also *Hills Bros Co. v. U. S.*, 1930 AMC 623). An example of this type of loss is the decay of a commodity such as potatoes. A test to be used in determining whether or not damage to or loss of cargo comes within Rule XII is to ascertain whether such damage or loss would have been sustained had the cargo remained in the vessel throughout the general average detention. If it would, then there are no grounds for making an allowance in general average. While the rule is broadly construed and is held to cover losses sustained as a result of cargo being placed in exposed places, such as on the beach, it does not cover losses incurred while in normal storage places ashore (for example, warehouses). Thus, if a fire destroyed the cargo while stored in warehouses ashore, the loss would not be considered to have been "necessarily caused in the act of discharging and storing." Pilferage losses incurred as a result of the forced discharge come within the intent of the rule, as would rainwater damage sustained during a forced discharge carried out in inclement weather. In short, any loss which can be considered to be the predictable consequence of the forced discharges is allowable in general average.

It is very seldom that the interpretation of individual York/Antwerp Rules comes before the courts, but Rule XII was interpreted by the Canadian courts in the *Oak Hill* (1970 AMC 227). In that case, the court held that loss of cargo (through admixture), even if sustained during a general average procedure (the discharge of cargo to refloat the vessel), was not recoverable in general average when due to an act of neglect on the part of the master and the general average cargo surveyor during an operation. In other words, the general average act of discharging cargo did not in itself result in the loss, which was, in fact, due to an intervening act of negligence.

Rule VIII of the York/Antwerp Rules also deals in part with damage to cargo during a forced discharge.

AMOUNT TO BE MADE GOOD FOR CARGO LOST OR DAMAGED BY SACRIFICE. Rule XVI of the York/Antwerp Rules lays down the method by which the amount to be made good to cargo is determined; it reads:

RULE XVI. AMOUNT TO BE MADE GOOD FOR CARGO LOST OR DAMAGED BY SACRIFICE. The amount to be made good as general average for damage to or loss of *cargo* sacrificed shall be the loss which has been sustained thereby based on the *value at the time of discharge, ascertained from the commercial invoice rendered to the receiver or if there is no such invoice from the shipped value. The value at the time of discharge shall include the cost of insurance and freight except insofar as such freight is at the risk of interests other than the cargo.*

When *cargo* so damaged is sold and the amount of the damage has not been otherwise agreed, the loss to be made good in general average shall be the difference between the net proceeds of sale and the net sound value *as computed in the first paragraph of this Rule.*

All previous versions of the York/Antwerp Rules have provided that cargo be valued both for allowances in general average and for contribution, on the basis of landed values at destination (based on gross wholesale market values). The obtaining of such values was time-consuming and often presented difficulties. It will be seen that the new version of Rule XVI stipulates that any amount to be made good in general average for cargo lost or damaged by sacrifice is to be based on the *invoice value* at the time of discharge (delivery), or in the words of the rule "the commercial invoice rendered to the receiver." If there is no such invoice, any amount to be made good is to be based on the shipped value including freight if guaranteed, vessel lost or not lost. In short, the value to be used is the actual cost of the cargo to the receiver. The object of the amendment is simplicity even at the expense, on rare occasions, of equity. For example, if a vessel is under general average at a port of loading and is so badly damaged that the voyage is abandoned there, under this new rule the allowance in general average will still be based on the invoice value of the goods including any guaranteed freight. Formerly, in such circumstances the cargo would be valued at the port of loading (which in the circumstances described has become "port of delivery"), that is to say, on its actual value at that port which in normal circumstances would be the invoice value (*excluding* freight). Thus, in the interest of simplicity, the new rule is to be strictly followed even though on certain rare occasions (such as that described) the result will not be one of strict equity.

Apart from the proviso regarding the use of invoice values as the basis for cargo allowances, the amount to be made good is the loss which the owner of the goods has sustained and, in computing that loss, deduction must be made of any subsequent loss which the goods would have suffered in any event had they not already been damaged by sacrifice. In Coe's words (Lowndes, 8th ed., pp. 324, 325):

> If goods jettisoned were either damaged at the time, or certain to become damaged before the end of the voyage (as, for instance, if the ship after being relieved by jettison was subsequently sunk or filled with water, and it is certain that damage would have been received by the sacrificed goods had they not been sacrificed), only the value which it is assumed this merchandise would have produced if it had not been jettisoned and had stood the vicissitudes of the voyage, is to be allowed. In this event, if similar goods are damaged, the amount allowed for the sacrificed goods is in practice based on the damaged value of the goods that arrive.

Computing the loss which the owner of the goods has sustained can sometimes present difficulties. An example of this is when the freight is at the risk of the vessel owner but is payable in full even though only a part of the cargo is delivered. Let us suppose that part of the cargo was jettisoned for the common safety; the full freight is payable but, in making an allowance for the cargo jettisoned, the value to be used should include the proportion of the freight applying to the cargo jettisoned (the value of the goods jettisoned having been enhanced by the freight paid). Nevertheless in such circumstances, since the entire freight was at the risk of the vessel (it not being certain at the time of the jettison that the vessel would arrive, or that any freight would ever be earned), contribution is assessed against the vessel owner upon the whole freight, less the deductions stipulated by the York/Antwerp Rules (*Christie* v. *Davis Coal & Coke Co.*, 95 Fed. Rep. 837).

The second paragraph of the rule applies when damaged goods are sold and provides for allowances to be made on a "salvage loss" basis unless the damage has been otherwise agreed.

In practice, the general average cargo surveyor usually agrees a percentage depreciation in value. This percentage is applied to the net sound value of the goods; that is, what would have been the value of the goods if sound, less the expenses which the owner of the goods would have had to incur to realize that value.

Rule XVII of the Association of Average Adjusters dealing with the same subject reflects the position under the York/Antwerp Rules, 1950, rather than the new 1974 rule and reads:

RULE XVII. ALLOWANCES FOR CARGO DAMAGED AND SOLD AND CONTRIBUTORY VALUE OF SAME. Where cargo is damaged, as a consequence of a general average act, and sold, and the extent of the loss has not been otherwise determined, the amount, if any, to be made good for same shall be based on the market value at the date of arrival or at the termination of the adventure (dependent on the facts) and shall be determined on the "salvage loss" basis, irrespective of the date of sale.

The contributory value of such cargo shall be based on the proceeds of sale to which shall be added any amount made good; deduction being made of charges incurred subsequent to the general average act, except such charges as are allowed in general average.

"The date of arrival" in the case of a vessel herself delivering all cargo saved shall be the last day of discharge; and in complex cases, this principle shall be followed as far as possible.

Thus, under the 1950 Rules or where the general average is stated in accordance with American law and practice, the market value at destination will still be used in computing cargo allowances in general average. An exception would be where cargo sacrificed in general average is replaced at the port of loading; in such circumstances, the amount to be made good is the actual cost of replacing the cargo (and not the market value at destination). As we have already seen under Rule XVI of the York/Antwerp Rules, 1974, the invoice value (including freight if guaranteed) will be used in such cases.

With regard to cargo allowances generally, cases sometimes arise where the damage is attributable to both the general average sacrifice and accidental causes, and it is difficult if not impossible to determine the damage sustained due to the general average act. The case of *Reliance Marine Insurance Co., Ltd.* v. *New York & Cuba Steamship Co.* (already referred to in connection with smoke damages) seems to establish that in such circumstances no part of the damage should be made good in general average.

Rule XIX of the York/Antwerp Rules deals with damage or loss caused to undeclared or wrongfully declared cargo, as follows:

RULE XIX. UNDECLARED OR WRONGFULLY DECLARED CARGO. Damage or loss caused to goods loaded without the knowledge of the shipowner or his agent or to goods wilfully misdescribed at time of shipment shall not be allowed as general average, but such goods shall remain liable to contribute, if saved.

Damage or loss caused to goods which have been wrongfully declared on shipment at a value which is lower than their real value shall be contributed for at the declared value, but such goods shall contribute upon their actual value.

The rule is self-explanatory and the punishment does indeed fit the crime. Fortunately, it is rarely necessary to invoke it.

When the danger which has led to a sacrifice of goods was caused by their unfitness for shipment, the cargo owner is not precluded from claiming contribution unless his conduct in shipping them was wrongful or negligent (*Greenshields* v. *Stephens* and *William J. Quinlan, supra.*).

Sacrifices of Freight

Rule XV of the York/Antwerp Rules reads:

RULE XV. LOSS OF FREIGHT. Loss of freight arising from damage to or loss of cargo shall be made good as general average, either when caused by a general average act, or when the damage to or loss of cargo is so made good.

Deduction shall be made from the amount of gross freight lost, of the charges which the owner thereof would have incurred to earn such freight, but has, in consequence of the sacrifice, not incurred.

The first paragraph of the rule lays down the circumstances under which loss of freight (at the risk of the shipowner) is to be made good in general average. While most freight allowances in general average arise as a result of a sacrifice of cargo, it is worth mentioning that if a vessel is so damaged *by a general average sacrifice* that she is unable to complete the voyage and deliver the cargo, the resultant loss of freight would be made good in general average.

The second paragraph of Rule XV stipulates that the party receiving the allowance must give credit for any charges which he would have incurred to earn the freight but which he had not incurred by reason of the general average sacrifice. As an example, let us take a case where cargo has been jettisoned for the common safety and the freight was at the risk of the shipowner. Under this rule, the shipowner would receive an allowance for the gross freight lost as a result of the jettison but would have to give credit for any expenses of earning the freight which, by reason of the jettison, he has not incurred, such as the cost of discharging the jettisoned cargo at destination (always assuming the cost of discharging cargo was for the account of the shipowner under the terms of the contract of affreightment).

Cases sometimes arise where, as a result of a jettison of cargo in the circumstances described above, the shipowner is able, on the same voyage, to take cargo in the space made vacant by reason of the jettison and thereby earn a new freight. In some such cases, it is the practice to credit the net new freight earned against the allowance in general average for the original freight lost. This is done only when the new cargo occupied the space made available because of the jettison and when there would have been no space available in which to load the new cargo if there had been no jettison. If the space utilized for the new cargo would have been available even if there had been no jettison, no credit should be given, as, in that event, the additional freight would not be a matter which concerned the general average regardless of the fact that the new cargo was loaded at a port of refuge. The earning of additional freight in such circumstances is regarded as merely an incidental advantage accruing to the shipowners.

A similar situation arises when cargo on which freight is at risk is damaged by a general average sacrifice and left behind at a port of refuge. The freight on any new cargo loaded at the port of refuge is subject to the same consideration described above.

This question of giving credit for new freight earned has to be carefully considered in each instance and is governed by the circumstances applying in each individual case. However, before new freight can be taken into account in general average at all, it is necessary to show that the space was made available solely by reason of *general average loss of or damage to cargo.*

Rule XIV of the Association of Average Adjusters of the United States is similar to Rule XV of the York/Antwerp Rules and reads, in part, as follows:

> RULE XIV. FREIGHT—CONTRIBUTORY VALUE AND AMOUNT MADE GOOD IN GENERAL AVERAGE . . . And when loss of freight at risk of the Shipowners or Charterers is allowed in general average, the allowance shall be for the net freight lost, to be ascertained by deducting from the gross freight sacrificed the expenses that would have been incurred, subsequent to the sacrifice, to earn it, but which, because of the sacrifice, have not been incurred.

GENERAL AVERAGE EXPENDITURE

We now come to the branch of general average which accounts for most of the claims for contribution—general average expenditure—or, to use the definition given in the *Star of Hope* (76 U. S. 203), "those (losses) which arise out of extraordinary expenses incurred for the joint benefit of ship and cargo."

Port of Refuge Expenses

The most common form of general average expenditure is the expenditure resulting from putting into ports of refuge. This expenditure comprises chiefly port charges and wages and maintenance of crew and is dealt with by Rules X and XI of the York/Antwerp Rules. Rule X reads as follows:

RULE X. Expenses at Port of Refuge, etc. (a) When a ship shall have entered a port or place of refuge, or shall have returned to her port or place of loading in consequence of accident, sacrifice or other extraordinary circumstances, which render that necessary for the common safety, the expenses of entering such port or place shall be admitted as general average; and when she shall have sailed thence with her original cargo or a part of it, the corresponding expenses of leaving such port or place consequent upon such entry or return shall likewise be admitted as general average.

When a ship is at any port or place of refuge and is necessarily removed to another port or place because repairs cannot be carried out in the first port or place, the provisions of this Rule shall be applied to the second port or place as if it were a port or place of refuge and the cost of such removal *including temporary repairs and towage* shall be admitted as general average. The provisions of Rule XI shall be applied to the prolongation of the voyage occasioned by such removal.

(b) The cost of handling on board or discharging cargo, fuel or stores whether at a port or place of loading, call or refuge, shall be admitted as general average, when the handling or discharge was necessary for the common safety or to enable damage to the ship caused by sacrifice or accident to be repaired, if the repairs were necessary for the safe prosecution of the voyage, *except in cases where the damage to the ship is discovered at a port or place of loading or call without any accident or other extraordinary circumstance connected with such damage having taken place during the voyage.*

The cost of handling on board or discharging cargo, fuel or stores shall not be admissible as general average when incurred solely for the purpose of restowage due to shifting during the voyage unless such restowage is necessary for the common safety.

Whenever the cost of handling or discharging cargo, fuel or stores is admissible as general average, *the costs of storage, including insurance if reasonably incurred, reloading and stowing of such cargo, fuel or stores shall likewise be admitted as general average.*

But when the ship is condemned or does not proceed on her original voyage, *storage expenses shall be admitted as general average only up to the date of the ship's condemnation or of the abandonment of the voyage or up to the date of completion of discharge of cargo if the condemnation or abandonment takes place before that date.*

Rule X (d) which dealt with substituted expenses has been deleted from the 1974 Rules; this will be commented on later when dealing with the general subject of substituted expenses.

It will be seen from Rule X that the expenses of entering a port of refuge or returning to a port or place of loading (in other words, port charges) are only admissible in general average when the port was entered "in consequence of accident, sacrifice, or other extraordinary circumstances, which render that necessary for the common safety." This phrase refers to the *physical safety* of the vessel and her cargo and not to the successful completion of the voyage. However, as we have seen in discussing Rule A, it is not necessary that the vessel be in the grip of immediate disaster before having recourse to a port of refuge. It is sufficient that, in the opinion of the master, it would be dangerous for the vessel to continue on her voyage. Nevertheless, even though the peril need not be immediately pending and can be merely anticipated, it must be real and substantial. The fact that a vessel deviates to a port outside the ordinary course of the voyage does not automatically constitute a general average act. For example, entry into a port of refuge merely to survey damage, repairs to which are not immediately necessary for seaworthiness, is not a general average act because in such circumstances the common adventure was not in peril. In short, fear of a future peril rather than the existence of a present peril is not sufficient unless the fear of a future peril is real and substantial and the future peril reasonably to be anticipated.

As to what constitutes an "accident" within the meaning of this rule has been the subject of much discussion. E. W. Reading, the distinguished British average adjuster, has written:

> The word "accident" has to be given its ordinary meaning, which may be said to be "something unexpected," and that definition could cover in some circumstances a happening which has resulted from wear and tear. For example, a shaft may break and the vessel may have to be towed to a port of refuge to effect repairs. Examination shows that the breakage was due to wear and tear. The ship has been maintained according to the standards of the Classification Society in which she has been registered and no one could have expected that the shaft would break at that particular time. Although wear and tear is the cause of the breakage, the happening was an accident and the port of refuge expenses should be recoverable in general average.

In short, when a vessel is obliged to proceed to a port of refuge (whether it is a port of call or not) because of a sudden and unexpected failure of a vital part due to wear and tear, a general average situation exists (*see* British Association of Average Adjusters report, 1952, p. 34). Or as another average adjuster has put it, the consequential general average act of putting into a port of refuge must be considered, not as the consequence of the wear and tear which resulted in a breakdown, but as an initial act in itself which has been brought about by a condition of peril. In other words, there is a general average situation whether the emergency giving rise to the voluntary act has arisen by unseaworthiness or wear and tear, although the question of contribution or non-contribution by cargo may be subject to contractual obligations. If this were not so, the whole principle of general average would be defeated (*see* British Association of Average Adjusters report, 1949, p. 7).

In practice, a liberal definition is given to the word "accident" and the reason for entering a port of refuge is regarded as accidental if it is clearly unexpected so far as the shipowner is concerned.

The expression, "other extraordinary circumstances," also presents some difficulty. It seems clear that it is intended to include only circumstances not ordinarily incidental to the voyage. In practice, it is held to cover shortage of fuel, lack of competent crew due to sickness or other reasons, necessity to restow cargo, or any other circumstances which endanger the vessel and her cargo. It does not include putting into port to shelter from heavy weather encountered during a voyage in a season when such weather is to be anticipated.

In deciding on the port of refuge, the master does not necessarily have to head for the nearest port but must in his discretion balance all factors, including the peril to his vessel and the repair facilities available (*Kansas City Fire & Marine Ins. Co.* v. *Dan Arias Shrimp Co.*, 1959 AMC 135).

Along similar lines, if a vessel is lying *unnavigable* at an anchorage in a roadstead or harbor where she may be, as Lowndes puts it (7th ed., p. 198), "in a sort of temporary safety" and could remain there indefinitely without danger, the anchoring can be considered to be merely the first step toward entering a port of refuge for repairs. Consequently the cost of moving the vessel into the port proper is allowable in general average. On the other hand, if a vessel which is able to navigate under her own power anchors in a place of safety at the entrance to a port of refuge to await a harbor pilot or tugs or the availability of a repair berth, the cost of the subsequent move from anchorage to berth follows the treatment of the cost of the operation which is subsequently carried out at the berth. The cost of the final move is, therefore, not automatically general average and may indeed be particular average or even for the shipowner's account depending on the circumstances.

When a vessel is moved to another port because repairs cannot be carried out at the first port of refuge, the last paragraph of Rule X (a) provides that the second port is to be treated as a port of refuge. Thus the wages of crew and fuel, etc., used during the removal to the second port of refuge (or repair port) and either back again to the port of refuge or, if the vessel continues her voyage, direct from the second port of refuge to a point equivalent to the original point of deviation, are recoverable in general average. This paragraph of the rule does not apply if repairs could be effected at the first port of refuge and the vessel was only moved to save expense and/or time. In such cases, the removal expenses might be recoverable in general average as a substituted expense under Rule F. However, in considering Rule X (a), the phrase "cannot be carried out" must be construed in a commercial sense. It not only covers the obvious case of a port where no physical facilities for repairs exist but would also cover a situation where conditions were such that an *indefinite and quite unreasonable delay* would be entailed. Take the case of a vessel which has entered a port of refuge in the Great Lakes shortly before the termination of navigation for the season. While repairs could physically be effected there, the time entailed would result in the vessel being shut in for the winter. If in such circumstances the vessel proceeds to a second port of refuge outside the Great Lakes for repairs, such a removal would come within the intent of Rule X (a) because repairs could not be carried out in a commercial sense at the first port of refuge.

It will be noted that the new addition to Rule X (a) makes it clear that if the vessel requires to be towed to the second port of refuge or if temporary repairs are necessary in connection with such a removal, the cost of the towage and/or temporary repairs is to be allowed in general average. In short, all expenses necessarily incurred to remove the vessel to the second port of refuge are to be treated as general average.

American law and practice (when the York/Antwerp Rules are not applicable) differs in that *if the vessel discharges her cargo at the first port before proceeding to the second port,* the costs of leaving the first port, proceeding to and entering the second (including any necessary temporary repairs or towage), leaving the second port after repairs, and reentering the first port are treated as part of the cost of repairs and apportioned accordingly. The wages and maintenance of crew throughout are, however, allowed in general average.

DISCHARGE OF CARGO AT PORTS OF REFUGE ETC. Rule X (b) provides that the cost of handling onboard or discharging cargo, fuel, or stores, whether at a port of loading, call, or refuge is allowable in general average: (1) when the handling or discharge is necessary for the common safety (that is, the physical safety of ship and cargo), or (2) to enable damage to the ship caused by sacrifice or accident to be repaired, if the repairs are necessary for the safe prosecution of the voyage. An important qualification to the latter has been introduced into the 1974 Rules. In those cases where the damage to the ship is merely *discovered* at the port or place of loading or call without any *"accident or extraordinary circumstance connected with such damage having taken place during the voyage"* (that is to say, subsequent to the commencement of loading of cargo), the act of handling or discharging cargo is not allowable in general average. In fact, under the new wording of this rule, a general average situation would not exist under the circumstances described (*see also* Rule XI (b)). As the chairman of the British Association of Average Adjusters, N. G. Hudson, commented in his address in 1973:

> In principle, in order that a port of call situation should qualify for general average allowance, both the detention at the port and the accident which gave rise to it should have occurred during the community of interest.

As has already been stated in Chapter 2, the effect of this amendment is to eliminate the extension of general average which had been introduced into the 1924 Rules. Under both those rules and the 1950 Rules, the accident which gave rise to the necessity of effecting repairs for the safe prosecution of the voyage need not have occurred during that specific voyage; it was sufficient that repairs were necessary for the safe prosecution of the voyage. In brief, the intent of the amendment is to reduce the possibility of cargo interests being involved in a general average situation without an accident having occurred subsequent to the loading of cargo.

Difficulties may arise in deciding whether there has, in fact, been an *"accident or extraordinary circumstance"* subsequent to the loading of cargo or whether there has been a mere "discovery" of damage. As previously indicated, a liberal definition has always been given to the word "accident" in a general average context—traditionally, something fortuitous or unexpected. It is suggested, therefore, that if something happens after the loading of cargo, such as the giving way of a pipe or a plate, there has been an "accident or extraordinary circumstance" within the meaning of Rule X (b). The fact that the giving way was the consequence of an accident which occurred on a previous voyage or indeed was the result of wear and tear is irrelevant. It is sufficient that the part in question was functioning satisfactorily whilst the vessel was loading cargo and that subsequent to the loading an accident occurred. It may be, of course, that contribution could not be enforced against cargo, but nevertheless a general average situation exists.

The type of general average situation which is excluded by Rule X (b) is that which arises when (after loading a cargo) a routine inspection of the vessel's hull or machinery reveals a *condition* which requires repairs.

This is a mere discovery of damage; there has been no accident. Even if the damage discovered was the result of a previous accident, unless that accident occurred subsequent to the loading of cargo, under the 1974 Rule X (b) there is no general average situation. If the damage which was discovered was accidental in nature there would have been a general average situation under the 1950 Rule X (b). On the other hand, what is the position if a routine inspection reveals a latent defect in the machinery which has become patent subsequent to the loading of cargo? Does that constitute an "accident"? It would seem that the mere "discovery" of a latent defect is not an accident in itself although if some unexpected incident or occurrence instituted the examination which disclosed the latent defect, the answer might be different. The facts must be closely scrutinized in each individual case in conjunction with the wording of the rule.

It might assist the reader in understanding the effect of the amendments to Rules X (b) and XI (b) to give a few illustrations:

(1) A vessel encounters heavy weather while proceeding to a loading port in ballast but is not thought to have sustained any damage. After loading her cargo, a plate gives way (apparently as a belated result of the heavy weather) and she is detained for repairs. The actual giving way of the plate constitutes an accident subsequent to the loading of cargo and there is a general average situation.

(2) In the same circumstances, if the vessel was actually leaking *before* the loading of cargo (even though such leakage had not been discovered at the time cargo was loaded), there is no general average situation at the loading port for there has been no accident subsequent to the loading of cargo; there has been a mere discovery of pre-existing damage.

(3) A vessel strands on the ballast passage to a loading port but is not thought to have sustained any damage, and cargo is loaded. When the vessel is preparing to leave, it is belatedly discovered that her rudder had been damaged in the stranding and she is detained for repairs. There is no general average situation because the rudder was damaged before the cargo was loaded and there has been no subsequent accident; there has been a mere discovery of pre-existing damage.

(4) After loading cargo, a vessel's engineers open up a unit of machinery; damage is found due to a foreign object passing through the unit and the vessel is detained for repairs. However, damage could only have happened when the machinery was operating, which was before the cargo was loaded. Consequently there has been no accident subsequent to the loading of cargo, and there is no general average situation.

(5) After loading cargo, a unit of machinery fails in operation while being warmed up preparatory to the vessel's departure, and the vessel is

detained for repairs. There has been an accident subsequent to the loading of cargo and there is a general average situation.

To sum up, under the York/Antwerp Rules, 1974, if an accident (even if it relates back to wear and tear or to the operation of a marine peril on a previous voyage) occurs subsequent to the loading of cargo, there is a general average situation at the port of loading or call. The question of enforcement of contribution against the cargo on board at the time of the accident is, of course, an entirely separate matter. It is interesting to note that in all the examples given, a general average situation would have existed under the York/Antwerp Rules, 1950, but only examples (1) and (5) create a general average situation under the York/ Antwerp Rules, 1974.

Rule X (c) extends the allowance in general average to include the cost of storing the cargo at the port of refuge and the cost of reloading. When such cargo is not reloaded, it is the practice to allow the storage charges in general average only until the vessel sails from the port of refuge (assuming the original voyage is continued). The theory is that, up to the time the vessel actually sails, the possibility of the cargo being reloaded still exists. After the vessel sails, all expenses in connection with the cargo left behind become special charges on that cargo—unless the cargo was left behind because of damage caused by a general average act, in which case the charges continue to be general average. In the event that the original voyage is abandoned, all general average allowances cease as from the time of the abandonment or the completion of discharge of cargo, whichever is the later. However, it must be stressed that community of interest between ship and cargo is not severed on completion of discharge unless each party bears its own charges from that time. The rewording of Rule X (c) in the 1974 Rules does not change the substance of the rule in any way.

In cases where the accident giving rise to the general average is of such a magnitude that the voyage is frustrated at a port of refuge, the wages and maintenance of crew are recoverable in general average up to the completion of the discharge of cargo as provided for in Rule XI (b). If the decision to abandon the voyage was taken before the discharge of cargo was commenced, the cost of discharging is necessarily incurred to deliver the cargo at the port of refuge and, depending on the terms of the contract of affreightment, the carrier or the concerned in cargo is required to bear the cost of discharge if the discharge was a normal operation. However, in many cases of this type the discharge of cargo is carried out in extraordinary circumstances and under abnormal conditions, such as discharging cargo at a berth which is not equipped for a discharging operation or when the vessel was actually in dry dock. In such unusual circumstances, it is quite obvious that the cost of the discharging operation is greatly enhanced and, indeed, is more of a salvage operation from the viewpoint of the concerned in cargo. In such cases, and assuming the contract of affreightment required the vessel owner to pay for the cost of discharge, it would be unreasonable to expect the vessel owner to bear more than the normal anticipated cost of discharging cargo; the extra cost, because of the abnormal circumstances involved in the discharge (that is, not due to the condition of the cargo but rather to the conditions of the discharge), is usually treated as a special charge on cargo whose value was preserved by the discharge. Indeed, there is some authority for the suggestion that in such cases the entire cost of discharge is a special charge on cargo when the voyage is justifiably abandoned short of destination (*Medina Princess*, 1965 1 L. L. R. 361).

It will have been observed that Rule X (c) of the York/Antwerp Rules provides for the allowance in general average of insurance on cargo discharged from the vessel at a port of refuge. It is highly desirable that any cargo discharged from the vessel should be insured against shore perils (including fire) and, if it is stored on lighters, also have effective marine insurance. The amount to be insured is the estimated value of the cargo in its sound or damaged condition, as the case may be. Such insurance should also contain a clause to the effect that it takes precedence over any other insurance effected on the goods because such insurance is for the benefit of the owners of the goods or the original insurers. Sometimes such insurances also incorporate a clause stipulating that in the event of damage to goods, the general average has first lien (on the proceeds of any claim under the insurance) for any unpaid salvage and/or general average or special charges. In other words, such insurance is *for the account of the general average* which must be protected in case such cargo is not insured or not fully insured. Furthermore, it ensures that such cargo (even if destroyed while stored ashore) will not be lost as a contributing interest to the general average. The original insurers of the cargo (if any) are substantial beneficiaries in the event of a claim under such insurances, and since the cargo has been exposed (as a result of the forced discharge) to additional risks, cargo underwriters are usually pleased to have this reinsurance at the expense of the general average. It has sometimes been suggested that such insurance is for the most part unnecessary since the shipowner is protected by the Hague Rules or their equivalent with the result that, if the forced discharge was reasonable, no liability would attach to the shipowner for any damage to cargo while separated from the vessel. This may or may not prove to be true in every case, but since such insurance is permitted (one might almost say encouraged) by the York/Antwerp Rules, a shipowner would be wise to insure such cargo. Indeed the practice is so well established that American courts have held that a shipowner, as bailee of the cargo, has the duty to effect such an insurance and in the event of a failure to do so is liable to the cargo owner for any cargo damaged or destroyed while in storage ashore at a port of refuge (*Mormacmar*, 1947 AMC 1611; *see also* 1950 AMC 2018, 1952 AMC 1088, 1954 AMC 691, and 1956 AMC 1028).

Putting the matter on a purely practical basis, it is perhaps better to argue about an insurance premium (which is seldom of any great amount) than to become involved in a major lawsuit following the destruction of cargo while temporarily stored ashore in the shipowner's custody.

Occasionally cargo discharged at a port of refuge as a general average act cannot be stored or reloaded due to lack of facilities and consequently has to be sold. Any loss by sale of cargo in such circumstances is allowable in general average since the loss was the direct consequence of the general average act of putting into the port of refuge and discharging the cargo. Sometimes cargo which has been discharged in order to effect repairs is damaged to such an extent as to be worthless and has to be dumped at the port of refuge. Under American practice, any expenses incurred in dumping such cargo at the port of refuge is allowed in general average. The entire operation of discharging the cargo, storing it, and either reloading it into the vessel or dumping it if worthless, is considered to be one continuous general average act, and the entire cost is treated accordingly. Internationally, the dumping of cargo at a port of refuge is only allowed in general average if the damage necessitating the dumping resulted from a general average act or was an inevitable consequence of the general average discharge at a port of refuge. Otherwise, dumping charges are treated as special charges on cargo.

Most international Protection and Indemnity clubs respond for the additional costs (over and above those which would have been incurred if the cargo had not been damaged) in discharging and disposing of damaged cargo, but only if the shipowner had no recourse to recover those costs from any other party. This protection and indemnity coverage applies to the discharge of damaged cargo whether it be at a port of refuge or at destination.

The treatment of the cost of discharging, storing, and reloading cargo at *a port or place of loading or call* as sanctioned by Rule X (b) and (c) illustrates the working of the so-called artificial general average.

RESTOWAGE OF CARGO AT A PORT OF REFUGE. We have already seen that the term "extraordinary circumstances" covers, *inter alia*, putting into a port of refuge to restow cargo if such a course is necessary for the common safety. Thus, the wages and provisions and cost of entering and leaving the port would be allowable in general average. But what of the actual cost of restowing the cargo? There had been considerable controversy over this expense in the United States. It will be seen that the last paragraph of Rule X (b)—which is new—clearly states that any handling or discharge of cargo, fuel, or stores which is incurred *solely* for the purpose of restowage due to the shifting of cargo during the voyage, is not allowable in general average. The rule goes on to make it clear that the allowance of any restowage which may be necessary for the common safety (such as to reduce a list to prevent a vessel capsizing) is not prohibited. However, once safety has been attained, the amount of any additional restowage would come within the exclusion.

The cost of restowing cargo at a port of refuge merely to enable the voyage to be completed is, consequently, an obligation of the shipowner under his contract of carriage.

WAGES AND MAINTENANCE OF CREW AT PORT OF REFUGE. Rule XI of the York/Antwerp Rules deals with the allowance of wages and maintenance of crew and other expenses incurred in port of refuge situations and reads as follows:

RULE XI. WAGES AND MAINTENANCE OF CREW AND OTHER EXPENSES BEARING UP FOR AND IN A PORT OF REFUGE, ETC. (a) Wages and maintenance of master, officers and crew reasonably incurred and fuel and stores consumed during the prolongation of the voyage occasioned by a ship entering a port or place of refuge or returning to her port or place of loading shall be admitted as general average when the expenses of entering such port or place are allowable in general average in accordance with Rule X (a).

(b) When a ship shall have entered or been detained in any port or place in consequence of accident, sacrifice or other extraordinary circumstances which render that necessary for the common safety, or to enable damage to the ship caused by sacrifice or accident to be repaired, if the repairs were necessary for the safe prosecution of the voyage, the wages and maintenance of the master, officers and crew reasonably incurred during the extra period of detention in such port or place until the ship shall or should have been made ready to proceed upon her voyage, shall be admitted in general average.

Provided that when damage to the ship is discovered at a port or place of loading or call without any accident or other extraordinary circumstance connected with such damage having taken place during the voyage, then the wages and maintenance of master, officers and crew and fuel and stores consumed during the extra detention for repairs to damages so discovered shall not be admissible as general average, even if the repairs are necessary for the safe prosecution of the voyage.

When the ship is condemned or does not proceed on her original voyage, *wages and maintenance of the master, officers and crew and fuel and stores consumed shall be admitted as general average only up to the date of the ship's condemnation or of the abandonment of the voyage or up to the date of completion of discharge of cargo if the condemnation or abandonment takes place before that date.*

Fuel and stores consumed during the extra period of detention shall be admitted as general average, except such fuel and stores as are consumed in effecting repairs not allowable in general average.

Port charges incurred during the extra period of detention shall likewise be admitted as general average except such charges as are incurred solely by reason of repairs not allowable in general average.

(c) For the purpose of this and other Rules, wages shall include all payments made to or for the benefit of the master, officers and crew, whether such payments be imposed by law upon the shipowners or be made under the terms or articles of employment.

(d) When overtime is paid to the master, officers or crew for maintenance of the ship or repairs, the cost of which is not allowable in general average, such overtime shall be allowed in general average only up to the saving in expense which would have been incurred and admitted as general average, had such overtime not been incurred.

Under this rule, wages and maintenance of crew and fuel and stores consumed during the prolongation of the voyage occasioned by a vessel entering a port of refuge or returning to her port of loading are allowable in general average when the expenses of entering such port are allowable within the terms of Rule X (a). In addition, when a vessel has entered or been detained in any port in consequence of accident, sacrifice, or other extraordinary circumstances which render that necessary for the common safety or to enable damage to the vessel caused by sacrifice or accident to be repaired, if the repairs are necessary for the safe prosecution of the voyage, the wages and maintenance of crew and fuel and stores consumed during the period or extra period of detention are also allowable in general average. A new proviso has been introduced in Rule XI (b) which, in effect, stipulates that in those cases where the damage to the ship is merely *discovered* at the port or place of loading or call without any *"accident or other extraordinary circumstance connected with such damage having taken place during the voyage"* (that is to say, subsequent to the commencement of loading of cargo), there shall be no allowance in general average for wages and maintenance of crew even though the repairs themselves may have been necessary for the safe prosecution of the voyage. This amendment to the rule is in line with the amendment of Rule X (b) discussed previously and restricts the so-called artificial general average detentions which had been introduced in the 1924 Rules. As previously stated, the object is to limit the circumstances under which cargo interests can become involved in a general average situation at a port of loading; an accident must have occurred subsequent to the loading of cargo.

When the voyage is abandoned, the period of detention ceases at that time unless the discharge of cargo is not then completed, in which case it continues until the discharge is completed. (This is similar to the position under American law; see the *Joseph Farwell*, 31 Fed. Rep. 844.) In practice (when the voyage is being abandoned), the wages and maintenance of crew, etc., are allowed up to the completion of discharge whether or not the cost of discharge is allowable in general average.

The meaning of "wages and maintenance" of crew has already been discussed in connection with particular average claims. The definitions given by the Advisory Committee of the British Association of Average Adjusters are those usually followed insofar as general average allowances are concerned. Thus, overtime payments in connection with normal duties such as watchkeeping at a port of refuge would be considered as wages and therefore allowable in general average while any overtime in connection with repairs (other than general average repairs) would not fall within that category. Thus, the treatment of overtime on repairs would follow the treatment of the repairs being effected.

Average adjusters are often called upon to deal with circumstances which are not precisely covered by the York/Antwerp Rules. As an example, it often happens that when a vessel strands, cargo is discharged into lighters during the refloating operations. After refloating, the vessel puts into a port of refuge to ascertain whether damage has been sustained and to obtain a certificate of seaworthiness. The cargo is then reloaded into the vessel at the port of refuge. While the wages and maintenance of the crew, etc., incurred during the reloading of the cargo do not exactly fall within the wording of Rule XI, they are within the intent of the rule. Indeed, such expenses appear to be recoverable as a direct consequence of the general average act of the forced discharge of cargo. In practice such allowances in general average are made and accepted without question.

The period during which wages and maintenance of crew are to be allowed in general average when a fire breaks out at port of call has been the subject of much discussion among average adjusters. It is the practice in the United States to commence such allowances at the time of the first act to extinguish the fire. This practice is based on the premise that the extra detention during the efforts to extinguish the fire comes within the wording of Rule XI (b), namely "extraordinary circumstances which rendered that [detention] necessary for the common safety."

Sometimes the detention at a port of refuge is extended for reasons unconnected with the original detention. For example, a vessel, while otherwise ready to proceed, might be delayed by ice conditions, fog, or weather conditions. Delays on account of fog or weather are held to the vessel owner's account, the delay being merely the ordinary act of prudent seamanship such as might be required on the voyage itself. On the other hand, delay due to ice conditions might be admissible in general average if it can be shown that such a delay was within the contemplation of the master at the time he decided to put into the port of refuge, in other words, when the extra delay was, in fact, the inevitable consequence of putting into that particular port at that particular time of the year. Occasionally a vessel is subjected to extra delay at the port of refuge while arrangements are made to obtain the release of the vessel from arrest by salvors. In such cases it is customary to allow the extra detention in general average. This may not be strictly in accord with Rule XI but American average adjusters have usually taken a broad view of such delays. The rationale behind such allowances is that, with the best will in the world, it takes time to provide salvors with security at a foreign port. Therefore, if the time taken is *reasonable* it is customary to allow wages, etc., of crew during such *reasonable* delay. (It would be unusual to allow a delay of more than two or three days solely for this purpose.) The reasoning is that when the master signs a salvage contract (the general average act) it is apparent that some delay may be unavoidable in providing security and that, therefore, such *reasonable and unavoidable* delay flows directly from the general average act. It should be stressed that any *unreasonable or avoidable* delay would not qualify for a general average allowance. Thus, if the delay is due *solely* to lack of funds or credit, the delay becomes *unreasonable* and such extension of the detention at a port of refuge would not qualify as general average.

In the event the York/Antwerp Rules do not apply, the allowance of wages of crew, etc., under American law and practice differs in several respects from Rule XI. Take the case of an accident occurring while a vessel is loading cargo (i.e., before she has broken ground on her voyage), as a result of which additional expenses, including wages of crew, are incurred. In the past, American courts have taken the view that the risk of such accidents (in the absence of any imminent peril to both ship and cargo) falls upon the shipowner and that the expenses arising are not within the orbit of general average (*Bowring* v. *Thebaud*, 42 Fed. Rep. 794, 56 Fed. Rep. 520). Thus, an accident at a port of loading which delayed the vessel while repairs necessary for the safe prosecution of the voyage were effected, but which did not place the vessel or cargo in any peril, might not give rise to general average under American law, although such a case would come within general average under Rule XI of the York/Antwerp Rules.

However, it must be pointed out that in *Bowring* v. *Thebaud* (which was decided prior to the introduction of the Harter Act), the court based its findings on the premise that the implied warranty of seaworthiness in American law extends to the time when the vessel actually breaks ground on the voyage and not merely to the time when she begins to load cargo; hence, where a vessel was pierced by an unknown obstruction when at the dock receiving cargo, there was a breach of warranty, the shipowners were solely responsible for damage to the cargo, and there was no general average. Gourlie, in his address as chairman of the Association of Average Adjusters of the United States in 1893, criticized the court's decision and expressed the opinion that whenever the association between vessel and cargo begins (i.e., *when loading of cargo commences*), then the reciprocal obligations of one to the other in general average begin at the same time.

The courts would, perhaps, reach the same conclusion as in *Bowring* v. *Thebaud* in cases where the Harter Act is applicable, because that act did not relieve a shipowner from the absolute warranty of the vessel's seaworthiness *on sailng*. However, with the introduction of the Carriage of Goods by Sea Act in 1936, this extreme doctrine of seaworthiness was discarded. The Harter Act required the shipowner to exercise due diligence to provide a seaworthy vessel up to the time the vessel broke ground on the voyage and, by virtue of the courts' harsh interpretation of the act, failure to do so deprived the carrier, *inter alia*, of any right to contribution in general average. On the other hand, the immunities granted by the Carriage of Goods by Sea Act are not restricted to a situation in which the vessel is in all respects seaworthy; the unseaworthiness is material only if loss or damage results from it (*Isbrandtsen Company* v. *Federal Insurance Co.*, 1952 AMC 1945). In other words, the shipowner's right to claim contribution is not debarred unless there is a causal connection between the failure to use diligence to make the vessel seaworthy and the accident which gave rise to the general average. In the words of one distinguished admiralty attorney:

> It thus appears that, while a shipowner cannot derive benefit from the exemptions contained in the Harter Act for the period from the loading of the cargo to the commencement of the voyage, it is otherwise under "Carriage of Goods by Sea Act" because it operates immediately upon the ship commencing to load the cargo and any movement she may make in connection with the loading of the cargo in going to other docks to load additional cargo within the confines of the harbor and before she breaks ground for the voyage, as well as during the course of the voyage. (Robert G. McCreary, Great Lakes Protective Association report, 1953)

Whatever the position might be under American law, there is no question that when the contract of affreightment provides for adjustment of general average in accordance with the York/Antwerp Rules, expenses at a loading port of the nature dealt with in Rules X and XI are properly allowable in general average.

Another departure from the code of general average laid down in the York/Antwerp Rules is to be found in the American practice of allowing wages of crew during a detention at sea, as, for example, while undergoing necessary repairs at sea (*May* v. *Keystone Yellow Pine Co.*, 117 Fed. Rep. 287) or as a result of having to put to sea to avoid a hurricane. Such acts are treated as being akin to putting into a port for refuge. The York/Antwerp Rules limit the allowance of wages, etc., to those incurred at "a port or place of refuge" and the English courts have interpreted "place" as "a locality having some or many of the characteristics of a port" (*Humber Conservancy Board* v. *Federal Coal & Shipping Co.*, 29 L. L. R. 177). American adjusters tend to give a more liberal interpretation to the words "place of refuge," as, for example, in treating a sheltered bay or anchorage as a "place of refuge" within the meaning of the rule.

In calculating the period of wages to be allowed in general average, American law provides that the general average detention commences at the time of the deviation of the vessel from her course until she is ready to resume her voyage (not, as is the case under the York/Antwerp Rules, until she regains her position on course). This is the rule of thumb and, at least, it has the advantage of simplicity, an attribute with which general average is not too liberally endowed. Allowances for fuel and engine stores are similarly dealt with when American law and practice applies to the exclusion of the York/Antwerp Rules. Although under American law and practice, the wages and maintenance of crew, etc., are allowed from the moment of deviation to a port of refuge, if the deviation covers a long distance and if during most of the deviation the vessel is in fact proceeding towards her original destination, it is the practice to allow in general average only the wages and maintenance of crew, etc., during the extra time arising from putting into the port of refuge.

In connection with allowances for wages of crew, etc., the Association of Average Adjusters of the United States has two rules of practice which affect all adjustments of general average, whether the adjustment is being stated in accordance with the York/Antwerp Rules or not. The first is Rule XII, which lays down the allowance to be made in respect of provisions of crew. A fixed rate is embodied in the rule, which is brought up to date from time to time to accord with the fluctuating cost of provisions. The rule reads as follows:

RULE XII. ALLOWANCE IN RESPECT OF PROVISIONS. When allowance is made in General Average for provisions of Masters, Officers and crews, the allowance shall be $8.00 per person per day for voyages beginning on or after October 2, 1980. For voyages beginning prior to October 2, 1980, the allowance shall be based on previous Rule XII.

The Rule shall apply to United States flag vessels in all instances and to vessels of other flags on voyages to and from United States ports, including Territories and Insular possessions, when the general average is stated in accordance with the laws and usages of the United States, even though such laws and usages may be modified by York/Antwerp Rules.

The second rule referred to is Rule XVIII which stipulates that in making allowances for wages and provisions in general average, a period of less than twelve hours shall be disregarded and a period of twelve hours or more shall be treated as a whole day. The text of the rule is as follows:

RULE XVIII. WAGES AND PROVISIONS—GENERAL AVERAGE. In making allowances for wages and provisions in General Average either under American law or York/Antwerp Rules a period of less than twelve hours, either alone or in excess of complete days, shall be disregarded and a period of twelve hours or more, either alone or in excess of a number of complete days, shall be treated as a whole day.

Although there is no rule on the subject, it is the practice in general average detentions involving large passenger liners to allow the wages of the entire crew, including the larger number of stewards, etc., employed solely in looking after passengers, when the adjustment is being stated in accordance with the York/Antwerp Rules (as would be the case if the bills of lading under which cargo was being carried stipulated such an adjustment). On the other hand, if the general average is being adjusted according to American law (as, for example, when a liner is on a pleasure cruise and carries no cargo), only the wages of those members of the crew responsible for the navigation and safety of the vessel are allowed.

Another rule of practice of the Association of Average Adjusters of the United States which, in certain circumstances, would affect general average in port of refuge cases is Rule I, which reads as follows:

RULE I. COMPENSATION AND EXPENSES OF MASTER. Where the voyage is broken up by reason of shipwreck or condemnation of the ship at a place short of the port of destination, the master shall be entitled to compensation from the general interests for the time necessarily occupied by him in transacting the business growing out of the disaster until his departure thence for the home port with the proceeds, general accounts and vouchers.

He shall also be entitled to a reasonable indemnification for his necessary expenses and services in returning to the home port when needed or required, by the peculiar circumstances of the case, to justify his acts at the place of disaster, or to give information, not otherwise afforded, to finally adjust and apportion the average charges to be paid by the general or special interests for whom such services are performed, to be determined by the nature of the case.

These rules shall apply whether the vessel be in ballast or with cargo.

If the shipowner dispatches a special representative to a port of refuge in the belief that such course is to the mutual benefit of both vessel and cargo, the expenses arising therefrom are properly allowable in general average (*Hobson* v. *Lord*, 92 U. S. 397).

PORT DUES AT A PORT OF REFUGE. Rule XI (b) of the York/Antwerp Rules stipulates that port charges incurred during the extra period of detention at a port of refuge are recoverable as general average except such charges as are incurred "solely by reason of repairs not allowable in general average." Some discussion in British adjusting circles was occasioned as to the correct interpretation of this paragraph of the rule. These discussions resulted in British adjusters accepting the view that only such extra charges as were incurred by reason of repairs should be charged to those repairs and that charges which were incurred as the result of putting into port, but which were extended in time by reason of repairs, remained general average. In other words, the basic daily charge of occupying a port or berth is allowable in general average and it is only an extra or additional charge—over and above the basic rate and incurred solely because of the repairs—that is excluded. For example, if a vessel repairs at a wharf, the wharfage is general average if it would have had to be incurred at that port even if no repairs were being effected. On the other hand, if the vessel could have remained at buoys in the river without incurring any expense but for the necessity to repair, the wharfage would follow the cost of repairs.

In the United States, the tendency seems to be to interpret Rule XI (b) in a like fashion. Where the York/Antwerp Rules do not apply, it is the practice of at least some adjusters in the United States to treat wharfage at a port of refuge as general average if any part of the cargo remains in the vessel; if, however, the cargo has been discharged at the time the wharfage is incurred, the wharfage is treated according to the nature of the work proceeding at the time.

CREDIT ALLOWANCE FOR NEW FREIGHT. As has been noted previously, the question of whether the general average should be credited with any new freight earned at a port of refuge is governed by the circumstances applying in each case.

In the case of the *Rosamond* (1940 AMC 195), the court held that it would be inequitable to permit the shipowner to benefit by the freight earned on new cargo loaded at a port of refuge and that if the net new freight exceeded the general average expenses, then no loss had, in fact, been sustained and no contribution was due from anyone. If the general average expenses exceeded the net new freight, then only the amount of the excess should be apportioned among the contributing interests.

The *Rosamond* case should not be followed blindly and is not a guide for all port of refuge cases for the following reasons. In that case, the charterers had chartered and paid for the entire ship and it was the shipowner (not the charterers) who filled up the space made vacant by the jettison and received the freight on the new cargo. In arriving at its decision, the court was no doubt influenced by these unusual circumstances. The principle laid down would hardly seem applicable to a vessel carrying a general cargo of several hundred separate shipments.

EXTRA EXPENSES FOLLOWING A FIRE ON SHIPBOARD. Following a fire, considerable extra expenses in connection with the handling of cargo are often incurred, some of which may be allowable in general average. Those extra expenses not admissible as general average may qualify as special charges on cargo. Special charges on cargo can be defined as extra expenses incurred solely on behalf of cargo which are not allowable in general average and which are chargeable to cargo under law, contract or otherwise.

For the discharge of cargo following a fire to be allowable in general average, the discharge must have either been necessary for the common safety or have been required to enable repairs necessary for the safe prosecution of the voyage to be carried out (*see* Rule X (b)). If the cargo is discharged for either of these reasons, the cost of discharging cargo, whether it be wet cargo (damaged as a result of the efforts to extinguish the fire) or burnt cargo, is allowable in general average. Until the vessel leaves the port of refuge to resume her voyage, all charges on cargo—such as wharfage, storage, or watching—are allowed in general average. However, when the vessel sails, leaving some damaged cargo behind (as is often the case), the charges on the cargo left behind follow the nature of the damage sustained—that is, all charges on *wet cargo* are general average but all charges on *burnt cargo* are, "special charges on burnt cargo." The special charges are subsequently apportioned among the various shipments of burnt cargo which were left behind at the port of refuge. If overtime is worked during the forced discharge, the extra cost is usually allowable in general average on the grounds that it was worked in the general interest; that is to say, the overtime may be justified because it was essential to have the discharge expedited to prevent increased damage to cargo or because there was still a possibility of the fire breaking out again.

Special charges are simply particular charges; they are charges incurred by the vessel owner on behalf of the owners of the cargo for the safety and preservation of the cargo. The separation and allocation of special charges in a general cargo case are largely matters of common sense. In most fire cases, for the sake of convenience all the special charges on burnt cargo are extended to one column so named. These special charges on burnt cargo are subsequently separated if they are of a varying nature. For example, some of the charges might apply exclusively to cotton shipments, others might be specific to tea, and so on. The various items in the special charges column are thus separated under as many headings as may be necessary. There is almost certain to be one class of charge (such as watching) which will apply to all the cargo left behind and this would be classified as "all cargo" (meaning, of course, all burnt cargo left behind). After the total of the special charges column has been separated under headings indicating the various categories of cargo in respect of which they were incurred, these categories may, in turn, have to be broken down into sub-categories, such as "Special Charges on Cotton—Bulk," "Special Charges on Cotton—Value," and "Special Charges on Cargo—Specific." The reason for this is that the charges for warehousing, say, 100 bales of cotton may be unaffected by the values of each individual bale—the warehouseman is simply selling space. This is called a "bulk charge." However, the cost of watchmen watching these 100 bales of cotton is a charge which is more equitably divided among the various shipments he is watching on a value basis—this is a "value charge." Other charges may have been incurred in respect of a specific shipment and will therefore have to be borne by that shipment only.

Having separated the various special charges, the next step is to *allocate* these charges to specific shipments. This is where the previous separation helps because quite obviously any "special charges on tea" will be payable by the burnt tea shipments left behind at the port of refuge and any "special charges on cotton," by the cotton shipments. The bulk items will be apportioned on a package or weight basis, and the value items on a value basis. There is no end to the various ramifications, but if the separation and allocation are approached step by step, the special charges will fall into place just as a jigsaw puzzle does. In carrying out this task, it is a good thing to put oneself in the position of the owners of the cargo: how would they expect the charges to be apportioned? Finally, it should be remembered that special charges levied against a shipment should be deducted in arriving at the contributory value of that shipment for general average purposes.

Very often, as a result of the fire and the efforts to extinguish same, the cost of discharge *at destination* is enhanced by reason of some of the cargo having been damaged—a salvage rate may be demanded by stevedores or the discharge itself may take longer than it would if the cargo had been sound. In such cases the practice is to ascertain the number of packages or other units damaged by water only and the number of packages or other units damaged by fire or fire and water. The *extra* cost of discharge is divided in that proportion: that applying to the water damage is allowed in general average; the balance of the extra cost is payable by the shipowner as an enhanced voyage expense unless the freight was at risk and insured, in which case the extra cost falling on the shipowner would be recoverable as a special charge on freight.

Inevitably following a fire in a cargo hold, the hold itself requires cleaning. It is usual to allow the entire cost of such cleaning in general average particularly if the agent used to extinguish the fire was water. It is considered that the necessity for cleaning is principally due to the extinguishing operations. In some cases it is also necessary to scrape and repaint the hold. In such circumstances, the scraping and/or painting is usually treated as having been made necessary as a result of the fire itself; such damage is therefore of an accidental and not a general average nature.

EXPENSES LIGHTENING A SHIP WHEN ASHORE. When a ship runs aground, it is very often necessary to lighten her by removing some of the cargo she is carrying. Expenses of this nature are dealt with by Rule VIII of the York/Antwerp Rules, as follows:

> RULE VIII. EXPENSES LIGHTENING A SHIP WHEN ASHORE, AND CONSEQUENT DAMAGE. When a ship is ashore and cargo and ship's fuel and stores, or any of them, are discharged as a general average act, the extra cost of lightening, lighter hire and reshipping (if incurred), and the loss or damage sustained thereby, shall be admitted as general average.

It should be noted that the requirements of Rule A must be met before the extra expenses, etc., mentioned in the rule are admissible as general average. If it is the normal procedure of a ship to discharge her cargo into lighters at or near the place where the vessel is ashore and, after lightening the ship, the lighters deliver the cargo to destination, the lighterage allowed under this rule must be reduced by the ordinary cost of lighterage.

Although the rule states that the loss or damage sustained during the discharge of cargo, etc., as a general average act is to be admitted as general average, this must be qualified. If the loss or damage is the result of a negligent act during the discharge, the chain of causation has been broken and such loss or damage would not be recoverable in general average (the *Oak Hill*, 1970 AMC 227). Thus, the sinking of a lighter during a lightening operation which was due to a separate accident not contemplated at the time of the general average act or which was not the inevitable result of the general average act would only be recoverable in general average in the most exceptional circumstances. For consequential damage of this nature to be recoverable in general average, the damage must have been the necessary (unavoidable) consequence of the general average discharge. The position is the same under American law and, as Coe remarks, the allowance in general average "includes damage by exposure while on lighters or in landing the cargo on the beach."

Substituted Expenses

So far, general average expenses per se have been discussed, but now we turn to a type of expenditure which, while not qualifying as general average in itself, becomes allowable as general average by virtue of having been incurred in lieu of expenditure which, if incurred, would have been allowable as general average. Such expenses are known as substituted expenses and have been described as expenses incurred in the interest of ultimate economy by adopting a course of action other than that which is apparently indicated. Although substituted expenses usually result in a saving to all the parties to the common adventure, they unfortunately have little support in American law, most of the recorded cases being opposed to such allowances (see *Hugg* v. *Baltimore & Cuba S. & M. Co.*, 35 Md. 414). One of the few exceptions is the case of *Bowring* v. *Thebaud* (42 Fed. Rep. 794) in which it was held that the extra cost of dry-docking with cargo on board was recoverable in general average as an expense substituted in place of the cost of discharging, storing, and reloading the cargo.

Fortunately, the York/Antwerp Rules incorporate the doctrine of substituted expenses, Rule F establishing the principle and Rule XIV dealing with a specific example of this type of expenditure. In accordance with the Rule of Interpretation, Rule F can be invoked only in circumstances not dealt with by the aforementioned numbered rule.

RULE F. Any extra expense incurred in place of another expense which would have been allowable as general average shall be deemed to be general average and so allowed without regard to the saving, if any, to other interests, but only up to the amount of the general average expense avoided.

It must be emphasized that before expenditure can qualify as a substituted expense, a real alternative must have existed which would have involved expenditure properly allowable in general average. Expense means the actual extra outlay of money involved in carrying out the substituted measures and, on the other hand, the outlays avoided thereby. The rule only deals with expenses; *losses* are not to be brought into consideration. In practice, substituted *losses* can be covered by special agreement.

It will be noted that Rule F provides for the allowance of substituted expenses without regard to the savings (if any) to other parties. Although the extra expense may result in a saving to interests other than the general average, the latter is usually the interest most directly concerned. The drafters of the York/Antwerp Rules therefore felt it to be a practical and not inequitable method to allow in general average the substituted expenses up to, but not exceeding, the amount saved to the general average. General average is thus in no worse a position and often in a better one than if the substituted expenses had not been incurred.

In many cases, substituted expenses consist of the cost of forwarding cargo to destination in lieu of retaining it at the port of refuge while the vessel effects repairs. In other cases, the substituted expense may be the cost of towing the vessel to destination in lieu of effecting repairs at a port of refuge. Rule X (d) of the York/Antwerp Rules, 1950, dealt specifically with such cases but has been eliminated from the 1974 Rules, leaving the cost of forwarding cargo to destination or the cost of towage to destination to be dealt with, as necessary, under the general terms of Rule F.

To qualify for treatment as substituted expenses, the towage or the forwarding must have been entered into with the intention of avoiding or saving general average expenditure; Rule F does not apply to situations where such steps are taken merely to avoid inconvenience or loss to one or more of the interests.

The "extra cost" of forwarding referred to in the rule is the additional cost incurred as a result of the towage, transshipment, or forwarding, over and above the cost that would be incurred if such towage, transshipment or forwarding was not carried out. In other words, the shipowner must give credit against the extra expenditure incurred for any ordinary voyage expenses which he has saved.

Contrary to the general provisions of Rule F, Rule X (d) of the 1950 Rules had stipulated that the extra cost of towage, transshipment, and forwarding (up to the amount of the extra expense saved) was to be payable by the several parties to the adventure in proportion to the extraordinary expense saved. Thus, if the shipowner had effected a saving in the cost of repairs, he was required to contribute to the substituted expense in respect of that saving. With the elimination of Rule X (d), this anomaly has been removed from the new rules and only the savings to general average are to be considered in applying the principle of substituted expenses.

It must be stressed that the allowance of forwarding expenses can be justified only if the carrier would have been entitled, in the particular circumstances prevailing, to retain the cargo at the port of refuge; otherwise no alternative would exist. This raises the question as to the circumstances under which the shipowner is or is not justified in abandoning a voyage. The question usually arises following a major accident as a result of which the vessel has been badly damaged, where even if it is economically possible to effect repairs, there is often a long delay involved. Here are two of the factors usually involved in the question under discussion: expense and delay. There is also occasionally a conflict of interest between ship and cargo—sometimes it is to the benefit of the shipowner to complete the voyage (as when the freight is only earned on delivery of the cargo or if only to recover the port of refuge expenses in general average)—and sometimes it is not (he may wish to scrap the badly damaged vessel). Cargo interests also have occasions when they do not wish to have their cargo held up during a long delay for repairs and in the process contribute to the shipowner's expenses in general average (they would rather take delivery at the port of refuge); on other occasions the cargo interests might insist on the vessel fulfilling the contract of affreightment by completing the voyage (as when the freight has been paid and is non-returnable).

The right of a shipowner to regard a contract of affreightment as frustrated defies precise definition. However, it is beyond question that the shipowner is required to take all reasonable and practical steps to complete the adventure—and whether the freight is prepaid and guaranteed or is payable at destination is irrelevant to this requirement. Generally speaking, following a major casualty, if the vessel can be repaired at a reasonable cost and in a reasonable time, it is the duty of the shipowner, as custodian of the cargo, to carry it to destination. On the other hand, if, for example, the cost of repairing the vessel would exceed her value when repaired, or if she is at a place where she cannot be repaired, the shipowner is prevented in a business sense from carrying the goods to destination, and he may justifiably abandon the voyage. However, the right to abandon the voyage is not influenced by the market value of the vessel alone; the amount of freight (whether guaranteed or at risk) to be earned by completing the voyage is also a factor. In considering the question, this revenue is often compared with the cost of effecting such repairs as are necessary to complete the voyage. Furthermore, if temporary repairs alone are necessary to complete the voyage and deliver the cargo, only the cost of these repairs would be compared with the repaired value of the vessel to determine whether the completion of the voyage is mandatory.

In any event, in considering a shipowner's right to abandon a voyage, it is not sufficient that a supervening event merely renders the terms of the contract of affreightment more expensive (*Christos*, 1966 AMC 1455). In short, it is only when a supervening event makes it *impossible* (either in a physical or commercial sense) to carry out a voyage charter that the contract of affreightment can be frustrated and abandoned without liability. When the supervening event only renders the completion of the voyage more expensive, or more difficult, the voyage must be completed without extra compensation. As the House of Lords has stated:

> A situation must arise which renders performance of the contract "a thing radically different from that which was undertaken by the contract" . . . It must be positively unjust to hold the parties bound (*Ocean Tramp Tankers Corp.* v. *V/O Sovfracht*, 1964 2 Q. B. 226).

It is undecided exactly how much the cost of completing the voyage may increase before frustration of the voyage is justified. A doubling of voyage costs because of an increase in Suez Canal charges was held not to be sufficient in the English courts (*Tsakiroglou & Co.* v. *Noblee Thorl G.m.b.H.*, 1960 2 Q. B. 318, *aff.* 1962 A. C. 93). It is submitted, however, that a commercial total loss of the voyage freight (such as when the cost of transshipment from a port of refuge is greater than the original voyage freight) would be a clear case of mercantile impossibility, as opposed to physical impossibility. The editors of Chalmer's *Marine Insurance Act, 1906* (8th ed., p. 92), suggest that since a merchant trades for profit, not for pleasure, the law will not compel him to carry on business at a loss. Presumably a shipowner is entitled to similar protection in cases in which the completion of the voyage would result in a *substantial* loss. It might be otherwise where an unexpected increase in voyage expenses merely resulted in a marginally unprofitable voyage.

In addition to the expense involved, another important factor to be considered in determining a shipowner's right to abandon a voyage is the distance already covered on the contemplated voyage when the supervening event takes place. A delay of even three to four months at the beginning of a long voyage might not justify the shipowner in abandoning that voyage. On the other hand, if a similar delay occurred when the vessel was almost at destination, it would not be reasonable to retain the cargo for that length of time. But here again, there is no reliable yardstick as to the length of delay which would justify abandonment of the voyage. In this connection, one English jurist is often quoted with approval; he had this to say:

The commercial frustration of an adventure by delay means, as I understand it, the happening of some unforeseen delay, without the fault of either party to a contract, of such a character as that by it, the fulfillment of the contract in the only way in which fulfillment is contemplated and practicable is so inordinately postponed that its fulfillment when the delay is over will not accomplish the only object or objects which both parties to the contract must have known that each of them had in view at the time they made the contract, and for the accomplishment of which object or objects the contract was made.

In other words, the common maritime adventure has ceased to be that originally contemplated.

It might be useful to consider the position following a *justifiable* abandonment or frustration of the voyage. If, as is probably the case, the vessel is under general average, all general average allowances will cease as from the date of the abandonment of the voyage or the date of completion of discharge of cargo at the port of frustration for future disposition, whichever is the later. If the freight was prepaid and guaranteed, the shipowner would not necessarily exercise any option which might be contained in the contract of affreightment to forward the cargo. He would give delivery of the cargo at the port of frustration and the cargo owner would have to forward it at his own expense (which forwarding expenses might be recoverable from cargo underwriters if the cargo was insured). However, until the cargo owner does take over the cargo, the shipowner is, of course, responsible as bailee for its safekeeping. If the cargo owner fails to take delivery within a reasonable time, the shipowner is entitled to sell the cargo for account of whom concerned although it will be obvious that no such drastic step should be taken without first making every endeavor to obtain the cargo owner's instructions. On the other hand, if the freight was payable at destination, the shipowner might very well decide to forward the cargo at his own expense to earn the original freight (in such circumstances the cost of forwarding might be recoverable from freight underwriters).

Needless to say, if a vessel is operating under a time charter and the time charterer enters into a separate contract with the concerned in cargo, it is the time charterer who is responsible for delivering the cargo to destination under the contract of affreightment, and it is therefore his responsibility to arrange for the transshipment of cargo if such a course is indicated.

To sum up: In determining whether a shipowner is justified in abandoning a voyage following a major accident (or, conversely, whether he is entitled to retain the cargo under general average), all the relevant facts of the situation have to be considered carefully. In particular, the following factors must be considered:

(1) The length of time necessary to effect repairs.

(2) The distance already covered on the chartered voyage coupled with the distance from destination.

(3) The cost of effecting such repairs as are necessary solely to complete the voyage.

(4) The facilities for repairs at the port of refuge.

(5) The freight earned or to be earned on the voyage.

(6) The nature of the storage facilities available at the port of refuge, assuming cargo has to be discharged to effect repairs.

(7) The nature of the cargo itself (that is to say, whether it could survive a long delay).

The shipowner and/or other parties to the adventure are entitled to take a reasonable time to develop all this information and to consider the conflicting interests of shipowner, cargo owner, and underwriters on ship, cargo, and freight. However, as soon as the person who alleges frustration has developed the necessary information, he must make his decision and notify all parties. He cannot plead absence of definite instructions from the concerned in cargo or their underwriters since the carrier has control of the cargo and is entitled to take whatever steps he considers appropriate and prudent.

In practice, Rule X (d) of the 1950 Rules was not often applied, as it had become a common practice for agreements to be prepared at the time of the general average act giving consideration to all the factors influencing the various parties to the adventure and stipulating what was, and what was not, to be allowed in general average. With the demise of Rule X (d), no doubt this practice will be even more prevalent. The object of a forwarding or non-separation of interest agreement is to obtain an extension of the treatment of forwarding expenses; to preserve the shipowner's rights to an allowance for wages and maintenance of crew after the forwarding of cargo; and to ensure that the cargo forwarded continues to contribute in general average. Usually, the fact that the shipowner is prepared to transship without charging a second freight to the concerned in cargo is used as a lever to obtain:

(1) The allowance of wages of crew, etc., while repairing as if there had been no separation of interests.

(2) The allowance of the cost of forwarding the cargo up to the saving in general average expenses as a result of the forwarding.

The cost of forwarding could either consist of a second freight, in which case a credit for voyage expenses saved should be given, or may be confined to the cost of discharging and reloading into the forwarding vessel that part of the cargo which had to be discharged for repairs and often the remainder of the cargo also. The saving to the general average will usually consist of the cost of storing that part of the cargo which would have had to be discharged at the port of refuge in order to effect repairs necessary for the safe prosecution of the voyage. The principle behind such forwarding agreements has been succinctly described by the distinguished British average adjuster C. T. Ellis as a *quid pro quo*, or "tit for tat." The "tit" was the fact that the cargo owner received his cargo earlier, and the "tat" was that the shipowner recovered the wages and maintenance of crew in general average (British Association of Average Adjusters report, 1965, p. 16).

In 1967 the British marine insurance market adopted a Standard Form of Non-Separation Agreement, which reads as follows:

> It is agreed that in the event of the vessel's cargo or part thereof being forwarded to original destination by other vessel, vessels or conveyances, rights and liabilities in general average shall not be affected by such forwarding, it being the intention to place the parties concerned as nearly as possible in the same position in this respect as they would have been in the absence of such forwarding and with the adventure continuing by the original vessel for so long as justifiable under the law applicable or under the Contract of Affreightment.
>
> The basis of contribution to general average of the property involved shall be the values on delivery at original destination unless sold or otherwise disposed of short of that destination; but where none of her cargo is carried forward in the vessel she shall contribute on the basis of her actual value on the date she completes discharge of her cargo.

It will be noted that this form is confined to the major question of general average allowances after the cargo has been forwarded. The treatment of the actual cost of forwarding is not dealt with, and any special arrangements in this connection would have to be the subject of a separate agreement. Otherwise, the cost of forwarding will now have to be dealt with in accordance with the provisions of Rule F.

When a vessel is operating under a time charter and the time charterer enters into separate contracts with cargo interests, difficulties and questions often arise as to the respective rights and obligations of the shipowner and the time charterer when the vessel is under general average. In such cases, the time charterer is responsible for delivering the cargo to destination under the contracts of affreightment and it is therefore his responsibility to arrange for the transshipment of cargo from a port of refuge if such a course is indicated. It follows that the forwarding expenses to be considered in general average are the extra expenses incurred by the time charterer, and such expenses will normally be confined to actual out-of-pocket expenses but would include any freight actually paid to a third party unconnected with the adventure.

It is, of course, open to the carrier and cargo interests to incorporate in non-separation of interest agreements any conditions which are mutually acceptable. The intention of such agreements is to avoid any disputes as to the liabilities; and if this purpose is to be achieved, the conditions must be equitable and the effect to be given to them in the general average adjustment should be clear and explicit.

It must again be emphasized that a forwarding or non-separation of interest agreement can only be justified if the carrier is entitled to hold the cargo under the original contract of affreightment. As we have seen, this and the interrelated question as to when the carrier (if so desiring) may legally abandon the voyage, is often extremely difficult to determine. In American forwarding agreements, cargo underwriters often insist on the inclusion of the following clause:

> It is understood that the amount charged to cargo under this agreement shall not exceed what it would have cost the cargo owners if cargo was delivered to them at [the port of refuge] and forwarded by them to destination.

This clause, commonly known as the Bigham clause, gives the concerned in cargo a guarantee that, come what may, by signing the non-separation of interest agreement he will never be called upon to contribute in general average more than the equivalent of a second freight. In other words, at the very worst, he will be placed in the same position as if he had taken delivery of his cargo at the port of refuge. The clause purports to reflect the legal position and no doubt it is an excellent solution from the point of view of cargo interests, guaranteeing them as it does the wisdom of hindsight. On the other hand, the shipowner is put in a nebulous position and no weight is given to the advantage accruing to cargo interests by reason of a prompt delivery without payment of a second freight.

In 1989 a non-separation agreement was approved by the Association of Average Adjusters of the United States and the American Institute of Marine Underwriters for general use in the American marine insurance market that reads as follows:

> NON-SEPARATION AGREEMENT. In the event that the cargo or any part thereof is forwarded to its original destination by the vessel owner or charterer using other vessels or land conveyances, rights and liabilities in general average shall not be affected, it being the

intention of the parties that they shall be, as nearly as possible, in the same position as if there had been no forwarding and the adventure had continued in the original vessel as long as justified by law and the contract of affreightment.

Contribution to general average shall be based upon values at the original destination except that cargo not forwarded to destination shall contribute on its value where disposed of and the vessel, if it carries none of the cargo to destination, shall contribute on its value at completion of discharge. Rule XVII York/Antwerp Rules, 1974, if applicable, remains fully in force.

It is understood that the amount charged to cargo under this agreement shall not exceed what it would cost the cargo owners if cargo was delivered to them at the port of refuge and forwarded by them to destination.

It will be seen that this agreement is based in part on the British marine insurance market form referred to previously. However, the American Bigham clause (*q.v.*) has been incorporated. The main advantages achieved by the use of such standard forwarding agreements is that prompt action can be taken with regard to the forwarding of cargo and some degree of international uniformity is established. However, the problem as to whether in fact the carrier is entitled to hold the cargo under the original contract of affreightment (and is therefore entitled to ask the concerned in cargo to subscribe to such an agreement) remains to be dealt with in each individual case. The inclusion of the Bigham clause places a ceiling on cargo interests' contribution under the forwarding agreement and shipowners in particular should in every case seek advice from their average adjusters and/or their admiralty attorneys before entering into such agreements with cargo interests.

Forwarding agreements were the subject of the address of the chairman of the British Association of Average Adjusters in 1965, R. C. Clancey, and the address is an excellent source of reference.

Following a breakdown at sea, the cost of towing a vessel to destination (on a per diem cost basis) is often allowed in general average under Rule F as a substitution for the greater expense of putting into a port of refuge en route, discharging her cargo, effecting repairs, and then resuming her voyage. When a vessel is towed to destination, the shipowner obviously saves considerable fuel expenses. However, the voyage inevitably takes longer under tow and the shipowner incurs additional wages of crew. It is the practice of average adjusters to offset the saving in fuel by what is usually the greater amount paid in wages of crew. The result is that, in most cases, the cost of towage to destination is the full cost of the towage without any credit having to be given for voyage expenses saved. It should, perhaps, be added that even in cases where the vessel's destination is in fact the nearest port with repair facilities, the cost of towage (less any savings to the shipowner) is invariably allowed in general average on the grounds that the towage was incurred in lieu of what would undoubtedly be a greater salvage award.

An example of a substituted expense coming within Rule F is overtime worked on repairs at a port of refuge. Such overtime is allowed in general average up to the general average expenses saved thereby, and without regard to the saving, if any, to other interests.

When American law and practice applies (and not the York/Antwerp Rules), the extra cost of overtime worked on repairs is apportioned between general and particular average savings in accordance with Rule X of the Association of Average Adjusters of the United States, which reads:

> RULE X. OVERTIME WORK—GENERAL, AND PARTICULAR AVERAGE SAVING APPORTIONMENT. The bonus or extra cost of overtime work on repairs shall be allowed in general and/or particular average up to the amount of the saving of drydock dues or other charges, which otherwise would have been incurred and allowed in general and/or particular average; and where the overtime work effects a savings both of general average expense (excluding general average repairs) and in the cost of repairs, the extra cost for overtime shall be apportioned over the general average expenses saved and the savings in the cost of repairs.
>
> The Adjuster shall insert a note in the average statement in explanation of the allowances made.

Another example of substituted expenses is the allowance in general average of the extra cost of air freight incurred in expediting the transportation of repair parts. The Association of Average Adjusters of the United States has a rule (Rule XXI) which reads in part as follows:

> RULE XXI. AIR FREIGHT . . . Nevertheless when shipment by air saves General Average expense, the extra cost of shipment by air over the cost of water and/or land conveyance, shall be allowed in General Average up to the expense saved.

The allowance of the extra cost of air freight as a substituted expense has sometimes been criticized on the grounds that air freight is now the normal, accepted, and universal method of transporting repair parts. However, even if it is conceded that we have now reached the point where air freight is the normal method of transporting repair parts (and this is difficult to substantiate as long as some parts move by land or sea), there still seems to be no valid reason why (when a vessel is under general average) cargo interests should not contribute to the cost of expediting the repairs and completing the adventure. It is submitted that regardless of whether or not the shipowner might incur such expenses even if the vessel were not under general average, this should not preclude such expenses from qualifying as extra expenses within the meaning of Rule F. In fact, the same principle is endorsed by Rule XIV of the York/Antwerp Rules in connection with temporary repairs.

The treatment of the extra cost of air freight as being a first charge on general average has been upheld by the Canadian courts in *Western Canada Steamship Co. v. Canadian Commercial Corp.* (1960 2 L. L. R. 313). In that case, an aircraft was chartered to fly a replacement tailshaft from Wales to Singapore, and the Canadian Supreme Court held that this was an extra expense incurred in place of the expense which would have been involved if the vessel had been required to remain at Singapore while a shaft was being sent out by sea.

The one example of substituted expenses specifically dealt with in the numbered rules is the treatment of temporary repairs to accidental damage. Rule XIV of the York/Antwerp Rules reads:

RULE XIV. TEMPORARY REPAIRS. Where temporary repairs are effected to a ship at a port of loading, call or refuge, for the common safety, or of damage caused by general average sacrifice, the cost of such repairs shall be admitted as general average.

Where temporary repairs of accidental damage are effected *in order to* enable the adventure to be completed, the cost of such repairs shall be admitted as general average without regard to the saving, if any, to other interests, but only up to the saving in expense which would have been incurred and allowed in general average if such repairs had not been effected there.

No deductions "new for old" shall be made from the cost of temporary repairs allowable as general average.

This rule deals with the effecting of temporary repairs in three different circumstances, namely: (1) for the common safety, that is, the physical safety of ship and cargo; (2) repairs of damage caused by general average sacrifice; (3) repairs of accidental damage to enable the adventure to be completed.

The first two categories are admissible as general average automatically, the first coming within the definition of general average as laid down in Rule A and the second being a direct consequence of a general average act. Temporary repairs coming within the third category are only allowable in general average as a substituted expense, up to the amount of the general average expenses saved thereby (without regard to the savings, if any, to other interests).

It must be stressed that where temporary repairs are effected at a port of refuge "merely to enable the adventure to be completed" (the third category above), they cannot be admitted in general average if permanent repairs were not possible at that port of refuge. In such circumstances, there was clearly no choice and the principle of substituted expenses could not apply. The temporary repairs would thus become part of the reasonable cost of permanent repairs. However, in such cases, if there was a practical alternative whereby the vessel could have been removed to a second port of refuge where permanent repairs could be carried out but instead temporary repairs are effected at the first port, it would be proper to treat the cost of the temporary repairs as a substituted expense. The question whether permanent repairs were or were not possible at the port of refuge would not affect the allowance in general average of temporary repairs effected either for the common safety or of damage caused by general average sacrifice (the first two categories covered by Rule XIV).

The words "*in order to*" in the second paragraph of the rule replace the words "merely to" in the 1950 Rules for the sake of clarity.

On the subject of temporary repairs, American law is even more generous than the York/Antwerp Rules, and the American attitude thereto is a good example of the "benefit of adventure" theory as opposed to the "attainment of safety" theory. In the United States, reasonable temporary repairs are treated as general average if they were necessary for the safe prosecution of the voyage, and it is immaterial whether or not permanent repairs could be effected at that time or place (*Shoe* v. *Craig*, 189 Fed. Rep. 227). However, Phillips stresses that temporary repairs must be of "no particular benefit to the shipowner, and leave him subject to the same expense in prosecuting the voyage, and subsequently making repairs, as if the same had not been made."

Temporary repairs to damage caused by a general average sacrifice which are effected after the general average voyage has been completed and the cargo delivered do not come within Rule XIV but may be allowable under Rule XVIII.

Sometimes it has been suggested that average adjusters accept without much investigation the alleged alternative course for which the substituted expenses are substituted: they are content to charge the lesser sum to general average under the strict terms of Rule F. It is true that the alternative course is often outrageously expensive. An example of this would be when the alternative is to charter a tanker for use as a storage vessel at a port of refuge when no storage facilities are available. The more economical alternative in such circumstances is to charter the tanker to take the cargo to destination, the cost of which is often allowed in general average either under the terms of a special agreement or as a substituted expense under Rule F. The greater the difference between the cost of the two alternatives, the more obvious it would seem for the cheaper one to be adopted. Taking a strictly legal view, however, it might be argued that the lesser cost ought not to be treated as a substituted expense because the alternative expenditure could not really be regarded as reasonable; in other words, that there was no real alternative. However, the principle of substituted expenses was no doubt incorporated into the York/Antwerp Rules for the purpose of avoiding the necessity of obtaining a special agreement in every case, and average adjusters customarily look at these matters from a practical, commercial viewpoint. This is not to say that average adjusters do not have a responsibility to see that the principle of substituted expenses is not abused. The whole purpose of general average is to extricate ship and cargo from the peril that threatens and, thereafter, from the commercial dilemma that often flows from the general average act. If the course adopted is reasonable and achieves its objective, ship and cargo interests are usually content to share the general average expenditure that has been incurred for the common safety and common benefit.

The chairman of the British Association of Average Adjusters in 1988, D. J. Wilson, dealt with the subject of substituted expenses in his somewhat controversial address to the association. The chairman emphasized that it was the average adjuster's duty to closely examine the alternative course of action put forward to justify the allowance in general average of the expenses actually incurred as substituted expenses. In particular, the normal contractual obligations of the carrier to the concerned in cargo should be considered and the allowance in general average of substituted expenses should not be based on "ludicrous" alternative courses of action. This danger has always been present and the chairman was correct to warn against the abuse of the principle of substituted expenses. However, most qualified average adjusters can be relied upon to interpret the York/Antwerp Rules in a manner which is equitable to both ship and cargo interests.

Commission and Interest

The object of a general average adjustment is to place all the parties to the adventure in the same position regardless of which of them initially sustained the loss or incurred the expenditure. To achieve this result it is not sufficient merely to reimburse the party who has suffered the financial loss. He may be out of pocket for a considerable time before collections are effected under the adjustment and the loss equalized. With this in mind, the York/Antwerp Rules provide for the allowance of commission and interest on disbursements and allowances.

Rule XX deals with commission and reads as follows:

RULE XX. PROVISION OF FUNDS. A commission of 2 percent of general average disbursements, other than the wages and maintenance of master, officers and crew and fuel and stores not replaced during the voyage, shall be allowed in general average, but when the funds are not provided by any of the contributing interests, the necessary cost of obtaining the funds required by means of bottomry bond or otherwise, or the loss sustained by owners of goods sold for the purpose, shall be allowed in general average.

The cost of insuring money advanced to pay for general average disbursements shall also be allowed in general average.

The commission accrues to the benefit of the party authorizing the expenditure and liable for its payment (usually the shipowner). However, if the funds for payment are provided in the first instances from general average deposits, the commission is credited to the depositors providing the funds. Similarly, if any other party to the adventure, or underwriters, provide the funds for payment, the commission on such advances is credited accordingly. In short, the allowance of advancing commission is to compensate the party or parties who either pledge their credit or actually provide the funds to pay general average disbursements. The rule is often particularly helpful in cases where, for one reason or another, the provision of funds in the first instance presents difficulties. It has been suggested that under Rule XX commission is only allowed on disbursements incurred during the voyage. In practice, average adjusters do not differentiate between general average disbursements or expenses incurred during the voyage and, for example, repair expenses incurred after the voyage in quantifying a general average sacrifice.

Under American practice (in the absence of the York/Antwerp Rules) a commission of $2\frac{1}{2}$ percent is allowed on general average disbursements for advancing funds (Gourlie, p. 429).

The last paragraph of Rule XX relates to the universal practice of insuring general average disbursements incurred at a port of refuge for the remainder of the voyage to destination. This is for the reason that, if the vessel and cargo were lost before delivery of the cargo at destination, the shipowner would have no way of collecting cargo's share of the general average. Alternatively, if the vessel or cargo sustains further damage on the voyage before reaching destination, the proportions payable by the vessel and cargo respectively would differ from the proportions payable by each on the basis of the values at the time the voyage was resumed. The general average disbursements to be insured comprise all the general average expenses incurred at the port of refuge, including wages and overtime of crew. The allowance in general average for provisions of crew and fuel and stores should not be insured unless they were actually replaced at the port of refuge. Nor should general average commission and interest or adjusting fees be insured. If damaged cargo is discharged at the port of refuge and delivered to its owners, it is advisable that any general average allowance to which that cargo is entitled be included as part of the general average disbursements to be insured.

In the event of any subsequent accident, the underwriters insuring the general average disbursements are liable for the amounts not recovered by reason of the contributory values of ship and cargo having been reduced or extinguished as a result of the subsequent accident. However, in adjusting claims under the average disbursements policy, it must be remembered that the insurance does not cover the proportion of *general average* attaching to the diminution in value of the property, but rather covers the proportion of the *general average disbursements* attaching thereto. In stating claims under the policy, therefore, only the proportion of the *general average disbursements insured* attaching to the diminution is recoverable. When the amount recoverable from the average disbursements underwriters has been ascertained, it is first applied to restore to the parties concerned the respective increase in their contributions, any balance afterwards being distributed pro rata to all contributors.

A set of clauses used in insuring general average disbursements in the United States is shown in Appendix E. To illustrate the practical application of the clauses, let us assume a case where general average expenditures at a port of refuge totaled $65,000 and was insured for that amount. Without any further accident, the general average would have been apportioned as follows:

Ship	$400,000	pays	$40,000
Cargo	200,000	pays	20,000
Freight at Risk, net	50,000	pays	5,000
	$650,000		$65,000

(or 10 percent contribution)

As a result of a subsequent accident, the values at destination were reduced and, in the absence of an insurance on average disbursements, the apportionment would have been made as follows:

Ship	$220,000	pays	$35,750
Cargo	140,000	pays	22,750
Freight at Risk, net	40,000	pays	6,500
	$400,000		$65,000

(or 16.25 percent contribution)

The claim on underwriters insuring average disbursements would be arrived at as follows:

Diminution in contributory values $250,000 at the original rate of contribution of 10 percent equals $25,000.

The apportionment of this amount and the final position would be:

	Would Pay	Did Pay	Excess Paid to Rank in Priority	Net Payment to Participate in General Distribution	General Distribution
Ship	$40,000	$35,750	—	$35,750	$12,210
Cargo	20,000	22,750	2,750	20,000	6,830
Freight at Risk	5,000	6,500	1,500	5,000	1,710
(net)	$65,000	$65,000	$4,250	$60,750	$20,750

Ship

To pay per adjustment	$35,750	
To receive credit for	12,210	
To pay	$23,540	
		$23,540

Cargo

To pay per adjustment	22,750	
To receive credit for $2,750 plus $6,830	9,580	
To pay	13,170	
		$13,170

Freight at Risk, net

To pay per adjustment	6,500	
To receive credit for $1,500 plus $1,710	3,210	
To pay	3,290	
		$3,290
		$40,000

General Average as above	$65,000
Less recovery from insurance on average disbursements	25,000
	$40,000

This American method of allocating the recovery from average disbursements underwriters among the different interests produces a slightly different result from that reached in the United Kingdom. In that country the recovery from the insurance on average disbursements ($25,000) is simply credited against the total general average ($65,000) and the resultant balance of $40,000 is apportioned over the final contributory values of ship, cargo, and freight ($400,000).

Advancing commission dealt with in Rule XX of the York/Antwerp Rules should not be confused with *collecting commission*—which is peculiar to American law and practice. A commission of 2½ percent is allowed in general average for *collecting and settling* the general average in all average adjustments where the general average is stated:

(1) In accordance with American law,

(2) According to the York/Antwerp Rules supplemented by American law or usage,

(3) According to the York/Antwerp Rules and the adventure terminates at a U.S. port including territories and insular possessions.

In *Barnard* v. *Adams* (10 How. 270), the U.S. Supreme Court said:

> The two and a half percent allowed for collecting the general average rests upon the usage and custom of merchants and average brokers. It [collecting] is a duty arising out of the unforeseen disaster and resulting directly from it.

The propriety of this commission was upheld by the U.S. Supreme Court in a case where vessel and cargo were of the same ownership (the *Gulf of Venezuela*, 1929 AMC 796). However, in ballast general average cases, collecting commission is customarily waived.

General average interest is dealt with by Rule XXI of the York/Antwerp Rules as follows:

RULE XXI. INTEREST ON LOSSES MADE GOOD IN GENERAL AVERAGE. Interest shall be allowed on expenditure, sacrifices and allowances charged to general average at the rate of *7 percent per annum*, until the date of the general average statement, due allowance being made for any interim reimbursement from the contributory interests or from the general average deposit fund.

There is a significant change in this rule, the rate of interest being increased from the 5 percent per annum allowed under the 1950 Rules to 7 percent per annum under the 1974 Rules. This is in accord with generally rising interest rates.

Unlike general average commission, general average interest is allowed on allowances as well as disbursements and accrues to the party who sustained the loss or made the disbursements. As the rule indicates, if any reimbursement is made by any of the other parties to the adventure, those parties are entitled to participate in the interest allowed in general average subsequent to the date of reimbursement.

Where the general average adjustment is prepared in accordance with American law and practice and where the York/Antwerp Rules do not apply, interest is allowed on general average disbursements and allowances for the estimated period of the outlay at the legal rate prevailing at the place of adjustment (*Sims* v. *Willing*, 8 Ser. L. R. 103; brig *Mary*, 1 Sprague 17). The Association of Average Adjusters of the United States has a rule to that effect, as follows:

RULE II. INTEREST ON ALLOWANCES IN GENERAL AVERAGE. Where allowances, sacrifices or expenditures are charged or made good in general average, interest shall be allowed thereon at the legal rate prevailing at the place of adjustment.

References to the "place of adjustment" refer to the laws and rules which prevail at the port of destination when the voyage is completed (Coe).

Unlike the interest allowed under the York/Antwerp Rules, interest allowed when the adjustment is prepared in accordance with American law is extended beyond the date of the general average adjustment to the estimated date when settlements should have been effected under the adjustment (usually some two or three months beyond the date of the general average adjustment).

When cargo is consigned to several ports of discharge having varying rates of interest, it is usual to allow interest at the rate prevailing at the last port of discharge for the reason that this is the "final" port of destination.

It is the practice of American average adjusters to allow (though not in general average) advancing commission and interest on special charges on cargo or freight on the same basis as on general average disbursements and allowances. However, collecting commission is not allowed on such items.

BASIS OF CONTRIBUTION

The interests which have been saved by the general average act (usually ship, cargo, and freight) are required to contribute to the general average on the basis of the value of the property saved, to which should be added any amounts made good in general average.

What has been saved by the general average act can be determined only at the completion of the adventure—insofar as cargo is concerned on the basis of its value at the port or ports of destination and insofar as the ship is concerned on the basis of its value at the last port to which any of the cargo on board at the time of the general average act is consigned.

In this connection, Rule G of the York/Antwerp Rules provides as follows:

RULE G. General average shall be adjusted as regards both loss and contribution upon the basis of values at the time and place when and where the adventure ends.

This rule shall not affect the determination of the place at which the average statement is to be made up.

Rule XVII of the York/Antwerp Rules deals more specifically with contributory values, as follows:

RULE XVII. CONTRIBUTORY VALUES. The contribution to a general average shall be made upon the actual net values of the property at the termination of the adventure *except that the value of cargo shall be the value at the time of discharge ascertained from the commercial invoice rendered to the receiver or if there is no such invoice from the shipped value. The value of the cargo shall include the cost of insurance and freight unless and insofar as such freight is at the risk of interests other than the cargo, deducting therefrom any loss or damage suffered by the cargo prior to or at the time of discharge. The value of the ship shall be assessed without taking into account the beneficial or detrimental effect of any demise or time charter party to which the ship may be committed.*

To *these* values shall be added the amount made good as general average for property sacrificed, if not already included, deduction being made from the freight and passage money at risk of such charges and crew's wages as would not have been incurred in earning the freight had the ship and cargo been totally lost at the date of the general average act and have not been allowed as general average; deduction being also made from the value of the property of all *extra* charges incurred in respect thereof subsequently to the general average act, except such charges as are allowed in general average.

Where cargo is sold short of destination, however, it shall contribute upon the actual net proceeds of sale, with the addition of any amount made good as general average.

Passenger's luggage and personal effects not shipped under bill of lading shall not contribute in general average.

As we have already seen in connection with Rule XVI, the abandonment of the use of landed values of cargo for allowances in general average and in assessing contributions to general average represents a great simplification in the adjustment of general average. The value to be used under the 1974 Rules is the *invoice value* at the time of discharge ("the commercial invoice rendered to the receiver"), that is to say, the cost to the receivers of cargo. If there is no such invoice, the shipped value is to be used. The term "shipped value" means the value of the cargo at the place of shipment. It does not necessarily mean the replacement cost to the shipper but rather the value to anyone at that time and place. The principle of using arrived values for contribution to general average should be maintained; therefore, the cost of getting the cargo to its destination should also be taken into account. In short, when cargo is shipped without an invoice being rendered to the receiver, the average adjuster must assess the contributory value as best he can from the shipped value (Lowndes & Rudolf, 10th Ed., p. 820). In either case, the freight is to be included if it has been prepaid or guaranteed, vessel lost or not lost. Special provision is made for those cases where cargo is sold short of destination. In such circumstances the actual net proceeds of sale form the basis in arriving at the cargo's contributory value. However, if any property has been sacrificed and made good in general average, such allowance must be added to the value of that interest because its value has been increased by the allowance made in general average. If this was not done, the property sacrificed would finish up in a more favorable position than the remaining interests. The rule does not deal with the computation of the contributory value of damaged cargo which is sold at destination. This omission has caused some difficulty among average adjusters but the consensus is that in such situations the contributory value should be the net proceeds of sale plus any amount made good in general average. The amount to be made good would, of course, be computed in accordance with Rule XVI.

Under Rule XVII, deductions must be made "from the *value of the property* of all extra charges incurred in respect thereof subsequently to the general average act." The deductions refer to all the property involved in the general average and authorizes, for example, the deduction from the value of the vessel of repairs effected at the port of refuge. The object of the rule in authorizing the deduction (*inter alia*) of the cost of all repairs effected to the vessel subsequent to the general average act is to avoid bringing into contribution money spent on the vessel after the general average act. However, it is submitted that this part of the rule is inapplicable in those rare cases where deduction of the cost of repairs carried out at the port of refuge would result in a contributory value which is less than the scrap value of the vessel at destination. It is fundamental that what was saved by the general average act is the value of the vessel in its condition at that time; it is further submitted that that value can never be less than the scrap value of the vessel at destination. In arriving at the scrap value, regard must be had to the location of the vessel vis-à-vis the highest and/or the nearest scrap market. Unless the vessel can carry cargo to the port where she is to be scrapped, the cost of removing the vessel to that port and the crew repatriation costs would also have to be taken into account. Usually it is also a requirement that the vessel be delivered to the ship-breakers gasfree.

It is also necessary in computing contributory values to deduct the contributions made to any subsequent general average on the same voyage.

Thus, if a second general average occurs on the same voyage and the relative values of vessel and cargo are changed, the second general average is apportioned first and the contributions paid by ship, cargo, and freight to that general average are deducted from the respective contributory values when apportioning the original general average.

One result of the principles established by Rules G and XVII is that a shipowner incurring general average expenditure runs the risk of losing the right to contribution to that expenditure if the contributing interests or part of them are lost before the completion of the voyage. (See *Chellew v. Royal Commission on the Sugar Supply,* 1921 2 K. B. 627, 1922 1 K. B. 12, in which it was held that the shipowner could not recover from the cargo in general average as no values remained at the termination of the adventure upon which to apportion it.) In practice, such general average expenditure (disbursements) is insured and the cost of the insurance is allowable in general average.

American law and practice is in accord with Rules G and XVII of the York/Antwerp Rules except insofar as the use of invoice values in arriving at the value of cargo is concerned. When general averages are stated in accordance with American law and practice, landed values of cargo will normally be used, as was the case under the York/Antwerp Rules, 1950.

Contributory Value of Ship

Rule XVII of the York/Antwerp Rules stipulates that contribution to a general average is to be made on the actual net values of the property at the termination of the adventure.

In the United States it is customary to base the vessel's contributory value on the sale prices of similar vessels which have been sold by their owners within a recent period, making such adjustments as may be necessary to reflect the age and condition of the particular vessel being valued: "the worth of the thing is the price it will bring" (the *Blanche C. Pendleton,* 1924 AMC 382). It has never been the practice to take into consideration any charter party under which the vessel may be operating—whether it be remunerative or otherwise. In other words, the value generally used is the value of the vessel in the open market as if she were a free vessel without reference to the benefit which might accrue under her existing contractual obligations. This is in accord with the law of damages, it being fundamental that the measure of damages to be applied is the market value of a lost ship, if it has a market value at the time of destruction. This value is to be established by contemporaneous sales. Other evidence of value, such as reproduction cost depreciated, may be resorted to only when no market value can be established (*Standard Oil Co.* v. *Southern Pacific Co.,* 268 U.S. 146). As already indicated, any repairs effected at a port of refuge are deducted. It will be noted that Rule XVII now states "the value of the ship shall be assessed without taking into account the beneficial or detrimental effect of any demise or time charter party to which the ship may be committed." This, in effect, introduces into the York/Antwerp Rules the American practice regarding ship valuations. In the United Kingdom the courts have taken into account favorable charters but ignored unfavorable charters in assessing the sound value of a vessel (the *Castor*, 1932 Prob. Div. 142; the *San Onofre*, 14 Asp. 74). International uniformity is, therefore, achieved by this addition to Rule XVII. With regard to ship valuations generally, the reader is again referred to the chairman's address to the Association of Average Adjusters of the United States in 1985.

When there are two general averages arising out of the same accident and the contributory value of cargo changes (as when a vessel has stranded entering a first port of discharge with cargo on board for ports beyond), the second general average (comprising detention expenses at the port of discharge) is apportioned first. The first general average (consisting of refloating expenses) is then apportioned and, as no new accident has intervened, the contributory value of the vessel is usually the same in both apportionments. Sometimes, however, there are two entirely unconnected general averages at two ports of refuge on the same voyage with the second general average arising as a result of a new accident. In such cases, if permanent repairs to the damage giving rise to the first general average have been effected at the first port of refuge, then the cost of such repairs is not deducted from the sound value of the vessel in arriving at the contributory value for the second general average. The reason for this will be obvious: the vessel has been made sound after the first accident giving rise to the first general average, and must contribute to the second general average on the basis of a sound vessel. The normal deductions and amounts made good arising out of the second accident and second general average will, of course, be applicable.

Contributory Value of Freight

Whether freight earned on the voyage is at the risk of the carrier (and therefore a contributor to the general average) depends on the freight clause in the contract of affreightment. In the United States, in the absence of some stipulation to the contrary, the cargo must be carried to destination before any freight is earned. Even if the freight is paid in advance (as is often the case), unless there is an express stipulation to the contrary such payment must be earned by the proper delivery of the cargo, otherwise it must be repaid (*Salina Cruz*, 1953 AMC 837). However, if the freight is earned on shipment, "vessel lost or not lost," it becomes guaranteed freight and is non-returnable even if, due to an accident, the cargo is never delivered at destination. Such prepaid and guaranteed freight in effect becomes part of the value of the cargo, and the carrier is not required to contribute to the general average in respect thereof.

Freight at the risk of the carrier (collect freight payable at destination only on delivery of the cargo) must contribute to general average. The question to be posed in arriving at the contributory value of freight is, "What has been saved by the general average act?" The answer is the freight at risk (namely, that which is only payable at destination on the delivery of the cargo) less the expense (subsequent to the general average act) of earning that freight.

Thus, in computing the contributory value of shipowner's freight at risk, deduction is made from the gross freight at risk of all port charges (including discharging expenses if paid by the shipowner) and crew's wages incurred subsequent to the general average act in order to earn that freight (that is, up to the completion of discharge of cargo). As Rule XVII of the York/Antwerp Rules puts it, "deduction being made from the freight . . . at risk, of such charges and crew's wages as would not have been incurred in earning the freight had the ship and cargo been totally lost at the date of the general average act and have not been allowed as general average." In practice, no deduction is made for provisions of crew or fuel and stores if supplies sufficient to complete the voyage were already on board at the time of the general average act. If, however, fuel is purchased after the general average act, such part of that fuel as is *actually used* in completing the adventure should be deducted in arriving at the contributory value of the freight. The expenses deducted from the gross freight at risk to arrive at the contributory value are known as contingent expenses (that is, expenses necessarily incurred subsequent to the general average act to bring the vessel to destination and so earn the freight).

In the case of a vessel under time charter carrying cargo shipped under bill of lading with the bill of lading freight guaranteed, vessel lost or not lost, the shipowner escapes contribution on his time hire. This for the reason that in such a case the freight is included in the value of the cargo. Where the bill of lading freight is at risk—that is, *not* guaranteed—an apportionment is made between the interest of the shipowner and the charterer, according to the respective amounts each has at risk. It is therefore important to ascertain what expenses are payable by the shipowner and charterer respectively under the terms of the charter. The contingent expenses to be deducted from the voyage or bill of lading freight at the risk of and earned by the charterer will usually be comprised of the *charter hire* paid from the time of the completion of the general average act up to the completion of the discharge plus the port charges paid by the charterer up to the completion of discharge.

Example:

Bill of lading or voyage freight at risk of charterer			$20,000
Deduct:	Charter hire	$9,000	
	Port charges	4,000	13,000
			$7,000

In the example given, the charter hire deducted from the charterer's freight at risk ($9,000) becomes the charter hire at the risk of the *shipowner*, and usually the only contingent expenses payable by the shipowner and to be deducted therefrom are the wages of crew from the time of the completion of the general average act up to the completion of discharge of cargo.

Example:

Charter hire at risk of shipowner		$9,000
Deduct:	Wages	3,000
		$6,000

When there are a number of speculative subcharters, it is important to understand that it is the final bill of lading freight which constitutes the basis for computing the total contributory value of freight. This contributory value may be subdivided as appropriate among the various charterers but the total contributory value of the freight must not be reduced. In other words, the total contributory value of the final bill of lading freight at risk cannot be affected by preceding subcharters, even if one of those charters proved to be unfavorable.

Rule XIV of the Association of Average Adjusters of the United States deals in part with the contributory value of freight and is similar to Rule XVII of the York/Antwerp Rules. The relevant part reads as follows:

RULE XIV. FREIGHT—CONTRIBUTORY VALUE AND AMOUNT MADE GOOD IN GENERAL AVERAGE. The contributory value of freight shall be the amount at risk of the Shipowners or Charterers and earned on cargo on board, to which shall be added the allowance in general average for net freight lost, and from the total shall be deducted the expenses (except those allowed in general average) incurred to earn it after the date of the general average act; and if there be any cargo on board on which the freight is not at the risk of the Shipowners or Charterers, the charges to be deducted from the freight at their risk shall be only those which would have been incurred if such cargo had not been aboard . . .

Where the general average is prepared in accordance with York/Antwerp Rules and there be any cargo on board on which the freight is not at risk of the Shipowners or Charterers, the deductions made from the freight at their risk to arrive at the contributory value of freight shall be determined in accordance with the principles set forth above.

With regard to the contributory value of freight generally, Coe writes:

> While the general rule is that amounts made good contribute to the general average, there is one exception in regard to freight which is worth mentioning. In stating the contributory value of freight under York/Antwerp Rules, it is the practice to add the amount made good for freight to the amount of freight collectible at destination, and then to deduct the wages, port charges, etc. The result in some instances is that where the vessel is making an expensive voyage with a small freight list, the expenses deducted exceed the freight collectible and the amount made good, and there is no contribution. The reason for this is that if the amount made good contributed regardless of the deduction for expenses, the shipowner would not be in as good a position as he would have been if the property of another had been sacrificed.

It will have been seen that this American practice to which Coe refers is embodied in Rule XIV of the Association of Average Adjusters of the United States.

Charter Hire

It has always been a matter of controversy as to whether, when a vessel is under a time charter, time charter hire should contribute to general average. In Congdon's words, "General average recognizes only the vessel, the cargo and the freight named in the bill of lading." As we have seen, it is the practice of average adjusters to divide the contribution due from the voyage or bill of lading freight at risk between the time charterer and the shipowner. However, when a vessel is time chartered and *the time charterer is carrying his own cargo* (as is often the case when the U. S. government is the time charterer), time charter hire is not brought into contribution. In any event, if the voyage or bill of lading freight is guaranteed, vessel lost or not lost, the shipowner escapes contribution on his time charter hire because, in such cases, the freight is included in the value of the cargo.

Time Charterers' Bunker Fuel

When a vessel is under time charter it is customary for the charterer to supply his own bunker fuel. Prior to 1981 it was not the practice in the United States to require such bunker fuel to contribute in general average. The reason for this was that the value of such bunkers was negligible in comparison with the value of the ship and her cargo. The phenomenal rise in the cost of fuel oil in the seventies altered the situation. In the case of very large vessels, the value of bunker fuel on board could then amount to as much as a million dollars and it was no longer equitable to exclude this property of time charterers from contribution in general average. When bunkers are owned by the shipowner, this is (or should be) reflected in the value of the ship for contribution in general average. Old practices die slowly and it was not until 1981 that the executive committee of the American Association of Average Adjusters issued a memorandum to members stating that the practice of many American average adjusters to disregard time charterers' fuel as a contributing interest in general average could no longer be justified. It was also pointed out that in valuing vessels for general average purposes the value of bunker fuel on board at the completion of a general average voyage should be taken into account if the fuel was the property of the vessel owner.

It must be mentioned that any allowance in general average for time charterers' bunkers consumed, for example, in resorting to a port of refuge, should be treated as a general average sacrifice and added to the value of the bunkers remaining at the termination of the voyage in arriving at the contributory value of the bunkers.

Contributory Value of Cargo

The obtaining of contributory values of cargo is much simpler under the York/Antwerp Rules, 1974, which as we have seen call for the use of invoice values. However, in those rare cases when the general average statement is being prepared in accordance with American law and practice (to the exclusion of the York/Antwerp Rules) or under the York/Antwerp Rules, 1950, it will still be necessary to obtain landed values. The contributory value of cargo in such cases is the market value at destination (including profit) less certain charges, such as collect freight (if not guaranteed, vessel lost or not lost), landing charges, cartage, selling charges, duty, and other charges which would not have been incurred if the cargo had been lost before arrival. Particular or special charges payable in respect of the goods should also be deducted (the *Eliza Lines*, 102 Fed. Rep. 184).

In cases where the voyage is abandoned at the loading port, the contributory value of the cargo is its value at that port.

The market value at a port is the wholesale value for which the goods can be sold at that port. It is not the amount of the invoice for which the consignee purchases the goods from the shipper, notwithstanding that the consignee might be able to duplicate the shipment by ordering it from the shipper and paying for it the amount of the original invoice. The value for general average purposes is the value of the goods themselves at the place where the voyage ends. The wholesale market value of the goods in any place is the value for which the consignee can sell his goods to the trade.

Rule XVII of the Association of Average Adjusters of the United States deals in part with the contributory value of cargo which has been damaged and sold.

ARBITRARY CONTRIBUTORY VALUE OF CARGO. When a vessel is bound to ports abroad where experience has proved that the obtaining of accurate market values is difficult, it is the practice in the United States to use what are known as "built-up values." By this method the market value is assumed to be the invoice value including shipping charges (but not insurance premium). To this is added 10 percent for profit and, finally, the prepaid freight. The markup of 10 percent is only an expedient method of arriving at the wholesale market value, and the fact that a shipment is not intended for resale does not in itself preclude the addition of the 10 percent. The 10 percent is not added where the goods have been manufactured to a special order and would be of little or no value to anyone other than the firm for which they have been especially made. As a matter of interest, in a Canadian case involving the assessment of the value of cargo not replaceable locally, the court added 15 percent for estimated profit *(Mormacsaga* v. *Crelinsten Fruit Co.,* 1969 AMC 1621).

When the adventure is abandoned at a port of refuge and the goods are forwarded to destination, their value at the port of discharge can be deduced from the value realized at destination (the *Eliza Lines,* 102 Fed. Rep. 184). Thus, in such cases the contributory value is assumed to be the value at the port of destination (the invoice value under the 1974 Rules) less the cost of forwarding.

Contribution in Excess of the Contributory Values

Having considered the method of arriving at the contributory values of the various interests, the moment seems appropriate to discuss the question of the maximum contribution which can properly be claimed from each interest. While there is no direct authority for the proposition that liability for general average contribution can never exceed the contributory value, the practical difficulties in the way of a successful recovery of a liability in excess of 100 percent from the concerned in cargo are considerable. Gilmore & Black (pp. 241–42) go further and consider such a claim would not be in keeping with the principles of general average. It is difficult to see why this should be so because it is surely equitable to expect the interests imperiled to respond for reasonable general average expenditure incurred in good faith even if the cost should ultimately prove to have exceeded the value of the property saved. Indeed, hull underwriters have accepted the principle by agreeing in the Sue and Labor clause of the American Institute Hull Clauses to bear expenses reasonably incurred in salving or attempting to salve the insured vessel, even when the attempt is unsuccessful and a total loss is paid under the policy.

An interesting discussion of this subject is included in the report of the British Association of Average Adjusters, 1945 (p. 13 *et seq.*). The general feeling was that, under English law, there was no reason why general average in excess of 100 percent of the value of the property saved should not be paid in full by the interests sought to be saved. It was agreed, however, that the practical difficulties in the way of collecting more than 100 percent from cargo interests were almost insurmountable; as a consequent practice, contributions due from cargo were limited to 100 percent of value saved and delivered. The right of the shipowner to collect the excess general average from his hull underwriters is discussed later.

RATES OF EXCHANGE

For want of a better opportunity, it seems convenient to deal now with the vexed question of rates of exchange insofar as general average is concerned. In this connection, Coe states:

> Large fluctuations in exchange give rise to many disputes because of divergence of opinions as to the rate of exchange which should be adopted in the conversion of general average disbursements in currencies other than that of the port of destination. These were resolved in the case of the *Arkansas* (*Det Forenede Dampskibsselskab* v. *Ins. Co. of North America*, 1929 AMC 581). Expenses were incurred at ports of distress in Norway and England and were settled by drafts for which the Danish owners paid Danish kroners. The vessel's destination was Boston, and the United States Circuit Court of Appeals held that the Danish kroners should be converted into United States dollars at the rate of exchange prevailing at the termination of the adventure. The Court pointed out that salvage awards must be an exception for it will seldom be that they can be made until after the date of the ship's arrival and often will not be earned till then. The inference is that the Court intended such payments in a currency other than that of the place of destination (and any others incurred after the arrival of the vessel) should be converted into United States dollars at the rate of exchange current at the time they were made.

In the case of American-owned vessels, the general average clause in the contract of affreightment frequently contains the following:

In such adjustment, disbursements in foreign currencies shall be exchanged into United States money at the rate prevailing on the dates made and allowances for damage to cargo claimed in foreign currency shall be converted at the rate prevailing on the last day of discharge at the port or place of final discharge of such damaged cargo from the ship.

The object of this clause is to enable the general average adjustment to be stated in U.S. currency, even in cases where the vessel is bound to foreign ports. There is some doubt as to whether the clause could be successfully enforced in a foreign country if the consignees of cargo in that country demanded an adjustment in the currency of destination. Rates of exchange as they affect general average were dealt with by the chairman of the Association of Average Adjusters of the United States, Charles S. Haight, in his address in 1965. He recommended that a practice be established whereby the rate to be adopted in exchanging general average expenditures in other countries to the currency of the adjustment be the rate prevailing on the dates the expenditures were made; it was suggested that an exception might be made to the rule in cases where it was evident that there would not have been an immediate conversion into the currency of the adjustment, even if there had been prompt settlement of the expenditures in the currency abroad.

In practice, American average adjusters usually draw up the general average adjustment in U.S. currency, the dollar having generally been one of the stronger international currencies. In exchanging expenditure into the currency of the adjustment, the *Arkansas* formula is followed; that is to say, the rate of exchange prevailing at the termination of the adventure is used unless the actual payment of the expenditure incurred was made after that date, in which case the rate of exchange prevailing at the time of payment is used. Most European average adjusters also follow this practice although there is a not inconsiderable minority who favor using the rate of exchange prevailing at the date of the general average adjustment (or settlement).

Whenever international currencies fluctuate violently there will inevitably be difficulties, and in some cases hardships, as a result of exchanging from one currency to another—and there would appear to be no entirely satisfactory solution to such problems. The guiding principle is to endeavor to provide the party who has suffered a financial loss as a result of the general average act with as exact an indemnity as possible, reducing to a minimum any fortuitous profit or loss arising from the fluctuation in the rate of exchange. This is often difficult if not impossible to achieve and the average adjuster can only consider the facts carefully in each case and endeavor to see that, as far as possible, equity is achieved.

TUG AND TOW

The same principles of general average which apply to a single ocean vessel apply also to a maritime adventure comprising a flotilla of vessels under tow. In the classic definition of general average in Rule A of the York/Antwerp Rules: "There is a general average act, when, and only when, any extraordinary sacrifice or expenditure is intentionally and reasonably made or incurred for the common safety for the purpose of preserving from peril the property involved in a common maritime adventure." The common maritime adventure envisaged by the York/Antwerp Rules is that existing between a vessel and its cargo. But what of the situation where a tug is towing (or pushing) several barges, each containing cargo? It should be noted that the property involved in a common maritime adventure must have been preserved from peril if a general average act is to be claimed. What then is the position if a fire breaks out on a barge at the end of a long tow—perhaps as much as a mile away from the tug—and general average sacrifices are made or general average expenditure incurred to save the *barge and its cargo*? It has been suggested that the tug (and any other vessels in the flotilla) should be brought into contribution if the tug was engaged in a contract of affreightment but not if it was engaged in a contract of towage. This contention appears to make a lottery out of general average. Yet that is what has been endorsed by one U.S. district court.

It has generally been the practice of average adjusters throughout the world to require only the vessel (or vessels) actually in peril, and therefore concerned in the general average act, to contribute to the general average together with its (or their) cargo. This practice was initially based on the *J. P. Donaldson* (167 U.S. 599) case in which the U.S. Supreme Court said:

> It is solely for the purpose of performing the contract of towage that the vessels towed are put under the control and management of the master of the tug. In all other respects, and for all other purposes, they remain under the control of their respective masters; and, in the case of unforeseen emergency, it is upon the master of each that the duty rests of determining what shall be done for the safety of his vessel and of her cargo. If the question arises whether it is safer for one of the barges to continue in tow, or to cut loose and anchor, the decision of that question ultimately belongs to her master, and not to the master of the tug. And if the question presented is either whether the barge should be run ashore for the purpose of saving her cargo, or else whether a part of the whole of the cargo of the barge should be sacrificed in order to save the rest of her cargo, or the barge itself, the decision of the question whether such stranding or jettison should not be made is within the exclusive control of the master of the particular

barge, and in no degree under the control of the master of the tug; and, in either case, *any right of contribution in general average cannot extend beyond that barge and her cargo.*

This decision has always been taken to establish that there is no community of interest between a tug and its tow insofar as general average is concerned. It is further submitted that even if the barges were unmanned and that consequently general average decisions had to be taken by the master of the tug, this would not alter the position. Since he was in charge of each barge, as well as the tug, the master would be carrying out a general average act for the benefit of that particular barge which was imperiled. In short, if only one barge and its cargo were in peril, it is they and they alone who benefited from the general average act and who must therefore contribute to the cost of their own salvation.

However, in a case involving a tug towing several barges, one court has drawn a distinction between situations where a tug is engaged in a contract of affreightment as opposed to situations where the contract was one of towage only. In *Sacramento Navigation Co. v. Salz* (1927 AMC 397), the U.S. Supreme Court had held that tug and tow, under common ownership while carrying a cargo under a contract of affreightment, constitute a single vessel by which the contract of transportation was effected. This was not a general average case at all; but in *Loveland 33* (1963 AMC 260), a lower court seized on the decision and suggested that by parity of reasoning the tug and barge constituted a single vessel for the purposes of general average contribution. Such a conclusion appears to ignore the fundamental principles of general average. Whether the tug was or was not proceeding under a contract of affreightment is not germane in determining whether the tug and other barges (if any) were involved in the general average act. If the tug and other vessels in the flotilla were not in peril, they cannot have been "preserved from peril" as required in the classic and universal definition of general average quoted earlier. Absent peril, they were not, in fact, involved in the general average act; the sacrifice or expenditure was not made or incurred for the common safety of the tug and other barges at all. It is true that these vessels were able to complete the contract of affreightment (assuming one existed) but this has nothing to do with general average. Indeed, for example, any indirect loss whatsoever is not admissible as general average (Rule C, York/Antwerp Rules). The same principle applies to any indirect gain.

General average cases very seldom come before the courts; consequently very few judges or, for that matter, very few admiralty lawyers are familiar with the subject. As one court admitted (*Jean LaFitte*, 1967 AMC 905):

It must be remembered that general average adjusting is a highly specialized field. Most often, differences are resolved by specially trained adjusters in non-legal forums. Consequently, judicial interpretation of general average adjustments is rare. The Court therefore finds that the opinions of general average adjusters are significant in a case such as this.

In a similar strain, in an arbitration, a leading admiralty lawyer and former average adjuster (acting as an arbitrator) had this to say (*J. Whitney*, 1968 AMC 995):

Although the principles of the law of general average were recognized by Mediterranean merchants in the days of Rhodes, they did not come to the attention of our American Courts until the 19th century. For the last hundred years, however, these principles have been subjected to interpretation and misinterpretation by Judges whose experience in the subject was too often nil or ill. Many cases, though correctly decided, contain misleading dicta which taken out of context have given the impression that almost any predicament may justify a general average. The result has been almost chaotic, especially with respect to the doctrine upon which the entire edifice has been erected, namely, *peril*.

When the courts do get involved, bad law is often the result. This is what happened in the *Loveland 33* case (*supra*). A tug and several barges of the same ownership were engaged in a contract of affreightment. One of the barges was concerned in an accident as a result of which only that barge and its cargo were in peril. The court, by the parity of reasoning previously mentioned, decided that the entire flotilla should be required to contribute to the barge's general average sacrifices and expenses even though the rest of the flotilla were never in danger. The court seized on the fact that the tug and barges were of common ownership, linked this fact to the basic transportation agreement, and then lost sight of general average principles in reaching its determination. It cannot be stated too strongly that the right to contribute in general average does not arise from any contract of affreightment but rather from a general rule of international maritime law. General average is not a creature of contract—it is applicable even if there be no contract. The contract of affreightment may stipulate as to how any general average is to be drawn up, but it does not affect the fundamental principles of contribution, namely, that the entire property must have been in peril—not merely, for example, individual units of a tow. It is a familiar doctrine that a tug and its tow are not engaged in a common maritime adventure in the relationship of carrier and cargo. In any event, as has already been stated, the existence of a common maritime adventure is only part of the requirements for general average. The editors of the latest edition (10th) of Lowndes & Rudolf (p. 66) describe the *Loveland 33* decision as "surprising" since at the time of the general average act no common danger threatened the whole adventure.

The same general average question was squarely before the courts in the case of the *Mohican* (1934 AMC 112). In that case, the suggestion that the *J. P. Donaldson* case was not applicable in cases where the tug was engaged in a contract of affreightment and not one of towage was rejected by the court, which stated:

> General Average has to do with relations between the carrying vessel and its cargo, and respondent has cited no cases indicating a widening of the scope of this relationship so as to include a tug towing such carrying vessel. The fact that the *Sacramento* case held the tug and tow together constituted the "vessel transporting merchandise" within Section 3 of the Harter Act for purposes of exemption from liability is not sufficient reason for holding them to be one vessel for purposes of General Average adjustment. The right to such an adjustment existed long before the enactment of the Harter Act, and under the Maritime Law it now exists independently of that Act. The law of General Average is not applicable to the relationship between a tug and her tow.

Such has been the view of textbook writers and the practice of average adjusters throughout the world for over 75 years. As Carver put it, "it seems doubtful whether rights of contribution can ever arise as between interests which are at risk upon separate ships" (9th ed., p. 605). The editors of the 8th edition of Lowndes & Rudolf echoed this view with the comment (p. 34):

> Ship and cargo are necessarily involved in a common adventure but what of ship A and the cargo in ship B? It is submitted that only in the most exceptional cases could it be said that such interests were involved in a common adventure.

Despite their usual practice, average adjusters do not preclude a tug and all the vessels in its tow being called upon to contribute in general average in exceptional circumstances. However, this could only arise when the tug and all the units of its tow were actually in peril. If the entire flotilla is threatened by a common danger—that is to say, all the vessels are in peril—the master of the tug is necessarily in control of tug, barges, and cargo. Any general average act initiated by him *for the common safety of the entire flotilla* (such as a request for salvage assistance) would require contribution from all. This would be the case whether the tug was engaged in a contract of affreightment or in a contract of mere towage. In short, the type of contract—towage or carriage—is not the deciding factor; the twin elements of physical danger and benefit to all should control. In every case it is necessary to consider carefully whether there was a common peril or merely a danger threatening one, or some, or all interests in the flotilla. As the U.S. Supreme Court put it in *Hobson* v. *Lord* (92 U.S. 397):

> Property not in peril requires no such sacrifice, nor that any extraordinary expense should be incurred; and property not saved from the impending peril is not required to pay any portion of such a loss or expenditure . . .

This sentiment was repeated by a well-known American average adjuster (Congdon, 1st ed., p. 10):

> It must always be borne in mind that the primary and indispensable requisite, and the very foundation upon which the law of general average is based, *is a common peril to be avoided* . . .

Congdon's stricture of 1913 was reiterated by the Committee on Rules and Practice of the Association of Average Adjusters of the United States in 1966 when it stated that the general practice in the United States is not to treat a tug and its tow as one vessel for the purpose of general average adjustment. Only if the entire flotilla is in peril and the general average sacrifice or expenditure is made or incurred for the safety of all are all units of the flotilla required to contribute in general average. This "flotilla doctrine" characterizing a tug and its tow as a single vessel applies only to claims based on contract, and general average is not a creature of contract.

This fascinating aspect of general average was the subject of K. W. Hext's address as chairman of the Association of Average Adjusters of Canada in 1984. The history of the practice of average adjusters on the West Coast of Canada and the United States is dealt with exhaustively in the address and an up-to-date viewpoint is provided. Subsequently, Hext, responding to a questionnaire from the European Average Adjusters' Association on the subject of tugs and their tows in general average situations, expressed the opinion that Canadian law was silent as to there being a possibility of general average involving both tug and tow and that on balance he thought that this would be an extension of the normal community of interest involving a vessel and its cargo. However, in his address to the Canadian association, Hext agreed that salvage rendered to a flotilla would seem to be an exception. In his words:

> Salvage would appear to be the exception since it arises as an external factor, namely services performed by a third party which are a matter

of fact. If those services relate to more than one vessel and are rendered jointly, then the salving party will look to those vessels to respond to his demand for recompense and there is little option but for each to respond rateabley, be it on a joint-values basis or as separate entities contributing to separate charges.

In his address Hext had referred with approval to the Canadian case of *Northland Navigation Co. Ltd.* v. *Patterson Boiler Works Ltd.* (1985 AMC 465), where a disabled tug cut its loaded tow adrift in heavy weather with knowledge that the tow would either strand or sink. However, the court's decision that the tug need not contribute in general average to the resultant expenditure to rescue the stranded barge and its cargo raises some doubts among average adjusters. In such situations the questions to be asked are whether the cutting adrift in itself was a general average act to save the tug alone, to save the barge and its cargo, or to save the tug, the barge, and its cargo. The facts in such cases have to be considered carefully and the general average adjusted accordingly. It is submitted that if, in the *Northland* case, the entire flotilla was in peril at the time the tug cut the towline, as appears to have been the case, the general average should have been stated on the tug and the expenditure incurred in salving the barge and its cargo allowed in that general average. This on the grounds that the stranding of the barge with its cargo was the direct consequence of the tug's general average act of cutting adrift (or sacrificing) the tow as the best chance of saving the most property. Given that situation, on grounds of equity alone, it would seem appropriate to bring the barge and its cargo into contribution with the tug (including amounts made good in general average). The result then would be that all parties would finish up bearing the general average proportionately based on the respective values of the property saved (including amounts made good in general average).

The topicality of this problem of tug and tow in general average situations was further demonstrated by the fact that in 1986 the chairman of the Association of Average Adjusters of the United States, L. A. Walsh, chose to tackle the subject in his address to the association. After a review of the general situation he supported the American adjusting practice of only bringing into contribution those vessels and their cargoes which were actually in peril at the time of the general average act. Other vessels not in peril should not contribute and it was irrelevant whether the tug and barge(s) are of the same ownership and acting in concert in providing a transportation service. The chairman also dealt with a new type of tug and tow in his address—the integrated tug-barge (ITB). This system consists of specially designed tugs and barges, so constructed that they are joined together to form a single unit. The joining or mating procedure is complex and the units are intended to work only as a matched set. The chairman reached the conclusion that ITBs were in fact one vessel and should be treated as such in general average situations.

In summary, in determining whether all units of a flotilla must contribute in general average, one must look to the question of peril rather than look to the contract of transportation; or, to give an average adjuster the last word, as Congdon wrote (1st ed., Pref. vi):

> General average has its foundation in equity . . . [and] is not dependent on contract.

SECURITY FOR CONTRIBUTION

A claim for general average contribution accrues and becomes enforceable upon the arrival of the ship at her port of destination and the delivery of the cargo, not upon the completion of the general average adjustment (*United States of America* v. *Atlantic Mutual Insurance Co.*, 1936 AMC 993).

The shipowner has a lien upon cargo for general average contributions due from cargo (*Wellman* v. *Morse*, 76 Fed. Rep. 573), and cargo has a similar lien on the ship (the *Odysseus III*, 1948 AMC 608).

It is the duty of the master (on behalf of the shipowner) to take security from cargo interests before delivering the cargo. Should he fail to do so, the shipowner may be liable for the whole general average if he is unable to enforce contribution from cargo *in personam* (see below) (*Heye* v. *North German Lloyd*, 33 Fed. Rep. 60). In practice, the responsibility devolves upon the average adjusters appointed by the shipowner.

In most cases of general average it is the shipowner who must look to cargo interests for security. Nevertheless, in those rare cases where it is obvious from the outset that the owners of a bulk cargo or a major cargo interest in a general cargo case will be substantial creditors in the ultimate settlement of the general average, such cargo interests might be justified in asking for security from the shipowner.

This is a very rare situation, not only because most cases of general average do not involve specific cargo interests with an obvious substantial balance to receive, but also because even in such cases the cargo interests invariably rely on the financial stability of the shipowner backed by his hull underwriters. However, when appropriate, there is no reason why cargo interests should not request the shipowner to provide them with general average security. Assuming the facts warrant such a request, it would not be unreasonable for shipowners to look to their hull underwriters to provide a suitable form of guarantee to a cargo interest. Of course, any guarantee from hull underwriters would be subject to policy conditions, and before providing such a guarantee the underwriters might require a counter-guarantee from the shipowner to cover any deductible average in the hull policy or any under-insurance which might exist.

General Average Security

General average security consists of an average agreement (sometimes called average bond) signed by the owners of each shipment (usually the consignees) and, in addition, a cash deposit. If the goods are insured in the United States by an insurance company whose security is satisfactory, it is usual to accept the unlimited guarantee of such company in lieu of a cash deposit. Sometimes the shipowner is also prepared to accept the unlimited guarantee of internationally known insurance companies in lieu of a cash deposit. The average agreement or average bond is an undertaking by the owner of the goods to pay the general average contribution, salvage, or special charges due in respect of that shipment and to furnish particulars of its value so as to enable an average adjustment to be prepared.

The York/Antwerp Rules do not go into the question of general average security in principle, but Rule XXII deals with the treatment of cash deposits and reads as follows:

> RULE XXII. TREATMENT OF CASH DEPOSITS. Where cash deposits have been collected in respect of cargo's liability for general average, salvage or special charges, such deposits shall be paid without any delay into a special account in the joint names of a representative nominated on behalf of the shipowner and a representative nominated on behalf of the depositors in a bank to be approved by both. The sum so deposited, together with accrued interest, if any, shall be held as security for payment to the parties entitled thereto of the general average, salvage or special charges payable by cargo in respect to which the deposits have been collected. Payments on account or refunds of deposits may be made if certified to in writing by the average adjuster. Such deposits and payments or refunds shall be without prejudice to the ultimate liability of the parties.

The European Association of Average Adjusters has expressed the view that the average adjuster should be one of the trustees required by Rule XXII (Thirteenth General Assembly, 1985).

Deposits in foreign currency collected by the shipowner or his agents abroad are usually deposited in trust accounts abroad and not remitted to the average adjuster in the United States. This is to avoid any loss in the face value of the deposits by reason of any fluctuations in rates of exchange. In such cases, the responsibility of the trustee is limited to making the deposit available at the place and in the form in which it was collected.

In some instances, the shipowner prefers to have the general average deposits changed into U.S. currency (if possible) and remitted to the United States. This is no doubt preferable from a business point of view but, by doing so, the shipowner becomes liable to the depositors in the event of any adverse movement in the rate of exchange.

The practical operation of Rule XXII has been criticized in the United States as being cumbersome in that deposit receipts have to be signed by two trustees, that any payment from a trust account would have to be approved by two trustees, and that refunds from deposits, when settlements are made under the adjustment, would also have to be approved by two trustees. As a result, contracts of affreightment in the United States sometimes exclude Rule XXII, and it is the general practice to place the deposits in a *trust account* in the average adjuster's name only. Thus, the object of Rule XXII (which is security for the depositors) is achieved without the inconvenience of a joint account and the extra work which is inevitable in connection with such accounts.

In his capacity as trustee, the average adjuster cannot, of course, disburse the trust fund in accordance with the general average adjustment until he is satisfied, *as trustee*, that the liability of cargo to contribute to the general average is proved beyond doubt.

It has been held that a trustee of general average funds is entitled to have the fund pay the legal expenses of opposing efforts to charge the general average fund with unjustifiable disbursements. Furthermore, it was held in the *Sudbury* (1934 AMC 1096) that the legal expense of successfully defending the general average fund against certain parties whose claims, although bona fide, are defeated should be assessed proportionately against all those participating in the general average, and not solely against those whose claims have been defeated. In that case, certain cargo interests unsuccessfully brought action against the general average adjusters and trustees, claiming that they were entitled to a greater allowance in general average than had been made. In the same case, the average adjusters and trustees themselves brought action against certain cargo interests who had not paid the general average contribution shown to be due from them in the general average statement. It was agreed that these legal expenses also should be borne by the trust fund as a whole, that is to say, all the interests involved in the general average.

Right to Sue for Contributions

The shipowner may sue the owner of cargo for a general average contribution, and it has been held by the courts that the time to sue for a general average contribution commences to run when the right to demand the contribution arises (i.e., on delivery of the cargo). The time is not postponed until an average adjustment is issued (*Transpac S. S. Co.* v. *Marine Office of America*, 1957 AMC 1070). The reverse is apparently true in Japan where the Japanese one-year statute of limitation starts to run from the date of the average adjustment (*Percy Jordan*, 1968 AMC 2195). In the *Percy Jordan*, it was pointed out that a general average agreement or bond is merely a substitute for the common law lien for general average which the shipowner has against the cargo, and consequently the shipowner's rights should be no greater than what they would be if he were asserting his lien.

In *Aga* (1968 1 L. L. R. 431), it was held that even though a guarantee may be given by cargo underwriters to obtain the delivery of cargo, this does not preclude the vessel owner from suing on the average bond.

The accrual of the right to contribution does not depend upon whether it could be enforced by a suit *in rem* against the ship or cargo, as the case may be. Such a right accrues if and when all the elements essential to its existence are present, regardless of whether the appropriate means of enforcement be a suit *in rem* or a suit *in personam* (see *United States of America* v. *Atlantic Mutual Ins. Co.*, (1936 AMC 993). In that case the court commented:

> Various means of enforcing such [general average] have become well recognized such as a suit *in rem* in admiralty against ship or cargo, a suit *in personam* in admiralty against shipowner or cargo owner, and an action at law or a suit in equity against shipowner or cargo owner.

Generally speaking, the statutory time limit within which the shipowner may claim general average contribution is governed by the laws of the port of destination. The time limit governing suits arising out of written contracts is applicable. In most states, the time limit is six years, but notable exceptions are California (four years), Delaware (three years), Florida (five years), Illinois (ten years), Louisiana (ten years), Maryland (three years), Texas (four years), and Virginia (five years).

However, insofar as U.S. government cargo is concerned, the courts have held that an action by private steamship owners and carriers of U.S. government cargo must be brought under the Suits in Admiralty Act and the time limit is two years (*States Marine Corp.* v. *United States of America*, 1955 AMC 990).

Therefore, it behooves the average adjuster to bear the question of time limitation carefully in mind. If it becomes apparent that collections under the general average adjustment cannot be completed within two years (in cases involving U.S. government cargo) or the number of years stipulated by the law of the place of discharge (in cases involving commercial cargo) from the time of delivery of the cargo, the shipowner ought to be so advised. The shipowner can then take the necessary legal steps to preserve his general average lien.

The general understanding on both sides of the Atlantic that the time limitation in general average commences to run from the date of delivery of cargo was put in doubt by the surprising decision of the English House of Lords (Privy Council) in the case of *Castle Ins. Co. v. Hong Kong Islands Shipping Co. Ltd.* (the *Potoi Chau*), 1983 2 L.R. 376. Their lordships decided that time limitation for general average contributions from cargo runs from the date of the general average adjustment—not from the date of delivery of cargo. The decision is based on the premise that the contract of carriage invariably contains an express clause dealing with general average and so brings the claim to general average contribution into the field of contract law. The consignee of cargo has therefore a contractual liability (as opposed to a common law liability) and the time limitation dates from the accrual of the cause of action. Furthermore, the lords took the view that as reference is made in the bill of lading (or charter party) to the adjustment of general average according to the York/Antwerp Rules this implies that average adjusters are to be used to quantify the general average contributions; thus there is no cause of action until the general average adjustment is issued. It is doubtful whether this decision of itself will have any effect on the long-established American law and practice whereby the time limitation runs from the date of delivery of the cargo. It may, of course, encourage litigation in the United States in the future should either a shipowner or cargo interests decide to challenge the prevailing law and practice.

Liability of Cargo to Contribute

Before dealing with the general question of enforcing general average contributions against cargo interests, it must be understood that this is an entirely separate matter which has no bearing on whether or not a general average situation exists. The sole criterion as to whether a general average situation exists is whether (to borrow the definition of general average embodied in the York/Antwerp Rules), (a) any extraordinary sacrifice or expenditure is intentionally and reasonably made or incurred for the common safety for the purpose of preserving from peril the property involved in a common maritime adventure, or (b) expenditure is incurred under the circumstances envisioned in Rules X and XI. Whether or not claim for contribution can be enforced against the concerned in cargo, or indeed from hull underwriters, has no bearing whatever on whether there is a valid general average situation. As the English courts have said, "the Rhodian Law, which in that respect is the law of England, bases the right of contribution not upon the cause of damage but upon its actual presence" (*Strang, Steel & Co. v. A. Scott & Co.*, 14 App. 601). The position is the same in the United States; thus, any failure on the part of the carrier to fulfill his contractual obligation cannot alter the character of the general average act whether or not the carrier is at fault. If all the necessary elements of general average are present, a statement of general average is prepared by an average adjuster showing the contribution due from the various interests; it is then that the question of enforcing contributions under the adjustment arises. Although such a statement is not conclusive on the question as to cargo interests' liability to contribute (*Empire Stevedoring Co. Ltd.* v. *Oceanic Adjusters Ltd. et al.,* 1971 AMC 795), it is prima facie evidence of the details, computations, and allocation of the general average (the *Clydewater,* 1967 AMC 1474).

EFFECT OF FAULT. To understand the position in American law regarding the liability of cargo to contribute to general average, it is necessary to refer briefly to the law relating to the carriage of goods by sea. With the growth of shipping in the nineteenth century, so inevitably grew the potential liabilities of shipowners to the owners of the cargo they carried. Shipowners throughout the world attempted to escape liability to cargo by introducing clauses of every description into their contracts of affreightment, exempting them from claims for damage to or loss of cargo, whether resulting from their own negligence or not. In the United States, however, the courts took the view that any attempt by a carrier to exempt himself from liability for a loss caused by the negligence of himself or his servants was contrary to public policy and, therefore, void (*Liverpool & Great Western Steam Co.* v. *Phoenix Ins. Co.,* 129 U.S. 397).

The result of this and similar rulings by the courts of the United States was to place American shipowners at a great disadvantage compared with their foreign competitors. In an attempt to find a satisfactory solution fair to both shipowners and cargo interests, the Harter Act was passed by Congress in 1893. The act prohibited a shipowner from including in his contract of carriage any clauses exempting him from liability for "loss or damage arising from negligence, fault or failure in proper loading, stowage, custody, care or proper delivery" of the cargo. It also prohibited any clauses weakening or lessening the carrier's obligation to exercise due diligence to provide a seaworthy vessel. Furthermore, the act, rather surprisingly at that time, stipulated that if the shipowner used due diligence to provide a seaworthy vessel, he was to be exempted from liability for damage or loss resulting from "faults or errors in navigation or in the management of said vessel." The act applied to all shipments "from or between ports of the United States and foreign ports."

Returning to the matter of cargo's liability to contribute in general average, it must be borne in mind that one of the fundamental principles of the law of general average is that a guilty party in a maritime adventure cannot collect general average contributions from the other interests concerned in the adventure, if it was his guilt (or that of his servants) which gave rise to the necessity for the general average act. Moreover, the law of general average (unlike the law of marine insurance) does not embrace the principle of *causa proxima et non remota spectator* (looking to the immediate cause of an accident and not to the remote cause). Thus, even though a general average situation arises as the result of an accident such as stranding or collision (the immediate cause), the law of general average is that if the stranding or collision arose because of negligent navigation on the part of the master or the crew (the remote cause), then the shipowner (the master and crew being the servants of the shipowner) is not entitled to a general average contribution from the other parties to the adventure. Furthermore, if (as a result of the accident or general average act) those other interests themselves sustained losses, then (because of the negligence of his servants) the shipowner is responsible for making good such losses.

The effect of the Harter Act on the rights of shipowners to contribution in general average immediately became an important issue. It was contended by shipowners that Section 3 of the act, by exempting the shipowner from liability to cargo owners (under certain circumstances) for damages resulting from negligence, at the same time permitted him to receive general average contributions from cargo interests. However, the Supreme Court held that the Harter Act did not automatically give any *affirmative rights* in any general average resulting from the negligence (the *Irrawaddy*, 171 U.S. 187). In other words, while the shipowner was not responsible to the cargo owners for damage resulting from his servants' negligence, he, nevertheless, could not expect the cargo to contribute to his own loss.

The *Irrawaddy* case was followed by the *Strathdon* (94 Fed. Rep. 206, 101 Fed. Rep. 600). A fire had broken out in the cargo of the *Strathdon* and, in extinguishing it, water was used, causing damage to both the vessel and the cargo. In the general average adjustment, all sacrifices were treated as general average, but the owners of the cargo contended that the fire was the result of negligence on the part of the shipowners, that the vessel's sacrifices should not be allowed, and that the vessel must contribute to the sacrifices of cargo. The court held that, because the cargo had demanded contributions in general average, the vessel was entitled to offset against the cargo's claim to the extent of the cargo's proportion of the shipowner's expenses and sacrifices. In the words of Coe:

> This led to a most unsatisfactory state of affairs. It put the application of the doctrine of general average on a basis of self interest, as, if the shipowner's contribution to the cargo's sacrifices proved to be less than the cargo's contribution to the ship's sacrifices, the particular

cargo owner interested refrained from claiming in general average—a situation quite opposed to the principles of equity upon which general average is founded. In cases of vessels with general cargoes, where the sacrifices had arisen from negligent navigation, and the cargo of some shippers had been sacrificed and others not, the complications that ensued were practically interminable.

NEGLIGENCE GENERAL AVERAGE CLAUSE OR JASON CLAUSE.

The situation provoked by the *Strathdon* case gave birth to the negligence general average clause which shipowners inserted in contracts of affreightment in an attempt to nullify the courts' decisions. The original version of such clauses was as follows:

> If the owner of the ship shall have exercised due diligence to make said ship in all respects seaworthy and properly manned, equipped and supplied, it is hereby agreed that in case of danger, damage or disaster resulting from fault or negligence of the pilot, master or crew in the navigation or management of the ship, or from latent or other defects, or unseaworthiness of the ship, whether existing at time of shipment, or at the beginning of the voyage, but not discoverable by due diligence, the consignee or owners of the cargo shall not be exempted from liability for contribution in general average or for any special charges incurred, but, with the shipowner, shall contribute in general average, and shall pay such special charges as if such danger, damage or disaster had not resulted from such fault, negligence, latent or other defects or unseaworthiness.

The legality of such clauses was immediately questioned in the case of the *Yucatan* (139 Fed. Rep. 894), and it was held that they were invalid because they were in conflict with the declared public policy.

The famous *Jason* case followed (225 U.S. 32) in which the Supreme Court upheld the validity of the general average negligence clause quoted above. It did so on the grounds that Section 3 of the Harter Act had, in effect, modified the public policy against clauses exempting shipowners from the consequences of their negligence and management of the vessel, thus removing the obstacle to the legality of such a clause. Thus, the general average negligence clause became known as the *Jason clause*.

The original version of the Jason clause was framed to meet the requirements of the Harter Act. Under that act, the exercise of due diligence to make the vessel seaworthy on sailing is a condition precedent to the shipowner claiming the protection of the act—and it is no assistance to the shipowner that the unseaworthiness had no causal connection with the general average act. Thus, in the event of the shipowner failing to exercise due diligence at the commencement of the voyage, he would not be entitled to contributions from the cargo in any general average which arose subsequently on the voyage even if the general average was a result of a peril of the sea unconnected with the unseaworthiness (the *Isis*, 1933 AMC 1565).

It has also been held by the courts that, under the Harter Act, if the accident giving rise to the general average occurs before the commencement of the voyage (for example, at loading berth before the vessel sails), the shipowner is not entitled to the immunities granted by the act and he is thus liable for the negligence of the master or crew. It follows that if the general average was the result of such negligence, the cargo is under no obligation to contribute (*Gilchrist* v. *Boston Ins.*, 223 Fed. Rep. 716).

With the passing of the Carriage of Goods by Sea Act (COGSA) in 1936 (to which act all bills of lading covering foreign trade to and from the United States are subject), the effect of unseaworthiness on general average claims was somewhat eased. This for the reason that the immunities granted by that act are not restricted to a situation in which the vessel is in all respects seaworthy (insofar as the due diligence of the shipowner can make her seaworthy). The unseaworthiness is only material if the loss or damage results from it (*Isbrandtsen Co.* v. *Federal Ins. Co.*, 1952 AMC 1945).

The present-day version of the Jason clause was framed to take advantage of the immunities granted by the Carriage of Goods by Sea Act, 1936, and reads as follows:

> In the event of accident, danger, damage, or disaster, before or after commencement of the voyage resulting from any cause whatsoever, whether due to negligence or not, for which, or for the consequences of which, the Carrier is not responsible by statute, contract or otherwise, the goods, shippers, consignees, or owners of the goods shall contribute with the Carrier in general average to the payment of any sacrifices, losses, or expenses of a general average nature that may be made or incurred, and shall pay salvage and special charges incurred in respect of the goods.

It would seem that the law is clear that a vessel owner is only entitled to recover general average contribution from cargo under circumstances where he would have a valid defense against a claim for damage to cargo asserted against him. Thus, if any claim for damage to cargo would fail, it follows under the terms of the new Jason clause that owner's claims for contribution in general average would succeed.

EXERCISE OF DUE DILIGENCE. The importance of the shipowner's obligation to exercise due diligence to provide a seaworthy vessel cannot be too strongly stressed. It is difficult to determine what constitutes the exercise of due diligence and the facts in each case must be considered on their merits.

Cargo underwriters in the United States are especially watchful on this subject and question the seaworthiness of the vessel and the exercise of due diligence whenever the facts warrant it. They are, no doubt, encouraged in this attitude by the traditional tendency of American courts to protect the rights of cargo interests.

The carrier's obligations regarding seaworthiness under the Carriage of Goods by Sea Act are as follows:

Section 3 (1) states:

The carrier shall be bound, before and at the beginning of the voyage, to exercise due diligence to:

(a) Make the ship seaworthy;

(b) Properly man, equip, and supply the ship;

(c) Make the holds, refrigerating and cooling chambers, and all other parts of the ship in which goods are carried, fit and safe for their reception, carriage and preservation.

Section 4 (1) states:

Neither the carrier nor the ship shall be liable for loss or damage arising or resulting from unseaworthiness unless caused by want of due diligence on the part of the carrier to make the ship seaworthy, and to secure that the ship is properly manned, equipped, and supplied, and to make the holds, refrigerating and cool chambers, and all other parts of the ship in which goods are carried fit and safe for their reception, carriage and preservation in accordance with the provisions of paragraph (1) of Section 3. Whenever loss or damage has resulted from unseaworthiness, the burden of proving the exercise of due diligence shall be on the carrier or other persons claiming exemption under this section.

Section 4 (2) lists the exemptions as follows:

Neither the carrier nor the ship shall be responsible for loss or damage arising or resulting from—

(a) Act, neglect, or default of the master, mariner, pilot, or the servants of the carrier in the navigation or in the management of the ship;

(b) Fire, unless caused by the actual fault or privity of the carrier;

(c) Perils, danger, and accidents of the sea or other navigable waters;

(d) Act of God;

(e) Act of war;

(f) Act of public enemies;

(g) Arrest or restraint of princes, rulers, or people, or seizure under legal process;

(h) Quarantine restrictions;

(i) Act or omission of the shipper or owner of the goods, his agent or representative;

(j) Strikes or lockouts, or stoppage or restraint of labor from whatever cause, whether partial or general: *Provided,* That nothing herein contained shall be construed to relieve a carrier from responsibility for the carrier's own acts;

(k) Riots and civil commotions;

(l) Saving or attempting to save life or property at sea;

(m) Wastage in bulk or weight or any other loss or damage arising from inherent defect, quality, or vice of the goods;

(n) Insufficiency of packing;

(o) Insufficiency or inadequacy of marks;

(p) Latent defects not discoverable by due diligence;

(q) Any other cause arising without the actual fault and privity of the carrier and without the fault or neglect of the agents or servants of the carrier but the burden of proof shall be on the person claiming the benefit of this exception to show that neither the actual fault or privity of the carrier nor the fault or neglect of the agents or servants of the carrier contributed to the loss or damage.

It has been held that the burden of proof of the exercise of due diligence is on the shipowner (the *Southwark,* 191 U.S. 1) and, furthermore, that the duty of the carrier to exercise due diligence cannot be delegated to others (*American Linseed Co.* v. *Norfolk S. S. Co.,* 32 Fed. Rep. (2nd) 281). The shipowner is, therefore, as much responsible for the negligence of the assistant engineer *before the voyage commences* as he is for the negligence of his own shore staff.

Under the Harter Act, the obligation to exercise due diligence must be complied with up to sailing from the loading port (*Erie* v. *St. Lawrence Corp.* v. *Barnes-Ames Co.,* 1931 AMC 1994), but the obligation may be revived if the vessel puts into a port of refuge where she comes under the control of the managing personnel of the owner such as a marine superintendent (the *Isis,* 1933 AMC 1565).

If, before or during the loading of cargo, the shipowner had knowledge of a defect which subsequently gave rise to the necessity for a general average act, it is not sufficient that he selected repairers of good reputation to carry out necessary repairs, for "there must be due diligence in the work itself, and not merely in the selection of agents to do the work"

(*Norddeutscher Lloyd* v. *Ins. Co. of North America*, 110 Fed. Rep. 420, 427).

Even in cases where latent defects become apparent during the voyage, it has been held by the courts that the shipowner's burden of proof of due diligence includes the burden of showing that the latent defect was not discoverable prior to the commencement of the voyage (the *Caledonia*, 157 U.S. 124).

It should be noted that most of the foregoing cases arose under the Harter Act and that they may not all be applicable to a situation governed by the Carriage of Goods by Sea Act.

In *Isbrandtsen Co.* v. *Federal Ins. Co. John W. Miller*, 1952 AMC 1945, 1953 AMC 1770), the vessel, after loading, was moved to an anchorage to await clearance and stranded due to negligent navigation on her way to the anchorage. The court held that, unlike the Harter Act, the Carriage of Goods by Sea Act does not require proof of seaworthiness in order to make available to the owner the exemptions granted by the act, *even though the accident occurred prior to the commencement of the voyage.* Another case concerned the effect of the Carriage of Goods by Sea Act where damage occurred as the vessel was leaving her loading berth. The court, citing *Isbrandtsen* v. *Federal Ins. Co. (supra)* took the view that the exemptions of the Carriage of Goods by Sea Act are available even before the commencement of the voyage, stating that if cargo "had been immediately damaged by the in-rush of water, the [COGSA] defense would have been absolute whether the ship was deemed to have been on her voyage, making ready for her voyage, or simply undocking preparatory to the voyage." The court, however, decided that case on the theory that the voyage had already commenced when negligent navigation caused a puncture in the shell plating, which later caused cargo damage during the voyage (the *Del Sud,* 1959 AMC 2143).

As we have seen, Section 3 (1) of COGSA imposes upon the carrier the duty to exercise due diligence to make the vessel seaworthy "before and at the beginning of the voyage." However, the exemptions contained in Section 4 (2) of COGSA are not conditioned upon such exercise of due diligence (as was the case under the Harter Act). On the basis of the decisions in the *John W. Miller* and the *Del Sud* cases, it appears that COGSA will be interpreted to hold that the owner is not responsible for the immediate results of exempted causes of damage occurring prior to the commencement of the voyage, although if unseaworthiness caused in such a manner is not repaired prior to the commencement of the voyage, the owner would be liable for any damage which might later result. It would follow that, for example, crew negligence after loading cargo but prior to the commencement of the voyage would come within the terms of the new

Jason clause and that contribution to any general average expenditure incurred at the port of loading as a result of such negligence would be enforceable against the concerned in cargo.

However, the question as to when the voyage can be said to have commenced in order to claim the exemptions enumerated in the Carriage of Goods by Sea Acts is debatable. In one case, a vessel loaded cargo at six different ports, all in the Puget Sound area, for ports in the Far East. It was held that the various passages from loading port to loading port were simply steps in the process of preparing for the trans-Pacific voyage, and that the shipowner's obligation to exercise diligence "before and at the beginning of the voyage" continued until the vessel broke ground at the last loading port. As a result, the court ruled the shipowner was liable for improper ballasting procedures which caused damage to cargo loaded at one of the first Puget Sound ports even though, it was admitted, the shipowner would not be liable if the same error had occurred "during the voyage" (*American Mail Line* v. *U.S.A.*, 1974 AMC 1536; *cf. Maxine Footwear Co. Ltd.* v. *Canadian Government Merchant Marine Ltd.*, 1959 2 L. L. R. 105).

With the greatest respect to this particular court it yet seems, to a mere average adjuster, to be inequitable for a shipowner to be held responsible for the immediate results of exempted causes of damage occurring subsequent to the loading of cargo merely because the damage occurred before actually leaving the final (or even the first) loading port. The U.S. Carriage of Goods by Sea Act (which applies to all contracts of carriage of goods in foreign trade to or from ports in the United States) covers the period from the time the goods are loaded to the time they are discharged from the vessel. It is thus effective from the time the goods are loaded regardless of whether the voyage has actually commenced. Based on this, the U. S. Court of Appeals for the Fifth Circuit reached the conclusion that the exemptions granted the carrier by the Carriage of Goods by Sea Act are unconditional both as to due diligence and in point of time. With regard to the use of the words "before and at the beginning of the voyage" the court observed that the use of "before and at" did not make the commencement of the voyage (whenever it was) any less a beginning. When the voyage began, it was the voyage and not the beginning of it which continued (the *Del Sud, supra*). The effect of this viewpoint is that any damage to cargo resulting from an excused act occurring after the commencement of loading of cargo (such as errors in the management and navigation of the vessel) would not be the responsibility of the shipowner. The two differing legal interpretations can be quite simply stated: one court considers that an error in management or navigation subsequent to the loading of cargo but prior to sailing on the projected voyage, which results in an unseaworthy condition, is a failure to exercise due diligence to make the vessel seaworthy at the commencement of the voyage. The converse legal viewpoint is that if the error is the *immediate cause of the damage*, it is excused and that, only if the error results in an unseaworthy condition which is not corrected, and which subsequently causes damage, the carrier is liable. So here again we have a legal tug of war as to the construction of the Hague Rules.

It is a very neat point which no doubt delights the legal mind but one which should be resolved on a commercial rather than a legal basis. The nature of maritime commerce is such that the parties involved have to endure the perils of the sea. But should they have to endure the vagaries of the law as well? It would seem to be within the spirit and intent of the Hague Rules that crew negligence (which is excused after sailing) should also be excused if it took place subsequent to the loading of cargo but before sailing (the *John W. Miller, supra*). The community of interest between vessel and cargo commences when cargo is loaded and, for general average purposes, the voyage begins at that time. On this interpretation (which has some legal support), any errors in navigation or management of the vessel (such as crew negligence) which occur after loading cargo but prior to sailing would come within the terms of the new Jason clause, and contribution to any general average expenditure incurred at the port of loading as a result of excepted perils would be enforceable against the concerned in cargo.

Even in cases where a fire gives rise to a general average situation, the shipowner's traditional statutory exemption from liability for loss or damage due to fire is subject to the caveat that the fire must not have been caused by the actual "fault or privity" of the carrier. This has been consistently watered down by some courts to the point where the "fault or privity" of a marine superintendent might be sufficient to deny the carrier the exemption (*American Mail Line* v. *Tokyo Marine*, 1959 AMC 2220). Nevertheless, it should be clearly stated that the words "fault or privity" as used in the Carriage of Goods by Sea Act refer to the "fault or privity" of the shipowner personally, as distinguished from neglect of subordinate employees or seagoing personnel. In the case of a corporate owner, the "fault or privity" of managing officers or responsible agents may be imputed to the corporation. Furthermore, the Carriage of Goods by Sea Act precludes recovery by cargo interests when the origin of a shipboard fire has not been proved and remains a matter of speculation; cargo claimants have the burden of proving the shipowner's personal fault ("fault or privity"). Incidentally, for all practical purposes the words "design or neglect" used in the so-called Fire Statute of the United States (46 U.S. Code, Sect. 182) have a similar meaning as the phrase "fault or privity" in the Carriage of Goods by Sea Act. The protection against losses by fire afforded the shipowner by both statutes is therefore identical. In the *Complaint of Ta Chi Navigation*

(Panama) Corp., S. A., for Exoneration from or Limitation of Liability (1982 AMC 1710) the court reached the same conclusion. The carrier need not prove that it exercised due diligence in order to invoke the provisions of either statute. The burden is on cargo to prove that the carrier's negligence either caused the fire or prevented its being extinguished.

What, then, are the circumstances in which there is no doubt that the carrier *can* successfully enforce general average contributions against cargo interests? For all practical purposes, the list is a very short one and comprises:

(a) Negligence of the crew or the servants of the carrier in the navigation or the management of the vessel during the voyage in question.

(b) Fire unless caused by the actual fault or privity of the carrier.

(c) Perils, dangers, and accidents of the sea (such as heavy weather, collision, or stranding) with or without negligent navigation.

(d) Latent defects not discoverable by due diligence.

(e) Any other cause arising without the actual fault and privity of the carrier and without the fault or neglect of the agents or servants of the carrier.

Rule D of the York/Antwerp Rules deals with the effect of fault and is as follows:

> RULE D. Rights to contribution in general average shall not be affected, though the event which gave rise to the sacrifice or expenditure may have been due to the fault of one of the parties to the adventure; but this shall not prejudice any remedies *or defences* which may be open against *or to* that party *in respect* of such fault.

The minor changes made in this rule are by way of clarification and are not intended to alter the original concept of the rule. It will be seen that Rule D expresses in general terms the proposition that rights to contribution are not affected, although the event giving rise to the general average act may be due to the fault of one of the parties to the adventure, but that this is without prejudice to any remedy open against the wrongdoer. In other words, the object of the rule is to keep all questions of alleged fault outside the adjustment. In practice, the rule's chief result is to preserve an innocent party's right of recovery in general average. In such circumstances, the innocent party (usually a cargo owner) is not barred from first receiving general average contributions to his loss from all the other parties to the adventure before proceeding against the guilty party for recovery of his damages.

In the United States, as we have already seen, it is necessary to include a Jason clause in contracts of affreightment, and the scope of Rule D is limited by the requirements of American law. Indeed, it has been suggested that Rule D is not valid in the United States because of the prohibition of a carrier contracting from the results of his own negligence.

To sum up, the burden of proof of the exercise of due diligence to provide a seaworthy vessel is a heavy one. Due diligence to make a vessel seaworthy, as interpreted by the American and English courts, means that every defect that due diligence can discover should be detected and remedied. The trend of legal decisions in recent years both in the United States and the United Kingdom has been to make this obligation applicable to everyone who has any part in any work carried out on the vessel. No less a person than Lord Devlin (in commenting on the *Muncaster Castle*, 1961 AMC 1357, in which the vessel owner was held responsible for negligence on the part of a reputable shiprepairer) has sympathized with vessel owners' feeling that the exemptions granted by the Hague Rules in 1924 (on which the Carriage of Goods by Sea Acts in both the United States and United Kingdom are based) have been whittled away to a point where (as Lord Devlin puts it) "the shipowner feels the present state of the law does not fairly represent the bargain made in 1924." In other words, although, by international agreement in 1924, the former absolute warranty of seaworthiness was abandoned in favor of what was thought to be a reduced requirement to exercise due diligence to provide a seaworthy vessel, the manner in which this requirement has been interpreted by the courts has, in effect, made the shipowner the guarantor of his vessel's seaworthiness.

Be that as it may, tea and sympathy are of little help to vessel owners or their Protection and Indemnity insurers who face ever-increasing difficulties in satisfying cargo interests as to the exercise of due diligence.

Nevertheless, in considering the liability of cargo to contribute in general average, it is well to remember that, as the chairman of the British Association of Average Adjusters in 1973, N. G. Hudson, pointed out:

> A cargo interest seeking to decline payment of a general average contribution on the ground of unseaworthiness, has to produce positive evidence:
>   (a) that the vessel was unseaworthy, and
>   (b) that the unseaworthiness was causally connected with the general average.
> If he establishes both these propositions, the burden of proof then shifts to the carrier who will have to prove that he had exercised due diligence to make the vessel seaworthy.

It would seem, therefore, that cargo interests are only justified in refusing to pay their contribution to general average when all of the following circumstances exist:

(1) The vessel was unseaworthy.

(2) There was a causal connection between the unseaworthiness and the general average.

(3) The shipowner was not diligent at the commencement of the voyage (that is, at the commencement of loading cargo) in that he failed to discover and correct the unseaworthiness. Furthermore, in determining whether the shipowner was diligent at the commencement of the voyage it should be remembered that "due diligence" within the meaning of the Carriage of Goods by Sea Act means no more than "reasonable care" (the *Southwark*, 191 U.S. 1). In particular, it does not mean that wisdom born of the event can be the measure of due diligence; indeed, the standard must be one of conduct rather than of consequences (*Standard Oil Co.* v. *Anglo-Mexican Petroleum Corp.*, 112 F. Supp. 630). While in cases of prima facie unseaworthiness the burden is on the shipowner to prove that he and his servants have exercised due diligence, it is not enough for cargo interests to say that if certain steps had been taken there would have been a better chance of discovering the unseaworthiness. As Lord Reid has put it (the *Amstelslot*, 1963 2 L. L. R. 223):

> There must be some compromise or balance in deciding what steps to take in any particular case, keeping in mind both the serious consequences which may flow from failure to detect a defect and the remoteness of the chance that such a defect may exist; for it would plainly be impracticable to make elaborate scientific tests for every defect which could possibly be present.

Or in the words of an American court, "Due diligence means doing everything reasonable, not everything possible. The term is practically synonymous with reasonable or ordinary care" (the *Hamildoc,* 1950 AMC 1973).

To put the matter in a few words, unless the shipowner could and should have anticipated and remedied the defect which gave rise to the necessity for the general average act, by the use of ordinary prudent methods, there has been no lack of due diligence.

General average adjustments are often referred to the Committee on Adjustments of the American Institute of Marine Underwriters for examination. This examination is primarily directed towards the accuracy of the adjustment itself, but the committee will, if necessary, give their opinion on the question of due diligence or lack thereof. Usually, a very reasonable attitude is taken towards this problem, but the committee acts in an advisory capacity only and will not even consider the question of due diligence if any of the individual cargo underwriters actually involved have instructed attorneys. Since more often than not counsel have been instructed at the time of the accident that gave rise to the general average, the good offices of the committee on the question of the exercise of due diligence are unfortunately not usually available.

The shipowner is faced with many problems in general average situations. Not the least of these is whether to take the step of declaring general average and thereby incur the cost of instructing average adjusters to obtain general average security from cargo interests and to prepare a general average adjustment; this is especially true in general cargo cases. On the one hand, the shipowner is obligated to protect all parties to the maritime adventure (including those cargo interests whose cargo may have been sacrificed). On the other hand, cargo interests often take the position that the shipowner failed to exercise due diligence to provide a seaworthy vessel, and sometimes are ultimately upheld. In that event, the cost of taking security from hundreds of cargo interests and preparing a general average adjustment (which may be substantial) will have been incurred in vain. Yet Protection and Indemnity clubs and underwriters are loath, at the time of the accident and/or at the time of declaration of general average, to reach a decision as to whether or not they will respond to the shipowner for cargo's share of the geneal average, thereby admitting cargo's allegations as to the vessel's unseaworthiness. This is true even though the early evidence may point to the unseaworthiness of the vessel having been a factor in the accident which led to the general average situation. Generally speaking, before Protection and Indemnity clubs and underwriters will respond for cargo's proportion of general average not recoverable from cargo interests, they require the shipowners (armed with a general average adjustment) to pursue the cargo interests for their contributions and obtain their refusal to pay. Indeed, in some cases they require the shipowner to sue the cargo interests under the general average adjustment to obtain contributions from cargo. This is really an intramarket problem between cargo underwriters and Protection and Indemnity underwriters but the unfortunate shipowner is caught in the middle. Such cases can also create problems when a negligent third party is ultimately pursued for all the damages resulting from the accident (including the general average expenses incurred). In one case a tort-feasor objected to the substantial cost of taking general average security and to the cost of preparing the general average adjustment; it was argued that the shipowner should have realized that he would be unable to recover from cargo interests in general average because he had failed to exercise due diligence to provide a seaworthy ship. Consequently he should not have proceeded with the preparation of a complete general average adjustment. The court, albeit with some reluctance, was constrained by precedent to affirm recovery for the general average adjustment expenses (the *Farida,* 1978 AMC 1267). The shipowner's dilemma is not so painful in single interest general average cargo cases when the cost of taking general average security and employing average adjusters is usually not so expensive.

If the Hamburg Rules, the result of the latest international convention on the carriage of goods by sea, ever come into effect, the shipowner's difficulty in enforcing contribution from cargo interests will become even more difficult. Under these rules (Art. 24, Sect. 2), the right of the carrier to *enforce* general average contributions against cargo owners is conditioned upon the carrier's freedom from liability "for loss of or damage to the goods" under the convention's main provisions. In principle this achieves the same result as is now achieved by the new Jason clause customarily included in contracts of affreightment (in conjunction, of course, with the Hague Rules). Put simply, a carrier is only entitled to recover general average contributions from cargo interests under circumstances where he would have a valid defense against a claim for damage to cargo asserted against him. Thus, if any claim for damage to cargo would fail, it follows, under the new Jason clause, that the carrier's claim for contribution would succeed. Art. 24, Sect. 2 of the Hamburg Rules adopts this principle and presumably renders the new Jason clause superfluous insofar as the Hamburg Rules are concerned. However, the Hamburg Rules substitute a general standard of carrier liability for the specific language of the Hague Rules which contain a whole catalogue of exemptions from liability. At the Hamburg Conference practically all these exceptions were swept away. Not only was the due diligence concept abandoned, but the major traditional defenses of errors in the navigation or of management of the vessel granted under the Hague Rules were abolished. Only those perils of the sea over which the carrier has no control (and he must *prove* he has no control) and a reduced fire exemption remain. The overall requirement of the Hamburg Rules that the carrier *prove* that "he, his servants or agents took all measures that could reasonably be required to avoid the occurrence and its consequences" (Art. 5, Sect. 1) is akin to *proving* the absence of negligence—often a difficult task. In short, the burden of proof is reversed—the carrier is guilty unless *he* proves himself innocent. As Annex II to the Hamburg Rules puts it, the liability of the carrier is based on the principle of presumed fault or neglect. This is where the new rules place a severe limitation on general average: to the extent that the carrier's traditional defenses under the Hague Rules are reduced by the Hamburg Rules, the situations in which general average contributions can be recovered from cargo owners will also be reduced.

The increased difficulty in enforcing general average contributions from cargo interests under the Hamburg Rules will be apparent. Indeed, some observers have expressed the opinion that if the rules become universal, they will result in the demise of general average as we know it today; it is said cargo interests will continually refuse to contribute and the difficulties involved in proving entitlement to contribution—namely that the shipowner took all measures that could reasonably be required to avoid the occurrence giving rise to the general average act—will result in the shipowner throwing in the towel. As the chairman of the Association of Average Adjusters of Canada, R. G. Chauvin, Q. C., has said, ". . . The Hamburg Rules do not alter international maritime law, as such, on the subject of general average, but they do . . . have a very real bearing . . . an impact of consequence, on the application of that law" (annual report, 1979).

However, the future of the Hamburg Rules, at this writing, is doubtful. They may never replace the Hague Rules on a universal basis. The institution of general average has been written off on so many occasions that one is tempted to echo Mark Twain's cable to the Associated Press: "The report of my death was an exaggeration."

WHEN CARGO CONTRIBUTES IN GENERAL AVERAGE

Generally speaking, cargo is brought in as a contributing interest to general average if it was on board at the time of the general average act, that is, at the time it was decided to make a sacrifice or incur an extraordinary expenditure within the meaning of Rule A or under the conditions envisioned in Rules X and XI of the York/Antwerp Rules (see *Percy R. Pyne*, 1926 AMC 1582). Thus, under Rules X (b) and XI (b) of the 1950 Rules, it was possible to load into a general average. For example, a vessel may have encountered heavy weather en route to her loading port and sustained damage without it being realized. After commencement of loading, damage is belatedly discovered (without any intervening accident) and repairs have to be effected which are necessary for the safe prosecution of the voyage, resulting in the vessel being delayed. In such circumstances, the cargo actually loaded on board the vessel at the time the decision (the general average act) is taken to effect repairs, is brought in as a contributing interest. For reasons discussed earlier, it is unlikely the contributions could be enforced against the cargo in such circumstances; nevertheless there is a bona fide general average situation under the 1950 Rules and the vessel owner would be able to collect the vessel's contribution from his hull underwriters, subject, of course, to policy conditions. It was with the intention of limiting general averages of this type that Rules X (b) and XI (b) were amended, and the reader is referred to the previous discussions as to the efficacy of the amendments. On the other hand, sometimes cargo is loaded as a matter of convenience after the decision to incur general average expenditure has been made but before the expenditure is actually incurred.

Such cargo would not be brought in as a contributing interest, and, if the general average expenditure were increased by reason of the presence of cargo loaded after the decision to incur general average expenditure was made, such increase in expenditure would be for the shipowner's account.

Separation of Interests at a Port of Refuge

If a cargo owner wishes to take delivery of his cargo at a port of refuge short of destination, he is entitled to do so in exchange for the usual documents of title and payment of full freight to the original destination, assuming he provides whatever general average security is required. The cargo must also be easily accessible to the shipowner without the incurring of additional expense.

American courts have held that on taking delivery the cargo owner is not liable to contribute to any general average expenses incurred after delivery is effected unless a special agreement is obtained to the contrary (*Domingo de Larrinaga*, 1928 AMC 64). Insofar as general cargo is concerned, this differs from the practice in the United Kingdom where, even if the owners of certain shipments take delivery at a port of refuge, that cargo still continues to contribute to general average expenditure incurred after delivery has been taken; this on the theory that it would be unfair to permit those interests to walk away from their general average obligations, bearing in mind the fact that their cargo was on board at the time of the general average act. Even in the United States, the community of interest between ship and cargo is not destroyed on completion of discharge of cargo at a port of refuge unless each party bears its own charges from that time. In other words, delivery must actually be taken by the owner of the cargo before there is any separation of interests. Thus, if cargo is sold by the shipowner at a port of refuge for account of whom concerned and the proceeds are retained by the shipowner for allocation in the general average adjustment, such cargo continues to contribute to all the general average expenses incurred at the port of refuge. In theory, the proceeds realized replace the cargo sold and continue to destination with the vessel; in short, as this shipment (or the proceeds realized in lieu) remained in the custody of the shipowner, the community of interest between the vessel and those shipments is not broken. Such cargo, though physically separated from the vessel, is still, as far as general average is concerned, constructively with it and such cargo is chargeable with its proportionate share of the general average expenses incurred at the port of refuge to complete the voyage.

The American law and practice as enunciated in the *Domingo de Larringa* was endorsed by the Canadian Federal Court, Trial Division, in *Ellerman Lines* v. *Gibbs, Nathaniel (Canada)*, 1984 AMC 2579. The court held that once a cargo owner has paid full freight to destination, he has the right to require the ocean carrier to discharge his goods at any intermediate port of call having facilities for such discharge. Thus the owner of cargo consigned to Toronto had no obligation to sign a non-separation of interest agreement requiring him to contribute in general average for expenses incurred after the cargo was discharged from carrier's disabled vessel and delivered to him at Montreal pursuant to court order. This decision was upheld by the Canadian federal court of appeals (1986 AMC 2217).

APPLICATION TO POLICIES OF INSURANCE

In textbooks on general average, it is customary to emphasize the fact that general average exists quite independently of marine insurance and that rights to contribution are unaffected by any insurance of general average contributions or lack of it. All of which is quite true, as the reader will already have gathered. Nevertheless, in practice, the various parties to the adventure are usually insured against general average contributions indeed, it would be most imprudent of them if they were not. It was, therefore, thought to be useful to include a few words on the application to the various policies of insurance on ship, cargo, and freight. It must always be remembered, however, that the insurers are merely assuming a liability which primarily falls on their assured.

Insurances on Ship

As we have seen, a valid general average can arise even though the accident causing the general average situation may have been due to wear and tear; it is sufficient that the vessel and/or cargo are rescued from peril as a result of a general average sacrifice or expenditure. In stating the claim on the hull policies for vessel's proportion of the general average, it must be remembered that "in the absence of express stipulation, the insurer is not liable for any general average loss or contribution where the loss was not incurred for the purpose of avoiding or in connection with the avoidance of a peril insured against" (Marine Insurance Act, Sect. 66 (6)). In other words, the subject-matter insured must have been in actual danger from a peril insured against before a claim can be established. Indeed, in an old American case it was held that general average expenditure occasioned solely and directly by unseaworthiness of the vessel, and not by perils of the sea or negligence of master or crew, was not covered by the usual marine insurance policy (the *Fort Bragg*, 1924 AMC 275). However, it is the established and accepted practice that even when a general average situation arises due to wear and tear, general average expenditures (such as port of refuge expenses, salvage services, etc.) are recoverable from hull underwriters on the grounds that such expenses were necessary to save the vessel from a future peril which might operate. "What is sacrificed in general average ought in my judgment to be treated in principle as lost by the peril *averted*" (*Montgomery* v. *Indemnity Mutual*, 1 Q. B. 1901). For example, the vessel, in its disabled state, might encounter heavy weather and either founder or run aground, in which case the hull underwriters would undoubtedly be liable for the loss thereby sustained. On the other hand, if a vessel with cargo sank as a result of a wear and tear situation, vessel's proportion of any future salvage expenses of a general average nature would not be recoverable from hull underwriters, because in those circumstances the salvage expenses were not incurred "in connection with the avoidance of a peril insured against." In point of fact, prior to the incurring of the salvage expenses, the vessel was lost due to wear and tear (an uninsured peril).

It is perhaps important to mention that "the liability of underwriters to pay general average attaches, not as of the date of injury to the vessel, but as of the date of the sacrificial act" (*Percy R. Pyne*, 1926 AMC 1582). In other words, liability for general average attaches to the underwriters on risk *at the time of the general average act,* that is to say, at the time the decision is taken to make an extraordinary sacrifice or incur an extraordinary expenditure rather than at the time of the accident (whether it be of a particular average nature or due to wear and tear) giving rise to the necessity for the general average act. In some instances the accident and the general average act may be simultaneous, but in others there may be a time lag with the result that the particular average claim (if any) arising from the accident may fall on one policy period, and the general average act (perhaps a *decision* to enter a port of refuge) may not take place until after a new policy period has attached. Thus, the resultant claim for general average expenditure would fall on the succeeding policy period. Again, however, it must be stressed that the claim for general average falls upon the policies operative *at the time of the general average act*; the date on which the vessel actually deviates, or on which the general average expenditure is actually incurred, or the period of the general average detention is not the criterion. All such expenses flow from the general average act. In some cases it may be that the general average act will coincide with the commencement of the general average deviation, but in others the actual deviation may not commence until some time after the master has made the decision to seek a port of refuge. It is the time of that decision which determines the policy period on which the subsequent general average expenditure is claimable.

In those cases where the particular average claim and the general average claim are shown on separate policies, only one deductible average is applied because both claims arose from the same accident. The deductible average is apportioned over the amounts of the particular average and general average claims falling on the respective hull policies.

American vessels are usually insured under the American Institute Hull form of policy or some variation thereof. This policy contains the following clause:

> General Average and Salvage shall be payable as provided in the contract of affreightment, or failing such provision or there be no contract of affreightment, payable at the Assured's election either in accordance with York/Antwerp Rules, 1950 or 1974 or with the Laws and Usages of the Port of New York. Provided always that when an adjustment according to the laws and usages of the port of destination is properly demanded by the owners of the cargo, General Average shall be paid accordingly.

This clause is self-explanatory and calls for no special comment. It is particularly important because, when a vessel is in ballast and under charter, American practice does not recognize the general average clause in the contract of affreightment as governing the adjustment of general average; thus, it will be seen that the above clause requires all general averages occurring while the vessel is in ballast to be adjusted either in accordance with the York/Antwerp Rules, 1950 or 1974, or in accordance with the laws and usages of the Port of New York, at the option of the assured.

The American Institute Hull Clauses continue:

> In the event of salvage, towage or other assistance being rendered to the Vessel by any vessel belonging in part or in whole to the same Owners or Charterers, the value of such services (without regard to the common ownership or control of the vessels) shall be ascertained by arbitration in the manner provided for under the Collision Liability clause in this Policy, and the amount so awarded so far as applicable to the interest hereby insured shall constitute a charge under this Policy.

This is a Sister Ship clause of the type referred to earlier and permits the assured to claim against his underwriters in respect of salvage or other services rendered by a sister ship, that is, the services he has rendered to his own property.

We now come to a most important clause, which reads:

> When the contributory value of the Vessel is greater than the Agreed Value herein, the liability of the Underwriters for General Average contribution (except in respect to amounts made good to the Vessel), or Salvage, shall not exceed that proportion of the total contribution due from the Vessel which the amount insured hereunder bears to the contributory value; and if, because of damage for which the Under-

writers are liable as Particular Average, the value of the Vessel has been reduced for the purpose of contribution, the amount of such Particular Average damage recoverable under this Policy shall first be deducted from the amount insured hereunder, and the Underwriters shall then be liable only for the proportion which such net amount bears to the contributory value.

This clause stipulates that, in ascertaining the amount of underwriters' liability for general average *expenses,* regard must be had to the insured value of the vessel. If the insured value is equal to, or exceeds, the sound value on which the contributory value of the vessel is based, the underwriter pays the whole amount of the general average contribution. On the other hand, if the insured value is less than the sound value, the underwriter only pays a proportion of the general average expenses. The clause also provides that if the contributory value of the vessel is reduced by a damage for which *these same underwriters* are liable as particular average, the amount of that particular average damage under the policy is to be deducted from the insured value and the underwriters are only liable for the proportion which such net amount bears to the contributory value. General average sacrifices ("amount made good to the vessel") are not affected by this clause and are recoverable from underwriters without regard to any underinsurance. If this clause were not in the policy, underwriters would be liable for the full general average contribution attaching to the vessel (i.e., both sacrifices and expenses) regardless of any underinsurance (*International Navigation Co.* v. *Atlantic Mutual Ins. Co.*, 108 Fed. Rep. 988). In arriving at the amount of the particular average damage payable by underwriters for deduction from the insured value in accordance with the above clause, any deductible average must be taken into consideration. In other words, the deduction should be net of the deductible average.

The policy requirements regarding any underinsurance reflect Sect. 73 of the Marine Insurance Act (*q.v.*). In applying this section of the Marine Insurance Act, average adjusters deduct from the insured value all losses and charges for which underwriters are liable and which have been deducted in arriving at the contributory values (*see* British Association of Average Adjusters Rule of Practice B33).

Any underinsurance of the vessel on hull and machinery policies can be rectified (insofar as liability for general average contributions is concerned) by effecting an insurance on excess liabilities. Such an insurance covers (*inter alia*):

General Average, Salvage and Salvage Charges not recoverable in full under the policies in Hull and Machinery by reason of the difference between the insured value of the Vessel as stated therein (or any reduced value arising from the deduction therefrom in process of adjustment of any claim which law or practice or the terms of the policies covering Hull and Machinery may have required) and the value of the Vessel adopted for the purpose of contribution to General Average, Salvage or Salvage Charges, the liability under this Policy being for such proportion of the amount not recoverable as the amount insured hereunder bears to the said difference or to the total sum insured against excess liabilities if it exceeds such difference.

As we have already seen, when general average expenditure exceeds the total arrived values of ship and cargo, the cargo is liable for general average only up to its contributory value. It has been held in the English courts (*Green Star Shipping Co.* v. *London Assurance*, 1933 1 K. B. 378) that in such circumstances the underwriters on ship are liable for the balance of the general average expenditure, even though it exceeded the contributory value of the ship on the grounds that this was the proportion of the general average expenditure which fell upon the shipowner. (Subsect. 4 of Sect. 66 of the Marine Insurance Act states that "where the assured has incurred a general average expenditure, he may recover from the insurer in respect of *the proportion of the loss which falls upon him.*") While the point has not been litigated in the United States, it is probable that American courts would reach a similar conclusion, namely, that in such circumstances the whole amount of the general average expenditure is recoverable from hull underwriters as representing the general average expenditure falling upon the shipowner, always provided that, when combined with any particular average claim, the entire claim does not exceed the insured value.

The American Hull form of policy also stipulates that general average shall be payable without deduction of thirds, "new for old." The effect of this is to make underwriters liable for any deductions "new for old" made by average adjusters in stating the general average in accordance with the York/Antwerp Rules or American law and practice.

General average has never been popular with shipowners, particularly general cargo carriers, because of the inconvenience to their customers (the cargo owners) of delaying the delivery of cargo while general average security is obtained. With the advent of container ships the difficulties involved have increased. Shipowners, of course, need to be reimbursed for the general average expenses they have incurred, and in 1979 the American Hull Insurance Syndicate made available a General Average Absorption clause (January 1, 1979) reading as follows:

> In consideration of additional premium paid it is understood and agreed that, subject to the terms and conditions of this Policy, cargo's

proportion of General Average (including Salvage, if any) not exceeding $ shall be recoverable hereunder, provided claim for contribution from all cargo has been waived by the Assured. It is also agreed that in these circumstances no collecting and settling commission will be recoverable hereunder in respect of either Vessel's or cargo's proportion of General Average.

The amount of the absorption is negotiable and, within the limitation of the amount agreed, the clause enables shipowners to make a prompt decision whether or not to declare general average. If they decide not to declare general average and cargo's proportion of the general average ultimately exceeds the amount stated in the clause they would have to absorb the excess as a business expense. Of course if the amount of the general average payable by cargo is estimated at the outset to be greatly in excess of the amount agreed in the Absorption clause, shipowners will not avail themselves of the concession and will declare general average in the usual way. There are various other versions of General Average Absorption clauses but they all seek to simplify and limit the number of general averages. The idea is to restrict declaration of general averages to major cases. However, when the general average expenditure and/or sacrifices of ship and/or cargo are substantial, the cost and inconvenience of preparing a general average adjustment, even with hundreds of cargo owners participating, is unavoidable if the shipowner and cargo owners (or their underwriters) are to be fully reimbursed. It should be noted that a General Average Absorption clause is unnecessary for owners of bulk carriers since the obtaining of general average security from one or two cargo owners is not a difficult or expensive task.

Insurances on Cargo

Most insurances on cargo include a general average clause along the following lines:

> General Average and Salvage Charges payable according to United States laws and usage and/or as per Foreign Statement and/or per York/Antwerp Rules (as prescribed in whole or in part) if in accordance with the contract of affreightment.

In short, cargo underwriters are agreeing to respond for any general average contribution falling on their assured as a result of a general average adjustment drawn up in accordance with the provisions in the contract of affreightment (usually in accordance with the York/Antwerp Rules).

Quite apart from any specific clause in the policy, American law expressly provides that cargo underwriters are only liable for the full general average contribution levied against their assured if the insured value of the cargo is equal to or exceeds the sound value on which the contributory value of cargo is based. This was laid down in *Gulf Refining Co.* v. *Atlantic Mutual Ins. Co.* (279 U. S. 708): the Court held that cargo owners were co-insurers with their underwriters in respect of the difference between the contributory value of the cargo and its insured value. This decision, in effect, embraces the general principle laid down in Sect. 73 (1) of the English Marine Insurance Act (*q.v.*). Leaving nothing to chance, cargo policies usually include a Contributory Value clause reading:

> This Company shall be liable for only such proportion of General Average and Salvage Charges as the sum hereby insured (less Particular Average for which this Company is liable hereunder, if any) bears to the Contributory Value of the Property hereby insured.

Thus, in the event of underinsurance the same procedure is followed in cargo insurance as in hull insurance.

Insurances on Freight

Insurances on freight also cover general average contributions, and the principle of underinsurance applies equally to freight.

In practice, the gross amount of freight at risk and not the net amount (or contributory value) is compared with the insured value of the freight to determine whether it is fully insured. Thus, where the sum insured is less than the gross freight at risk, the amount recoverable under the policy in respect of general average contributions is reduced in proportion to the underinsurance.

General Average Sacrifices

Unlike general average expenses, general average sacrifices are recoverable directly from the underwriters concerned.

In the case of the vessel, underwriters are liable for the full amount of the damage, any question of underinsurance being disregarded (the *St. Paul*, 100 Fed. Rep. 304). The assured may also claim the full amount of the general average sacrifice from his underwriters without first claiming the contributions due from any other interests involved in the maritime adventure. In such instances, the underwriters themselves are, by subrogation, entitled to the contributions due from other interests. The shipowner is, therefore, obligated to preserve his general average lien against the cargo. In cases where the vessel and cargo are owned by the same owner, the courts have held that the assured cannot recover from the underwriters on ship for any sacrifice made without first crediting the contribution due from cargo as general average (*Potter* v. *Providence & Washington Ins. Co.*, 4 Mason 298).

In the case of cargo and freight, any direct claim on underwriters for general average sacrifices is assessed on the basis of the insured value in accordance with normal adjusting procedure.

As we shall see later, most Protection and Indemnity insurers respond for cargo's share of general average in those cases where the shipowner is unable to enforce contribution against cargo by reason of a breach in the contract of carriage. However, as a general rule, Protection and Indemnity insurers are not liable for general average sacrifices; consequently, if the general average contribution due but uncollectible from cargo includes any sacrifices, the claim under the Protection and Indemnity coverage must be reduced accordingly.

SIMPLIFICATION OF GENERAL AVERAGE

From time to time the ancient, international law of general average comes under the close scrutiny of modern, computer-conscious underwriters and modern, container-conscious shipowners. The verdict is not always complimentary. This is easy to understand because, in spite of its basic simplicity, the declaration of general average inevitably delays delivery of cargo and causes various problems to all concerned in the voyage being prosecuted; it is, at best, a necessary evil, albeit an economic necessity. It is small wonder, therefore, that periodically, campaigns are instigated by well-meaning groups to simplify or even abolish general average. For all practical purposes it is impossible to abolish general average without first altering the common law of every maritime nation in the world—a formidable, if not impossible, task. Nor is it likely that the shipowners of the world would be agreeable to bearing the considerable financial burdens which would result from their foregoing their right to receive contributions to general average expenses incurred by them as bankers to the maritime adventure. As an institution, general average has stood the test of almost 2,000 years, an indication of its inherent fairness in distributing losses equitably amongst all the interests concerned in a maritime adventure.

Simplification of general average is another matter, and all connected with general average are in favor of this reform. However, even the limited goal of simplification presents great difficulties and has usually been approached through the medium of the York/Antwerp Rules.

Chapter 7

Salvage Expenses and Sue and Labor Charges

SALVAGE EXPENSES

Salvage expenses constitute an important type of expenditure which, while not, strictly speaking, general average, often become general average by reason of the circumstances in which they are incurred. Salvage has been defined by the English courts as "the compensation made to those by whose assistance a vessel or its cargo has been saved from impending peril or recovered from actual loss."

According to the Marine Insurance Act:

> "Salvage Charges" means the charges recoverable under maritime law by a salvor independently of contract. They do not include the expenses of services in the nature of salvage rendered by the assured or his agents, or any person employed for hire by them, for the purpose of averting a peril insured against. Such expenses, where properly incurred, may be recovered as particular charges or as a general average loss, according to the circumstances under which they were incurred. (Sect. 65 (2))

However, it should be noted that it has recently been held by the English court of appeals (reversing the lower court) that in English law there is no right to salvage remuneration where the service is rendered on nontidal inland waters (the *Goring*, 1987 2 L.R. 15).

Salvage has been defined by the American courts as

> . . . a service voluntarily rendered to save maritime property from impending peril at sea by those under no obligation to do so. (*Salvatore Nicastro* v. *Peggy B.*, 1960 AMC 914)

The English law relating to voluntariness of salvage services is stated in *Kennedy on Civil Salvage* (4th ed., p. 25), as follows:

> Voluntariness is an essential element of salvage in the sense that if a service is rendered solely under a pre-existing contractual or official

duty owed to the owner of the salved property, or solely in the interest of self preservation, it is not a salvage service. (Quoted with approval in the *Gregerso*, 1917 1 L. L. R. 220.)

Salvage charges proper (as defined by the Marine Insurance Act) result from the voluntary act on the part of a total stranger to the adventure and without a contract of any kind, as, for example, when a derelict vessel is picked up by another vessel and towed into port. The compensation paid to such voluntary salvors is not general average as defined by Rule A of the York/Antwerp Rules.

Thus, salvage services rendered by *volunteer* salvors without a contract of any kind (verbal or otherwise) are really pure salvage and not general average. Pure salvage (or salvage charges as defined by the Marine Insurance Act) represents the taking by the salvors of a part of the property. Thus, in effect, pure salvage answers the description of a particular average loss or a particular charge or special charge on the property salved (but *not* a Sue and Labor charge).

On the other hand, salvage by contract (that is, when salvors are engaged by the assured or his agents) represents the giving, not the taking, of a part of the property salved; such salvage is of the nature of general average under American law (under English law it could, of course, be a Sue and Labor charge if the vessel was in ballast).

Actually there are few instances where salvage services are rendered without a contract having been entered into, usually under a salvage agreement on a no cure—no pay basis. Services rendered under such contracts arranged by the assured, whether under Lloyd's or any other form of agreement, if they were incurred at a time of danger, are generally accepted as coming within the definition of general average under Rule A of the York/Antwerp Rules. If it is accepted that salvage under agreement is general average, then the values adopted by the arbitrator or courts in determining the salvage award must be regarded as being merely for the purpose of determining the amount to be paid for the salvage services. That is to say, in preparing the resultant statement of general average, the adjuster must reapportion the amount of the salvage over the values at destination as stipulated by the York/Antwerp Rules. This practice is, in fact, endorsed by Rule of Practice C 1 of the British Association of Average Adjusters, which reads as follows:

Expenses for salvage services rendered by or accepted under agreement shall in practice be treated as general average provided that such expenses were incurred for the common safety within the meaning of Rule "A" of the York/Antwerp Rules, 1924, or York/Antwerp Rules, 1950.

Some authorities in England feel that the Rule of Practice is contrary to English law on the subject of salvage. They point out that, for example, under Lloyd's Form of Salvage Agreement the master (or other authorized person signing the agreement) contracts only as agent for vessel and cargo, binding each separately and not collectively; thus, one party has not incurred liability for the common benefit as, the argument goes, is necessary before the salvage can be considered to be general average. Conversely, others point out that the Marine Insurance Act (Sect. 65) defines salvage charges as "charges recoverable under maritime law by a salvor independently of contract" and conclude that salvage services rendered under contract cannot come within the statutory definition of salvage. Be that as it may, it is the practice of British average adjusters to treat salvage services rendered under an agreement as general average.

Under American law, it is quite settled that if the salvage services *meet the requirements of general average*, the salvage award, however or whenever liquidated, is reapportioned on the basis of values at the termination of the adventure. In the case of the *Jason* (162 Fed. Rep. 56, 178 Fed. Rep. 414), the Supreme Court of the United States said:

> It seems to me, therefore, that this salvage expense, however or whenever liquidated, was something done for common benefit and therefore should under American law be brought into the general average adjustment . . . The test in general average is not what it was worth to each interest to procure its own salvation. That is no more to the point than the fact that some shippers of goods may prefer them to be lost rather than saved. The test is whether there was in law a voluntary sacrifice for the common benefit, and the moment salvage is paid or agreed to be paid on goods saved with the vessel, such sacrifice exists.

Or, as Congdon put it:

> When a salvage award is made either before or after the arrival of the adventure at destination, upon approximate values of vessel and cargo, such valuations do not control in the adjustment, the actual values at the port of destination being those upon which, in practice, the salvage expenses are apportioned.

Any doubt remaining regarding the worldwide practice of treating salvage services as general average was, for all practical purposes, set to rest by the introduction of Rule VI in the 1974 version of the York/Antwerp Rules. This reads as follows:

RULE VI. SALVAGE REMUNERATION. Expenditure incurred by the parties to the adventure on account of salvage, whether under contract or otherwise, shall be allowed in general average to the extent that the salvage operations were undertaken for the purpose of preserving from peril the property involved in the common maritime adventure.

It is an innovation for the York/Antwerp Rules to deal with salvage expenses, and it will be seen that the rule stipulates that all salvage expenses, *whether contractual or voluntary*, are now to be treated as general average. Thus, although voluntary salvage services rendered without a contract do not come within general average as defined by Rule A, because of the Rule of Interpretation, Rule VI is paramount and would seem to be conclusive regarding the allowance of all salvage services in general average. Certainly that was the intent of the conferees at Hamburg. Furthermore, whether or not the payment for the salvage services is initially settled separately by ship and cargo interests, "the aggregate of the liabilities" (as one of the early drafts of the rule called it) is to be reapportioned as general average if the services were incurred for the common safety of ship and cargo. In some cases this may result in the salvage award being reapportioned as general average over entirely different contributory values and thereby altering the incidence of payments as between ship and cargo. For example, regardless of the basis on which the salvage arbitrator may have arrived at the value of the vessel, the average adjuster, under Rule XVII of the York/Antwerp Rules, 1974, will have to recalculate the vessel's contributory value "without taking into account the beneficial or detrimental effect of any demise or time charter party." It may also be, of course, that the valuation of cargo accepted by the arbitrator is on a different basis from that required by Rule XVII of the York/Antwerp Rules, 1974.

It has been suggested that, in those cases where ship and cargo interests settle separately with the salvors on different terms, it should not be mandatory for the general average adjuster to have to reapportion these independent settlements as general average (see address by the chairman of the British Association of Average Adjusters in 1988, D. J. Wilson). However Rule VI of the York/Antwerp Rules, 1974, is quite explicit as to the treatment of such differential salvage payments. Moreover, the reason Rule VI was introduced into the York/Antwerp Rules in 1974 was to achieve international uniformity in the treatment and apportionment of salvage as general average and in particular to contract out of English law on the subject (*see also* paper by N. G. Hudson, a former chairman of the British Association of Average Adjusters, dealing with Rule VI and reprinted in Bulletin No. 5 [1989] of the Association of Average Adjusters of the United States).

When ship and cargo interests choose to be separately represented by attorneys at a salvage arbitration, the question arises as to whether the attendant legal expenses of both parties should be merged and allowed in general average, just as separate salvage awards made by the arbitrator to ship and cargo interests are merged and reapportioned as general average in accordance with Rule VI of the York/Antwerp Rules, 1974. Alternatively, should such legal expenses be treated as special charges on ship and cargo respectively? The practice in the London market is to meld and reapportion such legal expenses in general average. In the United States there is no uniform practice. As already stated, Rule VI was introduced in the York/Antwerp Rules in 1974 with the object of attaining international uniformity in the treatment of salvage as general average. Therefore it seems to the writer that all legal expenses incurred by the various parties should also be treated as general average and dealt with on the same basis as separate payments for salvage. This presupposes that the legal expenses of both ship and cargo were incurred solely in connection with the salvage award.

Arising out of the recent International Convention on Salvage, 1989 (*q.v.*), Rule VI of the York/Antwerp Rules, 1974, was amended. The new text of Rule VI reads:

(a) Expenditure incurred by the parties to the adventure in the nature of salvage, whether under contract or otherwise, shall be allowed in general average provided that the salvage operations were carried out for the purpose of preserving from peril the property involved in the common maritime adventure.

Expenditure allowed in general average shall include any salvage remuneration in which the skill and efforts of the salvors in preventing or minimizing damage to the environment such as is referred to in Art. 13, paragraph 1 (b) of the International Convention on Salvage, 1989 have been taken into account.

(b) Special compensation payable to a salvor by the shipowner under Art. 14 of the said Convention, to the extent specified in paragraph 4 of that Article or under any other provision similar in substance shall not be allowed in general average.

The new wording reflects the International Convention of Salvage, 1989 (*q.v.*) but does not change the practice followed by average adjusters when dealing with salvage under the original Rule VI of the York/Antwerp Rules, 1974. The new Rule VI simply endorses average adjusters' interpretation of the original rule and includes the safety net feature introduced into LOF in 1980. (The spirit of the safety net concept had been adopted by the international convention in Art. 14.) Incidentally, the amended Rule VI, for the first time in the long history of the York/Antwerp Rules, makes a specific reference to an international convention. The reference in the new rule to "any other provision similar in substance" would include, for example, LOF 1990.

The new text of the York/Antwerp Rules (that is including the new, amended Rule VI) is to be referred to as the York/Antwerp Rules, 1974 as amended 1990.

With the advent of the new international convention on Salvage, Lloyd's deemed it appropriate to revise and update Lloyd's open form of salvage agreement (LOF 1990) so that it fit in with the convention. Most of the amendments merely involve simplification of language but articles 1, 8, 13, and 14 of the convention are incorporated. Furthermore, while LOF 1980 dealt solely with oil spill damage, under LOF 1990 the presence of hazardous cargoes other than oil (such as nuclear waste, chemicals, liquid gas, etc.) may now qualify the salvors for the special compensation (safety net) provided by Art. 14 of the convention. The convention could take as long as ten years before it is ratified by the necessary number of nations and then comes into operation. Since as much as eighty percent of the world's salvage is conducted under Lloyd's open form, the inclusion of the main features of the International Convention of Salvage, 1989, into LOF 1990 enables the terms of the convention to be brought into effect sooner that they could be otherwise.

It should also be mentioned that the funding agreement (*q.v.*) within the London marine insurance market whereby payments made to salvors under the safety net feature of LOF 1990 and the International Convention of Salvage, 1989 (Art. 14) will be borne by Protection and Indemnity insurers and payments under Art. 13 relating to the vessel, will be borne by hull insurers, always subject to the respective policy conditions.

Since salvage expenses are invariably treated as general average, the ordinary rules regarding consequential damage are applicable. Thus, if the salvor's vessel *unavoidably* and *accidentally* collides with and damages the vessel being assisted, the resultant damage to that vessel is allowed in general average. Similarly if any cargo, stores, or equipment are pilfered during the salvage operations, such loss is made good in general average.

The obligation of a salvor after salvaging property is to "place it in a place of safety in which it would be available to the owner, subject to a libel *in rem* for salvage if desired" (the *Snow Maiden—Laurence H. Powers* v. *Frederick T. White,* 1957 AMC 2093). Until the salvor does redeliver the vessel in a place of safety, he has not completed the salvage services and is not entitled to an award (unless, of course, the vessel owner has accepted redelivery). As to what constitutes a place of safety has been before the British courts on several occasions. In the case of the *Glaucus* (81 L. L. R. 262), when that vessel was redelivered by one salvor at Aden and was subsequently towed to Suez by another vessel, it was held that towage from Aden to Suez also constituted salvage services; this on the grounds that at Aden the *Glaucus* was a damaged ship incapable of any maneuvers whatever under her own power and must, therefore, be regarded as still being in a position of danger. The question came before the courts again in the case of the *Troilus* (195 L. L. R. 467). That vessel lost her propeller and was towed by a sister ship to Aden. Another vessel was engaged to tow the *Troilus* from Aden to the United Kingdom and did so. The issue was whether the towage from Aden to the United Kingdom constituted salvage services or was merely towage services. The case went to the House of Lords and this highest British court considered that the question as to whether a vessel has reached a place of safety or not must depend on the facts of each case; among the factors to be taken into account should be facility for repairs at the place in question, the possibility of safely discharging and storing the cargo and of sending it on to its destination, and the danger of its deterioration. The services begun as salvage by the first vessel were continued by the second vessel because that was the safest, quickest, and most convenient method of towage. The fact that the *Troilus* could lie in physical safety at either Aden, Suez, or Port Said did not transform the services begun as salvage into mere towage. Thus, a ship taken from a position of danger to her ultimate destination may still be the subject of salvage, although on her voyage she is towed past ports at which she could lie in safety. There was an obligation on the master whose ship had suffered damage to do his best to preserve the ship and cargo and to bring both to their destination as cheaply and efficiently as possible, and the salvage lasted as long as the master acted reasonably for the combined benefit of ship and cargo.

From these decisions it appears that unless a vessel is at a port where she can effect repairs necessary for the safe prosecution of her voyage, she cannot be considered to be in a place of safety insofar as the completion of salvage services is concerned.

In the United States it has been held that the standard for determining salvage is not whether the peril is "imminent" but whether it is "reasonably to be apprehended" (tug *Nellie and Barges,* 1969 AMC 186). As another court put it, "immediacy of harm is not essential to salvage" (*Basic Boats v. U. S. A.,* 1973 AMC 522).

Once a salvor has brought the property salved to a place of safety, he will, naturally, not allow it to be removed until either his claim for salvage has been satisfied, or security has been provided. In practice, it is seldom possible to determine the amount of salvage to be paid without the delay of negotiation, arbitration, or legal proceedings, so that the usual course is for bail or other security to be given. The shipowner furnishes security in respect of the ship and also the freight at his risk. In the case of bulk cargoes, it is sometimes possible to arrange for the owners of the cargo to provide security direct to the salvor in respect of the cargo, or to counter-guarantee the shipowner if he furnishes security to the salvor in respect of the cargo. It used to be more usual, however, for the shipowner to give security in respect of the whole of the salved property. If a general cargo were involved, with many individual cargo owners, this course was more or less unavoidable. In giving security in respect of the cargo, the shipowner is protected by his general average lien on the cargo, which he can exercise before parting with the cargo at the termination of the voyage. When the security has been completed, and when whatever repairs may be necessary at the port of refuge have been carried out, the vessel proceeds on her voyage and on arrival at destination the shipowner delivers the cargo and, in substitution for his lien, receives average agreements signed by the consignees, coupled with deposits or average guarantees. In the United States, a salvor sometimes accepts letters of undertaking from the shipowner, if he is known to him, and letters of undertaking from cargo underwriters. If the salvor insists on additional security, it is usual for the vessel's insurance brokers to arrange with a bonding company to provide the necessary salvor's bond to cover the security demanded. This is done at a reduced rate so long as the vessel underwriters provide a letter of counter-indemnity to the bonding company. The Loss Payee clause in the latest (1977) version of the American Institute Hull Clauses authorizes underwriters to make direct payment (by way of reimbursement) to persons providing security for the release of the vessel in salvage cases.

A shipowner who has given security to a salvor for salvage services rendered to both ship and cargo has an insurable interest in the cargo for the contribution due from its owners (*Dodwell* v. *Munich Assurance Co.*, 123 Fed. Rep. 841, 128 Fed. Rep. 835). Thus, immediately after the salvage services are concluded, the vessel owner should effect an insurance on "general average and/or salvage disbursements" because even if the vessel were subsequently lost before completing her voyage, the salvor would still be entitled to a salvage award based on the salved values at the termination of the salvage services. However, for some time shipowners have found it increasingly difficult to collect general average contributions from cargo interests who have raised the defense of unseaworthiness at every opportunity. In this attitude they have been encouraged by the courts, who have tended to look very closely at the Hague Rules' exemptions and interpret very strictly the carrier's obligation to exercise due diligence to provide a seaworthy vessel at the commencement of the voyage. If and when the Hamburg Rules come into effect, the prospect of shipowners collecting promptly from cargo interests under general average guarantees will become even more remote (*see* Chapter 6). Consequently, it is unlikely that many shipowners will put up security to salvors on cargo interests' behalf. The result has been that salvors have had to obtain separate salvage security from the various cargo interests. In the case of general cargoes (and, in particular, containerized cargoes) this has resulted in salvors being faced with the considerable expense and difficulty of tracing hundreds and perhaps thousands of individual cargo owners. Very often the employment by salvors of an average adjuster to take such security has been the only solution. Once the shipowner has provided security in respect of the vessel, the salvor cannot detain it, and if the salvor is to preserve his lien against cargo he may have no alternative but to discharge and store the cargo until such time as security is obtained. Since the cargo, *in toto*, is often worth considerably more than the ship, this solution—expensive though it may be— cannot be lightly rejected by the salvor. In cases where it is not possible to salve the vessel but the cargo can be saved, the cost of the operation becomes a special or particular charge against such cargo. In such cases, the services of an average adjuster to collect security before releasing the cargo saved, to obtain salved values, and to apportion the salvage award are necessary and, indeed, invaluable to the salvor.

In 1989 the Association of Average Adjusters of the United States and the American Institute of Marine Underwriters addressed the problem of providing security to salvors on behalf of cargo interests and approved the following agreement for general use in the American marine insurance market.

> SALVAGE SECURITY AGREEMENT. In consideration of the vessel owner or other interested party(ies) providing salvage security to the Committee of Lloyds or others on behalf of the cargo described above, we hereby undertake to pay on demand any sum or sums including interest and costs that may be agreed with and/or awarded to the Salvor in respect of said cargo under the terms of Lloyd's Standard Form of "No Cure—No Pay" salvage agreement or other agreement of similar import. Payment(s) will not exceed, in total, the above cargo's proportion of the award or agreed settlement had cargo posted security directly to salvors.
>
> It is understood cargo's right to demand indemnification from the vessel owner and/or concerned P and I Club and/or other party(ies) is not prejudiced by this undertaking.

The thrust of the agreement is that cargo underwriters undertake to pay the salvor that part of any salvage award which falls on cargo that they insured. In essence, the agreement postpones any right which those cargo underwriters might have to obtain indemnification from the carrier or his Protection and Indemnity underwriters, etc. (as, for example, when there has been lack of due diligence to provide a seaworthy vessel and the necessity for the salvage operation arose because of that lack of diligence). In brief, legal arguments regarding any alleged unseaworthiness are to be deferred until after the salvor has been paid (*see* the discussion in Chapter 6 regarding the exercise of due diligence by shipowners in general average cases). The agreement is also in line with the spirit of Rule D of the York/Antwerp Rules (*q.v.*).

Sometimes, in spite of the salvor's best efforts, it is not possible to save either vessel or cargo. If the salvor was employed on a no cure—no pay contract, he simply licks his wounds and hopes for better luck next time; the shipowner and cargo owners collect total losses under their policies. However, if the salvor was operating on a daily rate basis without regard to the success or failure of the operation (which may very well be the case if the chances of success were remote from the outset), he still has to be paid by the shipowner who, in spite of collecting a total loss from his hull underwriters, remains out of pocket for the abortive salvage expenses. Hull underwriters, recognizing their assured's predicament, now include a clause in the hull policy which enables the shipowner to recover part of such expenses to the extent that they can be regarded as having been incurred in respect of the vessel. In other words, the abortive salvage expenses are apportioned over the estimated values of ship and cargo, and hull underwriters respond for the vessel's share. The shipowner is still out of pocket for cargo's share of such expenses unless the cargo underwriters can be traced and are in a benevolent frame of mind. While cargo underwriters may have a moral liability to the shipowner in such situations, they are not legally liable to make any contribution.

If the salvor does not enforce his lien against vessel and cargo before the voyage is completed and the cargo delivered, he is then left with the following courses of action. He may enforce his lien against the vessel *in rem* or against the vessel owner *in personam*, but only in respect of vessel's share of the salvage award. The salvor's lien against the cargo is reduced to an *in personam* suit against the cargo owner.

Very often salvage operations continue for an appreciable period of time. Sometimes the cargo is landed separately as a first step in the attempt to save the vessel. The problem of how to deal with these so-called complex salvage operations has always presented difficulties and each case must be dealt with on its merits.

Generally speaking, it is usual for the complete cost of complex salvage operations to be treated as general average—at least up to the point when the safety of *all* the property at risk has been attained. Thus, where the whole series of operations has been planned at the outset and undertaken with the object of saving both ship and cargo and is continuously carried out, the entire cost is general average (*McAndrews* v. *Thatcher*, 3 Wall. 347). In similar vein where, just before scuttling the vessel to extinguish a fire, part of the cargo was discharged into lighters and forwarded by another vessel, the separation was considered to have been not merely for the safety of the cargo discharged but also for the benefit of the ship and the remainder of the cargo; thus, the cargo so forwarded was chargeable with its proportionate share of the expense of salving the ship and the remainder of the cargo (*Reliance Marine Ins. Co.* v. *New York & Cuba Mail S. S. Co.,* 77 Fed. Rep. 317).

On the other hand, where part of the property is removed before salvage operations are commenced, solely for its own preservation (for example, a small shipment of high value such as bullion), and delivered to the consignees, the cost of removal is treated as a special charge on that cargo, which is not required to contribute to the subsequent salvage operations (*Pacific Mail S. S. Co.* v. *N. Y. H. & R. Minting Co.,* 74 Fed. Rep. 564). However, such shipments, *if on board the vessel when the salvage operations are commenced,* are liable to contribute to the entire cost of the salvage operations (the *St. Paul,* 86 Fed. Rep. 340).

In deciding the treatment of borderline cases, the more important factors to be considered include:

(1) Whether the cargo in question was separated because of some special characteristic, such as bullion which has a high ratio of value to bulk and weight, or perishables which deteriorate during delay, in other words, the real reason for its discharge.

(2) Whether the cargo in question was discharged before the regular salvors commenced their operations.

(3) Whether the accident occurred near destination.

(4) Whether the discharged cargo was ever reloaded.

When salvage expenses are treated as general average, it is the practice in the United States to give credit against the salvage award for any voyage expenses saved. In this connection, Rule V of the Association of Average Adjusters reads:

RULE V. CREDIT FOR EXPENSES SAVED ON SALVAGE SERVICES, ETC. Where salvage services are rendered to a vessel, or she becomes disabled and is necessarily towed to her port of destination, and the expenses of such towage are allowable in general average, there shall be credited against the allowance such ordinary expenses as would have been incurred, but have been saved by the salvage or towage services.

However, in applying this rule it is the practice of average adjusters to offset the savings in voyage expenses (usually fuel and stores, etc., by virtue of the salvor having towed the vessel towards destination) by the extra wages, etc., of the crew incurred as a result of the enhanced duration of the voyage due to the vessel being under tow.

When both the salving and the salved vessels belong to the same owner, he may claim salvage for the services rendered to the *cargo* in the salved ship. In this connection, the Salvage Act of 1912 provides that "the right to remuneration for assistance or salvage shall not be affected by common ownership of the vessels rendering and receiving such assistance or salvage services." The policies on the vessel may contain a Sister Ship salvage clause whereby the shipowner may claim against his underwriters in respect of the proportion of the salvage services applying to the sister ship—that is, the services he has rendered to his own property. The Sister Ship clause in the American Institute Hull Clauses reads:

> In the event of salvage, towage or other assistance being rendered to the Vessel by any vessel belonging in part or in whole to the same Owners or Charterers, the value of such services (without regard to the common ownership or control of the vessels) shall be ascertained by arbitration in the manner provided for under the Collision Liability clause in this Policy, and the amount so awarded so far as applicable to the interest hereby insured shall constitute a charge under this Policy.

In practice it is quite customary for the vessel owner to submit an invoice for the services rendered by the sister ship. This invoice is usually based on the actual operating expenses of the sister ship, including consumption of fuel and stores; wages, provisions, and overtime of the crew; any special bonus paid to the officers and crew; and the cost of marine insurance for the period involved plus any profits lost by the vessel owner by reason of the salvage services performed. The invoice setting forth the amount claimed is then submitted to the vessel and cargo underwriters and any other interests concerned in the salvage expenses for their agreement. Such a procedure obviates having to submit the question of salvage remuneration to arbitration, which can be quite a time-consuming procedure.

Unless otherwise agreed by contract, success is essential to any claim for salvage and no award can be granted where nothing was saved (the *Helena*, 1971 AMC 2270). Awards for salvage services are either mutually agreed upon between the salvors and the owners of the property salved or they may be decided by an arbitrator or by the courts.

The factors to be considered in arriving at the award were enumerated in the case of the *Blackwall* (77 U.S. 1) and the following is an extract from the opinion of the court:

> Courts of admiralty usually consider the following circumstances as the main ingredients in determining the amount of the award to be decreed for a salvage service:

(1) The labor expended by the salvors in rendering the salvage service.

(2) The promptitude, skill and energy displayed in rendering the service and saving the property.

(3) The value of the property employed by the salvors in rendering the service and the danger to which such property was exposed.

(4) The risk incurred by the salvors in securing the property from the impending peril.

(5) The value of property saved.

(6) The degree of danger from which the property was rescued.

Article 13 (1) of the International Convention on Salvage, 1989 (*q.v.*), enlarged on the "criteria for fixing the reward" as follows:

The reward shall be fixed with a view to encouraging salvage operations, taking into account the following criteria without regard to the order in which they are presented below:

(a) the salved value of the vessel and other property.

(b) the skill and efforts of the salvors in preventing or minimizing damage to the environment.

(c) the measure of success obtained by the salvor.

(d) the nature and degree of the danger.

(e) the skill and efforts of the salvors in salving the vessel, other property and life.

(f) the time used and expenses and losses incurred by the salvors.

(g) the risk of liability and other risks run by the salvors or their equipment

(h) the promptness of the services rendered.

(i) the availability and use of vessels or other equipment intended for salvage operations.

(j) the state of readiness and efficiency of the salvor's equipment and the value thereof.

It will be noted that an important new factor has entered into salvage operations and the assessment of salvage awards since the previous salvage convention of 1910—the protection of the environment.

The values to be taken into consideration in assessing the award are the values at the completion of the salvage operations. These values may or may not be the same as at the completion of the adventure (if the adventure is resumed). If the vessel happens to be sold immediately following the salvage services, it has been held that in arriving at her salved value, the following expenses can be deducted: port charges including any dry dock dues necessarily incurred to effect repairs for the common safety, dry-docking, etc., for inspection by potential purchasers, and, of course, the expenses of sale (the *Lamington,* 86 Fed. Rep. 675).

Insofar as the salved value of cargo is concerned, this, like the salved value of the vessel, is based on the actual value at the place where the salvage services are terminated and will usually be the invoice cost including freight if same was prepaid or guaranteed, vessel lost or not lost. If the freight was at the risk of the shipowner or charterer, this will contribute separately. From the basic cargo value, any damage and particular or special charges are deductible to arrive at the salved value. If freight is contributing separately, the contingent expenses necessary to earn such freight would be deductible. However, arbitrators generally have shown reluctance to accept that any deductions should be made from the value of either ship or cargo on account of "contingencies," that is to say, the risks inherent in the completion of the voyage. Nor is it the practice to deduct future general average contributions from the salved values. An exception to this would be where, after the salvor has redelivered the vessel at a place of safety, the vessel with its cargo is towed to destination. In such circumstances, the cost of towage (which would probably be allowable as general average) would be deductible from the ship value to arrive at the salved value; this on the grounds that the value of the ship at the place of safety where the salvage service terminated is the value at the place to which the ship is subsequently towed, less the cost of such towage. Furthermore, in arriving at the salved values, the expense is treated as one which has been incurred by the shipowner and not apportioned between ship and cargo—even though, ultimately, such an apportionment may be made in the general average adjustment.

A salvage award is not limited to any particular percentage of the value of the property salved and under unusual circumstances might even amount to the total value salved (*Barbara Lee—Invincible,* 1964 AMC 2314).

The International Convention on Salvage, 1989 (*q.v.*), states that "the rewards" exclusive of any interest and recoverable legal costs that may be payable thereon, shall not exceed the salved value of the vessel and other property (Art. 13 (3)).

Any damage negligently done by a salvor to a vessel while rendering salvage services is taken into account firstly by the salvage award being based on a salved value reduced by the damage, and secondly by deducting part or all of the damage from the salvage award. Furthermore, it has been held that the vessel owner is entitled to counterclaim for damages (including loss of profit, if any) arising from negligence of the salvor, and that such counterclaim is not restricted to the amount of the salvage award (the

Tojo Maru, 1971 1 L. L. R. 341). In essence, a salvor now has no right arbitrarily to reduce his liability for negligent work.

In these days of strict oil pollution laws, negligence during a salvage operation can have even more disastrous financial repercussions; nor can a salvor rely on the right to limit his liability as a vessel owner in such circumstances. It was held in the *Tojo Maru* case (*supra*) that a salvor may not limit his liability when a crew member of the salvage tug leaves the tug to perform work on the vessel being salved and negligently causes damage to that vessel. In such circumstances, the court decided that the negligent act was neither done in the "management" of the salvage tug nor was it an act or omission of a person "on board" the tug. This decision caused consternation among salvors, particularly in view of the possibility of enormous oil pollution liabilities arising out of salvage operations. This resulted in innumerable requests by salvors for indemnities before they would undertake salvage contracts. Ultimately, salvors' Protection and Indemnity underwriters were obliged to provide coverage against such liabilities.

When the International Convention on Limitation of Liability for Maritime Claims, 1976, came into effect, this difficulty for salvors was alleviated. The convention extends the right of limitation to salvor as such. Unfortunately, it is not likely to be ratified by the United States. It is to be hoped that if and when the American Limitation of Liability Act is revised, consideration will be given to protecting salvors, whose very efforts to salve a tanker and prevent oil pollution may, due to the conditions under which they are working, unhappily result in oil spills, with or without negligence.

In the United States, the amount to be paid for salvage services is often negotiated with the salvor by the Salvage Awards Committee of the American Institute of Marine Underwriters. The committee (which acts in an advisory capacity only) meets with representatives of the salvor, the average adjuster, and other interested parties and, after discussing the merits of the case, recommends the amount to be awarded the salvor. The award is subject to the approval of the shipowner, the ship and cargo underwriters concerned, and the salvor. Any substantial uninsured cargo interest would also have the right to object to the award.

Most salvage services are rendered on Lloyd's Standard Form of Salvage Agreement which was revised in 1972 (*see* Appendix G of the first edition of this book). However, because the universal fear of oil pollution had created many new difficulties for professional salvors, the form was again revised in 1980 (*see* Appendix G of the second edition of this book). Traditionally, under Lloyd's form, the services are undertaken on a no cure—no pay basis; in other words, there is no award unless the property is salved. While this no cure—no pay concept is retained in the 1980 form, there is one important deviation therefrom. If the property being salved is a tanker, laden or partly laden with a cargo of oil, and, without negligence on the part of the salvors,

(a) the services are not successful, or
(b) are only partially successful, or
(c) the salvor is prevented from completing the services,

the salvor shall nevertheless receive his "reasonably incurred expenses and an increment not exceeding 15 per cent of such expenses" but only if and to the extent that such expenses plus increment exceed any amount (award) otherwise recoverable under the salvage agreement. This important innovation (which has been described as a "safety net") ensures that the salvor of a laden or partly laden tanker will receive some reward for his services even if, through no fault of his own, he is not successful or only partially successful. Some such provision was essential to encourage professional salvors to continue to undertake salvage services to tankers notwithstanding the special difficulties now inherent in such operations. In the event the so-called safety net exception to the principle of no cure—no pay becomes likely to be applicable, the vessel owner is required to provide security to the salvor for his remuneration under the exception. Any ultimate payment to the salvor under this provision will be borne by Protection and Indemnity clubs and underwriters. Presumably as a *quid pro quo* for the new safety net feature, the salvor, in the new salvage agreement, specifically undertakes to "use his best endeavors to prevent the escape of oil from the vessel while performing the service of salving the subject vessel and/or her cargo bunkers and stores."

Several other important changes were included in the 1980 form:

(1) Provision is made for the salvage security, salved values, and salvage award to be given in any currency agreed to by the parties to the salvage agreement.

(2) Provision is made for an interim salvage award by way of payment on account against the final award.

(3) Provision is made for the salvor to claim salvage and enforce any award or agreement made between the salvor and the parties interested in the property salved against security provided under the salvage agreement in the name and on behalf of any subcontractors, including masters and members of the crews of vessels employed by him provided he indemnifies and holds harmless the owner of the property salved against all claims by or liabilities incurred to the said persons.

(4) The salvor is allowed to limit any liability to the owner of the subject vessel arising from the salvage services "to the extent provided by

English law and as if the provisions of the Convention on Limitation of Liability for Maritime Claims, 1976 were part of the law of England." (It should be noted that the 1980 form stipulates that English law is to govern the salvage agreement and the arbitration proceedings.)

Under the 1980 form, as under previous versions of the form, the master (as agent) contracts independently on behalf of the ship, cargo, and freight interests. On completion of the salvage services, the salvor, if he has not already done so, notifies the committee of Lloyd's as to the amount of security required, and the committee takes the necessary steps in this connection. Pending the completion of the security arrangements, the contractor (salvor) has a maritime lien on the property salved, which property must not be removed from the place of safety to which it has been taken by the contractor until such security has been provided. In due course, the arbitration procedure laid down in the form is followed. Solicitors are appointed to represent the property salved, salved values are agreed (if possible) with the solicitors representing the salvors, and the arbitrator appointed by the committee of Lloyd's hears both sides. After due consideration, the arbitrator's award is published. There is a right of appeal against the award but this must be made within 14 days (exclusive of Saturdays, Sundays, or other general holidays). If no appeal is lodged, the committee collects the sum awarded from the parties concerned and pays the salvor. Interest at a rate per annum to be fixed by the arbitrator is payable to the contractor from the expiration of 21 days (exclusive of Saturdays, Sundays, or other general holidays) from the date of publication of the award until the date of payment. If there is a default in payment, the award may be enforced against the security held by the committee. If an appeal is lodged, an arbitrator on appeal is appointed who subsequently issues his award. The award of the arbitrator on appeal is final and binding on all the parties concerned.

The long-established practice under Lloyd's Open Form (LOF) whereby the master (as agent) contracts independently on behalf of the ship, cargo, and freight interests was questioned in the case of the *Choko Star*. In that case the cargo owner was required to provide security of $2.15 million to salvors in respect of cargo alone and did so under protest. Cargo interests took the position that LOF was not binding on them; the master was not an agent of necessity, as it was clearly unreasonable for him to bind them in the circumstances prevailing. Cargo interests further maintained that the master could and should have communicated with them before entering into LOF; it was unreasonable to engage these salvors to deal with the casualty when local tug assistance (on a per diem basis) was all that was necessary. The cargo owners applied for an injunction restraining the salvors from proceeding with the salvage arbitration. The application was refused by the lower court and, on appeal, the English court of appeals held that under LOF the arbitral procedure had operated successfully worldwide for many decades; once security had been given, all parties knew and proceeded on the basis that in the absence of a settlement there would be an arbitration; that process should only be arrested in exceptional circumstances and unless there were such circumstances there should be no interference by the court with the normal, well-understood, and accepted procedures which resulted from LOF being signed (the *Choko Star,* 1987 1 L.R. 508). It is interesting to note that the International Convention on Salvage, 1989 (*q.v.*), specifically provides that the master shall have the authority to conclude contracts for salvage operations on behalf of the owner of the vessel and, furthermore, that the master or the owner of the vessel shall also have the authority to conclude such contracts on behalf of the owner of the property on board the vessel (Art. 6 (2)).

The fear of oil pollution coupled with the strict international legislation against oil pollution has made life difficult for professional salvors. In the past, the first priority of both the shipowner and the salvor was to save the distressed ship and its cargo. Now there is a new priority for both shipowners and salvors, particularly when dealing with loaded tankers, that is, to prevent or limit oil spills during the salvage operation. Indeed, it has been suggested that where there is a *risk* of oil pollution, salvors should be entitled to an enhanced award as a matter of public policy. Salvors (and others) have suggested that there should be either an extra fund earmarked for the prevention of oil pollution or that salvors should be guaranteed payment for services rendered in preventing or attempting to prevent oil pollution regardless of success or failure. This idea is, of course, contrary to the concept of no cure—no pay on which Lloyd's Form of Salvage Agreement is based. It must also be remembered that salvage services rendered under Lloyd's form are treated as general average, with the result that any increase in the amount of the salvage award because of the salvor's efforts to prevent or limit oil pollution during the salvage services would, in the normal course, be borne by ship and cargo underwriters. Such interests are not really liable for such extra payment and, indeed, such increments to salvors do not come within the definition of general average. The questions are: Who should bear the enhanced awards? And if the answer be hull underwriters, cargo underwriters, and Protection and Indemnity underwriters, then in what ratio?

The new 1980 Lloyd's Form of Salvage Agreement represented a compromise. While there has been no extra fund created for specific awards for pollution avoidance, the safety net feature (to be financed by Protection and Indemnity insurers) will at least ensure some payment to salvors for services rendered in preventing or attempting to prevent oil pollution, regardless of success or failure. In the case of *successful* salvage operations, arbitrators, in arriving at the amount of the award, will no doubt continue to take into account the services rendered by salvors in avoiding or reducing oil pollution. Absent any breakdown of such awards between salvage of property and oil pollution avoidance (which is apparently not contemplated), the awards will be apportioned as general average over vessel, cargo, and any other salved property in the usual way.

An arbitrator, in arriving at a salvage award, takes into account all the facts of the actual situation including the salvor's efforts to avert or reduce oil pollution. As a practical matter it would be almost impossible to quantify that part of the salvage award relating to the skill and "best endeavors" of the salvors in preventing or minimizing damage to the environment. Indeed one Lloyd's arbitrator has written (*Lloyd's Maritime and Commercial Law Quarterly,* February 1985, p. 41):

> . . . one could no more divorce those features from the overall assessment of remuneration than one can divorce other features such as the state of the weather or of the sea on particular days during the salvage service.

With this difficulty in mind a so-called funding agreement was entered into in the London marine insurance market between hull and cargo underwriters and the International Group of P & I clubs whereby the clubs agreed to accept liability for salvage awards made under the "safety net" provisions of Lloyd's Form of Salvage Agreement (1980) subject to a general acceptance by hull and cargo underwriters of an obligation to pay in full any property awards inclusive of any element of enhancement for preventing or minimizing damage to the environment. In the United States the American Hull Insurance Syndicate accepted this compromise in principle although there has been dissent by some individual American cargo underwriters and some American oil companies.

In these changing times, whenever a major accident occurs involving a loaded tanker, the interested parties are no longer limited to the shipowner, the cargo owner, and those who insure them. The whole world is watching with a critical eye, and those whose property is threatened if the salvage operation is not successful have as big a stake as those directly involved. It is apparently felt that the greater the potential reward to salvors, the more likely we are to avoid international disaster through oil pollution. In such situations salvors are also faced with other practical difficulties such as the reluctance of even major maritime countries to provide anchorages to damaged tankers for lightening purposes. Furthermore, as we have already seen, salvors are being held strictly liable for any oil spills attributable to negligence on their part and, as a result, may have difficulty in obtaining adequate coverage against oil pollution liabilities. These potential liabilities are so immense that it is understandable that salvors should be concerned—and on occasions decline to become involved in extreme cases where the prospect of a successful salvage operation with adequate remuneration is remote and not worth the risks involved. Some of these difficulties are, of course, beyond the scope of Lloyd's Form of Salvage Agreement but, nevertheless, LOF 1980 went a long way towards solving some of the salvage contractors' problems. LOF 1990 (*supra*), embracing as it does the new international salvage convention, continues the good work.

The chairman of the British Association of Average Adjusters in 1980, W. P. F. Bennett, dealt in his address with some of the questions faced by average adjusters in this area of salvage, general average, and oil pollution.

Occasionally contracts for salvage are arranged with *an agreed sum* to be paid only if the salvage efforts are successful. As long ago as 1856, the U.S. Supreme Court (*Post* v. *Jones*, 60 U.S. 150, 160, quoted by Baer in *Admiralty Law of the Supreme Court*) had this to say about such contracts:

> Where the stipulated compensation is dependent upon success, and particularly of success within a limited time, it may be very much larger than a mere *quantum meruit*.

> Indeed, such contracts will not be set aside unless corruptly entered into, or made under fraudulent representations a clear mistake or suppression of important facts, in immediate danger to the ship, or under other circumstances amounting to compulsion, or when their enforcement would be contrary to equity and good conscience.

> We are unable to assent to the general proposition laid down in some [cases] . . . that salvage contracts are within the discretion of the court, and will be set aside in all cases where, after the service is performed, the stipulated compensation appears to be unreasonable. If such were the law, contracts for salvage services would be of no practical value, and salvors would be forced to rely upon the liberality of the courts.

> A salvage contract is not objectionable, "when prudently entered into, upon the ground that it may result more or less favorably to the parties interested than was anticipated when the contract was made."

> We do not say that to impugn a salvage contract such duress must be shown as would require a court of law to set aside an ordinary contract; but where no such circumstances exist as amount to a moral compulsion, the contract should not be held bad simply be-

cause the price agreed to be paid turned out to be much greater than the services were actually worth. The presumptions are in favor of the validity of the contract.

If when the contract is made the price agreed to be paid appears to be just and reasonable in view of the value of the property at stake, the danger from which it is to be rescued, the risk to the salvors and the salving property, the time and labor probably necessary to effect the salvage, and the contingency of losing all in case of failure, this sum ought not to be reduced by an unexpected success in accomplishing the work, unless the compensation for the work actually done is grossly exorbitant.

The saving of human life (life salvage) without the saving of property does not entitle the salvor to an award, although life salvors are entitled to a fair share of the remuneration awarded for salving a vessel and her cargo. However, the courts may be reconsidering this attitude (*see* the recent case of *Peninsular & Oriental Steam Navigation Co.* v. *Overseas Oil Carriers Inc.*, 1977 AMC 283, which is discussed in Chapter 8). It should be noted, however, that the International Convention on Salvage, 1989 (*q.v.*), states that no remuneration is due from persons whose lives are saved but that a salvor of human life, who has taken part in the salvage operation, is entitled to a fair share of the payment awarded to the salvor for salving the vessel or other property or for minimizing damage to the environment (Art. 16).

A tug is bound by the contract of towage not to abandon both tow and contract when the tow gets into difficulties until reasonable resources of seamanship are exhausted. No claim for remuneration beyond the amount of the towage contract can lawfully be made by the tug until the obligation of that contract has been fulfilled as far as reasonably possible, or until the service claimed is shown to be outside of the contract (the *Joseph F. Clinton*, 250 Fed. Rep. 977). Thus, in *Waterman S. S. Corp.* v. *Shipowners & Merchants Towboat Co. Ltd.* (1953 AMC 125), it was held that when, through the parting of a hawser in a full gale, a vessel in tow went adrift and was rescued through the efforts of her tug, the services were beyond the scope of the towage contract and the tug was entitled to salvage. On the other hand, a tug which negligently strands a barge in tow may not have salvage from the cargo in the barge for extra standing by and extra towing (the *Mohican*, 1934 AMC 112).

As the court put it in *Franklin Sears* v. *American Producer, et al.* (1972 AMC 1647), whether a tug's services constitute salvage rather than towage depends on the existence of an apparent marine peril and the fact that the services were voluntary rather than the result of an existing duty or special contract.

The law in the United Kingdom is similar; to constitute a salvage service by a tug under contract to tow, two elements are necessary:

(1) That the tow is in danger by reason of circumstances which could not reasonably have been contemplated by the parties, and

(2) That risks are incurred or duties performed by the tug which could not reasonably be held to be within the scope of the contract.

Under American law, whether salvage services rendered under contract are general average or Sue and Labor charges is often difficult to determine. It can also be a very important question because Sue and Labor charges can be recovered in addition to a total loss while salvage charges in the nature of general average cannot. The question most frequently comes up when the salvage services are rendered to a vessel in ballast. In such cases it has been suggested that if the salvor has been hired by the assured or his agents for a *fixed sum* (even though on no cure—no pay terms), under American law the services come within the definition of both Sue and Labor charges and general average. Under English law they would, of course, be Sue and Labor. Thus, even if the value of the salved vessel proved to be less than the fixed sum payable to the salvors, underwriters would be liable under the Sue and Labor clause for the full amount paid for salvage in addition to a total loss. (Underwriters could, of course, take possession of the wreck.) However, if similar services are rendered on no cure—no pay terms with remuneration to be settled on a salvage basis, the resultant award is salvage (or general average under American law) and would not be recoverable by the assured in addition to a total loss. However, in such a case the salvage award applying to the vessel could not be more than the salved value of the vessel and (under American law) would be payable by underwriters as general average. If the vessel turned out to be a constructive total loss, the assured would presumably have abandoned the vessel to underwriters and the salvage award would be payable by whoever exercised ownership of the wreck.

The chairman of the Association of Average Adjusters of the United States in 1969, T. Livingstone, dealt with various practical problems arising out of contract salvage and the reader will find his address of great interest.

International Convention on Salvage, 1989

A new international salvage convention under the auspices of the International Maritime Organization (IMO) was considered and adopted at a diplomatic conference in London in 1989. This convention will "enter into force one year after the date on which 15 States have expressed their consent to be bound by it" (Art. 29). When ratified, the convention will supersede the existing international law of salvage as laid down in the Brussels Convention of 1910. Environmental considerations were the dominating factor behind the new convention. The main objective was to provide an adequate level of remuneration to salvors in all kinds of salvage operations. With adequate remuneration guaranteed it was hoped that salvors would be encouraged to undertake salvage even in cases where there was little or no chance of their succeeding in salving the ship and its cargo yet the environment was threatened. In such cases there might be no fund of salved property on which to base a salvage award in the normal manner. In view of this objective it is not surprising that that part of the new convention dealing with the method to be followed to adequately compensate and encourage salvors was the most important (and difficult) problem facing the conference in London.

The Comité Maritime International (CMI) had worked on a proposed salvage convention for several years and a draft convention had been approved at a CMI conference at Montreal in 1981. The matter was then referred to the Legal Committee of the International Maritime Organization (IMO), an organization of the United Nations. The draft salvage convention approved by the CMI at Montreal became the working document in preparing the final draft for submission to the diplomatic conference in London in 1989. In addressing the problem of providing special (guaranteed) remuneration to salvors for their efforts in preventing or minimizing damage to the environment, the diplomatic conference adopted the "safety net" approach introduced in Lloyd's Open Form of Salvage Agreement (LOF) in 1980, which approach had been endorsed by the CMI in 1981. The international convention in London adopted a special compensation clause (Art. 14) to ensure that salvors, even if they were unsuccessful in salving either ship or cargo but had prevented or minimized damage to the environment, would be suitably rewarded. This was what the so-called Lloyd's safety net did. Under the new convention any special compensation under Art. 14 is to be paid by the shipowners or their Protection and Indemnity (P&I) insurers (if any). Indeed this is the case under the London market's funding agreement. The draft convention prepared by the CMI had accepted the principle of rewarding salvors for efforts in preventing or minimizing damage to the environment, whether their efforts in saving the ship and its cargo were successful or not, and were aware of the funding agreement in this connection. However at the London convention dissenting cargo interests and others attempted, albeit unsuccessfully, to persuade the convention to modify the method by which the salvage award was to be funded by underwriters (the funding agreement). They objected to ship and cargo alone having to contribute to a successful salvage operation when during the course of that operation the salvor had prevented or minimized damage to the environment. They felt the shipowner or his P&I insurers should bear part of the award in such cases. As we have seen under the existing market agreement, the shipowner's liability underwriters (P&I) funded the special compensation payable under the safety net rule in those cases where no property was saved (a liability which technically would not fall on P&I insurers unless the oil pollution had resulted from their assured's negligence). Under the agreement the property underwriters (ship and cargo insurers) paid the salvage award for salving the ship and its cargo (including as a *quid pro quo* to the P&I insurers any enhancement in the salvage award which might have resulted from preventing or minimizing oil pollution). In this connection salvage arbitrators have said that in a successful salvage operation it is virtually impossible to quantify that part of the award appertaining to "preventing or minimizing" oil pollution. The gentleman's agreement or funding agreement referred to above had proven to be an equitable solution and one which had satisfied most insurers for almost a decade.

Art. 13 of the new convention (*supra*) gives the criteria for fixing the reward. In particular the reward is to be fixed with a view to encouraging salvage operations and must not exceed the salved value of the vessel and other property. Art. 14 deals with the thorny subject of special compensation to salvors and is probably the most important part of the convention from a marine insurance viewpoint. If the salvor has carried out the salvage operation with "skill . . . in preventing or minimizing damage to the environment . . ." (Art. 13) but has failed to earn a reward under Art. 13 "at least equivalent to the special compensation assessable in accordance with this article" (Art. 14) the salvor is entitled to special compensation *from the owner of the salved vessel* equivalent to his expenses. (Salvor's expenses means the out-of-pocket expenses reasonably incurred by the salvors, including a fair rate for equipment and personnel actually and reasonably used in the salvage operation [Art. 14 (3)].) Furthermore, if the salvor by his salvage operation has prevented or minimized damage to the environment, the special compensation payable by the shipowner to the salvor may be increased up to a maximum of thirty percent of the expenses incurred by the salvor. In addition, if the tribunal (arbitrator) deems it appropriate, the special compensation may be increased further, but in no event shall the total increase be more than 100 percent of the expenses incurred by the salvor. The total special compensation under Art. 14 is to be paid only "if and to the extent that such compensation is greater than any reward recoverable by the salvor under Art. 13." A common understanding (Attachment 1) was added to the International Convention on Salvage stating that, in fixing a reward under Art. 13 and assessing special compensation under Art. 14, the tribunal (arbitrator) does not need to fix a reward under Art. 13

up to the maximum salved value of the vessel, cargo, and any other property before assessing any special compensation under Art. 14. This apparently means that when the property salved is of limited value so that the special compensation approaches that value, two awards may be made: one against the property salved in the usual manner and the other for the balance of the salvor's expenses assessed under Art. 14. A further resolution (Attachment 2) was passed at the convention requesting an amendment to Rule VI (*q.v.*) of the York/Antwerp Rules, 1974. The object of this resolution was to ensure that *special compensation* paid under Art. 14 was not to be allowed in general average (that is to say, was not to be reapportioned as general average). In point of fact, this request made by the conference appears to have been unnecessary because Rule VI of the York/Antwerp Rules, 1974, already limits the allowance of salvage in general average "to the extent that the salvage operations were undertaken for the purpose of preserving from peril the *property* involved in the common maritime adventure." Thus special compensation payable to salvors under Art. 14 would not come within Rule VI and therefore could not be allowed and reapportioned in general average as the conference apparently feared. It should be again emphasized that the resolution refers only to the *special compensation* payable under Art. 14. Nevertheless, as stated earlier, Rule VI of the York/Antwerp Rules, 1974 has been amended to allay the fears expressed at the International Convention on Salvage, 1989.

It was not all good news for salvors because the convention stipulates that if the salvor is negligent and as a result of that negligence fails to prevent or minimize damage to the environment he may be deprived of the whole or part of any special compensation due under Art. 14.

It might be useful to summarize the effect of the International Convention on Salvage, 1989, when it is binding on the parties to a salvage contract. The salvage arbitrator, in assessing his award, may use either or both of two methods (depending on the nature and result of the salvage services rendered).

(1) Under Art. 13 he may assess his award against *the salved property* in the usual way but his award must not exceed the value of the salved property (ship and cargo). The award is to be independent of any special compensation which may be awarded to the salvor under Art. 14 and the award under Art. 13 is payable by the salved property (or their insurers) in proportion to their respective values in the usual way.

(2) Under Art. 14 the arbitrator may award the salvor a special compensation equivalent to his expenses for preventing or minimizing damage to the environment if his award under Art. 13 is not at least equivalent to the special compensation provided for in Art. 14. Art. 14 permits the arbi-

trator to increase the special compensation to the salvor (consisting of his expenses) by a maximum of 30 percent of the expenses incurred by the salvor. When it is appropriate, he may increase the special compensation further but in no event shall the total increase exceed the expenses incurred by the salvor. The total special compensation under Art. 14 is to be paid by the shipowner only if and to the extent that such compensation is greater than any award recoverable by the salvor under Art. 13.

It has to be said that the formula for assessing special compensation under Art. 14 is rather unwieldy and somewhat difficult to interpret. In any event as already stated the actual salvage contract in each individual case will prevail over the convention.

The complete text of the International Convention on Salvage, 1989, is to be found in Appendix H.

SUE AND LABOR CHARGES

Sue and Labor charges form a subdivision of the more general term, particular charges (or special charges). Particular charges are expenses incurred by, or on behalf of, the assured for the safety or preservation of the subject-matter insured, other than general average and salvage charges (Marine Insurance Act, Sect. 64 (2)). Sue and Labor charges are dealt with in Sect. 78 of the act, which reads:

(1) Where the policy contains a suing and laboring clause, the engagement thereby entered into is deemed to be supplementary to the contract of insurance, and the assured may recover from the insurer any expenses properly incurred pursuant to the clause, notwithstanding that the insurer may have paid for a total loss, or that the subject-matter may have been warranted free from particular average, either wholly or under a certain percentage.

(2) General average losses and contributions and salvage charges, as defined by this Act, are not recoverable under the suing and laboring clause.

(3) Expenses incurred for the purpose of averting or diminishing any loss not covered by the policy are not recoverable under the suing and laboring clause.

(4) It is the duty of the assured and his agents, in all cases, to take such measures as may be reasonable for the purpose of averting or minimizing a loss.

Sue and Labor charges arise when the assured, his servants, factors, or assigns incur expenditure to minimize or avert a loss which has occurred or is threatened. The loss minimized or averted must be one for which underwriters are liable and must arise out of the basic perils insured against and not be due to those perils especially covered by the collision clause (*Munson* v. *Standard Marine Ins. Co.*, 156 Fed. Rep. 44).

A Sue and Labor clause is included in most policies on ship, cargo, and freight and in the American Institute Hull Clauses reads as follows:

> And in case of any Loss or Misfortune, it shall be lawful and necessary for the Assured, their Factors, Servants and Assigns, to sue, labor and travel for, in, and about the defense, safeguard and recovery of the Vessel, or any part thereof, without prejudice to this insurance, to the charges whereof the Underwriters will contribute their proportion as provided below. And it is expressly declared and agreed that no acts of the Underwriters or Assured in recovering, saving or preserving the vessel shall be considered as a waiver or acceptance of abandonment.

The U.S. Supreme Court used these words (*Washburn Manufacturing Co.* v. *Reliance Marine Ins. Co.*, 179 U.S. 1):

> The public interest requires both the assured and assurer to labor for the preservation of the property, and to that end this provision is made so that it may be done without prejudice.

It should be noted that it is the duty of the assured to take such measures as may be reasonable to avert or minimize a loss. If he fails to act when he should have done, he incurs the risk of his claim for loss or damage being rejected in whole or in part (*Integrated Container Service* v. *British Traders Ins. Co. Ltd.*, 1984 1 L.R. 154).

The sue and labor clause was reviewed in *American Merchant Marine Ins. Co.* v. *Liberty Sand and Gravel Co.* (282 Fed. Rep. 514) when the court said:

> The original purpose of the suing and laboring clause in a policy of marine insurance was to permit the insured to take every measure in preserving his vessel without waiving his right later to tender abandonment and claim a total loss. As there enured to the insurer a corresponding benefit from the labor bestowed and money expended, it came about that the insurer, in order to stimulate the insured, assumed liability for a proportion of any reasonable expense incurred in preserving the subject insured from the operation of the perils insured against.

The court went on to say that the English cases on the subject have been followed without variation by the American courts.

For Sue and Labor charges to be properly claimable, the loss or misfortune must actually have occurred or commenced to operate. However, it is not essential for there to have been any actual loss or damage to the insured property as long as the charges were properly incurred to prevent such a loss at a time when the subject-matter insured is immediately and actively threatened *by an insured peril* (see *Reliance Ins. Co.* v. *Yacht Escapade, et al.,* 1961 AMC 2410). Nor is it necessary to show a benefit to underwriters, but only that the charges were incurred in good faith with the *intention* of averting a loss recoverable from them. As the English court of appeals has said, there is nothing in the Sue and Labor clause which requires the assured to show that a loss would "very probably" have occurred. The duty under Sect. 78 of the Marine Insurance Act was "to take such measures as may be reasonable for the purpose of averting or minimizing a loss" and those words imposed a duty to act in circumstances where a reasonable man intent on preserving his property would act; whether or not the assured could recover should depend upon the reasonableness of his assessment of the situation and the action taken by him; and since the right to recover expenses was corollary to the duty to act, the insured should be entitled to recover all extraordinary expenses reasonably incurred by him where he could demonstrate that a prudent assured person would incur expense of an unusual kind; this was the effect of the Sue and Labor clause (*Integrated Container Service Inc.* v. *British Traders Ins. Co. Ltd.,* 1984 1 L.R. 154). This case involved an "all risks" policy on containers which had been leased. The lessee was adjudged bankrupt and the insured owner of the containers incurred expenses locating and recovering the containers. The question was whether the recovery costs fell within the Sue and Labor clause in the policy or whether (as the insurer contended) they were solely incurred in a commercial undertaking to retrieve the containers from a bankrupt hirer. The court said that the true test applicable was whether or not in all the circumstances the assured had acted reasonably to avert a loss when there was a risk that insurers might have to bear it and the evidence showed that they did. For the Sue and Labor clause to cease to apply it was necessary for the (insured) goods to be restored to the custody and control of the assured to the extent that it could be said that they were no longer threatened by perils for which the assured was not responsible; the evidence showed that the containers were not free from the threat and perils and consequently the expenses claimed were properly incurred. A similar case came before an American court in *States Steamship Co.* v. *Aetna Insurance Co.,* 1985 AMC 2749. In that case a shipowner leased containers and subsequently became bankrupt. The container lessor incurred expenses in recovering the equipment which was scattered throughout the world at the time of the shipowner's bankruptcy. An "all risks" policy had been effected by the shipowner and the court held that underwriters were liable under the Sue and Labor clause for amounts paid by the shipowner-assured to reimburse the container lessor. The court described the English court of appeals decision (*supra*) as representing a well-reasoned approach to resolving questions concerning Sue and Labor clauses and bankruptcy. Another American court had previously held that an "all risks" policy on containers covered loss of the insured containers due to "mysterious disappearance," a cause not exempted under the policy. The insurance was against "total loss and constructive total loss" and the court found that, under the Sue and Labor clause, this permitted recovery of the cost of repairs made in order to prevent such a loss at a time when the insured equipment was immediately or actively threatened by an insured peril (*Northwestern National Ins. Co.* v. *Chandler Leasing Corp.*, 1982 AMC 1631).

Sue and Labor charges may not be added to particular average for franchise purposes. However, with the deductible average having for all practical purposes eliminated the voyage franchise concept of marine coverage, this has ceased to have any great significance. Most market forms provide for Sue and Labor charges to be subject to the deductible average clause and this has been criticized from time to time as not being in underwriters' best interest, the inference being that the assured might hesitate to Sue and Labor when such expenditure is subject to a deductible average. Underwriters naturally respond by pointing out that the assured is *obliged* to Sue and Labor and that any failure to do so might imperil the coverage provided. In this connection, the requirements of Sect. 78 (4) of the Marine Ins. Act were considered by the English courts (albeit *obiter*) in the *Gold Sky* (1972 2 L. L. R. 187). In that case it was alleged, *inter alia*, by underwriters that there had been a breach of duty by the assureds or their agents under Sect. 78 (4) to take reasonable steps for the purpose of averting or minimizing the loss, specifically that the *master and crew* had refused salvage assistance to their sinking vessel. In the course of the hearing it was suggested that Sect. 78 (4) was in conflict with Sect. 55 (2) (a) of the Marine Ins. Act which states, *inter alia*, that the assured is liable for any loss proximately caused by a peril insured against, even though the loss would not have happened but for the misconduct or negligence of the master or the crew. J. Mocatta, had this to say on the question:

> In my judgment it is clear that some meaning and effect must be given to the subsection [78 (4)]. On the other hand it is difficult to believe that it was intended to cut down the effect of sect. 55 (2) (a). Moreover the attempt to give it this effect by holding that any failure by the master or crew to act reasonably to avert or minimize a loss, when, during the currency of the cover, the subject-matter insured

appears about to suffer loss through an insured peril or has suffered some such loss which may increase or perhaps become total, would appear irrational. If a loss is recoverable by a shipowner owing to his master having unreasonably and negligently set a risky course, whereby the ship has suffered a gash in her plating from a rock which should have been given a wide berth, why should the shipowner be unable to recover in respect of subsequent loss, whether total or partial, due to subsequent unreasonable and negligent conduct by the master, such as, for example, continuing to his destination relying on his pumps coupled, perhaps, with wedging and the tightness of bulkheads, rather than putting into a nearby port of refuge for repairs? . . .

It will be noticed that in sect. 55 (2) (a) the words used are "but for the misconduct or negligence of the master or crew." . . . In contrast in sect. 78 (4) the words used are "It is the duty of the assured and his agents." The word "agents" is capable of a wide range of different meanings depending upon the context and circumstances in which it is used. The master of a ship is primarily the servant of her owner; his authority as master is strictly limited and in general he only has wide powers as an agent to bind his principal and employer in cases where he has to act as agent of necessity. Whilst the master of the *Gold Sky*, had he entered into a Lloyd's salvage agreement . . . would no doubt by so doing have bound the plaintiffs, I do not think it necessarily follows that, in the absence of instructions from his owners, the master of a vessel must be taken to be included within the words "the assured and his agents" in sect. 78 (4), so that a failure by the master to take such measures as may be reasonable will militate against his owners' claim against insurers. I think the words "his agents" should in the context and to avoid an acute conflict between two subsections of the Act be read as inapplicable to the master or crew, unless expressly instructed by the assured in relation to what to do or not to do in respect of suing and laboring. Many persons other than the master and members of the crew may be agents of the assured with the duty to act on his behalf in relation to suing and laboring.

It is interesting to note, however, that the court expressed the view that, if the defendant underwriter in the aforementioned case had been able to bring Sect. 78 (4) into play, he would be able to set off a counterclaim (that is to say, a counterclaim for the amount of the total loss paid under the policy less such expenses for general and particular average as would have been recoverable under the policy if the salvage service had been accepted and had been successful). In short, the application of such counterclaim would have reduced the claim under the policy, to that which, accepting underwriters' views, would have been recoverable had the assured sued and labored effectively.

Under American law, it is sometimes very difficult to draw a distinction between general average and Sue and Labor charges insofar as services rendered to a vessel are concerned. In English law, when a vessel is in ballast and not under charter at the time services are rendered to her for a fixed remuneration (say, in refloating the vessel following a stranding), there is no general average, the expenses under such circumstances being recoverable under the Sue and Labor clause. In the United States, it is submitted that in the above situation the assured has the right to claim the refloating expenses either as general average (because American law recognizes general average in ballast, regardless of whether the vessel is chartered or not) or as Sue and Labor expenses.

In insurances on cargo, the Sue and Labor clause is particularly important since there are many more occasions on which the assured is required, under the clause, to protect and preserve the cargo from further damage once an insured peril has operated. Reasonable expenses or charges incurred by the assured in carrying out this obligation are recoverable under the Sue and Labor clause.

An example of Sue and Labor charges in an insurance on cargo would be expenses incurred reconditioning and repacking goods, which were damaged by a peril insured against, to enable them to be sent on to destination in their original condition.

In the case of insurance on freight, the expenses of transshipping cargo in the event of a total loss of the insured vessel are recoverable under the Sue and Labor clause.

Policies of insurance usually include a clause stipulating that Sue and Labor charges—like general average charges—are subject to any underinsurance. The value insured must not be lower than the actual value of the vessel or the assured becomes his own insurer for the balance. The American Institute Hull Clauses include such a clause, which reads:

> In the event of expenditure under the Sue and Labor clause, the Underwriters shall pay the proportion of such expenses that the amount insured hereunder bears to the Agreed Value, or that the amount insured hereunder (less loss and/or damage payable under this Policy) bears to the actual value of the salved property, whichever proportion shall be less; provided always that their liability for such expenses shall not exceed their proportionate part of the Agreed Value.
>
> If claim for Total Loss is admitted under this Policy and sue and labor expenses have been reasonably incurred in excess of any proceeds realized or value recovered, the amount payable under this Pol-

icy will be the proportion of such excess that the amount insured hereunder (without deduction for loss or damage) bears to the Agreed Value or to the sound value of the Vessel at the time of the accident, whichever value was greater; provided always that Underwriters' liability for such expenses shall not exceed their proportionate part of the Agreed Value. The foregoing shall also apply to expenses reasonably incurred in salving or attempting to salve the Vessel and other property to the extent that such expenses shall be regarded as having been incurred in respect of the Vessel.

The clause provides that in the event of a claim for Sue and Labor expenses, underwriters' liability is to be arrived at by the application of either of the following formulae:

(a) The proportion of such expenses that the amount insured bears to the agreed (insured) value of the vessel, or

(b) The proportion of such expenses that the amount insured, less loss and/or damage payable under the policy, bears to the actual value of the salved property (that is to say, the value of the insured vessel in damaged condition).

Underwriters' liability is for the lesser of the two amounts arrived at as above.

The object and effect of these formulae is to subject Sue and Labor expenses to the same rules regarding underinsurance as are applicable to general average expenses. Thus, if the agreed value (insured value) is lower than the actual value of the vessel, the assured becomes his own insurer for the balance. Sometimes in practice these formulae are ignored when the Sue and Labor charges are incurred to avert or minimize a loss which would otherwise fall on the policy. An example of this would be expenses incurred in recovering (or attempting to recover) an anchor and cable, the loss of which would constitute a claim under the policy. If reasonably and prudently incurred by the assured or his agents, such expenses are usually paid in full without going into the question of whether or not such expenses are fully insured. The rationale for this special treatment is that, in such circumstances, the assured is "suing and laboring" to avoid a particular average loss or damage which would have resulted in a claim below the insured value and which would therefore have been unaffected by any underinsurance.

In extreme cases, where the assured elects to claim on a partial loss basis (even though the particular average claim amounts to as much as 100 percent of the insured value) and the vessel has a residual value prior to effecting the repairs, the above formulae will result in the assured either having to contribute to the Sue and Labor expenses incurred or perhaps not being able to recover them at all under the hull policy (even though he may be fully insured). By way of illustration, let us assume a vessel is insured for $100,000 and is damaged by an insured peril to the extent of $90,000; Sue and Labor expenses of $20,000 have been incurred to save the vessel and the salved vessel has a damaged value of $15,000. The assured elects to repair the vessel and submits a particular average claim for $90,000 plus the Sue and Labor expenses of $20,000. Applying formula (b), the agreed or insured value ($100,000) less damages payable under the policy ($90,000) gives a balance of $10,000 to be compared with the actual value of the salved property ($15,000). The hull underwriters would therefore be liable for only 10/15ths of the Sue and Labor charges of $20,000. On the other hand, if the cost of repairs (particular average claim) was $100,000, then it would follow that under the formula the hull underwriters would not be liable for any part of the Sue and Labor charges.

However, it is probable that any insurance on increased value of hull or excess liabilities would respond for that part of the Sue and Labor expenses not recoverable under the hull policy.

The above formulae only apply when the Sue and Labor expenses have been incurred as a result of an accident which has not resulted in a claim for total loss under the policy.

The Sue and Labor clause goes on to stipulate that if a claim for total loss has been paid under the policy and Sue and Labor expenses have been reasonably incurred in excess of any proceeds realized or value recovered, the amount payable under the policy is to be the proportion of such excess that the amount insured (without deduction for loss or damage) bears to the agreed (insured) value or the sound value of the vessel at the time of the accident, whichever value was greater.

The Sue and Labor clause concludes by making provision regarding expenses incurred in salving or attempting to salve the vessel and other property, that is, when the vessel is carrying cargo or property belonging to others. Such expenses are recoverable to the extent that they can be regarded as having been incurred in respect to the vessel. In other words, any expenses incurred in an unsuccessful general average act may be recoverable to the extent that they relate to the vessel. This provision visualizes a situation wherein the vessel and cargo are in difficulties and expenses are incurred by the assured in dispatching help to the scene. If these expenses are incurred in vain and the vessel and cargo are lost, the policy, in effect, provides for apportionment to be made over the estimated values (at the time the expenditure was incurred) of the vessel and other property involved, with hull underwriters accepting liability for the proportion of the Sue and Labor expenses (perhaps more properly describable as general charges or salvage expenses) applying to the vessel. Such estimated values would reflect any damage known to have been sustained by the vessel and/or the cargo at the time the expenses were incurred.

If it were not for this express provision in the policy, the assured would not be able to collect such expenses even though they were quite properly incurred with a view to saving the vessel and cargo. Since the expenditure was incurred to benefit both the vessel and cargo, it does not come within the heading of Sue and Labor. It was initially in the nature of general average but cannot be recovered under that heading either, because no property was saved. Furthermore, the hull underwriters, having paid a total loss, have extinguished their liability under the hull policies, except for such expenditure as can be recovered as Sue and Labor. Nor can the expenditure be classified as salvage, for the simple reason that no property was saved against which salvage could be awarded. It is, therefore, as a matter of equity that hull underwriters undertake to bear such expenses to the extent that they can "be regarded as having been incurred in respect of the vessel." This part of the Sue and Labor clause was dealt with in depth by the chairman of the British Association of Average Adjusters in 1985, G. S. Hughes, particularly with regard to the proportion of such expenses applying to cargo on board the doomed vessel. In essence, the shipowner's hope of recovering cargo's proportion of these expenses is entirely dependent on the generosity of his Protection and Indemnity Club (under the omnibus clause common to British Protection and Indemnity clubs). Hughes' address also dealt with other aspects of the Duty of Assured (Sue and Labor) clause in the latest English Institute Time Clauses, Hulls 1.10.83.

It should be noted that any claim for Sue and Labor expenses is limited to the insured (agreed) value. As the clause states, ". . . liability for such expenses shall not exceed (underwriters') proportionate part of the Agreed Value."

The Chairman of the Association of Average Adjusters in 1980 (E. A. Effrat), dealt with the Sue and Labor clause in his address to the Association.

The Sue and Labor clause is one of the most important clauses in a marine insurance policy. It often comes into play in constructive total loss cases: *see* Chapter 4.

Chapter 8

Liabilities to Third Parties

As we all know, potential liabilities to third parties have increased ten-fold in the last decade. In an illuminating address to the British Association of Average Adjusters in 1978, Chairman Lord Justice Roskill foresaw the inevitable results of the "law reformers" in an age of consumer protection. He said:

> So we enter the last quarter of this century with the law of negligence in a very different state from what it had been at the end—let alone at the beginning—of the first quarter. It cannot now be doubted that as a general principle a duty of care exists on a far wider basis than was originally thought to be the case and that underwriters are today carrying a much wider liability than is perhaps generally realized in the market, and that defences such as absence of duty of care or noncompliance with limitation periods have been struck from the hands of defendants and their insurers.

But, as Roskill further pointed out, "underwriters are not purveyors of blessings poured out freely from cornucopia. The greater the liabilities of the assured, the higher the premiums the underwriters will demand." And so it came to pass, with the marine insurance markets of the world inevitably involved.

Liabilities to third parties can and do arise in connection with all kinds of marine property. Consequently, it would be most unwise for any person or corporation interested in, or responsible for, insurable property to omit to insure their potential liabilities to third parties arising from maritime perils. In such insurances, the measure of indemnity, subject to any express provisions in the policy, is the amount paid or payable by the assured to such third party in respect of such liability (Marine Ins. Act, Sect. 74). Thus, if a carrier insures his liability in respect of cargo worth $40,000 for only $20,000 and the cargo is damaged to the extent of $20,000, he can recover the whole $20,000 (*Cunard* v. *Marten*, 2 K. B. 624). In effect, legal liability insurance is not subject to the rules applicable to underinsurance in other types of marine insurance although, of course, an assured's legal liability coverage is limited to the amount insured.

As we have seen, the perils of the sea are both many and varied and not the least serious of which is collision. A shipowner's liability arising out of a collision due to the negligent navigation of the vessel extends to include any accident involving his vessel in contact not only with another vessel, but with all floating or fixed objects, such as piers, buoys, docks, etc. Furthermore, liability may arise without actual contact, such as damage caused to property by the wash due to a vessel's excessive speed. On the other hand, it must be stressed that where no negligence is involved, there can be no liability to a third party. Even in the case of a moving vessel striking a stationary object, if the collision was an inevitable accident which human skill and a proper display of nautical skill could not have prevented, no liability would attach (the *Andros Tower*, 1961 AMC 1573).

The liabilities which a negligent vessel can incur may be classified under the following headings:

(1) *Torts*. This is the legal term for a wrong or an injury not arising out of contract, such as the damage done by one ship to another in collision.

(2) *Statutory powers*. Local statutory regulations may render a shipowner liable for damage to harbors, docks, etc., and for the cost of removing the wreck of his ship. Recently, liability for oil pollution has been imposed upon shipowners by governmental legislation.

(3) *Breach of contract*. Liability may arise under the contract of affreightment, e.g., in respect of unreasonable deviation, unseaworthiness, etc.

All these liabilities can be covered by insurance; collision liabilities are covered partly by normal hull insurance and covered partly by Protection and Indemnity insurance. The other liabilities are usually covered by Protection and Indemnity insurance.

COLLISION LIABILITIES

Prior to 1975, the American law in collision cases, where both vessels were found guilty of negligence which contributed to the collision, was that the resultant damages had to be borne *equally*, whatever the respective degrees of fault might be (the *Catharine*, 58 U.S. (17 How.), 170, 177-178). The Supreme Court was unanimous in adopting the equal division rule as being the most equitable and just and "as best tending to induce care and vigilance on both sides in navigation." This rule of equal division of property damage (even though one of the vessels may have been much more at fault than the other) had been firmly established in the United States since 1855.

As recently as 1952, the Supreme Court said (*Halcyon Lines* v. *Haenn Ship Ceiling & Refitting Corp.*, 342 U.S. 282).:

> Where two vessels collide due to the fault of both, it is established admiralty, doctrine that mutual wrongdoers shall share equally the damages sustained by each, as well as personal injury and property damages inflicted on innocent third parties.

However, in 1975 the Supreme Court reversed itself and adopted the principle of proportionate liability (*U.S.A.* v. *Reliable Transfer*, 1975 AMC 541). The Court said:

> We hold that when two or more parties have contributed by their fault to cause property damage in a maritime collision or stranding liability for such damage is to be allocated among the parties proportionately to the comparative degree of their fault, and that liability for such damages is to be allocated equally only when the parties are equally at fault or when it is not possible fairly to measure the comparative degree of their fault.

In reaching this conclusion, the Supreme Court commented that the courts of every other major maritime nation had long since abandoned the rule of the equal division of property damage, whenever both parties were found to be guilty of contributing fault, whatever the relative degree of their fault may have been.

The Court was referring to the fact that most other maritime countries are signatories to the Brussels Collision Convention of 1910, a convention which provides that where collision is due to mutual fault, damages are apportioned according to the degree of fault of each vessel. However, under the terms of the convention, there is no joint and several liability to third parties for property damage. This is contrary to a basic principle of law in the United States, that when an innocent person is injured by the contributory negligence of two or more persons, he can recover his entire damages from any one of them or from all of them jointly. This principle is known as "the joint and several liability of joint tort-feasors." The Brussels Convention abolishes this principle in regard to claims by third parties for damage to vessels, or to their cargoes, or to the effects or other property of crews, passengers, or other persons on board—that is, all property damage caused by the collision. Thus, innocent property claimants can only recover from the non-carrying vessel to the extent that that vessel was at fault for the collision, as will be explained later (*see infra*).

The Brussels Convention retains the principle of joint and several liability insofar as claims for loss of life and personal injury are concerned.

In such an event, the claimants may recover in full from either vessel, subject to the right to limit liability, and the owner of that vessel can obtain contribution from the other vessel for his proportion of the loss. Since *Reliable Transfer (supra)*, claims for loss of life and personal injury are treated similarly in the United States, that is to say, on a proportionate liability basis. Prior to *Reliable Transfer*, the paying vessel had automatically recouped 50 percent of the amounts paid to settle such claims (*Tulane Law Review*, Vol. 43, No. 3, p. 683).

Let us consider the position under the Brussels Collision Convention in a both-to-blame collision case where, for example, the liability of the carrying vessel involved in the collision is adjudged to be 75 percent and that of the other vessel 25 percent. In such a situation, the cargo owner can recover only 25 percent of his loss from the non-carrying vessel. Furthermore, because of permissible provisions against negligent navigation in the contract of affreightment between the carrying vessel and the owner of the cargo being carried (*see* Carriage of Goods by Sea Act), the latter cannot recover the remaining 75 percent of his loss. Nor does the non-carrying vessel have any right of recourse against the carrying vessel with respect to payments to cargo. It should be noted, however, that there is such recourse if one vessel pays more than its proportionate share of death or injury claims.

The law in the United States is different. It has always been a fundamental principle of the American courts that it is contrary to public policy to permit common carriers to stipulate against the consequences of their own or their employees' negligence. In spite of the modification of this attitude, as evidenced by the provisions of the Harter Act and the U.S. Carriage of Goods by Sea Act, the American courts continue to look with disfavor on "unreasonable" conditions in bills of lading.

Prior to the passing of the Harter Act in 1893, the Supreme Court held that an innocent cargo owner was not bound to pursue both colliding vessels, even though both might be at fault, but was entitled to judgment against one for the entire amount of his damages (the *Atlas,* 93 U.S. 302). The Harter Act exempted the carrier from responsibility for damage or loss resulting from errors in navigation, with the result that the cargo owner could no longer recover from the carrying vessel damages resulting from a negligent collision. However, the Supreme Court subsequently ruled that the Harter Act did not restrict or affect the rights of a cargo owner against the non-carrying vessel in both-to-blame collision cases (the *Chattahoochee,* 173 U.S. 540). Consequently, in such cases a cargo owner can recover from the non-carrying vessel the full amount of his loss. It follows that the non-carrying vessel can thereafter include the amount so paid in his claim against the carrying vessel and recover a proportionate share of same according to the degree of fault of the carrying vessel. The result is that the carrying vessel indirectly pays a proportionate share of the loss sustained by the cargo it is carrying, even though the contract of affreightment might contain provisions against liability for damage to cargo consequent on negligent navigation. There is also the anomaly of a vessel entirely at fault for a collision being protected against any claims by the cargo she is carrying by reason of protective provisions in the contract of affreightment, while if the same vessel were only partly to blame for the collision, she indirectly becomes liable for a proportionate share of the damage to cargo.

Ironically, the *Reliable Transfer* decision did not involve a collision between vessels and did not involve innocent third parties. There has been much speculation as to whether the new apportionment rule affects innocent cargo's recovery from the non-carrying vessel. The consensus is that it does not. Indeed, court decisions since *Reliable Transfer* have held that innocent cargo is still entitled to a 100 percent recovery from the non-carrying vessel despite the percentage apportionment of fault and that such liability is joint and several *(Complaint of Flota Mercante Grancolombiana S.A.,* 440 F. Supp. 704; *Complaint of Malaysia Overseas Line Ltd.,* 1976 AMC 1287; the *Anco Princess,* 1978 1 L. L. R. 3); *Allied Chemical Corp. v. Hess,* 1982 AMC 1271.

Both-to-Blame Collision Clause

Shipowners and their Protection and Indemnity underwriters somewhat naturally considered this state of affairs unsatisfactory and, in an attempt to remedy the position, the Both-to-Blame Collision clause was introduced into contracts of affreightment. The clause reads as follows:

> If the ship comes in collision with another ship as a result of the negligence of the other ship and any act, neglect or default of the master, mariner, pilot or the servants of the carrier in the navigation or in the management of the ship, the owners of the goods carried hereunder will indemnify the carrier against all loss or liability to the other or non-carrying ship or her owners insofar as such loss or liability represents loss of, or damage to, or any claim whatsoever of the owners of said goods, paid or payable by the other or non-carrying ship or her owners to the owners of said goods and set-off recouped or recovered by the other or non-carrying ship or her owners as part of their claim against, the carrying ship or carrier. The foregoing provisions shall also apply where the owners, operators or those in charge of any ship or ships or objects other than, or in addition to, the colliding ships or objects are at fault in respect of a collision or contact.

The effect of the clause is to bring American law into line with the provisions of the Brussels Convention by protecting the shipowner against liability for any part of the loss sustained by the cargo being carried. The clause does not come into operation unless the cargo has enforced its claim against the non-carrying vessel for 100 percent of its damages and that vessel has in turn recovered a proportion of such damages from the carrying vessel.

The Both-to-Blame Collision clause was in use for some time without its validity being ruled upon. However, in 1952 a decision was handed down by the Supreme Court ruling the clause invalid insofar as common carriers are concerned (*United States of America* v. *Atlantic Mutual Ins. Co.*, 1952 AMC 659). The effect of this decision will be apparent. Any claim enforced by the cargo against the non-carrying, vessel and thereafter included by that vessel in its claim to be divided with the carrier will result in the latter bearing part of the loss sustained by the cargo he is carrying. As a result of the prevailing law, such a payment falls on the Protection and Indemnity underwriters. The Both-to-Blame Collision clause has, however, been found valid when incorporated in a charter party (*American Union Transport* v. *U.S.A.*, 1976 AMC 1480).

Cargo policies in the United States contain a Both-to-Blame Collision clause which reads:

> Where goods are shipped under a Bill of Lading containing the so-called "Both to Blame Collision" Clause, this Company agrees as to all losses covered by this insurance, to indemnify the Assured for this Policy's proportion of any amount (not exceeding the amount insured) which the Assured may be legally bound to pay to the shipowners under such clause. In the event that such liability is asserted the Assured agree to notify this Company who shall have the right at their own cost and expense to defend the Assured against such claim.

The intent of the clause is to indemnify the assured in respect of any amount which the assured may be legally bound to pay to the carrier under the Both-to-Blame Collision clause in the contract of affreightment. It will be noted that the cargo underwriter reserves the right to oppose the validity of the clause.

Single Liability

As between the owners of the colliding vessels, where both vessels are to blame, there are not two liabilities each to the other but only one single liability, that is, the obligation of the owner suffering the lesser damages to make payment to the other of the difference between one-half (or other adjudged proportion) of their respective damages. In other words, the owner of the vessel that has the greater financial liability pays the other the difference between their respective financial liabilities (the *North Star*, 106 U.S. 17). There is no reason to believe that this ancient rule of "single liability" has been affected in any way by *Reliable Transfer (supra)*. The rule of single liability came into being under the old mathematical division of damages. *Reliable Transfer* effects no real change as to the nature of the liability, i.e., a single liability; the vessel with the lesser damages (by monetary amount and proportion of fault) should still have a "single liability" to the vessel having the greater.

In the United States, in arriving at these financial liabilities, the physical damage sustained by both vessels and the liabilities for damage suffered by third parties (including cargo damage, death, and personal injury claims, etc.) are taken into account (*in re* the diesel tanker *A. C. Dodge Inc.*, 1961 AMC 233). However, only those damage items which have been paid or will be certainly payable warrant inclusion in the division of damages. Thus, in *Olson v. Marine Leopard* (1966 AMC 1064), when limitation of liability by the non-carrier rendered its damages (the amount payable to cargo claimants) uncertain and wholly contingent upon recovery of a sum representing an interest in the non-carrying lost vessel, the court held that cargo's claim was too speculative to warrant inclusion in the division of damages. In that case it was doubtful which vessel would be the creditor on a single liability settlement on the basis of hull damages: although the *Olson* was a total loss it was not highly valued, and the *Marine Leopard* had extensive damage. Thus, as *Marine Leopard's* cargo's claim was not likely to be settled in full, if at all, the court held that until *Olson's* limitation fund (which would comprise principally any balance payable by *Marine Leopard* to *Olson*) was established, *Marine Leopard's* cargo's claim was too speculative to warrant inclusion in the division of the damages.

Limitation of Liability

The law of the United States (the Limitation of Liability Act, 1851) grants a shipowner the right to limit his liability for the damage arising out of a collision (provided the collision occurred without his privity or knowledge). The present law permits a shipowner to limit his liability in cases involving damage to property only, to the value of the vessel at the end of the voyage on which the collision occurred plus the freight actually earned on the voyage. (Whether the freight was prepaid and guaranteed or was at risk is immaterial in this connection.) If the vessel is lost as a result of the collision or is lost before the intended voyage is completed, the "value of the owner's interest is only the value of his interest in the wreck, which may be nothing" (the *Scotland*, 105 U.S. 24; the *City of Norwich*, 118 U.S. 468). The reverse is also true, for if the vessel is repaired at a port of refuge and thereafter completes her voyage, her value for limitation purposes would seem to be her repaired value (the *Lara*, 1947 AMC 27). However, even if the vessel is lost, any prepaid or guaranteed freight would constitute the limitation fund, such freight having in fact been earned on the voyage.

In certain circumstances, the limitation fund of a vessel wrecked as a result of an accident will include any amount recovered from another party responsible for the accident. Thus, if a vessel involved in a both-to-blame collision is a total loss and is also the net creditor on a "single liability" basis, the recovery from the debtor vessel must be surrendered as part of the creditor vessel's limitation fund. In other words, an element of a shipowner's interest in the vessel is the value of its claim against a tort-feasor for damaging it and thereby reducing its value (*O'Brien* v. *Miller,* 168 U.S. 287 (1897); see also *Oliver J. Olson & Co.* v. *S. S. Marine Leopard,* 356 F2d 728 (1966)).

In cases where personal injury claims are concerned in addition to property claims, there is a deviation from the aforementioned procedure. In such cases, if the limitation fund computed as above is insufficient to pay all claimants in full and the proportion of the fund available for the payment of claimants in respect of personal injury claims is less than $60 per ton of the vessel's gross tonnage, the limitation fund must be increased so that there is $60 per gross ton available for claims of that nature. This special treatment for personal injury claimants was introduced in the 1935 Limitation of Liability Act and the amount of $60 per gross ton was based on a rough estimate of the value of the American merchant marine fleet in 1935. Inflation has been rampant since then and the statutory limits were brought up to date in 1981 by the enactment of an amendment increasing the $60 per gross ton figure to $420 per gross ton.

One result of this method of arriving at the limitation fund is that if one of the colliding vessels is sunk in the collision and the wreck has no value and no freight is earned, the owner, by limiting his liability, escapes liability for the collision (insofar as property claims are concerned), even if his vessel was at fault, because there is no limitation fund.

There is some authority under American law for the premise that innocent parties are entitled to priority in the limitation fund. Thus, if the damage to cargo on the colliding vessel is substantial, the owners of that cargo would have a prior claim on the limitation fund. They may even be entitled to the entire amount of the limitation fund to the exclusion of the colliding vessel's claim since the cargo interests were innocent and the colliding vessel (in a both-to-blame situation) was partially at fault for the collision. This principle of innocent claimants is supported in the case of the *George W. Roby* (111 Fed. Rep. 601). Gilmore and Black (p. 726) state that the authorities stand principally for the proposition that a claimant whose ship was at fault in a collision will be subordinated to cargo and personal injury claims. Nevertheless, they express the opinion (p. 724) that "the question whether maritime lien priorities are to be observed in the distribution of the limitation fund is one on which it would be unwise to speak with dogmatic finality."

Those countries which are signatories to the 1957 Brussels Convention on Limitation of Liability also grant shipowners the right to limit liability, but the amount of the limitation fund is fixed at 1,000 gold franc units (approximately $67) per gross ton for property claims alone plus an additional 2,100 gold franc units (approximately $140) per gross ton in cases where loss of life and personal injury claims are involved. In the event that the fund of $140 per ton proves insufficient to satisfy the loss of life and personal injury claims in full, the balance of those claims ranks with the property claims in the distribution of the fund of $67 per ton. The tonnage of a vessel is placed at a minimum of 300 tons for contributory purposes. One result of the convention is that the shipowner is not relieved of his liability if his vessel is a total loss as a result of the collision.

Opponents of limitation of liability are numerous and often attack in particular the size of the limitation fund. As a result, a new international convention on limitation of liability for maritime claims, drawn in 1976 under the auspices of the United Nations, increased the amount of the fund based, again, on a tonnage formula. While the United States delegation did not sign this convention, it endorsed it in principle, objecting mainly that the limits of liability were still too low. This seems a strange attitude when the prevailing U.S. law can result in no fund at all. The Maritime Law Association of the United States has spent considerable time and effort at attempting to produce a proposed new American limitation of liability statue based on the 1976 international convention, but with increased limits of liability. The association's efforts have not yet borne fruit within the U.S. Congress, which is also still attempting to introduce a bill acceptable to the conflicting interests of shipowners, seamen, and marine liability underwriters, among others. The objective of all these amendments and proposed amendments to shipowners' limitation rights is, of course, to increase the limitation fund available to claimants and thereby to discourage attacks on the principle of limitation itself. Marine liability underwriters are in favor of adequate limits that can be enforced strictly; they insist, however, that some limit must be placed on shipowners' liability.

It will have been noted that a prerequisite before the right to limit liability can be claimed is that the collision must have occurred without the shipowner's privity or knowledge. In the United States, limitation proceedings (that is, application to the courts for permission to limit liability) must be commenced within six months from receipt of the first written notice of the claim. A plea for exoneration from, or limitation of, liability must be supported by an ad interim stipulation of value bond. This is provided by a bonding company who will require hull underwriters to provide countersecurity in the form of the 1955 Short Form Letter of Indemnity discussed later under "The Arrest of Ships" (*q.v.*). The burden of proof in a limitation of liability proceeding—as was determined in *Pennsylvania* (1957 AMC 2277)—is on the petitioner, including the burden of proving lack of knowledge, or of the means of knowledge, on the part of managerial employees that the vessel was unseaworthy. A perusal of this case will give the reader some idea of how heavy this burden has become. Thus:

> Liability may not be limited under the statute where the negligence causing the loss is that of an executive officer, manager or superintendent whose scope of authority includes supervision over the phase of the business out of which the loss or injury occurred.

The court held a port engineer to be a managerial employee.

More recently, in *Elna II* v. *Mission San Francisco* (1960 AMC 221, 1961 AMC 1878), a shipowner was denied the right to limit liability for damages arising out of a tanker explosion resulting from a collision, where the owner had not gas-freed the tanker before undertaking the short ballast voyage on which the collision occurred.

The courts have continued to impute to the shipowner the "privity or knowledge" of his servants in ever descending areas of importance. To quote only two recent cases:

> The party seeking exoneration from or limitation of liability has the burden of proof . . . [I]ts burden is to establish that the negligence . . . was not that "of an executive officer, manager or superintendent whose scope of authority includes supervision over the phase of the business out of which the loss or injury occurred" . . . [It] must show that its management personnel did not have "privity or knowledge" . . . (*In re Allied Towing Corp.,* 409 F. Supp. 180), and
>
> With the duty to make inquiry "the measure" of the knowledge "is not what the owner knows, but what he is charged with finding out" (*In re Farrell Lines Inc.,* 378 F. Supp. 1354).

In the latter case, a shipowner was denied limitation of liability where command procedures for a bridge approach were insufficient and uncoordinated.

In short, if a shipowner or his managerial employees have personally participated in, or were aware, or should have been aware, of the fault or negligence which caused the accident, the shipowner is not entitled to limit his liability.

The courts have been particularly loath to permit limitation of liability in cases involving death or personal injury claims. This was demonstrated in the case of the *Mormackite* (1958 AMC 1497, 1960 AMC 185). The trial court denied a shipowner's petition to limit liability for deaths, personal injury, and loss of cargo resulting from the capsizing of his vessel. On appeal, this was affirmed as to death and personal injury claims but modified to allow the shipowner to limit as against cargo. Similar difficulties were encountered in the United Kingdom and in his address to the British Association of Average Adjusters in 1987 the chairman, Mr. Justice Sheen, graphically described the situation as it existed prior to the international 1976 Limitation Convention which came into force in the United Kingdom in December 1986.

Shipowners and their insurers are entitled to know where they stand on limitation of liability and should not be subject to each individual judge's interpretation of "privity or knowledge." The international Limitation of Liability Convention of 1976 appears to recognize this by making limitation more difficult to break. In that convention, limitation would be granted unless the claimant could prove that the loss resulted from a personal act or omission of the shipowner, committed with intent to cause such loss or recklessly and with knowledge that such loss would probably result. Such a yardstick is in line with the tradition in marine insurance of excluding coverage for "any loss attributable to the wilful misconduct of the assured" (Marine Insurance Act, 1906, Sect. 55 (2) (a)).

A charterer who shall "man, victual and navigate" the vessel "at his own expense or by his own procurement" is deemed to be an "owner" within the meaning of the Limitation of Liability Act. Thus, bareboat or demise charterers may limit their liability under the act, but the usual time charterer or voyage charterer who does not man, victual, and navigate does not have the protection of the act. Because of this, most hull policies contain a so-called Charterer's Limitation clause whereby no person making a claim under the policy may recover more than could the vessel owner. Damages in excess of the owner's putative liability are borne by the charterer, not the insurers. It follows that underwriters insuring charterer's liabilities must assess their premiums accordingly. However, the Convention on Limitation of Liability for Maritime Claims, 1976, specifically grants the right of limitation to any type of charterer. In modern commerce a time charterer is often responsible for all the operating rights and obligations, and it is an anomaly that time charterers should be cast in the role of second-class citizens in the shipping world.

In the United States, tugs, barges, and similar craft are in a favored position insofar as limitation of liability is concerned. Their owners are exempt from the supplementary liability of $60 per ton with respect to death and personal injury claims. Furthermore, a tug owner seeking limitation for collision damage to a third party, caused solely by fault of the tug, need not surrender the tug's tow, also owned by him (*Liverpool-Brazil and River Plate S. N. Co.* v. *Eastern District Terminal,* 251 U.S. 48). An innocent tow will only become part of the limitation fund if she is of the same ownership as the negligent tug *and* has injured a third party with whom the common owner of tug and tow has a *contractual relationship* (*Tulane Law Review*, Vol. 43, No. 3, p. 618). If the court rules that a guilty tug's innocent tow is to be surrendered, it would seem that the court's object in so ruling is to increase the limitation fund; but it is submitted that the liability remains solely with the guilty tug. Thus the entire payment out of the fund would fall on the *tug's* liability underwriters and none on the *tow's* underwriters. There seems little merit to the suggestion that because the value of the tow is included in the tug's limitation fund, the portion of the liability attached to that portion of the fund should be payable by the tow's liability underwriters. If this were so, it would be a case of guilt by association or liability without fault. It is submitted that including the tow's value in the limitation fund is no different than including pending freight in the tug's basic limitation fund; both are merely a means of establishing a fund. Once the amount of the fund is established, any payments from the fund fall on the guilty vessel's underwriters. In short, it is that vessel that has limited its liability, whatever formula is used in arriving at the amount of the limitation fund.

It has been held that where limitation is granted with respect to a claim for cargo damaged aboard a LASH barge prior to loading onto the mother vessel, the petitioner must surrender the value of the mother vessel and all LASH barges consigned to the voyage as well as pending freight for cargo aboard any of them (*Agrico Chemical Co. and Continental Insurance Co.* v. *Atlantic Forest et al.,* 1979 AMC 801). Here again, it is submitted that regardless of the number of vessels included in the limitation fund, any payments from the fund fall on the guilty vessel's underwriters.

In the United Kingdom it has been held that a salvor may not limit his liability when a crew member of the salvage tug leaves that vessel to perform work on the vessel being salved and negligently causes damage to the vessel. In such circumstances, the court decided that the negligent act was neither done in the "management" of the tug nor was it an act or omission of a person "onboard" the tug (the *Tojo Maru,* 1971 1 L. L. R. 341). This decision understandably caused consternation among salvors, particularly in view of the possibility of extensive oil pollution liability arising out of salvage operations. As a result, innumerable salvors requested indemnity before they would undertake salvage contracts. Ultimately, salvors' Protection and Indemnity underwriters were obliged to provide coverage against such liabilities. It is interesting to note that the latest international Convention on Limitation of Liability for Maritime Claims, 1976 (which is not yet in effect), extends the right of limitation to salvors. Furthermore, the English Merchant Shipping (Oil Pollution) Act of 1971, which is designed to give effect to the International Convention on Civil Liability for Oil Pollution Damage, specifically relieves from liability for fuel oil pollution "any person performing salvage operations with the agreement of the owner."

The chairman of the Association of Average Adjusters of the United States in 1960, Nicholas J. Healy, III, made the subject of his address: "The proposed changes in the laws relating to the limitation of liability of shipowners." The reader will do well to study his remarks, although thirty years later the proposed changes have made little headway in the United States.

To sum up, the fundamental purpose of the Limitation of Liability Act is to encourage the development of American merchant shipping by limiting a vessel owner's liability for maritime disasters occasioned without his privity or knowledge to the value of his interest (*Panoceanic Faith*, 1971 AMC 1163).

Collision Clause

Partial coverage for liability for collision damages is afforded by the Collision clause included in most hull policies.

In the American Institute Hull Clauses, the Collision clause reads as follows:

And it is further agreed that:

(a) if the Vessel shall come into collision with any other ship or vessel, and the Assured or the Surety in consequence of the Vessel being at fault shall become liable to pay and shall pay by way of damages to any other person or persons any sum or sums in respect of such collision, the Underwriters will pay the Assured or the Surety, whichever shall have paid, such proportion of such sum or sums so paid as their respective subscriptions hereto bear to the Agreed Value, provided always that their liability in respect to any one such collision shall not exceed their proportionate part of the Agreed Value;

(b) in cases where, with the consent in writing of a majority (in amount) of Hull Underwriters, the liability of the Vessel has been contested, or proceedings have been taken to limit liability, the Underwriters will also pay a like proportion of the costs which the Assured shall thereby incur or be compelled to pay.

When both vessels are to blame, then, unless the liability of the owners or charterers of one or both such vessels becomes limited by law, claims under the Collision Liability clause shall be settled on the principle of Cross-Liabilities as if the owners or charterers of each vessel had been compelled to pay to the owners or charterers of the other of such vessels such one-half or other proportion of the latter's damages as may have been properly allowed in ascertaining the balance or sum payable by or to the Assured in consequence of such collision.

The principles involved in this clause shall apply to the case where both vessels are the property, in part or in whole, of the same owners or charterers, all questions of responsibility and amount of liability as between the two vessels being left to the decision of a single Arbitrator, if the parties can agree upon a single Arbitrator, or failing such agreement, to the decision of Arbitrators, one to be appointed by the Assured and one to be appointed by the majority (in amount) of Hull Underwriters interested; the two Arbitrators chosen to choose a third Arbitrator before entering upon the reference, and the decision of such single Arbitrator, or of any two of such three Arbitrators, appointed as above, to be final and binding.

Provided always that this clause shall in no case extend to any sum which the Assured or the Surety may become liable to pay or shall pay in consequence of, or with respect to:

(a) removal or disposal of obstructions, wrecks or their cargoes under statutory power or otherwise pursuant to law;

(b) injury to real or personal property of every description;

(c) the discharge, spillage, emission or leakage of oil, petroleum products, chemicals or other substances of any kind or description whatsoever;

(d) cargo or other property on or the engagements of the Vessel;

(e) loss of life, personal injury or illness.

Provided further that exclusions (b) and (c) above shall not apply to injury to other vessels or property thereon except to the extent that such injury arises out of any action taken to avoid, minimize or remove any discharge, spillage, emission or leakage described in (c) above.

This clause covers the assured, or the surety against liability and costs arising out of actual collision with another ship or vessel. It is a separate contract added to the policy contract, and coverage under it is limited to the insured value of the vessel plus costs, if incurred, with the consent in writing of the majority (in amount) of hull underwriters. Like Sue and Labor charges, claims under the Collision clause are recoverable in addition to a total loss paid under the basic policy contract.

As between the owners of the colliding vessels, where both vessels are to blame, there are not two liabilities each to the other, but only one single liability: that is, the obligation of the owner suffering the lesser damages to make payment to the other of the difference between his proportion of the damages of the other vessel and the latter's proportion of the damages of his. In other words, the owner of the vessel that has the greater financial liability pays the other the difference between their respective liabilities, but as a *single* liability, the liability of the one vessel to the other. If this principle of single liability were adopted in adjusting claims under marine insurance policies, the result would be that the owner of the vessel who had received that single payment on balance from the other vessel would have had no claim under the Collision clause of his own hull policy for any portion of the amount deducted from his recovery for damage done to the other vessel, because he will not actually have paid anything to the owner of that vessel.

It was to correct this shortcoming in the law and in coverage that the cross liabilities provision was added to the Collision clause in the hull policy. This paragraph provides that when both vessels are to blame, then *unless the liability of the owners of one or both vessels becomes limited by law*, claims under the Collision clause shall be settled on the principle of cross liabilities as though each vessel had been compelled to pay to the other vessel such proportion of that vessel's damages as may have been properly allowed in ascertaining the balance or sum payable by or to the assured in consequence of the collision. The result benefits the assured by enabling him to collect part of his demurrage claim from the other vessel (to the extent that that vessel was liable for the collision) and also to collect under the Collision clause his liability for that vessel's damages. The concession of claiming from underwriters on the basis of cross liabilities is only available to the assured in cases where neither vessel has *effectively* limited liability. This principle of cross liabilities is merely an agreed device for settlement of claims under the Collision clause of the policy. By agreement, it is assumed (fictitiously, if you will, but by express policy provision) that there are dual liabilities and dual payments although at law there is but a single liability. Similar cross liabilities provisions are included in Protection and Indemnity policies.

Sometimes, by agreement between the parties, liabilities arising out of a collision are settled by each vessel bearing its own damages and perhaps making agreed payments to any third party claimants (such as personal injury claimants, cargo owners, etc.). Such agreements are known as "hands-off" settlements; they are not to be considered as single liability settlements but rather as indicating an agreed division of liabilities between the colliding vessels. It is the practice of American average adjusters to calculate the overall percentages of liability which are actually being borne by the respective vessels as a result of this type of settlement. The claims on underwriters arising out of the collision are then adjusted in accordance with the cross liability provisions customarily included in both hull and Protection and Indemnity policies or club rules.

Because this concession of adjusting claims under the Collision clause of the hull policy on a cross liabilities basis is not applicable if the liabilities of one or both colliding vessels become *limited by law*, it is important to understand exactly what is meant by this provision. It frequently happens that in the case of a serious collision the *potential* liability of each vessel exceeds the amount to which the vessel owner may be entitled to limit his liability under the limitation statutes and, in such cases, *both* vessels often institute proceedings for limitation of liability. Nevertheless, after the case is concluded by litigation or settlement, it may well be that the total actual liabilities of each vessel fall below the amount to which each vessel's owner is entitled to limit its liability. Furthermore, it is the single liability balance payable by the debtor vessel which is the criterion which determines whether the debtor vessel's liability has been *limited by law* within the meaning of the Collision clause. That a shipowner has been granted the right to limit does not in itself mean that his liability has been *limited by law*. Only if the final settlement on a single liability basis between the colliding vessels is reduced or cancelled by reason of the insufficient limitation fund of the debtor vessel to meet the single liability settlement can it be said that that vessel's liability has been *limited by law*. In short, if the debtor vessel has a limitation fund sufficient to discharge its single liability to the other vessel, i.e., the imbalance owing, there has been no *effective* limitation of liability and a cross liabilities settlement under the Collision clause would be permissible. Thus, the principle to be applied in adjusting the claims between the two vessels might, under their hull policies, differ radically from the single liability principle which would be applied by the court in the collision case itself

In arriving at the balance between the claims of the two vessels (that is, the single liability), it must be remembered that under U.S. law (unlike the law of those countries who are signatories to the Brussels Collision Convention) cargo claimants can recover *in full* from the non-carrying vessel. The non-carrying vessel then adds its payment to cargo claimants to its own hull damage and any other damages it has sustained before the final balance is struck. Effectively, it shifts to the carrier a portion of its debt to the cargo owner. A similar state of affairs exists insofar as loss of life and personal injury claimants are concerned: any such payment made by either vessel is included in that vessel's damages prior to arriving at the single liability settlement.

In the United Kingdom, the setoff in ascertaining the single liability is confined to the immediate damages sustained by the respective vessels (including demurrage claims, if any) and does not include any loss of life and personal injury claims or cargo claims arising out of the collision. It is only the single liability balance due from one vessel to the other that ranks on the debtor vessel's limitation fund, and any loss of life and personal injury claims or cargo claims rank separately on the same limitation fund. Even when, in a both-to-blame collision case with both vessels equally to blame, a cargo claim was settled in full in accordance with American law, it was held by an English court that only 50 percent of the amount paid was to be credited in the distribution of that vessel's limitation fund (the *Giacinto Motta*, 1977 2 L. L. R. 221). Thus, in accordance with English law and practice, there may also be a claim under the Collision clause for any payment ultimately made in respect of loss of cargo in the other vessel.

Partly because the United States is not a signator to the Brussels Collision Convention, and partly because of the concept of innocent third parties having priority to limitation funds, the practice in the United States is somewhat different. Any payments made to innocent third parties in respect of loss of life and personal injury and/or arising out of damage to cargo lose their identity and become part of the respective vessel's collision damages before the single liability between the vessels is calculated.

Whether collision claims are adjusted for insurance purposes on a cross liabilities basis (when there has been no *effective* limitation) or on a single liability basis (because liability has been *limited by law*) can make a great difference to the respective liability underwriters, both hull and Protection and Indemnity. This was demonstrated in the case of diesel tanker *A. C. Dodge Inc.* v. *Stewart* (1966 AMC 1746, *aff'd* 1967 AMC 1689). In the collision litigation between the *Dodge* and the *Michael*, both vessels were held at fault, with the *Dodge* entitled to limitation. On a single liability basis, the *Michael* was the creditor, but the *Dodge*'s limitation fund was nil, that vessel being a total loss. The hull claim of the *Dodge* (a total loss) was in excess of $800,000 and that of the *Michael* $462,000. However, since the *Michael* had paid third-party claimants some $650,000, its total damages were greater than the total damages of the *Dodge*. In a novel approach, the *Dodge* sued its Protection and Indemnity and other liability underwriters for one-half the difference between the hull claim of the *Michael* and its own *hull claim*. The *Dodge* argued that were it not for the third-party loss of life and injury claims and its own cargo claim, the *Dodge*, having suffered the greater hull damage, would have recovered this amount from the *Michael*. In short, the *Dodge* maintained that it was entitled to a settlement on a cross liabilities basis from the Protection and Indemnity underwriters because, as net creditor on the hull claims, its right to limit liability was meaningless. The Protection and Indemnity policies did, in fact, include the usual cross liabilities clause, but Judge Cannella pointed out in his decision that the cross liabilities principle in the Protection and Indemnity policy is governed by the limitations and conditions established in the hull policy's Collision clause. With the liability of the *Dodge* effectively limited, the hull policy's Collision clause denied a cross liabilities settlement; therefore, the Protection and Indemnity policy's cross liabilities provision was equally inoperative.

To sum up: Firstly, limitation of liability is only applied after the balance has been struck and the single liability determined; secondly, limitation is only *effective* when that balance exceeds the statutory limit. Once this happens and the limiting vessel's actual liabilities are reduced to a fixed sum under the limitation statute (that is, *limited by law*), there is no longer any basis for the principle of cross liabilities. The claim under the policies must therefore be adjusted on the basis of the single liability as actually fixed by the court's decree. Accordingly, the owner of the vessel which has sustained the greater physical damage and who, therefore, receives a payment on balance from the colliding vessel does not have any claim under the Collision clause in his policy of insurance in respect of the physical damage done to the colliding vessel.

The Collision clause provides for arbitration of all questions of responsibility and of the amount of liability when two vessels of the same ownership are involved in a collision. This is necessary because an owner cannot be legally liable to himself. This Sister Ship collision provision places the owners of the two sister ships in the same position vis-à-vis their insurers as if the ships were separately owned. As a result, the shipowner can include demurrage (if any) in the claim of each ship. In sister ship collisions where one of the vessels is patently responsible for the collision, it is customary to request underwriters' permission to state the claim for damage to the innocent vessel on the policies covering the guilty vessel. This obviates the necessity of resorting to the arbitration procedure provided for in the Collision clause. On the other hand, if no demurrage claims are involved, claims arising from sister ship collisions are often stated as particular average on the respective vessels' policies and the liability question is not pursued. However, where there is any doubt as to the question of liability for the collision and demurrage claims involved, the arbitration procedure has to be followed.

The Collision clause includes a proviso or exceptions paragraph specifically excluding coverage for the following:

(a) removal or disposal of obstructions, wrecks or their cargoes under statutory powers or otherwise pursuant to law;

(b) injury to real or personal property of every description;

(c) the discharge, spillage, emission or leakage of oil, petroleum products, chemicals or other substances of any kind or description whatsoever;

(d) cargo or other property on or the engagements of the Vessel;

(e) loss of life, personal injury or illness.

Provided further that exclusions (b) and (c) above shall not apply to injury to other vessels or property thereon except to the extent that such injury arises out of any action taken to avoid, minimize or remove any discharge, spillage, emission or leakage described in (c) above.

These exclusions are absolute and apply whether the items enumerated are paid by the insured vessel as a direct liability consequent on the collision or whether they are paid by and included in the colliding vessel's provable damages.

Exclusion (a) eliminates all claims for removal of wrecks or their cargoes, etc. As we have seen, the decision of the U.S. Supreme Court in *Wyandotte Trans. Co.* v. *U. S.* (1967 AMC 2553) places a heavy burden on the owner of a wrecked vessel to remove the wreck. With this in mind it is clear that, whatever the circumstances, the expenses of wreck removal, etc., are not recoverable under the Collision clause.

The object of sections (b) and (c) (as qualified by the final paragraph of the amendment) is to veto all claims arising from oil pollution, etc., following a collision *except pollution expenses relating to other vessel or property thereon.* Even pollution expenses relating to other vessels are barred if they arise out of any action taken to avoid, minimize, or remove oil pollution hazards (as, for example, expenses incurred removing oil from the sea or the shore or deliberately destroying a vessel to prevent pollution).

Exclusion (d) is self-explanatory. In any event, by virtue of the provisions of the Carriage of Goods by Sea Act, the carrying vessel would not normally be liable to her own cargo; however, under American law where both vessels are at fault, cargo being carried by a vessel involved may recover in full from the non-carrying vessel, and the carrying vessel is obliged to repay to the non-carrying vessel its proportionate liability for the damages sustained by the carrying vessel's cargo. It is this indirect liability of the carrying vessel which is excluded by the Collision clause.

Exclusion (e) is also self-explanatory. Hull underwriters do not cover loss of life, personal injury, or illness claims which like the other exclusions in the proviso paragraph of the Collision clause) come within the orbit of Protection and Indemnity insurance.

It must be stressed that a claim on underwriters under the Collision clause can only arise when there has been an actual collision between the insured vessel and some other vessel. To constitute a collision there must be a striking together of two vessels and this involves an actual contact of one with another. If one vessel strikes another with any part of her fabric, whether hull or materials, a collision within the meaning of the clause is considered to have occurred. However if, for example, a tug was assisting a vessel with a line on her and she was pulled over and sank, any liability incurred by the vessel as a result of the accident would not be recoverable under the Collision clause in the vessel's hull policies, since there had been no collision.

What constitutes "any other ship or vessel" has already been considered. This is a question of fact to be determined in each individual case.

When a tug and tow, operating as a unit, are involved in a collision with another vessel, the question as to whether the tug or the tow is liable depends upon its individual wrongdoing (*Harbor Towing Corp.* v. *Atlantic Mutual Ins. Co.*, 1951 AMC 1070). In England, it was held in one well-known case (the *Niobe*, 1891, A. C. 41) that if the tow was in charge of the navigation and was herself at fault for the collision, the tug was, in effect, merely the propelling mechanism of the tow and that they were one vessel. In that case, the Collision clause in the tow's hull policy was held to cover the tow's liability for the collision between the tug and another vessel even though the tow herself was not in actual contact with the colliding vessel. This decision has been criticized by American courts (*Western Transit Co.* v. *Brown*, 161 Fed. Rep. 869, and *Coastwise Steamship Co.* v. *Home Ins. Co.*, 161 Fed. Rep. 871), and it is doubtful whether it will be followed.

Insurances on freight usually contain a Freight Collision clause which protects the shipowner in the event that he becomes liable to pay collision damages in respect of the freight (arising out of the law relating to the limitation of liability in the United States). The Freight Collision clause is only operative when the value of the vessel and freight adopted for the limit of liability exceeds the insured value of the vessel.

As we have seen, the Collision clause is a separate contract which provides coverage against certain liabilities to third parties. This additional contract provides that underwriters will indemnify the assured against certain claims for damage consequent on the insured vessel colliding with another vessel. This indemnification is limited to a sum not exceeding the insured (or agreed) value in the policy. Generally speaking, in the absence of any special provision, a policy against liabilities to third parties does not render underwriters liable for the costs incurred by the assured in defending a claim made upon him. Thus, in the Collision clause, express provision is made regarding legal expenses; a further indemnity is added by the inclusion of the following words:

> (b) in cases where, with the consent in writing of a majority (in amount) of Hull Underwriters, the liability of the Vessel has been contested, or proceedings have been taken to limit liability, the Un-

derwriters will also pay a like proportion of the costs which the Assured shall thereby incur or be compelled to pay.

Furthermore, the full amount of such legal expenses is payable in addition to the maximum collision liability (that is, the insured or agreed value) and is unlimited in amount.

In stating claims under the Collision clause in both-to-blame collision cases, it is necessary to separate the legal expenses into three categories: *General, Attack,* and *Defense.*

(1) *General.* These are the costs of *testing or determining liability,* that is to say, the cost incurred in the endeavor to establish liability and up to the time liability is established. This category would include investigation, interviewing witnesses, attending hearings, preparing for the trial (insofar as the question of liability is concerned) including both the efforts to prove that the other vessel was liable and the efforts to prove that our vessel was *not* liable. Also included would be any other costs which cannot be attributed specifically to *Attack* or *Defense* as dealt with below. In most cases, this category will comprise the major portion of the attorney's account.

The average adjuster ultimately divides general costs between attack and defense in accordance with Rule of Practice XX of the Association of Average Adjusters, which reads as follows:

RULE XX. APPORTIONMENT OF LEGAL COSTS AND/OR OTHER EXPENSES IN COLLISION CASES. In cases involving collisions, the legal costs and/or other expenses incurred to determine liability either by court action, arbitration or determination by consent of the parties shall be apportioned rateably over the full provable damages, excluding interest and costs, of the claim and counterclaim which have been or would have been allowed.

Nothing contained in this rule shall affect those legal costs and/or other expenses incurred specifically for the purpose of defense or recovery which shall be charged accordingly.

Under this rule the general costs (that is, all costs incurred up to the time liability is actually established) are apportioned over the full claims which it is considered would have been established; that is, the full amounts really at stake on each side. The eventual result is of no moment; each party's interest in the proceedings must necessarily be for the full amount of their claim. Although the final liability may be settled at, say, 75/25 it is assumed that each party entered into the proceedings with a view to recovering 100 percent of their own claim. However, when a vessel *effectively* limits liability, this rule is superseded: such costs are apportioned over the agreed claim of one vessel and the share of the limited liability fund attaching to the other.

(2) *Attack (or Costs of Recovery)*. These are the costs of prosecuting the claim against the other side. In this category would fall the preparing, serving, and filing of the libel, and obtaining security from the other vessel; examining the documents submitted in support of the damages to the subject vessel; obtaining proofs or supports as necessary, including fees paid witnesses engaged solely for the purpose of proving the damages of our vessel as distinguished from expenses incurred in connection with the question of liability. Any costs incurred in attacking the other vessel's right to limit liability or the size of the limitation fund would also fall within this category.

The average adjuster ultimately apportions attack costs over the various items of the claim which have been actually recovered. If the recovery efforts were unsuccessful, these attack costs are apportioned over the interests that would have benefited by a successful outcome.

(3) *Defense*. These are the costs of defending the claim of the other side. This would include the receiving and answering of the libel filed by the other side, providing the other side with security, examining the other side's damages and any expenses incurred challenging the damages of the other side. Any costs incurred in filing limitation proceedings on behalf of the subject vessel would also fall within this category.

The average adjuster ultimately charges defense costs to the interests benefited or intended to be benefited by these costs: the hull underwriters in respect of those third party claims which are covered by the Collision clause, and the Protection and Indemnity underwriters in respect of claims which are covered by them.

The reader's attention is also directed to Rule 13 of the Association of Average Adjusters of Canada's Rules of Practice for the Great Lakes (Appendix D); this rule deals with the division of legal expense in a similar fashion to that described above.

If legal expenses are incurred in successfully defending a large potential collision claim, such expenses are apportioned over the potential provable claim and the deductible average in the policy (if any). The assured thus bears that proportion of the legal expenses which would have applied to the deductible average had the defense been unsuccessful and a collision claim had resulted. On the other hand, if the defense of a collision claim merely succeeds in reducing a potential collision claim from, say, $20,000 to $10,000 and the legal expenses are $4,000, no part of the resultant claim of $14,000 would be recoverable under a policy providing for a deductible average of $15,000.

Provable Damages in Collision Cases

It might be useful to include some general remarks regarding provable damages in collision cases.

The owner of a damaged vessel has an obligation to minimize his damages; he must, therefore, defer repairs which are not immediately necessary for seaworthiness until the vessel's next regularly scheduled dry docking or repair period. If this is done then none of the common repair expenses (such as pilotage, towage, gas-freeing, etc.) are claimable from the guilty vessel as collision damages, at least to the extent that they would have had to be incurred in any event. This also means that no part of the time required on dry dock for owner's or other average work is claimable from the other side, only the excess time on dry dock (if any) solely necessary because of the collision damage. The same considerations apply to claims for loss of use arising out of the collision damage repairs.

On the other hand, if the collision damage repairs are immediately necessary for seaworthiness, the shipowner can take advantage of the emergency dry-docking by advancing classification surveys and performing any repair work for his own account (provided it was not immediately necessary for seaworthiness) without bearing any part of the common charges. Similarly, this non-essential owner's work does not prevent the shipowner from collecting his loss of use in full from the offending vessel.

If a new accident occurs before the collision damage repairs are effected—an accident which requires immediate dry-docking—and the collision repairs are effected concurrently, it is the new accident which bears the cost of the common dry-docking and against which any claim for loss of use falls. Thus, for the purpose of the claim against the colliding vessel, the collision damage repairs do not bear any common charges, nor is any claim for loss of use enforceable.

In short, the treatment of common charges in terms of provable damages differs from the treatment of common charges in stating claims under marine insurance policies.

In assessing provable damages in collision cases, problems sometimes arise when rates of exchange have to be applied. Should the claims of the respective parties (say, one in dollars, the other in lire) be set off against the other: (a) at the time of the collision or (b) several years later when the claims of both parties have been agreed in their own currencies? The English admiralty court decided in favor of method (b) in *Transoceanica Francesca & Nicos V* (1987 2 L.R. 155).

The general rule in admiralty is that interest will be allowed in collision cases as part of just compensation for the wrong done (*Sinclair Refining Co.* v. *Green Island*, 1970 AMC 1117). Any such interest allowed becomes part of the damages awarded (Roscoe: *Damages in Maritime Collisions*, 1909, p. 29; Hurd: *Marine Insurance Liabilities*, 2d ed., pp. 86, 100, 111). The reason for allowing interest on damages is that the claimant was out of pocket to the extent of those damages and has therefore lost the ability to earn interest on his capital. This is the theory of restitution (See also *Seminole Asphalt Refining Co.* v. the *M.V. Delbert, Jr., et al.* (1987 AMC 2230), where the insured tug owner, found liable in a collision action for $344,000 plus interest, was covered by underlying insurance up to a $250,000 limit and the excess liability insurer was to bear the $94,000 difference and all interest awarded by the judgment.)

For a discussion of "General Average Contributions as Provable Damages in Collision Cases," see the author's paper published in the *Tulane Law Review*, Vol. 51, No. 4, pp. 839-65.

PROTECTION AND INDEMNITY INSURANCE

Protection and Indemnity insurance (in the form of mutual clubs) was introduced in the United Kingdom in the second half of the nineteenth century to cover those liabilities not covered at all (or only partially covered) by the standard hull marine insurance policies of the day. At that time, collision liabilities were only covered by hull policies on payment of an additional premium, and such coverage was limited to three-fourths. (It is still the general practice in the United Kingdom for hull policies to provide coverage for only three-fourths collision liability.) Furthermore (as is still the case today), the mid-Victorian hull policy did not cover other and more important third party liabilities at all. Such liabilities, particularly loss of life and personal injury, were increasing due to the growth in passenger services coupled with changes in the law whereby injured persons and their dependents were enabled to institute actions for damages against shipowners (the Fatal Accidents Act, 1846, commonly known as Lord Campbell's Act). While there is no doubt that shipowners looked to the new mutual protection associations (as they were then known) for coverage of collision liabilities not provided by their hull policies, it would appear that the chief reason for the formation of these clubs (as they came to be known) was to provide protection against claims for loss of life, personal injury, and excess collision liability (*Tulane Law Review*, Vol. 43, No. 3, p. 467). As a result of social and other legislation, new liabilities had been imposed on shipowners; this trend continued, and Protection and Indemnity clubs and underwriters were continually required to add new risks to the coverage they provided.

Shipowners' exposure to legal liabilities also increased rapidly in the United States but such liabilities were invariably insured in the London market. Indeed, it was not until 1917 that a market was developed in the United States for this type of insurance. At that time the British government's wartime regulations handicapped the British Protection and Indemnity market's insurance of neutral fleets. Necessity became the mother of invention and the first American Protection and Indemnity association was formed to fill the void.

Whatever may have been the original impetus behind Protection and Indemnity insurance, it is still important to remember that in arranging Protection and Indemnity insurance it is essential that such insurance covers those liabilities specifically excluded from the hull policy, by the proviso clause included in the collision clause. Protection and Indemnity insurance must also pick up shipowners' liabilities not dealt with at all in the hull policy, which is primarily an insurance against physical damage to the subject-matter insured. Such liabilities are always increasing, the most recent example of this being the new international legislation against oil pollution.

It is interesting to note that, unlike the British Protection and Indemnity clubs, all of which have their own (albeit similar) rules, American clubs and underwriters, generally speaking, use a standard form of policy. This includes a general clause under which the underwriter (or club) agrees "to indemnify the assured against any loss, damage or expense which the assured shall become liable to pay and shall pay by reason of the fact that the assured is the owner (or operator, manager, charterer, mortgagee, trustee, receiver or agent, as the case may be) of the insured vessel" and which results from the liabilities, risks, events, occurrences, and expenditures as set forth in the policy. Thus, in considering the extent of coverage afforded by the individual policy clauses, it is important that they be read in conjunction with the general clause. For example, the Protection and Indemnity insurer has no obligation to indemnify (for compulsory wreck removal expenses) when the assured's "innocent" barge sank solely because of the negligence of the towing tug. Under the Wreck Act the tug is solely liable for the government's removal costs and the Protection and Indemnity insurance on the barge did not cover any liability of the assured as tug owner (*St. Paul Fire & Marine Ins. Co.* v. *Vest Transportation Co.,* 1982 AMC 450). Nevertheless, too much can be made of the stipulation that only liabilities incurred "as owner" of the insured vessel are covered. All this means is that there must be some connection between the liability being claimed and the ownership, etc., of the insured vessel.

It will also be noted that the coverage provided is strictly one of indemnity and not direct liability; the assured must first have been legally liable to pay and have paid the loss, damage, or expense before the Protection and Indemnity underwriter is himself liable under the policy. Thus, under New York statutory law, underwriters are not directly liable to the judgment creditor of a bankrupt assured (*Cucurillo* v. *American Steamship Owners Mutual Protection and Indemnity Association,* 1969 AMC 2334). See also *Ali Galeb Ahmed* v. *American Steamship Mutual Protection and Indemnity Association* (1981 AMC 897). However, in these days of direct action statutes against underwriters it is doubtful whether, outside New York state, courts would permit Protection and Indemnity underwriters to hide behind such a shield. It is probable that in most states when a third party obtains judgment against a bankrupt assured, he could recover from the assured's Protection and Indemnity underwriters.

Indeed the basic principle of indemnity which has always been fundamental to Protection and Indemnity insurance world-wide (hence the name) was recently challenged in the English court of appeals in two consolidated cases. British Protection and Indemnity clubs had always included "pay to be paid" clauses which stipulated that the member (assured) must have paid the liability covered under the club rules (policy) before he had any right to be indemnified. The court held that the "pay first" provision could not be used to defeat an action by a third party claimant under the English Third Parties (Rights against Insurers) Act, 1930. (This act enabled injured third party claimants to proceed directly against an insolvent wrongdoer's liability insurers.) See *Newcastle P & I Assoc.* v. *Firma C-Trade S.A. (the Fanti) and Socony Mobil Oil, Colne and Others* v. *West of England Ship Owners Mutual Insurance Assoc. Ltd. (the Padre Island),* 1989 1 L.R. 239. Predictably, the British Protection and Indemnity clubs appealed this decision to the House of Lords and at the time of writing the outcome is eagerly awaited. If the court of appeals is upheld, one effect of this English decision would be to make British Protection and Indemnity clubs subject to direct action suits as is the case in those states of the United States which have direct action statutes (*q.v.*). However, in the United States a recent decision of the Eleventh Circuit Court of Appeals held that a Protection and Indemnity club could not be joined as a defendant in a personal injury suit under Florida law because no such joinder is permitted where the policy is one of indemnity (*Weeks* v. *Beryl Shipping Inc.,* 1988 AMC 2187). This decision would presumably prevent a claimant from suing a Protection and Indemnity club in Florida. As this book goes into print it is learned that the House of Lords reversed the court of appeals in the *Fanti/Padre Island* case referred to above. Thus the Protection and Indemnity clubs' time honored position that the member's contractual right to indemnity was subject to the member (assured) being liable to pay the loss and further, that the member had discharged that liability by payment was upheld. It also appears that the Lord's decision preserves Protection and Indemnity clubs' and insurers' traditional shield against any direct action by third party claimants.

Some of the liabilities covered by Protection and Indemnity insurance are summarized below, the form of insurance used being that of the American Steamship Owners Mutual Protection and Indemnity Association, Inc., which is representative of American Protection and Indemnity coverage.

Loss of Life, Injury, and Illness

This coverage includes liability for loss of life, personal injury to and illness of any person including the crew, stevedores, passengers, or any other person on board the insured vessel; it also covers a liability to persons injured on shore as a result of negligence on the part of the vessel or her crew. There is one major exclusion and that is liability to an employee (other than a seaman) under any compensation act. Such risks are usually the subject of separate liability insurance. Where personal injury claims under the Protection and Indemnity coverage arise out of handling cargo for the insured vessel, the liability commences from the time of receipt by the assured of the cargo on dock or wharf, or on craft alongside for loading, and continues until due delivery from dock or wharf of discharge or until discharge from the insured vessel onto a craft alongside.

Masters and members of the crews of vessels (seamen) are not covered under state workers' compensation laws nor under the Long-shoremen's and Harbor Workers' Compensation Act (*q.v.*). They are subject to admiralty or general maritime law and, if injured, have the right to sue their employers for damages if the injury resulted from any breach by their employers of the warranty of seaworthiness of the vessel. Such proceedings are in the nature of employer's liability suits. Seamen also have the right to transportation, wages, and maintenance and cure (regardless of fault). They are also subject to the Merchant Marine Act of 1920, known as the Jones Act (*U.S. Code,* Title 46) which in essence applies the provisions of the federal Employers' Liability Act to seamen. It should be noted that everyone employed on board a vessel is deemed to be a seaman if connected with the operation or welfare of a vessel while in navigable waters. Claims brought under the Jones Act are not like the periodic benefits and medical expenses paid to workers injured in the course of their employment regardless of fault; they are seamen's tort suits for damages against an employer (the shipowner).

In his excellent pamphlet, *Protection and Indemnity Insurance,* Henry I. Bernard wrote (p. 6):

A shipowner is obligated to pay what is called "maintenance and cure" plus wages to the end of the voyage if a seaman is disabled from illness or injury. He does not have to prove that there was negligence on the part of the shipowner to be entitled to maintenance and cure. All he need show is that he became disabled while in the service of the ship, excepting disability caused by his own wilful misconduct.

A seaman obtains maintenance and cure immediately he is disabled. If he is disabled at sea he received his maintenance and cure on board the vessel (board, keep and such medical aid as is available and wages). Maintenance and cure may continue during his disability after he is put ashore. If he is an inpatient at a Marine or private hospital such hospitalization is considered to be his maintenance and cure. If he is an outpatient he receives medical care, plus an allowance for food and lodging.

It will be seen therefore that "maintenance" constitutes a living allowance (usually $35 per diem) while "cure" covers nursing and medical expenses. Furthermore, the liability is absolute, regardless of fault and without regard to the cause of the injury. Indeed, the U.S. Supreme Court has said that the shipowner's obligation to pay maintenance and cure is so broad that "negligence or acts short of culpable misconduct on the seaman's part will not relieve him of the responsibility" (*Aguilar* v. *Standard Oil Co.*, 318 U.S. 724). Moreover, the burden is on the vessel owner to prove such gross misconduct and that such misconduct was the sole and proximate cause of his disability (*Gulledge* v. *U.S.A.*, 1972 AMC 1187). Generally speaking, maintenance and cure terminates when the maximum cure has been effected, while wages are recoverable up to the completion of the voyage on which the injury or illness occurred (*Farrell* v. *United States*, 336 U.S. 511).

The seaman's right to maintenance and cure for injuries suffered in the course of his service to his vessel extends to injuries suffered while on shore leave. In such cases the American courts have concluded that seamen on shore leave are still in the service of their vessel "subject to the call of duty as a seaman, and earning wages as such" (*Aguilar* v. *Standard Oil Co.*, *supra*). However, a shipowner's obligation to provide maintenance and cure extends only to disabilities incurred while a seaman is "answerable to the call of duty," that is, under some binding obligation to serve. Thus, maintenance was denied to a marine diver injured in a brawl ashore at a time when he was not under any obligation to serve on a vessel and when his employer was not obliged to rehire him, even though he was subject to recall to work and would have been willing to return (*Thomas E. Baker* v. *Ocean Systems*, 1972 AMC 287).

Nevertheless, it is well established that the maintenance and cure obligation is equally applicable to injuries actually received on land "during the period of relaxation while on shore as to those received while reaching it" (*Warren* v. *United States*, 340 U.S. 523). The determining factor as to whether a seaman is in the service of the vessel and answerable to the call of duty at the time of the accident depends on the particular facts and circumstances of each case. In short, there must be a clear legal obligation on the part of both the seaman and the shipowner: the former must be obligated to answer the call of duty in the service of his vessel, and the latter must be obligated to pay him and therefore provide maintenance and cure. In the case of *Baker* v. *Ocean Systems* quoted above, it was held that it was not sufficient that the seaman was subject to being called back to work, the crux of the matter being that he was a free agent and was under no *obligation* to return.

Bernard (p. 10) goes on to say:

In addition to maintenance and cure, a seaman is entitled to recover damages if he is injured or becomes ill:

   (1) as a result of negligence on the part of the employer,

   (2) if the vessel is unseaworthy, or,

   (3) if the injury or illness is caused by the fault of a fellow servant (a fellow servant meaning another employee).

Also, dependents of a seaman who is killed by reason of negligence or fellow servant fault are entitled to damages.

Cases involving negligence are by far the most difficult to deal with because there is no fixed schedule of allowances to be paid for damages. These cases are for the most part settled through negotiations between the seamen and the underwriters or the employing owners. In the majority of the more serious cases the injured seaman engages a lawyer through whom settlement negotiations are conducted.

Damages mean the amount of money to which a seaman is entitled over and above the allowance for maintenance and cure. The amount of damages is based on the extent of injuries, length of disability, loss of earnings, and the degree of pain and suffering.

As already noted, it is generally accepted that most injuries to crew members are covered whether sustained afloat or ashore (*Aguilar* v. *Standard Oil Co., supra*). This on the theory that the crew member is still in service of the ship when ashore for recreation or other purposes (*Warren* v. *United States, supra*; *Tulane Law Review*, Vol. 43, No. 3, p. 510).

Burial expenses are recoverable when reasonably incurred by the assured for the burial of any seaman, although such claims were usually subject to a limit of $500. However, this age of inflation applies equally to the cost of dying and Protection and Indemnity insurers generally accept all burial expenses reasonably incurred.

In dealing with claims from all other persons (such as passengers, stevedores, etc.), the amount of damages depends on the extent of the injuries, loss of earnings, the degree of pain and suffering, length of disability, and, in the case of death, the pecuniary loss to the next of kin (Bernard, *supra*).

The shipowner's liability for loss of life and personal injury arising out of unseaworthiness has been greatly extended during this century. In 1920, the U.S. Congress passed the Jones Act (*supra*) which permitted a seaman injured in the course of his employment by the negligence of the shipowner, master, or fellow crew members to recover damages for his injuries; it also abolished contributory negligence as a defense. Prior to the Jones Act, the proximate cause of any injury was relevant, and if the claimant's negligence had contributed to his injury, his claim would fail. Under the act, contributory negligence (if any) only results in a reduction or mitigation of damages. Furthermore, seamen had not been able to claim damages when injured as a result of negligence on the part of the shipowner, master, or fellow crew member. The Jones Act altered all this and in very short order longshoremen also were held to be "seamen" entitled to sue under the act (*Seas Shipping Co.* v. *Sieracki,* 328 U.S. 85). Under the Jones Act the shipowner is required to exercise reasonable care, but the courts have clearly established that, quite independently of their obligation under the act, shipowners have the non-delegable duty to furnish a seaworthy vessel. Furthermore, this duty is absolute and not predicated upon negligence (*Machnich* v. *Southern S. S. Co.*, 321 U.S. 96); nor is the duty to furnish a seaworthy vessel satisfied by due diligence. In the context of personal injury suits, the term "unseaworthiness" includes practically all types of operating negligence in the navigation and management of the ship (Gilmore & Black, p. 252). It was not long before this liability for unseaworthiness was extended to include almost all workers, including stevedores injured while working on board vessels and, later, stevedores injured on shore (*Gutierrez* v. *Waterman S. S. Corp.*, 373 U.S. 206). As Justice Harlan of the U. S. Supreme Court put it (*Moragne* v. *States Marine Lines,* 1970 AMC 967):

> The unseaworthiness doctrine has become the principal vehicle for recovery by seamen for injury or death, overshadowing the negligence action made available by the Jones Act, and it has achieved equal importance for longshoremen and other harbor workers to whom the duty of seaworthiness was extended because they perform work on the vessel traditionally done by seamen.

It should be noted, however, that the mere capacity to float or move across navigable water does not necessarily make a structure of a Jones Act vessel. The Fifth Circuit Court of Appeals upheld a district court finding that a floating "work punt" utilized solely as a work platform for pile driving activities and neither designed nor used for navigation was not a Jones Act vessel (*Bernard* v. *Binnings Construction Co.*, 1985 AMC 784).

The term "unseaworthiness" is very widely construed when assessing liability for loss of life and personal injury. Thus, when a crew member slips as a result of soap, oil, or grease on floor, deck, or steps, the accident may well be adjudged to be the result of the vessel's "unseaworthiness." At the other end of the scale, a seaman with a vicious disposition and a willingness to fight may also render a vessel "unseaworthy." In one recent case, when a longshoreman was injured as a result of slipping on beans which had spilled from bags being discharged, it was held that the vessel was "unseaworthy" (*Frank Burrage* v. *Flota Mercante Grancolombiana, S. A.*).

The implied warranty of absolute seaworthiness in the United States to seamen and others doing work traditionally performed by seamen, coupled with the traditionally high damages awarded by American courts, inevitably results in liabilities for death and personal injury being a very substantial part of payments under Protection and Indemnity policies.

The Longshoremen's and Harbor Workers' Compensation Act (LHWCA) was enacted in 1927 for the benefit of maritime workers who service vessels but who do not qualify as seamen (they do not do work normally done by seamen). Such workers are not covered by state workmen's compensation laws and therefore have no remedy against their employers. The act provides fixed compensation for disability or death of an employee but only if the disability or death results from an injury occurring on the navigable waters of the United States (including any adjoining pier, wharf, dry dock, terminal, building way, marine railway, or other adjoining area customarily used by an employer in loading, unloading, repairing, dismantling, or building a vessel) (Sect. 903). Under the act the term "employee" means any person engaged in maritime employment including longshoremen, harbor workers, ship repairers, shipbuilders, and ship-breakers (Sect. 902). Such workers are sometimes referred to as "brown water" employees as opposed to "blue water" seamen. Although the act provides a statutory compensation award against the employer of these workers, it also preserves their right to bring tort actions for damages against any third party (such as the shipowner). Masters and crew members of any vessel are specifically excluded from coverage under the act (Sect. 902).

For many years shipowners complained bitterly about the state of the law, particularly insofar as it permitted longshoremen to proceed against them on grounds of "unseaworthiness." Under LHWCA as it existed prior to 1972, workers injured on or by a vessel could bring a so-called third party action against the vessel with a right to recover if the vessel was "unseaworthy." This resulted in vessel owners bringing indemnity actions against the employers of the injured workers (such as shipyards, stevedores, etc.). In an attempt to reduce this widespread litigation, the U.S. Congress amended the LHWCA in 1972, eliminating suits by longshore-men against a shipowner based *solely* on the "unseaworthiness" of the ves-sel. However, longshoremen, under the act, can still sue shipowners for injuries resulting from the direct negligence of the owners. In short, "un-seaworthiness" per se is removed as a basis for longshoremen's suits against shipowners. The so-called warranty of workmanlike service said to be owed by maritime contractors to vessel owners was also eliminated, thereby affecting vessel owners' indemnity actions. It is doubtful whether vessel owners gained any more on the swings than they lost on the round-abouts as a result of the amendments to the LHWCA. Furthermore, in 1979 the U.S. Supreme Court, in a majority decision, held that the U.S. Congress in enacting the 1972 amendments to the LHWCA did not intend to impose a proportionate-fault rule so as to change the judicially created admiralty rule that the shipowner can be made to pay all the damages not due to the longshoreman's own negligence. Thus, where injury to a longshoreman is occasioned by the combined negligence of shipowner, stevedore, and in-jured longshoreman, the liability of the shipowner is not restricted only to that proportion of fault—and the shipowner could be made to pay all the damages not due to the injured longshoreman's own negligence (*Edmonds* v. *Compagnie Generale Transatlantique,* 99 S. Ct. 2753).

Life salvage is also covered under this section of the Protection and Indemnity policy, but the coverage is more apparent than real because, generally speaking, under maritime law the saving of human life without the saving of property does not entitle the salvor to an award. However, life salvors are entitled to a fair share of the remuneration awarded for salving a vessel and her cargo. The International Convention on Salvage, 1989, endorsed this long-time practice (*see* "Salvage Expenses" in Chapter 7). In other words, if a salvor, while in the process of saving maritime property, also saves human life, the latter factor will be taken into consideration in assessing the salvage award and, indeed, two separate awards may be made to the salvor. Nevertheless, even if the amount by which the award is in-creased because of the saving of human life is shown separately, the entire amount or amounts awarded would be payable by the underwriters on ves-sel and cargo (always assuming the policies covered salvage) (*see* the *Bos-worth,* 1962 1 L. L. R 483.) However, the court in that case agreed that specific sums payable *solely* in respect to saving life at sea would be recov-erable under normal Protection and Indemnity coverage. For example, where an assured paid another vessel for pouring oil on the sea to assist in saving the insured vessel's crew, such a payment would be recoverable. In a more recent American case, a vessel picked up the crew of a ship which was on fire in the Pacific. After two unsuccessful attempts to tow the vessel to port, she left the scene. Eight days later a salvage tug located the burning vessel, successfully brought her into port, and in due course received a property salvage award. It was held that the first vessel was not entitled to recover life salvage out of the property salvage award. In order to recover life salvage under 46 U.S.C., Sect. 729, a life salvage claimant must forego the opportunity to engage in the really profitable work of property salvage; in this particular case, the evidence showed that, despite their best efforts, the life salvage claimants were incapable of becoming property salvors. Furthermore, the life salvage was too remote in time (8 days) from the successful property salvage effort (*North America*, 1970 AMC 1742).

Passenger liners are often required to go to the assistance of other vessels in order that the ship's doctor can attend to injured seamen; the result is a considerable annual loss by way of deviation expenses. Such assistance does not constitute "life salvage" and the expenses incurred are not recoverable from Protection and Indemnity underwriters. Any claim could only lie against the vessels to whom the services had been rendered but such claims are not legally enforceable. Furthermore, Protection and Indemnity underwriters take the position that unless their assured is legally liable to pay for the services rendered, there is no coverage. As vessels which assist other vessels, either in saving human life from the sea or in rendering medical assistance, have no legal claim for the services rendered, there can be no claim under Protection and Indemnity insurance.

If a vessel has an injured or sick seaman on board and arranges to rendezvous with a liner, thereby *herself* incurring some deviation expenses, the vessel of which the injured seaman is a crew member may be able to recover her deviation expenses from her Protection and Indemnity underwriters. On the other hand, the liner which went to the assistance of the seaman has no claim for deviation expenses either against the vessel assisted or from the liner's own Protection and Indemnity underwriters. Such services come under the category of moral obligations.

However, in the words of Nicholas J. Healy (*Annual Survey of American Law—Admiralty and Shipping*, New York University School of Law, 1978):

> A significant step toward judicial recognition of a right to life salvage when there is no saving of property was taken by the Second Circuit in *Peninsular & Oriental Steam Navigation Co.* v. *Overseas Oil Carriers, Inc.* (1977 AMC 283). Here in response to a radio request, a passenger vessel deviated to take on board an ailing seaman from a tanker having no medical staff. Reasoning that where its admiralty jurisdiction is invoked a district court may consider quasi-contractual claims, the court held the passenger vessel's owners entitled to the

reasonable value of the services rendered. The trial judge was therefore found in error in applying the "questionable doctrine" of life salvage in denying the owners of the passenger vessel a recovery for the extra fuel costs incurred in coming to the aid of the ailing seaman.

Nevertheless, this "questionable doctrine" was endorsed by the International Convention on Salvage, 1989 (*see* "Salvage Expenses" in Chapter 7).

Repatriation Expenses

Liability for expenses reasonably incurred in necessarily repatriating any member of the crew or any other person employed on board the insured vessel is covered under the basic Protection and Indemnity policy. However, any such expenses incurred due to the expiration or voluntary termination of the shipping agreement are not recoverable unless, of course, caused by sea perils. Any repatriation expenses due to shipwreck, injury, illness, or any other fortuitous occurrence would be recoverable.

Collision

This coverage is for liability for loss or damage arising from collision of the insured vessel with another ship or vessel where the liability is such as would not be covered by the four-fourths collision clause in the American Institute Hull Clauses. The risks covered under the Collision clause of the American Protection and Indemnity policy form are therefore limited to those risks excluded by the so-called proviso (or exclusions) clause in the Hull Collision clause. These risks include the expenses for which the assured is liable in respect of his vessel for raising, removing, or destroying the wreck of another ship or vessel or her cargo, and damage done by another ship or vessel to any harbor, wharf, pier, stage, or similar structure in consequence of the insured vessel having been in collision with another vessel. Also recoverable under this clause are payments for damage to the cargo of the insured vessel by the non-carrying vessel involved in the collision and included by that vessel in her counterclaim against the insured or carrying vessel in accordance with American law. The Protection and Indemnity coverage does not extend to any liability, direct or indirect, in respect of the engagements of or the detention or loss of time of the insured vessel. The policy contains a Cross Liabilities clause and a Sister Ship clause similar to those included in the Collision clause in the American hull form of policy.

The meaning of the exclusion from Protection and Indemnity coverage of "such damages as are recoverable under the collision clause" (in the hull policy) was considered by the court in *Steamship Mutual Underwriting Assoc. Ltd.* v. *George H. Landry* (1960 AMC 54). It was contended by the Protection and Indemnity Association that its coverage did not operate as an excess collision policy when the amount insured under the American Institute Time (Hulls) form of policy did not satisfy a collision liability because the insured value was less than the vessel's actual value. It was further contended by the association that it covered liabilities not covered at all by the American Institute Time (Hulls) form and did not cover liability for amounts in excess of that coverage. The court held that the Protection and Indemnity Association remained liable for so much of the shipowner's liability as exceeded the maximum values which might be covered by a standard hull policy without special riders.

As a result of this decision, most Protection and Indemnity clubs and underwriters reworded their rules or policies by stipulating that no liability attached to them for any loss, damage, or expenses which would be payable under the terms of the American hull form of policy (or similar hull coverage) whether or not the vessel was fully covered by such insurance sufficient in amount to pay such loss, damage, or expense in full. In other words, it was put beyond doubt that basic Protection and Indemnity insurance does not provide excess collision coverage. However, sometimes, by mutual agreement, a Protection and Indemnity policy will be endorsed to provide excess coverage.

Oil pollution arising from a collision, which as we have seen is largely excluded from the coverage provided by hull underwriters, is another potentially heavy risk in respect of which vessel owners look to their Protection and Indemnity coverage for protection. It would seem appropriate, therefore, to review the entire subject of oil pollution.

Oil Pollution

Protection and Indemnity clubs and underwriters have always protected their assureds against any legal liability arising out of oil pollution. However, it used to be that, in accordance with normal Protection and Indemnity requirements, the oil pollution must have resulted from the assured's negligence. Furthermore, in the past, tankers were not as big as they are today and, indeed, the transportation and consumption of oil was on a much smaller scale. Consequently, oil pollution claims were relatively insignificant and certainly not the subject of international scrutiny.

Oil pollution is an emotional subject; while everyone likes the convenience and products which the oil industry makes possible, no one likes tar on his feet or on his property. Furthermore, the study and protection of the environment have become phenomena of the times. Consequently, much of the national and international legislation which exists was developed following emergency situations and under the emotional and critical eyes of the people of a country whose national resources were threatened or thought to be threatened.

It all began in 1967 when the *Torrey Canyon*, fully laden with oil on her maiden voyage, stranded off the coast of England, causing widespread oil pollution along the coasts of both England and France. After the vessel had been declared a total loss, the British government decided to bomb the wreck in an attempt to prevent further pollution, a measure that was only partially successful. The British and French governments eventually accepted £3 million in full and final settlement of all claims, including private claims which they had paid. Things have never been the same since, for it was under the impetus of this disaster that the thicket of oil pollution legislation grew and flourished throughout the maritime world.

The international oil companies and tanker owners reacted with the Tanker Owners Voluntary Agreement Concerning Liability for Oil Pollution—better known as TOVALOP. This purely voluntary program was started in 1969 and most deep-sea tanker tonnage, including the large Russian tanker fleet, now participates. Oil pollution, it seems, is no respecter of iron curtains. It is important to stress that TOVALOP deals solely with *clean-up costs*—not third party liability claims. Under the agreement, tanker owners agree to reimburse *governments* for their clean-up costs unless the vessel concerned can prove that no negligence was involved. This was the first step towards the strict liability concept of today. TOVALOP members (tanker owners) are also encouraged to instigate clean-up operations themselves, regardless of fault, in the knowledge that if they do so the reasonable costs of such voluntary clean-ups are covered by TOVALOP. Under TOVALOP, the limits covered are $100 per gross ton (of the offending vessel) with a maximum of $16.8 million. The agreement is administered by the International Tanker Owners Pollution Federation and the liabilities and obligations under TOVALOP are insured by the International Tanker Indemnity Association (ITIA) in conjunction with the international Protection and Indemnity clubs.

At a much later date, by which time it had become apparent that the amount available under TOVALOP for clean-up following a major oil spill would probably not be sufficient to do the job, the oil industry introduced a new scheme: the Contract Regarding an Interim Supplement to Tanker Liability for Oil Pollution—better known as CRISTAL. While TOVALOP is an agreement among tanker owners, membership in CRISTAL is confined to cargo owners and, indeed, is limited to oil companies engaged in the production, refining, or marketing of oil. Its objective is *firstly* to provide *additional* compensation to governments or other third parties suffering pollution damage and which they cannot fully recover from the owner of the offending vessel because of that vessel's limit of liability. *Secondly,*

CRISTAL (like TOVALOP) seeks to encourage voluntary clean-up and will reimburse the tanker owner (or his Protection and Indemnity club) in respect of the tanker owner's own clean-up costs after remedies available under other regimes have been exhausted. It will be seen that CRISTAL is not likely to operate if the offending tanker has a very large gross tonnage since, in that event, the tanker's limit of liability would probably be sufficient to cover third party claims. Furthermore, in the case of such large vessels, *clean-up costs* would have to exceed $16.8 million before CRISTAL would operate—an unlikely event. On the other hand, in the case of smaller vessels, CRISTAL can be a very large and helpful contributor, because such smaller vessels' limitation funds might not be sufficient to cover either *clean-up costs* or third party claims in full. However, before CRISTAL can operate at all, the vessel carrying the oil cargo must be a member of TOVALOP and the cargo being carried must be owned by a CRISTAL member (that is, a major oil company). The incident giving rise to the pollution must be one where the vessel owner is, or would be, liable under the International Civil Liability Convention, to be dealt with later. The limits under CRISTAL are somewhat complicated. A maximum figure of $36 million is often mentioned but the maximum compensation under CRISTAL is really $36 million less the amount paid by a vessel owner in respect of his own clean-up and less the amount paid by the vessel owner in respect of third party claims. CRISTAL is, in effect, a "bumbershoot" program created by the oil industry to operate in major oil spills involving their members, with the object of helping both governments and third party claimants in meeting pollution clean-up costs and helping tanker owners in providing compensation for property damage. In short, CRISTAL, although available only in certain circumstances, is designed to supplement the amount of compensation available after other sources of compensation have been exhausted. A fund is maintained for the settlement of claims and replenished by calls on cargo owners. Thus, by creating CRISTAL the oil industry hoped to convince public opinion throughout the world that it was willing to make a large financial contribution toward the war against pollution.

The introduction of TOVALOP (by tanker owners) and CRISTAL (by the oil industry) was, perhaps, to a large degree a public relations exercise with the hope of obviating the necessity for countries importing oil to introduce more onerous pollution legislation. If so, it was a case of too little, too late. More likely, in the ecology-conscious atmosphere prevailing, nothing could have stopped the rush to legislation. The maritime nations, goaded by public outcry, lost no time in introducing severe pollution laws. Since most of these laws require the vessel owner himself to clean up the oil spill, the voluntary nature of the steps to be taken as envisaged by

TOVALOP has largely ceased to exist. Liability under the prevailing local law will probably be strict (rather than based on fault) with limits of liability in excess of TOVALOP. Thus the value of TOVALOP is reduced, although TOVALOP does cover some areas where the International Civil Liability Convention does not apply (such as the mere threat of pollution as opposed to actual pollution). Moreover, TOVALOP covers a spill from a vessel in ballast while the Civil Liability Convention only applies when vessels are carrying oil cargoes. Furthermore, many countries who are not yet parties to the Civil Liability Convention continue to rely on TOVALOP and CRISTAL.

In most areas of the world outside the territorial waters of the United States, the International Civil Liability Convention will probably govern *all claims* following a major oil spill. This international oil pollution convention was held in 1969—its full title is the International Convention on Civil Liability for Oil Pollution Damage—more commonly known as CLC. This convention has been ratified by most of the major maritime nations of the world, although, predictably, not by the United States, which has its own version (or versions) of pollution legislation. CLC came into operation in 1975, at which time the required number of nations had ratified the convention. The Civil Liability Convention applies to vessels carrying oil in bulk as cargo—but where oil is being so carried CLC extends to pollution caused by leakage of bunkers of such vessels. A vessel carrying more than 2,000 tons of such cargo must obtain a government certificate testifying that there is available in respect of the vessel adequate insurance or other security to meet the convention liabilities. This applies at all times to vessels registered in contracting states and to all other vessels when calling at contracting states' ports. Furthermore, in the event of any claims arising, there is a right of direct action against the insurer. The limit of liability under the convention was approximately $160 per limitation ton with a maximum of approximately $17 million; this applies globally to all pollution claims arising out of one particular incident and includes the cost of clean-up performed by the vessel owner himself. The limitation figures in CLC are expressed in gold francs and therefore fluctuate when exchanged into other currencies, particularly in these days of inflation and floating currencies. The dollar, equivalents given are therefore only approximate. Liability under CLC is strict, the only defenses being an act of God, an act of war, deliberate damage by a third party, or sole negligence on the part of a government or other authority regarding the upkeep of lights or other navigational aids. The CLC was amended in 1984 in an attempt to keep pace with inflation and also to provide a more adequate fund to deal with major oil spills. Under this 1984 protocol a vessel owner carrying oil in bulk may limit his liability to approximately $136 per limitation ton or approximately $62 million maximum for one occurrence at the rates of exchange prevailing in 1984.

The fund established under CLC is supplemented by the Compensation Fund Convention of 1971. This new Fund Convention was to be financed by a tonnage charge on oil cargoes; it was designed to provide compensation in those cases where no liability for pollution damages arose under the CLC or where the owner was unable to meet his obligations in full or in those cases where the claims and expenses exceeded the vessel owner's limit of liability under CLC. The object of creating this additional fund was to persuade countries who might otherwise not ratify CLC to do so. (Some countries, including the United States, had expressed the view that the limitation under CLC was not large enough.) The Fund Convention entered into force in 1978 but relatively few countries have ratified it. It is, in effect, the intergovernmental counterpart of CRISTAL in the same way as the Civil Liability Convention is the counterpart of TOVALOP. The Fund Convention supplemented the original CLC maximum fund for a single pollution incident ($17 million) to approximately $46 million. Nevertheless, there were continuing doubts as to the adequacy of the limits available in the event of a major oil spill. In 1984, with this in mind, there was (as we have seen) a protocol to the CLC increasing the liability limit under that convention to $62 million. At the same time (1984) a protocol to the Fund Convention was also adopted increasing the combined potential recovery under both CLC and the Fund Convention to approximately $140 million with a possible increase to $208 million depending on the aggregate of oil imports of those nations ratifying the protocols.

When CLC does not apply (as where the spill occurs in the navigable waters of a country, such as the United States, which has not ratified the convention), it is necessary to look to the local law. What then is the position in the United States? In no country in the world has there been more concern shown by both the government and the people than has been the case here. The first manifestation of this concern was the Water Quality Improvement Act of 1970 (amended in 1972 to become the Federal Water Pollution Control Act). This act also introduced the principle of strict liability "without regard to whether any such act or omission was or was not negligent." Except where a spill from a vessel was the result of an act of God, an act of war, negligence by the United States, or an act or omission by a third party, the owner of the vessel causing pollution is liable for the costs of clean-up incurred by the *U.S. government*. The original act stipulated limits of liability of $100 per gross ton up to a maximum of $14 million. Thus, even contributory negligence on the part of a vessel owner would make him liable under the act. Furthermore, the act required any vessel over 300 tons gross, using any port or place in the United States or the navigable waters of the United States, to establish and maintain evidence of financial responsibility up to the limits of liability stipulated to meet the liability to the U.S. government to which such vessel could be subjected for the discharge of oil into or upon the navigable waters of the United States or adjoining shorelines. The navigable waters of the United States include the U.S. portions of the Great Lakes and the St. Lawrence Seaway.

In 1977 and 1978, the Clean Water Act amended the limits of liability of the owner or operator of the offending vessel as follows:

Inland oil barges:	$125 per gross ton or $125,000, whichever is greater.
Tankers:	$150 per gross ton or $250,000, whichever is greater.
Other vessels:	$150 per gross ton with no floor

The amendments also removed the previous overall $14 million ceiling on liability.

Unlike the international convention (CLC), the Water Quality Improvement Act (and its successors, the Federal Water Pollution Control Act and Clean Water Act) deals only with the *U.S. government's claim for clean-up costs*; private claims are not affected at all by this legislation. Thus, while the international convention's limit of approximately $160 per limitation ton (with a ceiling of approximately $17 million) applies to all claims, government and private, made against a vessel, the Water Quality Improvement Act (and its successors) applies only to government claims—leaving private interests (such as fishing industries and individual property owners) unlimited in their claims for compensation (subject, of course, to any limitation rights which might be available to vessel owners in the ordinary course). As in the case of the international convention (CLC), direct action is permitted against insurers, but such insurers may invoke all the rights and defenses which would have been available to the vessel owners. The act is wider than the international convention (CLC) in that it applies not only to tankers but also to dry cargo vessels; the act also applies to demise or time charterers while the CLC does not. However the federal act is like the CLC in that it requires vessels to have on board a certificate issued by the Federal Maritime Commission evidencing that it has satisfactorily established its financial responsibility.

The limitation of liability under the federal act is not applicable if the spill was caused as a result of negligence or wilful misconduct within the privity and knowledge of the vessel owner. If wilful misconduct within the vessel owner's privity and knowledge is established, the owner is liable for the full cost of clean-up without regard to the gross tonnage limitation or the ceiling limitation under the act. The meaning of "negligence or wilful misconduct within the privity or knowledge of the vessel owner" was considered in the case of the tug *Ocean Prince* (584 F2d 1151, 2nd. Cir. 1978): the court defined wilful misconduct as "an act, intentionally done, with knowledge that the performance will probably result in injury or done in such a way as to allow an inference of a reckless disregard of the probable consequences." In another case the court pointed out that although the element of privity and knowledge is the same under both the Limitation of Liability Act and the Federal Water Pollution Control Act, the degree of negligence which precludes limitation of liability under the two statutes is different; under the Pollution Control Act the negligence or misconduct must be *wilful*. Thus, a barge owner's haphazard inspection practices made him privy to an unseaworthy condition, thus justifying denial of limitation, but did not amount to a "wilful misconduct" under the Pollution Control Act sufficient to vitiate the $100 per gross ton limit on the federal government's claim for oil spill removal costs (*Complaint of Steuart Transportation Co.*, 1979 AMC 1187).

The Water Quality Improvement Act was amended to become the federal Water Pollution Control Act primarily to extend the act to cover pollution caused by the discharge not only of oil but also of other *"hazardous substances."* The amendments to the original act also authorized the U.S. Coast Guard to "summarily remove, and, if necessary, destroy" any vessel creating a "substantial threat of a pollution hazard." This authorization raised the question as to the marine insurance coverage for such a loss (assuming the vessel was not already a constructive total loss at the time she was destroyed by governmental authority). Vessel underwriters ultimately agreed to accept such risks if the necessity for destruction arose as a result of an insured peril in the marine policies. Accordingly, a Deliberate Damage (Pollution Hazard) clause was attached to the basic hull policy. Indeed, the last two versions of the American Institute Hull Clauses incorporate such a clause in the policy itself. The clause covers loss of or damage to the insured vessel directly caused by governmental authorities acting for the public welfare. The objective must have been to prevent or mitigate a pollution hazard, or threat thereof, *resulting directly from damage to the vessel for which the underwriters are liable under the policy.* There is a proviso that such act of governmental authorities must not have resulted from want of due diligence by the assured to prevent or mitigate such hazard or threat.

American cargo policies usually incorporate a similar endorsement extending coverage to include loss of or damage to the insured cargo caused by governmental authorities acting for the public welfare to prevent or mitigate a pollution hazard or threat thereof. There is a proviso that the accident or occurrence creating the situation which required such governmental action would have resulted in a recoverable claim under the policy if the cargo insured had sustained physical loss or damage as a direct result of such accident or occurrence.

Disappointment has been expressed in marine insurance circles that the U.S. government has chosen to proceed unilaterally in addressing itself to the problem of oil pollution. In particular, by not ratifying the international convention (CLC), the United States is thought to be out of step with most of the other major maritime countries of the world. One result is that new domestic legislation has already been deemed necessary to extend the federal Water Pollution Control Act in order to cover third party liabilities and to increase the existing limits of liability. Such legislation is now pending in the U.S. Congress. Indeed, as early as 1973 it was thought necessary to introduce the Trans-Alaska Pipeline Authorization Act (TAPA). This act applies to vessels loading oil from the Trans-Alaska pipeline and provides a $14 million limit of liability *regardless of the vessel's size*. Even though it appears that only very large tankers will load at Valdez, it has been suggested that this act would apply to smaller craft, including barges, which may receive oil from the tankers which had loaded at Valdez. Under the act all vessels, regardless of size, must provide evidence of financial responsibility in the sum of $14 million—an apparent absurdity in the case of smaller vessels. This has naturally caused consternation among the oil pollution insurers of such small craft. Furthermore, TAPA reduces the defenses available to vessel owners to acts of war and negligence of the government or the damaged party. In addition, the act covers all damages including clean-up costs, sustained by any person, public or private. Many of the innovations introduced in TAPA (with an assist from CLC) will no doubt be incorporated in the new (and hopefully overall) federal act now being worked on by the U.S. Congress. The failure of the U.S. government to ratify CLC has made this piecemeal approach to oil pollution legislation more or less inevitable.

Furthermore, the Supreme Court has affirmed the right of individual states to enact their own regulations covering oil pollution matters and many states have already done so. The result has been a substantial increase in the number of oil pollution claims to which a vessel owner is exposed. He may be liable not only to the federal government for clean-up expenses under the federal acts but to state and third party claimants also. This raises the question as to whether such manifold risks are insurable. The marine insurance profession had hoped that the CLC convention would be universally adopted by the principal maritime countries rather than have individual countries proceed with more onerous legislation which might be uninsurable and therefore self-defeating. The CLC is insurable largely because of safeguards in favor of the vessel owner and his insurers, such as an insurable limit of liability which applies to *all claims* arising from a specific oil spill (not limited to government clean-up costs) and a limitation fund to which *all claims* are directed even if the spill involves more than one country (as in the case of the *Torrey Canyon*). It will be seen that insurers know where they stand regarding their total liability exposure under the international convention (CLC), whereas in countries not subscribing to the international convention they cannot calculate with accuracy the total exposure and, as a result, may not be able to offer insurance beyond a certain amount. The international group of Protection and Indemnity clubs (with which the American Steamship Owners Mutual Protection & Indemnity Association, Inc., is affiliated) currently have a limit of $400 million on the maximum coverage for oil pollution arising out of one incident. It is to be hoped that the new federal act, when it emerges, will at least be overriding and dispose of all the uncertainties.

The certification procedures required under both the federal Water Pollution Control Act and the international convention (CLC) have created quite an administrative burden. Fortunately, adequate insurance against oil pollution liabilities is acceptable as proof of financial responsibility by the Federal Maritime Commission (under the federal Water Pollution Control Act) and by the governments of other maritime countries (under the international convention—CLC). In the case of oceangoing vessels entered in Protection and Indemnity clubs, such clubs will supply the necessary evidence of adequate insurance.

In the United States, the fact that, under the Water Pollution Control Act, every vessel over 300 gross tons (including barges) must establish financial responsibility to the Federal Maritime Commission, brought about the formation of the Water Quality Insurance Syndicate. The various domestic insurance companies who insured many of the smaller craft operating in U. S. navigable waters against Protection and Indemnity risks were not prepared to assume these new and severe oil pollution risks without receiving additional premiums. The Water Quality Insurance Syndicate was, therefore, set up by these companies initially to cover only vessel owners' liabilities under the Water Quality Improvement Act (as it then was) and, of course, to undertake (on behalf of its assureds) the task of providing evidence of financial responsibility to the Federal Maritime Commission. In the event of an oil spill, the Water Quality Insurance Syndicate encourages its assureds immediately to undertake clean-up costs themselves (without waiting for the U.S. government to undertake the operation itself). However, if the oil spill is of such a magnitude that it is obvious that the clean-up costs will exceed the liability under the act for that particular vessel, the U.S. government should be asked to undertake the operation. The reason for this will be obvious: the Water Quality Insurance Syndicate is only liable for the insured vessel's statutory limit of liability (which in the case of small craft would not amount to a very large sum) and if more than this limitation amount were spent on the clean-up, the vessel owner would be out of pocket for the excess since the assured would have no recourse to the U.S. government for reimbursement. Another instance where the Water Quality Insurance Syndicate would require its assureds to leave the spill to be cleaned up by the U.S. government would be when the leaking vessel was a dumb barge in tow of a tug of different ownership and where the tug had negligently stranded the barge, thus causing the spill. In such a case the barge owner (the assured) should request the U.S. government to clean up the spill and look to the owners of the tug for statutory reimbursement. The Water Quality Insurance Syndicate now offers additional coverage against third party liabilities arising from oil spills, that is to say, liabilities outside the Federal Water Pollution Control Act.

To sum up, the coverage available against the many and varied oil pollution statutes and liabilities is almost as varied as the legislation on the subject. A tanker owner has available to him ITIA (for TOVALOP coverage), the Protection and Indemnity clubs (including TOVALOP) for overall coverage, and the Water Quality Insurance Syndicate (for more limited overall coverage). *In extremis,* in certain circumstances, he may look to CRISTAL for a lifeline. Of course excess oil pollution liability insurance is also available in the London market, although capacity problems are ever present because of that market's substantial involvement in the re-insurance of the international Protection and Indemnity clubs. Vessel owners should seek the advice of their marine insurance brokers as to the oil pollution insurance program most suited to their particular needs. However, it must be clearly understood that potential oil pollution clean-up costs and potential third party liabilities are enormous—and only so much is insurable. The trend of some legislation towards absolute and unlimited liability can only be described as unrealistic and more punitive than constructive. In this connection, a further difficulty arises in the United States where some states have their own pollution laws which operate in addition to the federal act. In some instances, states with such legislation have sought to require vessel owners to provide evidence of financial responsibility on top of the security given to the federal government, a procedure which the international Protection and Indemnity clubs have resisted strenuously. As previously stated, at present the major international Protection and Indemnity clubs provide coverage for oil pollution up to a maximum of $400 million, which is said to represent the maximum re-insurance available to the clubs. There is no insurance available for unlimited liability and beyond this fixed sum a vessel owner would be without coverage. One has to say that it is pointless for governments to introduce legislation which could result in financial disaster to the perhaps unlucky vessel owner who is involved in a major oil spill but who could not in any way maintain the ecological balance or protect the environment. Like spilt milk, spilt oil cannot be undone.

To repeat the obvious, the occurrence of a large oil spill usually results in a widespread public outcry and a demand for immediate action. However, it is essential that the consequent actions be both appropriate and reasonable. The ideal solution to the problem would lie in a combination of public relations and technical expertise. To ensure that the best possible approach is taken, a shipowner whose vessel is involved in a major casualty resulting in oil pollution should immediately contact both his liability and hull underwriters whose representatives will be able to advise as to the best course to be pursued and where the best technical help is to be found in that particular area. Everyone involved should cooperate fully with the government concerned and make every effort to avoid antagonizing public opinion. There is no question that the vessel owner and his insurers carry a heavy responsibility in such cases—in particular they must avoid giving any grounds for allegations of lack of interest. On a more optimistic note, very often what appears to be a major oil spill dissipates itself, for, contrary to popular belief, oil does in fact disappear in time at sea. This is not to say that oil pollution is not a major problem in the world today. No matter what care and precautions are taken, no matter what legislation is passed, sooner or later a supertanker will break up following an accident and cause a monumental pollution problem. What *can* be done is to attempt to mitigate the adverse results of oil spills.

The oil industry, in conjunction with the marine insurance profession, is doing everything possible to provide the financial and technical assistance which will be required.

After almost a decade without major oil spills in American waters, a series of spills during the first half of 1989 (including the largest-ever American incident when the *Exxon Valdez* spewed eleven million gallons of crude oil off the Alaskan coast) raised new concerns about the shortcomings of clean-up technology, and the weaknesses of existing emergency response plans, and focused further attention on the existing liability laws. Oil spill liability had been languishing in the U.S. Congress for fourteen years, the burning question being which existing laws were to be applied. The federal Clean Water Act regulates clean-up costs but the parties involved in the oil spill could be sued under state laws by property owners, fishermen, and tourism businesses affected by the incident. The question has always been whether federal oil spill legislation preempted state liability laws. It is on this issue that previous attempts to legislate comprehensive federal liability laws have foundered for more than a decade. Both oil and maritime interests have said that they cannot accept state oil spill laws in addition to federal (or for that matter international) programs. However, it must be emphasized that the vast majority of oil spills, large and small, are the result of human error, and that from an environmental viewpoint once oil is spilt no amount of legislation or money can restore the status quo. As long as the world is dependent on oil for energy, certain risks have to be borne and it is futile to think that more punitive monetary legislation will solve the problem of oil spills; all it would accomplish would be to raise the cost of oil to the consumer. Furthermore, as has been stated previously, only so much liability insurance is available in the marine insurance markets of the world. Consquently there must be some international limitation of liability available to shipowners if oil is to be transported by sea at all.

Nevertheless, spurred on by the *Exxon Valdez* disaster and the outraged public reaction to the environmental damage caused, the U.S. Congress quickly completed and passed the Oil Pollution Act of 1990 which became law in August 1990. The new act sets the limits of liability for tanker vessels at $1,200 per gross ton or, for a vessel over 3,000 tons, $10 million *whichever is greater*. Limitation will not be permitted if gross negligence or wilful misconduct or violation of a safety requirement or operating regulation were involved in the accident giving rise to the pollution. There is a requirement for evidence of financial responsibility which may present difficulties for the international Protection and Indemnity clubs who customarily provide certificates of financial responsibility on behalf of their members. Under the new act, these members are now exposed to much greater potential liabilities, not only to the federal government, but also to state and local governments as well. After a major oil spill the potential liabilities could be so great as to make insurance of such risks uninsurable beyond the $400 million ceiling per incident currently provided by the Protection and Indemnity clubs. A final shock to shipowners is the requirement that, beginning in 1995, all *new* tankers are required to have double hulls and by the year 2015, all vessels carrying oil in U.S. waters will be required to have double hulls. The U.S. Coastguard has been given the task of promulgating regulations under the provisions of the act. The new regulations are not expected to be issued before October 1991. When this is done, the full effect on the shipping, marine insurance, and oil industries under what appears to be a punitive and unrealistic regime, will be better able to be evaluated

Damage Caused Otherwise than by Collision

Liability for loss of or damage to any other vessel or craft, or to property onboard such other vessel or craft caused otherwise than by collision of the insured vessel with another vessel or craft, is also covered by the basic Protection and Indemnity policy. Bernard (p. 32) lists the types of claims covered under this heading as follows:

(1) Damage resulting from the insured vessel proceeding at excessive speed in narrow or crowded waters creating a wash sufficient to cause another vessel to break loose from its moorings or being damaged by being forced against other vessels or structures.

(2) Damages caused by propeller suction created as a result of power dock trials.

(3) Dropping cargo on lighters, barges or other vessels alongside the insured vessel.

(4) Causing another vessel to go ashore or to collide with a third vessel by crowding or through improper navigation.

This coverage usually incorporates a Sister Ship clause with the stipulation that the Protection and Indemnity underwriters only respond for loss or damage which is not covered under any other insurance.

Damage to Dock, Buoys, Etc.

Liability for damage to "any dock, pier, jetty, bridge, harbor, breakwater, structure, beacon, buoy, lighthouse, cable, or to any fixed or movable object or property whatsoever, except another vessel or craft or property on another vessel or craft, or to property on the insured vessel unless property on the insured vessel is elsewhere covered herein" is one of the more important coverages provided by Protection and Indemnity clubs and underwriters. Included in this coverage is the assured's *legal liability* for oil pollution, whether arising from a collision or not, but this would not in itself cover clean-up expenses voluntarily incurred as envisaged under TOVALOP. To provide such additional coverage, Protection and Indemnity insurers added a further clause to their policies (*see* Section on "Discharge of Oil or Other Substance" hereafter).

Wreck Removal

The general position regarding wreck removal expenses has been discussed previously. Such claims can be very costly and the risk is usually covered by Protection and Indemnity insurance. The assured is protected against the cost of raising or removing the wreck of the insured vessel or the cargo on board (when such removal is compulsory), to the extent that it would not be recoverable under the American Institute Hull Clauses and a policy written on the American Institute Increased Value and Excess Liabilities clauses. Credit is to be given for the value of any salvage recovered as a result of the removal. This coverage may be subject to limitations enumerated in the conditions of insurance. For instance, it is often stipulated that the assured shall be liable for any expenses incurred in removing the wreck of the insured vessel from his own premises. However, the

American Steamship Owners Mutual Protection and Indemnity Association does respond for such expenses if liability for the removal of the wreck of the insured vessel would have been imposed upon the assured by law if the wreck had been upon property belonging to another. In short, wreck removal from the assured's own property is given the same treatment by the American club as if it had been on the property of others.

As we have seen, Protection and Indemnity insurers only provide coverage for wreck removal expenses when "such removal is compulsory by law." In most cases this qualification presents no difficulty because the Wreck Statute invariably applies (*see* Chapter 4). If not, it is likely some state statute or other local law will require the owner of the wreck to remove it. The Fifth Circuit Court of Appeals, sitting *en banc,* found that wreck removal is not "compulsory by law" within the meaning of a Protection and Indemnity policy absent a clear, present, and unconditional duty imposed by statute or judicial decision (*Continental Oil Co.* v. *Bonanza Corp. and Republic Ins. Co.,* 1983 AMC 2059).

It must also be remembered that (as stated previously) Protection and Indemnity insurance covers wreck removal expenses only if incurred by the assured "as owner of the vessel named herein." Thus the insurer had no obligation to indemnify when the assured's "innocent" barge sank solely because of the negligence of the towing tug. Under the Wreck Act the tug was solely liable for the government's removal costs and the Protection and Indemnity insurance on the barge did not cover any liability of the assured as tug owner (*St. Paul Fire & Marine Ins. Co.* v. *Vest Transportation Co.,* 1982 AMC 450).

The assured is usually also covered (although not under this clause) if he is legally liable for removing the wreck of any other vessel, if such removal flows from any of the various liabilities against which he is indemnified.

Liability for Loss of or Damage to Cargo, Etc.

The policy covers "liability for loss of or damage to or in connection with cargo or other property (except mail or parcel post) including baggage and personal effects of passengers, to be carried, carried, or which has been carried on board the insured vessel" subject to certain stated exclusions.

As is to be expected, Protection and Indemnity clubs and underwriters require their assureds to avail themselves of the protection of such statutes as the Harter Act and the Carriage Of Goods by Sea Act. These or similar acts protect the carrier against liabilities arising from errors in the navigation or management of the insured vessel (always subject to the exercise of due diligence). However, the term "navigation or management of the ship" has been consistently construed not to include negligence in the care and custody of cargo, since both the aforementioned acts obligate the carrier to "properly and carefully load, handle, stow, carry, keep, care for, and discharge the goods carried" (*Larsen* v. *Insurance Company of North America,* 1965 AMC 2576).

Most cargo claims paid under this coverage result from either shortages, improper stowage, or unseaworthiness of the vessel. The requirement to provide a seaworthy vessel in the context of carriage of cargo is somewhat less onerous than is the case in a personal injury context since the requirement is not absolute. Under the Carriage of Goods by Sea Act, 1936, "neither the carrier nor the ship shall be liable for loss or damage arising or resulting from unseaworthiness unless caused by want of *due diligence* on the part of the carrier to make the ship seaworthy." However, as discussed previously in connection with general average, the duty to exercise due diligence to make the ship seaworthy has been narrowly construed by the courts. Furthermore, although under the Carriage of Goods by Sea Act the duty of furnishing a seaworthy vessel is not absolute, it is the duty of the carrier to prove that due diligence was used to make the vessel seaworthy (*Sears, Roebuck & Co.* v. *American President Lines, etc.,* 1971 AMC 2255). For a general discussion of the law relating to the carriage of goods by sea, the reader is directed to Chapter 9.

Any unauthorized deviation of a vessel results in the carrier losing the benefit of the protective clauses included in the contract of carriage and, in effect, becoming the insurer of the cargo. Since this could result in very heavy claims from cargo interests, the Protection and Indemnity policy requires the assured to separately insure his liability arising out of any deviation which is known to him in time to cover the risk. On the other hand, if the assured is not privy to the deviation, the coverage under the basic Protection and Indemnity policy holds good.

Fines and Penalties

The policy covers "liability for fines and penalties for the violation of any laws of the United States, or of any State thereof, or of any foreign country; provided, however, that the Association (or underwriter) shall not be liable to indemnify the assured against any such fines or penalties resulting directly or indirectly from the failure, neglect or fault of the assured or its managing officers to exercise the highest degree of diligence to prevent a violation of any such laws."

In the international war against smuggling drugs, some countries confiscate vessels in lieu of or in addition to levying fines. Subject to the caveat regarding due diligence of the assured shipowner some Protection and Indemnity insurers will respond to innocent shipowners for the market value of insured vessels which are so confiscated.

Mutiny and Misconduct

The policy covers "liability for expenses incurred in resisting any unfounded claim by a seaman or other person employed on board the insured vessel, or in prosecuting such person or persons in case of mutiny or other misconduct; not including, however, costs of successfully defending claims elsewhere protected in this policy." It should be noted that the policy covers only expenses for such claims.

Bernard (p. 45) clarifies this:

> For example, a seaman may bring a claim against a shipowner for wages alleged to be due him. If it should develop that the seaman's claim is meritorious the P. & I. underwriter pays neither the claim nor any expenses incurred by the shipowner. But, if the shipowner establishes that the seaman's claim has no merit, or to use the policy term, unfounded, then the P. & I. underwriter pays the expenses incurred in resisting the claim.
>
> Likewise, in a case involving mutiny, the P. & I. policy covers only the expenses incurred in prosecuting the person or persons involved.

Quarantine Expenses

This coverage embraces "liability for extraordinary expenses, incurred in consequence of the outbreak of plague or other disease on the insured vessel, for disinfection of the vessel or of persons on board, or for quarantine expenses, not being the ordinary expenses of loading or discharging, nor the ordinary wages or provisions of crew or passengers; provided, however, that no liability shall exist hereunder if the vessel be ordered to proceed to a port where it is known that she will be subjected to quarantine."

Bernard (p. 46) comments:

> For the shipowner to obtain recovery under this provision of the policy the expenses must be of extraordinary nature. The policy, however, does not cover expenses incurred if the vessel is proceeding to a port where it is known that she will be subject to quarantine, nor the ordinary expenses incurred to prevent sickness or disease such as vaccination of crew or passengers, nor for the ordinary expenses of fumigation required after the carriage of certain types of cargo.

Claims of this nature are few and far between.

Putting in Expenses

Port charges incurred solely for the purpose of putting in to land an injured or sick seaman or passenger and the net loss to the assured in respect of bunkers, insurance, stores, and provisions as the result of the deviation are recoverable under the usual form of Protection and Indemnity insurance.

Cargo's Proportion of General Average

The American Protection and Indemnity policy covers the liability for cargo's proportion of general average (which would include contract salvage) insofar as the assured is not entitled to recover same "from any other source." This goes farther than the British Protection and Indemnity clubs' coverage, which is limited to the proportion of any salvage or general average expenses assessed against cargo but which the assured has not been able to recover from the concerned in cargo by reason of the assured's breach of the contract of affreightment. Such a breach would be the assured's failure to exercise due diligence to make the vessel seaworthy at the inception of the voyage. Thus if, for example, cargo's proportion of general average is not recoverable because of insolvency on the part of the cargo owner or because the statute of limitations had been allowed to operate, it would be recoverable under American Protection and Indemnity coverage even though there had been no breach of the contract of affreightment on the part of the assured. Similarly, any shortage or loss of general average contribution due to fluctuations in rates of exchange would also be recoverable under the American form of policy. Such claims would not be recoverable under the British clubs' rules.

The American coverage under this category is dependent upon the inclusion of a general average negligence clause in the contract of affreightment.

Protection and Indemnity clubs and underwriters generally do not respond for any part of the general average contribution which related to sacrifices of the vessel (see "Risks Excluded" in the basic American policy). The reason for this exclusion is that Protection and Indemnity insurance is a liability insurance and does not cover the vessel physically. Thus, in calculating the amount payable under this coverage, any vessel sacrifices included in cargo's proportion of the general average (such as repairs, fuel, and stores, etc.) must be deleted.

An important coverage is provided under this section of the policy when the assured, under the principle of cross liabilities, has become liable to the non-carrying vessel for the proportion of his own cargo's general average contribution. In such circumstances the assured can recover the amount included by the colliding vessel in its claim by way of offset.

Some British Protection and Indemnity clubs also respond for the excess amount of the ship's proportion of salvage or general average when the ship (although fully insured) has been valued for salvage or general average purposes at a figure in excess of the insured value. For example, a ship may be fully insured at the time of the accident giving rise to the salvage or general average, but before the voyage is completed the value of the ship had increased sharply to a figure much above the insured value at the time of the accident. Naturally hull underwriters are only liable for that part of the ship's proportion of salvage or general average corresponding to the insured value. Such situations are rare and have to be specially considered by the club. However, if the club reaches the conclusion that the assured was fully insured *at the time of the accident,* the claim for excess salvage or general average is usually paid.

Discharge of Oil or Other Substance

Liability for "expenses arising out of action taken in compliance with the laws of the United States or any state or subdivision thereof or of any country to avoid damage from, or to minimize or remove, any discharge, spillage, emission or leakage of oil, petroleum products, chemicals or other substances" is now specifically enumerated in American Protection and Indemnity policies. This extension covers liabilities arising from the types of oil pollution legislation discussed earlier.

Expenses of Investigation and Defense

Because policies covering marine liabilities to third parties do not automatically make underwriters liable for legal expenses incurred by the assured in defending a claim, it is usual for such insurances to make special provision for the coverage of legal expenses. Thus in Protection and Indemnity and other marine liability policies it is customary to include legal expenses among the liabilities covered (*see,* for example, SP-23 and SP-38 policy forms). Legal expenses are therefore on exactly the same footing as all the other enumerated classes of coverage.

Such expenses can be very heavy; the policy clause dealing with same reads:

> Liability for costs, charges and expenses reasonably incurred and paid by the assured in connection with any liability insured under this policy, subject, however, to the same deduction that would be applicable under this policy to the liability defended; provided that if any liability is incurred and paid by the assured as aforesaid, the deduction shall be applied to the aggregate of the claim and expenses; and provided further that the assured shall not be entitled to indemnity from expenses unless they were incurred with the approval in writing of the Association, or the Association shall be satisfied that such approval could not have been obtained under the circumstances without unreasonable delay, or that the expenses were reasonably and properly incurred; and provided further that any suggestion or approval of counsel, or incurring of expenses in connection with liabilities not insured under this policy, shall not be deemed an admission of the Association's liability.

Protection and Indemnity coverage includes the legal expenses incurred by the assured in defending claims which, if successful, would be
recoverable from the Protection and Indemnity insurer. However, there is
no coverage for legal expenses in excess of the policy limit (*Wills Lines* v.
Aetna Ins. Co., 1960 AMC 394). In other words, the maximum liability
under a Protection and Indemnity policy for each claim (inclusive of legal
expenses) is the policy limit. This was underscored recently in *Darville* v.
Rahming Shipping (1988 AMC 1782). The court held that defense costs,
even though paid by the underwriters rather than the assured, must be deducted from the policy limits. On the other hand, when claims *in excess of
the policy limit* are defended successfully, the entire defense costs are recoverable (if less than the policy limit) (the *Mirimar,* 1931 AMC 984). The
amount by which a total claim (including legal expenses) exceeds the
amount insured would have to be borne by the assured or would be recoverable under any excess liability coverage he might have (see also *Geehan*
v. *Arlington,* 1976 AMC 2510; and *Board of Commissioners of the Port of
New Orleans* v. *Rachel Guidry,* 1977 AMC 791).

To sum up: It is the law and practice in Protection and Indemnity
insurance for legal expenses incurred in defending a liability covered by
the policy to be treated as part of the overall claim. That claim (inclusive of
legal expenses) is limited by the amount insured in the primary policy. A
lonely dissent from this preponderant law and practice is to be found in the
case of *Allstate Ins. Co.* v. *St. Paul Fire & Marine Ins. Co.* (1985 AMC
2103). In that case the court held that as the primary policy failed to include
any specific limit on the insurers' liability for legal investigation and defense costs there could be no "excess" legal costs for which excess underwriters would be responsible, even though they ultimately bore 97 percent
of the assured's legal liability. Hence the court found that the primary
insurers' claim that excess underwriters should contribute *pro rata* to the
expenses incurred in contesting the liability had no merit.

The basic Protection and Indemnity policy usually includes a general
clause stating that any expenses incurred by the assured in the interest of
underwriters and with their authority will be reimbursed.

It should be mentioned that deductible averages are customarily applicable to several of the types of claims covered in the basic policy, and
reference must be made to the specific policies in this connection.

General Conditions and Limitations

The basic Protection and Indemnity policy concludes with various general
conditions and limitations. These include stipulations that prompt notice of
any claims be given, that underwriters are not to be liable for any claim not
presented within one year after payment by the assured, that suits are not

maintainable against underwriters unless commenced within two years after the loss, etc. The assured is required to cooperate with underwriters both in the settlement and defense of claims.

One important provision is that which excludes assumed contractual liabilities. However, the acceptance of towage contracts customarily in use, resulting in liabilities being placed upon the shipowner for which he would not otherwise be liable, does not affect the assured's right of recovery under the Protection and Indemnity policy. Thus, if the master of a tug goes aboard the insured vessel to act as pilot under the so-called Pilotage clause in the towage contract, he becomes the servant of the ship. If a claim arises as a result of negligence on the part of the tug master while acting as pilot, any right of recovery under the Protection and Indemnity policy would not be affected.

A double insurance clause is also incorporated in the policy excluding coverage where there is other insurance in effect which covers the loss. In *Joseph A. Ladrique* v. *Montegut Auto Marine Service* (1978 AMC 2272), such an "escape" clause negating contribution "on the basis of double insurance or otherwise" was held valid. In that case it was decided that full liability should be borne by the assured's general liability underwriters whose policy merely provided that it would be "excess above insured's other available and collectible insurance." Faced with "other insurance," "escape," or "no contribution" clauses on overlapping policies, courts will extend full protection to the assured and work out some equitable adjustment between the underwriters *(Tulane Law Review*, Vol. 43, No. 3, p. 627). As one court put it: "It is a disfavored approach to resolve disputes among insurance carriers on the basis of dogmatic reliance on the other insurance clauses of respective policies without regard to the intent of the parties as manifested in the overall pattern of insurance coverage." Perhaps because of this attitude, in most cases where double insurance does exist and the assured has difficulty in collecting from either insurer, it is customary for the underwriters concerned in the double insurance to compromise the matter.

As we have seen, liability under the basic or primary Protection and Indemnity policy in respect of any one accident or occurrence is limited to the amount insured. Hence, it is desirable to effect excess Protection and Indemnity insurance (that is, excess of the basic coverage) and/or "bumbershoot" coverage. The standard bumbershoot policy protects the insured, with certain specified exclusions, against (1) Protection and Indemnity risks of whatsoever nature whether or not covered by the underlying Protection and Indemnity insurance (primary and excess); (2) general average, collision liabilities, salvage, salvage charges, and Sue and Labor arising from any cause whatsoever; and (3) all other legal and contractual liabilities of whatsoever nature for personal injury, death, or property damage (whether by vessel or otherwise). As to losses covered by the underlying insurances, the bumbershoot policy responds only after the limits of the underlying insurances are exhausted; as to losses not covered by other insurance, the bumbershoot responds initially subject to the deductible specified (*Tulane Law Review*, Vol. 43, No. 3, p. 676). Sometimes a "dip down" clause is included so that bumbershoot underwriters "dip down" below the underlying coverage in specific cases. To give an example: the typical American hull policy contains a clause stipulating that no (assured) person making a claim under the policy shall be entitled to recover to a greater extent than would the vessel owner, were he the assured named in the policy. Thus, if an assured named in the policy is not entitled to limit liability (such as a time charterer under existing U.S. law), hull underwriters will only respond for the amount to which the owner of the vessel, as an assured, could have limited and claimed under the policy. If the bumbershoot policy contains a dip down clause, bumbershoot underwriters will respond for the excess amount owed by the assured charterer who cannot limit, notwithstanding that the underlying hull policy has not been exhausted and that, therefore, but for the dip down provision, bumbershoot underwriters would not be concerned.

The Protection and Indemnity policy concludes with a list of excluded risks, one of the most important being "any loss, damage, sacrifice or expense of a type, character or kind which would be payable under the terms of a policy written on the American Institute Hull Clauses and a policy written on the American Institute Increased Value and Excess Liabilities Clauses whether or not the insured vessel is fully covered under those policies by insurance and excess insurance sufficient in amount to pay in full and without limit all such loss, damage, sacrifice or expense." As explained previously, the object of the latter part of the clause is to avoid any liabilities arising out of the *Landry* decision (*supra*) and to ensure that Protection and Indemnity insurance is not to be construed as providing excess collision coverage.

Among the exclusions is any liability arising from the insured vessel towing any other vessel or craft, unless such towage was to assist such other vessel or craft in distress to a port or place of safety. This exception is not, however, to apply to loss of life, injury, and illness claims covered by the section "Loss of Life, Injury, and Illness" above, that is to say, crew members, etc., of the insured vessel.

If a tug is the subject-matter of the Protection and Indemnity insurance, in determining the coverage under the section on "Wreck Removal," (*supra*) the tug is deemed to be insured under the American Institute Tug form instead of the American Institute Hull Clauses, etc. Similarly, the exclusions referred to in the previous paragraph would be those claims payable under the American Institute Tug form. In the case of a tug, it is further stipulated that the coverage described in the section "Collision" is such as would not be provided by the Collision clause in the American Institute Tug form. Protection and Indemnity policies on tugs also specifically exclude "loss of or damage to any vessel or vessels in tow and/or their cargoes, whether such loss or damage occurs before, during or after actual towage." This exception does not apply to claims arising from loss of life, injury, and illness dealt with in the above section "Loss of Life, Injury, and Illness," that is to say, crew members, etc., of the insured tug.

The final paragraph in the Protection and Indemnity policy excludes all war risks, which, if required, must be the subject of a separate insurance.

Protection and Indemnity policies used to contain a Privity clause voiding the policy in the event of a loss resulting from the "fault or privity" of the assured. However, privity of the shipowner was so strictly construed by the court in the case of the *Morro Castle* (1941 AMC 243) that such clauses were omitted from Protection and Indemnity policies thereafter. As a result, underwriters usually accept claims arising from any improper condition of the vessel even though management might be aware of such condition.

In one of the rare cases where a Protection and Indemnity club raised the question of privity vis-à-vis a member, the English court of appeals said (the *Eurysthenes,* 1976 2 L. L. R. 171):

> For the owners to lose their cover it must be shown that the ship was sent to sea in an unseaworthy condition and that this was done with the privity of the assured. "Privity" means "with knowledge and consent."
>
> . . . [T]he assured only loses his cover if he has consented to or concurred in the ship going to sea when he knew or believed that it was in an unseaworthy condition.

It must always be remembered that the object of Protection and Indemnity insurance is to protect the assured against legal liabilities. The harsh legal interpretation of unseaworthiness (particularly in loss of life and personal injury cases in the United States) is such that if a privity clause were included in a Protection and Indemnity policy, it would often have the effect of depriving the assured of the very coverage he needs and is purchasing. Liabilities to third parties rarely occur without some degree of negligence that may well concurrently constitute unseaworthiness or lack of due diligence or even wilful misconduct on the assured's part. Thus the inclusion of any warranty of seaworthiness or of due diligence in a Protection and Indemnity policy would limit or defeat the purpose of the insurance from the start.

FREIGHT, DEMURRAGE, AND DEFENCE ASSOCIATIONS

Many British Protection and Indemnity clubs have a separate club or association to assist shipowners in making claims against another party. The main purpose of such associations is to cover and reimburse members for the legal expenses incurred in prosecuting such claims (even though the risk itself is one that is borne by the member). The legal expenses in respect of which the member is covered include those arising out of claims for unpaid freight, demurrage claims, breach of contracts of affreightment, supply of inferior fuel or equipment, negligent repairs, improper loading or discharge, and disputes under building contracts. A very common type of claim would be for the proportion of legal expenses applying to the member's claim for demurrage against the other side in a collision case, either in effecting or attempting to effect a recovery of demurrage. Such insurance is very seldom encountered in the United States.

MISCELLANEOUS INSURANCE AGAINST LIABILITIES TO THIRD PARTIES

Maritime Service Contractors' Liabilities

The oil drilling industry in the United States is serviced by a veritable army of contractors who supply personnel to offshore oilfields ranging from oil technicians to cooks and other crew members. These men are transported to and from their workplace by fleets of crew boats, jack-up barges, etc., which vessels themselves have to be serviced. The presence of so many so-called brown water maritime workers inevitably results in many liability claims. Such claims are usually brought against everyone even remotely connected with the operation in progress at the time of the particular accident that resulted in the loss of life of or personal injury to the unfortunate worker bringing the claim. Such cases are variously brought under the Jones Act (in the hope that the court will accept the claimant as a seaman), the Longshoremen's and Harbor Workers' Compensation Act (LHWCA), the general maritime law, or on grounds of the unseaworthiness of any watercraft involved. The contractors who provide such services, like all contractors, take out (a) standard Workmen's Compensation and Employers Liability and (b) Comprehensive General Liability policies to protect themselves against all such liabilities. These are, of course, basically nonmarine policies known in the American insurance industry as casualty policies. However, it is advisable for practitioners of marine insurance to have at least a general understanding of what these nonmarine policies cover.

The Workmen's Compensation and Employers' Liability (WC-EL) policy is in two sections, A and B. Section A (Workmen's Compensation insur-

ance) provides coverage for the statutory obligation of an employer to provide benefits for employees (regardless of fault) as required by the
workmen's compensation law of any state and (if the policy is so endorsed)
benefits as required by the Longshoremen's and Harbor Workers' Compensation Act. Section B (Employers' Liability insurance) provides coverage
for the liability of an employer for damages arising from death and personal injury claims following accidents involving their employees (including coverage for the liability of an employer under Admiralty law). One
frequently used standard endorsement (Amendments to Coverage B Endorsement—Maritime) extends or limits coverage (as the case may be) and
includes a stipulation that the WC-EL insurance shall not attach if there is
in force a Protection and Indemnity or similar policy which would cover
the same claim.

The Comprehensive General Liability (CGL) policy is a standard liability policy form used throughout the insurance industry. Coverage A covers bodily injury and Coverage B property damage. The policy contains a
Watercraft Exclusion clause and if it is to cover liabilities arising out of the
ownership of any watercraft this clause must be deleted or suitably
amended. The CGL policy only protects against third party liabilities, including contractual liabilities arising from "hold harmless" and indemnity
agreements. It does not, of course, cover suits brought by employees.

Since the maritime aspect of service contractors' operations is often
only a minor part of their overall business, many such contractors elect to
cover their potential maritime liabilities by amending their existing general
liability insurances to specifically include marine risks. This obviates the
necessity of taking out the more specialized Protection and Indemnity insurance which is geared to cover the liabilities of vessel owners, is more
expensive, and perhaps provides more coverage than is necessary for service contractors' quasi-maritime operations. Such amended general liability policies thus become in part marine insurance policies covering as they
do maritime liabilities. Nevertheless, if such contractors own or operate a
fleet of vessels in connection with their operations they should certainly
take out Protection and Indemnity insurance. However, in practice contractors owning small fleets often switch back and forth between Protection
and Indemnity policies and WC-EL policies to cover their maritime risks
(including Jones Act seamen's claims).

Shipbuilder's Liabilities

A shipbuilder, under the American Institute Builder's Risk form of policy
protects himself, *inter alia*, against liabilities for damages arising out of
risks covered by the collision and Protection and Indemnity clauses. The
Protection and Indemnity clauses read as follows:

It is further agreed that if the Assured shall by reason of his interest in the Vessel, or the Surety in consequence of its undertaking, become liable to pay any sum or sums in respect of any responsibility, claim, demand, damages, and/or expenses arising from or occasioned by any of the following matters or things during the currency of this Policy, that is to say:

(a) Loss of or damage to any other vessel or goods, merchandise, freight, or other things or interests whatsoever on board such other vessel, caused proximately or otherwise by the Vessel, insofar as the same is not covered by the Collision Liability clause in this Policy; but the foregoing shall not be construed to cover liability in excess of the amount recoverable under the Collision Liability clause;

(b) Loss of or damage to any goods, merchandise, freight or other things or interests whatsoever, other than as aforesaid, whether on board the Vessel or not, which may arise from any cause whatsoever; provided that this subparagraph (b) shall not include Builder's gear, material or cargo on the Vessel;

(c) Loss of or damage to any harbor, dock (graving or otherwise), slipway, way, gridiron, pontoon, pier, quay, jetty, stage, buoy, telegraph cable or other fixed or movable thing whatsoever, or to any goods or property in or on the same, howsoever caused;

(d) Loss of life of or bodily injury to, or illness of any person (other than an employee of the Assured under this Policy);

(e) Payments made on account of life salvage;

(f) Any attempted or actual raising, removal or destruction of the wreck of the Vessel or the cargo thereof or any neglect or failure to raise, remove or destroy the same; however, for the purpose of this paragraph only, the Assured shall be deemed liable for expenses, after deducting any proceeds of the salvage, actually incurred by the Assured in removing the wreck of the vessel from any place owned, leased or occupied by the Assured;

(g) Any sum or sums for which the Assured may become liable or incur from causes not hereinbefore specified, but which are recoverable under the Protection and Indemnity policy form known as Lazard No. SP 23;

the Underwriters will pay the Assured or the Surety such proportion of such sum or sums so paid, or which may be required to indemnify the Assured or the Surety for such loss, as their respective subscriptions bear to the Agreed Value. Where the liability of the Assured has been contested with the consent in writing of a majority (in amount) of the Underwriters, the Underwriters shall have the option of naming the attorneys who will defend the vessel and the Assured and will also pay a like proportion of the costs which the Assured shall thereby incur or be compelled to pay; provided that the total liability of the Underwriters under all sections of these Protection and Indemnity clauses in respect of any one accident or series of accidents arising out of the same event is limited to the Amount Insured Hereunder, plus costs as hereinabove provided.

Notwithstanding anything to the contrary contained in these Protection and Indemnity clauses, the Underwriters shall not be liable for nor indemnify the Assured against any sum(s) paid with respect to any loss, damage, cost, liability, expense, fine, or penalty of any kind or nature whatsoever, and whether statutory or otherwise, imposed on the Assured directly or indirectly in consequence of, or with respect to, the actual or potential discharge, emission, spillage, or leakage upon or into the seas, waters, land or air, of oil, fuel, cargo, petroleum products, chemicals or other substances of any kind or nature whatsoever. This exclusion, however, shall not apply to sums paid or payable, or liability of the Assured, for the physical loss of the property discharged, emitted, spilled, or leaked, provided that such sums are covered elsewhere under the terms and conditions of this Policy.

In the event that Sections 182 to 189, both inclusive, of U. S. Code, Title 46, or any existing law or laws determining or limiting liability of shipowners and carriers, or any of them, shall, while this Policy is in force, be modified, amended or repealed, or the liabilities of shipowners or carriers be increased in any respect by legislative enactment, the Underwriters shall have the right to cancel the insurances afforded by these Protection and Indemnity clauses upon giving thirty (30) days' written notice in the manner prescribed in the Non-Payment of Premium clause; in the event of such cancellation, Underwriters shall make an appropriate return of premium.

Underwriters' liability under these Protection and Indemnity clauses shall in no event exceed that which would be imposed on the Assured by law in the absence of contract.

It will be noted that Protection and Indemnity claims are limited to the insured value of the vessel or hull under construction plus legal costs as provided by the policy (underwriters have the option of naming attorneys to defend the vessel). Furthermore, loss of life, bodily injury to, or illness of employees of the assured are not covered; such liabilities would be covered by the shipbuilder's workmen's compensation insurance.

A shipbuilder also very often insures against any liability he may incur for breach of contract or to a subcontractor.

Ship Repairer's Liability Insurance

When a vessel is undergoing repairs, the potential liabilities of the ship repairer are very extensive. Ship repairers therefore usually effect an insurance against their legal liability "from any cause whatsoever" for loss, damage, or expense to vessels which are being repaired by them. This type of insurance is an insurance not on specific property but primarily against liabilities to third parties arising out of repairs effected at the assured's yard or elsewhere.

One widely used form of insurance against Ship Repairers' Liability gives the assured very wide coverage including the following:

(a) Loss, damage, or expense (including demurrage) to vessels, etc., for which the repairer is responsible or, to use the words of the policy, "legally liable." This includes the consequences of defective repairs.

(b) Loss, damage, or expense (including demurrage) to property of others caused by such vessels, etc., and for which the repairer is responsible.

(c) Loss, damage, or expense to property of the assured (the ship repairer) caused by such vessels, etc., or as a result of negligence of anybody engaged there to or from any casualty or accident.

(d) Legal expenses incurred with the approval of underwriters.

Moreover, the policy is liable up to the full amount insured in respect of any one accident in each of the classes of damage or expense enumerated. Thus, if an accident involved, say, three vessels and a dock, the amount of the insurance can be collected under the policy in respect of each vessel and in respect of the dock (resulting in a possible claim totaling four times the sum insured).

This form does not cover:

(a) Liability for loss of life or personal injury (risks of this nature are usually covered by the ship repairer's other liability insurances).

(b) Shipyard property covered by another policy.

(c) If liability to another vessel is caused by collision with a powered vessel belonging to the assured or its tow, the assured's vessels are deemed to be fully insured under a policy containing a 4/4ths collision clause amended to include tower's liabilities. Thus, the policy will only respond for any excess not collectible under such mandatory policies.

(d) Any damage discovered later than six months from date of redelivery.

Insurances of this nature are construed very broadly in the United States and respond, for example, for the cost of re-doing defective or unskillful repairs as well as for the cost of correcting errors in plans or faulty design. In fact, the policy guarantees the workmanship of the assured's personnel. This is rationalized by pointing to the wording of the policy which covers "the legal liability of the assured from any cause whatsoever."

This type of insurance invariably includes a Deductible Average clause and, generally speaking, the deductible average applies to each separate accident or occurrence. Legal expenses are not considered to be subject to the deductible average.

Although such insurances normally do not contain a Sue and Labor clause, underwriters usually respond for charges of that nature, such as overtime charges avoiding potential claims for demurrage, and the expenses of extinguishing fires on shipboard (subject to the limit of the insured value).

When damage repairs are effected by the assured, profit is sometimes excluded although it can be contended that underwriters' measure of indemnity is the reasonable cost of repairs which would, of course, include normal profit. In recent years, American underwriters insuring a ship repairer's legal liabilities have accepted normal profit as being part of the measure of indemnity under such policies. It is customary for underwriters' surveyor to agree the cost of repairs with the ship repairer, and this is usually regarded as being conclusive in that respect as between the assured and his underwriters.

The American Institute Ship Repairer's Liability Clauses (November 3, 1977) do not provide such wide coverage as the broker's policy quoted above. In particular, the cost of defending any suit against the assured is only recoverable if the amount of the claim exceeds the deductible under the policy; furthermore, the deductible average is applicable to all legal expenses. Specific exclusions from coverage include claims for demurrage; the expense of re-doing work improperly performed by or on behalf of the assured or the cost of replacement of materials furnished in connection therewith; the cost of repairing, replacing, or renewing any faultily designed part; and for any expenditure incurred by reason of a betterment or alteration in design.

It should be noted that virtually all ship repairers in the United States include in their repair contracts a so-called Red Letter clause which limits the repairers' liability to $300,000. The following is a typical example of such clauses:

> . . . We undertake to perform work on vessels . . . only upon condition that we shall not be liable in respect to any one vessel, directly or indirectly in contract [or in] tort . . . to its owners, charterers or underwriters for any injury to such vessel, its cargo, equipment or movable stores, or for any consequences thereof, unless such injury is caused

by our negligence or the negligence of our employees and in no event shall our aggregate liability to all such parties in interest, for damage sustained by them, as a result of such injury, exceed the sum of $300,000.00.

In connection with the accident and/or indemnity and/or insurance clauses, if any, contained in your specifications, relating to liability for personal injuries, please note that we do not agree to same, insofar as they undertake to impose any liability or any obligation to take out or maintain insurance beyond the liabilities or the obligations to insure imposed upon us by law.

Clauses of this nature have been held to be valid and "not unconscionable or against public policy or made between parties of unequal bargaining capacity." In short, these clauses have been held to be distinguishable from the rule applicable to towage contracts (see *Alcoa Corsair*, 1966 AMC 1030, 1967 AMC 2578). As the Ninth Circuit Court of Appeals put it, "a red letter exculpatory clause in a shipyard repair agreement is enforceable, even though the Supreme Court's 1955 decision in *Bisso* invalidates such provisions in towage contracts" (*Morton & Kent* v. *Zidell Explorations*, 1983 AMC 2929).

Tower's Liabilities

A tugboat owner, in addition to being faced with many of a vessel owner's normal liabilities, has a wide exposure to possible liabilities to the vessel being towed or assisted. These potential liabilities are so extensive that it was customary for tugboat owners to include exculpatory clauses in their towage contracts. Indeed, in the United Kingdom and the territorial waters of the British Commonwealth, the U.K. Standard Towage Contract has been in use for some forty years. Under the provisions of these conditions, from the period commencing when the tug is in a position to receive orders direct from the hirer's vessel to pick up ropes and lines until the final orders of the hirer's vessel to cast off lines have been carried out, the owner of the vessel, as the hirer of the tug, literally assumes the burden of all the tug's liabilities for any damage, loss of life, or injury including negligence at any time on the part of the tug owner's servants or agents. It is with the knowledge that vessel owners may be obliged to accept such towage contracts in foreign ports that the American Institute Hull Clauses include the following clause:

This insurance shall not be prejudiced by reason of any contract limiting in whole or in part the liability of pilots, tugs, towboats, or their owners when the Assured or the agent of the Assured accepts such contract in accordance with established local practice.

Where in accordance with such practice, pilotage or towage services are provided under contracts requiring the Assured or the agent of the Assured:

(a) to assume liability for damages resulting from collision of the vessel insured with any other ship or vessel, including the towing vessel, or

(b) to indemnify those providing the pilotage or towage services against loss or liability for any such damages,

it is agreed that amounts paid by the Assured or Surety pursuant to such assumed obligations shall be deemed payments "by way of damages to any other person or persons" and to have been paid "in consequence of the Vessel being at fault" within the meaning of the Collision Liability clause in this Policy to the extent that such payments would have been covered if the Vessel had been legally responsible in the absence of any agreement. Provided always that in no event shall the aggregate amount of liability of the Underwriters under the Collision Liability clause, including this clause, be greater than the amount of any statutory limitation of liability to which owners are entitled or would be entitled liability under any contractual obligation referred to in this clause were included among the liabilities subject to such statutory limitations.

In the United States, the position regarding exculpatory clauses in towage contracts is quite different: various courts (including the Supreme Court) recognize that when a tug is actually towing other craft, the control of both the vessels in tow and the cargo being carried therein passes from the barge and cargo owners to the tugboat owner and have refused to allow the tugboat owner to exculpate himself from his own negligence. In *Bisso* v. *Inland Waterways Corp.* (1955 AMC 899), the Supreme Court, on grounds of public policy, invalidated contracts releasing towers from all liability for negligence. On the other hand, it has been held that the public policy considerations behind the *Bisso* decision do not invalidate a provision in a barge's marine hull policy under which the barge's underwriters waived their right of subrogation against the towing tug (*Port Everglades Towing Co., Ltd.*, 1972 AMC 316). In similar vein, a cargo owner's agreement in a towing contract to obtain a waiver from its insurers of their subrogation rights against defendant towing company is not the same as an exemption from liability for negligent towage and is not void as against public policy (*Tenneco Oil Co.* v. tug *Tony, et al.*, 1971 AMC 2336; *Fluor Western, Inc.* v. *G & H Offshore Towing Co., Inc.*, 1972 AMC 406). Nor does the Supreme Court's decision in *Bisso* invalidate contracts requiring the owner of the tow to take out full hull insurance on its vessel and to name the towing company as an additional assured with a waiver of subrogation against it (*Dillingham Tug & Barge Corp.* v. *Collier et al.,* 1984 AMC 1990). In *Bisso* the Court did, however, distinguish negligent pilotage from negligent towage; thus a Pilotage clause (in a case involving pilotage and not towage), exonerating from liability the towing company supplying the negligent pilot, is valid. The American courts' negative attitude to exculpatory clauses was criticized by the chairman of the Association of Average Adjusters, Eugene Underwood, in his address to the association in 1970 when he humorously referred to such decisions as "Sons of Bisso." The distinguished dissent notwithstanding, the law appears to be quite settled. American courts have generally held steadfastly to the rule, although in the words of Charles E. Lugenbahl "there is some indication that the courts are reassessing this view as indirect exculpation is now possible in America by virtue of insuring arrangements" ("The Law of Tug and Tow," the continuing Legal Education Society of B. C., the University of B. C., April 1979). The reader is also referred to the discussion of "Release of Liability Agreements" in Chapter 12.

Consequently, tower's liabilities for property damage to the vessel in tow, its cargo, piers, docks, etc., whether caused by the towboat *or the tow* are customarily insured under a Tower's Liability policy or a Tower's Liability endorsement to the tugboat's hull policy. Vessels regularly engaged in towing other craft usually incorporate in their hull coverage a Collision clause which includes tower's liability. Such a clause reads in part as follows (American Institute Tug form, August 1, 1976):

> And it is further agreed that:
> (a) if the Vessel hereby insured shall come into collision with any other vessel, craft or structure, floating or otherwise (including her tow); or shall strand her tow or shall cause her tow to come into collision with any other vessel, craft or structure, floating or otherwise, or shall cause any other loss or damage to her tow or to the freight thereof or to the property on board, and the Assured, or the Surety, in consequence of the insured Vessel being at fault, shall become liable to pay and shall pay by way of damages to any other person or persons any sum or sums, we, the Underwriters, will pay the Assured or the Surety, whichever shall have paid, such proportion of such sum or sums so paid as our subscriptions hereto bear to the value of the Vessel hereby insured, provided always that our liability in respect of any one such casualty shall not exceed our proportionate part of the value of the Vessel hereby insured . . .

It will be seen that if the insured vessel collides with any other vessel, craft, or structure, floating or otherwise (including her tow), or strands her tow or causes her tow to come into collision with any other vessel, craft, or structure, floating or otherwise, underwriters will reimburse the assured for any payments made by way of damages consequent on the fault of the insured vessel.

However, such clauses also contain a proviso excluding liability for removal of obstructions under statutory powers, loss of life or personal injury, and claims resulting from oil pollution. Most Protection and Indemnity policies also exclude claims for loss of life and personal injury arising out of towage operations (other than crew members and passengers of the insured vessel); to obtain such towage liability coverage, it is necessary to modify the policy by reinstating the coverage lost as a result of the standard towage exclusion.

It must be stressed that Tower's Liability clauses require fault or liability on the part of the tug as a prerequisite for payment under the policy, and the burden of proving such fault is on the aggrieved party (the tow). Nevertheless, circumstances surrounding a claim may be such as to warrant an inference of negligence on the tug's part, thereby shifting the burden of proof.

In the United States, an action by a tow against a tug lies in tort, not contract, and the tow must prove negligence on the part of the tug as being the proximate cause of the loss (*South* v. *Moran Towing & Transportation Co.*, 1965 AMC 2559). Under the American doctrine of the personification of the vessel, the tug may herself be a wrongdoer when there is a fault chargeable to her, and a suit may be brought against the tug *in rem*. Under this personification theory, a vessel may be held liable *in rem* under circumstances where her owner is not personally liable, which is contrary to the position under English law. As another distinguished American attorney, Wilbur H. Hecht, pointed out, this does not mean that the mere fact that one vessel strikes and damages another vessel or property makes her liable for the injury. There must be some fault on the part of the colliding vessel (Papers on *Marine Insurance Matters,* Vol. III, Institute of London Underwriters, p. 40):

> ... The fact that a vessel while in tow of a tug is in collision does not of itself charge the tow with fault and create a maritime lien against her. The test in such case is if there is fault chargeable to the tow. In the usual towage situation the navigation of the flotilla will be under the supervision of the tug and where the tow is brought into collision with another vessel or other property due solely to fault on the part of the tug, there is no liability on the tow.

In short, the innocent tow of a negligent tug is not subject to *in rem* liability when her tug causes her to collide or do damage (the *Eugene Moran*, 212

U.S. 466, 474). In such circumstances, the injured third party must look to the tug or her owners for recovery (*Tulane Law Review*, Vol. 43, No. 3, p. 618). The English courts seem more inclined to regard the relation entered into by an ordinary towage contract as that of master and servant, with the tow (the hiring master) liable for the negligence of the servant tug.

Mr. Hecht further commented that the American concept of a vessel as a juristic person is of particular importance in tug and tow law because it can affect the division of damages in a tort case where there is fault chargeable to both tug and tow. Thus, under American law, where the tug and tow are at fault for a collision jointly with other blameworthy craft, the common owner of tug and tow must bear one share of the loss for each blameworthy vessel in the flotilla (Papers on *Marine Insurance Matters*, p. 43).

Very often during towage operations, tug captains board the vessel being towed or assisted and act as docking and undocking pilots. If such pilots are negligent and their negligence results in damage to the vessel being towed or to third parties (such as damage to the cargo in the vessel being towed or damage to a wharf or pier), the aggrieved party could recover from the towing company *in personam* (as employer of the negligent pilot) even though the tug herself was not negligent and, consequently, was not liable to an *in rem* action. The foregoing presupposes that the vessel being assisted was using her own propelling power; on the other hand, if a tug captain goes aboard a dumb barge to direct the towage operation, he does not thereby divorce himself from his tug, which remains liable *in rem* for his negligence. To cover all such liabilities, it is usual for the tower's liability insurers to cover the legal liability of either the insured tug (*in rem*) or the assured (*in personam*), or both, for any negligent act of the tug captain (as docking pilot) while conducting the operation of docking or undocking the tow, or while acting as harbor pilot.

To cover the situation when the vessel being towed is making use of her own propelling power, it is customary to include a Pilotage clause in the towage contract. Such clauses stipulate that the docking pilot is acting solely as the servant of the owner of the vessel he is piloting and is subordinate to and under the direction and control of the master of that vessel. This precludes any *in personam* liability attaching to the towing company for any damage to the vessel being towed which might be caused by the docking pilot's negligence.

It should be understood that the Pilotage clause (which has been in use in one form or another for over fifty years) was intended to reflect the *fact* that the towing company did not *furnish* pilots or pilotage in cases where the vessel being assisted was using her own propelling power. In other words, the clause was not intended to be a private contract but was rather a declared limitation by the towing company on the work and duties its servants were permitted to undertake. The latest version of the Pilotage clause reads as follows:

> We do not furnish pilots or pilotage to vessels making use of or having available their own propelling power so that whenever any licensed pilot, or a captain of any tug which is furnished to or is engaged in the service of assisting a vessel making use of or having available her own propelling power, participates in directing the navigation of such vessel, or in directing the assisting tugs, from on board such vessel or from elsewhere, it is agreed that he becomes the borrowed servant of the vessel assisted and her owner or operator for all purposes and in every respect, his services while so engaged being the work of the vessel assisted, her owner and operator, and being subject to the exclusive supervision and control of the vessel's personnel. Any such service performed by any such person is beyond the scope of his employment for us and neither those furnishing the tugs or lending any such person, nor the tugs, their owners, agents, charterers, operators or managers shall be liable for any act or omission of any such person. The provisions of this paragraph may not be changed or modified in any manner whatsoever except by written instrument signed by an officer of this company.

The validity of the principle which the Pilotage clause seeks to enunciate was, in fact, upheld by the Supreme Court in *Sun Oil Co.* v. *Dalzell Towing Co., Inc.* (287 U.S. 291), and the latest version of the clause represents a new attempt to put beyond doubt the fact that the pilots become *exclusively* the servants of the assisted vessel. It remains to be seen whether some courts will continue to ignore this basic premise that the pilot is a "loaned employee" who becomes the employee of the assisted vessel *for all purposes* when piloting a vessel under its own power (*see* Alex L. Parks, *Law of Tug, Tow and Pilotage*, "Harbor Pilotage.") In short, it remains to be seen whether even the latest version of the Pilotage clause will provide adequate protection to towing companies, particularly in cases involving third party claimants. Of course, when moving dead ships, any pilotage clause in the towage contract would be valueless.

A further discussion of the complexities involved in providing adequate insurance coverage to towboat owners will be found in Chapter 12.

Charterer's Liability Insurance

Such insurances cover the legal and/or contractual liability of the assured (the charterer of a vessel or vessels) resulting from an accident involving the vessel or vessels named in the policy.

To ascertain the extent of a charterer's contractual liability to the chartered vessel, it is necessary to refer to the relevant charter party. The legal and/or contractual liabilities which charterer's liability insurance covers usually include failure to provide a safe berth, third party liabilities for property damage (including liability to cargo), personal injury, loss of life, etc.

The coverage provided extends to consequential losses or damages for which the assured is held legally liable including, *inter alia*, demurrage, removal of wreck, etc. Legal expenses and costs incurred with underwriters' approval in defending and/or investigating claims are also covered.

Charterer's liability insurances (particularly on tankers) usually exclude seepage and pollution; it is often difficult to obtain such coverage. In this connection, it must be remembered that under American law charterers have no right to limit their liability. Since charterer's liability for oil pollution would probably be a contractual liability to the vessel owner under the charter party, it is usual for underwriters granting such coverage to insist on the use of a charter party form which places the minimum responsibility on the charterer.

Charterer's liability insurances are usually subject to a deductible average each accident or occurrence. In one such insurance with a deductible applicable to "any one loss, accident or disaster," it was held that the charterer could reasonably expect that damage to the ship's deck by repeated contacts of a grab bucket during the discharge of scrap cargo would constitute a single event or occurrence. The court felt that if the insurer intended each individual contact to be a separate accident, the policy should have said so in precise language. (*E. B. Michaels and Ralph Michaels* v. *Mutual Marine Office*, 1979 AMC 1673).

Charterer's liability insurances are not subject to an implied warranty of seaworthiness and cover the liability of the charterer for loss of cargo even if due to unseaworthiness of the vessel with owner's privity (*Martin & Robertson* v. *Orion Ins. Co.*, 1971 AMC 515).

Second Seamen's Policy

During World War II the U.S. government provided certain benefits to seamen in accordance with the U.S. Department of Commerce, Maritime Administration, Second Seamen's War Risk policy. After the war the American seamen's unions apparently thought it desirable that their members continue to receive such benefits, particularly since many of the risks covered were equally present in peacetime conditions. As a result, most American flag shipowners are required by their labor contracts to provide such coverage and to purchase this insurance in the commercial marine insurance market. Since the premium is paid by the shipowner, the courts have held that payments made under the Second Seamen's policy may be offset by the shipowner against any damage awards made against the shipowner in respect of the same loss (*Moore-McCormack Lines, Inc.* v. *Richardson*, 1962 AMC 804).

This type of insurance is written on the basis of the U.S. government standard form referred to above. In brief, the policy covers against loss of life, disability (including dismemberment and loss of function), loss or damage to personal effects, and detention and repatriation benefits arising from the perils and causes stated in the policy. These are war risks, stranding, sinking, or breakup of the vessel, explosion or fire causing loss or substantial damage to the vessel, collision by the vessel, or contact with another external substance (including ice but excluding water), irrespective of whether the same are caused by risks of war or warlike operations or by marine risks or perils. It is stipulated that the word "vessel" shall include any waterborne conveyance used to transport the insured to and from the vessel in which he is employed and shall also include any airborne conveyance used to transport the insured pursuant to instructions or permission of underwriters. The period of coverage is from the time "such person signs the articles or enters into a contract of employment for the voyage of the aforesaid vessel . . . until such person shall be returned to a place within continental United States . . . unless sooner terminated by desertion, discharge, etc. . . . If it is established . . . that the insured's vessel has been destroyed or abandoned as a result of a risk or peril insured against herein and that the insured has survived such an event . . . monthly benefits shall be paid as provided."

The benefits payable under the policy include:

Loss of life:	$5,000
Total disability:	$100 a month during hospitalization in the continental United States: otherwise $150 a month until $5,000 is paid up to $2,500 more if disabled from all work, business, or occupation.

In addition, the Second Seamen's policy covers loss or damage to personal property such as personal effects, carpenter's tools, and navigational instruments.

For a brief discussion of this specialized and unusual policy, the reader is directed to the *Tulane Law Review,* Vol. 43, No. 3, pp. 610, 675.

Insurances on Excess Liabilities

As we have seen, under the Disbursements clause in the American Institute Hull Clauses, the assured is permitted to effect additional total loss insurances on "Disbursements . . . Excess or Increased Value of Hull and Machinery, etc.," up to 25 percent of the agreed (or insured) value. However, although insurances against excess liabilities are often coupled with total loss coverage, they do not have to be; coverage *solely* against excess liabilities is not limited by the disbursements warranty and therefore can be unlimited in amount. The relevant clauses in the American Institute Increased Value and Excess Liabilities Clauses (November 3, 1977) read as follows:

(2) GENERAL AVERAGE AND SALVAGE not recoverable in full under the policies on Hull and Machinery by reason of the difference between the Agreed Value of the Vessel as stated therein (or any reduced value arising from the deduction therefrom in process of adjustment of any claim which law or practice or the terms of the policies covering Hull and Machinery may have required) and the value of the Vessel adopted for the purpose of contribution to General Average or Salvage, the liability under this Policy being for such proportion of the amount not recoverable as the amount insured hereunder bears to the said difference or to the total amount insured against excess liabilities if it exceed such difference.

(3) SUE AND LABOR CHARGES not recoverable in full under the policies on Hull and Machinery by reason of the difference between the Agreed Value of the Vessel as stated therein (or any reduced value arising from the deduction therefrom of any claim which the terms of the policies covering Hull and Machinery may have required) and the value of the Vessel adopted for the purpose of ascertaining the amount recoverable under the policies on Hull and Machinery, the liability under this Policy being for such proportion of the amount not recoverable as the amount insured hereunder bears to the said difference or to the total amount insured against excess liabilities if it exceed such difference.

(4) COLLISION LIABILITY (including Costs) not recoverable in full under the Collision Liability clause (including the Pilotage and Towage extension) in the policies on Hull and Machinery by reason of such liability exceeding the Agreed Value of the Vessel as stated therein, in which case the amount recoverable under this Policy shall be such proportion of the difference so arising as the amount hereby insured bears to the total amount insured against excess liabilities.

As we have seen, vessel's contribution to general average and/or salvage charges are recoverable in full from hull underwriters only when the insured value of the vessel (less particular average, if any) is sufficient to cover the contributory value; in other words, when the contributory value is equalled or exceeded by the insured value (less particular average, if any). Clause (2) above provides coverage for such unrecovered contributions.

Clause (3) similarly covers Sue and Labor charges.

Clause (4) covers excess collision liabilities; such claims arise when the insured value of the vessel in the hull policies is less than the assured's total liability for damages falling under the Collision clause. It covers the assured for the difference between the insured value of the vessel and the actual damages paid and falling under the Collision clause (subject, of course, to the total amount insured against excess liabilities).

The liabilities under (2), (3), and (4) separately, in respect of any one claim, must not exceed the amount insured by the policy or policies covering such excess liabilities.

Insurance on excess liabilities protects the shipowner against any underinsurance on the vessel for collision liabilities and underinsurance for general average and salvage contributions, and enables him to collect Sue and Labor charges which would not otherwise be recoverable because of underinsurance. Such insurance is an economical shield against underinsurance in these particular areas.

Legal Expenses

Because policies covering liabilities to third parties do not automatically make underwriters liable for legal expenses incurred by the assured in defending a claim, it is usual for such insurances to make special provision for the recovery of legal expenses. If legal expenses are incurred in successfully defending a claim, the expenses are apportioned over the damages (which would have been provable) and the deductible average respectively, with the assured bearing the proportion applying to the deductible average. However, liability policies sometimes cover legal expenses in full without the application of a deductible, provided the expenses were incurred with the consent of underwriters.

Direct Action Statutes

Several states in the United States have direct action statutes which permit claims to be pursued directly against underwriters for damages recoverable against a shipowner, even though such damages may exceed that shipowner's limitation fund. The startling philosophy (from underwriters' viewpoint) behind such statutes is that liability insurance is for the benefit of the injured party rather than for the protection of the assured.

The Supreme Court attempted to solve the limitation-direct action conflict in *Maryland Casualty Co.* v. *Cushing* (347 U.S. 409). While the Court could not reach overall agreement, it did unanimously reach the conclusion that the Limitation of Liability Act was intended to afford protection to shipowners and not insurers because the U.S. Congress had not mentioned the latter in the act. In a compromise decision, the direct actions were enjoined until the amount of the limitation fund was established; after the fund had been disbursed to the claimants and the shipowner was assured the full benefit of his insurance, the claimants could proceed directly against the insurer for any additional claims up to the policy limit.

Legal decisions since *Cushing* have not given underwriters any solace. In *Olympic Towing Corp. v. Nebel Towing Co.* (1969 AMC 1571), the court granted limitation of liability to the vessel owner (the assured) but denied limitation to the insurers. In that case, it was held that under the Louisiana Direct Action Statute, limitation was a personal defense available only to the vessel owner and bareboat charterer and not available to their insurers. In other words, under this interpretation of the direct action statute, underwriters are required to respond for liabilities in excess of the limitation fund subject, of course, to policy limits. This particular statute becomes part of every insurance policy, including protection and indemnity policies, having effect in Louisiana; it has been held applicable to a suit for injuries sustained by a seaman on the high seas (*Session v. Leslie Savoie and Midcontinent Underwriters*, 1971 AMC 1910). Thus it may be contended that a right of direct action exists in Louisiana when either (a) the accident takes place in that state or (b) the insurance contract is written or delivered therein (*Tulane Law Review*, Vol. 43, No. 3, p. 362.)

However, the Fifth Circuit Court of Appeals sitting *en banc* in 1986 recanted from its decision in *Olympic Towing Corp. v. Nebel Towing Co.* In the case before the court the rules of the Protection and Indemnity club provided that "When a Member for whose account a ship is entered in this Class, is entitled to limit his liability, the liability of the Class shall not exceed the amount of such limitation . . ." The court held that this rule was a policy defense, and not a statutory defense, and the Louisiana Direct Action Statute is specifically subject to all policy defenses that are not in violation of public policy, and thus the Protection and Indemnity underwriters were able to limit their liability. A minority of the court considered that it was contrary to the public policy of Louisiana to treat such policy defenses as valid conditions of coverage for purposes of the direct action statute (*Crown Zellabach Corp. v. Ingram Industries and London Steamship Owners' Mutual Insurance Association*, 1986 AMC 1471).

The right of direct action is somewhat naturally opposed by underwriters, except in cases of the bankruptcy of the assured, since it leaves underwriters without any form of defense against claims. It has been held, however, that ship repairers' legal liability underwriters, even though sued under a direct action statute, are entitled to avail themselves of a so-called

Red Letter clause in a ship repair contract, limiting the contractor's liability for negligence to $300,000. The court (*Alcoa S. S. Co.* v. *Charles Ferran & Co., et al.*, 1971 AMC 1116) held that such a defense "results from the nature of the obligation" and is not "personal" to the repairer (distinguishing *Nebel Towing* where the statutory limitation of liability was held to be a "personal defense" not available to underwriters).

In summation, it is unlikely that underwriters will willingly accept the principle of direct action unless it is with the understanding that they are entitled to all the defenses at law the defendant assured has available to him and that they are permitted to invoke all the conditions of the policy as issued to the assured. In this connection, it is interesting to note that the international Limitation of Liability Convention of 1976 provides: "An insurer of liability for claims subject to limitation in accordance with [this statute] shall be entitled to the benefits of [this statute] to the same extent as the assured himself." If a similar statute were to be introduced in the United States, it would overrule *Maryland Casualty Co.* v. *Cushing,* and would preempt all direct action statutes by enabling liability underwriters to stand in the shoes of their assureds.

The Arrest of Ships and the Steps to be Taken to Obtain their Release

There are two types of admiralty libels or suits—the *in personam* suit and the *in rem* suit. The *in personam* suit is self-explanatory: it is a suit against a named person or corporate person. The *in rem* suit is peculiar to admiralty law and to understand it one must also understand the concept of "maritime lien." A maritime lien is a privileged claim upon maritime property. For example: following a collision, maritime law gives the aggrieved party— and usually both parties consider themselves the aggrieved party—a privileged claim or maritime lien against the colliding vessel. This lien is enforced by filing a libel against the offending vessel. Such a proceeding is called a suit *in rem;* the vessel in which a lien is claimed is then taken into the custody of the court, or "arrested." In other words, the plaintiff arrests the ship to compel the defendant to appear or to provide security to answer the claim (which may or may not prove to be well founded). This is known as the procedure of admiralty arrest.

The arrest of a ship puts a very effective pressure on her owner to provide bail or security for the amount of the libel and thereby obtain the release of his ship from arrest. The plaintiff, by the arrest of the ship, immediately obtains security for his claim. If he is ultimately successful in his suit, he can enforce judgment by selling the ship (if she has remained under arrest), or by recovering against the bail or security if the ship has been released. In most cases the defendant obtains the release of his ship by providing acceptable security either in the shape of a letter of undertaking or by providing a *release of libel bond*, otherwise known as a surety bond or bail bond. For a sample form of a letter of undertaking, the reader is directed to *Tulane Law Review*, Vol. 43, No. 3, p. 614.

Another example of a maritime lien occurs when salvage services are rendered to a vessel. Once the salvor has brought the property to a place of safety he will, naturally, not allow it to be removed until either his claim for salvage has been satisfied, or security has been provided. Very often this security takes the form of a salvor's bond (or surety bond or bail bond) for the amount of the security demanded by the salvor. Most salvage operations worldwide are performed under the terms of Lloyd's Open Form of Salvage Agreement and the 1980 version of this form stipulates that, unless otherwise agreed by the parties, security shall be given to the Committee of Lloyd's in a form approved by the committee. The committee requires guarantors to obtain insurance from Lloyd's syndicates to indemnify the committee and the contractor (salvor) against the default of the guarantors. A nonresident of the United Kingdom will need to find a person, firm, or corporation resident in the United Kingdom acceptable to the committee of Lloyd's who is willing to lodge an insured guarantee on his behalf. This will often be the London insurance broker who placed the insurance on the salved property. Whoever gives security is entitled to a fee which is usually one percent of the amount guaranteed.

Arrangements can be made with a bonding company to provide release of libel bonds and salvor's bonds. The bonding company requires almost full collateral for the amount of the bond furnished. This collateral can take several forms, namely: (1) a letter of indemnity from underwriters, (2) cash or Treasury bearer bonds, (3) a financial statement showing a liquid position satisfactory to the bonding company.

The letter of indemnity signed by underwriters insuring the type of claim being asserted is the major type of collateral furnished in most cases.

The letters of indemnity take two basic forms: the so-called 1955 Short Form and the form offered in the past by the American Hull Insurance Syndicate. The material difference between these forms is that the former contains the so-called waiver clause reading:

> Notwithstanding the foregoing, we hereby agree, in consideration of the issuance of this Bond to waive any defense we might have under the vessel's policies on Hull and Machinery and/or Increased Value in respect of any breach of warranty, written or implied.

The inclusion of this clause enables the underwriters who furnish it to obtain a reduced rate of premium. London Hull and Protection and Indemnity underwriters readily agree to furnish the 1955 Short Form letter of indemnity as do American underwriters, including in recent years the American Hull Insurance Syndicate.

As the surety bond provides that the bonding company must pay any interest allowed by the court, the letter of indemnity must include a similar provision. Because of the interest feature, as the amount of the bond approaches the amount insured, care must be taken not to ask underwriters to sign a letter which might commit them to a payment in excess of the insured value.

If the insurance policies contain a deductible average, the bonding companies require collateral to cover it, as underwriters' letters of indemnity are restricted to policy coverage. Such collateral takes the form of cash (or Treasury bearer bonds). In lieu of the cash deposit, the bonding company may accept an indemnity from the assured, if the bonding company is satisfied that the assured is financially solvent. This determination is made by their viewing the latest financial statement of the assured and by checking the assured's credit rating with Dun & Bradstreet and other credit rating sources.

Under hull policies, sometimes it is possible to avoid the cash deposit and/or financial inquiry by applying the deductible to the particular average portion of the claim, leaving the collision claim free of deductible requirements.

In cases where a salvor's bond is required, a similar procedure is followed.

A bond premium is charged by the bond company in the United States. In the United Kingdom it is customary for Protection and Indemnity clubs to provide bail or other security to avoid the arrest of their members' vessels (subject of course to countersecurity being provided). The shipowners are charged commission on the amount of the bail or security at one percent.

While, in general, marine insurance underwriters assist their assureds in providing security, it has been held that, absent any express provision in the policy, there is no "certain and specific evidence of custom within the marine insurance industry" which requires an underwriter to post security in limitation actions if by doing so he risks exposure beyond the policy limits in related nonlimitation actions. Instead, the underwriter was required to deposit policy proceeds in the registry of the court in connection with owner's petition for limitation of liability. This action was held by the appeals court to be within the equitable powers of the district court (*New York Marine Managers* v. *Helena Marine Service,* 1986 AMC 662).

Collision Lien Insurance

As we have seen, the law of the United States permits a vessel owner to limit his liability for property damaged to the value of the vessel at the end of the voyage on which the accident occurred plus the pending freight.

This facet of American limitation law has led to some doubt as to the value of security given by the colliding vessel at a port short of destination.

For instance, if the colliding vessel proceeds on her voyage after having given security and is subsequently lost, there is some doubt as to the value of the security. In such a case there is a possibility that the vessel could limit her liability to the pending freight only. The question is whether security posted for the release of a vessel short of her ultimate destination would replace the vessel herself to the extent that if the vessel were lost prior to reaching her destination, the arresting claimant would be protected against such loss in terms of the lost vessel's limitation fund.

Apparently the answer cannot be given with any certainty, and consequently it has been the practice in such cases to place collision lien insurance. The insurance is effected by the claimant on the arrested vessel against any total loss or diminution in value of that vessel for the period commencing with her release from arrest to the completion of her voyage. Such an insurance would only respond in the event that the insured vessel is held liable for the collision and to the extent that the amount available for the satisfaction of the claim against the insured vessel is diminished or exhausted by reason of loss, damage, or expenses to the insured vessel arising out of perils insured under the American hull form of policy and American War Risk clauses. The measure of indemnity is the amount by which the assured's recovery, if any, for damages resulting from the collision is so diminished or exhausted. The cost of effecting collision lien insurance is treated as a legal expense and falls into the category of "Attack" ("Costs of Recovery") as discussed previously.

THE CHANNELS OF COMMUNICATION

The insurance of a shipowner's liabilities is a complex subject, and liability underwriters should be kept closely advised of potential claims and all developments at all times. In particular, immediately following a major marine casualty, counsel should be appointed by the assured not only to protect his own interest but, perhaps more importantly, to protect the interest of the liability underwriters since it is they who must foot the bill. Thus, in the case of a collision, hull underwriters, Protection and Indemnity underwriters, and any other liability underwriters would be involved. The assured's insurance broker will have advised the underwriters concerned regarding the casualty, and arrangements will have been made for the attendance of a surveyor to represent the underwriters. If any cargo damage has been sustained, a surveyor should also be appointed to survey and report on such damage. If general average expenditure has been incurred, the average adjusters will arrange any insurance that may be necessary and supervise the obtaining of general average security from cargo interests. Counsel will, of course, have exchanged security with the attorneys representing the colliding vessel.

It is imperative that counsel (through the insurance broker) keep underwriters fully and promptly advised as to the facts and figures involved, give his opinion as to the liability question, and advise them regarding steps that may need to be taken in the event a petition for limitation of liability is deemed necessary. If applicable, collision lien insurance will be placed by the insurance broker. Counsel's reports on these and other matters are forwarded by the insurance broker to underwriters not only for their information but also in case they should have any special instructions to give. When loss of life and personal injury claims are involved, it is usual for counsel representing the Protection and Indemnity underwriters to negotiate settlements, but here again it is essential that counsel keep those underwriters fully and promptly advised so that they may keep their loss reserves up to date. There is nothing more calculated to raise an underwriter's blood pressure than to hear from counsel at the very last minute that an injury case can be settled for a certain figure, only to find that he has an inadequate file with no previous recommendations. Yet he is expected to give instructions in a vacuum. This is not the way for attorneys to win friends and influence underwriters.

In due course the average adjusters will produce an average adjustment setting forth the particular average claim for damage to the vessel and apportioning any general average expenses or allowances and any special charges over vessel and cargo interests. Counsel will find this average adjustment of considerable assistance, setting forth as it does most of the disbursements arising out of the accident. The average adjustment will not include any claim for loss of use, which will have to be calculated by the attorneys. Payments made under the average adjustment by hull underwriters (that is, particular average damage and the vessel's proportion of any general average) and by the individual cargo receivers or their underwriters in respect of any general average contributions or special charges will rank with all other claims participating in any limitation fund. In those cases where the shipowner is not entitled to recover general average contributions from cargo interests (because of failure to provide a seaworthy vessel), such contributions are recoverable from Protection and Indemnity underwriters, and consequently those underwriters would participate in the other side's limitation fund. The importance of assistance which the average adjuster can give attorneys in the preparation of the list of claims to share in the limitation fund cannot be overemphasized. Furthermore, when the limitation fund has been apportioned among the various claimants—shipowner, hull underwriters, Protection and Indemnity underwriters, and cargo interests—the services of the average adjuster may be necessary to see that the proper parties are credited with the amounts recovered.

Chapter 9

Subrogation and Double Insurance

SUBROGATION

Subrogation has been defined as the right by which an underwriter, having settled a loss, is entitled to place himself in the position of the assured, to the extent of acquiring all the rights and remedies in respect of the loss which the assured may have possessed. However, although it is true that an insurer acquires no interest in a claim of the assured against a third party until subrogated to the rights of the assured, his ability to bring suit on his own behalf prior to subrogation is merely limited. The doctrine of subrogation does not prevent the insurer from taking whatever steps believed necessary, such as impleading a third party, if he is sued on the insured's claim (*Welded Tube* v. *Hartford Fire*, 1973 AMC 555).

Section 79 of the Marine Insurance Act deals with the rights of the insurer on payment of a loss:

> (1) Where the insurer pays for a total loss, either of the whole, or in the case of goods of any apportionable part, of the subject-matter insured, he thereupon becomes entitled to take over the interest of the assured in whatever may remain of the subject-matter so paid for, and he is thereby subrogated to all the rights and remedies of the assured in and in respect of that subject-matter as from the time of the casualty causing the loss.
>
> (2) Subject to the foregoing provisions, where the insurer pays for a partial loss, he acquires no title to the subject-matter insured, or such part of it as may remain, but he is thereupon subrogated to all rights and remedies of the assured in and in respect of the subject-matter insured as from the time of the casualty causing the loss, insofar as the assured has been indemnified, according to this Act, by such payment for the loss.

The rights to which underwriters are entitled on payment of a total loss are of two kinds: rights of ownership (by abandonment) of whatever remains of the subject-matter insured, and rights against third parties (by subrogation). There is no obligation on the part of underwriters to exercise these rights and sometimes it is not to their advantage to do so. If rights of ownership are exercised by underwriters, they must also take over any liabilities which attach to the property. An example of this would be the liability of removing a wreck, the cost of which might prove to exceed the value of the wreck. Where an insurance company pays a loss in full and assumes control of the vessel, the insurance company becomes the owner of the vessel, just as a purchaser who buys the wreck from the owner after the disastrous event (*Wong* v. *Utah Home Fire Ins. Co.*, 1960 AMC 649). However, if the insurer, although paying a total loss, decides not to exercise rights of ownership, this in no way affects his subrogation rights. As a distinguished British average adjuster has remarked, such rights arise because the marine insurance policy is one of indemnity. The assured, if he has a right against a third party, cannot make a profit out of his misfortune and must hand over to the underwriter anything which mitigated his loss (E. W. Reading, British Association of Average Adjusters' report, 1951, p. 33). It is, therefore, important to distinguish between the rights of ownership (which may or may not be exercised) and the rights of subrogation.

Following abandonment, if the thing abandoned proves to be of greater value than the amount paid to the assured, the underwriter is still entitled to retain possession of the whole proceeds. On the other hand, subrogation, as opposed to abandonment, can never entitle the insurer to recover more than he has paid the assured. This was the finding of the court in the *Livingstone* (130 Fed. Rep. 746). In that case, a vessel, the insured value of which was less than her real value, was sunk by collision, and the underwriters paid for a total loss. Afterwards, the assured recovered the amount of her real value as damages from the vessel in fault, and the court held, reversing the decision of the district court, that the insurers were only entitled to receive the amount which they had actually paid, with interest. "The title of the insurers, by virtue of the valued policies, abandonment and conveyance, to the physical property and to salvage may well be conceded, as may also their right to share in the property to the extent of full and complete reimbursement for all losses paid by them incident to the insurance. We are truly convinced that equity and good sense do not require the court to go further and permit them to realize an enormous profit from the transaction. No controlling authority compels such a decision; no principle of equity requires it." (*See also* the *St. Johns*, 101 Fed. Rep. 469: ". . . The insurer's right of subrogation in equity could not extend beyond recoupment or indemnity for the actual payments to the assured . . .")

In other words, the right of the assured to recover damages from a third party is not one of the rights which are incidental to the subject-matter insured.

The position is the same in the United Kingdom; under subrogation, underwriters are not entitled to participate in any recovery in excess of the amount actually paid by them. In *Yorkshire Ins. Co. Ltd. v. Nisbet Shipping Co. Ltd.* (1961 1 L. L. R. 479), it was held that the shipowners could retain the amount recovered in excess of the amount paid by underwriters. This excess arose because the vessel (which was a total loss) was worth slightly more than her insured value. Not only was a full recovery effected but the recovery was greatly increased by virtue of a windfall resulting from the devaluation of the pound sterling. The court commented that in relation to a contract of marine insurance the doctrine of subrogation was no more than a convenient way of referring to those terms which were to be implied to give business efficacy to an agreement, whereby the assured should be fully indemnified and never more than fully indemnified by the insurer. If before the insurer had paid, the assured recovered from some third party a sum in excess of the actual loss, he could recover nothing from the insurer because he had sustained no loss; but it had never been suggested that the insurer could recover from the assured the amount of the excess. It was difficult to see why a term should be implied which would involve a fundamentally different result merely because the insurer had already paid for the loss before the assured had recovered any sum from the third party.

However, under English practice, underwriters are entitled to the full amount of any recovery from third parties if it does not exceed the amount paid in settlement. Indeed, in the English Institute Time clauses (Hull) it is stipulated that recoveries against any claim which is subject to the applicable deductible average shall be credited to underwriters in full to the extent of the sum by which the claim, unreduced by any recoveries, exceeds the deductible.

U.S. law takes an entirely different view of the manner in which the principle of subrogation should be applied. In *Aetna Ins. Co. v. United Fruit Co.* (1938 AMC 710), counsel for underwriters maintained that the principle as laid down in Sect. 79 of the Marine Insurance Act was correct—namely, that the valuation in a hull policy was controlling in the distribution of recoveries from third parties—and the underwriters were entitled to full reimbursement on the basis of the agreed value before the assured could share in any such recovery. On the other hand, opposing counsel argued that the recovery from the wrongdoer should be distributed on principles of subrogation with equity and justice and that the equitable principles of subrogation were not changed by the agreed valuation in the policies. The Supreme Court held that the insurer's rights of recovery rested upon subrogation unaffected by the valuation clause in the policy and upheld the rule that the insurer is entitled to subrogation only after the insured is appropriately indemnified. The valuation clause did not foreclose proof of actual value as a step in measuring the insurer's recovery by way of subrogation.

The Supreme Court's decision was invoked in a more recent case (*Nils Risdal, et al.* v. *Universal Ins. Co.*, 1964 AMC 1894) where a vessel. was insured for $30,000 although worth $60,000. The court held that owners were coinsurers to the extent of the uninsured $30,000. Coinsurance has been defined as "a relative division of the risk between the insurer and the insured, depending upon the relative amount of the policy and the actual value of the property insured" *(Couch on Insurance*, 1962). The insurance policy was silent as to coinsurance and subrogation. When under a valued hull policy a ship is undervalued, and with respect to its actual value is underinsured, the insured is a coinsurer with the insurance company. The court referred to *Aetna Insurance Co.* v. *United Fruit Co.*, in which the Supreme Court had said of a valued policy: ". . . The valuation clause in its usual form does not operate as an estoppel or by agreement to foreclose proof that actual value exceeds agreed value when the question is of the insurer's right to subrogation . . . beyond its controlling effect in determining the insurance liability, the clause does not operate to exclude proof of actual value when relevant." The court concluded that since the risk retained by the owners was in the same amount as that assumed by the insurers, they were entitled to an equal share of the recovery. There was nothing that entitled the insurer to be made whole at the expense of the insured. It would be inequitable to make him the beneficiary of that portion of the amount recovered which was attributable to the uninsured loss.

A similar position exists insofar as cargo insurances are concerned. In the case of *Standard Oil of New Jersey* v. *Universal Ins. Co.* (1933 AMC 675, 1644), it was held that an assured was coinsurer in respect to the excess of the actual value of cargo over the insured value and was, therefore, entitled to share rateably with the underwriters in a recovery obtained from a colliding ship.

It will be seen that the effect of subrogation in the United States is different from that in England. Let us take as a simple example the case of a vessel insured for $1 million but actually worth $1.5 million. Let us assume the vessel was lost in a collision and underwriters paid a total loss of $1 million. If, subsequently, a recovery of $100,000 was effected from the colliding vessel (the limit of that vessel's liability), the shipowner, under American law, would be entitled to participate in the recovery of $100,000 on the grounds that he had not been fully reimbursed. On the other hand, under English law, the underwriters (and not the shipowner) would be entitled to the entire recovery.

Underwriters are not entitled to claim from third parties anything that the assured might not have claimed. This was endorsed by the courts in

M. V. M. Inc. v. *St. Paul Fire & Marine Ins. Co. and U. S. Lines* (1958 AMC 341). In that case, it was held that if neither the owner of the cargo nor the cargo insurer has sued the carrier within the year permitted by the Carriage of Goods by Sea Act, the cause of action is extinguished. A cargo underwriter does not become subrogated to a cargo damage claim until he has paid the loss; if he contests his liability for the loss, he cannot sue the ocean carrier upon the contingency that he may be compelled to pay the loss and may eventually become subrogated.

When two vessels of the same ownership collide, underwriters have no rights against the owner because the owner could not have sued himself and consequently had no rights to transfer to the underwriters (*Augusta* v. *Detroit*, 1925 AMC 756).

On the other hand, Phillips points out that "the rights of an underwriter cannot be affected by any contract made by the assured with another underwriter or any other person, except so far as the assured is supposed to reserve the right of making such other contract, and the underwriter to subscribe the policy under an implied condition that the assured may avail himself of such right" (Subsect. 1715). These sentiments are echoed by Arnould (13th ed., Sect. 1240A) who more succinctly states that the insurer's rights of subrogation must not be impaired or diminished by dealings of the assured with other persons.

Subrogation rights are very important to cargo underwriters because the assured (cargo owner) will often have rights against the carrier in respect of cargo claims which have been settled by cargo underwriters. Most cargo policies contain an Assignment and Impairment of Recovery clause reading as follows:

> Warranted by the Assured that the assignment of this Policy or of any insurable interest therein or the subrogation or any right thereunder to any party, without the consent of this Company, shall render the insurance affected by such assignment or subrogation, void. It is also warranted that in case of any agreement or act by the Assured, prior or subsequent hereto, whereby any right of recovery of the Assured for loss of or damage to any property insured hereunder, against any Carrier or Bailee, is released, impaired or lost, which would on acceptance of abandonment or payment of a loss by this Company have inured to its benefit, but for such agreement or act, this Company shall not be bound to pay any loss, but its right to retain or recover the premium shall not be affected. Should the right of recovery of the Assured be contested or denied by the aforesaid Carrier or Bailee, then this Company shall advance to the Assured the amount of the loss (otherwise recoverable hereunder) as a loan without interest

pending a determination of Carrier's or Bailee's liability; the Company further agrees to bear all the expense of any suit brought in the name of the Assured or of the owners of the insured merchandise, or otherwise to enforce the liability of the Carrier or Bailees. The repayment of the loan to the Company is conditional upon, and only to the extent of, any net recovery from the Carrier or Bailee received by the Assured or owner of the insured merchandise.

It is essential, therefore, that in every instance of loss or damage to cargo, the assured should send immediate written notice of claim to the carrier, holding him responsible; as we have seen, a copy of this notification is required in support of the assured's claim under the cargo policy. Upon payment of the loss, the cargo underwriter becomes subrogated to the assured's rights against the carrier. Whether or not the carrier is liable is governed in part by common law, the bill of lading contract, and statutory enactments as interpreted by the courts.

Under most cargo policies the assured is also specifically required to report all claims promptly. If a belated claim is received and subrogation rights have been affected by the failure to report promptly, underwriters would be justified in initially declining the claim. However, given an acceptable explanation of the breach of notice of loss, such claims are usually negotiated and any loss of subrogation rights reflected in the settlement.

Recoveries from third parties play such an important role in cargo insurance that it is desirable to have a working knowledge of the law relating to the carriage of goods by sea. The basic concept of an ocean carrier's liability has been summarized by an American court (the *Willdomino*, 300 Fed. 5) as follows:

A carrier, of goods by water like a carrier by land is an insurer, and though no actual blame is imputable to it, it is absolutely liable, in the absence of a special contract limiting its liability, for all damages sustained by the goods entrusted to its care unless the damage is occasioned by the act of God, the public enemy, the public authority, the fault of the shipper, or the inherent nature of the thing shipped.

Although the law was similar in all maritime countries, shipowners invariably protected themselves from virtually all liability by inserting exculpatory clauses in their contracts of affreightment. The U.S. Harter Act of 1893 sought to prevent such abuses by means of a compromise: a nondelegable duty to exercise due diligence to provide a seaworthy vessel was imposed on shipowners and, if this duty was discharged, the shipowner in exchange was entitled to avoid liability to cargo resulting from certain enumerated causes, notably negligent management and navigation of the vessel. The Harter Act was, in fact, also a compromise between the strict U.S. carrier law and the more liberal English freedom of contract.

In an attempt to develop a universal, international system to deal with the allocation of liabilities between carriers and cargo interests, an international convention was held in 1924 which culminated in the Hague Rules. These rules, which were based substantially on the Harter Act, were widely adopted with varying minor amendments. They came into effect in 1931 and can be said to have regulated the international carriage of goods by sea for fifty years. The Hague Rules represent a compromise between carrier and cargo interests and result in an apportionment of risks and liabilities between the carrier's liability underwriters (Protection and Indemnity) and the cargo owners' underwriters. In 1936, the U.S. Congress passed the Carriage of Goods by Sea Act based substantially on the Hague Rules.

While the Hague Rules have served the international shipping community well, changing conditions have made the 1924 package limitation of £100 or U.S. $500 obsolete. There were also difficulties in defining a "package." These and other problems were dealt with in the Visby amendments to the Hague Rules in 1968; these amendments to the Hague Rules constitute a trade-off of increased liability limits for other provisions needed by shipowners. Apart from increasing the package limitation recovery amounts to approximately U.S. $800 per package or $1.10 per lb., whichever is higher, the question of whether a container is a package for limitation purposes was resolved by stating that the number of packages enumerated in the bill of lading as being packed within the container will be the number of packages or units for limitation purposes. However, the carrier is not entitled to benefit from the limits of liability "if it is proved that the damage resulted from an act or omission of the carrier done with intent to cause damage, or recklessly and with knowledge that damage would probably result." The Visby amendments are now in effect in those countries whose governments have ratified them; they have never been submitted for ratification to the U.S. Senate although the Maritime Law Association of the United States recommended that the amendments be ratified.

In any event, the concessions made in the Visby amendments did not satisfy the developing countries who, under the auspices of UNCTAD (United Nations Conference on Trade and Development) and UNCITRAL (United Nations Commission on International Trade Law), succeeded in producing a new carriage of goods by sea convention, the Hamburg Rules, 1978. Under these rules the carrier's exemption for errors in the navigation and management of the vessel is eliminated. The Hamburg Rules substitute a general standard of carrier liability for the specific language of the Hague Rules, a language which stipulates a whole catalogue of exemptions from liability. At the Hamburg conference practically all these exemptions were swept away. Not only was the due diligence concept abandoned, but the major traditional defenses of errors in the navigation or management of the vessel granted under the Hague Rules were abolished. Only those perils of the sea over which the carrier has no control (and he must *prove* he has no control) and a watered-down fire exemption remain. The overall requirement of the Hamburg Rules that the carrier *prove* that "he, his servants or agents took all measures that could reasonably be required to avoid the occurrence and its consequences" (Art. 5, Sect. 1) is akin to *proving* the absence of negligence—often a difficult task. In short, the burden of proof is reversed—the carrier is guilty unless *he* proves himself innocent. As Annex II to the Hamburg Rules puts it, the liability of the carrier is based on the principle of presumed fault or neglect. The Hamburg Rules will not become operative until one year from the date of deposit of the twentieth instrument of ratification, and it remains to be seen whether they will become operative. If the Hamburg Rules do come into effect, there will then be three conventions governing the carriage of goods by sea: the original Hague Rules (or variations thereof), the Hague-Visby Rules, and the Hamburg Rules. As one admiralty attorney jocularly put it, the resultant confusion is likely to result in a lifetime "endowment" for lawyers.

In his address to the British Association of Average Adjusters in 1978 (previously referred to in Chapter 6), Lord Justice Roskill referred to "the recent proposals [the Hamburg Rules] to alter the Hague Rules." What was proposed, he said, was the imposition upon shipowners and their Protection and Indemnity associations of liabilities hitherto borne by cargo interests and their insurers. He viewed with some concern the proposal that loss of or damage to cargo caused by negligent navigation or some other negligent act should cease to be an excepted peril. The law had always distinguished between the fault of the shipowner himself (actual fault or privity) and the shipowner's responsibility for the negligence of his servants. For the former he must remain responsible; for the latter he had historically always been allowed to disclaim responsibility. The Hague Rules had worked well for fifty years and should not be changed lightly.

Ten years later the Hamburg Rules are still not operative, although it is thought they might be in force on a limited scale by the early 1990s.

Waivers of Subrogation

When a tug enters into a contract to tow a barge, it is quite customary for the owner of the tug to require that the barge's hull, cargo, and Protection and Indemnity underwriters waive subrogation against the tug. Insofar as the barge is concerned this can be done by including a Waiver of Subrogation clause in the barge's policies or, more deviously, by including the owner of the tug as an assured in the barge's policies. In either case, the result is that the barge underwriters can have no subrogation rights against the tug and are thus responsible, subject to policy conditions, for the acts of the barge crew, the tug owner, and their respective agents for damage to the barge. Such waivers of subrogation have been held valid and not void as against public policy (*Port Everglades Towing Co., Ltd.*, 1972 AMC 316).

Sometimes the owner of the tug also stipulates in the towage contract that he is to have the benefit of the insurances on the barge. The object of this latter requirement also is to cut off the subrogation rights of the tow or the cargo underwriters against the tower. In *Dillingham* v. *Collier* (1984 AMC 1990), it was held that the Supreme court's decision in *Bisso (supra)*, invalidating exculpatory provisions in towing contracts, does not apply to contracts requiring the owner of the tow to take out full hull insurance on its vessel and to name the towing company as an additional assured with a waiver of subrogation against it. However, the validity of Benefit of Insurance clauses in towage contracts is uncertain in view of the *Bisso* decision (*see* Chapter 8). Furthermore, the effect of such clauses can be nullified by the use of a loan receipt by the tow's underwriters (*see infra*). It should also be noted that although a Waiver of Subrogation clause in the policies and/or the other exculpatory stratagems noted above prevent the underwriters on the barge pursuing a negligent tug, It would not prevent the barge's owner himself taking such legal action, at least to the extent of his uninsured interest, absent any release from the tow or express provision in the towage contract (*see* Chapter 12 for a further discussion of Release of Liability agreements).

Under the American hull form of policy, underwriters waive right of subrogation against affiliated companies but this waiver does not apply in the event of a collision with a vessel owned or controlled by an affiliated company. The reason for this is that underwriters are not prepared to waive subrogation rights in collision cases involving an affiliate's vessel presumably in case the affiliate's vessel is uninsured or insured with other underwriters. Thus, if all affiliated companies are to be protected, it is essential that they be named as assureds in all policies, especially if there is any likelihood of any of the affiliate's vessels being uninsured. The use of Affiliated Companies clauses obviates the necessity of listing, in many cases, numerous affiliates as additional assureds. The practice of naming affiliates as assureds is to prevent an insurer, after paying a claim under the policy, from proceeding under subrogation (where applicable) against other members of the assured's corporate family. The clause achieves this. However, most Affiliated Companies clauses include a proviso that subrogation is not waived against any affiliated company if that company is itself insured against the liability asserted.

Loan Receipts

Occasionally underwriters prefer to advance the amount of a loss to an assured in exchange for a loan receipt. Such payments have been held by the courts to have the legal status of a loan and not a payment of the loss. By signing the loan receipt, the assured acknowledges the money as a loan, without interest, *repayable to the underwriter only in the event of the loss being recovered elsewhere and then only to the extent of the recovery.*

The loan receipt is often resorted to by underwriters when they wish to bring suit in the assured's own name to recover the loss from another source. This avoids the necessity of the insurer bringing an action in his own name as subrogee with such disadvantages as might result to a named insurance company plaintiff (see *American Dredging Co.* v. *Federal Ins. Co.,* 1970 AMC 1163).

Such agreements usually supply the assured promptly with money to the full extent of the indemnity to which he is entitled in respect of the loss while preserving to the underwriters any claims which the assured may have against other parties.

Recoveries

In dealing with recoveries from third parties, when the original claim has been paid under a hull insurance policy and was subject to a deductible average, the principle of coinsurance is followed. Thus the net recovery (after deducting the costs incurred in effecting the recovery, such as legal expenses, etc.) is apportioned in the first instance over the items in respect of which the recovery was made; thereafter, the recovery applying to the claim paid under the hull policy is apportioned between the underwriters and vessel owners, the latter participating on the basis of the deductible average. This principle and practice is underscored in the Deductible Average clause included in the American hull form of policy. In that clause it is specifically stated that "a recovery from other interests and/or parties shall not operate to exclude claims under this insurance provided the aggregate of such claims arising out of one separate accident if unreduced by such recovery amounts to said sum." Practical difficulties can arise in allocating the proportion of recoveries applicable to deductible averages and the chairman of the British Association of Average Adjusters in 1986, K. Wood, devoted much of his address to the association to such problems.

It sometimes happens that legal and other expenses are incurred in attempting unsuccessfully to effect a recovery. In such cases, the costs of attempting recovery are apportioned between underwriters and the assured on the basis described above.

The principle of coinsurance is not followed when a recovery is effected in respect of protection and indemnity or other legal liability claims which have previously been paid subject to a deductible average. In such cases, the underwriters are entitled to the entire recovery until they have been made whole, and the assured only participates after the underwriters have been fully reimbursed. Consequently, in the event of expenses having been incurred in attempting unsuccessfully to effect a recovery, all such expenses are borne by the underwriters. In short, insofar as protection and indemnity and other legal liability coverage is concerned, the insured is not regarded as being a coinsurer to the extent of the deductibles applying to such claims. The reason for this is that Protection and Indemnity insurers cover their assured's ultimate liability which would reflect any amounts payable by or recoverable from other parties; in other words, legal liability insurers are only liable for the ultimate net claims after all avenues of recovery have been exhausted, less any deductible average. Sometimes, when a policy covers both hull and protection and indemnity risks, a clause is included specifically stating that the recoveries received subsequent to a loss settlement under the policy shall be applied as if recovered prior to such settlement.

Any policies written on "policy proof of interest" (P.P.I.) or "full interest admitted" (F.I.A.) terms are usually agreed to be "without benefit of salvage" (W.B.S.). That is to say, that on payment of a loss under such policies (usually Increased Value or Disbursements policies), underwriters are not entitled to participate in any proceeds which might be realized from the sale of the wreck following payment of a total loss. However, in the United States, this does not exclude such underwriters from sharing in *a recovery from a third party.* It is otherwise in the United Kingdom, where no subrogation rights at all exist in connection with such policies because (as we have seen earlier) all P.P.I., etc., policies are illegal in that country. Thus, in the United States, when a payment of a total loss under hull and increased value policies is made and a recovery is subsequently effected from a third party, both hull and increased value underwriters participate in the recovery even though the increased value policy was on a P.P.I. or similar basis. However, in the United Kingdom, the increased value underwriters would not participate in the recovery.

In the United States, legal expenses are not recoverable from the other side. In the United Kingdom, when a party is successful in a legal action, it is customary for him to recover part of the costs (legal expenses) he has incurred. His solicitor's account is "taxed" by the court and he recovers this amount from the other side; he has to bear the balance of the account himself and these unrecovered costs are known as solicitor and client costs. Generally speaking, if a party is successful, he recovers his taxed costs from the other side; if he is unsuccessful, he has to pay the taxed costs of the other side.

The question as to whether the insurers of a shipment of cargo could (by way of subrogation) claim interest in addition to the amount which they had paid their assured came before the English courts in *H. Cousins & Co. Ltd.* v. *D & C Carriers Ltd.* (1970 2 L. L. R. 397). It was held that the reference in Sect. 70 (1) of the Marine Insurance Act, 1906, to the "subject-matter insured" was a reference to the goods; the plaintiffs' claim against the defendants for the loss of the goods was a claim in respect of the subject-matter insured; the resulting judgment for their loss and a sum by way of interest was a single judgment based on a single cause of action; and the insurers were subrogated to the plaintiffs' right to sue for the loss of the goods and also interest.

It has been held that a legal liability underwriter insuring a terminal operator against risk of lost cargo is not entitled to share in gains from unclaimed "found" cargo. Thus, in the absence of any "fresh" consideration, the terminal operator's promise to its insurer that it would apply the sale proceeds of unclaimed fish cargo against litigated shortage claim by the owner-consignee of another fish cargo is unenforceable. The proceeds did not constitute "salvage" (*Insurance Co. of North America* v. *Korean Frontier,* 1978 AMC 2102).

As we have already seen in *Yorkshire Ins. Co. Ltd.* v. *Nisbet Shipping Co. Ltd.* (1961 1 L. L. R. 479), it has been held that an assured is entitled to any windfall which may result from fluctuations in rates of exchange subsequent to payment of a claim by an insurer and prior to the recovery being effected. However, in that case, a full recovery was effected and the insurers were made whole; the excess recovery which arose due to exchange fluctuations accrued to the assured.

DOUBLE INSURANCE

Double insurance is legal in the United States, but intentional double insurance would be rather pointless, being, as Phillips puts it, "a mere insurance of the solvency of each set of underwriters, by the policies of the others, for he can recover but one indemnity from all" (Subsect. 206).

The Marine Insurance Act deals with double insurance as follows:

> Where two or more policies are effected by or on behalf of the assured on the same adventure and interest or any part thereof, and the sums insured exceed the indemnity allowed by this Act, the assured is said to be overinsured by double insurance.
>
> Where the assured is over-insured by double insurance—

(a) The assured, unless the policy otherwise provides, may claim payment from the insurers in such order as he may think fit, provided that he is not entitled to receive any sum in excess of the indemnity allowed by this Act;

(b) Where the policy under which the assured claims is a valued policy, the assured may give credit as against the valuation for any sum received by him under any other policy without regard to the actual value of the subject-matter insured;

(c) Where the policy under which the assured claims is an unvalued policy he must give credit, as against the full insurable value, for any sum received by him under any other policy;

(d) Where the assured receives any sum in excess of the indemnity allowed by this Act, he is deemed to hold such sum in trust for the insurers, according to their right of contribution among themselves. (Sect. 32), and

Where the insured is over-insured by double insurance, each insurer is bound, as between himself and the other insurers, to contribute rateably to the loss in proportion to the amount for which he is liable under his contract.

If any insurer pays more than his proportion of the loss, he is entitled to maintain an action for contribution against the other insurers, and is entitled to the like remedies as a surety who has paid more than his proportion of the debt. (Sect. 80)

Double insurance cannot arise unless the policies cover the same interest—that is, the same insurable interest. Specifically, there is double insurance whenever two or more insurances are effected on the same subject matter by or on behalf of the same assured and the total of the insurances exceeds the value expressed in the policies, or the highest value if different values are used. When double insurance does exist, the assured may collect under the policies in any order he chooses but is limited to the amount of the insured value or the highest value if different values are used in the respective policies.

American common law on the subject of double insurance is similar to English law as is evidenced by Sect. 2489 of the *Law of Insurance* (2nd ed.) by Joseph A. Joyce, which reads as follows:

If several policies of Marine insurance are issued upon the same property and risk, and contain no clause as to apportionment of the liability of the insurers, the rule in England and the common-law rule in the United States is, that the insured may recover a proportionate part of the loss from each of the insurers, or he may recover the entire amount from any one of the insurers, and the insurer may demand contribution from the others. Where several policies are issued by different insurers upon the same property, they are, as between themselves, sureties.

In *Thurston* v. *Koch* (4 Dall. 348), the court said:

Such being the law of England as to double insurances before and at the commencement of our regulation, which divides the loss ratably among the insurers. It was also the law of this country, and is so now. It is of authoritative force, and must govern the present case. Besides, if the court were at liberty to elect a rule, I should adopt the English regulation, which divides the loss ratably among the insurers. It is the most convenient, equal, and consonant to natural justice, and has been practiced upon nearly half a century by the first commercial nation in the world.

Notwithstanding the position under American common law, it has been the practice in the United States *in cargo insurances* to give precedence to earlier policies. Indeed, a double insurance clause is usually included in *cargo policies* along the following lines:

If an interest insured hereunder is covered by other insurance which attached prior to the coverage provided by this Policy, then this Company shall be liable only for the amount in excess of such prior insurance; the Company to return to the Assured premium equivalent to the cost of the prior insurance at this Company's rates.

A similar double insurance clause was apparently included in early policies on vessels but has long since been omitted.

Open cargo policies invariably contain an Other Insurance clause along the same lines. Such a clause might read:

(a) If an interest insured hereunder is covered by other insurance which attached prior to the coverage provided by this policy, then this Company shall be liable only for the amount in excess of such prior insurance; the Company to return to the Assured premium equivalent to the cost of the prior insurance at this Company's rates.

(b) If an interest insured hereunder is covered by other insurance which attached subsequent to the coverage provided by this policy, then this Company shall nevertheless be liable up to the full amount of its insurance without right to claim contribution from the subsequent Insurers.

(c) Other insurance upon the property of same attaching date as the coverage provided by this policy shall be deemed simultaneous and this Company will be liable only for a rateable contribution to the loss or damage in proportion to the amount for which this Company would otherwise be liable under this policy, and will return to the Assured an amount of premium proportionate to such reduction of liability.

It will be seen that this clause prescribes formulae for dealing with double insurance based on the date of attachment of the respective policies.

Absent such a clause, the English method of dealing with double insurance would be followed as it coincides with American common law on the subject (*see* Phillips, Subsect. 361).

It is interesting to note that, at an International Law Conference held at Buffalo in 1899, the English rule dealing with double insurance was preferred as against the rule and/or practice in the United States and in European continental companies.

More recently in *American Dredging Company* v. *Federal Ins. Co.* (1970 AMC 1163), the court set forth the result of double insurance as follows:

> Where two policies of insurance cover the same risk, the insured may recover the full amount of the loss from either insurer. By the same token, the insured is entitled to recover only once for the same loss. Once full payment for loss has been made, the right of the insured to recover against co-insurers of the same risk is extinguished. All that remains is the right of the insurer who has paid the loss to its assured to pro rate contributions from co-insurers.

Under the common law rule, the usual method of apportioning a claim for total loss when there has been double insurance is as follows:

> Assuming one policy has been placed for $150,000 and another on the same subject-matter for $200,000, the first policy would bear 50 percent of the common amount ($150,000) or $75,000. The second policy would also bear $75,000 plus the excess over the policy for the smaller amount, viz. $50,000 or a total of $125,000. A grand total of $200,000 would then be paid by underwriters insuring the same risk.

The method to be used in apportioning a claim when there has been double insurance came before the English court of appeals in 1976 in *Commercial Union Assurance Co. Ltd.* v. *Hayden* (1977, 1 Q.B. 804). In that case the Commercial Union Insurance Co. Ltd. insured a firm under a public liability policy with a limit of £100,000, and a Lloyd's syndicate (represented by Mr. Hayden) had also insured the firm for a maximum of £10,000 for any one occurrence. Each policy contained a clause providing, "if at the time of any claim arising under this section there shall be any other insurance covering the same risk . . . the company shall not be liable for more than its rateable proportion thereof." A claim for personal injuries was made against the firm for £4,425 which was settled by Commercial Union with the agreement of Lloyd's. Lloyd's maintained that liability should be divided on a "maximum liability" basis; that is, that maximum liability on the respective policies being £100,000 and £10,000, their liability would be ten-elevenths of every claim. Commercial Union maintained that division should be on an "independent liability" basis whereby any claim up to £10,000 would be divided equally, but on a claim for say £40,000 the company's independent liability would be for £40,000 and Lloyd's for £10,000; thus, the apportionment would be in ratio four to one, that is, the company would pay £32,000 and Lloyd's £8,000. Commercial Union appealed against the judgment of Mr. Justice Donaldson in the lower court in favor of Lloyd's. Lord Justice Cairns said that the problem was one of construction of the clause, and it could not be said that as a matter of language either construction was preferable to the other. There was no English authority directly on the point although it appeared that the maximum liability approach is adopted universally in North America irrespective of whether the insurance covers property or liability. His lordship approached the problem as one not governed by authority binding on the court: he asked himself which meaning was more likely to be intended by reasonable businessmen. Since it was not to be supposed that when either policy was issued the insurer knew that another policy would cover the same risk, his lordship found the "independent liability" basis was much more realistic in its results. Any loss up to £10,000 would be shared equally and it was only on larger losses that the proportion of the company's share to that of Lloyd's increased until, with a loss of £100,000 or more, ten-elevenths of the liability fell on the company. It seemed artificial to use the limits under the two policies to adjust liability in respect of claims which were within the limits of either policy. Lord Justice Stephenson and Lord Justice Lawton concurred in that the appeal should be allowed.

In the United States, liability policies (including most Protection and Indemnity policies) invariably contain "other insurance" clauses, also known as "escape" clauses, "cover elsewhere" clauses, "exclusion" clauses, "no contribution" clauses, or "pro rata" clauses. Such clauses are framed to allow that particular insurer to escape coverage when other insurance covers the same risk. The difficulty is that invariably the other policy or policies also contain escape clauses. It is not surprising therefore that one court has described such clauses as being "mutually repugnant," since their literal effect would leave the insured without any insurance at all. Courts, of course, will not allow this to happen. Generally speaking, when two or more policies cover the same risk and all have "other insurance" clauses, courts have tended to prorate or apportion the claims falling within the coverage of the respective policies. However, in deciding how this is to be done, close attention is given to the wording of the respective "other insurance" clauses. One court has said that "it is a disfavored approach to resolve disputes among insurance carriers on the basis of dogmatic reliance on the 'other insurances' clauses of respective policies without regard to the intent of the parties as manifested in the overall pattern of insurance coverage" (*Lloyd's* v. *Firemen's Fund and Eagle Star Insurance Co.*, 1976 AMC 856). Another court dealt with a situation where one insurance company provided a Protection and Indemnity policy containing an escape clause by which that company would not provide cover "on the basis of double insurance or otherwise." A second insurance company provided a comprehensive general liability policy to the same assured; this contained an exclusion clause which provided that if, at the time of the loss, the assured had other available and collectible insurance then the general liability insurance would only apply as excess above the assured's other available and collectible insurance. The court found that both these "other insurance" clauses were only to be given effect when an insured party has other insurance on the same liability. According to the court the effect of the two clauses was very different: the Protection and Indemnity policy's escape clause relieved those insurers of liability altogether while the general liability insurer's "excess clause" merely limited their liability. The court held that the Protection and Indemnity policy's escape clause was valid and therefore that policy escaped liability. Thus, as far as the general liability policy was concerned, there was no other coverage available which could operate to activate its "excess clause" and the general liability policy must bear the full liability (*Joseph A. Lodrigue* v. *Mantegut Auto Marine Insurance*, 1978 AMC 2272). Another court faced with two similar clauses favored prorating the claim over both policies on the basis of the monetary limits of each policy (*Rini* v. *Transocean Contractors*, 1981 AMC 1128).

The only conclusion to be drawn from these decisions (and there are no doubt many others) is that no matter how cleverly lawyers draw up "other insurance" clauses there is but one certainty and that is that courts will protect the insured and that individual courts will have their own ideas as to how claims are to be prorated among insurers of the same risk, if at all.

It may be helpful to summarize the effects of double insurance: American common law and English common law are identical; that is to say, however many insurances are effected the assured may claim from any one of the insurers and that insurer is entitled to a rateable contribution from the others (the 1800 case of *Thurston* v. *Koch*, 4 Dall. (4 U.S.) 348, solidified contribution among insurers as the American common law in cases of double insurance.)

In hull insurance (i.e., property insurance), the established practice when two policies cover the same insurable interest, for example, one for $150,000 and another for $200,000, is for both policies to bear one-half of the common amount of $150,000, i.e., $75,000 each and the policy covering the larger amount would pay in addition the excess of the common amount, or $50,000. Thus each policy bears one-half of the amount which is doubly insured and the larger policy pays the whole of the amount which is not doubly insured.)

However, insofar as cargo insurance is concerned (i.e., property insurance) it has been the practice in the United States to give precedence to policies which were placed earlier; that is to say, the insurance which attached first responds. A Double Insurance clause is usually included in American cargo policies giving effect to this practice, and thereby contracting out of the American common law as it applies to double insurance. If the assured's claim on the cargo policy placed first exceeds the amount insured by that policy, the cargo policy placed later acts only as excess coverage. If two cargo policies were effected on the same date, the claim is divided between them using the same method as is customary in hull insurance (*supra*).

Turning to liability insurance, difficulties can arise. In such insurances there are no insured or agreed values, only a limit of liability. Futhermore, the extensive use of "other insurance" clauses makes it difficult to ascertain whether double insurance exists. If it does, there is no settled basis for contribution under liability, as contrasted with property, insurance. However, there are two suggested methods of apportioning or prorating claims among liability insurers:

(1) The "maximum liability" basis; that is, if two liability policies were issued, one for $10,000 and another for $100,000, their respective liabilities would be one-eleventh and ten-elevenths of each and every claim.

(2) The "independent liability" basis. On this basis and given the same policies as above, any claim up to $10,000 would be divided equally (i.e., similar to the American and English common law practice for dealing with double insurance). If the claim was in excess of $10,000 (say, $40,000) then the respective insurers' independent liability would be for $10,000 and $40,000 respectively. The apportionment would therefore be in the ratio of one to four. Thus the $10,000 policy would pay $8,000 (one-fifth) and the $100,000 policy $32,000 (four-fifths).

The independent liability basis is invariably used in property insurance in the United States. As we have seen, in 1977 the English court of appeals decided that the independent liability method was correct, being more "realistic in its results." Any loss up to the amount covered by both policies would be shared equally and it was only on larger losses that the larger limit of one of the policies came into play so that, on the figures given above, with a loss of $100,000 ten-elevenths of the liability would fall on the policy insuring $100,000 and one-eleventh on the policy insuring $10,000. The court commented that it seemed artificial to use the limits under the two policies to adjust liability in respect of claims which were within the limits of either policy.

However, it must again be stressed that in cases of double insurance, and subject to the limits of the respective policies, the assured, in the first instance, is entitled to claim in full from whichever insurer he chooses without regard to the subsequent division of the claim among the various insurers.

Chapter 10

Miscellaneous Insurances of a Special Nature

SHIPBUILDING INSURANCES

Under most building contracts the vessel, as it is constructed, and all materials, etc., allocated to the "new building" become the property of the builders; furthermore, the vessel is at the risk of the builders until delivered to her ultimate owner. Invariably the delivery is effected afloat after satisfactory trials and the builder is responsible for her trial trip. Consequently, the builder is exposed to various third party liabilities and must protect himself by appropriate insurance. Thus, although the coverage provided by Builder's Risks clauses (*see* Appendix A) is basically an insurance against physical loss or damage to the hull insured, it is wider in many respects than that provided by the usual hull insurances. In particular, since builders cannot become members of shipowners' Protection and Indemnity clubs, it is essential that builders be provided with coverage against such liabilities.

Most Builder's Risks insurances are effected on "all risks" terms and cover "all risks of physical loss of or damage to the subject-matter insured." However, the term "all risks" must not be taken too literally for it is basic that even under such wide terms, underwriters' liability is normally confined to fortuitous damage or loss and does not cover any loss, damage, or expense which is inevitable at the inception of the risk.

In general, Builder's Risks policies cover:

(a) Any damage to the vessel (or parts destined for it and not yet on the vessel but in the custody of the yard) caused by some accident, casualty, or fortuitous event.

(b) "Accidents" in the building of the vessel by the employees of the yard, such as damage caused by negligence of workmen.

(c) *Consequential damage* due to errors in design, manufacture, or workmanship.

(d) In case of failure of launch, all subsequent expenses incurred in completing the launch.

(e) All claims are payable without deductions "new for old."

(f) Protection and indemnity risks.

Builder's Risks policies do not cover:

(a) Loss or expenditure incurred *solely* in remedying errors or neglect in design or manufacture (for in those cases there has been no accident causing damage to the subject-matter insured).

(b) Replacement of parts improperly fabricated in the first instance.

(c) War risks.

(d) Loss through delay.

The measure of indemnity is the reasonable cost of replacing or repairing the *damaged* material. The existence of "damage" is usually broadly interpreted; thus, underwriters have responded for corrective measures in cases where, for example, lifeboat davits have been negligently installed in reverse position or where a boiler casing has been negligently installed too close to enter. On the other hand, if a plate is fabricated too big, there is no damage; conversely, if it is fabricated too small, there is damage.

The policy is not intended to cover damage which does not arise out of and during the normal course of construction; thus, if negligence of builders results in damage after delivery, it falls on the policies then in effect (subject, of course, to those policies' conditions). As an example, when a vessel sank more than 100 miles from the construction site, after delivery and the expiration of the policy, the insurer was not liable even though the cause of the sinking may have been due to defective construction during the policy period (*Richard Rydman and Ins. Co. of North America* v. *Martinolich*, 1975 AMC 1005). Nevertheless, another court stated that the uncertain meaning of the term "delivery" should be construed against the insurer and that the mere transfer of custody was not determinative. In that case, insurers were held liable when the insured vessel capsized while being towed from the original construction site to water of sufficient depth to permit completion of the work (*Ahto Walter* v. *Marine Office of America*, 1976 AMC 1471).

Under most Builder's Risks policies, partial losses were customarily payable irrespective of percentage, but the conventional trend is towards a specified deductible average (or excess) for each accident or occurrence. The latest American Institute Builder's Risks clauses (February 8, 1979) contain a Deductible clause along the lines of the American Institute Hull form of policy.

In general, the format of this latest Builder's Risks form follows that of the basic hull form edited to reflect the subject-matter of the insurance. However, the following refinements should be noted:

(1) Although the policy includes an "all risks" clause, it stipulates that "in the event that faulty design of any part or parts should cause physical loss of or damage to the vessel, this insurance shall not cover the cost or expense of repairing, replacing or renewing such part or parts, nor any expenditure incurred by reason of betterment or alteration in design."

(2) No claim for total loss (actual or constructive) shall exceed the policy's proportion of the value of the vessel at the stage of her construction at time of loss . . . The policy shall also pay its proportion of any physical loss or damage to material insured hereunder and not yet installed in the vessel.

While the American Institute Builder's Risks clauses embody the War, Strikes, and Related Exclusions clause it is customary to attach an addendum (American Hull Insurance Syndicate #1) which reinstates coverage for damage caused by strikers, riots, vandalism, malicious acts, etc.

The Protection and Indemnity section of the policy has been discussed earlier (*see* Chapter 8).

It was not long after the 1979 version of the American Institute Builder's Risks clauses was issued that underwriters felt it necessary to re-evaluate their position in the light of the courts' increasingly liberal interpretation of "all risks" insuring conditions. In 1981 Addendum No. 2 was added to the 1979 Builder's Risks clauses which reads as follows:

HULL RISKS

Lines 61-62 of the attached policy are hereby deleted and the following substituted therefor:

Subject to the provisions of exclusion (b) of the following paragraph, in the event that faulty design of any part or parts should cause physical loss of or damage to the Vessel this insurance shall not cover the cost or expense of repairing, replacing or renewing such part or parts, nor any expenditure incurred by reason of a betterment or alteration in the design. Faulty design shall include, but not be limited to, errors, omissions or deficiencies in plans, drawings, specifications or calculations.

Further, Underwriters shall not pay for any loss, damage or expense caused by or arising in consequence of:

(a) faulty workmanship, or the installation or use of improper or defective materials, unless resulting in destruction, deformation, breaking, tearing, bursting, holing or cracking of the Vessel, or any other like condition, and which loss, damage or expense is not otherwise excluded under the terms and conditions of the War, Strikes and

Other Exclusions Clause of the attached policy; provided that Underwriters in no event shall respond for the cost or expense of repairing, replacing or renewing any improper or defective materials;

(b) faulty production or assembly procedures even if constituting faulty design.

SUBROGATION

The following provision is added after line 205 of the attached policy:

In case of any agreement or act, past or future, by the Assured whereby any right of recovery of the Assured against any person or entity is released or lost to which these Underwriters on payment of loss would be entitled to subrogation but for such agreement or act, this insurance shall be vitiated to the extent that the right of subrogation of these Underwriters has been impaired thereby; and in such event the right of these Underwriters to retain or collect any premium paid or due hereunder shall not be affected.

ALL OTHER TERMS AND CONDITIONS REMAIN UNCHANGED.

Essentially, the changes effected by the addendum are as follows:

Faulty Design: There has been added to this section a list of several functions which are incidental to the overall design itself. The purpose of the change is to distinguish the treatment in the policy of faults in performing such functions from the faulty workmanship coverage.

Faulty Workmanship, Etc.: This clause excludes damage resulting from faulty workmanship unless resulting in destruction, etc., of a part itself, in which case the cost of repairing or renewing the part plus consequential damage, if any, is recoverable. This change is principally intended to eliminate the "do over" type of claim based on mere discovery. However, even if improper or defective materials are used and result in destruction, etc., the cost of repairing or replacing such materials is not recoverable, only the consequential damage, if any.

Faulty Production or Assembly Procedures: Damage occurring in consequence of the use of such procedures is excluded even if they could be construed as being part of the design. Under this clause there is no coverage for either the part itself or for any consequential damage.

Subrogation: A specific provision regarding subrogation has been added which is self-explanatory.

By adding this addendum to the Builder's Risks policy, underwriters hoped to maintain and protect the traditional risk, or accidental cause of loss, concept and stop what had become a trend towards treating insurers as virtual guarantors of the success of ship construction ventures. While the intent had always been to offer a broad form of "all risk" protection to builders, underwriters felt it was essential to re-establish that this intent was to protect the builder only from those accidental losses which were beyond his reasonable means to avoid.

Examples of the manner in which Builder's Risks insurance has been extended in recent years is to be found in the English Institute clauses adopted in 1963. For the first time, shipbuilders were specifically enabled to recover in respect of any part condemned solely in consequence of a latent defect discovered during the period of the insurance. In this respect, the coverage is broader than that provided by some forms and, in fact, goes beyond the "all risks" concept of insurance which rules out loss or damage caused by the inherent vice or nature of the subject-matter insured.

To sum up, to justify a claim under a Builder's Risks policy, there must have been an accident which has resulted in loss or damage to the subject-matter insured. However, in such insurances it is customary to give a very wide meaning to the word "accident"; for example, a loss may be regarded as accidental if it is clearly unexpected as far as the builder is concerned. Nevertheless, the loss must not have been inevitable, for underwriters cover risks and not certainties. Using this wide interpretation of the word "accident," damage caused by negligent or improper workmanship during the actual construction of the insured vessel would be construed as an "accident." Perhaps the best test of all is whether or not the damage was inevitable at the inception of the risk.

It is self evident that when the insured peril (for example, negligence of the builder's workmen), *and* the resultant damage to the insured vessel take place and are revealed during the period covered by the Builder's Risks policy, the claim for repairs will fall on that policy. This is true even if the full extent of the damage is not realized and corrected until after the vessel has left the builder's yard, that is, after the Builder's Risks policy has terminated. As long as the insured peril operated and caused some damage during the currency of the Builder's Risks policy, all the repairs necessary to correct the problem are recoverable under that policy. This is not a case of extending the Builder's Risks policy, but rather of fulfilling an ongoing obligation to repair the damage which had been known to exist during the term of that policy. This is in line with average adjusting practice—namely, that if damage caused by an insured peril is revealed during the currency of a policy and *inevitably* progresses thereafter (without any lack of diligence on the part of the assured), the entire claim falls on the policy in effect at the time the initial damage was discovered. In short, an assured is entitled to a complete repair. Conversely, if a builder negligently installs a pump during the construction of a vessel but the damage is not discovered until after the vessel has left the yard, there is no coverage under the Builder's Risks policy. The claim for repairs to the pump would fall on the navigating policy in effect at the time the damage became patent (subject, of course, to the terms and conditions of that policy). The same is true if a latent defect became patent after delivery of the vessel to its owner.

INSURANCE OF OFFSHORE OIL DRILLING RIGS

The growth in the last decade of offshore oil drilling has created a vast new industry of enormous potential. The operators of offshore rigs are seeking not only oil but also gas and sulphur. The value of the rigs themselves ranges from $3 million to $70 million and are of various types, as follows:

(1) *Self-contained or tender-assisted fixed platforms.* These fixed platforms are built on the ocean floor and are used when a large number of wells can be drilled from one location.

(2) *Floating vessels.* These vessels are anchored and the wells are drilled over the side or through a hole in the center of the vessel.

(3) *Mobile rigs.* Some of these rigs have legs which are lowered and rest on the bottom of the ocean, and then raise the platform clear of the water. Others have a separate lower hull which is filled with water to make it submerge and rest on the bottom.

Oil rigs are subject to many hazards and most are insured in the London marine insurance market either on a Named Peril form or under "all risks" conditions.

In the Named Peril form, the *main risks* covered are:

Fire	Heavy Weather
Lightning	Capsizing
Explosion (above the surface)	Negligence
Blowout*	Perils of the sea (stranding, collisions,
Cratering**	jettisons, washing overboard)
Hurricane	Pull-in and collapse of derrick

*Blowouts occur when the underground pressures become greater than the downward pressure exerted by the column of drilling mud put in while the hole is being drilled.

**Cratering is the result of oil, water, or gas forcing itself to the surface outside the hole casings.

(Cover is normally provided only for continuous eruption—if eruption is not continuous, it is merely what is known as a "kick.")

Additional Coverage

Collision clause.

Sue and Labor clause (but underwriters not liable for fire-extinguishing materials lost or destroyed in fire-fighting, blow-out, or cratering).

Salvage expense and sue and labor on drill-stem in the hole. (Underwriters usually have in their policy a clause to the effect that they will be liable for no greater proportion of expense than the value of the drill-stem below the surface of the ground at the time of loss bears to the total value of the drill-stem and the value of the hole, and that in no event shall they be liable for more than the cash value of the drill-stem below the surface of the ground at the time of the loss.)

N.B. It is customary for insurances on Oil-Drilling Rigs to contain a deductible average.

Adjusting Practices

In adjusting claims, the following must be borne in mind:

When the drill-stem becomes stuck in the hole because of a peril insured, work is done to recover the drill-stem, but at the same time the workers are recovering the hole, so the owner of the hole must pay his proportionate part of the expense.

When dealing with the actual oil rig, loss should be paid only on the replacement value new less depreciation.

No deductions "new for old" on hull.

Any expense incurred in connection with plugging and abandoning a well after a major casualty is usually not recoverable because the operator is invariably obligated to do this in the end, regardless of the casualty.

Exclusions

A list of *exclusions* usually appears in the policy, *viz*:

Wear and tear.

Deterioration.

Neglect by assured to take reasonable measure to save and preserve the property insured.

Explosion of engines, boilers, and similar types of apparatus.

Delay or loss of use.

Damage or loss caused by intentional sinking of the barge for operational use.

Faulty workmanship.
Faulty material.
Error in design.
Loss of blueprints, etc.
Loss of mud and chemicals.
Damage or loss to casing while in use or to casing and tubing while in well.

Property Usually Covered

Hull
Rig
Equipment
Tools
Supplies
Drill–stem
Casing
Tubing

⎫ Either on Drilling barge or in barges alongside (i.e., to be used for job in hand)

Drill-stem in the well
being drilled

(Named perils form also gives cover up to 25 percent of the total insured value of the equipment referred to above on equipment which is situated elsewhere but also allocated for the particular job.)

The above is based largely on the London *"named peril" form.*

The other London form used is the *all risks form.* There are only two major differences from the named peril form. These are:

(1) Underwriters cover "all risks of direct physical loss or damage to the property insured."

(2) In addition to the exclusions under the "named peril" form is the exclusion of liability for loss or damage to drilling equipment rigged up at drilling locations caused by negligence of employees of the assured.

Extraneous Coverages Which Underwriters Are Asked to Undertake

Among the various types of extraneous coverage which an assured may purchase are the following:

Removal of wreck or debris.
Expense of regaining control of well.
Loss of use or occupancy.
Mortgage protection.
Property damage (above ground and underground).

Loss of hole or well.

Liability under various compensation acts, etc.

Coverage for various types of comprehensive general liabilities (umbrella or bumbershoot coverage).

The insurance of offshore oil drillings rigs is a highly specialized subject and in most cases the coverage is specially designed to meet the assured's requirements, subject, of course, to the premium paid. Thus, the basic London forms are often amended. A particular policy may, for example, contain an earthquake exclusion or stipulate that there shall be no abandonment to underwriters of any of the property insured, or not limit the coverage on equipment situated elsewhere to 25 percent of the total insured value. The concession of no deductions "new for old" is sometimes extended to apply to the actual oil rig; that is to say, the drilling machinery and drilling equipment. Such equipment is deemed to be part of the hull and machinery and the insured value is computed accordingly.

MORTGAGEE'S INTEREST INSURANCE

A mortgagee has an insurable interest in respect of any sum due or to become due under the mortgage (Sect. 14 (2) of the English Marine Insurance Act). In the United States prior to 1960, it was usual for mortgagees of large oceangoing vessels to protect their interest by requiring the mortgaged vessels to be insured by their owners (the mortgagors) against marine and war perils on as wide terms as were available in the marketplace. Mortgagees also required that they be named as an assured in the marine and war risk policies and as a loss payee under those policies. At that time the possibility of a mortgagor scuttling the mortgaged vessel was generally considered too remote to require mortgagees to protect their interest with separate mortgagee's interest insurance. As for the possibility of the mortgagee losing the coverage afforded by the mortgagor's hull policies due to a breach of warranty by the assured-shipowner, it was apparently also thought by mortgagees to be too remote to insure against. Mortgagees no doubt relied upon the good faith of hull underwriters not to enforce such breaches against innocent mortgagees. This was certainly the attitude of the mortgagees who financed large oceangoing vessels at that time. Yet in 1970 it was held that an "innocent" mortgagee named as a co-assured with the mortgagor-shipowner could have no better rights under the policy than a "guilty" mortgagor (the *Padre Island,* 1970 AMC 600).

Early in the 1960s, direct mortgagee's interest insurance had been introduced in the American marine insurance market principally to accommodate the U.S. Maritime Administration (the American Institute Marad

Title XI Mortgagee Form 4/1/62; *see* Appendix A). Prior to that time, not even the so-called standard union mortgage clauses commonly used in fire policies in the United States had been written into marine hull insurance policies (*see* fn. 5, *Ionian Shipping Co.* v. *British Law Insurance Co.*, 1970 AMC 1112). Under the Marad Title XI form very wide coverage was given to the U.S. Maritime Administration in its capacity as an innocent mortgagee. The form insured against any nonpayment by hull underwriters resulting from "any act of or omission by the Mortgagor . . . or breach of any warranty. . ." It even covered nonpayment under the shipowner's policies when the claim rejection resulted from a peril not insured under the shipowner's policy. Thus even a loss by scuttling was covered and this was understood to be the case by all concerned at the time. However, the good faith inherent in all marine insurance contracts was such that many American shipowners (mortgagors) considered such insurance not only unnecessary but also that it was a reflection on the integrity of the U.S. marine insurance market and on the moral integrity of American shipowners (the *New York Times*, 3/7/65).

In 1963 an American Institute Single Interest Mortgagee (7/1/63) form was introduced for use by commercial mortgagees in cases unconnected with the Maritime Administration (*see* Appendix A). This form requires an underlying hull form and insures only against the nonpayment by hull underwriters when that nonpayment results from any act of, or omission by, the assured-mortgagor named in the hull policy, or from breach of any warranty in the hull policy. As a condition precedent to any claim under the mortgagee's interest policy, the underwriters of the hull policy must have denied the claim and the assured-mortgagor must have instituted suit against the hull underwriters to collect the claim. Unlike the Marad form, this form makes no reference to the coverage of nonpayment by the underlying hull underwriters when the nonpayment resulted from a peril not insured against in the hull policy (such as scuttling). To determine the extent of coverage it is therefore necessary to consider the words "nonpayment by (hull underwriters) . . . which non-payment results from any act of, or omission by the assured named in the hull policy or breach of any warranty." There can be no doubt that the intent was to preserve for the mortgagee the coverage which an assured-mortgagor (shipowner) had under the hull policy but which he (the shipowner) might forfeit because of any act or omission or because of any breach of warranty. For example, the shipowner might breach the warranty of seaworthiness or any warranties as to employment or trading, etc. Such breaches of warranty might render the policy void from the time of the breach, in which case even a loss caused by an insured peril after the breach would not be recoverable by the assured-shipowner under the hull policy. However, in such situations, under the mortgagee's interest policy, the mortgagee would be rendered innocent of such breaches by the mortgagor and be able to collect under that policy (to the extent of the unimpaired original policy coverage). Similarly, a breach of the due diligence proviso in the Inchmaree clause in the hull policy by the assured-shipowner resulting in his not being able to collect claims falling under that clause would not impair the mortgagee's right of recovery of such claims under his own single interest policy. Thus it seems that mortgagee's interest insurances, in excusing to the mortgagee "any act or neglect" of the vessel owner, is referring to acts in the management or operation of the vessel. In fact such insurance is often referred to as breach of warranty (B.O.W.) insurance. However, even though the Institute single interest form does not specifically import new perils, such as scuttling, into the policy, it has been accepted by some American Institute members and insurance brokers that the form was intended to cover innocent mortgagees against scuttling. This is based on the theory that, if the mortgagee is not privy to the scuttling, then the loss, insofar as he is concerned, is caused by a peril of the sea (sinking) and not by scuttling. This concept is further discussed below.

Smaller banks and loan associations in their role as mortgagees of smaller vessels, such as fishing vessels, were never as sanguine as to their mortgagor's integrity as were the larger banks who dealt primarily with big, established, and responsible corporate entities. Consequently mortgagees of smaller craft invariably sought added protection from their mortgagors' hull underwriters (who themselves very often occupied a relatively minor position in the marine insurance hierarchy). This added protection was usually given to the mortgagee by way of an endorsement to the hull policy. While there is no official mortgagee's interest endorsement in marine insurance, such endorsements are often based on the so-called standard or union mortgagee clause used in fire insurance. In consideration of an additional premium, such endorsements usually start with an admission of seaworthiness as between the insurer and the mortgagee and go on to say that the interest of the mortgagee shall not be impaired or invalidated by an act or omission or neglect of the mortgagor or by any failure to comply with any warranty or condition over which the mortgagee has no control. The endorsement sometimes contains a specific proviso that the loss, in the absence of such act or neglect or breach of warranty or condition, must have been a loss recoverable under the policy. Such a proviso appears to indicate that, whatever the nature of the mortgagor's act or neglect, etc., the mortgagee's right of recovery under the endorsement is limited to the coverage provided by the hull policy to which the endorsement is attached. Indeed this appears to be the case in fire insurance. Thus *Couch on Insurance* states that "in view of the applicability of other policy provisions, a mortgagee claiming under a standard mortgage clause asserts his right subject to all the terms and conditions of the contract of insurance except those which are expressly waived in the mortgage clause" and "the standard or union mortgage clause thus operates as an independent contract only for the limited purpose of preventing the defeating of the insurance by the act of the insured alone, but does not in any other way affect the terms of the policy" Sect. 42:731). This also was the view of a federal court in California which found that a mortgagee's endorsement (albeit with a proviso clause) adds no insured perils to those listed in the policy. The endorsement served only to avoid a loss of coverage that the owner, master, agent, or crew might otherwise cause by breaching the policy terms or conditions. The decision by the Fifth Circuit in *Ingersoll Rand Financial Corp.* v. *Employers of Wausau (infra)* was found to be distinguishable because of the existence of the proviso clause (*Ennia General Ins. Co.* v. *V & W Seafood Enterprises*, 1987 AMC 1488). Thus it seems that at least the possibility exists of underwriters having to pay even for losses deliberately caused where the basic standard or union mortgage clause is used without the proviso clause specifically limiting coverage under the endorsement to losses recoverable under the policy itself.

It has been suggested by one highly respected textbook writer that an innocent mortgagee is in a stronger position insofar as mortgagee's interest coverage is concerned if the insurance is effected separately by the mortgagee himself with the coverage stated in specific terms (presumably rather than by way of an endorsement to the vessel owner's hull policy). Otherwise, if mortgagee's interest is merely protected by an endorsement to the hull policy, that endorsement should be specific as to coverage (Howard B. Hurd: *Marine Insurance*, 2d ed., London 1952). Hurd had the "peril" of scuttling in mind in making these remarks.

Most single interest mortgagee's interest policies in use in the London marine insurance market required that until nonliability under the underlying hull policy was determined, either by litigation or by the passage of a year or even longer from the date of the hull underwriter's declination of coverage, mortgagee's interest underwriters were not required to respond. In short, the nonliability of the hull underwriters had to be demonstrated before the mortgagee's interest underwriters responded. This question as to when the cause of action against mortgagee's interest underwriters arises came before the English courts in the *Alexion Hope* (1987 1 L.R. 60, 1988 1 L.R. 311). On the facts of that particular case the court of appeals held that the cause of action arose when (1) an average adjustment had been issued and (2) hull underwriters had declined to pay.

Mortgagees have argued that (absent any specific stipulations in the policy regarding time of payment along the lines described above) mortgagee's interest insurance is payable at the time of the loss (if covered by the terms of the policy) whether or not the mortgagee has in fact suffered or will suffer a loss of security. Such payment to the mortgagee reduces the mortgage debt and any surplus is held for the benefit of the mortgagor. This view was upheld in *Walter* v. *M.O.A.* (1977 AMC 1471), and is based on fire insurance cases.

It is submitted that the words "any act" (of the mortgagor) in mortgagee's interest insurance and similar endorsements to hull policies may not have been intended to imply the introduction of a new peril (such as scuttling) into the policy for the benefit of innocent mortgagees. However, in recent times, because of a dramatic increase in the frequency of scuttlings, banks, as mortgagees, often obtain specific coverage against scuttling and some brokers in the London market have produced forms to this end. Once such form which came before the English commercial court insured the mortgagee against nonpayment by hull underwriters when the nonpayment resulted from deliberate, negligent, or accidental act or omission of the owner-mortgagor, including the deliberate or negligent casting away or damaging of the vessel or by reason of some breach of warranty. The coverage was subject to the insured mortgagee not having been privy to the circumstances causing the loss (*Continental Illinois National Bank* v. *Bathurst*, 1985 1 L.R. 625). It should be noted that what was at that time a very unusual and specific coverage of an innocent mortgagee against scuttling was twice repeated in this particular policy. This appears to support the view that if such unique coverage against scuttling is required, the mortgagee's interest insurance should clearly say so.

However, some mortgagees contend that the words "any act" (of the shipowner-mortgagor) used in the usual type of mortgagee's interest insurances or in endorsements to the shipowner-mortgagor's hull policies does embrace scuttling and that, therefore, the mortgagee, being innocent of such scuttling, can collect such claims under the mortgagee's interest insurance or under the hull policy endorsement as if they were ordinary sinkings (a peril of the seas). The difficulty with this contention is that the proximate cause of such losses remains scuttling, which is not a peril of the seas. ("The possibility of scuttling is not a peril of the seas; it is a peril of the wickedness of man and would have to be mentioned expressly in the policy, like barratry or pirates, in order that the assured should recover from the underwriter in respect of it"—*P. Samuel & Co.* v. *Dumas*, (1924) 18 L. L. R. No. 7 p. 211). Mortgagees further argue that the so-called Bill of Lading clause ("innocent cargo owners" clause) introduced into cargo policies following *Samuel* v. *Dumas* is analogous to mortgagee's interest policies and/or endorsements to hull policies. This is not a true analogy; the "innocent cargo owners" clause in cargo policies refers to the "wrongful act or misconduct" of the shipowner (which would embrace scuttling) for which, under the clause, the innocent cargo-assured is excused and which enables him to collect under his cargo policy even if the vessel was scuttled. The words "wilful misconduct of the assured" are used in Sect. 55 (2) (a) of the English Marine Insurance Act to specifically exclude, *inter alia*, scuttling as an insured peril. In any case, the innocent cargo owner (unlike the innocent mortgagee of a vessel) is unconnected with the shipowner and has effected an insurance on a different subject-matter (cargo). He is in fact truly innocent of any connection whatsoever with the shipowner or the scuttling.

In a recent case, mortgagees successfully challenged this contention that a mortgagee cannot recover for a loss caused by a peril not covered by the hull policy taken out by the mortgagor-shipowner. The court held that the standard or union mortgagee clause (an endorsement to the hull policy creates a separate contract of insurance between the insurer and the mortgagee and this clause provided that the interest of the mortgagee shall not be impaired "by any act of, or omission or neglect of" the mortgagor-owner. In that case the negligent acts and omissions had resulted in the theft of the insured vessel. The court based its decision on its opinion that the standard mortgagee's clause was a separate undertaking between the mortgagee and the insurer, which contract was measured by the terms of the mortgage clause itself; furthermore, that when the mortgagee was not guilty himself of any breaches of policy conditions, he could recover for a loss sustained by the mortgaged property (even though the risk be excluded from the policy coverage) when any act of the mortgagor had caused or contributed to the loss resulting from an excluded risk. (The cause of the loss was the theft of the insured vessel and it had been agreed that this was not a risk covered by the hull policy.) See *Ingersoll Rand Financial Corp. v. Employers of Wausau* (1986 AMC 1109).

It will be seen that mortgagee's interest insurance remained in a rather confused state. To ensure coverage for events resulting from the wilful misconduct of the mortgagor-shipowner, mortgagees would be wise to take out a separate policy covering their own interest and not rely on an endorsement of the mortgagor's hull policy. Furthermore, such single interest mortgagee's policies should specifically include the "peril" of scuttling so that both insurers and insureds can have no doubt as to the existence of this unique (in terms of marine insurance) coverage. If underwriters do accept a mortgagee's interest endorsement to the mortgagor's hull policy, they should indicate their understanding of the effect of the endorsement. If their intent is not to cover scuttling, a proviso should be included in the endorsement to that effect.

In 1986, no doubt with these uncertainties in mind, the London market issued new Institute Mortgagees Interest Clauses—Hulls, 30/5/86 (*see* Appendix A). Perhaps bowing to the inevitable, the new clauses specifically cover, *inter alia*, losses or damages "by virtue of any alleged deliberate, negligent or accidental act or omission . . . of the Owners . . . of the vessel . . . including the deliberate or negligent casting away . . . of the vessel . . . without the privity of the Assured: (that is, without the privity of the mortgagee). The vexed question as to when payment is to be made under the mortgagee's interest policy, when there has been a nonpayment or reduced payment under the mortgagor's hull policy, is specifically addressed in Clause 8. This clause stipulates that there shall be deemed to be a nonpayment by the underwriters of the owner's (mortgagor's) policies (a) when a final court judgment is delivered in favor of those underwriters or (b) at such earlier time when the assured (mortgagee) can demonstrate to the satisfaction of mortgagee's interest underwriters that there is no reasonable prospect of the mortgagors succeeding in the claim against the underwriters of the mortgagor's policies. At that time the assured-mortgagee is required to present his claim to the mortgagee's interest underwriters, which claim shall be payable within three calendar months from the date on which a properly documented claim was submitted. The Institute clauses are in the form of an open cover and in effect a mortgagee (such as a bank) is required to declare all its loans ("without exception") made on vessels. This might not always be convenient to the assured. However, no doubt Lloyd's brokers will continue to find underwriters who are willing to insure mortgagee's interests on an individual basis and even under the broker's own form of policy as long as it is substantially based on the official Institute clauses.

One thing that all parties concerned in mortgagee's interest insurance are agreed on is that the sum insured is the unpaid principal amount of a valid mortgage held by the assured on the vessel, reducing *pro rata* to the extent of payments made on account of the mortgage indebtedness. The policy also usually insures interest earned and unpaid to date of loss. The total of the unpaid balance including interest must not exceed the sum insured (*see* American Institute Single Interest Mortgagee Form, Appendix A). The London Institute form describes the indemnity provided by the policy as being the outstanding indebtedness under the loan at the time for payment under Clause 8 (assuming that that amount was less than the unrecoverable claim under the mortgagor's policies).

BILLS OF LADING INSURANCE

With the advent of the carriage of cargo in containers, a new concept of insuring cargo emerged. It was felt by some shippers that the cost of transporting cargo could be reduced if one party were designated to assume the burden of both the carrier's potential liabilities and insurance against physical loss of or damage to cargo. The result was some experimentation with "bills of lading insurance." This type of cargo insurance is accomplished by the carrier filing a tariff under which the normal legal liabilities assumed by carriers are increased over and above those imposed by law under a domestic bill of lading; an appropriate surcharge is then made for issuing such insured bills of lading (*see* further discussion of bills of lading insurance in Chapter 12 under "Carriage of Cargo"). The bills of lading insurance therefore imposes on the carrier a liability nearly commensurate with that of an insurer. It has been the practice of the carriers who issue insured bills of lading to in turn insure their liabilities to cargo in the commercial marine insurance market.

Sometimes carriers offered their customers a choice of either arranging their own insurance or opting for "insured bills of lading" coverage. The cost of the latter was built into the freight rate charged. The usual form of open cargo policy was used with the subject-matter insured described as "upon merchandise of others while in the custody of the assured and for which valid bills of lading, dock receipts or other documents evidencing receipt of merchandise for shipment has been issued by the assured." The assured in such policies was necessarily the carrier, for account of whom it may concern, with losses payable to the legal holders of the shipping documents referred to above. The named assured (the shipowner or carrier) was in effect acting as agent "as their interest may apply" and "for account of whom it may concern" (that is, for account of those cargo owners who elected to be insured).

However, it should be noted that when a shipowner or carrier takes out an open policy to cover the goods of his shippers, the policy is limited to the interest which it was originally intended to insure, that is, physical loss or damage to cargo. In particular, unless specific provision is made, such insurances do not cover the shipowner's or the carrier's personal risks or legal liabilities. The insurances are effected solely for the protection of other principals, not on their own behalf or for any interest of their own (*Scott* v. *Globe*, 1896 1 Comm. Cas. 370). Thus the Bill of Lading, etc., clause ("seaworthiness admitted" clause) relates only to the contract of insurance between the underwriter and the insured cargo owner. The shipowner and the carrier, although named as assureds "for account of whom it may concern," can hardly be construed as "innocent cargo owners" who are the parties intended to be protected by the "seaworthiness admitted" clause. Indeed there are cases in England supporting the right of underwriters, by way of subrogation, to pursue the shipowner or carrier in whose name, as agent only, the policy had been effected (the *Yasin*, 1979 2 L.R. 258).

The use of "insured bills of lading" is in the main confined to American carriers operating in domestic trades, and the American marine insurance market was never very enthusiastic about this new form of cargo insurance. Most major shippers prefer to arrange their own insurance of cargo and to stand on their own individual loss records rather than be merged with other shippers who might not be so loss-control conscious. Moreover, the coverage provided by the carrier to cargo owners under insured bills of lading is not the equivalent of an "all risks" Warehouse to Warehouse policy; in order to have his interest fully protected, a prudent cargo owner would need to obtain a Difference in Conditions policy with a Warehouse to Warehouse provision. Such a policy would respond for any loss or damage not provided for under the insured bills of lading coverage. So many steps to obtain complete coverage inevitably increase the total cost of the insurance required and in effect defeat the intent of bills of lading insurance.

INSURANCE OF CONTAINERS

In the 1960s with the advent of container ships and the intermodal transportation of goods, it became necessary for insurances to be devised to cover the large number of containers (and allied equipment) at risk throughout the world. Containers needed to be insured not only while at sea but also while being transported on land and while stored in container parks. In 1969 the London market introduced various container clauses: the Institute Container Clauses, Time (All Risks), the Institute Container Clauses, Time (Total Loss, etc.), and the Institute War and Strikes Clauses, Containers—Time.

In the United States no market container forms existed and since containers are more akin to cargo than to ships it became the practice to use open cargo policy forms, suitably adapted, to insure containers. Most shipowners leased containers from container companies and under the terms of such leases the lessee (shipowner) was usually obligated, at the termination of the lease, to return the containers to the lessor in good condition, normal wear and tear excepted, and to be liable for any loss or damage. Very often the lessor also required shipowners to insure the containers while in their possession. This concept of the lessee of containers being responsible for the maintenance, repair, and insurance of the containers is similar to the long-term bareboat charter of ships. Such insurances on containers are usually open policies effected against "all risks" of physical loss or damage with a deductible average applicable to "each and every occurrence" (or similar wording). Often the deductible is not to be applied to the total loss of a container whilst ashore unless the occurrence is within a terminal area or container park, the inference being that the deductible in general is intended to be applicable to losses of catastrophic proportions (as when a container vessel sinks at sea with many containers lost or when a fire destroys a container park full of containers). There is usually a limit of loss "by any one vessel or by any one usual connecting conveyance or at any one place at any one time." This type of clause has been held not to be applicable to the bankruptcy of the carrier, which could not be invoked as triggering the recovery limit in the clause. Thus there was no limited fund for which all the cargo container lessors, making claims against the policy to recover for damages allegedly arising from the bankruptcy, were competing. The plain language of the clause limits it to incidents which occurred at one place and one time, or on one vessel or conveyance (*Interpool Ltd. v. U.S. Fire Ins. Co.,* 553 F. Supp. 385 (1983)).

A prudent owner of containers (the lessor) also effects insurance on his containers (which may be leased to many different shipowners). The lessor's insurance is generally on an "all risks" open policy based on the usual open cargo policy form. Since the terms of the lease invariably make the lessee responsible for the return of the leased containers in good condition, fair wear and tear excepted, in theory the lessor only needs coverage under his own insurance for "off-lease" containers. However, he usually incorporates contingency insurance into his open policy. Such insurance covers his interest in containers lost or damaged while in the lessee's possession when, for one reason or another, the lessee does not (or is unable to) comply with the lease and reimburse the lessor. In essence, this contingency aspect of the lessor's policy is intended to insure the default of the lessee; the default may be due to bankruptcy or lack of appropriate insurance to cover physical loss or damage to the containers, or any other reason. Once the lessee fails to meet his obligation under the lease, the lessor has an insurable interest under the contingency aspect of his own open policy. Container policies covering this contingency risk usually include a clause to the effect that, with regard to leased containers, claims are payable only after due diligence has been exercised by the insured (lessor) to recover from the lessee or the lessee's insurers. A reasonable definition of due diligence in this context is that, once the lessor-assured has taken every possible step to recover the containers and/or to be indemnified by the lessee or the lessee's insurers, the lessor is then entitled to collect his claim from his own contingency insurers (subject to proof of quantum). The lessor is certainly not required to await the outcome of any legal suit which he might have filed against the lessee and/or the lessee's insurers before collecting from his own insurers. Needless to say, the lessor's insurers (on payment of the claim) would be subrogated to any recovery which might ultimately be effected from the lessee's insurers.

Some container leasing companies also offer a damage protection plan to their lessees. Such plans cover the lessee against payments for damage to the containers under the terms of the lease. For an additional payment per day per container, the lessor agrees to absorb damage payments under the lease. If such plans are in effect the container leasing company often incorporates stop loss coverage in his own open policy. For an additional premium the policy is extended to indemnify the assured (lessor) for financial loss sustained through the damage protection plan. This protection is usually in excess of a prearranged amount. Once the repairs paid for by the lessor under the damage protection plan exceed the amount designated in the policy, any excess payments are recoverable under the policy.

All policies on containers include Sue and Labor clauses (*q.v.*). These clauses are particularly important in container insurances; by their very nature containers can be misplaced and claimed as missing only to subsequently turn up (often months or even years later). Often the cost of tracing and recovering missing containers (especially when large numbers are involved) can be considerable. In a claim which came before the English courts it was argued by the container insurers that expenditure incurred in tracing and recovering containers following the bankruptcy of the lessee did not come within the Sue and Labor clause in the policy but was rather incurred in "a commercial undertaking to retrieve the containers from a bankrupt hirer." This viewpoint was rejected by the court of appeals. The court said that the true test applicable was whether or not in all the circumstances the assured had acted reasonably to avert a loss when there was a risk that insurers might have to bear it and the evidence showed that they did (*Integrated Container Service* v. *British Traders Ins. Co.*, 1984 1 L.R. 154) This case was referred to with approval by an American court in a similar situation. The court held that expenses incurred by the container lessors in recovering the insured equipment scattered throughout the world at the time of the shipowner's bankruptcy were recoverable under the shipowner-lessee's container policy (*States Steamship Co.* v. *Aetna Ins. Co.*, 1985 AMC 2749).

The cost of recovering missing containers is sometimes defined in container policies as expenses incurred from the point of abandonment to the assured's nearest leasing depot, and would include any storage charges, etc., which might have had to be paid to repossess the containers.

For a full discussion of the Sue and Labor aspect of these two container policy cases, see Chapter 7.

INSURANCE OF YACHTS

Yachts are usually insured on "all risks" terms. There is no standard nationwide yacht policy and most brokers and insurance companies have their own forms. Once such form in general use is the Hansen All Risks Yacht form.

The warranties and general conditions section of this policy includes a Private Pleasure warranty which stipulates that the insured vessel is to be used solely for private pleasure purposes and is not to be hired or chartered except with underwriters' permission.

The hull section of the policy provides coverage against all risks of physical loss or damage to the property from any external cause. A deductible amount is usually stipulated which is applicable to hull claims other than total or constructive total losses. No deductible is applicable to claims under the Running Down clause (Collision clause). Any equipment separated from the vessel and laid up on shore is covered but only to an amount not exceeding 50 percent of the sum stated under the heading "Amount of Insurance"; the insured amount attaching to the insured yacht is decreased by the amount covered in respect of the separated equipment. Repairs to the hull are to be paid without deduction, new for old, except that underwriters are only liable for the cost of repairs to sails, covers of canvas, or other like material, or a reasonable value in lieu of repairs. A Strikes clause is included which covers loss or damage to the insured vessel caused by strikes, etc., or caused by vandalism or persons acting maliciously. The usual type of Running Down (Collision) clause is included. An important clause gives coverage, as assureds, to members of the immediate family of the assured who are domiciled with the assured, and who may be operating the insured yacht with the prior permission of the assured.

There is a list of specific exclusions, including theft or mysterious disappearance of equipment or accessories, other than boats and launches and their motors, unless occurring in conjunction with the theft of the entire yacht or unless there be visible evidence of forcible entry. Other exclusions are losses caused by ice and/or freezing, and mechanical breakdown or derangement of machinery.

The form also incorporates Protection and Indemnity (liability) insurance and this section duplicates the clause in the hull section which gives coverage to members of the assured's immediate family who may be operating the insured yacht with the prior permission of the assured.

There is a separate omnibus clause in the policy which stipulates that whenever the word "assured" is used in connection with the liability coverage provided (that is to say, in the Running Down clause in the hull section and in the Protection and Indemnity section) it includes in addition to the named assured "any person, firm, corporation or other legal entity who may be operating the vessel with the prior permission of the named assured, but does not include a charterer or a paid member of the crew of the insured vessel or a person, firm, corporation or other legal entity or any agent or employee thereof, operating a shipyard, boat repair yard, marina, yacht club, sales agency, boat service station or similar organization."

The object of this clause is to take care of any liability which might fall on any friends or relatives operating the yacht with the prior permission of the named assured. However, it does not extend liability coverage to persons acting in a professional capacity, such as a paid master and crew, or shipyards, boat repair yards, marinas, yacht clubs, sales agencies, boat service stations, etc. Such persons and organizations are assumed to have their own liability insurance.

This yacht form of policy concludes with sections dealing with medical payments insurance and federal Longshoremen's and Harbor Worker's Compensation insurance.

In summary, such "all risks" yacht policies are intended not only to provide comprehensive coverage against physical loss or damage to the yacht but also to protect the assured and his friends and relations against the liabilities inherent in the ownership or operation of such vessels. However, it should be noted that coverage provided others under the policy (that is, other than the named assured) does not cover their possible liability to the named assured.

In recent years, in an attempt to simplify marine insurance for the layman, it has become the practice of American yacht underwriters to issue what are described as "plain language policies for boat owners." Indeed, there is a market form now in common use (Yacht Policy—New All Risk Plain Language Clauses). This is not an official Institute policy form but it represents the marine hull market's attempt to produce a policy which laymen can understand. These policies are not intended to vary the customary "all risks" coverage, and in the "plain language" policy referred to above, the coverage is expressed as follows:

Causes of Loss That Are Covered:

> We will cover accidental direct physical loss or damage from any cause. We will also cover physical damage that is directly caused by any defect in the yacht that could not have been discovered by a reasonably thorough inspection. However we will not cover the cost of repairing or replacing any defective part.

The last sentences are a "plain language" translation of part of the traditional Inchmaree (or Additional Perils clause). While it is laudable to attempt to write a marine insurance policy in language yacht owners can understand, such attempts are fraught with pitfalls. The standard official market forms in general use are understood by the professionals in the world marine insurance markets (insurance brokers, or agents as they are sometimes called, underwriters, and most commercial yacht owners). There are over one hundred years of court decisions to look to in the event of any disputes arising as to coverage, etc. Translating yacht policies into so-called plain language is a difficult, and can be a dangerous, task. For example, it was argued by a corporate yacht owner in one recent case that the historical interpretation of the Inchmaree clause (*q.v.*) was inapplicable because the policy was marketed as a "plain language" policy. Fortunately, the court in that case was not persuaded. It was found that that particular "plain language" ("We will . . . pay for a loss caused by any hidden defect in the hull or machinery, but not the cost to repair or replace the defective part.") had the same meaning as the traditional Inchmaree clause (*Hubbard Broadcasting* v. *Continental Ins. Co.*). While it was "plain language" to the court it was apparently not "plain language" to the assured. One philosopher has said, "Truth calls a spade a spade" but unfortunately marine insurance does not lend itself to such a simple approach.

INSURANCE OF FISHING VESSELS

Special clauses are used for the insurance of fishing vessels. Such clauses are usually based on the standard clauses for the insurance of ocean hulls, suitably amended. Fish (catch), bait, cargo, fishing tackle, nets, power-boats, dories, skiffs, any kind of fishing equipment, and aircraft are all usually not considered to be part of the subject-matter insured and any deliberate sacrifices of these items are usually specifically excluded from general average. There is invariably a trading warranty in the policy although any breach of such a warranty is held covered subject to notice being given to the underwriters as soon as possible and subject to an additional premium as required. Protection and Indemnity risks are often incorporated into the policy along the lines of Builder's Risk and yacht policies. Two forms in general use to insure fishing vessels are the AHAB (American Institute) form and the California Fishing Vessels form. Both these forms are named perils policies.

LOSS OF EARNINGS INSURANCE

Loss of time and delay are two factors which are in general excluded from marine insurance coverage. However, with the advent of larger oil tankers following World War II and the practice of chartering these vessels for long periods of time, often before the vessels were even constructed, a demand arose for insurance to protect vessels' future earnings should the vessels sustain accidental damage preventing them from continuing to earn hire. Very often the vessels were mortgaged to banks and the effecting of insurances against loss of earnings ensured that their owners would be able to continue to meet payments to the mortgagees.

This type of insurance may be called insurance of Loss of Hire, Loss of Earnings, or Loss of Profits but, call it what you will, it is an insurance against a ship operator's failure to earn monies accruing from the use of a vessel due to a marine casualty preventing the insured vessel from operating. Loss of Earnings insurance is principally for the owner's account—that is, the owner is the assured, and in most cases he has a mortgage to repay.

Policies are written showing the sum insured per day as a valued amount, thus simplifying underwriters' actual liability in the event of a claim. The sum payable per day should bear a reasonable relation to the actual *net* daily loss on an off-hire period, and underwriters are generally becoming more reluctant to insure more than about 80 percent of the gross earnings of the vessel.

There are many different Loss of Earnings forms in existence but the purpose of all forms is to indemnify the assured, following a marine casualty to his vessel, for excess of so many days up to an agreed limit of number of days for any one accident and in all. While there are variations of this, a popular limit is 91 days, excess of 14 days. Sometimes there is another layer on top of this first layer, such as 91 days, excess of 105 days. Generally speaking, the excess (or deductible) of 14 days is the lowest underwriters will grant.

Underwriters' liability may commence from either the actual date of the casualty or the commencement date of the subsequent repairs, should the vessel not have been prevented from earning hire at the time of the casualty.

The question of granting coverage for slow steaming due to an insured peril is a delicate issue but most forms in use grant it. While it is not expressly mentioned in the American market's Loss of Hire form (*see* Appendix A), slow steaming is intended to be covered under the form. In fact, it is safe to say that slow steaming is covered in all cases unless expressly excluded.

For obvious reasons, the Perils clause in Loss of Earnings insurance is very often much broader than that provided by the basic American hull form of policy. For example, the mere breakdown of machinery is often covered with the proviso that the breakdown has not resulted from wear and tear or want of due diligence by the assured. The peril "breakdown of machinery" seldom appears in marine insurance policies (other than in loss of earnings policies). The peril "breakdown of electrical machinery" does appear in the American Institute Hull policy (Inchmaree clause) and in practice has always been considered to require a breakdown in operation; it does not cover the mere discovery of a faulty condition or latent defect. Insofar as loss of earnings coverage is concerned, a similar yardstick has usually been applied although a failure in the machinery resulting in a vessel having to proceed to a port of repair is usually considered to be a breakdown within the meaning of Loss of Earnings insurance. In other words there does not have to be a complete breakdown. Breakdown of machinery was interpreted by the Australian courts in *Sun Alliance* v. *N.W. Iron Co.,* (N.S.W.L.R. 1974). It was held that there had been a breakdown of machinery whilst in use even though the breakage (cracks) was not discovered until the machinery was stopped for regular maintenance. It appears that to avoid a claim submitted under the wide coverage of "breakdown of machinery," underwriters would need to sustain the argument not only that there had been no breakdown in operation but also that there was in fact a mere discovery of a fault or latent defect.

The American Loss of Hire clauses require the assured to incur any expenses which would reduce underwriters' liability, such expenses if reasonably incurred being for underwriters' account.

It is the custom in Loss of Hire insurances to limit the claim to full periods of 24 hours, no allowance being made for parts of a day. Sometimes the term used in the policy is "24 consecutive hours"; in this case, should the loss of hire from one accident comprise two or more separate periods, the odd hours and minutes of each period cannot be added together to make a day (they do not constitute 24 consecutive hours).

Generally speaking, in Loss of Earnings claims the assured is required to prove that he has, in fact, lost hire due to a marine casualty, and a Simultaneous Repairs clause is often included in the policy. Such a clause in the American Loss of Hire form states that if the vessel is laid up for damage repairs caused by a peril insured against and other repairs including but not limited to owner's repairs are carried out simultaneously therewith, as much time as is common to both classes of work in excess of the deductible period shall be divided equally between underwriters and the assured. Furthermore, in the event the time necessary to effect damage repairs is extended in any way by reason of concurrent repairs, such additional time is for the assured's account. The object of the Simultaneous Repairs clause is to allocate the time lost to those repairs actually causing or contributing to the loss of hire.

The words "other repairs including but not limited to owner's repairs, etc.," are meant to refer to *other repairs which contributed to the loss of earnings*; they may be

(a) Owner's repairs immediately necessary for seaworthiness (i.e., repairs which do not result in a loss of earnings claim because they were not necessitated by a *peril enumerated in the loss of earnings policies*) or repairs to accidental damage which are not immediately necessary for seaworthiness and in respect of which the assured does not choose to submit a claim under the loss of earnings policies, or

(b) Repairs immediately necessary for seaworthiness which result in a claim under another loss of earnings policy covering a different period of time.

In Loss of Earnings insurances it is more or less assumed that the vessel is engaged on a time charter party, but by stipulating a fixed amount per day (valued policy) this form of insurance may also be used for ships engaged on other contracts of affreightment. If such insurance is effected for a vessel while tramping, some provision must be made in the policy for a proper method of ascertaining whether, in fact, any hire is lost or not. Generally speaking, a claim for loss of time is not allowable if the repairs are effected during the period for which the ship is not under any freight engagement, unless the repairs were commenced immediately following the termination of a contract of affreightment and the ship sails for the purpose of entering on a new contract of affreightment within a short period after the completion of repairs.

The American form of policy is designed for long-term chartered vessels only (either time or contract). The insurance is intended to be one of indemnity except that it is subject to an agreed allowance per diem; i.e., the assured must prove a loss but not how much loss.

It will be appreciated that often the owner of a ship which is tramping cannot show what he has lost except by stating that he would have earned some freight if the vessel had not been laid up by reason of a casualty. This situation has led to so much difficulty that it is rare to find a vessel which is insured for loss of earnings which is not under charter. Many policies state that the vessel must be under charter, although there is sometimes a clause added to the effect that if a charter is cancelled during an insurance, the vessel shall be deemed to be earning hire for the balance of the policy period.

One way of avoiding this difficulty of proving a loss when the insured vessel is not under time charter is to include the words "or being offered for charter" in the policy preamble.

In conclusion, it should be stated that Loss of Earnings insurance is very much a question of practice and is liable to differ from underwriter to underwriter, while the varying forms of coverage call for varying interpretations.

The chairman of the Association of Averge Adjusters in 1990, M. L. Rahn, chose Loss of Earnings as the subject of his address to the association. Little is written on this subject and the address is particularly welcome and informative dealing as it does with practical problems encountered by average adjusters when adjustinmg such claims.

REINSURANCE

Phillips defines reinsurance as being a contract whereby one party, called the reinsurer, in consideration of a premium paid to him, agrees to indemnify the other against the risk assumed by the latter, by a policy in favor of a third party (Subsect. 374). The reinsurance may be against all or a part of the risks that have been assumed by the reinsured in the original policy (Subsect. 376). The original assured cannot assert any interest in a policy of reinsurance (Subsect. 404).

In practice, reinsurance falls into two main categories: facultative (or optional) and treaty. Facultative (risk-by-risk) insurance is direct or special reinsurance, usually of individual risks; in most instances, the ceding company shares the risk with the reinsurers on a participating basis. Treaty reinsurance is obligatory in that one party binds itself to pass business to another party, who in turn undertakes to accept it, in advance, on an obligatory basis. The reinsurer therefore shares in the business activity of the ceding company as a kind of partner. This obligatory assumption in advance of contingent liabilities at a fixed premium enables the ceding company to accept risks in excess of its own capacity. The reinsurer himself may place part of the business with further parties. Such reinsurance of reinsurers is called retrocession.

Treaty reinsurances fall into various categories. A *quota share (or part of) treaty* is an arrangement whereby the reinsurer accepts a predetermined percentage of all risks falling within the scope of the treaty (usually all business of a particular class). A *surplus treaty* stipulates that the ceding company and reinsurer have an agreed scale of limits with varying degrees of participation. Thus, in certain categories the ceding company retains most of the risk while in others there is a low level of retention. *An excess of loss treaty* may provide for the ceding company to pay in full any loss up to a certain sum with the reinsurer liable for the excess. A *stop loss treaty* is an arrangement whereby the ceding company accepts liability for a certain loss ratio (that is, the percentage arrived at by applying the losses for a year to the premium income) so that no liability falls on the reinsurer until the loss ratio is reached. The reinsurer is thus responsible for the losses in excess of the agreed loss ratio. However, such insurances are always subject to a limit beyond which the reinsurer's liability does not extend.

Policies of reinsurance contain a Reinsurance clause of which the following are common examples:

Being a reinsurance subject to the same claims and conditions as the original policy and to pay as may be paid thereof.

This reinsurance is subject to such risks, valuations and conditions, usual or unusual as are or may be taken or granted by the Reassured, including any alterations, amendments or extensions to which the Reassured may hereafter agree without notice to the Reinsurers, and to pay as may be paid by the Reassured, liable or not liable . . ."

The Ceding Company reserves to itself the sole right to settle all losses, whether by way of compromise or "ex gratia" payments or otherwise, and all settlements shall be unconditionally binding of the Reinsurer . . ."

Such clauses are sometimes referred to as "follow the fortune" or "pay as may be paid" clauses.

Reinsurance has been described as a transaction between gentlemen, and disputes between ceding companies and reinsurers are very rare. Nevertheless, disputes do occasionally arise, and such a dispute was litigated in *Insurance Company of North America* v. *United States Fire Ins. Co.* (1971 AMC 1891). In that case, the insured property (fertilizer) had been initially shipped in bulk from interior U.S. ports to Gulfport, Miss., where under the conditions of sale it was to be bagged prior to loading for shipment to the United Kingdom. The basic question was whether the reinsurer (the defendant) reinsured the loss sustained at a time when the fertilizer was partly bagged and partly in the process of being bagged at a warehouse in Gulfport, preparatory to further overseas shipping. The reassured (the plaintiff) maintained that the "follow the fortune" clause (the text of which was the same as the second reinsurance clause quoted above) put the question beyond doubt, referring to *Western Assurance Co. of Toronto* v. *Poole* (1903 1 K. B. 376) in which the court had defined such a clause to mean that:

> The reinsurer, when called upon to perform his promise, is entitled to require the reassured first to show that *a loss of the kind reinsured* has in fact happened; and secondly that the reassured has taken all proper and business-like steps to have the amount of it carefully ascertained. That is all. He must then pay . . . He has promised "to pay as may be paid thereon." Such is, in my opinion, the meaning and effect of these reinsurance policies. (Emphasis added.)

On the other hand, the reinsurer, in denying liability, contended that it reinsured a specific policy concerning goods in transit; that the goods were not in transit when destroyed, and that the plaintiff, by means of subsequent binders, increased the risk, making it one not reinsured by the defendant. In finding for the defendant, the court commented:

> Plaintiffs emphasis on the phrase "liable or not liable," in the above-quoted clause from the reinsurance contract, as binding defendant reinsurer to pay, in effect whenever the reinsured decides, unilaterally, to pay its assured is misplaced. It would be an unwarranted and indeed tortured construction of that clause to hold a reinsurer bound, for example, to pay if the prime insurer paid monies to its insured on a claim completely without the scope of the policy and not in good

faith. This construction is implicitly accepted by plaintiff in its argument in its brief that "where the loss sustained is, in the judgment of the primary insurer, *one reasonably covered under the primary policy* the reinsurer is bound to pay." [Emphasis added.] This argument supports defendant's contention that before its obligation to pay arises the claim paid by its assured must be reasonably encompassed within the bounds of the policy.

While the "follow the fortune" clause is certainly a broad one, it is clear that the reinsurer is liable only for "a loss of the kind reinsured" (*Western Assurance Co. of Toronto* v. *Poole, supra*). To determine what type of loss was reinsured, we must turn to the original insurance contract. Construction of the latter contract reveals that it covered "shipments," "voyages connecting consignees" and goods while "in transit." The examination before trial of Transammonia's president makes it crystal clear that the bagging process was not necessary to the transit of the cargo. The intent of the parties to the original insurance contract, showing that the bagging operation was not covered by the original contract, is borne out by the plaintiffs subsequent issuance of two binders covering the merchandise while at Gulfport, Mississippi. The president of Transammonia, in his deposition, testified that the binders were issued at his request for coverage on the bagging operation and that as far as he was concerned, the goods lost or damaged in Gulfport were insured by reason of the binders.

The stoppage and bagging of the cargo at Gulfport was an interruption in the transit of the goods and created a shore risk not insured under plaintiff's original insurance contract.

In short, this decision underscores the fact that while treaty reinsurance implies the advance acceptance of future risks, those risks must not deviate from the risks originally contemplated at the time the treaty was arranged; furthermore, that a following clause is not to be construed as a blank check.

To summarize, while there are many other facets of reinsurance, the role of the treaty reinsurer is to provide the ceding company with sound and continuing reinsurance cover on a long-term basis and so permit its operation to take place without undue fluctuation of results. The role of the facultative (or special) reinsurer is merely to shoulder part of an individual risk which, for one reason or another, the original insurer wishes to share.

For a fascinating insight into the operation of the largest marine reinsurance market in the world (London) the reader is directed to a law case involving a Lloyd's underwriter (*General Accident Fire and Life Assurance Corp.* v. *Peter William Tanter,* 1984 1 L. L. R. 58).

Chapter 11

Marine Insurance Claims on the Great Lakes

The Great Lakes of North America form not only the largest body of fresh water in the world but are also the most important unit of inland waterway. This in spite of the fact that, due to the freezing up of the lakes and connecting waters during the winter months, "lakers," generally speaking, operate only between April 1 and December 15.

Policies of marine insurance have been especially adapted to cover vessels trading exclusively on the lakes.

AMERICAN INSTITUTE GREAT LAKES HULL CLAUSES

The American Institute Great Lakes Hull Clauses, which were revised under date of March 9, 1978, warrant that the insured vessel shall be confined to the waters, bays, harbors, rivers, canals, and other tributaries of the Great Lakes, not below Prescott/Ogdensburg. Previous versions of these clauses stipulated that navigation of the insured vessel should be restricted to between April 1 and December 15, both days inclusive, with underwriters to be given prompt notice of the commencement of such navigation. In the latest version of the clauses, the dates have been deleted and blank spaces substituted to permit the insertion of an agreed season of navigation.

Navigation prior to and subsequent to the season of navigation is held covered provided:

(a) prompt notice is given to the underwriters,

(b) any amended terms of cover and any additional premium required by the underwriters are agreed to by the assured, and,

(c) prior approval of each sailing is obtained from the United States Salvage Association, Inc. (presumably, now from the Salvage Association (London)).

The vessel may discharge inward cargo, take in outward cargo, retain cargo on board, and move in port during the period she is in winter lay-up. For purposes of this provision, such of the following places as are designated by a single numeral shall be deemed one port: (1) Duluth—Superior; (2) Detroit—Dearborn—River Rouge—Ecorse—Wyandotte—Windsor; (3) Kingston—Portsmouth.

It is further warranted that the vessel be properly moored in a safe place and under conditions satisfactory to the underwriters' surveyor during the period of winter lay-up.

The Lakes clauses include a similar Deductible Average clause to that included in the American Institute Hull Clauses with the added proviso that claims arising from damage by ice while the vessel is on a voyage or moving in port (excepting claim for total loss) shall be subject to a deductible of $50,000 or 10 percent of the agreed value, whichever is the smaller, but in any event not less than the deductible stipulated in the basic deductible average clause, the deductible to be applied to each accident. However, like the American Institute Hull Clauses, it is agreed that all ice damage which occurs during a single sea passage between two successive ports is to be treated as though due to one accident.

General average and salvage claims are to be adjusted in accordance with the contract of affreightment, or (failing such provision or there being no contract of affreightment) in accordance with the York/Antwerp Rules, 1950 or 1974, or as per American or Canadian Lake adjustment (American Lake adjustments are often referred to as "the application of American law on the Lakes").

The Lakes form of policy also stipulates that if repairs have not been executed within 15 months from the date of the accident, underwriters shall not be liable for any increased cost of repairs by reason of such repairs being executed after 15 months from the date of the accident.

In other respects, the American Institute Great Lakes Hull Clauses are similar to the American Institute Hull Clauses.

CANADIAN BOARD OF MARINE UNDERWRITERS GREAT LAKES HULL CLAUSES

A Canadian form of policy for use on the Great Lakes was issued for the first time by the Canadian Board of Marine Underwriters in 1971. These Great Lakes Hull Clauses are similar in most respects to the American clauses with the following notable exceptions.

The navigational season is limited to the period from midnight, March 31, to midnight, December 15, but any breach of this warranty is held covered.

The deductible average is not to be applied to "claims arising under the Sue and Labor Clause, nor claims for salvage expenses, or general average." It has long been Lakes practice not to apply any deductible average to Sue and Labor expenses although such practice would, of course, be subject to any specific provision in the policy to the contrary. Reflecting this Lakes practice, Rule 3 of the Rules of Practice for the Great Lakes of the Association of Average Adjusters of Canada stated that "there shall be no deductible average applied to claims arising under the Sue and Labor Clause." This practice of giving preferential treatment to Sue and Labor claims was defended stoutly by the Canadian marine insurance market for some years but, as the practice in other marine insurance markets was to apply deductible averages to all claims of whatever nature, this practice became increasingly difficult to justify. Because the American Institute Great Lakes Hull clauses of 1978 specifically provided that any deductible was to be applied to all claims including Sue and Labor claims, the Association of Average Adjusters of Canada in 1982 deleted Rule 3 (*supra*) of their Rules of Practice for the Great Lakes.

A special penalty on claims for damage to machinery which results from negligence of the crew is introduced in the Canadian clauses. This clause reads as follows:

> In the event of a claim for loss of or damage to any boiler, shaft, machinery or associated equipment, arising from any of the causes enumerated in the Additional Perils (Inchmaree) clause, lines 106 to 115 hereunder, attributable in part or in whole to negligence of Master, Officers or Crew and recoverable under this insurance only by reason of the said Clause, then the Assured shall, in addition to the deductible, also bear in respect of each accident or occurrence an amount equal to ten percent of the balance of such claim, but not to exceed a further $50,000. This clause shall not apply to a claim for total or constructive total loss of the vessel.

The effect of this clause is to make the assured a coinsurer insofar as machinery claims arising from the negligence of the crew are concerned. The object is to encourage shipowners to exercise a greater control over negligent personnel and thereby reduce the number of such claims.

The exclusion of any allowance in particular average for wages of crew (except in removing the vessel for average repairs) is modified by the following words: "except when the Crew are employed in lieu of shore or other labor with the view to minimizing expense."

LAKE PRACTICE

Perhaps because they compose a unique system of inland water transportation, the Great Lakes have produced a unique collection of local practices in connection with the adjustment of claims. This is known as "Lake practice," to which brief reference has already been made.

Lake practice is a relic of the early days of marine insurance on vessels plying exclusively on the Great Lakes. These Rules of Practice are in many cases rough and ready, albeit practical, and originated much as did the customs of Lloyd's in the early days of marine insurance in England. From time to time they have been criticized as being, in some instances, vague and illogical.

Nevertheless, shipping interests on the Lakes have resisted various attempts to modernize lake practice and bring it more into line with present-day American adjusting practice. In this connection, the Great Lakes Protective Association—an insurance organization composed of vessel owners which carries a substantial percentage of the value of vessels entered in the association in its insurance fund—made the following comments in its annual report of 1938:

> In recent years there has been a disposition on the part of underwriters to modify Lake time clauses in order to make them conform more closely to ocean policies. In addition, there has also been more or less of an effort to substitute ocean practices for Lake practices. The Association believes these tendencies should be opposed and that every effort should be made to preserve the practices which have arisen on the Great Lakes over a number of years, inasmuch as they are adapted to our own peculiar needs. Vessel operation on the Great Lakes in the case of the ordinary bulk carriers is necessarily confined to the lakes, and many of the practices followed on the ocean serve no useful purpose here. Our method of handling matters involving marine insurance may seem strange to ocean underwriters, but it must be borne in mind that our problem is one that has developed through years of experience on the Great Lakes, so that the practices which have developed through the years should be preserved.

Such part of the nebulous Lake practice as embodied in written form appears in the Rules of Practice of the Great Lakes Protective Association (G.L.P.A.). Among the more interesting are the following (most of which are self-explanatory):

(2) *Deductions from cost of repairs in adjusting general average.* In adjusting claims for general average, repairs to be allowed in general average shall not be subject to deductions in respect of "new for old."

(5) *Deferment of repairs for convenience of owner* (See No. 14). Where repairs of known damage are deferred for the convenience of the owner beyond the vessel's navigation season, any increase in the claim against Underwriters resulting from such deferment shall be borne by

the owner, except increase in ship repairers' charges occurring during the 15-month period under the Limitation of Date of Repair or Claim clause. Nevertheless, if it can be established that such deferment resulted in a saving to the Underwriters, such increased costs, up to the amount of the saving effected, may be included in the claim. Notwithstanding the foregoing, repairs to damages resulting from disasters occurring subsequent to November 1, and effected during the following winter season shall not be considered as deferred repairs.

(7) *Interest and commissions in general average.* Interest or commissions on allowances, sacrifices or expenditures are not allowable in General Average in ballast cases or in cases involving the carriage of bulk cargoes unless the bill of lading or contract of affreightment covering the particular shipment expressly refers to the York-Antwerp rules or some other set of rules providing for interest or commissions.

The G.L.P.A. has also commented on the rule as follows:

We considered it advisable to refrain from adopting any rule covering general cargo and thus have confined Rule 7 to "in ballast" cases or cases involving the carriage of bulk cargoes.

This rule applies to cases covered by American Lake Adjustment; it does not apply if the bill of lading or contract of affreightment covering the particular shipment expressly refers to the York-Antwerp Rules or some other set of rules providing for interest or commissions.

(8) *Valuation of contributing interest in general average.* The contributory values for general average involving the carriage of bulk cargoes, unless the bill of lading or contract of affreightment covering the particular shipment expressly refers to the York-Antwerp rules or other rules requiring appraisals or other determinations of value, shall be based upon the full agreed insurance valuation of the vessel appearing in the regular hull insurance policies excluding any increased value or excess liabilities insurance on the said vessel, the insured value of cargo or its invoice value if uninsured including guaranteed freight paid or payable, and the gross amount of freight at risk and earned less one-half.

(10) *Wages & provisions in general average*

(A) Where cargo is lightered, wages and provisions are allowable while the cargo is being reloaded.

(B) In making allowances for wages and provisions in General Average at a port or place of refuge, a period of less than 12 hours, either alone or in excess of a number of complete days, shall be disregarded and a period of 12 hours or more, either alone or in excess of the number of complete days, shall be treated as a complete day.

(11) *Apportionment of common expense when repairs are made.* Common expense for making repairs such as moving the vessel to and from a repair yard, towage, docking and undocking, dry-dock charges and other expenses which are common and required by both classes of work, shall be apportioned between the owner and the Underwriters when a vessel is dry-docked and/or undergoes repairs:

(A) For owner's account and damage previously unknown is discovered chargeable to Underwriters for which repairs are concurrently made; or

(B) For survey and/or repairs chargeable to Underwriters and repairs for owner's account are concurrently made which are immediately necessary for the seaworthiness or the continued operation of the vessel even though the necessity for such owner's repairs was previously unknown.

A classification survey, although it is for the owner's account, shall not be considered as requiring the apportionment of common expenses under this Rule since classification societies defer such surveys for the owner's convenience and the entire amount of the common expense shall be chargeable to the Underwriters unless repairs are concurrently made for owner's account which are immediately necessary for seaworthiness or the continued operation of the vessel.

When as a matter of convenience an owner takes advantage of the vessel being at a repair yard for Underwriters' repairs and makes repairs or has maintenance work performed for owner's account not immediately necessary for seaworthiness or the continued operation of the vessel, the entire amount of the common expense shall be chargeable to the Underwriters.

It is of interest to record that, under American Lake adjustment, common charges have been *apportioned* in certain circumstances; that is to say, the common charges are divided with owners, each accident bearing an equal proportion. It has been suggested that this method (which is contrary to normal adjusting procedures whereby the common charges are *divided equally* between the owner and the underwriters) came about due to the well-established practice on the Lakes of deferring as much work as possible to the winter months when navigation was closed. It may also derive from the lack of annual dry-dockings because American Bureau of Shipping and U.S. Coast Guard regulations only require inspection on dry dock of a Great Lakes vessel once in five years. Consequently, damages arising from many accidents are often repaired at the same time during the dry-docking period.

(12) *Maintenance of class charges.* Some adjusters have included two Maintenance of Class charges of the American Bureau of Shipping in their adjustments of Particular Average damage, one at the time preliminary survey of the damage was held and one at the time permanent repairs are made at the shipyard. This practice is not justified, the original service relating merely to the determination of whether or not the vessel is seaworthy to continue in operation without making immediate repairs, the postponement being for the convenience of the owner to permit the ship to continue in operation without making permanent repairs until some later date. It would appear as though the services relate more to obtaining a Certificate of Seaworthiness and therefore entirely for the benefit of the owner and an expense which he should bear, except where it can be established that the services resulted in an ultimate saving to the Underwriters, as provided for in the latter part of the following rule:

When a vessel meets with an accident which a survey discloses has not affected her seaworthiness and a certificate to that effect is issued by a Classification Society surveyor, granting permission to postpone permanent repairs until a later date, and a second survey for Maintenance of Class is made when repairs are finally carried out, the Underwriters will recognize only the second Maintenance of Class charge, unless it develops that the services result in an ultimate saving to the Underwriters, in which event the extra expense may be asserted in an amount up to the saving effected.

(14) *Repairs not made within 15-month period* (See No. 5). When repairs are not made within the fifteen-month period and for the convenience of the owner an extension is granted to defer repairs beyond this period, the Underwriters will only pay their proportion of the reasonable cost of what repairs would have amounted to had repairs been made within the fifteen-month period. For example: In a case where permission is given an owner to defer repairs beyond the fifteen-month period and in the meantime shipyard costs for labor and material have increased and repairs are made, such extra cost will be disallowed. Nevertheless, if it can be established that such deferment resulted in a saving to the Underwriters, such increased costs, up to the amount of the saving effected, may be included in the claim.

In connection with these rules G.L.P.A. has commented as follows:

When it has been possible to do so, shipowners have deferred repairs of damage sustained during the navigation season to the winter months when the ship would be idle in any event thus avoiding loss of use. However, repairs during the winter months for the owner's convenience have entailed increased expenses because of winter weather and the status of the vessel (such as towage charges for "no steam," icebreaking, etc.). Consequently, it has been the practice for many years under American Lake Adjustment to disallow such extra charges which result from deferment of the repairs for the owner's convenience.

Rule 5 should not be confused with the 15-month limitation period on repairs formerly contained in the Lake Time Hull Policy which is dealt with in Rule 14. The concept in the latter rule is that underwriters should not be required to pay higher labor and material costs because the owner has been given permission to defer repairs beyond the 15-month period. It has nothing to do with the owner's choice of the time of year in which the repairs are to be made. Rule 5 applies to special added expenses incurred by deferring repairs to the winter months other than increases in labor and material cost whereas Rule 14 applies to increased costs in labor and material when the owner has been granted permission to defer repairs beyond the 15-month limitation in the policy.

(15) *Commencement and termination of a voyage.* Navigating risk shall attach when a vessel, light or loaded, sails on the first voyage of the season by breaking ground for the voyage in complete readiness for the voyage with the present intention of immediately quitting the port. Conversely, port risk shall attach at the time a vessel reaches its final port of destination at the close of the navigating season subject to the provision of the Trading Warranty and Season of Navigation clause in the Association's Certificate which provides: "A vessel may discharge inward cargo, take in outward cargo, retain cargo on board, and move in port during the period she is in Winter lay-up. For purposes of this provision, such of the following places as are designated by a single numeral shall be deemed one port: (1) Duluth—Superior, (2) Detroit—Dearborn—River Rouge—Ecorse—Wyandotte—Windsor, (3) Kingston—Portsmouth.

It is interesting to note that in 1978 subscribers of the Great Lakes Protective Association approved the substitution of the Liner Negligence clause in lieu of the Inchmaree clause in the association's Certification of Participation.

Insofar as general average is concerned, Lake practice is, to some extent, subject to modification in cases where the contract of affreightment stipulates that general average is to be adjusted according to the York/Antwerp Rules but, as the usual Lakes form of bill of lading makes no provision regarding the method of adjusting general average, such cases are not frequent.

In 1971 the Association of Average Adjusters of Canada issued their own Rules of Practice for the Great Lakes using the Great Lakes Protective Association Rules as a basis. Most of the Canadian rules are similar to those of the G.L.P.A. but Rules 5-8 and 11 differ in certain respects, while the G.L.P.A. has an additional Rule 14. The Canadian Rule 5 is more liberal than the combined Rules 5 and 14 of the G.L.P.A. in that the Canadian rule permits the allowance of the cost of repairs in full whether or not they are effected after the close of navigation and provided they are carried out within the 15-month limitation period. The G.L.P.A. makes a distinction between the increased cost of repairs effected following the close of navigation (for example, additional expenses because of winter weather and the status of the vessel, such as extra "no steam" towage charges, icebreaking, etc.) and the extra cost caused by increases in the cost of labor and material because repairs are deferred beyond the 15-month period.

The intent of the Canadian Rule 6, dealing with temporary repairs, is similar to that of the G.L.P.A. but goes on to deal with general average situations.

Canadian Rule 7, dealing with the allowance of interest and commission in general average, is identical with the G.L.P.A. rule insofar as ballast cases and cases involving bulk cargoes are concerned. However, the Canadian rule also provides for the allowance of interest and commission in cases involving general cargo (or package freight cargo, as it is sometimes called on the Great Lakes).

Canadian Rule 8, dealing with the valuation of contributing interests in general average, is similar to that of the G.L.P.A. but, in addition, stipulates that electronic or other equipment not included in the vessel's insured value shall contribute on a value based on its insured value or, if uninsured, upon its actual value.

Canadian Rule 11, dealing with the apportionment of common repair expense, differs from that of the G.L.P.A. in only one (albeit important) respect. The Canadian rule provides for an equal division between the owner and underwriters whereas, as stated previously, the G.L.P.A. rule provides for an apportionment. Thus, when a division of common charges is required under the rule and there are, say, three accidents being dealt with for underwriters' account and the owner effects repairs for his account which are immediately necessary within the terms of the rule, the Canadian rule would call for fifty percent of the common charges to be borne by the owner and the remaining half apportioned one-third to each accident. On the other hand, under the G.L.P.A. rule, the owner would only bear 25 percent of the common expenses with 25 percent being charged to each of the three accidents.

The complete Rules of Practice for the Great Lakes of the Association of Average Adjusters of Canada and those of the Great Lakes Protective Association are shown in Appendices D and C.

Chapter 12

Marine Insurance on the Rivers, Harbors, and Coastal and Inland Waterways of the United States

The waterways of the United States constitute a vast system serving large areas of the country. They are dominated by the Mississippi River and its navigable tributaries, which in themselves provide almost one-third of the United States with a cheap and efficient means of transportation. The system has received a tremendous impetus since 1940 by virtue of the advances made in controlling floodwaters, reinforcing banks of rivers, the charting and marking of channels, and the advances in towboat technology and design. Most cargo is carried by large flotillas of barges usually pushed by tugs. The volume of cargo is so immense and the marine insurance covering it is so important to the operators that the whole facet of marine insurance as it is applied to vessels operating in these waters must be examined.

The vast majority of river business is placed with the local offices of national domestic companies and very often both vessel and cargo are insured with the same underwriter. It is a highly specialized business and one in which the insurance broker in particular is required to exhibit all the expertise of his profession if he is to provide his client with complete coverage against the many perils and unique situations common to river navigation. While most of the rules and practices of marine insurance already dealt with are applicable to river business, there are many situations unique to smaller craft and, in particular, to tugs and their tows. Moreover, this chapter will serve in some respects as a revision course—an application of the fundamental rules and practices of marine insurance to the special problems encountered on the rivers, harbors, and coastal and inland waterways of the United States.

HULL INSURANCE

While the standard American Institute Hull Clauses are sometimes used for insuring vessels trading on the domestic waterways of the United States, these clauses are primarily intended for the insurance of oceangoing vessels; to avoid the use of numerous amendments, there are many other policy forms perhaps more suitable for vessels plying these waterways, particularly tugs.

The American Institute of Marine Underwriters has produced a form based on the standard American ocean hull form of policy, the Coastwise and Inland Hull Clauses, November 2, 1972. With minor exceptions, it closely follows the standard ocean hull form and is obviously intended for vessels having their own propulsion and carrying cargoes. In the Perils clause, the traditional "perils of the seas" coverage is replaced by perils "of the waters named herein." More importantly, a seaworthiness clause is included which reads:

> The underwriters shall not be liable for any loss, damage or expense arising out of the failure of the Assured to exercise due diligence to maintain the vessel in a seaworthy condition after attachment of the policy; the foregoing, however, not to be deemed a waiver of any warranty of seaworthiness implied at law.

Such a clause is frequently used in insurances on small craft operating on inland waters although, in fact, it simply reiterates the legal position in the United States regarding seaworthiness. Underwriters insuring river craft apparently feel that the river vessel owner has a closer connection with operating personnel and a greater direct control of the day-to-day operation of his vessel than does the owner of an oceangoing vessel. They therefore consider it reasonable to insist on the owner maintaining his vessel in a seaworthy condition. For the same reason, river policies often include a special cancellation clause which the underwriter can invoke if the incidence of losses proves catastrophic and he wishes either to get off the risk or to negotiate an increased premium. The institute policy also stipulates that there shall be no other insurance against physical loss of or damage to the vessel (other than against war risks). The Collision clause is similar to that included in the standard hull form of policy and, therefore, tower's liabilities are not covered (the form not being intended for tugs). There is a Litigation and Defense clause which grants underwriters the option of naming the attorneys to represent the assured in any litigation between the assured and third parties which involves underwriters.

Provision is made for the insertion of a trading warranty confining the insured vessel to a specific area. Any breach of the trading warranty specified in the policy results in the suspension of the policy. However, on the return of the vessel *in a seaworthy condition* to within the limits specified in the trading warranty, the policy re-attaches (*see* Adventure clause). Similar provisions are customary in most hull policy forms intended for use by smaller craft operating on coastal or inland waterways.

The American Institute of Marine Underwriters also has a form specially intended for tugs, the American Institute Tug form, August 1, 1976, which also closely follows the standard American hull form of policy. The perils are once again described as "perils of the waters named herein"; Seaworthiness, Limitation of Insurance, Cancellation, and Litigation clauses are also included. An innovation is the inclusion of a Watchman clause, reading as follows:

> It is agreed that when this vessel is tied up or moored, it shall be at all times in charge of a watchman in the employ of the Assured, whose duty it shall be to make careful examination of the Vessel throughout at reasonable intervals, including inspection of the bilges.

Small craft are often tied up alongside the riverbank or in staging areas and this clause seeks to ensure that the insured vessel will never be left unattended during such periods. The Collision clause in this tug policy is, of course, extended to cover tower's liabilities, which aspect of coverage will be discussed later. It is worth noting that earlier versions of this tug form did not include, in their Perils clause, coverage of loss by assailing thieves or barratry (possibly because such vessels were more accessible to thieves than are oceangoing vessels). Whatever the reason for the omission, the latest version does include such coverage.

There are other tug forms in use including the McClelland 1706 and McClelland 2139 clauses which include an Inchmaree clause extended to cover "other causes of whatsoever nature arising either on shore or otherwise, howsoever, causing loss or injury to the property hereby insured." In other words, an "all risks" policy.

The Taylor hull form—1953 (Rev. 70), SP-39C, is used extensively on the rivers to insure both tugs and barges. It is a named perils policy augmented by the Inchmaree clause; it follows much of the format of the standard hull form of policy, omits the seaworthiness clause discussed above, and has no Watchman or Cancellation clauses. Nor is there any exclusion regarding scraping and painting the vessel's bottom. A Collision clause is included which is extended to provide limited tower's liability coverage. (This extension would, of course, be deleted when the subject-matter insured is a barge.)

Most insurance brokers, however, have their own River hull forms and, since much river business is placed with a single underwriter and is highly competitive, brokers are usually able to persuade underwriters to accept their particular form. These forms all follow much the same format, with the traditional sea perils being redescribed as "perils of the inland seas and waters." They are named perils policies with the insured perils augmented by the Inchmaree clause. Indeed, the Liner Negligence clause is making its appearance in River policies although originally it was never intended for small craft. A Seaworthiness clause is often included. Sometimes the usual exclusion regarding the recovery of the cost of scraping and painting the vessel's bottom is omitted, presumably because small craft are often not registered in a classification society or are not subject to periodic dry-docking. Furthermore, as they usually operate in fresh water, bottom painting is less important an item than it is with oceangoing vessels.

It is not usual or necessary for vessels operating on the rivers and inland waterways to insure against all war risks. However in these turbulent times it is desirable that coverage be obtained against vandalism, sabotage, malicious mischief, strikers, labor disturbances, etc. This can be achieved by attaching the American Institute Srikes, Riots and Civil Commotions endorsement (Hulls) to the basic policy.

HULL COVERAGE EXTENDED TO INCLUDE TOWER'S LIABILITIES

If the vessel to be insured is a tug, care must be taken to ensure that adequate tower's liability coverage is provided. This can be achieved by adding endorsements to the basic Collision clause in the hull policy for the extent of coverage required. Alternatively, a towboat owner, as we have seen, has several other hull forms available to him which not only provide coverage of the towboat itself but which also include Collision clauses extended to cover tower's liabilities.

The American Institute Tug form (August 1, 1976) previously discussed includes a Collision clause extended to provide almost complete tower's liability protection; that is to say, if the insured vessel comes into collision with any other vessel, craft, or structure, floating or otherwise (including her tow), or strands her tow or causes her tow to come into collision with any other vessel, craft, or structure, floating or otherwise, or causes any other loss or damage to her tow or to the property on board, then any liability of the insured vessel arising from such events is covered. A Sister Ship collision clause is included; without it, the tower's liability coverage would be worthless if the insured tug was towing a barge of the same ownership. The inclusion of a Sister Ship clause means that the common assured of both tug and tow can claim for damage to his own barge (including loss of use) under the tug policy as a tower's liability claim. If he is also the owner of any cargo being carried by the barge, he may also include any claim for damage to cargo in any claim against the tug's underwriters for tower's liability. He may prefer to claim all these items under the tug policy if the deductible average in the tug policy is less than the particular average deductible under the barge policy—or the barge and its cargo may not be insured. On the other hand, if the barge and its cargo are insured, the common owner may not wish to pay an additional premium for inclusion of a Sister Ship clause. It is in considering such questions that the expertise of the insurance broker comes into play. It should be noted that the Institute Tug form does not cover any liability arising as a result of the tug causing another vessel to strand or collide without an actual collision involving the insured tug or its tow. Such coverage must, therefore, be provided by the Protection and Indemnity policy if this tug form is used.

A tug form in use on the West Coast (Tug Hull Form 1955) not only includes the extensive coverage against tower's liability provided by the Institute tug form but in addition responds for liability to third parties if the insured vessel or its tow causes another vessel to strand or collide without actually being involved in a collision themselves.

On the Western Rivers and on the U.S. Gulf Coast a commonly used form is the Taylor hull form—SP-39C, referred to previously. This policy only covers tower's liability arising out of a collision between the tow and other vessels and excludes the tug's liability for damage to the tow and its cargo; it does not cover liabilities arising out of collisions with fixed objects. In its basic form it would be, for example, suitable for an assured who tows his own barges and transports his own cargo and separately insures them accordingly. However, by the use of endorsement SP-39D, full tower's liability coverage (complete with Sister Ship clause) can be obtained, including the tug's liability for damage to the tow and its cargo.

It must be remembered, however, that all these Collision clauses, extended though they may be to cover tower's liabilities, still contain one version or another of the basic Collision clause proviso specifically excluding liability for loss of life and personal injury claims, wreck removal, oil pollution, etc. These liabilities must, therefore, be covered elsewhere.

PROTECTION AND INDEMNITY

It will have been noted that the liabilities arising out of towage operations can be covered in a variety of ways; but if the necessary coverage is not fully provided by tower's liability endorsements in the hull policy, it is all-important that Protection and Indemnity insurance fills the void. Certain of the traditional Protection and Indemnity coverages are included in *some* of the tower's liability extensions discussed previously (such as *liabilities* arising from striking a fixed object or as a result of having caused another vessel to strand, etc., without the insured vessel having been in collision). However, as stated above, the proviso or exclusions clause in the Collision clause (amended as necessary to coincide with the additional coverage granted under the tower's liability extension) is still operative.

Protection and Indemnity form SP-23 dovetails with the basic Collision clause in the standard ocean hull policy (that is, without any tower's liability extension) to cover those risks which are excluded by the proviso clause. It also covers the traditional Protection and Indemnity risks *simpliciter* (that is: loss of life and personal injury claims, collision with fixed objects, damage other than by collision, etc.). However, this form contains a Towage Exclusion clause which must be deleted or modified as necessary if the subject-matter insured is a tug. If the Collision clause in the hull policy has been extended to cover tower's liabilities, the SP-23 form will need to be carefully examined to take cognizance of the increased liabilities being assumed under the hull policy and which will therefore no longer need to be covered by the Protection and Indemnity policy. Occasionally liability for loss of life and personal injury, and cargo liability coverage are deleted from the Protection and Indemnity policy, and if this is done such liabilities must be covered elsewhere.

Protection and Indemnity form SP-38 is more limited in coverage than SP-23. It does not, for example, cover

(a) claims for loss of or damage to cargo, or

(b) cargo's proportion of general average or salvage not recoverable from any other source, both of which are covered under form SP-23.

In other respects form SP-38 provides similar coverage to form SP-23. A Protection and Indemnity form which excludes cargo claims (as does SP-38) is used where liability to cargo is covered elsewhere (either under the Tower's Liability clause in the hull policy in the case of a tug, or by a separate policy covering legal liability to cargo). Both form SP-23 and form SP-38 contain a clause stipulating that if the assured has any interest other than as a shipowner, the underwriter will not be liable to any greater extent than if the assured were the shipowner and as such entitled to all the rights of limitation to which a shipowner is entitled. This is similar to the Charterer's Limitation clause in the standard American hull clauses which was discussed earlier. It is important, therefore, if the assured is a time charterer (and so not entitled to limitation rights under the prevailing American law), that he make provision for alternative coverage to respond in cases where the owner would have been entitled to limit his liability. In that situation, under the above clause, underwriters would only be liable for the amount to which the shipowner himself would have been able to limit, not what had to be paid because the charterer could not limit his liability. It should also be mentioned that form SP-23 contains a clause stipulating that underwriters are not liable for any claim which would be recoverable under the standard [name to be inserted] hull form of policy "if the vessel were fully covered by such insurance sufficient in amount to pay such claim." This wording is similar to the clause litigated in the much criticized *Landry* decision (*q.v.*) and, if that case were to be followed in other circuits, could be construed as covering excess collision liabilities, a construction which was never intended. (Protection and Indemnity underwriters had intended to cover only those collision liabilities not covered at all by the Collision clause in the basic hull policy, that is to say, those liabilities excluded by the proviso paragraph in that clause. They never intended to assume liability for amounts in excess of the basic coverage provided in the Collision clause.) For some unknown reason, form SP-23 was not amended to make this intention clear following the *Landry* decision. It is interesting to note, however, that although form SP-38 (unlike form SP-23) does not affirmatively include collision liability coverage, it quite clearly *excludes* excess collision liability "whether or not the vessel . . . is actually covered by such insurance and regardless of the amount thereof" (lines 61-62).

In arranging complete coverage against tower's liability, all eventualities must be considered, and it is usually necessary to arrange additional Protection and Indemnity coverage and excess liabilities coverage. In this connection the following should be borne in mind:

(a) Since those liabilities covered under the hull policy are limited to the insured value of the tug, bumbershoot or other excess liabilities insurance should be effected (most Protection and Indemnity insurance policies do not cover *excess* liabilities, only those liabilities not covered at all by the primary hull insurance).

(b) Since the Collision clause in the basic hull policy, even when amended to cover tower's liabilities, specifically excludes loss of life and personal injury claims, and since standard Protection and Indemnity policies exclude all towage-related claims of that nature (other than loss of life and personal injury claims of passengers and crew members of the tug), such policies should be amended to include the coverage lost as a result of the towage exclusion. The Towage Exclusion clause, invariably included in Protection and Indemnity policies, excludes "any loss, damage or expense, or claim arising out of or having relation to the towage of any other vessel or craft." It follows that if tower's liability Protection and Indemnity coverage is required, this clause must be deleted; that is to say, the policy must be modified to extend to towing operations.

If special provisions are not made in the Protection and Indemnity policy, a bumbershoot policy covering all risks and liabilities not covered by other insurance should be effected.

Unless other insurance arrangements have been made, the Protection and Indemnity policy on a dumb barge should cover the liability of the barge owner to the cargo being carried. It might also be necessary for the barge owner to effect excess coverage against legal liability to cargo since the cargo coverage under the Protection and Indemnity policy will be limited to the amount insured under that policy and, furthermore, will not cover any assumed contractual liabilities (such as may be incorporated into an insured bill of lading). The normal Protection and Indemnity policy only covers those liabilities to cargo which are imposed by law.

CARRIAGE OF CARGO

In considering the insurance of cargo and the possibilities of effecting recoveries from carriers for loss of or damage done to cargo, it is important to consider the carrier-shipper relationship. This relationship differs from a tower-towee relationship. On the Rivers there are two major types of carriers: the public or common carrier and the contract or private carrier. In general, a common carrier is a carrier engaged in the transportation of two or more cargoes for different owners. Therefore, in River practice when two or more cargoes for different consignees are carried in separate barges but towed by one towboat, that towboat would probably be considered a common carrier. Common carriers sometimes issue an insured bill of lading. This is accomplished by the carrier filing a tariff under which the liabilities assumed by the carrier are increased over and above those imposed by law under a domestic bill of lading; an appropriate surcharge is then made for issuing such insured bills of lading. The tariff provisions are deemed to be incorporated into the terms and conditions of the insured bill of lading. The carrier in turn usually seeks protection by way of a cargo liability policy rather than by relying on coverage under his Protection and Indemnity policy. The reason for this as stated before: the Protection and Indemnity policy only responds for the legal liability of the assured as imposed by law—it does not cover assumed contractual liabilities. Thus, if the carrier, by issuing an insured bill of lading, voluntarily assumes a greater liability, he is not covered by the Protection and Indemnity underwriter for such increased contractual liability. In any event, the amount insured under the Protection and Indemnity policy may be insufficient, and even if the common carrier issues a normal bill of lading he may prefer to insure his liability under a cargo liability policy.

However, most cargo moving on the Rivers is in the area of the so-called contract or private carriage. A cargo owner charters an entire barge under a private contract and the towboat owner's responsibilities in these circumstances are merely that of a tower. In such circumstances, cargo insurance is arranged by and written for the account of the individual cargo owner.

When, then, does a carrier, either private or common, become a mere tower? In general, if a towboat owner also owns the barges in which the cargo is carried, or if the towboat owner is the person chartering the barges from their owners, he is a carrier and not a tower. As a carrier, the towboat owner's liability to the cargo being carried is limited by the terms of the Harter Act or the Carriage of Goods by Sea Act, whichever is applicable. On the other hand, if the towboat owner enters into an agreement with a shipper to transport the shipper's cargo in a barge chartered from the barge owner by the shipper, he is considered a tower with a towing contract.

Most River cargoes are insured by their owner on F.P.A. conditions. This restricted coverage leaves the cargo owner self-insured to some extent and, consequently, an enthusiastic partner with underwriters in subrogation actions against carriers whenever possible.

RELEASE OF LIABILITY AGREEMENTS

Assessing potential liabilities or assessing the possibility of recoveries is made more difficult by the common practice on the Rivers of granting release of liability agreements. Insofar as towage contracts are concerned (that is, where a towboat is towing—or pushing—a tow which is not owned or chartered by the tower), towboat owners use various methods of shifting the risk of the venture to the tow. One such method is to obtain a waiver of subrogation from the tow's hull and Protection and Indemnity underwriters and from the underwriters insuring the cargo being carried. However, it should be noted that this method only protects the tower from liability for damage to tow and cargo to the extent that those interests have been paid by their underwriters. It does not, for example, prevent the owner of the tow from suing the tower for any *loss of use* of the tow arising from an insured peril. A second method is to have the tower named as an additional assured in the hull and Protection and Indemnity policies on the tow, and in the cargo policy, with the result that those underwriters are unable to subrogate against their own (albeit additional) assured (the tower). This has the same effect as a waiver of subrogation and, in addition, may offer some coverage for liabilities to third parties (through the tow's hull and/or Protection and Indemnity policies). However, being named as an assured in the Protection and Indemnity policy on the tow will not protect the tower against liability for loss or damage to cargo since that policy does not cover the liability (negligence) of the tower. Similarly, being named as an assured in the hull policy on the barge will not protect the tower against claims arising under the Collision clause in that policy, because that clause does not insure the liability for the assured against negligent operation of the towing vessel (*Harbor Towing Corp.* v. *Atlantic Mutual Ins. Co.,* 1951 AMC 1070). Thus, while waivers of subrogation and being named as additional assured afford the tower some protection against claims for damage to the tow or its cargo, the tower may still have liability exposure to the tow or its cargo for the reasons given and also to the extent of any deductible in the tow's policies or by reason of limited insuring conditions on the cargo.

Notwithstanding these shortcomings, the tower's exposure to liability for damage to the tow or its cargo is frequently dealt with in the towage contract along the foregoing lines. Although it is apparently settled that such clauses in towage contracts (requiring the owner of the tow to insure it and to name the tower and the towing vessel as assured with waiver of subrogation) are valid and enforceable, it may be necessary for the towage contract to contain "reciprocal" insurance undertakings by the tower (*Twenty Grand Offshore v. West India Carriers,* 1974 AMC 2254). Insofar as contracts of affreightment (as opposed to towage contracts) are concerned, exculpatory clauses are valid and enforceable (*Kerr-McGee Corp.* v. *Law,* 1973 AMC 1667). In private carriage the parties are free to contract with respect to the liability of the carrier for loss of or damage to cargo or with respect to the insurance thereon, as they see fit.

It may be appropriate to repeat that being named as an additional assured often does little more than act as a waiver of subrogation by the insurer against the additional assured. For example, it has been held that a barge owner, named as an additional assured in the towing tug's hull policy, is not entitled to recover indemnity from the insurer for liability arising out of the barge's sole fault in damaging a bridge. The barge was neither listed in the tug policy nor covered by its Collision and Tower's Liability clause (*State of Louisiana v. Louisiana Towing Co. et al.,* 1984 AMC 2674). In another case although an oil drilling company was named as an additional assured under a Protection and Indemnity policy taken out by a crew boat owner, it was held that the policy covered only claims arising out of the operation of the crew boat, not claims based on the drilling company's independent negligence in failing to provide a safe means of access to its drilling rig (*John C. Gryar* v. *Odeco Inc.,* 1982 AMC 143). In still yet another case a tug owner was specifically included as a named assured in the towed barge's Protection and Indemnity policy. The tug negligently brought the barge into collision with a bridge without any fault on the part of the barge. The court held that the policy did not cover the tug's liability for negligence where there was no fault on the part of the insured vessel (the barge) (*N.Y. & L.B.R.R.* v. *U.S.,* 1976 AMC 2253).

To sum up: Whatever basic tower's liability insurance is carried, whatever risk-shifting device is used, a comprehensive general liability policy is essential. The standard bumbershoot policy, for example, protects the assured, *inter alia* and with certain specified exclusions, against Protection and Indemnity risks of whatsoever nature whether or not covered by the underlying Protection and Indemnity insurance. It also covers other basic liabilities on an excess basis and all other legal and contractual liabilities of whatsoever nature for personal injury, death, and property damage (whether by vessel or otherwise).

ADJUSTMENT OF CLAIMS

With regard to the practical side of adjusting claims the following should be noted:

(1) Most barges and towboats do not follow regular dry-docking schedules; operating in fresh water as they do, it is accepted by underwriters that the question of their being due for dry-docking does not usually arise. Generally speaking, River vessels are normally only dry-docked at intervals of five years or even longer. While certain River vessels come under the U.S. Coast Guard and American Bureau of Shipping regulations and do have to maintain regular dry-docking schedules, underwriters apparently turn a blind eye to the question as to whether or not these vessels were due for dry-docking at the time damage repairs are effected.

(2) General average is frowned upon, and when general average statements cannot be avoided they are kept as simple as possible. Generally speaking, wages and provisions of crew (if any), fuel and stores, and commission and interest are ignored. Apportionment of the general average is invariably made on the basis of the insured values of vessel and cargo. The controversial question as to whether all vessels in a tow should be brought into contribution has never raised its ugly head on the Rivers.

(3) When legal expenses and surveyor's fees are incurred in defending a third party claim in excess of the deductible average applying to such claims, and the claim is ultimately defeated or otherwise falls below the deductible average; the legal expenses, etc., are usually recoverable in full from underwriters. That is to say, they are not apportioned between underwriters' and owner's respective interests.

So-called River practice appears to be even more nebulous than Lakes practice and can be summed up as being a very simple approach to claims with little or no formal adjustment of claims. Of course, when the insurance of River craft is written on ocean conditions (such as the American hull form) regard must be had to the standard policy conditions. Nevertheless, River practices must be followed in such matters as dry-docking, legal expenses, etc. In short, the average adjuster must use his discretion in many areas, with the emphasis always on simplicity.

Actually, because of this practical approach to claims and because more often than not claims are adjusted by the insurance company underwriting the risk, average adjusters are little known on the Rivers. This is a pity, because while the vast majority of claims may not require the average adjuster's expertise, major accidents on the rivers can produce as many, and more, problems regarding coverage, the steps to be taken following a constructive total loss, limitation of liability, wreck removal, etc., as the most involved blue water casualty. It is a short-sighted policy on the part of insurance companies and their assureds not to instruct average adjusters, in addition to attorneys, when faced with major casualties involving complex marine insurance questions. By their training, average adjusters are accustomed to take a practical, commercial approach to such problems rather than a legalistic approach. Furthermore, while average adjustments may have no legal status, they are seldom questioned in the courts, and even if the average adjuster's solution is not acceptable to all parties, the average adjustment will form a basis for negotiation, and, if the adjuster was consulted at the outset, the steps taken will have followed the basic tenets of marine insurance.

Chapter 13

Punitive Damages

It is with some diffidence that a subject which is anathema to marine insurers is introduced in this third edition. However, the possibility of additional punitive damage awards, either directly against insurers on the grounds of bad faith or in the shape of increased awards to third party claimants by way of punishment of the insured shipowner, is unhappily a new "peril" facing underwriters. In fact, punitive damages are very much a feature of American jurisprudence although not often encountered elsewhere in the world of marine insurance. In practice, the inclusion of punitive damages in suits against shipowners or their insurers (often in the millions of dollars) has become a tool of American lawyers, particularly when representing the injured party in death and personal injury suits. While punitive damages in marine insurance cases are rarely actually awarded, the mere threat of such a tremendous potential exposure causes alarm and consternation in the hearts of even the strongest underwriters. The purpose of punitive damages in third party suits is said to be to deter offenders from similar offenses in the future and therefore they should only be awarded if there has been proven a reckless disregard for the safety of others or where an injury or death has been wilfully caused.

Punitive damages in maritime cases are the progeny of products liability cases in which field the principle of strict liability prevails rather than liability based on fault. In 1967 the marine insurance community was made aware of the advent of punitive damages in admiralty when a federal court stated that the cause of action for punitive damages had always been recognized as an actionable right in admiralty. So said the U.S. District Court for the Northern District of Ohio in holding the owners of the *Cedarville* liable for punitive damages arising out of the deaths of several seamen following the collision of that vessel with another vessel. The court held that because the corporate vessel owner had vested sole and exclusive discretion in the captains of its vessels and because the captain of the *Cedarville* endeavored to beach his ship without evacuating the crew (characterized by the court as "an outrageous, indeed horrendous, act of misconduct") the master's actions "were tantamount to those of the board of directors" of the company. On that basis punitive damages were decreed against the corporate vessel owner. To the great relief of marine insurers everywhere the court of appeals reversed the district court on the question of punitive damages on the grounds that company officials sitting hundreds of miles away had no obligation to countermand the decisions of the master "who was on the scene and in the middle of an emergency." The court commented that punitive damages are not recoverable against the owner of a vessel in addition to compensatory damages unless it can be shown that the owner authorized or ratified the acts of the master either before or after the accident. However, punitive damages may be recoverable if the acts complained of were those of an unfit master and the owner was reckless in employing him (the *Cedarville,* 1967 AMC 1965, 1969 AMC 252). In similar vein another court held that a shipowner was not liable for punitive damages to a cargo owner for stowing his shipment on deck when underdeck stowage had been stipulated in the bills of lading. The court stated that cargo interests had failed to establish the requisite "gross negligence, or actual malice or criminal indifference" (the *Oliver Drescher,* 761 F2d 855, 861, 2d Circuit 1985).

While claims for punitive damages under maritime law may have originated with loss of life and personal injury cases (third party situations), admiralty attorneys were quick to realize its potential in first party cases. Marine underwriters (hull, cargo, and Protection and Indemnity) suddenly found themselves subject to claims for punitive damages allegedly for "bad faith" (often defined as an unreasonable denial of a claim). Needless to say, such first party actions against insurers are subject to a different standard of culpability. The test to be applied in a first party bad faith action is whether the insurer's conduct was reasonable in the circumstances prevailing; the assured must prove that the insurer's refusal to pay policy benefits was unreasonable. Therefore, to justify a claim for punitive damages against an insurer, the assured must prove bad faith on the part of the insurer. In a suit brought in California—a state which has the reputation of being receptive to claims for punitive damages—a federal court applied a federal standard to the proof of malice required to support an award of punitive damages and rejected the use of the more liberal California state standard. The court held that under federal general maritime law an award of punitive damages was proper only when the act complained of was not only deliberate and unreasonable but was also done with a malicious and wrongful intent. Even under California law, claimants must show more than bad faith (that is, an unreasonable refusal to pay the insurance proceeds) in order to maintain a claim for punitive damages. It must be established that the insurer is guilty of oppression, fraud, or malice, that the insurer intended to harm the claimants, or that the insurer acted in conscious disregard of the rights or safety of claimants. The punitive damage cause of action was dismissed (*Ennia* v. *V. & W. Seafood,* 1987 AMC 1488).

However, underwriters are not always so fortunate. In a case concerning a cargo policy, an action was brought in a Louisiana state court against underwriters for failure to respond for the total loss of an offshore jacket being carried as cargo on a barge in tow of two tugs. The tugs lost control of the barge in heavy weather and the jacket went overboard. Although the tow had been approved by the U.S. Salvage Association (as required by the policy) underwriters declined liability on the grounds that the assured was aware that the tow was unsafe. Thereafter, the assured instituted suit against underwriters for the amount of the policy plus an award for defamation. Applying state law, the court held underwriters liable for the total loss of the jacket and found that the reason given by underwriters for declining the claim (namely, that the assured was aware that the tow was unsafe) was defamatory. Underwriters had failed to prove that the assured knew the tow was unsafe; the words used were issued with malice and with reckless disregard of whether it was false or not. The court awarded punitive damages against underwriters for defamation in the amount of $1 million (*Oceanic Contractors* v. *British Underwriters,* 1981 AMC 1264). While the case was under appeal a negotiated settlement was reached which involved the dropping of the claim for punitive damages. This case is a classic example of how claims for punitive damage can be used as a catalyst. The claim for the total loss of the jacket which had been declined by underwriters amounted to over $24 million and the possibility of underwriters having also to respond to punitive damages of $1 million was no doubt a factor in enabling the assured to obtain payment in full under the policy. Such coercive threats with the object of forcing payment of what seem to insurers to be debatable claims are on the increase and apparently are considered acceptable tactics by some assureds and/or their attorneys. One can only say that the Edwardians' noble concept of marine insurance as evidenced by the English Marine Insurance Act of 1906 ("a contract of marine insurance is a contract based upon the utmost good faith"—Sect. 17) has become somewhat tarnished in the eighty years which have elapsed since the act was formulated. However much one might regret this, it is clear that, in the United States at least, the threat of punitive damages will continue to have a salutary effect on insurers' decisions as to whether or not to decline what in their view are doubtful claims. In the not so distant past one leading American insurance company used to run advertisements saying that they looked for reasons to pay claims rather than looking for grounds on which to turn them down. During the last twenty years most insurers' attitude to claims has hardened. No doubt this is due to the heavy losses sustained by marine insurers in general during that period. Perhaps, therefore, blame for the increase in claims for punitive damages should not be assigned solely to anxious assureds and their advocates (attorneys).

Before leaving the unhappy subject of punitive damages it must be reported that the question as to whether Protection and Indemnity insurers are liable for third party punitive damages awarded by courts against their assureds was widely discussed in 1967 following the *Cedarville* case (*supra*). "Punitive" or "exemplary" damages have no relationship to "compensatory" or "pecuniary" damages. They are allowed on the grounds of public policy and not because the plaintiff has suffered any monetary damages for which he is entitled to reimbursement. Most Protection and Indemnity policies and club rules agree to indemnify the assured against any "loss, damage or expense" arising out of liability for loss of life or personal injury. It would seem, therefore, that any punitive damages awarded against the assured would constitute a "loss, damage or expense" within the meaning of Protection and Indemnity policies or club rules. The only possible restriction against insurance protection for such punitive damages would be on the grounds that coverage of this type would offend against public policy. The consensus within the marine insurance profession was (and is) that the wanton or wilful negligence necessary for any award of punitive damages is not sufficient to constitute deliberate injury from an intentional act, such as is needed to justify forfeiture of insurance coverage. Furthermore, even when corporate employees have been responsible for wilful negligence giving rise to the award of punitive damages, the corporation would be able to protect itself and its innocent shareholders from the consequences of its employee's wilful negligence. Protection and Indemnity insurers and clubs have therefore always proceeded on this assumption and, since they are selling protection to their assureds, have made no attempt, generally speaking, to exclude punitive damages from the coverage they provide. However, in 1983 a revision of the American Institute of Marine Underwriters Protection and Indemnity clauses (June 2, 1983) for the first time specifically excluded "liability imposed on the assured as punitive or exemplary damages, however described." This belated amendment not only illustrates the concern of underwriters regarding the increase in suits for punitive damages but also would appear to be a tacit admission that, without such a policy exclusion, punitive damages would be recoverable under Protection and Indemnity policies. As the Institute Protection and Indemnity form is the only form with such an exclusion, it is seldom used by shipowners and their brokers, who somewhat naturally prefer forms SP-23 and SP-38, which do not include any such exclusion. (These forms, while not official market forms, are in general use in the United States.) Nor do the major international Protection and Indemnity clubs specifically exclude punitive damages from the coverage they provide. As long as shipowners are faced with the possibility of such awards to third parties they will need and insist on complete coverage from their Protection and Indemnity insurers.

It must be noted, however, that one federal district court in Louisiana has found that Protection and Indemnity insurers are not liable for the punitive damages awarded to an injured seaman. This is on the grounds that an award for punitive damages was not an award "on account" of injury and that "by definition, punitive damages go beyond compensation for bodily injury" (*Smith* v. *Front Lawn Enterprises,* 1987 AMC 1130). No doubt sooner or later higher courts will have to come to grips with this aspect of punitive damages. Nevertheless, it is submitted that, absent any express exclusion in the policy, any award for punitive damages in respect of claims otherwise covered is payable by underwriters for the reasons given previously. However, this is, and will continue to be, a volatile subject.

To end on a more optimistic note, generally speaking and under federal maritime law, a punitive damage award is appropriate only when the act complained of is not only deliberate and unreasonable, but done with an intent to injure (actual malice). The difficulty is that very often claims involving punitive damages are brought in state courts and, bearing in mind the possible effect of *Wilburn* (*q.v.*), insurers cannot always rely on the federal maritime law standard being applied to such claims.

Marine Insurance Clauses

American Institute Hull Clauses

(June 2, 1977)

To be attached to and form a part of Policy No. .... of the ....

The terms and conditions of the following clauses are to be regarded as substituted for those of the policy form to which they are attached, the latter being hereby waived, except provisions required by law to be inserted in the Policy. All captions are inserted only for purposes of reference and shall not be used to interpret the clauses to which they apply. | 1 2 3

ASSURED

This Policy insures .... | 4 5

.... hereinafter referred to as the Assured. | 6 7 8

If claim is made under this Policy by anyone other than the Owner of the Vessel, such person shall not be entitled to recover to a greater extent than would the Owner, had claim been made by the Owner as an Assured named in this Policy.

Underwriters waive any right of subrogation against affiliated, subsidiary or interrelated companies of the Assured, provided that such waiver shall not apply in the event of a collision between the Vessel and any vessel owned, demise chartered or otherwise controlled by any of the aforesaid companies, or with respect to any loss, damage or expense against which such companies are insured.

LOSS PAYEE

Loss, if any, payable to .... | 9 10

.... or order. | 11

Provided, however, Underwriters shall pay claims to others as set forth in the Collision Liability clause and may make direct payment to persons providing security for the release of the Vessel in Salvage cases. | 12 13

VESSEL

The Subject Matter of this insurance is the Vessel called the .... or by whatsoever name or names the said Vessel is or shall be called, which for purposes of this insurance shall consist of and be limited to her hull, launches, lifeboats, rafts, furniture, bunkers, stores, supplies, tackle, fittings, equipment, apparatus, machinery, boilers, refrigerating machinery, insulation, motor generators and other electrical machinery. | 14 15 16 17

516

In the event any equipment or apparatus not owned by the Assured is installed for use on board the Vessel and the Assured has assumed responsibility therefor, it shall also be considered part of the Subject Matter and the aggregate value thereof shall be included in the Agreed Value.

Notwithstanding the foregoing, cargo containers, barges and lighters shall not be considered a part of the Subject Matter of this insurance.

DURATION OF RISK

From the .... day of .... 19 .... , ... time

to the .... day of .... 19 .... , ... time.

Should the Vessel at the expiration of this Policy be at sea, or in distress, or at a port of refuge or of call, she shall, provided previous notice be given to the Underwriters, be held covered at a pro rata monthly premium to her port of destination.

In the event of payment by the Underwriters for Total Loss of the Vessel this Policy shall thereupon automatically terminate.

AGREED VALUE

The Vessel, for so much as concerns the Assured, by agreement between the Assured and the Underwriters in this Policy, is and shall be valued at .... Dollars.

AMOUNT INSURED HEREUNDER

.... Dollars.

DEDUCTIBLE

Notwithstanding anything in this Policy to the contrary, there shall be deducted from the aggregate of all claims (including claims under the Sue and Labor clause and claims under the Collision Liability clause) arising out of each separate accident, the sum of $ .... unless the accident results in a Total Loss of the Vessel in which case this clause shall not apply. A recovery from other interests, however, shall not operate to exclude claims under this Policy provided the aggregate of such claims arising out of one separate accident if unreduced by such recovery exceeds that sum. For the purpose of this clause each accident shall be treated separately, but it is agreed that (a) a sequence of damages arising from the same accident shall be treated as due to that accident and (b) all heavy weather damage, or damage caused by contact with floating ice, which occurs during a single sea passage between two successive ports shall be treated as though due to one accident.

PREMIUM

The Underwriters to be paid in consideration of this insurance .... Dollars being at the annual rate of .... per cent., which premium shall be due on attachment. If the Vessel is insured under this Policy for a period of less than one year at pro rata of the annual rate, full annual premium shall be considered earned and immediately due and payable in the event of Total Loss of the Vessel.

RETURNS OF PREMIUM

Premium returnable as follows:

Pro rata daily net in the event of termination under the Change of Ownership clause;

Pro rata monthly net for each uncommenced month if it be mutually agreed to cancel this Policy;

For each period of 30 consecutive days the Vessel may be laid up in port for account of the Assured,

.... cents per cent. net not under repair, or

.... cents per cent. net under repair;

provided always that

(a) a Total Loss of the Vessel has not occurred during the currency of this Policy;

(b) in no case shall a return for lay-up be allowed when the Vessel is lying in exposed or unprotected waters or in any location not approved by the Underwriters;

(c) in the event of any amendment of the annual rate, the above rates of return shall be adjusted accordingly;

(d) in no case shall a return be allowed when the Vessel is used as a storage ship or for lightering purposes.

If the Vessel is laid up for a period of 30 consecutive days, a part only of which attaches under this Policy, the Underwriters shall pay such proportion of the return due in respect of a full period of 30 days attaching hereto bears to 30. Should the lay-up period exceed 30 consecutive days, the Assured shall have the option to elect the period of 30 consecutive days for which a return is recoverable.

NON-PAYMENT OF PREMIUM

In event of non-payment of premium 30 days after attachment, or of any additional premium when due, this Policy may be cancelled by the Underwriters upon 10 days written or telegraphic notice sent to the Assured at his last known address or in care of the broker who negotiated this Policy. Such proportion of the premium, however, as shall have been earned up to the time of cancellation shall be payable. In the event of Total Loss of the Vessel occurring prior to any cancellation or termination of this Policy full annual premium shall be considered earned.

ADVENTURE

Beginning the adventure upon the Vessel, as above, and so shall continue and endure during the period aforesaid, as employment may offer, in port or at sea, in docks and graving docks, and on ways, gridirons and pontoons, at all times, in all places, and on all occasions, services and trades; with leave to sail or navigate with or without pilots, to go on trial trips and to assist and tow vessels or craft in distress, but the Vessel may not be towed, except as is customary or when in need of assistance, nor shall the Vessel render assistance or undertake towage or salvage services under contract previously arranged by the Assured, the Owners, the Managers or the Charterers of the Vessel, nor shall the Vessel, in the course of trading operations, engage in loading or discharging cargo at sea, from or into another vessel other than a barge, lighter or similar craft used principally in harbors or inland waters. The phrase "engage in loading or discharging cargo at sea" shall include while approaching, leaving or alongside, or while another vessel is approaching, leaving or alongside the Vessel.

The Vessel is held covered in case of any breach of conditions as to cargo, trade, locality, towage or salvage activities, or date of sailing, or loading or discharging cargo at sea, provided (a) notice is given to the Underwriters immediately following receipt of knowledge thereof by the Assured, and (b) any amended terms of cover and any additional premium required by the Underwriters are agreed to by the Assured.

PERILS

Touching the Adventures and Perils which the Underwriters are contented to bear and take upon themselves, they are of the Seas, Men-of-War, Fire, Lightning, Earthquake, Enemies, Pirates, Rovers, Assailing Thieves, Jettisons, Letters of Mart and Counter-Mart, Surprisals, Takings at Sea, Arrests, Restraints and Detainments of all Kings, Princes and Peoples, of what nation, condition or quality soever, Barratry of the Master and Mariners and of all other like Perils, Losses and Misfortunes that have or shall come to the Hurt, Detriment or Damage of the Vessel, or any part thereof, excepting, however, such of the foregoing perils as may be excluded by provisions elsewhere in the Policy or by endorsement thereon.

ADDITIONAL PERILS (INCHMAREE)

Subject to the conditions of this Policy, this insurance also covers loss of or damage to the Vessel directly caused by the following:

Accidents in loading, discharging or handling cargo, or in bunkering;

Accidents in going on or off, or while on drydocks, graving docks, ways, gridirons or pontoons;

Explosions on shipboard or elsewhere;

Breakdown of motor generators or other electrical machinery and electrical connections thereto, bursting of boilers, breakage of shafts, or any latent defect in the machinery or hull, (excluding the cost and expense of replacing or repairing the defective part);

Breakdown of or accidents to nuclear installations or reactors not on board the insured Vessel;

Contact with aircraft, rockets or similar missiles, or with any land conveyance;

Negligence of Charterers and/or Repairers, provided such Charterers and/or Repairers are not an Assured hereunder;

Negligence of Masters, Officers, Crew or Pilots;

provided such loss or damage has not resulted from want of due diligence by the Assured, the Owners or Managers of the Vessel, or any of them. Masters, Officers, Crew or Pilots are not to be considered Owners within the meaning of this clause should they hold shares in the Vessel.

DELIBERATE DAMAGE (POLLUTION HAZARD)

Subject to the conditions of this Policy, this insurance also covers loss of or damage to the Vessel directly caused by governmental authorities acting for the public welfare to prevent or mitigate a pollution hazard, or threat thereof, resulting directly from damage to the Vessel for which the Underwriters are liable under this Policy, provided such act of governmental authorities has not resulted from want of due diligence by the Assured, the Owners, or Managers of the Vessel or any of them to prevent or mitigate such hazard or threat. Masters, Officers, Crew or Pilots are not to be considered Owners within the meaning of this clause should they hold shares in the Vessel.

CLAIMS (GENERAL PROVISIONS)

In the event of any accident or occurrence which could give rise to a claim under this Policy, prompt notice thereof shall be given to the Underwriters, and:

(a) where practicable, the Underwriters shall be advised prior to survey, so that they may appoint their own surveyor, if they so desire;

(b) the Underwriters shall be entitled to decide where the Vessel shall proceed for docking and/or repair (allowance to be made to the Assured for the actual additional expense of the voyage arising from compliance with the Underwriters' requirement);

(c) the Underwriters shall have the right of veto in connection with any repair firm proposed;

(d) the Underwriters may take tenders, or may require in writing that tenders be taken for the repair of the Vessel, in which event, upon acceptance of a tender with the approval of the Underwriters, an allowance shall be made at the rate of 30 per cent. per annum on the amount insured, for each day or pro rata for part of a day, for time lost between the issuance of invitations to tender and the acceptance of a tender, to the extent that such time is lost solely as the result of tenders having been taken and provided the tender is accepted without delay after receipt of the Underwriters' approval.

Due credit shall be given against the allowances in (b) and (d) above for any amount recovered:

(1) in respect of fuel, stores, and wages and maintenance of the Master, Officers or Crew allowed in General or Particular Average;

(2) from third parties in respect of damages for detention and/or loss of profit and/or running expenses;

for the period covered by the allowances or any part thereof.

No claim shall be allowed in Particular Average for wages and maintenance of the Master, Officers or Crew, except when incurred solely for the necessary removal of the Vessel from one port to another for average repairs or for trial trips to test average repairs, in which cases wages and maintenance will be allowed only while the Vessel is under way. This exclusion shall not apply to overtime or similar extraordinary payments to the Master, Officers or Crew incurred in shifting the Vessel for tank cleaning or repairs or while specifically engaged in these activities, either in port or at sea.

General and Particular Average shall be payable without deduction, new for old.

The expense of sighting the bottom after stranding shall be paid, if reasonably incurred especially for that purpose, even if no damage be found.

No claim shall in any case be allowed in respect of scraping or painting the Vessel's bottom.

In the event of loss or damage to equipment or apparatus not owned by the Assured but installed for use on board the Vessel and for which the Assured has assumed responsibility, claim shall not exceed (1) the amount the Underwriters would pay if the Assured were owner of such equipment or apparatus, or (2) the contractual responsibility assumed by the Assured to the owners or lessors thereof, whichever shall be less.

No claim for unrepaired damages shall be allowed, except to the extent that the aggregate damage caused by perils insured against during the period of the Policy and left unrepaired at the expiration of the Policy shall be demonstrated by the Assured to have diminished the actual market value of the Vessel on that date if undamaged by such perils.

GENERAL AVERAGE AND SALVAGE

General Average and Salvage shall be payable as provided in the contract of affreightment, or failing such provision or there be no contract of affreightment, payable at the Assured's election either in accordance with York-Antwerp Rules 1950 or 1974 or with the Laws and Usages of the Port of New York. Provided always that when an adjustment according to the laws and usages of the port of destination is properly demanded by the owners of the cargo, General Average shall be paid accordingly.

In the event of salvage, towage or other assistance being rendered to the Vessel by any vessel belonging in part or in whole to the same Owners or Charterers, the value of such services (without regard to the common ownership or control of the vessels) shall be ascertained by arbitration in the manner provided for under the Collision Liability clause in this Policy, and the amount so awarded so far as applicable to the interest hereby insured shall constitute a charge under this Policy.

When the contributory value of the Vessel is greater than the Agreed Value herein, the liability of the Underwriters for General Average contribution (except in respect to amounts made good to the Vessel), or Salvage, shall not exceed that proportion of the total contribution due from the Vessel which the amount insured hereunder bears to the contributory value, and if, because of damage for which the Underwriters are liable as Particular Average, the value of the Vessel has been reduced for the purpose of contribution, the amount of such Particular Average damage recoverable under this Policy shall first be deducted from the amount insured hereunder, and the Underwriters shall then be liable only for the proportion which such net amount bears to the contributory value.

TOTAL LOSS

In ascertaining whether the Vessel is a constructive Total Loss the Agreed Value shall be taken as the repaired value and nothing in respect of the damaged or break-up value of the Vessel or wreck shall be taken into account.

There shall be no recovery for a constructive Total Loss hereunder unless the expense of recovering and repairing the Vessel would exceed the Agreed Value. In making this determination, only expenses incurred or to be incurred by reason of a single accident or a sequence of damages arising from the same accident shall be taken into account, but expenses incurred prior to tender of abandonment shall not be considered if such are to be claimed separately under the Sue and Labor clause.

In the event of Total Loss (actual or constructive), no claim to be made by the Underwriters for freight, whether notice of abandonment has been given or not.

In no case shall the Underwriters be liable for unrepaired damage in addition to a subsequent Total Loss sustained during the period covered by this Policy.

SUE AND LABOR

And in case of any Loss or Misfortune, it shall be lawful and necessary for the Assured, their Factors, Servants and Assigns, to sue, labor and travel for, in, and about the defense, safeguard and recovery of the Vessel, or any part thereof, without prejudice to this insurance, to the charges whereof the Underwriters will contribute their proportion as provided below. And it is expressly declared and agreed that no acts of the Underwriters or Assured in recovering, saving or preserving the Vessel shall be considered as a waiver or acceptance of abandonment.

In the event of expenditure under the Sue and Labor clause, the Underwriters shall pay the proportion of such expenses that the amount insured hereunder bears to the Agreed Value, or that the amount insured hereunder (less loss and/or damage payable under this Policy) bears to the actual value of the salved property, whichever proportion shall be less; provided always that their liability for such expenses shall not exceed their proportionate part of the Agreed Value.

If claim for Total Loss is admitted under this Policy and sue and labor expenses have been reasonably incurred in excess of any proceeds realized or value recovered, the amount payable under this Policy will be the proportion of such excess that the amount insured hereunder (without deduction for loss or damage) bears to the Agreed Value or to the sound value of the Vessel at the time of the accident, whichever value was greater; provided always that Underwriters' liability for such expenses shall not exceed their proportionate part of the Agreed Value. The foregoing shall also apply to expenses reasonably incurred in salving or attempting to salve the Vessel and other property to the extent that such expenses shall be regarded as having been incurred in respect of the Vessel.

COLLISION LIABILITY

And it is further agreed that:
(a) if the Vessel shall come into collision with any other ship or vessel, and the Assured or the Surety in consequence of the Vessel being at fault shall become liable to pay and shall pay by way of damages to any other person or persons any sum or sums in respect of such collision, the Underwriters will pay the Assured or the Surety, whichever shall have paid, such proportion of such sum or sums so paid as their respective subscriptions hereto bear to the Agreed Value, provided always that their liability in respect to any one such collision shall not exceed their proportionate part of the Agreed Value;

132
133
134
135
136
137
138
139
140
141
142
143
144
145
146
147
148
149
150
151
152
153
154
155
156
157
158
159
160
161
162
163

(b) in cases where, with the consent in writing of a majority (in amount) of Hull Underwriters, the liability of the Vessel has been contested, or proceedings have been taken to limit liability, the Underwriters will also pay a like proportion of the costs which the Assured shall thereby incur or be compelled to pay.

When both vessels are to blame, then, unless the liability of the owners or charterers of one or both such vessels becomes limited by law, claims under the Collision Liability clause shall be settled on the principle of Cross-Liabilities as if the owners or charterers of each vessel had been compelled to pay to the owners or charterers of the other of such vessels such one-half or other proportion of the latter's damages as may have been properly allowed in ascertaining the balance or sum payable by or to the Assured in consequence of such collision.

The principles involved in this clause shall apply to the case where both vessels are the property, in part or in whole, of the same owners or charterers, all questions of responsibility and amount of liability as between the two vessels being left to the decision of a single Arbitrator, if the parties can agree upon a single Arbitrator, or failing such agreement, to the decision of Arbitrators, one to be appointed by the Assured and one to be appointed by the majority (in amount) of Hull Underwriters interested; the two Arbitrators chosen to choose a third Arbitrator before entering upon the reference, and the decision of such single Arbitrator, or of any two of such three Arbitrators, appointed as above, to be final and binding.

Provided always that this clause shall in no case extend to any sum which the Assured or the Surety may become liable to pay or shall pay in consequence of, or with respect to:

(a) removal or disposal of obstructions, wrecks or their cargoes under statutory powers or otherwise pursuant to law;

(b) injury to real or personal property of every description;

(c) the discharge, spillage, emission or leakage of oil, petroleum products, chemicals or other substances of any kind or description whatsoever;

(d) cargo or other property on or the engagements of the Vessel;

(e) loss of life, personal injury or illness.

Provided further that exclusions (b) and (c) above shall not apply to injury to other vessels or property thereon except to the extent that such injury arises out of any action taken to avoid, minimize or remove any discharge, spillage, emission or leakage described in (c) above.

PILOTAGE AND TOWAGE

This insurance shall not be prejudiced by reason of any contract limiting in whole or in part the liability of pilots, tugs, towboats, or their owners when the Assured or the agent of the Assured accepts such contract in accordance with established local practice.

Where in accordance with such practice, pilotage or towage services are provided under contracts requiring the Assured or the agent of the Assured:

(a) to assume liability for damage resulting from collision of the Vessel insured with any other ship or vessel, including the towing vessel, or

(b) to indemnify those providing the pilotage or towage services against loss or liability for any such damages,

it is agreed that amounts paid by the Assured or Surety pursuant to such assumed obligations shall be deemed payments "by way of damages to any other person or persons" and to have been paid "in consequence of the Vessel being at fault" within the meaning of the Collision Liability clause in this Policy to the extent that such payments would have been covered if the Vessel had been legally responsible in the absence of any agreement. Provided always that in no event shall the aggregate amount of liability of the Underwriters under the Collision Liability clause, including this clause, be greater than the amount of any statutory limitation of liability to which owners are entitled or would be entitled if liability under any contractual obligation referred to in this clause were included among the liabilities subject to such statutory limitations.

522

CHANGE OF OWNERSHIP

In the event of any change, voluntary or otherwise, in the ownership or flag of the Vessel, or if the Vessel be placed under new management, or be chartered on a bareboat basis or requisitioned on that basis, or if the Classification Society of the Vessel or her class therein be changed, cancelled or withdrawn, then, unless the Underwriters agree thereto in writing, this Policy shall automatically terminate at the time of such change of ownership, flag, management, charter, requisition or classification; provided, however, that:

(a) if the Vessel has cargo on board and has already sailed from her loading port, or is at sea in ballast, such automatic termination shall, if required, be deferred until arrival at final port of discharge if with cargo, or at port of destination if in ballast;

(b) in the event of an involuntary temporary transfer by requisition or otherwise, without the prior execution of a written agreement by the Assured, such automatic termination shall occur fifteen days after such transfer.

This insurance shall not inure to the benefit of any transferee or charterer of the Vessel and, if a loss payable hereunder should occur between the time of change or transfer and any deferred automatic termination, the Underwriters shall be subrogated to all of the rights of the Assured against the transferee or charterer in respect of all or part of such loss as is recoverable from the, transferee or charterer, and in the proportion which the amount insured hereunder bears to the Agreed Value.

The term "new management" as used above refers only to the transfer of the management of the Vessel from one firm or corporation to another, and it shall not apply to any internal changes within the offices of the Assured.

ADDITIONAL INSURANCES

It is a condition of this Policy that no additional insurance against the risk of Total Loss of the Vessel shall be effected to operate during the currency of this Policy by or for account of the Assured, Owners, Managers, Operators or Mortgagees except on the interests and up to the amounts enumerated in the following Sections (a) to (g), inclusive, and no such insurance shall be subject to P.P.I., F.I.A. or other like term on any interests whatsoever excepting those enumerated in Section (a); provided always and notwithstanding the limitation on recovery in the Assured clause a breach of this condition shall not afford the Underwriters any defense to a claim by a Mortgagee who has accepted this Policy without knowledge of such breach:

(a) DISBURSEMENTS, MANAGERS' COMMISSIONS, PROFITS OR EXCESS OR INCREASED VALUE OF HULL AND MACHINERY, AND/OR SIMILAR INTERESTS HOWEVER DESCRIBED, AND FREIGHT (INCLUDING CHARTERED FREIGHT OR ANTICIPATED FREIGHT) INSURED FOR TIME. An amount not exceeding in the aggregate 25% of the Agreed Value.

(b) FREIGHT OR HIRE, UNDER CONTRACTS FOR VOYAGE. An amount not exceeding the gross freight or hire for the current cargo passage and next succeeding cargo passage (such insurance to include, if required, a preliminary and an intermediate ballast passage) plus the charges of insurance. In the case of a voyage charter where payment is made on a time basis, the amount shall be calculated on the estimated duration of the voyage, subject to the limitation of two cargo passages as laid down herein. Any amount permitted under this Section shall be reduced, as the freight or hire is earned, by the gross amount so earned. Any freight or hire to be earned under the form of Charters described in (d) below shall not be permitted under this Section (b) if any part thereof is insured as permitted under said Section (d).

(c) ANTICIPATED FREIGHT IF THE VESSEL SAILS IN BALLAST AND NOT UNDER CHARTER. An amount not exceeding the anticipated gross freight on next cargo passage, such amount to be reasonably estimated on the basis of the current rate of freight at time of insurance, plus the charges of insurance. Provided, however, that no insurance shall be permitted by this Section if any insurance is effected as permitted under Section (b).

(d) TIME CHARTER HIRE OR CHARTER HIRE FOR SERIES OF VOYAGES. An amount not exceeding 50% of the gross hire which is to be earned under the charter in a period not exceeding 18 months. Any amount permitted under this Section shall be reduced as the hire is earned under the charter by 50% of the gross amount so earned but, where the charter is for a period exceeding 18 months, the amount insured need not be reduced while it does not exceed 50% of the gross hire still to be earned under the charter. An insurance permitted by this Section may begin on the signing of the charter.

(e) PREMIUMS. An amount not exceeding the actual premiums of all interest insured for a period not exceeding 12 months (excluding premiums insured as permitted under the foregoing Sections but including, if required, the premium or estimated calls on any Protection and Indemnity or War Risks and Strikes insurance) reducing pro rata monthly.

(f) RETURNS OF PREMIUM. An amount not exceeding the actual returns which are recoverable subject to "and arrival" or equivalent provision under any policy of insurance.

(g) INSURANCE IRRESPECTIVE OF AMOUNT AGAINST:—Risks excluded by War, Strikes and Related Exclusions clause; risks enumerated in the American Institute War Risks and Strikes Clauses; and General Average and Salvage Disbursements.

WAR STRIKES AND RELATED EXCLUSIONS

The following conditions shall be paramount and shall supersede and nullify any contrary provisions of the Policy.

This Policy does not cover any loss, damage or expense caused by, resulting from, or incurred as a consequence of:

(a) Capture, seizure, arrest, restraint or detainment, or any attempt thereat; or

(b) Any taking of the Vessel, by requisition or otherwise, whether in time of peace or war and whether lawful or otherwise; or

(c) Any mine, bomb or torpedo not carried as cargo on board the Vessel; or

(d) Any weapon of war employing atomic or nuclear fission and/or fusion or other like reaction or radioactive force or matter; or

(e) Civil war, revolution, rebellion, insurrection, or civil strife arising therefrom, or piracy; or

(f) Strikes, lockouts, political or labor disturbances, civil commotions, riots, martial law, military or usurped power; or

(g) Malicious acts or vandalism, unless committed by the Master or Mariners and not excluded elsewhere under this War Strikes and Related Exclusions clause; or

(h) Hostilities or warlike operations (whether there be a declaration of war or not) but this subparagraph (h) not to exclude collision or contact with aircraft, rockets or similar missiles, or with any fixed or floating object, or stranding, heavy weather, fire or explosion unless caused directly by a hostile act by or against a belligerent power which act is independent of the nature of the voyage or service which the Vessel concerned or, in the case of a collision, any other vessel involved therein, is performing. As used herein, "power" includes any authority maintaining, naval, military or air forces in association with a power.

If war risks or other risks excluded by this clause are hereafter insured by endorsement on this Policy, such endorsement shall supersede the above conditions only to the extent that the terms of such endorsement are inconsistent therewith and only while such endorsement remains in force.

230
231
232
233
234
235
236
237
238

239
240
241
242
243
244
245
246
247
248
249
250
251
252
253
254
255

American Institute

INCREASED VALUE AND EXCESS LIABILITIES CLAUSES
(November 3, 1977)

To be attached to and form a part of Policy No. .... of the ....

The terms and conditions of the following clauses are to be regarded as substituted for those of the policy form to which they are attached, the latter being hereby waived, except provisions required by law to be inserted in the Policy. All captions are inserted only for purposes of reference and shall not be used to interpret the clauses to which they apply.

ASSURED

This Policy insures .... hereinafter referred to as the Assured.

If claim is made under this Policy by anyone other than the Owner of the Vessel, such person shall not be entitled to recover to a greater extent than would the Owner, had claim been made by the Owner as an Assured named in this Policy.

Underwriters waive any right of subrogation against affiliated, subsidiary or interrelated companies of the Assured, provided that such waiver shall not apply in the event of a collision between the Vessel and any vessel owned, demise chartered or otherwise controlled by any of the aforesaid companies, or with respect to any loss, damage or expense against which such companies are insured.

This insurance shall not be prejudiced by reason of any contract limiting in whole or in part the liability of pilots, tugs, towboats, or their owners when the Assured or the Agent of the Assured accepts such contract in accordance with established local practice.

LOSS PAYEE

Loss, if any, payable to .... or order.

Provided, however, Underwriters shall pay claims to others as set forth in the Collision Liability clause and may make direct payment to persons providing security for the release of the Vessel in Salvage cases.

On **INCREASED VALUE AND EXCESS LIABILITIES** of the Vessel called the ....
(or by whatsoever name or names the said Vessel is or shall be called).

	Line
	1
	2
	3
	4
	5
	6
	7
	8
	9
	10
	11
	12
	13
	14
	15
	16
	17

AMOUNT INSURED HEREUNDER

.... Dollars.

DURATION OF RISK

From the .... day of .... 19......, ... time

to the .... day of .... 19......, ... time.

Should the Vessel at the expiration of this Policy be at sea, or in distress, or at a port of refuge or of call, she shall, provided previous notice be given to the Underwriters, be held covered at a pro rata monthly premium to her port of destination.

In the event of payment by the Underwriters for Total Loss of the Vessel this Policy shall thereupon automatically terminate.

PREMIUM

The Underwriters to be paid in consideration of this insurance ....

.... Dollars being at the annual rate of .... per cent, which premium shall be due on attachment. If the Vessel is insured under this Policy for a period of less than one year at pro rata of the annual rate, full annual premium shall be considered earned and immediately due and payable in the event of Total Loss of the Vessel.

RETURNS OF PREMIUMS

Premium returnable as follows:

Pro rata daily net in the event of termination under the Change of Ownership clause;

Pro rata monthly net for each uncommenced month if it be mutually agreed to cancel this Policy;

For each period of 30 consecutive days the Vessel may be laid up in port for account of the Assured,

.... cents per cent. net not under repair, or

.... cents per cent. net under repair;

provided always that:

(a) A Total Loss of the Vessel has not occurred during the currency of this Policy;

(b) In no case shall a return for lay-up be allowed when the Vessel is lying exposed or unprotected waters or in any location not approved by the Underwriters;

(c) In the event of any amendment of the annual rate, the above rates of return shall be adjusted accordingly;

(d) In no case shall a return be allowed when the Vessel is used as a storage ship or for lightering purposes.

If the Vessel is laid up for a period of 30 consecutive days, a part only of which attaches under this Policy, the Underwriters shall pay such proportion of the return due in respect of a full period of 30 days as the number of days attaching hereto bears to 30. Should the lay-up period exceed 30 consecutive days, the Assured shall have the option to elect the period of 30 consecutive days for which a return is recoverable.

NON-PAYMENT OF PREMIUM

In event of non-payment of premium 30 days after attachment, or of any additional premium when due, this Policy may be cancelled by the Underwriters upon 10 days written or telegraphic notice sent to the Assured at his last known address or in care of the broker who negotiated this Policy. Such proportion of the premium, however, as shall have been earned up to the time of cancellation shall be payable. In the event of Total Loss of the Vessel occurring prior to any cancellation or termination of this Policy full annual premium shall be considered earned.

ADVENTURE

Beginning the adventure upon the Vessel, as above, and so shall continue and endure during the period aforesaid, as employment may offer, in port or at sea, in docks and graving docks, and on ways, gridirons and pontoons, at all times, in all places, and on all occasions, services and trades; with leave to sail or navigate with or without pilots, to go on trial trips and to assist and tow vessels or craft in distress, but the Vessel may not be towed, except as is customary or when in need of assistance, nor shall the Vessel render assistance or undertake towage or salvage services under contract previously arranged by the Assured, the Owners, the Managers or the Charterers of the Vessel, nor shall the Vessel, in the course of trading operations, engage in loading or discharging cargo at sea, from or into another vessel other than a barge, lighter or similar craft used principally in harbors or inland waters. The phrase "engage in loading or discharging cargo at sea" shall include while approaching, leaving or alongside, or while another vessel is approaching, leaving or alongside the Vessel.

The Vessel is held covered in case of any breach of conditions as to cargo, trade, locality, towage or salvage activities, date of sailing, or loading or discharging cargo at sea, provided (a) notice is given to the Underwriters immediately following receipt of knowledge thereof by the Assured, and (b) any amended terms of cover and any additional premium required by the Underwriters are agreed to by the Assured.

COVERAGE

This insurance covers only:

(1) **TOTAL LOSS (ACTUAL OR CONSTRUCTIVE) OF THE VESSEL** directly caused by Perils of the Seas, Men-of-War, Fire, Lightning, Earthquake, Enemies, Pirates, Rovers, Assailing Thieves, Jettisons, Letters of Mart and Counter-Mart, Surprisals, Takings at Sea, Arrests, Restraints and Detainments of all Kings, Princes and Peoples, of what nation, condition or quality soever, Barratry of the Master and Mariners and of all other like Perils, Losses and Misfortunes that have or shall come to the Hurt, Detriment or Damage of the Vessel, or any part thereof, excepting, however, such of the foregoing perils as may be excluded by provisions elsewhere in the Policy or by endorsement thereon. It shall also cover Total Loss (actual or constructive) directly caused by the following:--

Accidents in loading, discharging or handling cargo, or in bunkering;

Accidents in going on or off, or while on drydocks, graving docks, ways, gridirons or pontoons;

Explosions on shipboard or elsewhere;

Breakdown of motor generators or other electrical machinery and electrical connections thereto, bursting of boilers, breakage of shafts, or any latent defect in the machinery or hull, (excluding the cost and expense of replacing or repairing the defective part);

43
44
45
46

47
48
49
50
51
52
53
54

55
56
57

58
59
60
61
62
63

64
65
66
67
68
69

Breakdown of or accidents to nuclear installations or reactors not on board the insured Vessel;

Contact with aircraft, rockets or similar missiles, or with any land conveyance;

Negligence of Charterers and/or Repairers, provided such Charterers and/or Repairers are not an Assured hereunder;

Negligence of Masters, Officers, Crew or Pilots;

provided such loss or damage has not resulted from want of due diligence by the Assured, the Owners or Managers of the Vessel, or any of them. Masters, Officers, Crew or Pilots are not to be considered Owners within the meaning of this clause should they hold shares in the Vessel.

Subject to the conditions of this Policy, this insurance also covers Total Loss (actual or constructive) of the Vessel directly caused by governmental authorities acting for the public welfare to prevent or mitigate a pollution hazard, or threat thereof, resulting directly from damage to the Vessel for which the Underwriters are liable under this Policy, provided such act of governmental authorities has not resulted from want of due diligence by the Assured, the Owners, or Managers of the Vessel or any of them to prevent or mitigate such hazard or threat. Masters, Officers, Crew or Pilots are not to be considered Owners within the meaning of this clause should they hold shares in the Vessel.

In ascertaining whether the Vessel is a constructive Total Loss the Agreed Value in the policies on Hull and Machinery shall be taken as the repaired value and nothing in respect of the damaged or break-up value of the Vessel or wreck shall be taken into account.

There shall be no recovery for a constructive Total Loss hereunder unless the expense of recovering and repairing the Vessel would exceed the Agreed Value in policies on Hull and Machinery. In making this determination, only expenses incurred or to be incurred by reason of a single accident or a sequence of damages arising from the same accident shall be taken into account, but expenses incurred prior to tender of abandonment shall not be considered if such are to be claimed separately under the Sue and Labor clause in said policies.

Provided that the policies on Hull and Machinery contain the above clauses with respect to the method of ascertaining whether the Vessel is a constructive Total Loss (or clauses having a similar effect), the settlement of a claim for Total Loss under the policies on Hull and Machinery shall be accepted as proof of the Total Loss of the Vessel under this Policy; and in the event of a claim for Total Loss being settled under the policies on Hull and Machinery as a compromised total loss, the amount payable hereunder shall be the same percentage of the amount hereby insured as the percentage paid on the amount insured under said policies.

Should the Vessel be a constructive Total Loss but the claim on the policies on Hull and Machinery be settled as a claim for partial loss, no payment shall be due under this Section (1).

Full interest admitted; the Policy being deemed sufficient proof of interest.

In the event of Total Loss, the Underwriters waive interest in any proceeds from the sale or other disposition of the Vessel or wreck.

(2) **GENERAL AVERAGE AND SALVAGE** not recoverable in full under the policies on Hull and Machinery by reason of the difference between the Agreed Value of the Vessel as stated therein (or any reduced value arising from the deduction therefrom in process of adjustment of any claim which law or practice or the terms of the policies covering Hull and Machinery may have required) and the value of the Vessel adopted for the purpose of contribution to General Average or Salvage, the liability under this Policy being for such proportion of the amount not recoverable as the amount insured hereunder bears to the said difference or to the total amount insured against excess liabilities if it exceed such difference.

70
71
72
73
74
75
76
77
78
79
80
81
82
83
84
85
86
87
88
89
90
91
92
93
94
95
96
97
98
99
100

(3) **SUE AND LABOR CHARGES** not recoverable in full under the policies on Hull and Machinery by reason of the difference between the Agreed Value of the Vessel as stated therein (or any reduced value arising from the deduction therefrom of any claim which the terms of the policies covering Hull and Machinery may have required) and the value of the Vessel adopted for the purpose of ascertaining the amount recoverable under the policies on Hull and Machinery, the liability under this Policy being for such proportion of the amount not recoverable as the amount insured hereunder bears to the said difference or to the total amount insured against excess liabilities if it exceed such difference.

(4) **COLLISION LIABILITY** (Including Costs) not recoverable in full under the Collision Liability clause (including the Pilotage and Towage extension) in the policies on Hull and Machinery by reason of such liability exceeding the Agreed Value of the Vessel as stated therein, in which case the amount recoverable under this Policy shall be such proportion of the difference so arising as the amount hereby insured bears to the total amount insured against excess liabilities.

Underwriters' liability under (1), (2), (3) and (4) is separate and shall not exceed the amount insured hereunder in any one section in respect of any one claim.

NOTICE OF CLAIM

When it becomes evident that any accident or occurrence could give rise to a claim under this Policy, prompt notice thereof shall be given to the Underwriters.

CHANGE OF OWNERSHIP

In the event of any change, voluntary or otherwise, in the ownership or flag of the Vessel, or if the Vessel be placed under new management, or be chartered on a bareboat basis or requisitioned on that basis, or if the Classification Society of the Vessel or her class therein be changed, cancelled or withdrawn, then, unless the Underwriters agree thereto in writing, this Policy shall automatically terminate at the time of such change of ownership, flag, management, charter, requisition or classification; provided however, that:

(a) if the Vessel has cargo on board and has already sailed from her loading port, or is at sea in ballast, such automatic termination shall, if required, be deferred until arrival at final port of discharge if with cargo, or at port of destination if in ballast;

(b) in the event of an involuntary temporary transfer by requisition or otherwise, without the prior execution of a written agreement by the Assured, such automatic termination shall occur fifteen days after such transfer.

This insurance shall not inure to the benefit of any transferee or charterer of the Vessel and, if a loss payable hereunder should occur between the time of change or transfer and any deferred automatic termination, the Underwriters shall be subrogated to all of the rights of the Assured against the transferee or charterer in respect of all or part of such loss as is recoverable from the transferee or charterer, and in the proportion which the amount insured hereunder bears to the Agreed Value.

The term "new management" as used above refers only to the transfer of the management of the Vessel from one firm or corporation to another, and it shall not apply to any internal changes within the offices of the Assured.

101
102
103
104
105
106
107
108
109
110
111
112
113
114
115
116
117
118
119
120
121
122
123
124
125
126
127

WAR, STRIKES AND RELATED EXCLUSIONS

The following conditions shall be paramount and shall supersede and nullify any contrary provisions of the Policy.   128

This Policy does not cover any loss, damage or expense caused by, resulting from, or incurred as a consequence of: 129

(a) Capture, seizure, arrest, restraint or detainment, or any attempt thereat; or   130

(b) Any taking of the Vessel, by requisition or otherwise, whether in time of peace or war and whether lawful or otherwise; or   131

(c) Any mine, bomb or torpedo not carried as cargo on board the Vessel; or   132

(d) Any weapon of war employing atomic or nuclear fission and or fusion or other like reaction or radioactive force or matter; or   133

(e) Civil war, revolution, rebellion, insurrection, or civil strife arising therefrom, or piracy; or   134

(f) Strikes, lockouts, political or labor disturbances, civil commotions, riots, martial law, military or usurped power; or 135

(g) Malicious acts or vandalism, unless committed by the Master or Mariners and not excluded elsewhere under this War Strikes and Related Exclusions clause; or   136, 137

(h) Hostilities or warlike operations (whether there be a declaration of war or not) but this subparagraph (h) not to exclude collision or contact with aircraft, rockets or similar missiles, or with any fixed or floating object, or stranding, heavy weather, fire or explosion unless caused directly by a hostile act by or against a belligerent power which act is independent of the nature of the voyage or service which the Vessel concerned or, in the case of a collision, any other vessel involved therein, is performing. As used herein "power" includes any authority maintaining naval, military or air forces in association with a power.   138, 139, 140, 141, 142

If war risks or other risks excluded by this clause are hereafter insured by endorsement on this Policy, such endorsement shall supersede the above conditions only to the extent that the terms of such endorsement are inconsistent therewith and only while such endorsement remains in force.   143, 144

American Institute

Hull War Risks and Strikes Clauses

(Including Automatic Termination and Cancellation Provisions)

For Attachment to American Institute Hull Clauses

December 1, 1977

To be attached to and form a part of Policy No. .... of the ....
....

This insurance, subject to the exclusions set forth herein, covers only those risks which would be covered by the attached Policy (including collision liability) in the absence of the WAR, STRIKES AND RELATED EXCLUSIONS clause contained therein but which are excluded thereby and which risks shall be construed as also including: 1

1. Any mine, bomb or torpedo not carried as cargo on board the Vessel; 2

2. Any weapon of war employing atomic or nuclear fission and/or fusion or other like reaction or radioactive force or matter; 3

3. Civil war, revolution, rebellion, insurrection, or civil strife arising therefrom; 4

4. Strikes, lockouts, political or labor disturbances, civil commotions, riots, martial law, military or usurped power; 5

5. Malicious acts or vandalism to the extent only that such risks are not covered by the attached Policy; 6

6. Hostilities or warlike operations (whether there be a declaration of war or not) but this paragraph (6) shall not include collision or contact with aircraft, rockets or similar missiles, or with any fixed or floating object, or stranding, heavy weather, fire or explosion unless caused directly by a hostile act by or against a belligerent power which act is independent of the nature of the voyage or service which the Vessel concerned or, in the case of 7

8

9

10

11

12

13

14

15

a collision, any other vessel involved therein, is performing. As used herein, "power" includes any authority maintaining naval, military or air forces in association with a power.

EXCLUSIONS

This insurance does not cover any loss, damage or expense caused by, resulting from, or incurred as a consequence of:

a. Any hostile detonation of any weapon of war described above in paragraph (2);

b. Outbreak of war (whether there be a declaration of war or not) between any of the following countries: United States of America, United Kingdom, France, the Union of Soviet Socialist Republics or the People's Republic of China;

c. Delay or demurrage;

d. Requisition or preemption;

e. Arrest, restraint or detainment under customs or quarantine regulations and similar arrests, restraints or detainments not arising from actual or impending hostilities;

f. Capture, seizure, arrest, restraint, detainment, or confiscation by the Government of the United States or of the country in which the Vessel is owned or registered.

HELD COVERED AND OTHER PROVISIONS

The held covered clause appearing under the heading ADVENTURE in the attached Policy is deleted and the following clause substituted therefore:—

"Subject to the provisions of the Automatic Termination and Cancellation Clauses below, held covered in the event of any breach of conditions as to loading or discharging of cargo at sea, or towage or salvage activities provided (a) notice is given to the Underwriters immediately following receipt of knowledge thereof by the Assured, and (b) any amended terms of cover and any additional premium required by the Underwriters are agreed to by the Assured."

If at the natural expiry time of this insurance the Vessel is at sea, this insurance will be extended, provided previous notice be given to the Underwriters, for an additional premium at a rate to be named by the Underwriters, until midnight Local Time of the day on which the Vessel enters the next port to which she proceeds and for 24 hours thereafter, but

in no event shall such extension affect or postpone the operation of the Automatic Termination and Cancellation Clauses 40
below. 41

Warranted not to abandon in case of capture, seizure or detention, until after condemnation of the property insured. 42
The provisions of the attached Policy with respect to constructive Total Loss shall apply only to claims arising from 43
physical damage to the Vessel. 44

AUTOMATIC TERMINATION AND CANCELLATION CLAUSES

A. This insurance and any extension thereof, unless sooner terminated by the provisions of section B or C, shall terminate 45
automatically upon and simultaneously with the occurrence of any hostile detonation of any nuclear weapon of war 46
as defined above, wheresoever or whensoever such detonation may occur and whether or not the Vessel may be 47
involved. 48

B. This insurance and any extension thereof, unless sooner terminated by the provisions of section A or C, shall termi- 49
nate automatically upon and simultaneously with the outbreak of war, whether there be a declaration of war or not, 50
between any of the following countries: United States of America, United Kingdom, France, the Union of Soviet 51
Socialist Republics or the People's Republic of China. 52

C. This insurance and any extension thereof, unless sooner terminated by section A or B, shall terminate automatically 53
if and when the Vessel is requisitioned, either for title or use. 54

D. This insurance and any extension thereof may be cancelled at any time at the Assured's request, or by Underwriters 55
upon 14 days' written notice being given to the Assured, but in no event shall such cancellation affect or postpone 56
the operation of the provisions of sections A, B or C. Written or telegraphic notice sent to the Assured at his (its) 57
last known address shall constitute a complete notice of cancellation and such notice mailed or telegraphed to 58
the said Assured, care of the broker who negotiated this insurance, shall have the same effect as if sent to the 59
said Assured direct. The mailing of notice as aforesaid shall be sufficient proof of notice and the effective date 60
and hour of cancellation shall be 14 days from midnight Local Time of the day on which such notice was mailed or 61
telegraphed as aforesaid. Underwriters agree, however, to reinstate this insurance subject to agreement between 62
Underwriters and the Assured prior to the effective date and hour of such cancellation as to new rate of premium 63
and/or conditions and/or warranties. 64

RETURNS OF PREMIUM

65 The RETURNS OF PREMIUM clause of the attached Policy is deleted and the following substituted therefore:—

66 "In the event of an automatic termination or cancellation of this insurance under the provisions of sections

67 A, B, C or D above, or if the Vessel be sold, pro rata net return of premium will be payable to the Assured,

68 provided always that a Total Loss of the Vessel has not occurred during the currency of this Policy. In no

69 other event shall there be any return of premium."

70 THIS INSURANCE SHALL NOT BECOME EFFECTIVE IF, PRIOR TO THE INTENDED TIME OF ITS ATTACHMENT, THERE

71 HAS OCCURRED ANY EVENT WHICH WOULD HAVE AUTOMATICALLY TERMINATED THIS INSURANCE UNDER THE

72 PROVISIONS OF SECTIONS A, B, OR C HEREOF HAD THIS INSURANCE ATTACHED PRIOR TO SUCH OCCURRENCE.

American Institute Great Lakes Hull Clauses

(MARCH 9, 1978)

To be attached to and form a part of Policy No. .... of the ....

The terms and conditions of the following clauses are to be regarded as substituted for those of the policy form to which they are attached, the latter being hereby waived, except provisions required by law to be inserted in the Policy. All captions are inserted only for purposes of reference and shall not be used to interpret the clauses to which they apply.

ASSURED

This Policy insures 1

.... 2

.... herinafter referred to as the Assured. 3

If claim is made under this Policy by anyone other than the Owner of the Vessel, such person shall not be entitled to recover to a greater 4
extent than would the Owner, had claim been made by the Owner as an Assured named in this Policy. 5

Underwriters waive any right of subrogation against affiliated, subsidiary or interrelated companies of the Assured, provided that such waiver 6
shall not apply in the event of a collision between the Vessel and any vessel owned, demise chartered or otherwise controlled by any of the 7
aforesaid companies, or with respect to any loss, damage or expense against which such companies are insured. 8

LOSS PAYEE

Loss, if any, payable to 9

.... 10

.... or order. 11

Provided, however, Underwriters shall pay claims to others as set forth in the Collision Liability clause and may make direct payment to 12
persons providing security for the release of the Vessel in Salvage cases. 13

VESSEL

The Subject Matter of this insurance is the Vessel called the 14
or by whatsoever name or names the said Vessel is or shall be called, which for purposes of this insurance shall consist of and be limited to 15
her hull, launches, lifeboats, rafts, furniture, bunkers, stores, supplies, tackle, fittings, equipment, apparatus, machinery, boilers, refrigerating 16
machinery, insulation, motor generators and other electrical machinery. 17

In the event any equipment or apparatus not owned by the Assured is installed for use on board the Vessel and the Assured has assumed responsibility therefor, it shall also be considered part of the Subject Matter and the aggregate value thereof shall be included in the Agreed Value.

Notwithstanding the foregoing, cargo contaniers, barges and lighters shall not be considered a part of the Subject Matter of this insurance.

DURATION OF RISK

From the .... day of .... 19......, ... C.S.T.

to the .... day of .... 19......, ... C.S.T.

Should the Vessel at the expiration of this Policy be in distress or at a port of refuge, she shall be held covered to her port of destination, provided previous notice is given to the Underwriters and additional premium required by Underwriters is agreed to by the Assured.

In the event of payment by the Underwriters for Total Loss of the Vessel this Policy shall thereupon automatically terminate.

AGREED VALUE

The Vessel, for so much as concerns the Assured, by agreement between the Assured and the Underwriters in this Policy, is and shall be valued at .... Dollars.

AMOUNT INSURED HEREUNDER

.... Dollars.

DEDUCTIBLE

Notwithstanding anything in this Policy to the contrary, there shall be deducted from the aggregate of all claims (including claims under the Sue and Labor clause and claims under the Collision Liability clause) arising out of each separate accident, the sum of $ ...., unless the accident results in a Total Loss of the Vessel in which case this clause shall not apply. A recovery from other interests, however, shall not operate to exclude claims under this Policy provided the aggregate of such claims arising out of one separate accident if unreduced by such recovery exceeds that sum. For the purpose of this clause each accident shall be treated separately, but it is agreed that (a) a sequence of damages arising from the same accident shall be treated as due to that accident and (b) all heavy weather damage which occurs during a single sea passage between two successive ports shall be treated as though due to one accident.

PROVIDED, however, that claims arising from damage by ice while the Vessel is on a voyage or moving in port (excepting claim for Total Loss) shall be subject to a deductible of $50,000. or 10% of the Agreed Value, whichever is the smaller, but in no event less than the amount stated above, in respect of each accident. It is agreed that all ice damage which occurs during a single sea passage between two successive ports shall be treated as though due to one accident.

PREMIUM

The Underwriters to be paid in consideration of this insurance:

(a) a Port Risk premium of $ ...., being at the annual rate of .... per cent., which shall be due on attachment, and

(b) a Navigating premium calculated from the date of sailing during the Season of Navigation at daily pro rata of the Season Navigating rate of .... per cent., which shall be due at commencement of navigation.

The Composite rate (combined Port Risk and Navigating rate) for this insurance is .... per cent. Additional premiums, if any, shall be due at commencement of the risk for which such additional premiums have been assessed.

Full premium (Port Risk, Navigating for the entire Season of Navigation and any additional premium due) shall be considered earned in the event the Vessel becomes a Total Loss during the term of this Policy.

RETURNS OF PREMIUM

Port Risk and/or Navigating premium returnable as follows:

Pro rata daily net in the event of termination under the Change of Ownership clause;

Pro rata monthly net for each uncommenced month if it be mutually agreed to cancel this Policy;

Pro rata daily net of the Navigating rate for each period of 15 consecutive days between the dates as set forth in the Season of Navigation, both days inclusive, C.S.T. that the Vessel may be laid up in port and for which Navigating premium has been paid; provided always that:

(a) a Total Loss of the Vessel has not occurred during the currency of this Policy;

(b) in no case shall a return for lay-up be allowed when the Vessel is lying in exposed or unprotected waters or in any location not approved by the Underwriters;

(c) in no case shall a return be allowed when the Vessel is used for lightering purposes.

If, for account of the Assured, the Vessel is laid up for a period of 15 consecutive days, a part only of which attaches under this Policy, the Underwriters shall pay such proportion of the return due in respect of a full period of 15 days as the number of days attaching hereto bears to 15. Should the lay-up period exceed 15 consecutive days, the Assured shall have the option to elect the period of 15 consecutive days for which a return is recoverable.

NON-PAYMENT OF PREMIUM

In event of non-payment of the Port Risk or Navigating premium within 30 days after their respective due dates or of any additional premium when due, this Policy may be cancelled by the Underwriters upon 10 days written or telegraphic notice sent to the Assured at his last known address or in care of the broker who negotiated this Policy. Such proportion of the premium, however, as shall have been earned up to the time of cancellation shall be payable. In the event of Total Loss of the Vessel occurring prior to any cancellation or termination of this Policy full premium (Port Risk, Navigating for the entire Season of Navigation and any additional premium due) shall be considered earned.

TRADING WARRANTY AND SEASON OF NAVIGATION

Warranted that the Vessel shall be confined to the waters, bays, harbors, rivers, canals and other tributaries of the Great Lakes, not below Prescott/Ogdensburg, and shall engage in navigation only between .... and ...., both days inclusive, C.S.T. (referred to in this Policy as the Season of Navigation). Underwriters to be given prompt notice of the commencement of such navigation.

537

Navigation prior and subsequent to the Season of Navigation is held covered provided (a) prompt notice is given to the Underwriters and (b) any amended terms of cover and any additional premium required by the Underwriters are agreed to by the Assured.

Warranted that any sailing before April 1st and subsequent to December 15th, C.S.T. shall be subject to prior approval of United States Salvage Association, Inc.

The Vessel may discharge inward cargo, take in outward cargo, retain cargo on board, and move in port during the period she is in Winter lay-up. For purposes of this provision such of the following places as are designated by a single numeral shall be deemed one port: (1) Duluth — Superior (2) Detroit — Dearborn — River Rouge — Ecorse — Wyandotte (3) Kingston — Windsor — Portsmouth.

WINTER MOORINGS

Warranted that the Vessel be properly moored in a safe place and under conditions satisfactory to the Underwriters' surveyor during the period the Vessel is in Winter lay-up.

ADVENTURE

Beginning the adventure upon the Vessel, as above, and so shall continue and endure, subject to the terms and conditions of this Policy, as employment may offer, in port or at sea, in docks and graving docks, and on ways, gridirons and pontoons, at all times, in all places, and on all occasions, services and trades; with leave to sail or navigate with or without pilots, to go on trial trips and to assist and tow vessels or craft in distress, but the Vessel may not be towed, except as is customary or when in need of assistance, nor shall the Vessel render assistance or undertake towage or salvage services under contract previously arranged by the Assured, the Owners, the Managers or the Charterers of the Vessel.

The Vessel is held covered in case of any breach of conditions as to towage or salvage activities, provided (a) notice is given to the Underwriters immediately following receipt of knowledge thereof by the Assured, and (b) any amended terms of cover and any additional premium required by the Underwriters are agreed to by the Assured.

PERILS

Touching the Adventures and Perils which the Underwriters are contented to bear and take upon themselves, they are of the Seas, Men-of-War, Fire, Lightning, Earthquake, Enemies, Pirates, Rovers, Assailing Thieves, Jettisons, Letters of Mart and Counter-Mart, Surprisals, Takings at Sea, Arrests, Restraints and Detainments of all Kings, Princes and Peoples, of what nation, condition or quality soever, Barratry of the Master and Mariners and of all other like Perils, Losses and Misfortunes that have or shall come to the Hurt, Detriment or Damage of the Vessel, or any part thereof, excepting, however, such of the foregoing perils as may be excluded by provisions elsewhere in the Policy or by endorsement thereon.

ADDITIONAL PERILS (INCHMAREE)

Subject to the conditions of this Policy, this insurance also covers loss of or damage to the Vessel directly caused by the following:

Accidents in loading, discharging or handling cargo, or in bunkering;

Accidents in going on or off, or while on drydocks, graving docks, ways, gridirons or pontoons;

Explosions on shipboard or elsewhere;

Breakdown of motor generators or other electrical machinery and electrical connections thereto, bursting of boilers, breakage of shafts, or any latent defect in the machinery or hull, (excluding the cost and expense of replacing or repairing the defective part); 97 98

Breakdown of or accidents to nuclear installations or reactors not on board the insured Vessel; 99

Contact with aircraft, rockets or similar missiles, or with any land conveyance; 100

Negligence of Charterers and/or Repairers, provided such Charterers and/or Repairers are not an Assured hereunder; 101

Negligence of Master, Officers, Crew or Pilots; 102

provided such loss or damage has not resulted from want of due diligence by the Assured, the Owners or Managers of the Vessel, or any of them. Masters, Officers, Crew or Pilots are not to be considered Owners within the meaning of this clause should they hold shares in the Vessel. 103 104

DELIBERATE DAMAGE (POLLUTION HAZARD)

Subject to the conditions of this Policy, this insurance also covers loss of or damage to the Vessel directly caused by governmental authorities acting for the public welfare to prevent or mitigate a pollution hazard, or threat thereof, resulting directly from damage to the Vessel for which the Underwriters are liable under this Policy, provided such act of governmental authorities has not resulted from want of due diligence by the Assured, the Owners, or Managers of the Vessel or any of them to prevent or mitigate such hazard or threat. Masters, Officers, Crew or Pilots are not to be considered Owners within the meaning of this clause should they hold shares in the Vessel. 105 106 107 108 109

CLAIMS (GENERAL PROVISIONS)

In the event of any accident or occurrence which could give rise to a claim under this Policy, prompt notice thereof shall be given to the Underwriters, and: 110 111

(a) where practicable, the Underwriters shall be advised prior to survey, so that they may appoint their own surveyor, if they so desire; 112

(b) the Underwriters shall be entitled to decide where the Vessel shall proceed for docking and/or repair (allowance to be made to the Assured for the actual additional expense of the voyage arising from compliance with the Underwriters' requirement); 113 114

(c) the Underwriters shall have the right of veto in connection with any repair firm proposed; 115

(d) the Underwriters may take tenders or may require in writing that tenders be taken for the repair of the Vessel, in which event, upon acceptance of a tender with the approval of the Underwriters, an allowance shall be made at the rate of 30 per cent. per annum on the amount insured, for each day or pro rata for part of a day, for time lost between the issuance of invitations to tender and the acceptance of a tender, to the extent that such time is lost solely as the result of tenders having been taken and provided the tender is accepted without delay after receipt of the Underwriters' approval. 116 117 118 119 120

Due credit shall be given against the allowances in (b) and (d) above for any amount recovered: 121

(1) in respect of fuel, stores, and wages and maintenance of the Master, Officers or Crew allowed in General or Particular Average; 122

(2) from third parties in respect of damages for detention and/or loss of profit and/or running expenses; for the period covered by the allowances or any part thereof. 123 124

539

125 No claim shall be allowed in Particular Average for wages and maintenance of the Master, Officers or Crew, except when incurred solely for
126 the necessary removal of the Vessel from one port to another for average repairs or for trial trips to test average repairs, in which cases wages
127 and maintenance will be allowed only while the Vessel is under way. This exclusion shall not apply to overtime or similar extraordinary payments to
128 the Master, Officers or Crew incurred in shifting the Vessel for tank cleaning or repairs or while specifically engaged in these activities, either in
129 port or at sea.

130 General and Particular Average shall be payable without deduction, new for old.

131 The expense of sighting the bottom after stranding shall be paid, if reasonably incurred especially for that purpose, even if no damage be found.

132 No claim shall in any case be allowed in respect of scraping or painting the Vessel's bottom.

133 In the event of loss or damage to equipment or apparatus not owned by the Assured but installed for use on board the Vessel and for which
134 the Assured has assumed responsibility, claim shall not exceed (1) the amount the Underwriters would pay if the Assured were owner of such
135 equipment or apparatus, or (2) the contractual responsibility assumed by the Assured to the owners or lessors thereof, whichever shall be less.

136 No claim for unrepaired damages shall be allowed, except to the extent that the aggregate damage caused by perils insured against during
137 the period of the Policy and left unrepaired at the expiration of the Policy shall be demonstrated by the Assured to have diminished the actual
138 market value of the Vessel on that date if undamaged by such perils.

139 If repairs have not been executed within 15 months from the date of the accident, Underwriters shall not be liable for any increased cost
140 of repairs by reason of such repairs being executed after 15 months from the date of the accident.

GENERAL AVERAGE AND SALVAGE

141 General Average and Salvage shall be payable as provided in the contract of affreightment, or failing such provision or there be no contract
142 of affreightment, payable at the Assured's election either in accordance with York-Antwerp Rules 1950 or 1974 or as per American or Canadian
143 Lake adjustment. Provided always that when an adjustment according to the laws and usages of the port of destination is properly demanded by
144 the owners of the cargo, General Average shall be paid accordingly.

145 In the event of salvage, towage or other assistance being rendered to the Vessel by any vessel belonging in part or in whole to the same
146 Owners or Charterers, the value of such services (without regard to the common ownership or control of the vessels) shall be ascertained by
147 arbitration in the manner provided for under the Collision Liability clause in this Policy, and the amount so awarded so far as applicable to the
148 interest hereby insured shall constitute a charge under this Policy.

149 When the contributory value of the Vessel is greater than the Agreed Value herein, the liability of the Underwriters for General Average contribu-
150 tion (except in respect to amounts made good to the Vessel), or Salvage, shall not exceed that proportion of the total contribution due from the Vessel
151 which the amount insured hereunder bears to the contributory value; and if, because of damage for which the Underwriters are liable as Particular
152 Average, the value of the Vessel has been reduced for the purpose of contribution, the amount of such Particular Average damage recoverable under
153 this Policy shall first be deducted from the amount insured hereunder, and the Underwriters shall then be liable only for the proportion which
154 such net amount bears to the contributory value.

540

TOTAL LOSS

In ascertaining whether the Vessel is a constructive Total Loss the Agreed Value shall be taken as the repaired value and nothing in respect of the damaged or break-up value of the Vessel or wreck shall be taken into account.

There shall be no recovery for a constructive Total Loss hereunder unless the expense of recovering and repairing the Vessel would exceed the Agreed Value. In making this determination, only expenses incurred or to be incurred by reason of a single accident or a sequence of damages arising from the same accident shall be taken into account, but expenses incurred prior to tender of abandonment shall not be considered if such are to be claimed separately under the Sue and Labor clause.

In the event of Total Loss (actual or constructive), no claim to be made by the Underwriters for freight, whether notice of abandonment has been given or not.

In no case shall the Underwriters be liable for unrepaired damage in addition to a subsequent Total Loss sustained during the period covered by this Policy.

SUE AND LABOR

And in case of any Loss or Misfortune, it shall be lawful and necessary for the Assured, their Factors, Servants and Assigns, to sue, labor and travel for, in, and about the defense, safeguard and recovery of the Vessel, or any part thereof, without prejudice to this insurance, to the charges whereof the Underwriters will contribute their proportion as provided below. And it is expressly declared and agreed that no acts of the Underwriters or Assured in recovering, saving or preserving the Vessel shall be considered as a waiver or acceptance of abandonment.

In the event of expenditure under the Sue and Labor clause, the Underwriters shall pay the proportion of such expenses that the amount insured hereunder bears to the Agreed Value, or that the amount insured hereunder (less loss and/or damage payable under this Policy) bears to the actual value of the salved property, whichever proportion shall be less; provided always that their liability for such expenses shall not exceed their proportionate part of the Agreed Value.

If claim for Total Loss is admitted under this Policy and sue and labor expenses have been reasonably incurred in excess of any proceeds realized or value recovered, the amount payable under this Policy will be the proportion of such excess that the amount insured hereunder (without deduction for loss or damage) bears to the Agreed Value or to the sound value of the Vessel at the time of the accident, whichever value was greater; provided always that Underwriters' liability for such expenses shall not exceed their proportionate part of the Agreed Value. The foregoing shall also apply to expenses reasonably incurred in salving or attempting to salve the Vessel and other property to the extent that such expenses shall be regarded as having been incurred in respect of the Vessel.

COLLISION LIABILITY

And it is further agreed that:

(a) if the Vessel shall come into collision with any other ship or vessel, and the Assured or the Surety in consequence of the Vessel being at fault shall become liable to pay and shall pay by way of damages to any other person or persons any sum or sums in respect of such collision, the Underwriters will pay the Assured or the Surety, whichever shall have paid, such proportion of such sum or sums so paid as

541

their respective subscriptions hereto bear to the Agreed Value, provided always that their liability in respect to any one such collision shall not exceed their proportionate part of the Agreed Value;

(b) in cases where, with the consent in writing of a majority (in amount) of Hull Underwriters, the liability of the Vessel has been contested, or proceedings have been taken to limit liability, the Underwriters will also pay a like proportion of the costs which the Assured shall thereby incur or be compelled to pay.

When both vessels are to blame, then, unless the liability of the owners or charterers of one or both such vessels becomes limited by law, claims under the Collision Liability clause shall be settled on the principle of Cross-Liabilities as if the owners or charterers of each vessel had been compelled to pay to the owners or charterers of the other of such vessels such one-half or other proportion of the latter's damages as may have been properly allowed in ascertaining the balance or sum payable by or to the Assured in consequence of such collision.

The principles involved in this clause shall apply to the case where both vessels are the property, in part or in whole, of the same owners or charterers, all questions of responsibility and amount of liability as between the two vessels being left to the decision of a single Arbitrator, if the parties can agree upon a single Arbitrator, or failing such agreement, to the decision of Arbitrators, one to be appointed by the Assured and one to be appointed by the majority (in amount) of Hull Underwriters interested; the two Arbitrators chosen to choose a third Arbitrator before entering upon the reference, and the decision of such single Arbitrator, or of any two of such three Arbitrators, appointed as above, to be final and binding.

Provided always that this clause shall in no case extend to any sum which the Assured or the Surety may become liable to pay or shall pay in consequence of, or with respect to:

(a) removal or disposal of obstructions, wrecks or their cargoes under statutory powers or otherwise pursuant to law;

(b) injury to real or personal property of every description;

(c) the discharge, spillage, emission or leakage of oil, petroleum products, chemicals or other substances of any kind or description whatsoever;

(d) cargo or other property on or the engagements of the Vessel;

(e) loss of life, personal injury or illness.

Provided further that exclusions (b) and (c) above shall not apply to injury to other vessels or property thereon except to the extent that such injury arises out of any action taken to avoid, minimize or remove any discharge, spillage, emission or leakage described in (c) above.

CHANGE OF OWNERSHIP

In the event of any change, voluntary or otherwise, in the ownership or flag of the Vessel, or if the Vessel be placed under new management, or be chartered on a bareboat basis or requisitioned on that basis, or if the Classification Society of the Vessel or her class therein be changed, cancelled or withdrawn, then, unless the Underwriters agree thereto in writing, this Policy shall automatically terminate at the time of such change of ownership, flag, management, charter, requisition or classification; provided, however, that:

(a) if the Vessel has cargo on board and has already sailed from her loading port, or is at sea in ballast, such automatic termination shall, if required, be deferred until arrival at final port of discharge if with cargo, or at port of destination if in ballast;

(b) in the event of an involuntary temporary transfer by requisition or otherwise, without the prior execution of a written agreement by the Assured, such automatic termination shall occur fifteen days after such transfer. 213 214

This insurance shall not inure to the benefit of any transferee or charterer of the Vessel and, if a loss payable hereunder should occur between the time of change or transfer and any deferred automatic termination, the Underwriters shall be subrogated to all of the rights of the Assured against the transferee or charterer in respect of all or part of such loss as is recoverable from the transferee or charterer, and in the proportion which the amount insured hereunder bears to the Agreed Value. 215 216 217 218

The term "new management" as used above refers only to the transfer of the management of the Vessel from one firm or corporation to another, and it shall not apply to any internal changes within the offices of the Assured. 219 220

ADDITIONAL INSURANCES

It is a condition of this Policy that no additional insurance against the risk of Total Loss of the Vessel shall be effected to operate during the currency of this Policy by or for account of the Assured, Owners, Managers, Operators or Mortgagees except on the interests and up to the amounts enumerated in the following Sections (a) to (g), inclusive, and no such insurance shall be subject to P.P.I., F.I.A. or other like term on any interests whatever excepting those enumerated in Section (a); provided always and notwithstanding the limitation on recovery in the Assured clause a breach of this condition shall not afford the Underwriters any defense to a claim by a Mortgagee who has accepted this Policy without knowledge of such breach: 221 222 223 224 225 226

(a) DISBURSEMENTS, MANAGERS' COMMISSIONS, PROFITS OR EXCESS OR INCREASED VALUE OF HULL AND MACHINERY, AND/OR SIMILAR INTERESTS HOWEVER DESCRIBED, AND FREIGHT (INCLUDING CHARTERED FREIGHT OR ANTICIPATED FREIGHT) INSURED FOR TIME. An amount not exceeding in the aggregate 25% of the Agreed Value. 227 228 229

(b) FREIGHT OR HIRE, UNDER CONTRACTS FOR VOYAGE. An amount not exceeding the gross freight or hire for the current cargo passage and next succeeding cargo passage (such insurance to include, if required, a preliminary and an intermediate ballast passage) plus the charges of insurance. In the case of a voyage charter where payment is made on a time basis, the amount shall be calculated on the estimated duration of the voyage, subject to the limitation of two cargo passages as laid down herein. Any amount permitted under this Section shall be reduced, as the freight or hire is earned, by the gross amount so earned. Any freight or hire to be earned under the form of Charters described in (d) below shall not be permitted under this Section (b) if any part thereof is insured as permitted under said Section (d). 230 231 232 233 234 235 236

(c) ANTICIPATED FREIGHT IF THE VESSEL SAILS IN BALLAST AND NOT UNDER CHARTER. An amount not exceeding the anticipated gross freight on next cargo passage, such amount to be reasonably estimated on the basis of the current rate of freight at time of insurance, plus the charges of insurance. Provided, however, that no insurance shall be permitted by this Section if any insurance is effected as permitted under Section (b). 237 238 239 240

(d) TIME CHARTER HIRE OR CHARTER HIRE FOR SERIES OF VOYAGES. An amount not exceeding 50% of the gross hire which is to be earned under the charter in a period not exceeding 18 months. Any amount permitted under this Section shall be reduced as the hire is earned under the charter by 50% of the gross amount so earned but, where the charter is for a period exceeding 18 months, the amount insured need not be reduced while it does not exceed 50% of the gross hire still to be earned under the charter. An insurance permitted by this Section may begin on the signing of the charter. 241 242 243 244 245

(e) PREMIUMS. An amount not exceeding the actual premiums of all interests insured for a period not exceeding 12 months (excluding premiums insured as permitted under the foregoing Sections but including, if required, the estimated calls or premium on any Protection and Indemnity or War Risks and Strikes insurance) reducing pro rata monthly. — 246 247 248

(f) RETURNS OF PREMIUM. An amount not exceeding the actual returns which are recoverable subject to "and arrival" or equivalent provision under any policy of insurance. — 249 250

(g) INSURANCE IRRESPECTIVE OF AMOUNT AGAINST. Risks excluded by the War, Strikes and Related Exclusions clause; risks enumerated in the American Institute War Risks and Strikes Clauses; and General Average and Salvage Disbursements. — 251 252

WAR, STRIKES AND RELATED EXCLUSIONS

The following conditions shall be paramount and shall supersede and nullify any contrary provisions of the Policy. — 253

This Policy does not cover any loss, damage or expense caused by, resulting from or incurred as a consequence of: — 254

(a) Capture, seizure, arrest, restraint or detainment, or any attempt thereat; or — 255

(b) Any taking of the Vessel, by requisition or otherwise, whether in time of peace or war and whether lawful or otherwise; or — 256

(c) Any mine, bomb or torpedo not carried as cargo on board the Vessel; or — 257

(d) Any weapon of war employing atomic or nuclear fission and/or fusion or other like reaction or radioactive force or matter; or — 258

(e) Civil war, revolution, rebellion, insurrection, or civil strife arising therefrom, or piracy; or — 259

(f) Strikes, lockouts, political or labor disturbances, civil commotions, riots, martial law, military or usurped power; or — 260

(g) Malicious acts or vandalism, unless committed by the Master or Mariners and not excluded elsewhere under this War, Strikes and Related Exclusions clause; or — 261 262

(h) Hostilities or warlike operations (whether there be a declaration of war or not) but this subparagraph (h) not to exclude collision or contact with aircraft, rockets or similar missiles, or with any fixed or floating object, or stranding, heavy weather, fire or explosion unless caused directly by a hostile act by or against a belligerent power which act is independent of the nature of the voyage or service which the Vessel concerned or, in the case of a collision, any other vessel involved therein, is performing. As used herein, "power" includes any authority maintaining naval, military or air forces in association with a power. — 263 264 265 266 267

If war risks or other risks excluded by this clause are hereafter insured by endorsement on this Policy, such endorsement shall supersede the above conditions only to the extent that the terms of such endorsement are inconsistent therewith and only while such endorsement remains in force. — 268 269 270

544

American Institute
BUILDER'S RISKS CLAUSES
(FEB. 8, 1979)

To be attached to and form a part of Policy No. .... of the ....

The terms and conditions of the following clauses are to be regarded as substituted for those of the policy form to which they are attached, the latter being hereby waived, except provisions required by law to be inserted in the Policy. All captions are inserted only for purposes of reference and shall not be used to interpret the clauses to which they apply.

ASSURED

This Policy insures .... hereinafter referred to as the Assured.   1

If claim is made under this Policy by anyone other than the Owner of the Vessel, such person shall not be entitled to recover to a greater extent than would the Owner, had claim been made by the Owner as an Assured named in this Policy.   2 3 4

Underwriters waive any right of subrogation against affiliated, subsidiary or interrelated companies of the Assured, provided that such waiver shall not apply in the event of a collision between the Vessel and any vessel owned, demise chartered or otherwise controlled by any of the aforesaid companies, or with respect to any loss, damage or expense against which such companies are insured.   5 6 7

LOSS PAYEE

Loss, if any, payable to .... or order.   8 9

Provided, however, Underwriters shall pay claims to others as set forth in the Collision Liability or the Protection and Indemnity clauses and may make direct payment to persons providing security for the release of the Vessel in Salvage cases.   10 11

SUBJECT MATTER

The Subject Matter of this insurance (herein referred to as the Vessel) is the hull, launches, lifeboats, rafts, furniture, bunkers, stores, tackle, fittings, equipment, apparatus, machinery, boilers, refrigeration machinery, insulation, motor generators and other electrical machinery, ordnance, munitions, and appurtenances, including materials, plans, patterns and moulds, staging, scaffolding and similar temporary construction (to the extent only that the cost   12 13 14

of any of the foregoing is included in the Agreed Value) incorporated in or allocated to Hull No. .... Type   15

building at the yard of the Builder at   16

In the event of any material change in the specifications or design of the Vessel from that originally represented to the Underwriters, such change is held covered provided (a) notice is given to the Underwriters immediately following such change, and (b) any amended terms of cover and any additional premium required by the Underwriters are agreed to by the Assured.   17 18 19

This Policy insures only while the Vessel (ashore or afloat) is at the building location named above; while in transit within the port of construction to and from such location; and while on trial trips (including proceeding to and returning from the trial course), as often as required, within a distance by   20 21 water of 250 nautical miles of the port of construction, or held covered at an additional premium to be named by the Underwriters in the event of deviation of voyage, provided prompt notice thereof is given to the Underwriters.

DURATION OF RISK

From the .... day of .... 19 .... time,

to the .... day of .... 19 .... time
or until delivery, if delivered at an earlier date.

In the event of delivery not being effected by the aforesaid expiration date, this Policy may be extended at .... per month, provided prompt notice be given to the Underwriters but not for more than .... months from the date of original attachment, but held covered for an additional period of time provided prompt notice is given the Underwriters and any amended terms of cover and any additional premium required by the Underwriters are agreed to by the Assured; provided, however, in no case shall this Policy extend beyond delivery of the Vessel.

In the event of payment by the Underwriters for Total Loss of the Vessel this Policy shall thereupon automatically terminate.

PREMIUM

The Underwriters to be paid in consideration of this insurance ....

.... Dollars being at the rate of .... per cent., which premium shall be due on attachment.

RETURNS OF PREMIUM

In the event of delivery prior to the expiration date, or any extension thereof, to return pro rata daily of .... cents per cent. net per month.

AGREED VALUE

The Vessel, for so much as concerns the Assured and the Underwriters in this Policy, is and shall be valued at the completed contract price plus the value of materials and equipment destined for the Vessel but not included in such price. If no amount is stated for such materials and equipment, Underwriters shall have no liability for any loss, damage or expense thereto or in connection therewith, and such materials and equipment shall not be deemed a part of the Vessel.

The Agreed Value is provisionally declared as $ ...., being the contract price of $ .... and $ .... for materials and equipment destined for the Vessel but not included in the contract price.

ESCALATION

In the event of any increase or decrease in the cost of labor or materials, or in the event of any change in the specifications or design of the Vessel (not constituting a material change for purposes of the held covered provisions of the Subject Matter clause), the Agreed Value shall be adjusted accordingly, but any increase shall be limited to .... per cent. of the Agreed Value as provisionally declared, and the Amount Insured shall be adjusted proportionately; provided that the Assured shall pay premium at the full Policy rate on the total construction cost of the Vessel of this insurance, but the Underwriters shall in no event be liable under this Policy for more than the Agreed Value provisionally declared plus said percentage thereof.

546

22
23
24
25
26
27
28
29
30
31
32
33
34
35
36
37
38
39
40
41
42
43
44
45
46
47
48

AMOUNT INSURED HEREUNDER

In the event of a claim becoming payable under this Policy, the Underwriters shall not be liable for a greater proportion thereof than the Amount Insured Hereunder bears to the Agreed Value.

DEDUCTIBLE

Notwithstanding anything in this Policy to the contrary, there shall be deducted from the aggregate of all claims (including claims under the Sue and Labor, Collision Liability, and Protection and Indemnity clauses) arising out of each separate accident, the sum of $ ...., unless the accident results in a Total Loss of the Vessel in which case this clause shall not apply. A recovery from other interests, however, shall not operate to exclude claims under this Policy provided the aggregate of such claims arising out of one separate accident if unreduced by such recovery exceeds that sum. For the purpose of this clause each accident shall be treated separately, but it is agreed that (a) a sequence of damages arising from the same accident shall be treated as due to that accident and (b) all heavy weather damage, or damage caused by contact with floating ice, which occurs during a single sea passage between two successive ports shall be treated as though due to one accident.

PART I — HULL SECTION

HULL RISKS

This Policy insures against all risks of physical loss of or damage to the Vessel occurring during the currency of this Policy, except as hereinafter provided.

In the event that faulty design of any part or parts should cause physical loss of or damage to the Vessel, this insurance shall not cover the cost or expense of repairing, replacing or renewing such part or parts, nor any expenditure incurred by reason of betterment or alteration in design.

DELIBERATE DAMAGE (Pollution Hazard)

Subject to the terms and conditions of this Policy, this insurance also covers loss of or damage to the Vessel directly caused by governmental authorities acting for the public welfare to prevent or mitigate a pollution hazard, or threat thereof, resulting directly from damage to the Vessel for which the Underwriters are liable under this Policy, provided such act of governmental authorities has not resulted from want of due diligence by the Assured, the Owners, or Managers of the Vessel or any of them to prevent or mitigate such hazard or threat. Masters, Officers, Crew or Pilots are not to be considered Owners within the meaning of this clause should they hold shares in the Vessel.

FAILURE TO LAUNCH

In case of failure to launch, the Underwriters shall bear, up to the Amount Insured Hereunder, their proportion of all necessary expenses incurred in completing launch.

GENERAL AVERAGE AND SALVAGE

General Average and Salvage shall be payable as provided in the contract of affreightment, or failing such provision or there be no contract of affreightment, payable at the Assured's election either in accordance with York-Antwerp Rules, 1950 or 1974 or with the Laws and Usages of the Port of New York. Provided always that when an adjustment according to the laws and usages of the port of destination is properly demanded by the owners of the cargo, General Average shall be paid accordingly.

In the event of salvage, towage or other assistance being rendered to the Vessel by any vessel belonging in part or in whole to the same Owners or Charterers, the value of such services (without regard to the common ownership or control of the vessels) shall be ascertained by arbitration in the manner provided for under the Collision Liability clause in this Policy, and the amount so awarded so far as applicable to the interest hereby insured shall constitute a charge under this Policy.

When the contributory value of the Vessel is greater than the Agreed Value herein, the liability of the Underwriters for General Average contribution (except as provided in the Vessel), or Salvage, shall not exceed that proportion of the total contribution due from the Vessel which the amount insured hereunder bears to the contributory value; and if, because of damage for which the Underwriters are liable as Particular Average, the value of the Vessel has been reduced for the purpose of contribution, the amount of such Particular Average damage recoverable under this Policy shall first be deducted from the Amount Insured Hereunder, and the Underwriters shall then be liable only for the proportion which such net amount bears to the contributory value.

TOTAL LOSS

There shall be no recovery for a constructive Total Loss under this Policy unless the expense of recovering and restoring the Vessel (as insured hereunder) to the stage of her construction at time of loss would exceed her value at such stage of construction (which value shall be taken to be the cost of labor actually expended by the Builder in the construction of the Vessel and material actually incorporated therein at the time of loss, including accrued overhead and profit on such labor and material, not exceeding the Agreed Value). In making this determination only expenses incurred or to be incurred by reason of a single accident or a sequence of damages arising from the same accident shall be taken into account, but expenses incurred prior to tender of abandonment shall not be considered if such are to be claimed separately under the Sue and Labor clause.

No claim for Total Loss (actual or constructive) shall exceed this Policy's proportion of the value of the Vessel at the stage of her construction at time of loss as computed in the manner set forth in the preceding paragraph. This Policy shall also pay its proportion of any physical loss or damage to material insured hereunder and not yet installed in the Vessel.

In no case shall the Underwriters be liable for unrepaired damage in addition to a subsequent Total Loss sustained during the period covered by this Policy, or any extension thereof.

SUE AND LABOR

And in case of any Loss or Misfortune, it shall be lawful and necessary for the Assured, their Factors, Servants and Assigns, to sue, labor and travel for, in and about the defense, safeguard and recovery of the Vessel, or any part thereof, without prejudice to this insurance, to the charges whereof the

548

Underwriters will contribute their proportion as provided below. And it is expressly declared and agreed that no acts of the Underwriters or Assured in recovering, saving or preserving the Vessel shall be considered as a waiver or acceptance of abandonment. 97 98

In the event of expenditure under the Sue and Labor clause, the Underwriters shall pay the proportion of such expenses that the Amount Insured Hereunder bears to the Agreed Value, or that the Amount Insured Hereunder (less loss and/or damage payable under this Policy) bears to the actual value of the salved property; whichever proportion shall be less; provided always that their liability for such expenses shall not exceed their proportionate part of the Agreed Value. 99 100 101 102

If claim for Total Loss is admitted under this Policy and sue and labor expenses have been reasonably incurred in excess of any proceeds realized or value recovered, the amount payable under this Policy will be the proportion of such excess that the Amount Insured Hereunder (without deduction for loss or damage) bears to the Agreed Value or to the sound value of the Vessel at the time of the accident, whichever value was greater; provided always that Underwriters' liability for such expenses shall not exceed their proportionate part of the Agreed Value. The foregoing shall also apply to expenses reasonably incurred in salving or attempting to salve the Vessel and other property to the extent that such expenses shall be regarded as having been incurred in respect of the Vessel. 103 104 105 106 107 108

PART II — LIABILITY SECTION

COLLISION LIABILITY 109

And it is further agreed that:

(a) if the Vessel shall come into collision with any other ship or vessel, and the Assured or the Surety in consequence of the Vessel being at fault shall become liable to pay and shall pay by way of damages to any other person or persons any sum or sums in respect of such collision, the Underwriters will pay the Assured or the Surety, whichever shall have paid, such proportion of such sum or sums so paid as their respective subscriptions hereto bear to the Agreed Value, provided always that their liability in respect to any one such collision shall not exceed their proportionate part of the Agreed Value; 110 111 112 113 114

(b) in cases where, with the consent in writing of a majority (in amount) of Hull Underwriters, the liability of the Vessel has been contested, or proceedings have been taken to limit liability, the Underwriters will also pay a like proportion of the costs which the Assured shall thereby incur or be compelled to pay. 115 116 117

When both vessels are to blame, then, unless the liability of the owners or charterers of one or both such vessels becomes limited by law, claims under the Collision Liability clause shall be settled on the principle of Cross-Liabilities as if the owners or charterers of each vessel had been compelled to pay to the owners or charterers of the other of such vessels such one-half or other proportion of the latter's damages as may have been properly allowed in ascertaining the balance or sum payable by or to the Assured in consequence of such collision. 118 119 120 121

The principles involved in this clause shall apply to the case where both vessels are the property, in part or in whole, of the same owners or charterers, all questions of responsibility and amount of liability as between the two vessels being left to the decision of a single Arbitrator, if the parties can agree upon a single Arbitrator, or failing such agreement, to the decision of Arbitrators, one to be appointed by the Assured and one to be appointed 122 123 124 by the majority (in amount) of Hull Underwriters interested; the two Arbitrators chosen to choose a third Arbitrator before entering upon the reference, and the decision of such single Arbitrator, or of any two of such three Arbitrators, appointed as above, to be final and binding.

Provided always that this clause shall in no case extend to any sum which the Assured or the Surety may become liable to pay or shall pay in consequence of, or with respect to:

(a) removal or disposal of obstructions, wrecks or their cargoes under statutory powers or otherwise pursuant to law;

(b) injury to real or personal property of every description;

(c) the discharge, spillage, emission or leakage of oil, petroleum products, chemicals or other substances of any kind or description whatsoever;

(d) cargo or other property on or the engagements of the Vessel;

(e) loss of life, personal injury or illness.

Provided further that exclusions (b) and (c) above shall not apply to injury to other vessels or property thereon except to the extent that such injury arises out of any action taken to avoid, minimize or remove any discharge, spillage, emission or leakage described in (c), above.

PROTECTION AND INDEMNITY

It is further agreed that if the Assured shall by reason of his interest in the Vessel, or the Surety in consequence of its undertaking, become liable to pay and shall pay any sum or sums in respect of any responsibility, claim, demand, damages, and/or expenses arising from or occasioned by any of the following matters or things during the currency of this Policy, that is to say:

(a) Loss of or damage to any other vessel or goods, merchandise, freight, or other things or interests whatsoever on board such other vessel, caused proximately or otherwise by the Vessel, insofar as the same is not covered by the Collision Liability clause in this Policy; but the foregoing shall not be construed to cover liability in excess of the amount recoverable under the Collision Liability clause;

(b) Loss of or damage to any goods, merchandise, freight or other things or interests whatsoever, other than as aforesaid, whether on board the Vessel or not, which may arise from any cause whatsoever; provided that this subparagraph (b) shall not include Builder's gear, material or cargo on the Vessel;

(c) Loss of or damage to any harbor, dock (graving or otherwise), slipway, way, gridiron, pontoon, pier, quay, jetty, stage, buoy, telegraphic cable or other fixed or movable thing whatsoever, or to any goods or property in or on the same, howsoever caused;

(d) Loss of life of, or bodily injury to, or illness of any person (other than an employee of an Assured under this Policy);

(e) Payments made on account of life salvage;

(f) Any attempted or actual raising, removal or destruction of the wreck of the Vessel or the cargo thereof or any neglect or failure to raise, remove or destroy the same; however, for the purpose of this paragraph only, the Assured shall be deemed liable for expenses, after deducting any proceeds of the salvage, actually incurred by the Assured in removing the wreck of the Vessel from any place owned, leased or occupied by the Assured;

(g) Any sum or sums for which the Assured may become liable or incur from causes not hereinbefore specified, but which are recoverable under the Protection and Indemnity policy form known as Lazard No. SP 23;

the Underwriters will pay the Assured or the Surety such proportion of such sum or sums so paid, or which may be required to indemnify the Assured or the Surety for such loss, as their respective subscriptions bear to the Agreed Value. Where the liability of the Assured has been contested with the consent in writing of a majority (in amount) of the Underwriters, the Underwriters shall have the option of naming the attorneys who will defend the Vessel and the Assured and will also pay a like proportion of the costs which the Assured shall thereby incur or be compelled to pay; provided that the total liability of the Underwriters under all sections of these Protection and Indemnity clauses in respect of any one accident or series of accidents arising out of the same event is limited to the Amount Insured Hereunder, plus costs as hereinabove provided.

Notwithstanding anything to the contrary contained in these Protection and Indemnity clauses, the Underwriters shall not be liable for nor indemnify the Assured against any sum(s) paid with respect to any loss, damage, cost, liability, expense, fine, or penalty of any kind or nature whatsoever, and whether statutory or otherwise, imposed on the Assured directly or indirectly in consequence of, or with respect to, the actual or potential discharge, emission, spillage, or leakage upon or into the seas, waters, land or air, of oil, fuel, cargo, petroleum products, chemicals or other substances of any kind or nature whatsoever. This exclusion, however, shall not apply to sums paid or payable, or liability of the Assured, for the physical loss of the property discharged, emitted, spilled, or leaked, provided that such sums are covered elsewhere under the terms and conditions of this Policy.

In the event that Sections 182 to 189, both inclusive, of U.S. Code, Title 46, or any existing law or laws determining or limiting liability of shipowners and carriers, or any of them, shall, while this Policy is in force, be modified, amended or repealed, or the liabilities of shipowners or carriers be increased in any respect by legislative enactment, the Underwriters shall have the right to cancel the insurances afforded by these Protection and Indemnity clauses upon giving thirty (30) days' written notice in the manner prescribed in the Non-Payment of Premium clause; in the event of such cancellation, Underwriters shall make an appropriate return of premium.

Underwriters' liability under these Protection and Indemnity clauses shall in no event exceed that which would be imposed on the Assured by law in the absence of contract.

PART III — GENERAL PROVISIONS

CLAIMS

A. In the event of any accident or occurrence which could give rise to a claim under PART I of this Policy, prompt notice thereof shall be given to the Underwriters, and:

(a) where practicable, the Underwriters shall be advised prior to survey, so that they may appoint their own surveyor, if they so desire;

(b) the Underwriters shall be entitled to decide where the Vessel shall proceed for docking and/or repair (allowance to be made to the Assured for the actual additional expense of the voyage arising from compliance with the Underwriters' requirement);

(c) the Underwriters shall have the right of veto in connection with any repair firm proposed;

(d) the Underwriters may take tenders or may require in writing that tenders be taken for the repair of the Vessel, in which event, upon acceptance of a tender with the approval of the Underwriters, an allowance shall be made at the rate of 30 per cent. per annum on the amount insured, for each day or pro rata for part of a day, for time lost between the issuance of invitations to tender and the acceptance of a tender, to the extent that such time is lost solely as the result of tenders having been taken and provided the tender is accepted without delay after receipt of the Underwriters' approval; 182 183 184

(e) due credit shall be given against the allowances in (b) and (d) above for any amount recovered: 185
    (1) in respect of fuel, stores, and wages and maintenance of the Master, Officers or Crew allowed in General or Particular Average; 186 187
    (2) from third parties in respect of damages for detention and/or loss of profit and/or running expenses; 188
        for the period covered by the allowances or any part thereof. 189

No claim shall be allowed in Particular Average for wages and maintenance of the Master, Officers or Crew, except when incurred solely for the necessary removal of the Vessel from one port to another for average repairs or for trial trips made only to test average repairs, in which cases wages and maintenance will be allowed only while the Vessel is under way. This exclusion shall not apply to overtime or similar extraordinary payments to Officers or Crew members incurred in shifting the Vessel for tank cleaning or repairs or while specifically engaged in these activities, either in port or at sea. 190 191 192 193

General and Particular Average shall be payable without deduction, new for old. 194

The expense of sighting the bottom after stranding shall be paid, if reasonably incurred especially for that purpose, even if no damage be found. 195

No claim shall in any case be allowed in respect of scraping or painting the Vessel's bottom. 196

No claim for unrepaired damages shall be allowed, except to the extent that the aggregate damage insured against under the Policy and left unrepaired at the expiration thereof shall be demonstrated by the Assured to have diminished the actual market value of the Vessel on that date if undamaged. 197 198

B. In the event of any occurrence which may result in a loss, damage or expense for which the Underwriters are or may become liable under PART II of this Policy the Assured will give prompt notice thereof and forward to the Underwriters as soon as practicable after receipt thereof all communications, processes, pleadings and other legal papers or documents relating to such occurrence. 199 200 201

No action shall lie against the Underwriters under PART II of this Policy for the recovery of any loss sustained by the Assured unless such action is brought against the Underwriters within one year after the final judgment or decree is entered in the litigation against the Assured, or in case the claim against the Underwriters accrues without the entry of such final judgment or decree, unless such action is brought within one year from the date of the payment of such claim by the Assured. 202 203 204 205

NON-PAYMENT OF PREMIUM

In event of non-payment of premium 30 days after attachment, or of any additional premium when due, this Policy may be cancelled by the Underwriters upon 10 days written or telegraphic notice sent to the Assured at his last known address or in care of the broker who negotiated this Policy. Such proportion of the premium, however, as shall have been earned up to the time of cancellation shall be payable. In the event of Total Loss of the Vessel occurring prior to any cancellation or termination of this Policy full premium shall be considered earned. 206 207 208 209

WAR, STRIKES AND OTHER EXCLUSIONS

The following conditions shall be paramount and shall supersede and nullify any contrary provisions of the Policy. 210

This Policy does not cover any loss, damage, liability or expense caused by, resulting from, or incurred as a consequence of: 211

(a) Capture, seizure, arrest, restraint or detainment, or any attempt thereat; or

(b) Any taking of the Vessel, by requisition or otherwise, whether in time of peace or war and whether lawful or otherwise; or

(c) Any mine, bomb or torpedo not carried as cargo on board the Vessel; or

(d) Any weapon of war employing atomic or nuclear fission and/or fusion or other like reaction or radioactive force or matter; or

(e) Civil war, revolution, rebellion, insurrection, or civil strife arising therefrom, or piracy; or

(f) Strikes, lockouts, political or labor disturbances, civil commotions, riots, martial law, military or usurped power; or

(g) Malicious acts or vandalism, unless committed by the Master or Mariners and not excluded elsewhere under this War Strikes and Related Exclusions clause; or

(h) Hostilities or warlike operations (whether there be a declaration of war or not) but this subparagraph (h) not to exclude collision or contact with aircraft, rockets or similar missiles, or with any fixed or floating object, or stranding, heavy weather, fire or explosion unless caused directly by a hostile act by or against a belligerent power which act is independent of the nature of the voyage or service which the Vessel concerned or, in the case of a collision, any other vessel involved therein, is performing. As used herein, "power" includes any authority maintaining naval, military or air force in association with a power; or

(i) Delay or disruption of any type whatsoever, including, but not limited to, loss of earnings or use of the Vessel, howsoever caused, except to the extent, if any, covered by the Collision Liability or the Protection and Indemnity clauses of this Policy; or

(j) The firing or testing of any weapon of war from, by or on the Vessel. This exclusion is in addition to and is not to be considered in whole or part as a substitution for or modification of any other exclusion herein set forth; or

(k) Damage to docks, slipways, tools or any other property of the shipyard not intended to be incorporated in the Vessel, except as covered in Lines 12 through 16, and any damage to slipways occurring during a successful launch; or

(l) Any nuclear incident, reaction, radiation or any radioactive contamination, whether controlled or uncontrolled, and whether the loss, damage, liability or expense be proximately or remotely caused thereby, or be in whole or in part caused by, contributed to, or aggravated by the risks and liabilities insured under this Policy, and whether based on the Assured's negligence or otherwise; or

(m) Placing the Vessel in jeopardy as an act or measure of war taken in the actual process of a military engagement, including embarking or disembarking troops or material of war in the immediate zone of such engagement; and any such loss, damage, liability or expense shall be excluded from this Policy without regard to whether the Assured's liability in respect thereof is based on negligence or otherwise, and whether in time of peace or war.

212
213
214
215
216
217
218
219
220
221
222
223
224
225
226
227
228
229
230
231
232
233
234
235
236
237

American Institute
SHIP REPAIRERS LIABILITY CLAUSES
(November 3, 1977)

To be attached to and form a part of Policy No. .... of the ....

The terms and conditions of the following clauses are to be regarded as substituted for those of the policy form to which they are attached, the latter being hereby waived, except provisions required by law to be inserted in the policy.

1. This Policy insures ....

.... (hereinafter referred to as the Assured).

2. Policy Period: From .... to .... 12:01 A.M. Standard Time at the Assured's premises as stated in Clause 3.

3. In consideration of the payment of premium as hereinafter provided, and subject to the limits of liability, exclusions, conditions and other terms of this Policy, this Company agrees to pay on behalf of the Assured all sums which the Assured, as Ship Repairer, shall become legally obligated to pay:

A. By reason of the liabilities imposed upon the Assured by law for physical loss of or damage to watercraft and their equipment, cargo, or other interests on board, occurring only while such watercraft are in the care, custody or control of the Insured for the purpose of repair or alteration at ....

.... or while such watercraft are being moved via inland waters for a distance not in excess of .... miles in connection with repairs or alteration;

B. By reason of the liabilities imposed upon the Insured by law as damages because of property damage caused by a watercraft covered under "A" above while in the care, custody, or control of the Assured and being navigated or operated away from premises described in "A" above within permitted waters by an employee or employees of the Assured or in tow of a tug not owned by or demise chartered to the Assured. It is a condition of this Clause 3B that any employee of the Assured engaged in the navigation of a watercraft described herein shall possess such license as is required by the United States Coast Guard or any other applicable regulatory authority to perform the duties being carried out by said employee;

C. For the cost of defending any suit against the Assured on any claim based on a liability or an alleged liability of the Assured covered by this insurance if the amount of the claim hereunder exceeds the amount deductible under this Policy, but this Company shall not be liable for the cost or expense of prosecuting or defending any suit unless the same shall have been incurred with the written consent of this Company. This Company, however, reserves the right to conduct the defense of any actions or suits at its own expense. The cost and expense of prosecuting any claim in which the Assured shall have an interest by subrogation or otherwise, shall be divided between the Assured and this Company, proportionately to the amounts which they would be entitled to receive, respectively, if the suit should be successful.

4. The maximum liability of this Company on account of any one occurrence shall be:

A. $ .... with respect to each watercraft including its equipment, cargo, and other interests on board covered by Clause 3A;

B. $ .... any one occurrence with respect to liability covered by Clause 3B;

C. The legal costs, fees and expenses covered by Clause 3C.

The maximum aggregate liability of this Company on account of any one occurrence with respect to the coverage afforded under Sections 4 A, B and C above shall be $ ....

5. The Assured, by acceptance of this Policy, agrees to keep an accurate record of all Gross Charges for operations covered under the terms and conditions of this Policy, which record shall be open to examination by representatives of this Company at all times during business hours, during the term of this Policy or thereafter, and further agrees to report to this Company on or before the last day of each month the total amount thereof (collected and uncollected) for the preceding month or such period of time as is within the term of this Policy: the earned premium hereunder to be computed thereon at the rate of $ .... per each $100.00 and applied against the Deposit Premium until same is exhausted, following which all further earned premium shall be due and payable to this Company at time of filing the report on which the earned premium is due: and any unearned premium, being the amount by which the Deposit Premium exceeds the earned premium, shall be refunded upon expiration or cancellation of this Policy. This Company shall have the right of setoff against the claims payable under this Policy of any premiums due hereunder. It is agreed that, except in the event of cancellation of this Policy by this Company, the Minimum Premium hereunder shall be $ .... The Deposit Premium, payable upon attachment of this Policy, shall be $ ....

6. **NOTWITHSTANDING THE FOREGOING**, it is hereby expressly understood and agreed that this Policy does not cover against nor shall any liability attach hereunder for:

A. The first $ .... of any claim or claims, including legal fees and expenses, arising out of the same occurrence and insured against hereunder;

B. Death or personal injury;

555

C. Any liability assumed under contract or otherwise in extension of the liability which would have been imposed upon the Assured by law in the absence of contract;

D. Loss, damage or expense arising in connection with work on any vessel which has carried flammable or combustible liquid in bulk as fuel or cargo or any vessel which has carried flammable compressed gas in bulk, unless such work is done in accordance with the requirements of the rules and regulations of the National Fire Protection Association applicable to such work;

E. Demurrage, loss of time, loss of freight, loss of charter and/or similar and/or substituted expenses;

F. Loss, damage or expense which may be recoverable under any other insurance inuring to the benefit of the Assured except as to any excess over and above the amount recoverable thereunder;

G. Collision liability, tower's liability or liabilities insured against under the customary forms of hull or protection and indemnity policies arising out of the operation of any watercraft owned by, or demise chartered to, the Assured or any affiliated or subsidiary concern or party;

H. Loss of or damage to property owned, leased to, or in the possession of the Assured (other than watercraft which are in the custody of the Insured for the purpose of repair or alteration) or utilized by the Assured in its business as a ship repairer;

I. Loss of or damage to watercraft placed in the care, custody, or control of the Assured for the purpose of storage regardless of whether any work is also to be performed on the watercraft; provided that this exclusion shall not apply to any physical loss or damage to the watercraft (otherwise covered under this Policy) resulting directly from repairs or alterations to said watercraft carried out during such storage period;

J. The expense of redoing the work improperly performed by or on behalf of the Assured or the cost of replacement of materials, parts or equipment furnished in connection therewith;

K. The cost or expense of repairing, replacing or renewing any faultily designed part or parts which cause(s) loss of or damage to the watercraft, or for any expenditure incurred by reason of a betterment or alteration in design;

L. Any loss of or damage to watercraft occurring while in the care, custody or control of the Assured and otherwise covered under Section 3A hereof, but not discovered within sixty days of the delivery of the watercraft to the owner or demise charterer, or within sixty days after work is completed, whichever first occurs;

M. Loss, damage or expense caused by, resulting from or incurred by:

(a) Capture, seizure, arrest, taking, restraint, detainment, confiscation, preemption, requisition or nationalization, and the consequences thereof or any attempt thereat, whether in time of peace or war and whether lawful or otherwise ;

(b) Any weapon of war employing atomic or nuclear fission and/or fusion or other reaction or radioactive force or matter, or by any mine, bomb or torpedo;

(c) Hostilities or warlike operations (whether there be a declaration of war or not), but the phrase, "hostilities or warlike operations (whether there be a declaration of war or not)" shall not exclude collision or contact with aircraft, rockets or similar missiles or with any fixed or floating object, stranding, heavy weather, fire or explosion unless caused directly (independently of the nature of the voyage or service which the watercraft concerned or in the case of a collision, any other vessel involved therein, is performing) by a hostile act by or against a

52
53
54
55
56
57
58
59
60
61
62
63
64
65
66
67
68
69
70
71
72
73
74
75
76
77
78
79
80
81
82

belligerent power; for the purposes of the foregoing, power includes any authority maintaining navy, military or air forces in association with a power. In addition to the foregoing exclusions this insurance shall not cover any loss, damage or expense to which a warlike act or the use of military or naval weapons is a contributing cause, whether or not the Assured's liability therefore is based on negligence or otherwise, and whether in time of peace or war. The embarkation, carriage and disembarkation of troops, combatants, or materiel of war, or the placement of the watercraft in jeopardy as an act or measure of war taken in the actual process of a military engagement, with or without the consent of the Assured, shall be considered a warlike act for the purposes of this Policy.

(d) The consequences of civil war, revolution, rebellion, insurrection, military or usurped power, the imposition of martial law, or civil strife arising therefrom, or piracy, or from any loss, damage or expense caused by or resulting directly or indirectly from the act or acts of one or more persons, whether or not agents of a sovereign power, carried out for political or terrorist purposes, and whether any loss, damage or expense resulting therefrom is accidental or intentional.

(e) Malicious acts or vandalism, strikes, lockouts, political or labor disturbances, civil commotions, riots, or the acts of any person or persons taking part in such occurrence or disorder;

N. The firing or testing of any weapon of war on the watercraft;

O. Any nuclear incident, reaction, radiation or any radioactive contamination, whether controlled or uncontrolled, and whether the loss, damage, liability or expense be proximately or remotely caused thereby, or be in whole or in part caused by, contributed to, or aggravated by the risks and liabilities insured under this Policy, and whether based on the Assured's negligence or otherwise;

P. Any sums paid with respect to any loss, damage, cost, liability, expense, fine or penalty of any kind or nature whatsoever and whether statutory or otherwise, incurred by or imposed on the Assured, directly or indirectly, in consequence of, or with respect to, the actual or potential discharge, emission, spillage, or leakage upon or into the seas, waters, land or air, of oil, petroleum products, chemicals or other substances of any kind or nature whatsoever. This exclusion, however, shall not apply to sums paid or payable, or liability of the Assured, for the physical loss of the property discharged, emitted, spilled or leaked, provided that such sums, or such liability, are (is) covered else-where under the terms and conditions of this Policy.

7. A. In the event of an occurrence with respect to which insurances are afforded under this Policy, written notice containing particulars sufficient to identify the Assured and also reasonably obtainable information with respect to the time, place and circumstances thereof, and the names and addresses of available witnesses, shall be given by or for the Assured to this Company as soon as practicable.

B. If claim is made or suit is brought against the Assured, the Assured shall immediately forward to this Company every demand, notice, summons or other process received by him or his representative.

C. The Assured shall cooperate with this Company and, upon this Company's request, assist in making settlements, in the conduct of suits and in enforcing any right of contribution or indemnity against any person or organization who may be liable to the Assured because of injury or dam-age with respect to which insurance is afforded under this Policy; and the Assured shall attend hearings and trials and assist in securing and giving evidence and obtaining the attendance of witnesses. This Policy shall be void and of no force or effect, in respect of any accident or

557

occurrence, in the event the Assured shall make or shall have made any admission of liability either before or after such accident or occurrence in the event the Assured shall interfere in any negotiations of this Company for settlement or in any legal proceedings in respect of any claim for which this Company is or may be liable under this Policy.

8. It is expressly understood and agreed that no liability shall attach under this Policy until the liability of the Assured has been determined by final judgment against the Assured or by agreement between the Assured and the plaintiff with the written consent of this Company. In the event the Assured shall fail or refuse to settle any claim as authorized by this Company, the liability of this Company to the Assured shall be limited to the amount for which settlement could have been made.

9. No action shall lie against this Company for the recovery of any loss sustained by the Assured unless such action be brought against this Company within one year after the final judgment or decree is entered in the litigation against the Assured, or in case the claim against this Company accrues without the entry of such final judgment or decree, unless such action be brought within one year from the date of the payment of such claim, provided, however, that where such limitaiton of time is prohibited by the law of the State wherein this Policy is issued, then and in that event no action under this Policy shall be sustainable unless commenced within the shortest limitation permitted under the law of such State.

10. This Policy may be cancelled either by the Company or by the Assured giving 30 days' written or telegraphic notice to the other. Notice by the Company may be sent to the Assured's last known address, or in care of the broker who negotiated the placement of this Policy or the broker of record at the time the aforesaid notice is given.

TAYLOR HULL FORM

TAYLOR
1953
(Rev. 70)

1   In consideration of the premium and the stipulations, terms and conditions hereinafter mentioned, this Company
2   does hereby insure:

3   Assured

4

5

6   Whose address is

7   Loss, if any, payable to

8

9

10   Upon the   called

11   Her hull, tackle, apparel, engines, boilers, machinery, appurtenances, equipment, stores, boats and furniture

12   From the   day of   19   Beginning and ending

13   Until the   day of   19   at noon Standard Time
                                       at place of issuance.

14	AMOUNT INSURED HEREUNDER	RATE	PREMIUM	AGREED VALUATION
	$	%	$	$

15   Touching the adventures and perils which this Company is contented to bear and take upon itself, they are
16   of the waters named herein, fire, lightning, earthquake, assailing thieves, jettisons, barratry of the master and
17   mariners and all other like perils that shall come to the hurt, detriment or damage of the vessel named herein.

18   This insurance also covers loss of or damage to the vessel named herein caused by explosion on shipboard or
19   elsewhere.

This insurance also covers loss of or damage to the vessel named herein directly caused by:

Accidents in loading, discharging or handling cargo, or in bunkering;

Accidents in going on or off, or while on drydocks, graving docks, ways, marine railways, gridirons or pontoons;

Breakdown of motor generators or other electrical machinery and electrical connections thereto, bursting of boilers, breakage of shafts, or any latent defect in the machinery or hull, (excluding the cost and expense of replacing or repairing the defective part);

Breakdown of or accidents to nuclear installations or reactors not on board the vessel named herein;

Contact with aircraft, rockets or similar missiles, or with any land conveyance;

Negligence of charterers and/or repairers, provided such charterers and/or repairers are not assured(s) hereunder;

Negligence of master, mariners, engineers or pilots;

provided such loss or damage has not resulted from want of due diligence by the assured, the owners or managers of the vessel, or any of them.

General average, salvage and special charges payable as provided in the contract of affreightment, or failing such provision, or there be no contract of affreightment, payable in accordance with the laws and usages of the port of New York. Provided always that when an adjustment according to the laws and usages of the port of destination is properly demanded by the owners of the cargo, general average shall be paid in accordance with same.

And it is further agreed that if the vessel named herein and/or her tow, if any, shall come into collision with any other ship or vessel other than her tow, if any, and the assured in consequence of the vessel named herein being at fault shall become liable to pay and shall pay by way of damages to any other person or persons any sum or sums in respect of such collision, this Company will pay its proportion of such sum or sums so paid as the amount insured hereunder bears to the agreed valuation of the vessel named herein, provided always that this Company's liability in respect of any one such collision shall not exceed the amount insured hereunder. And in cases where the liability of the vessel named herein has been contested or proceedings have been taken to limit liability, with the consent in writing of this Company, this Company will also pay a like proportion of the costs which the assured shall thereby incur, or be compelled to pay; but when both vessels are to blame, then, unless the liability of the owners of one or both such vessels becomes limited by law, claims under this Collision Liability Clause shall be settled on the principle of cross-liabilities as if the owners of each vessel had been compelled to pay to the owners of the other of such vessels such one-half or other proportion of the latter's damages as may have been properly allowed in ascertaining the balance or sum payable by or to the assured in consequence of such collision. Provided always that this clause shall in no case extend to any sum which the assured may directly, indirectly, or otherwise incur or become liable to pay or shall pay for: removal, destruction or abatement of, or any attempt or failure or neglect to remove, destroy or abate obstructions or wrecks and/or their cargoes or any hazard resulting therefrom; loss of, or damage to, or expense, including demurrage and/or loss of use thereof, in connection with any fixed or movable object, property or thing of whatever nature (excepting other vessels and property thereon); loss of or damage to her tow; cargo, baggage or engagements of the vessel named herein or of her tow; or for loss of life of, or injury to, or illness of, any person. And provided also that in the event of any claim under this clause being made by anyone other than the owners of the vessel named herein, he shall not be entitled to recover in respect of any liability to which the owners of the vessel as such would not be subject, nor to a greater extent than the owners would be entitled in such event to recover.

In case of any loss or misfortune it shall be lawful and necessary for the assured, their factors, servants and assigns, to sue, labor and travel for, in and about the defense, safeguard and recovery of the vessel named herein, or any part thereof, without prejudice to this insurance, to the charges whereof this Company will contribute as hereinafter provided. It is agreed that the acts of the assured or this Company, or their agents, in recovering, saving and preserving the property insured in case of disaster shall not be considered a waiver or an acceptance of an abandonment, nor as affirming or denying any liability under this policy; but such acts shall be considered as done for the benefit of all concerned, and without prejudice to the rights of either party.

Warranted that in case of any casualty or loss which may result in a claim under this policy the assured shall give this Company prompt notice thereof and reasonable opportunity to be represented on a survey of the damage, each party to name a surveyor, which two surveyors shall proceed to draw specifications as to the extent of the damage and the work required to make the damage good. If the two surveyors agree, such specifications shall be binding on both this Company and the assured, subject nevertheless to policy terms and conditions and the question of whether or not the disaster and resulting loss or damage are covered by this policy. In the event the two surveyors cannot agree, they must select an umpire, and in the event they cannot agree upon an umpire, either party hereto may apply to the United States District Court for the district in which the home port of the vessel named herein is located for the appointment of an umpire, pursuant to the United States Arbitration Act. The decision of the umpire so appointed shall have the same force and effect as the specifications aforesaid. When specifications have been drawn in either of the modes aforesaid, if the Company shall be dissatisfied with the terms which the assured may obtain for the repair of the damage as specified by said survey, then this Company may require the surveyors or the umpire to submit the specifications prepared as aforesaid to such shipyard, repair men, boat builders and shipwrights, as may be selected by such surveyors or the umpire, with a request for bids for such repairs. If after reception of such bids, the assured shall elect to accept some other bid than that of the lowest bidder, this Company shall be liable only for its proportion of so much of the sum actually expended to effect repairs specified by the surveyors for its account as does not exceed said lowest bid. In no event however shall this Company respond for an amount actually expended by the assured in excess of its proportion of the amount actually expended in effecting such repairs.

With respect to physical loss or damage to the vessel named herein this Company shall be liable only for such proportion of such loss or damage as the amount insured hereunder bears to the agreed valuation.

In the event of expenditure under the sue and labor clause, this Company will pay the proportion of such expenses that the amount insured hereunder bears to the agreed valuation of the vessel named herein, or that the amount insured hereunder, less loss and/or damage payable under this policy, bears to the actual value of the salved vessel, whichever proportion shall be less.

When the contributory value of the vessel named herein is greater than the agreed valuation stated herein the liability of this Company for general average contribution (except in respect of amount made good to the vessel) or salvage shall not exceed that proportion of the total contribution due from the vessel that the amount insured hereunder bears to the contributory value; and if because of damage for which this Company is liable as particular average the value of the vessel has been reduced for the purpose of contribution, the amount of the

98 particular average claim under this policy shall be deducted from the amount insured hereunder and this Com-
99 pany shall be liable only for the proportion which such net amount bears to the contributory value.

100 The sum of $........ shall be deducted from the total amount of any or all claims (including claims
101 for sue and labor, collision liability, general average and salvage charges) resulting from any one accident. This
102 deduction does not apply to claims for total or constructive total loss. For the purpose of this clause each accident
103 shall be treated separately, but it is agreed that a sequence of damages arising from the same accident shall be
104 treated as due to that accident.

105 In case of loss, such loss to be paid in thirty days after satisfactory proof of loss and interest shall have
106 been made and presented to this Company, (the amount of any indebtedness due this Company from the assured
107 or any other party interested in this policy being first deducted).

108 Upon making payment under this policy the Company shall be vested with all of the assured's rights of re-
109 covery against any person, corporation, vessel or interest and the assured shall execute and deliver instruments
110 and papers and do whatever else is necessary to secure such rights.

111 Any agreement, contract or act, past or future, expressed or implied, by the assured whereby any right of re-
112 covery of the assured against any vessel, person or corporation is released, decreased, transferred or lost which
113 would, on payment of claim by this Company, belong to this Company but for such agreement, contract or act shall
114 render this policy null and void as to the amount of any such claim, but only to the extent and to the amount that
115 said agreement, contract or act releases, decreases, transfers, or causes the loss of any right of recovery of this
116 Company, but the Company's right to retain or recover the full premium shall not be affected.

117 This Company shall have the option of naming the attorneys who shall represent the assured in the prosecution
118 or defense of any litigation or negotiations between the assured and third parties concerning any claim, loss or inter-
119 est covered by this policy, and this Company shall have the direction of such litigation or negotiations. If the assured
120 shall fail or refuse to settle any claim as authorized by the Company, the liability of the Company to the assured
121 shall be limited to the amount for which settlement could have been made.

122 It is a condition of this policy that no suit, action or proceeding for the recovery of any claim for physical
123 loss of or damage to the vessel named herein shall be maintainable in any court of law or equity unless the same
124 be commenced within twelve (12) months next after the calendar date of the happening of the physical loss or
125 damage out of which the said claim arose. Provided, however, that if by the laws of the state within which this
126 policy is issued such limitation is invalid, then any such claim shall be void unless such action, suit or proceeding
127 be commenced within the shortest limit of time permitted, by the laws of such state, to be fixed herein.

128 In event of damage, cost of repairs to be paid without deduction of one-third, new for old.

129 If claim for total loss is admitted under this policy and sue and labor expenses have been reasonably incurred in
130 excess of any proceeds realized or value recovered, the amount payable under this policy will be the proportion of
131 such excess that the amount insured hereunder (without deduction for loss or damage) bears to the agreed valuation
132 or the sound value of the vessel named herein at the time of the accident, whichever value was greater.

133 It is a condition of this insurance that this Company shall not be liable for unrepaired damage in addition
134 to a total or constructive total loss.

135 No recovery for a constructive total loss shall be had hereunder unless the expense of recovering and re-
136 pairing the vessel named herein shall exceed the agreed valuation.

137 In ascertaining whether the vessel named herein is a constructive total loss the agreed valuation shall be
138 taken as the repaired value, and nothing in respect of the damaged or break-up value of the vessel or wreck shall
139 be taken into account.

140 In the event of total or constructive total loss, no claim to be made by this Company for freight, whether
141 notice of abandonment has been given or not.

142 Any deviation beyond the navigation limits provided herein shall void this policy; but on the return of the
143 vessel in a seaworthy condition, within the limits herein provided, this policy shall reattach and continue in full
144 force and effect, but in no case beyond the termination of this policy.

145 Warranted by the assured that there shall be no other insurance covering physical loss or damage to the
146 vessel named herein other than that which is provided in lines 15 through 33 hereof but permission is granted
147 to carry other insurance of whatever kind or nature not covered by this policy or additional amounts of insurance
148 of the kind or nature covered by this policy other than as provided in lines 15 through 33.

149 This insurance shall be void in case this policy or the vessel named herein, shall be sold, assigned, transferred
150 or pledged, or if there be any change of management or charter of the vessel, without the previous consent in
151 writing of this Company.

152 Notwithstanding anything to the contrary contained in this policy, this insurance is warranted free from
153 any claim for loss, damage or expense caused by or resulting from capture, seizure, arrest, restraint or detainment;
154 or the consequences thereof or of any attempt thereat, or any taking of the vessel, by requisition or otherwise,
155 whether in time of peace or war and whether lawful or otherwise; also from all consequences of hostilities or war-
156 like operations (whether there be a declaration of war or not), but the foregoing shall not exclude collision or
157 contact with aircraft, rockets or similar missiles, or with any fixed or floating object (other than a mine or
158 torpedo), stranding, heavy weather, fire or explosion unless caused directly (and independently of the nature of
159 the voyage or service which the vessel concerned or, in the case of a collision, any other vessel involved therein,
160 is performing) by a hostile act by or against a belligerent power, and for the purpose of this warranty "power",
161 includes any authority maintaining naval, military or air forces in association with a power; also warranted free,
162 whether in time of peace or war, from all loss, damage or expense caused by any weapon of war employing atomic
163 or nuclear fission and/or fusion or other reaction or radioactive force or matter.

164 Further warranted free from the consequences of civil war, revolution, rebellion, insurrection, or civil strife
165 arising therefrom, or piracy.

166 If war risks are hereafter insured by endorsement on the policy, such endorsement shall supersede the above
167 warranty only to the extent that their terms are inconsistent and only while such war risk endorsement remains
168 in force.

169 Warranted free of loss or damage in consequence of strikes, lockouts, political or labor disturbances, civil
170 commotions, riots, martial law, military or usurped power or malicious acts.
171 Either party may cancel this policy by giving ten days' notice in writing; if at the option of this Company
172 pro rata rates, if at the request of the assured short rates, will be charged—and arrival.

173 NAVIGATION LIMITS—SPECIAL CONDITIONS—ENDORSEMENTS, ETC.

174 Attached to and made part of Policy No. _____ of the

TAYLOR
1953
(Rev. 70)

TAYLOR HULL FORM TOWER'S LIABILITY ENDORSEMENT   SP-39 D

Endorsement to be attached to and made a part of Policy No.

of the

issued to

It is hereby mutually understood and agreed that the Collision Liability Clause appearing in lines 39 to 60, inclusive, of the form to which this endorsement is attached, is deemed deleted and that the following Collision Liability/Towers Liability Clause shall be substituted therefor:

And it is further agreed that if the vessel named herein shall come into collision with any other vessel, craft or structure, floating or otherwise (including her tow); or shall strand her tow or shall cause her tow to come into collision with any other vessel, craft or structure, floating or otherwise, or shall cause any other loss or damage to her tow or to the freight thereof or to the property on board, and the assured, in consequence of the vessel named herein being at fault, shall become liable to pay and shall pay by way of damages to any other person or persons any sum or sums, this Company will pay its proportion of such sum or sums so paid as the amount insured hereunder bears to the agreed valuation of the vessel named herein, provided always that the liability of this Company in respect of any one such casualty shall not exceed the amount insured hereunder. And in cases where the liability of the vessel named herein has been contested or proceedings have been taken to limit liability, with the consent in writing of this Company, this Company will also pay a like proportion of the costs, which the assured shall thereby incur or be compelled to pay; but when both vessels are to blame, then, unless the liability of the owners of one or both of such vessels becomes limited by law, claims under this clause shall be settled on the principle of cross liabilities, as if the owners of each vessel had been compelled to pay to the owners of the other of such vessels such one-half or other proportion of the latter's damage as may have been properly allowed in ascertaining the balance or sum payable by or to the assured in consequence of such casualty. It is hereby further agreed that the principles involved in this clause shall apply to the case where two or more of the vessels involved are the property, in part or in whole, of the same assured, all questions of responsibility and amount of liability as between such vessels being left to the decision of a single arbitrator, if the parties can agree upon a single arbitrator, or failing such agreement, to the decision of arbitrators, one to be appointed by the assured, and one to be appointed by this Company, the two arbitrators so chosen to choose a third arbitrator before entering upon the reference, and the decision of such single or of any two of such three arbitrators, appointed as above, to be final and binding. Provided always that this clause shall in no case extend to any sum which the assured may directly, indirectly or otherwise incur or become liable to pay or shall pay for: removal, destruction or abatement of, or any attempt or failure or neglect to remove, destroy or abate obstructions or wrecks and/or their cargoes or any hazard resulting therefrom; cargo, baggage or engagements of the vessel named herein; or for loss of life of, or injury to, or illness of, any person. And provided also that in the event of any claim under this clause being made by anyone other than the owners of the vessel named herein, he shall not be entitled to recover in respect of any liability to which the owners of the vessel as such would not be subject, nor to a greater extent than the owners would be entitled in such event to recover.

In consideration of the reduced rate at which this insurance is written this policy, under its Collision Liability/Towers Liability provisions appearing in the preceeding paragraph, excludes any claim for loss of, damage to, or expense in connection with vessel(s) (or their cargo) in tow of the vessel(s) named herein which vessel(s) (or their cargo) in tow are owned by or bareboat chartered to

All other terms and conditions remain unchanged.

PROTECTION AND INDEMNITY

Amount Insured $ ....
Premium $ ....
Rate ....

.... hereinafter called the Assured;

....

Loss, if any, payable to ....

.... or order

In the sum of .... Dollars

at and from the .... day of ...., 19...., at.................... time

until the .... day of ...., 19...., at.................... time
against the liabilities of the Assured as hereinafter described, and subject to the terms and conditions hereinafter set forth,

in respect of the vessel called the .... (Tonnage..................) or by whatsoever other names the
said vessel is or shall be named or called.

In consideration of the Stipulations Herein Named and of ....

.... Dollars, being Premium at the rate of ....

The Assurer hereby undertakes to make good to the Assured or the Assured's executors, administrators and/or successors, all
such loss and/or damage and/or expense as the Assured shall as owners of the vessel named herein have become liable to pay and
shall pay on account of the liabilities, risks, events and/or happenings herein set forth:

Loss of Life,
injury and
illness

　　(1) **Liability for loss of life of, or personal injury to, or illness of, any person, excluding, however, unless otherwise
agreed by endorsement hereon,** liability under any Compensation Act to any employee of the Assured, (other than
a seaman) or in case of death to his beneficiaries or others.

566

Protection hereunder for loss of life or personal injury arising in connection with the handling of cargo of the vessel named herein shall commence from the time of receipt by the Assured of the cargo on dock or wharf or on craft alongside the said vessel for loading thereon and shall continue until delivery thereof from dock or wharf of discharge or until discharge from the said vessel on to another vessel or craft.

Hospital, medical, or other expenses

(2) Liability for hospital, medical, or other expenses necessarily and reasonably incurred in respect of loss of life of, personal injury to, or illness of any member of the crew of the vessel named herein or any other person. Liability hereunder shall also include burial expenses not exceeding Two Hundred ($200) Dollars, when necessarily and reasonably incurred by the Assured for the burial of any seaman of said vessel.

Repatriation expenses

(3) Liability for repatriation expenses of any member of the crew of the vessel named herein, necessarily and reasonably incurred, under statutory obligation, excepting such expenses as arise out of or ensue from the termination of any agreement in accordance with the terms thereof, or by mutual consent, or by sale of the said vessel, or by other act of the Assured. Wages shall be included in such expenses when payable under statutory obligation, during unemployment due to the wreck or loss of the said vessel.

Damage to other vessel or property on board caused by collision

(4) Liability for loss of, or damage to, any other vessel or craft, or to the freight thereof, or property on such other vessel or craft, caused by collision with the vessel named herein, insofar as such liability would not be covered by full insurance under the ....(including the four-fourths running-down clause).

Principle of cross-liabilities to prevail

(a) Claims under this clause shall be settled on the principle of cross-liabilities to the same extent only as provided in the running-down clause above mentioned.

(b) Claims under this clause shall be divided among the several classes of claims enumerated in this policy and each class shall be subject to the deduction and special conditions applicable in respect of such class.

(c) Notwithstanding the foregoing, if any one or more of the various liabilities arising from such collision has been compromised, settled or adjusted without the written consent of the Assurer, the Assurer shall be relieved of liability for any and all claims under this clause.

Damage to other vessel or property on board not caused by collision

(5) Liability for loss of or damage to any other vessel or craft, or to property on such other vessel or craft, not caused by collision, provided such liability does not arise by reason of a contract made by the assured.

Where there would be a valid claim hereunder but for the fact that the damaged property belongs to the Assured, the Assurer shall be liable as if such damaged property belonged to another, but only for the excess over any amount recoverable under any other insurance applicable on the property.

Damage to docks, piers, etc.

(6) Liability for damage to any dock, pier, harbor, bridge, jetty, buoy, lighthouse, breakwater, structure, beacon, cable, or to any fixed or movable object or property whatsoever, except another vessel or craft, or property on another vessel or craft.

Where there would be a valid claim hereunder but for the fact that the damaged property belongs to the Assured, the Assurer shall be liable as if such damaged property belonged to another, but only for the excess over any amount recoverable under any other insurance applicable on the property.

Removal of wreck

(7) **Liability for cost or expenses of, or incidental to, the removal of the wreck of the vessel named herein when such removal is compulsory by law, provided, however, that:**

    (a) There shall be deducted from such claim for cost or expenses, the value of any salvage from or which might have been recovered from the wreck, inuring, or which might have inured, to the benefit of the Assured.

    (b) The Assurer shall not be liable for such costs or expenses which would be covered by full insurance under the .... arising out of hostilities or war-like operations, whether before or after declaration of war.

Cargo

(8) **Liability for loss of, or damage to, or in connection with cargo or other property, excluding mail and parcel post, including baggage and personal effects of passengers, to be carried, carried, or which has been carried on board the vessel named herein:**

Provided, however, that no liability shall exist under this provision for:

Specie, bullion, precious stones, etc.

    (a) Loss, damage or expense arising out of or in connection with the custody, care, carriage or delivery of specie, bullion, precious stones, precious metals, jewelry, silks, furs, bank notes, bonds or other negotiable documents or similar valuable property, unless specially agreed to and accepted for transportation under a form of contract approved, in writing, by the Assurer.

Refrigeration

    (b) Loss of, or damage to, or in connection with cargo requiring refrigeration unless the space, apparatus and means used for the care, custody, and carriage thereof have been surveyed by a classification surveyor or other competent disinterested surveyor under working conditions before the commencement of each voyage and found in all respects fit, and unless accepted for transportation under a form of contract approved, in writing, by the Assurer.

Passengers' effects

    (c) Loss, damage, or expense in connection with any passenger's baggage or personal effects, unless the form of ticket issued to the passenger shall have been approved, in writing, by the Assurer.

Stowage in improper places

    (d) Loss, damage, or expense arising from stowage of underdeck cargo on deck or stowage of cargo in spaces not suitable for its carriage, unless the Assured shall show that every reasonable precaution has been taken by him to prevent such improper stowage.

Deviation

    (e) Loss, damage, or expense arising from any deviation, or proposed deviation, not authorized by the contract of affreightment, known to the Assured in time to insure specifically the liability therefor, unless notice thereof is given to the Assurer and the Assurer agrees, in writing, that such insurance is unnecessary.

Freight on cargo short delivered

    (f) Freight on cargo short delivered, whether or not prepaid or whether or not included in the claim and paid by the Assured,

Misdescription of Goods

(g) Loss, damage, or expense arising out of or as a result of the issuance of Bills of Lading which, to the knowledge of the Assured, improperly describe the goods or their containers as to condition or quantity.

Failure to surrender Bill of Lading

(h) Loss, damage, or expense arising out of delivery of cargo without surrender of Bill of Lading.

And provided further that

(aa) Liability hereunder shall in no event exceed that which would be imposed by law in the absence of contract.

Protective clauses required in contract of affreightment

(bb) Liability hereunder shall be limited to such as would exist if the Charter Party, Bill of Lading or Contract of Affreightment contained the following clause (in substitution for the clause commonly known as the Jason Clause):

"In the event of accident, danger, damage or disaster before or after commencement of the voyage, resulting from any cause whatsoever, whether due to negligence or not, for which, or for the consequences of which, the shipowner is not responsible, by statute or contract or otherwise, the shippers, consignees or owners of the cargo shall contribute with the shipowner in general average to the payment of any sacrifices, losses or expenses of a general average nature that may be made or incurred, and shall pay salvage and special charges incurred in respect of the cargo."

When cargo is carried by the vessel named herein under a bill of lading or similar document of title subject or made subject to the Carriage of Goods by Sea Act, April 16, 1936, liability hereunder shall be limited to such as is imposed by said Act, and if the Assured or the vessel named herein assumes any greater liability or obligation than the minimum liabilities and obligations imposed by said Act, such greater liability or obligation shall not be covered hereunder.

Limit per package

When cargo is carried by the vessel named herein under a charter party, bill of lading or contract of affreightment not subject or made subject to the Carriage of Goods by Sea Act, April 16, 1936, liability hereunder shall be limited to such as would exist if said charter party, bill of lading, or contract of affreightment contained the following clauses: a clause limiting the Assured's liability for total loss or damage to goods shipped to Two Hundred and Fifty ($250) Dollars per package, or in case of goods not shipped in packages, per customary freight unit, and providing for pro rata adjustment on such basis for partial loss or damage; a clause exempting the Assured and the vessel named herein from liability for losses arising from unseaworthiness, even though existing at the beginning of the voyage, provided that due diligence shall have been exercised to make the vessel seaworthy and properly manned, equipped, and supplied; a clause providing that the carrier shall not be liable for claims in respect of cargo unless notice of claim is given within the time limited in such Bill of Lading and suit is brought thereon within the limited time prescribed therein; and such other protective clauses as are commonly in use in the particular trade; provided the incorporation of such clauses is not contrary to law.

The foregoing provisions as to the contents of the Bill of Lading and the limitation of the Assurer's liability may, however, be waived or altered by the Assurers on terms agreed, in writing.

Assured's own cargo

(cc) Where cargo on board the vessel named herein is the property of the Assured, such cargo shall be deemed to be carried under a contract containing the protective clauses described in the preceding paragraph, and such cargo shall be deemed to be fully insured under the usual form of cargo policy, and in case of loss thereof or damage thereto the Assured shall be insured hereunder in respect of such loss or damage only to the extent that they would have been covered if said cargo had belonged to another, but only in the event and to the extent that the loss or damage would not be recoverable under a cargo policy as hereinbefore specified.

569

(dd) The Assured's liability for claims under Custody Cotton Bills of Lading issued under the conditions laid down by the Liverpool Bill of Lading Conference Committee, is covered subject to previous notice of contract and payment of an extra premium of two (2¢) cents per ton gross register per voyage, but such additional premium shall be waived provided every bale is re-marked at port of shipment on another portion of the bale.

(ee) No liability shall exist hereunder for any loss, damage or expense in respect of cargo or other property being transported on land or on another vessel.
No liability shall exist hereunder for any loss, damage or expense in respect of cargo before loading on or after discharge from the vessel named herein caused by flood, tide, windstorm, earthquake, fire, explosion, heat, cold, deterioration, collapse of wharf, leaky shed, theft or pilferage unless such loss, damage or expense is caused directly by the vessel named herein, her master, officers or crew.

(9) Liability for fines and penalties, including expenses necessarily and reasonably incurred in avoiding or mitigating same, for the violation of any of the laws of the United States, or of any State thereof, or of any foreign country; provided, however, that the Assurer shall not be liable to indemnify the Assured against any such fines or penalties resulting directly or indirectly from the failure, neglect, or default of the Assured or his managing officers or managing agents to exercise the highest degree of diligence to prevent a violation of any such laws.

(10) Expenses incurred in resisting any unfounded claim by the master or crew or other persons employed on the vessel named herein, or in prosecuting such persons in case of mutiny or other misconduct.

(11) Liability for extraordinary expenses resulting from outbreak of plague or other contagious disease, including such expenses incurred for disinfection of the vessel named herein or persons on board, or for quarantine, but excluding the ordinary expenses of loading and/or discharging, and the wages and provisions of crew and passengers; each claim under this provision is subject to a deduction of Two Hundred ($200) Dollars. It is provided further, however, that if the vessel named herein be ordered to proceed to a port when it is or should be known that calling there will subject the vessel to the extraordinary expenses above mentioned, or to quarantine or disinfection there or elsewhere, the Assurer shall be under no obligation to indemnify the Assured for any such expenses.

(12) Net loss, due to deviation incurred solely for the purpose of landing an injured or sick seaman in respect of port charges incurred, insurance, bunkers, stores, and provisions consumed as a result of the deviation.

(13) Liability for, or loss of, cargo's proportion of general average, including special charges, in so far as the Assured cannot recover same from any other source; subject however, to the exclusions of Section (8) and provided, that if the Charter Party, Bill of Lading, or Contract of Affreightment does not contain the quoted clause under Section 8 (bb) the Assurer's liability hereunder shall be limited to such as would exist if such clause were contained therein.

(14) Costs, charges, and expenses, reasonably incurred and paid by the Assured in defense against any liabilities insured against hereunder in respect of the vessel named herein, subject to the agreed deductibles applicable, and subject further to the conditions and limitations hereinafter provided.

GENERAL CONDITIONS AND/OR LIMITATIONS

Warranted that in the event of any occurrence which may result in loss, damage and/or expense for which this Assurer is or may become liable, the Assured will use due diligence to give prompt notice thereof and forward to the Assurer as soon as practicable after receipt thereof, all communications, processes, pleadings and other legal papers or documents relating to such occurrences.

Marginal notes:

Cotton Bills of Lading

Land transportation not included

Customs, immigration or other fines or penalties

Mutiny or other misconduct

Extraordinary expenses in case of quarantine, etc.

Deviation for purpose of landing injured or ill

Cargo's proportion of general average

Costs and charges

Prompt notice of claim

Settlement of claims	The Assured shall not make any admission of liability, either before or after any occurrence which may result in a claim for which the Assurer may be liable. The Assured shall not interfere in any negotiations of the Assurer, for settlement of any legal proceedings in respect of any occurrences for which the Assurer is liable under this policy; provided, however, that in respect of any occurrence likely to give rise to a claim under this policy, the Assured are obligated to and shall take steps to protect their (and/or the Assurer's) interests as would reasonably be taken in the absence of this or similar insurance. If the Assured shall fail or refuse to settle any claim as authorized by Assurer, the liability of the Assurer to the Assured shall be limited to the amount for which settlement could have been made.
Assured to assist with evidence in defense, etc.	Whenever required by the Assurer the Assured shall aid in securing information and evidence and in obtaining witnesses and shall cooperate with the Assurer in the defense of any claim or suit or in the appeal from any judgment, in respect of any occurrence as hereinbefore provided.
Law costs	The Assured shall not be liable for the cost or expense of prosecuting or defending any claim or suit unless the same shall have been incurred with the written consent of the Assurer, or the Assurer shall be satisfied that such approval could not have been obtained under the circumstances without unreasonable delay, or that such costs and charges were reasonably and properly incurred, such cost or expense being subject to the deductible. The cost and expense of prosecuting any claim in which the Assurer shall have an interest by subrogation or otherwise, shall be divided between the Assured and the Assurer, proportionately to the amounts which they would be entitled to receive respectively, if the suit should be successful
	The Assurer shall be liable for the excess where the amount deductible under this policy is exceeded by (A) the cost of investigating and/or successfully defending any claim or suit against the Assured based on a liability or an alleged liability of the Assured covered by this insurance, or (B) the amount paid by the Assured either under a judgment or an agreed settlement based on the liability covered herein including all costs, expenses of defense and taxable disbursements.
Subrogation	The Assurer shall be subrogated to all the rights which the Assured may have against any other person or entity, in respect of any payment made under this policy, to the extent of such payment, and the Assured shall, upon the request of the Assurer, execute all documents necessary to secure to the Assurer such rights.
Cover elsewhere	The Assurer shall be entitled to take credit for any profit accruing to the Assured by reason of any negligence or wrongful act of the Assured's servants or agents, up to the measure of their loss, or to recover for their own account from third parties any damage that may be provable by reason of such negligence or wrongful act.
	Provided that where the Assured is, irrespective of this insurance, covered or protected against any loss or claim which would otherwise have been paid by the Assurer, under this policy, there shall be no contribution by the Assurer on the basis of double insurance or otherwise.
Assignments	No claim or demand against the Assurer under this policy shall be assigned or transferred, and no person, excepting a legally appointed receiver of the property of the Assured, shall acquire any right against the Assurer by virtue of this insurance without the expressed consent of the Assurer.
Actions against Assurers	No action shall lie against the Assurer for the recovery of any loss sustained by the Assured unless such action is brought against the Assurer within one year after the final judgment or decree is entered in the litigation against the Assured, or in case the claim against the Assurer accrues without the entry of such final judgment or decree, unless such action is brought within one year from the date of the payment of such claim.
Time limitation	The Assurer shall not be liable for any claim not presented to the Assurer with proper proofs of loss within six (6) months after payment thereof by the Assured.

571

At the expiration of this policy, the Assurer is to return .... for each thirty (30) consecutive days during the term of this insurance the vessel may be laid up in a safe port; or .... for each thirty (30) consecutive days during the term of this insurance the vessel may be laid up in a safe port without loading and/or discharging and without crew or cargo on board, provided the Assured give written notice to the Assurer as soon as practicable after the commencement and the termination of such lay-up period.

Cancellation provisions:

(a) If the vessel named herein should be sold or requisitioned and this policy be cancelled and surrendered, the Assurer to return .... for each thirty (30) consecutive days of the unexpired term of this insurance.

(b) In the event of non-payment of premium within sixty (60) days after attachment, this policy may be cancelled by the Assurer upon five (5) days' written notice being given the Assured.

(c) In the event that Sections 182 to 189, both inclusive, of U. S. Code, Title 46, or any other existing law or laws determining or limiting liability of shipowners and carriers, or any of them, shall, while this policy is in force, be modified, amended or repealed, or the liabilities of shipowners or carriers be increased in any respect by legislative enactment, the Assurer shall have the right to cancel said insurance upon giving thirty (30) days' written notice of their intention so to do, and in the event of such cancellation, make return of premium upon a pro rata daily basis.

Notwithstanding anything to the contrary contained in this policy, no liability attaches to the Assurer:

For any loss, damage, or expense which would be payable under the terms of the .... form of policy on hull and machinery, etc., if the vessel were fully covered by such insurance sufficient in amount to pay such loss, damage, or expense.

For any loss, damage or expense sustained by reason of capture, seizure, arrest, restraint or detainment, or the consequence thereof or of any attempt thereat; or sustained in consequence of military, naval or air action by force of arms, including mines and torpedoes or other missiles or engines of war, whether of enemy or friendly origin; or sustained in consequence of placing the vessel in jeopardy as an act or measure of war taken in the actual process of such military engagement, including embarking or disembarking troops or material of war in the immediate zone of such engagement; and any such loss, damage and expense shall be excluded from this policy without regard to whether the Assured's liability therefor is based on negligence or otherwise, and whether before or after a declaration of war.

For any loss, damage, or expense arising from the cancellation or breach of any charter, bad debts, fraud of agents, insolvency, loss of freight hire or demurrage, or as a result of the breach of any undertaking to load any cargo, or in respect of the vessel named herein engaging in any unlawful trade or performing any unlawful act, with the knowledge of the Assured.

For any loss, damage, expense, or claim arising out of or having relation to the towage of any other vessel or craft, whether under agreement or not, unless such towage was to assist such other vessel or craft in distress to a port or place of safety, provided, however, that this clause shall not apply to claims under this policy for loss of life or personal injury to passengers and/or members of the crew of the vessel named herein arising as a result of towing.

For any claim for loss of life or personal injury in relation to the handling of cargo where such claim arises under a contract of indemnity between the Assured and his sub-contractor.

It is expressly understood and agreed if and when the Assured under this policy has any interest other than as a shipowner in the vessel or vessels named herein, in no event shall the Assurer be liable hereunder to any greater extent than if such Assured were the owner and were entitled to all the rights of limitation to which a shipowner is entitled.

Unless otherwise agreed by endorsement to this policy, liability hereunder shall in no event exceed that which would be imposed on the Assured by law in the absence of contract.

Liability hereunder in respect of any one accident or occurrence is limited to the amount hereby insured.

Attached to and forming part of Policy No.   of

PROTECTION AND INDEMNITY CLAUSES

1 Assured

2 Address

3

4

5 Loss, if any, payable to

6

7 From the .... day of .... 19..........   Beginning and ending
8 Until the .... day of .... 19..........   at noon Standard Time
                                                               at place of issuance.

9 Amount hereby insured $ .... Rate .... % Premium $ ....

10 In consideration of the premium and subject to the warranties, terms and conditions herein mentioned, this Com-
11 pany hereby undertakes to pay up to the amount hereby insured and in conformity with lines 5 and 6 hereof,

12 such sums as the assured, as owner of the
13 shall have become legally liable to pay and shall have paid on account of:

14 Loss of life of, or injury to, or illness of, any person;

15 Hospital, medical, or other expenses necessarily and reasonably incurred in respect of loss of life of, in-
16 jury to, or illness of any member of the crew of the vessel named herein;

17 Loss of, or damage to, or expense in connection with any fixed or movable object or property of whatever
18 nature;

19 Costs or expenses of, or incidental to, the removal of the wreck of the vessel named herein when such
20 removal is compulsory by law; provided, however, that there shall be deducted from such claim the value
21 of any salvage recovered from the wreck by the assured;

22 Fines and penalties, including expenses reasonably incurred in attempting to obtain the remission or mitiga-
23 tion of same, for the violation of any of the laws of the United States, or of any state thereof, or of any
24 foreign country; provided, however, that this Company shall not be liable to indemnify the assured against
25 any such fines or penalties resulting directly or indirectly from the failure, neglect, or default of the as-

26 sured or his managing officers or managing agents to exercise the highest degree of diligence to prevent a
27 violation of any such laws;

28 Costs and expenses, incurred with this Company's approval, of investigating and/or defending any claim
29 or suit against the assured arising out of a liability or an alleged liability of the assured covered by this
30 policy.

31 Notwithstanding the foregoing this Company will not pay for:

32 The first $ of claims covered by lines 14, 15, 16, 28, 29 and 30 nor for the first $

33 of claims covered by any other parts of this policy, but, in no event shall the deductible exceed $
34 each occurrence. (For the purpose of this clause, each occurrence shall be treated separately, but a series
35 of claims hereunder arising from the same occurrence shall be treated as due to that occurrence.)

36 Loss of, or damage sustained by the vessel named herein or her tackle, apparel, furniture, boats, fittings,
37 equipment, stores, fuel, provisions or appurtenances;

38 Loss resulting from cancellation of charters, non-collectibility of freight, bad debts, insolvency of agents
39 or others, salvage, general average, detention, loss of use or demurrage of the vessel named herein;

40 Any loss, damage, expense or claim with respect to any vessel or craft in tow of the vessel named herein
41 and/or cargo thereon; provided this exclusion shall not apply to salvage services rendered in an emergency
42 to a ship or vessel in distress, nor to loss of life and/or injury to, or illness of any person;

43 Any claim for loss of, damage to, or expense in respect of cargo on board the vessel named herein;

44 Any claim arising directly or indirectly under the Longshoremen's and Harbor Workers' Compensation
45 Act or any workmen's compensation act of any state or nation;

46 Any liability assumed by the assured beyond that imposed by law; provided however that if by agree-
47 ment, or otherwise, the assured's legal liability is lessened, then this Company shall receive the benefit of
48 such lessened liability.

49 Any loss, damage or expense sustained by reason of any taking of the vessel by requisition or other-
50 wise, civil war, revolution, rebellion, or insurrection, or civil strife arising therefrom, capture, seizure,
51 arrest, restraint or detainment, or the consequences thereof or of any attempt thereat; or sustained in con-
52 sequence of military, naval or air action by force of arms; or sustained or caused by mines or torpedoes or
53 other missiles or engines of war, whether of enemy or friendly origin; or sustained or caused by any weapon
54 of war employing atomic fission or atomic fusion or radioactive material; or sustained in consequence of
55 placing the vessel in jeopardy as an act or measure of war taken in the actual process of a military engage-
56 ment, including embarking or disembarking troops or material of war in the immediate zone of such engage-
57 ment; and any such loss, damage and expense shall be excluded from this policy without regard to whether
58 the assured's liability in respect thereof is based on negligence or otherwise, and whether in time of peace
59 or war.

575

60 Any loss, damage, expense or claim collectible under the
61 form of policy, whether or not the vessel named herein is actually covered by such insurance and regardless
62 of the amount thereof.

63 Warranted that in the event of any occurrence which could result in a claim under this policy the assured
64 promptly will notify this Company upon receiving notice thereof and forward to this Company as soon
65 as practicable all communications, processes, pleadings or other legal papers or documents relating to such oc-
66 currence.

67 Whenever required by this Company, the assured shall aid in securing information and evidence and in obtaining
68 witnesses and shall cooperate with this Company in the defense of any claim or suit or in the appeal from any
69 judgment.

70 This Company shall have the option of naming the attorneys who shall represent the assured in the prosecution
71 or defense of any litigation or negotiations between the assured and third parties concerning any claim covered
72 by this policy, and shall have the direction of such litigation or negotiations. If the assured shall fail or refuse
73 to settle any claim as authorized by this Company, the liability of this Company shall be limited to the
74 amount for which settlement could have been made. The assured shall at the option of this Company
75 permit this Company to conduct, with an attorney of this Company's selection, at this Company's cost and expense
76 and under its exclusive control, a proceeding in the assured's name to limit the assured's liability to the extent,
77 and in the manner provided by the present and any future statutes relative to the limitation of a shipowner's
78 liability.

79 Liability hereunder in respect of loss, damage, costs, fees, expenses or claims arising out of or in consequence of
80 any one occurrence is limited to the amount hereby insured. (For the purpose of this clause each occurrence
81 shall be treated separately, but a series of claims hereunder arising from the same occurrence shall be treated
82 as due to that occurrence.)

83 The assured shall not make any admission of liability, either before or after any occurrence which could
84 result in a claim for which this Company may be liable. The assured shall not interfere in any negotia-
85 tions of this Company, for settlement of any legal proceedings, in respect of any occurrence for which this
86 Company may be liable under this policy; provided, however, that in respect of any occurrence likely to give rise
87 to a claim under this policy, the assured is obligated to and shall take such steps to protect his and/or the
88 Company's interests as would reasonably be taken in the absence of this or similar insurance.

89 Upon making payment under this policy this Company shall be vested with all of the assured's rights of recovery
90 against any person, corporation, vessel or interest and the assured shall execute and deliver such instruments
91 and papers as this Company shall require and do whatever else is necessary to secure such rights.

92 No action shall lie against this Company for the recovery of any loss sustained by the assured unless such
93 action is brought within one year after the entry of any final judgment or decree in any litigation against the
94 assured, or in the event of a claim without the entry of such final judgment or decree, unless such action is
95 brought within one year from the date of the payment of such claim.

576

96 No claim or demand against this Company under this policy shall be assigned or transferred, and no person
97 shall acquire any right against this Company by virtue of this insurance without the express consent of this
98 Company.

99 It is expressly understood and agreed if and when the assured has any interest other than as a shipowner in
100 the vessel named herein, in no event shall this Company be liable hereunder to any greater extent than if the
101 assured were the sole owner and entitled to petition for limitation of liability in accordance with present and
102 future law.

103 Where the assured is, irrespective of this policy, covered or protected against any loss or claim which would
104 otherwise have been paid by this Company, under this policy, there shall be no contribution or participation by
105 this Company on the basis of excess, contributing, deficiency, concurrent, or double insurance or otherwise.

106 The navigation limits in the policy covering the hull, machinery, etc. of the vessel named herein are considered
107 incorporated herein.

108 This insurance shall be void in case the vessel named herein, or any part thereof, shall be sold, transferred or
109 mortgaged, or if there be any change of management or charter of the vessel, or if this policy be assigned or
110 pledged, without the previous consent in writing of this Company.

111 Either party may cancel this policy by giving ten days' notice in writing; if at the option of this Company
112 pro rata rates, if at the request of the assured short rates, will be charged—and arrival.

113 SPECIAL CONDITIONS — WARRANTIES — ENDORSEMENTS, ETC.

114 Attached to and made part of Policy No.   of the

LOSS OF CHARTER HIRE FORM
(August, 1961)

To be attached to and form a part of Policy No. _____ of the _____

Insuring _____

FOR ACCOUNT OF THEMSELVES

Loss, if any, payable to _____ or order.

From noon _____ 19 _____ to noon _____ 19 _____

Standard Time at place of issuance.

INTEREST INSURED

On account of loss of charter hire to pay $ _____ (part of $ _____ insured this

interest) for each day of 24 consecutive hours in excess of _____ days (of 24 consecutive hours

each) up to a maximum of _____ days of 24 consecutive hours each that the _____

(hereinafter referred to as the "Vessel") is prevented

PERILS

from earning hire (in whole or in part) as a direct result of physical loss or damage to the Vessel occurring during the term of this Policy, or a sequence of such losses or damages arising from the same accident during said term. provided that such loss or damage is directly caused by a peril insured against under the American Institute Time (Hulls) December 1, 1959 form of policy, subject to the F. C. & S. Clause therein.

The phrase "same accident" shall be deemed to include all heavy weather damage occurring on one passage as defined in the said form of policy.

LIMIT OF LIABILITY

There shall be no further liability under this insurance after the per diem sum herein agreed upon has been paid

by these Underwriters for a total of _____ days of 24 consecutive hours each, amounting in all to a maximum

1
2
3
4
5
6
7
8
9
10
11
12
13
14
15
16

liability of _____

dollars $ _____ (Part of _____ dollars $ _____ insured this interest).

Rate _____ Premium $ _____

REINSTATEMENT
All claims for which Underwriters are liable hereunder shall, to the extent thereof, reduce the limit of liability under this Policy from the date of the physical loss or damage to the Vessel. However, this Policy may be reinstated to its original limit of liability under such terms and conditions as are named by Underwriters in writing.

HELD COVERED
Should the Vessel at the expiration of this Policy be at sea or in distress, or at a port of refuge or of call, this insurance shall, provided previous notice be given to the Underwriters, be continued at a pro rata daily premium to her port of destination.

WARRANTY OF CLASS
Warranted that the Vessel's class will be maintained during the currency of this Policy.

TRADING WARRANTIES
Subject to American Institute Trading Warranties but held covered in case of any breach of warranty as to cargo, trade, locality or date of sailing provided notice be given by the Assured immediately after such breach or proposed breach is known to the Assured and any additional premium required be then agreed upon.

CONDITIONS PRECEDENT TO CLAIM
NOTWITHSTANDING THE FOREGOING, the liability of Underwriters hereunder is subject to the following terms and conditions:

A. (1) NO CLAIM SHALL BE PAID UNDER THIS POLICY FOR LOSS OF HIRE due to the occurrence of a physical loss or damage, unless by reason of the accident on which the claim is based the Vessel:

(a) actually goes off hire under the current charter thereon or the charterer, under the terms of said charter, successfully claims a diminution of hire; or

(b) is unable to be tendered under the binding charter thereon and the charterer by reason thereof elects to cancel said charter, or the charterer agrees to a deferred delivery date, in consequence of which cancellation or deferred delivery date the owner has actually sustained a loss of hire; and

(2) NO CLAIM SHALL BE PAID UNDER THIS POLICY FOR LOSS OF HIRE in consequence of a deferred lay-up for repairs (during or after the Policy term) necessitated by a physical loss or damage occurring during the term of this Policy unless the Vessel is precluded from:

(a) continuing to perform under a then current charter thereon in consequence of which the owner has actually sustained a loss of hire under the terms and conditions of the said charter; or

(b) being tendered to a charterer under a then binding charter thereon and by reason thereof the said charter is cancelled under the terms thereof, or the charterer agrees to a deferred delivery date and the Assured has actually sustained a loss of hire in consequence of said cancellation or deferred delivery date; Provided that if the deferred repairs are carried out promptly after the termination of any charter on the Vessel and the Vessel is fixed and sails for a loading port within thirty days after completion of repairs, the claim shall be adjusted by these Underwriters without regard to the conditions of this Subsection A (2).

B. (1) Underwriters in no event shall pay hereunder for loss of hire for a number of days in excess of the remaining term of the current charter on the Vessel and the term(s) of any charter or sequence of charters immediately following and cancelled or deferred as in (A) above.

(2) If this insurance attaches or expires during a passage as defined in the American Institute Time (Hulls) December 1, 1959 form of policy, heavy weather damage occurring on the same passage but outside the period covered by this insurance may be added for the purpose of calculating the loss provided the damage sustained during the period covered hereunder has not been repaired during the passage, but only the proportion of the loss arising from damage occurring during the currency of this insurance shall be payable hereunder.

(3) If at the time a claim is presented to Underwriters and is otherwise collectible hereunder but the Assured cannot prove an actual loss of hire by reason of the fact that the charter on the Vessel is for a stipulated number of consecutive voyages over a stated period of time or requires the owner to lift a stipulated amount of cargo over a stated period, Underwriters will adjust and pay such claims on the basis of an estimation of the number of days of hire which the Assured can reasonably be expected to lose by the expiration of the consecutive voyage charter or contract of affreightment by reason of the physical loss or damage to the Vessel giving rise to the claim hereunder.

(4) If the loss of hire arises out of a claim by the charterer for diminution of hire as provided for in A(1)(a) above, notwithstanding the terms and conditions of this Policy, these Underwriters shall not be liable hereunder for a sum per diem in excess of the difference between the charter hire and the hire diminished as provided in A(1)(a) above, but in no event exceeding the per diem liability of these Underwriters set forth first above in this Policy.

C. No claim shall be paid under this Policy if:

(1) The Vessel becomes an absolute, constructive, compromised or arranged total loss under the Marine Hull and Machinery policies thereon. If the Vessel be uninsured for such interest, then for purposes of determining whether such a loss occurred it shall be assumed that the Vessel was insured under the American Institute Time (Hulls) December 1, 1959 form of policy for the fair market value thereof at the time of the loss.

(2) Repairs with respect to which a claim arises under this Policy are not completed within 24 months from the expiry of the term of this Policy.

TOTAL LOSS
AND
TIME TO
REPAIR

580

SIMULTANEOUS REPAIRS

D. (1) If the Vessel is laid up : 78

   (a) for damage repairs caused by a peril insured against hereunder and Assured's repairs (necessary for 79
seaworthiness or classification repairs due under periodic inspection requirements) are carried out simul- 80
taneously therewith; or 81

   (b) for Assured's repairs (necessary for seaworthiness or classification repairs due under periodic inspection 82
requirements) and damage repairs caused by a peril insured against hereunder are carried out simulta- 83
neously therewith; 84

as much time as is common to both classes of work in excess of the deductible period shall be divided equally 85
between Underwriters and Assured. 86

Provided that, if the time necessary to effect damage repairs is extended in any way by reason of concurrent 87
repairs, such additional time to be entirely for Assured's account. 88

For the purposes of this clause, classification repairs shall be deemed due at the time such repairs are recom- 89
mended by the Vessel's Classification Society or at any time thereafter. 90

TEMPORARY REPAIRS

   (2) In the event that temporary repairs to the Vessel are made (at a time and place when permanent 91
repairs could have been effected) and by reason thereof a claim is paid hereunder, these Underwriters shall not be 92
liable under this Policy for a further claim in consequence of making said temporary repairs permanent (so-called 93
permanent repairs) unless the Assured can demonstrate that by so doing Underwriters have not incurred a greater 94
loss than would have been the case if the permanent repairs were made at the time the temporary repairs were 95
effected as aforesaid. 96

DUE DILIGENCE OF ASSURED

   (3) The Assured shall effect, or cause to be effected, all repairs (temporary or permanent) with due 97
diligence and dispatch. Underwriters to have the right to require the Assured to incur any expense which would 98
reduce Underwriters' liability under this Policy provided such expense is for Underwriters' account. 99

INTERRUPTION OF REPAIRS

E. There shall be deducted from any claim, otherwise payable hereunder, the period of time, if any, that the 100
Vessel is precluded from earning hire by reason of : 101

   (1) Delay in the commencement or completion of repairs caused by or arising out of the capture, seizure, 102
arrest, restraint or detainment or of any attempt thereat, or any taking of the Vessel by requisition or otherwise, 103
whether in time of peace or war and whether lawful or otherwise, insurrection, rebellion, revolution, civil war, 104
any weapon of war or device employing atomic fission, fusion or radioactive force whether in time of peace or war, 105
hostile or warlike action by any government or any authority maintaining or using military, 106
naval or air forces or by any agent of any such government power or authority; or 107

   (2) Immobilization of the Vessel by ice or by the blocking or closing of natural or artificial arteries of 108

109
110
111
112
113
114
115
116
117
118
119
120
121
122
123
124
125
126
127
128
129
130
131
132
133
134
135
136
137
138
139
140
141

navigation, which preclude the commencement or completion of such repairs or the resumption of the normal operations of the Vessel.

OTHER INSURANCE

F. The liability under this Policy shall not exceed the sum insured hereunder, nor shall these Underwriters be liable for a greater proportion of any loss than the insurance hereunder shall bear to all insurance, whether valid or not, and whether collectible or not, covering in any manner the loss insured against by this Policy.

SUBROGATION

G. (1) In the event of any accident the Assured agrees to subrogate to these Underwriters all rights for recovery of loss of use or earnings of the Vessel for any period for which Underwriters have made payments under this Policy which the Assured may have against any other person or entity (including charterers) with respect to said accident. Said subrogation to be limited to the amount paid by Underwriters hereunder and to be distributed pro rata with the Assured's claim for demurrage (if any) during said period.

(2) In case of any agreement or act, past or future, by the Assured, except as is customary and necessary in the case of so-called pilotage agreements, whereby any right of recovery of the Assured against any person or entity is released or lost to which these Underwriters on payment of loss would be entitled to subrogation but for such agreement or act, this insurance shall be vitiated to the extent that the right of subrogation of these Underwriters has been impaired thereby; and in such event the right of these Underwriters to retain or collect any premium paid or due hereunder shall not be affected.

AUTOMATIC TERMINATION

H. (1) In the event that at any time during the term of this Policy the current charter on the Vessel expires or is cancelled or terminated for any reason whatsoever and the Vessel does not immediately go on charter, unless otherwise agreed to in writing by these Underwriters, this Policy shall automatically terminate, no notice to the Assured being necessary or required. The Assured will be entitled to pro rata return of premium in the event of such cancellation provided that no claim has been paid or is payable under this Policy. Underwriters to retain a minimum premium of thirty days.

CANCELLATION FOR NON-PAYMENT OF PREMIUM

(2) In the event of non-payment of premium within thirty days after attachment, this Policy may be cancelled by Underwriters by giving a five-day written notice of such cancellation. Written notice mailed to the Assured at the last known address of the Assured shall constitute a complete notice of cancellation and this Policy shall be null and void at noon on the fifth day after such notice shall have been mailed. A written or telegraphic notice sent through the brokers who negotiated the insurance or by them, at the request of Underwriters, shall operate to effect cancellation in the same manner as if sent directly by Underwriters. Such proportion of the premium on a daily pro rata basis as shall have been earned up to the time of such cancellation shall be due and payable immediately but in the event that a claim has been paid or is payable under this Policy full premium shall be deemed earned.

MUTUAL CANCELLATION AND LAY-UP RETURNS

(3) In the event of mutual cancellation Underwriters to return pro rata daily net premium provided no claim has been paid or is payable under this Policy. Underwriters, however, to retain a minimum premium of thirty

days. If the Vessel is laid up for more than thirty consecutive days at the request of a charterer, and not for any repairs which could give rise to a claim under this Policy, Underwriters to return one-third of daily pro rata net premium for the lay-up period provided that no claim has been paid or is payable under this Policy, and arrival.

(4) In the event of any change, voluntary or otherwise, in the ownership of the Vessel, or if the Vessel be placed under new management or be chartered on a bareboat basis or requisitioned on that basis, then, unless the Underwriters agree thereto in writing, this Policy shall thereupon become cancelled from time of such change in ownership or management, charter or requisition. A pro rata net daily return premium shall be made, provided that no claim has been paid or is payable under this Policy. Underwriters to retain a minimum premium of thirty days.

I. The Assured shall:

(1) As soon as practicable, report to these Underwriters every occurrence which may result in a claim under this Policy and, if the Vessel is covered by hull and machinery insurance, the Assured, again if practicable, shall file with Underwriters a copy of any notice of such occurrence given by it under the Marine hull and machinery policies on the Vessel; and

(2) give reasonable notice to these Underwriters of the time and place of any survey required by reason of an accident which could give rise to a claim under this Policy; and

(3) if required and if necessary for adjustment of a claim hereunder produce for examination all books of account, bills, invoices, ship's logs and accounts, charters or contracts of affreightment, or certified copies thereof if the originals are lost, at such reasonable time and place as may be designated by these Underwriters or their representatives, and shall permit extracts and copies thereof to be made.

J. Any dispute arising hereunder shall be submitted to arbitration at New York, New York. All questions (whether as to liability or amount thereof) shall be left to the decision of a single arbitrator, if the parties can agree upon a single arbitrator or failing such agreement, to the decision of arbitrators, one to be appointed by the Assured and one to be appointed by these Underwriters — the two arbitrators chosen to choose a third arbitrator before entering upon the reference and the decision of such single, or of any two of such arbitrators, appointed as above, to be final and binding and may be made a rule of the Court.

Marginal captions are inserted for purposes of convenient reference only and are not to be deemed a part of this Policy.

The terms and conditions of this form are to be regarded as substituted for those, if any, of the policy form to which it is attached, the latter being hereby waived, except provisions required by law inserted in the Policy.

This insurance is for account of _____

and the concerned (owners, underwriters or whoever they may be) in the property in the case of

the _____

Loss, if any, payable to._____

1. On disbursements and/or general average, and/or salvage, and/or other charges, and/or liabilities assumed or incurred, applicable to ship, cargo and freight.

2. Against "all risks" excluding, however, those risks excepted by the current F.C.&S. Warranty except to the extent such risks are covered under the current American Institute War Risk Clauses.

3. At and from _____

to _____, and in respect to the ship until completion of the discharge of cargo at the final port of destination, and in respect to the cargo and freight until actually delivered to the consignees at final destination (including in the interior), except as regards cargo which is not so delivered and is sold because of damages or charges or other reasons when the risk shall continue until sold, wherever sold.

4. With leave to call at any ports or places in any order, for any purpose whatsoever, and to drydock with or without cargo aboard, and including all liberties and privileges as per contracts of affreightment.

5. To cover afloat, ashore and elsewhere wheresoever the property is or may be located, including in or on other vessels or craft also during transportation ashore by whatever means. Under and/or on deck.

6. Seaworthiness of vessel and/or craft admitted.

7. To cover against total loss and increased liability of vessel and/or freight and/or cargo (including cargo left behind or discharged enroute) for said disbursements, etc. (as above) owing to any subsequent diminution in contributory values.

Diminution in value to be any subsequent loss of or damage to the property including general average and/or salvage and/or other charges and/or other liabilities.

8. In the event of claim for total loss to pay only the amount of disbursements and/or charges and or liabilities assumed or incurred.

In the event of claim for increased liability owing to diminution in value the amount payable shall be ascertained by applying to the diminution in value the percentage the salvage and/or general average and/or other charges and/or liabilities would have been of the original contributory values if there had been no diminution in the latter; also, in the event of diminution in value to pay any further amount which may be necessary to fully indemnify the concerned.

Without benefit of any other insurance.

9. The wrongful act or misconduct of any of the concerned in the adventure or their servants causing a loss is not to defeat the recovery on this policy by innocent assured if the loss in the absence of such wrongful act or misconduct would have been a loss recoverable on the policy.

10. If the cargo or any part thereof be shipped by or transhipped to another vessel or vessels, or be carried beyond or discharged short of destination, or in the event of deviation, change of voyage or vessel, or any interruption, or other variation of the voyage or risk, this insurance shall nevertheless continue to cover until safe arrival and delivery at final destination, provided prompt notice be given the insurers when such facts are known to the assured, and an additional premium paid if required.

11. It is further agreed that the terms and conditions contained in the foregoing clauses shall override anything that may be at variance or contradictory thereto in the policy to which these clauses are attached.

12. Interest admitted and policy proof thereof.

American Institute

SINGLE INTEREST MORTGAGEE FORM

July 1, 1963

ASSURED

To be attached to and form a part of Policy No. .... of the ....

....

Insuring .... ,

as Mortgagee, for account of themselves, for the interest described below, said Mortgagee being herein referred to as "the Assured".

INTEREST

Upon the interest of the Assured, as mortgagee of the vessel ....

(hereinafter referred to as "the Vessel").

LOSSES PAYABLE

Loss, if any, payable to Assured or order.

SUM INSURED

.... Dollars.

Part of .... Dollars insured this interest, being the unpaid principal amount of a valid mortgage held by the Assured on the Vessel, reducing pro rata to the extent of payments made on account of the mortgage indebtedness. This Policy also insures interest earned and unpaid to date of loss, which, however, with the unpaid balances, shall not exceed the sum insured hereunder.

TERM

At and from the .... day of .... , 19....... , ... time

to the .... day of .... , 19....... , ... time.

PREMIUM

These Underwriters to be paid in consideration of this insurance $ .... ,

being at the rate of .... % per annum of the sum initially at risk hereunder.

**CANCEL-
LATION**

This Policy (other than for non-payment of premium) may be cancelled by either party on 30 days' notice in writing. Such notice, when given by these Underwriters, shall be deemed to have been given at such time as written notice shall have been mailed to the Assured at its last known address or telegraphic notice sent thereto. A written or telegraphic notice sent through the brokers who negotiated this Policy or by them, at the request of these Underwriters, shall operate to effect cancellation of this Policy in the same manner as if sent directly by these Underwriters. Net unearned premium to be returned in the event of cancellation by either party as aforesaid.

In the event of non-payment of premium 30 days after attachment, this Policy may be cancelled by these Underwriters upon five days' written notice being given the Assured in the form provided for above. Such proportion of the premium, however, as shall have been earned up to the time of such cancellation shall be due and payable; but in the event of payment by these Underwriters of the sum insured hereunder by reason of non-payment by underwriters of the Hull Policy of a claim asserted thereunder for any liability, loss, damage or expense of, to or in respect of the Vessel occurring or arising prior to cancellation, the full annual premium shall be deemed earned.

TERMINATION

Unless otherwise agreed to in writing by these Underwriters, the insurance afforded by this Policy shall terminate in the event that there has been a change, voluntary or otherwise, in the ownership of the Vessel or it has been placed under new management or chartered on a bareboat basis or requisitioned on that basis.

**CONDITIONS
OF ATTACH-
MENT AND
DURATION
OF RISK**

1. It is a condition of this insurance that during the term of this Policy:

   (a) the Vessel is covered by policies of insurance on the form and in the amount specified below:

   (b) the Assured is named as a loss payee in the policies above described, which are herein referred to collectively and separately and defined as "the Hull Policy".

(Continued on following page)

RISKS INSURED AGAINST

2. This Policy insures only against the non-payment by underwriters of the Hull Policy, of a claim asserted thereunder for any liability, loss, damage or expense occurring or arising during the term of this Policy, which non-payment results from any act of, or omission by, the assured(s) named in the Hull Policy, or breach of any warranty, express or implied, in the Hull Policy other than breach of the warranty contained in the F. C. & S. Clause thereof;

PROVIDED that such act or omission or breach of warranty occurred without the consent or privity of the Assured.

EXCLUSIONS

3. The insurance afforded by this Policy does not cover:

(a) the non-payment of a claim for any liability, loss, damage or expense, or any part thereof:

(i) collectible under the Hull Policy or which would be collectible thereunder except for the in-solvency of the underwriters thereon; or

(ii) not recoverable under the Hull Policy by reason of any deductible or franchise included therein; or

(iii) which has been satisfied, repaired or discharged prior to payment of a claim hereunder; or

(b) any claim of the Assured arising solely out of the insolvency of the owner of the Vessel.

In no event shall these Underwriters indemnify or contribute to, pro rata or otherwise, underwriters of the Hull Policy.

CONDITIONS PRECEDENT TO CLAIM

4. As a condition precedent to any claim hereunder, unless waived by these Underwriters:

(a) the underwriters of the Hull Policy must have denied the claim for any liability, loss, damage or expense which is the subject of a claim hereunder, and

(b) the Assured shall have instituted suit against such underwriters to collect such claim.

SUBROGATION OF UNDERWRITERS

5. (a) These Underwriters, upon payment of a loss under this Policy, shall, to the extent of such payment, be subrogated to all of the rights of the Assured under the Hull Policy, the Mortgage on the Vessel and any note or bond secured thereby, and under any other instrument taken by the Assured as security for the repayment of the mortgage indebtedness. On the request of these Underwriters, the Assured shall excute and

deliver all documents necessary to effect a valid assignment of the said policy, mortgage, note or bond, and any other instrument taken by way of security as aforesaid, and of all the right, title and interest of the Assured therein. Any net sum recovered by these Underwriters in excess of the amount due to them by reason of their rights of subrogation as aforesaid shall be held for the account of the Assured.

(b) If any event occurs which does or could give rise to a claim under this Policy, the Assured shall not in any way, whether by act or failure to act, impair these Underwriters' rights of subrogation as aforesaid. Any claim under this Policy shall be reduced to the extent that such rights of subrogation have been impaired.

6. (a) The Assured shall, as soon as practicable, report to these Underwriters any denial of liability by the underwriters of the policies described in Clause "1" hereof for a claim thereunder which denial could result in a claim under this Policy.

(b) Whenever requested, the Assured shall arrange for attendance at any hull survey of a surveyor appointed by these Underwriters.

The terms and conditions of this Policy are to be regarded as substituted for those of the policy to which it is attached, the latter being hereby waived, except provisions required by law to be inserted in this Policy.

Marginal captions are inserted for purposes of convenient reference only and are not to be deemed part of this Policy.

NOTICE OF POSSIBLE CLAIM AND SURVEY

589

American Institute
MARAD-TITLE XI—
MORTGAGEE FORM
April 1, 1962

ASSURED

To be attached to and form a part of Policy No. _____ of the _____

insuring _____

_____ (Mortgagee)

and the United States of America, represented by the Secretary of Commerce, acting by and through the Maritime Administrator ("Assureds"), for account of themselves, as their respective interests may appear.

LOSSES PAYABLE

Losses payable to the Mortgagee and the United States of America, represented by the Secretary of Commerce, acting by and through the Maritime Administrator, as interest may appear, or order.

SUM INSURED

Part of $_____ insured this interest, being the unpaid principal amount _____ Dollars.

of a mortgage ("Mortgage") on the Vessel _____ ("the Vessel")

in respect of which a Contract of Insurance of Mortgage ("Mortgage Insurance Contract") was issued under Title XI, Merchant Marine Act, 1936, as amended, said sum insured reducing pro rata to the extent of payments made on account of the unpaid principal amount of the Mortgage unless paid with funds advanced by the Secretary of Commerce.

TERM

At and from the _____ day of _____ 19___, _____ time

to the _____ day of _____ 19___, _____ time.

PREMIUM

Underwriters to be paid in consideration of this insurance $_____

being at the rate of _____ %.

590

("Mortgagor") shall be directly liable to these Underwriters for all premiums under this Policy and there shall be no recourse against the Assureds for payment of premiums.

CANCELLATION

This Policy may be cancelled:

(a) if payment of premiums as above provided is not made by the Mortgagor within thirty (30) days after attachment, by these Underwriters giving to the Mortgagor and the Assureds five (5) days' notice of such cancellation. Written or telegraphic notice to said Assureds and the Mortgagor at their last known address (in the case of the United States of America: Attention Chief, Division of Insurance) shall constitute a complete notice as required under this clause and cancellation shall become effective five (5) days after receipt thereof by the United States of America. Such cancellation shall be without prejudice to claims and premiums earned and due for the period this Policy is in force and to any claim pending on the date of cancellation. A written or telegraphic notice sent through the brokers who negotiated the insurance or by them, at the request of these Underwriters, shall operate to effect cancellation in the same manner as if sent by these Underwriters direct, and

(b) by the Assureds giving to these Underwriters five (5) days' written notice of such cancellation.

TERMINATION

If at any time the liability of the Secretary of Commerce under the Mortgage Insurance Contract has terminated, other than by payment of the insurance provided for thereunder, this Policy shall automatically terminate, no notice to the Assureds being required. If practicable, the Assureds shall give prompt notice to these Underwriters of any such automatic termination.

In the event of cancellation or automatic termination of this Policy as above provided, net unearned premium shall be returned to the Mortgagor by these Underwriters.

CONDITIONS OF ATTACHMENT AND DURATION OF RISK

1. It is a condition of this Policy (subject always to the operation of the first proviso of Clause "2" hereof) that:

(a) the Vessel is insured under policies of marine Protection and Indemnity insurances and marine policies on Hull and Machinery, such policies being herein referred to, respectively, as "P & I Policies" and "Hull and Increased Value Policies", and collectively, as "Owner's Policies". All Owner's Policies shall be in form and amount satisfactory to the Maritime Administrator and the hull policy shall be no less comprehensive than the American Institute Time (Hulls) Form or similar clauses. Upon request of these Underwriters, full details concerning Owner's Policies will be furnished by the Maritime Administrator; and

(b) there shall be included in the Owner's Policies the Loss Payable Clause required under the terms of the Mortgage.

(Continued on following page)

2. This Policy insures only against the non-payment by underwriters on the Owner's Policies of a claim asserted thereunder for any liability, loss, damage or expense of, to or in respect of the Vessel, occurring or arising during the term of this Policy, which non-payment results from:

(a) any act of or omission by the Mortgagor or any agent thereof (other than non-payment of premium), or breach of any warranty, express or implied, in the said policies other than breach of the warranty contained in the F. C. & S. Clause thereof; or

(b) the fact that the accident or other occurrence out of which such liability, loss, damage or expense arose was caused by a peril not insured under the Hull and Increased Value Policies except for a peril insured against but excluded from said policies by the F. C. & S. Clause thereof; or

(c) the insufficiency in amount of the insurances described in Clause "1" hereof to satisfy claims of third parties against the Vessel resulting in a judicial sale of the Vessel, in which sale the lien of the Mortgage has been expunged in whole or in part;

PROVIDED that notwithstanding the conditions of Clause "1(a)" hereof it is agreed that should the Owner's Policies be rendered void from inception, or at any time during the policy term, by reason of an act or omission of the Mortgagor or any agent thereof, coverage hereunder shall not be affected and claims shall be payable hereunder as if the Owner's Policies had attached and remained in force during the policy term. Nothing in this provision, however, shall be deemed to require these Underwriters to assume any liabilities of underwriters under the Owner's Policies; and

PROVIDED further that such act or omission or breach of warranty referred to in "(a)" and "(b)" above occurred without the consent or privity of the Assureds.

3. The insurance afforded by this Policy does not cover:

(a) the non-payment of a claim for any liability, loss, damage or expense, or any part thereof, of, to or in respect of the Vessel;

(i) collectible under the Owner's Policies or which would be collectible thereunder except for the insolvency of the underwriters thereon; or

(ii) not recoverable under the Owner's Policies by reason of any deductible or franchise included therein; or

(iii) which has been repaired or made good by the Mortgagor prior to payment of claim hereunder

592

unless such repairs have been made or liabilities or expenses paid with funds advanced by the Secretary of Commerce

    (aa) pursuant to any terms of the Mortgage providing that the lien thereof shall attach to and cover such advances which shall be added to the outstanding indebtedness under the Mortgage, or

    (bb) with respect to which the Assureds will obtain the note or other evidence of such advance described in Clause "4(b)" hereof; or

  (b) any claim of the Assureds arising solely out of the insolvency of the Mortgagor.

In no event shall these Underwriters indemnify or contribute to, pro rata or otherwise, underwriters on the Owner's Policies.

As a condition precedent to any claim hereunder, unless waived by these Underwriters, the Assureds must have

  (i) received from the underwriters on the P & I Policies or the Hull and Increased Value Policies, as the case may be, denial of claim for any liability, loss, damage or expense which is the subject of a claim hereunder, and

  (ii) the Assureds or either must have instituted suit against such underwriters to collect such claim.

4. (a) These Underwriters, upon payment of a claim under this Policy, shall, to the extent of such payment, be subrogated to the rights of the Assureds

  (i) against the underwriters on the Owner's Policies,

  (ii) against the Mortgagor under the Mortgage,

  (iii) under any other instrument taken as security for the repayment of the principal amount of the Mortgage (except for the Mortgage Insurance Contract) and

  (iv) under any note or other evidence of indebtedness taken by the Assureds in exchange for the advance by the Assureds of funds paid by these Underwriters.

PROVIDED that such subrogation rights of these Underwriters as are herein provided

  (i) shall be subordinate to all claims of the Assureds in respect of their rights and interest referred to in Clause "4(b)" hereof, whether existing at or after the time of payment of a claim hereunder,

(ii) shall not prevent the taking of any action referred to in Clause "4(b)" hereof, and,

(iii) without the prior written consent of Assureds, shall not be exercised until the Assureds are made whole. The Assureds agree to cooperate with these Underwriters in the exercise of their subrogation rights provided the Assureds shall have first received indemnity satisfactory to them to protect against all cost, expenses and liability which may ensue therefrom.

(b) It is further agreed that any action which the Assureds may take in respect of their rights and interest

(i) in the Mortgage,

(ii) in any other instrument evidencing the indebtedness secured thereby,

(iii) in any collateral or security or policies of insurance held by the Assureds (unless in conflict with the terms of Clause "1" hereof) or

(iv) in the Mortgage Insurance Contract, or any action taken in accordance with Title XI of the Merchant Marine Act, 1936, as amended, shall not be deemed to affect the insurance under this Policy;

PROVIDED that if any such action entails the advance of funds by the Assureds to the Mortgagor, the Assureds will obtain from the Mortgagor, at least to the extent that such advance is equal to claims paid or to be paid by these Underwriters, a promissory note or other written evidence of such advance stating the obligation of the Mortgagor to repay the indebtedness evidenced thereby. These Underwriters shall, subject to the terms hereof, be subrogated to all rights of the Assureds under said note or evidence of indebtedness.

NOTICE OF CLAIM

5. The Assureds shall, as soon as practicable, report to Underwriters on this Policy

(a) any denial of liability by the underwriters on the Hull and Increased Value Policies for a claim thereunder, which denial could result in a claim under this Policy,

(b) any occurrence which may result in a loss under the P & I Policies or under the running-down clause of the Hull and Increased Value Policies in an amount in excess of the sums insured thereunder, and

(c) any accident or occurrence which could give rise to a claim under Clause "2(b)" hereof.

The terms and conditions of this form are to be regarded as substituted for those of the Policy to which it is attached, the latter being hereby waived, except provisions required by law to be inserted in the Policy.

594

Marginal captions are inserted for purposes of convenient reference only and are not to be deemed part of this Policy.

INSTITUTE MORTGAGEES INTEREST CLAUSES

HULLS

This contract is subject to English law and practice

1 SUBJECT-MATTER INSURED

1.1 This contract commences on.............and is to insure, subject to the conditions stated herein, the interest of.............as first mortgagees, in vessels to be declared for periods not in excess of 12 months each declaration.

1.2 This contract does not cover the interest of any other party and is not assignable or otherwise transferable.

2 DECLARATIONS

Subject to the provisions of Clause 3 it is a condition of this contract that the Assured must declare, without exception, and the Underwriters must accept, all interest by way of first mortgage in any vessel or vessels, giving provisional notice of the name(s) of the vessel(s) and their owner(s) and the amount(s) of the loan(s).

3 SUM INSURED

This contract is for an open amount not to exceed...............in respect of any one vessel unless specially agreed. In the event of loss after provisional but before final declaration the basis of valuation shall be the amount of the loan not exceeding the sound market value of the vessel at the time of the granting of the loan.

4 WARRANTIES

It is warranted in respect of each vessel that:

4.1 Hull and Machinery Policies on terms equivalent to Institute Time Clauses Hulls or American Institute Hull Clauses and where applicable Increased Value Policies equivalent to Institute Time Clauses—Hulls Disbursements and Increased Value (Total Loss Only including Excess Liabilities) or American Institute Increased Value and Excess Liabilities Clauses, also War Risks Policies equivalent to Institute War and Strikes Clauses Hulls—Time and full Protection and Indemnity Risks (hereafter referred to as "the Owners' Policies and Club Entries") have been taken out and shall be maintained throughout the currency of this contract.

4.2 the Owners' Policies and Club Entries, warranted in 4.1 above, shall be taken out and maintained in respect of each vessel at all times for an insured value and limit of liability not less than the amount insured hereunder of the amount of the outstanding loan.

4.3 each of the Owners' Policies and Club Entries is endorsed to the extent of the Assured's interest.

5 CHANGE OF OWNERSHIP OR CONTROL

This insurance will terminate automatically at the time of any change of ownership, management or control, of which the Assured hereunder has knowledge or privity, unless the Assured gives prompt notice of such change in writing to the Underwriters hereon and agrees to pay an additional premium, if required.

6 INDEMNITY

6.1 This contract is to indemnify the Assured for loss resulting from loss of or damage to or liability of each vessel which is prima facie covered by the Owners' Policies or Club Entries but in respect of which there is subsequent non-payment (or reduced payment which is approved in advance by the Underwriters hereon).

6.1.1 by reason of any act or omission of any one or more of the Owners, Operators, Charterers or Managers of the vessel or their servants or agents including breach or alleged breach of warranty or condition whether expressed or implied or non-disclosure or alleged non-disclosure of any fact or circumstances of any kind whatsoever.

6.1.2 by virtue of any alleged deliberate, negligent or accidental act or omission or any knowledge or privity of any one or more of the Owners, Operators, Charterers or Managers of the vessel or their servants or agents, including the deliberate or negligent casting away or damaging of the vessel or the vessel being unseaworthy.

6.2 **The cover provided under Clause 6.1 above shall only apply while any such act, omission, non-disclosure, breach of warranty or conditions, knowledge or privity occurs or exists without the privity of the Assured.**

6.3 The indemnity payable hereunder shall be an amount equal to whichever shall be the least of

6.3.1 the unrecoverable claim or part thereof under Owners' Policies and or Club Entries

6.3.2 the outstanding indebtedness under the declared loan at the time for payment under Clause 8 hereof

6.3.3 the sum insured.provided that if the subject-matter insured is not fully insured hereunder by reason of Clause 3 or otherwise, the indemnity shall be reduced in proportion to the under-insurance.

7 EXCLUSIONS

7.1 Excluding the Assured's legal costs and expenses incurred in relation to any claim under Hull Policies and or Club Entries.

7.2 In no case shall this insurance cover loss damage liability or expense arising from:

7.2.1 the relevant Owners Policies or Club Entries having been lawfully terminated by the Underwriters thereof due to non-payment of premium or call

7.2.2 insolvency or financial default of any of the Underwriters of the Owners' Policies or Club Entries

7.2.3 inability of any party to transmit funds

7.2.4 any fluctuation in exchange rates

7.2.5 the operation of any franchise deductible or provision or self-insurance.

8 TIME FOR PAYMENT

8.1 There shall be deemed to be a non-payment by the Underwriters of the Owner's Policies and/or Club Entries

8.1.1 when a final court judgement is delivered in favour of those Underwriters, or

8.1.2 at such earlier time as the Assured can demonstrate to the satisfaction of the Underwriters hereon that there is no reasonable prospect of the Owners and or Assured succeeding in the claim against the Underwriters of the Owners' Policies and/or Club Entries. In the event of disagreement between the Assured and the Underwriters hereon this issue shall be referred to a sole arbitrator to be agreed upon between the Underwriters hereon and the Assured.

8.2 Thereafter the Assured shall formally present their claim hereunder and any amount recoverable hereunder shall be payable within three calendar months of the date on which the Assured shall have presented their properly documented claim to the Underwriters of this contract.

9 SUBROGATION

9.1 Upon payment to the Assured of a claim hereunder the Underwriters shall be subrogated to all the rights and remedies of the Assured in respect of such payment.

9.2 It is a condition of this contract they any payment(s) by the Underwriters shall not be applied by the Assured in or towards discharge or satisfaction of the outstanding indebtedness.

10. DUTY OF ASSURED (SUE & LABOUR)

10.1 It is a condition of this insurance that the Assured shall give notice in writing to the Underwriters hereon of any circumstances which may give rise to a claim under this contract and shall thereafter keep the Underwriters fully informed of all developments.

10.2 It is the duty of the Assured and their servants and agents to take such measures as may be reasonable for the purpose of averting or minimising a loss which would be recoverable under this contract.

10.3 Except as provided in Clause 7.1 the Underwriters will reimburse charges properly and reasonably incurred by the Assured their servants or agents for such measures provided that if the subject-matter insured is not fully insured by reason of Clause 3 or otherwise, the indemnity shall be reduced in proportion to the under-insurance.

10.4 Measures taken by the Assured or the Underwriters with the object of averting or minimising a loss which would be recoverable under this contract shall not be considered as a waiver or acceptance of a claim or otherwise prejudice the rights of either party.

10.5 The sum recoverable under this Clause 10 shall be in addition to the loss otherwise recoverable under this contract.

11 CANCELLATION

This contract may be cancelled by either the Underwriters or the Assured giving thirty days notice in writing. Notice to commence from midnight of the day when it is issued but such cancellation shall not apply to any risks which have attached in accordance with the cover granted hereunder before the cancellation becomes effective.

12 AUTOMATIC TERMINATION AND NOTICE OF CANCELLATION—WAR AND STRIKES RISKS

Cover hereunder in respect of the risks which are covered by the Institute War and Strikes Clauses Hulls—Time 1/10/83 shall terminate

12.1 automatically upon the occurrence of any of the events mentioned in Clauses 5.2.1 and 5.2.2 of the Termination Clause in the Institute War and Strikes Clauses Hulls—Time 1/10/83

12.2 in respect of any vessel

12.2.1 automatically in the event of the vessel being requisitioned either for title or use

12.2.2 7 days after the Underwriters of Owner's War Risks Insurances, or any of them have given notice of cancellation or

12.2.3 7 days after the Underwriters hereon have given notice of cancellation in respect of the said risks.

12.3 Cancellation in accordance with Clauses 12.2.2 or 12.2.3 shall become effective on the expiry of 7 days from midnight of the day on which the notice of cancellation is given. The Underwriters agree however to reinstate this insurance subject to agreement between the Underwriters and the Assured prior to the expiry of such notice of cancellation as to new rate of premium and/or conditions and/or warranties.

Rules of Practice of Association of Average Adjusters of the United States

I. COMPENSATION AND EXPENSES OF MASTER
Adopted February 17, 1885

Where the voyage is broken up by reason of shipwreck or condemnation of the ship at a place short of the port of destination, the master shall be entitled to compensation from the general interests for the time necessarily occupied by him in transacting the business growing out of the disaster until his departure thence for the home port with the proceeds, general accounts and vouchers.

He shall also be entitled to a reasonable indemnification for his necessary expenses and services in returning to the home port when needed or required, by the peculiar circumstances of the case, to justify his acts at the place of disaster, or to give information, not otherwise afforded, to finally adjust and apportion the average charges to be paid by the general or special interests for whom such services are performed, to be determined by the nature of the case.

These rules shall apply whether the vessel be in ballast or with cargo.

II. INTEREST ON ALLOWANCES IN GENERAL AVERAGE
Adopted April 21, 1885

Where allowances, sacrifices or expenditures are charged or made good in general average, interest shall be allowed thereon at the legal rate prevailing at the place of adjustment.

III. DECK LOAD JETTISON
Adopted October 9, 1894

Where cargo consisting of one kind of goods is in accordance with a custom of trade, carried on and under deck, that portion of the cargo loaded on deck shall be subject to the same rules of adjustment in case of jettison and expenses incurred, as if the same were laden under deck.

IV. LOSS OF FREIGHT ON CARGO SACRIFICED
Adopted January 16, 1900

Rescinded October 9, 1913: rescission to take effect December 9, 1913.

V. CREDIT FOR EXPENSES SAVED BY SALVAGE SERVICES, ETC.
Adopted October 9, 1902

Where salvage services are rendered to a vessel, or she becomes disabled and is necessarily towed to her port of destination, and the expenses of such towage are allowable in general average, there shall be credited against the allowance such ordinary expenses as would have been incurred, but have been saved by the salvage or towage services.

VI. CREDITS FOR OLD MATERIAL
Adopted October 13, 1910

Where old material is replaced by new, credit shall be given in the average statement for the value of proceeds of the old material, or, if there is no credit, the Adjuster shall insert a note in explanation.

VII. APPROVAL OF REPAIR ACCOUNTS
Adopted October 13, 1910

All repair accounts shall be examined, when practicable, by the owners' surveyor and a surveyor for underwriters before the statement is issued.

The Adjuster shall insert a note in the average statement that this has been done and the result of same.

VIII. SCRAPING AND PAINTING BOTTOM OF VESSEL
Adopted October 13, 1910; Rescinded October 5, 1961.

IX. DRYDOCKING CHARGES AND EXPENSES INCIDENTAL TO DRYDOCKING—PARTICULAR AVERAGE
Adopted October 13, 1910

When a vessel is drydocked:

(1) For owners' account and repairs are found necessary for which underwriters are liable and which can only be effected in drydock; or

(2) For survey and/or repairs for which underwriters are liable and repairs for owners' accounts are made which are immediately necessary for her seaworthiness, or she is due for ordinary drydocking (in accordance with the owners' custom), the cost of removing the vessel to and from the drydock, of docking and undocking, and as much of the dock dues as is common to both classes of work, shall be divided equally between the owners and underwriters.

When the vessel is drydocked for underwriters' account and the owners avail of her being in drydock to scrape and paint or to do other work for their own account which is not immediately necessary for seaworthiness, all the expenses incidental to the drydocking of the vessel shall be charged to the underwriters.

The Adjuster shall insert a note in the average statement in explanation of the allowances made.

X. OVERTIME WORK—GENERAL AND PARTICULAR AVERAGE SAVINGS—APPORTIONMENT
Adopted October 13, 1910; Amended October 14, 1937

The bonus or extra cost of overtime work on repairs shall be allowed in general and/or particular average up to the amount of the saving of drydock dues or other charges, which otherwise would have been incurred and allowed in general and/or particular average; and where the overtime work effects a savings both of general average expense (excluding general average repairs) and in the cost of repairs the extra cost for overtime shall be apportioned over the general average expenses saved and the savings in the cost of repairs.

The Adjuster shall insert a note in the average statement in explanation of the allowances made.

XI. TEMPORARY REPAIRS—PARTICULAR AVERAGE
Adopted October 13, 1910

The cost of reasonable temporary repairs shall be allowed:
When made in order to effect a saving in the cost of permanent repairs;
When complete repairs cannot be made at the port where the vessel is;
When the material or parts necessary for permanent repairs are unobtainable
   at the port where the vessel is, except after unreasonable delay.

The Adjuster shall insert a note in the average statement in explanation of the allowances made.

XII. ALLOWANCE IN RESPECT OF PROVISIONS
Adopted October 13, 1910; Amended 1913, 1917, 1920, 1922, 1923, 1930, 1942, 1947, May 19, 1952, October 1, 1970, October 6, 1976 & October 1, 1980

When allowance is made in General Average for provisions of Masters, Officers, and crews, the allowance shall be $8.00 per person per day for voyages beginning on or after October 1, 1980. For voyages beginning prior to October 6, 1976, the allowance shall be based on previous Rule XII.

The Rule shall apply to United States flag vessels in all instances and to vessels of other flags, on voyages to and from United States ports, including Territories and Insular possessions, when the general average is stated in accordance with the laws and usages of the United States, even though such laws and usages may be modified by York/Antwerp Rules.

XIII. ALLOWANCES IN GENERAL AVERAGE FOR REPAIRS TO VESSELS
Adopted April 10, 1913; Amended October 5, 1961 & October 4, 1979

Repairs to be allowed in general average shall not be subject to deductions in respect of "new for old" where old materials or parts are replaced by new unless the ship is over fifteen years old in which case there shall be a deduction of one third. The deductions shall be regulated by the age of the ship from the 31st December of the year of completion of construction to the date of the general average act, except for insulation, life- and similar boats, communications and navigational apparatus and equipment, machinery and boilers for which the deductions shall be regulated by the age of the particular parts to which they apply.

The deductions shall be made only from the cost of the new material or parts when finished and ready to be installed in the ship.

No deduction shall be made in respect of provisions, stores, anchors and chain cables.

Drydock and slipway dues and costs of shifting the ship shall be allowed in full.

The costs of cleaning, painting or coating of bottom shall not be allowed in general average unless the bottom has been painted or coated within the twelve months preceding the date of the general average act in which case one half of such costs shall be allowed.

XIV. FREIGHT—CONTRIBUTORY VALUE AND AMOUNT MADE GOOD IN GENERAL AVERAGE
Adopted October 9, 1913; Amended October 11, 1939 & October 11, 1950

The contributory value of freight shall be the amount at risk of the Shipowners or Charterers and earned on cargo on board, to which shall be added the allowance in general average for net freight lost, and from the total shall be deducted the expenses (except those allowed in general average) incurred to earn it after the date of the general average act; and if there be any cargo on board on which the freight is not at risk of the Shipowners or Charterers the charges to be deducted from the freight at their risk shall be only those which would have been incurred if such cargo had not been aboard.

And when loss of freight at risk of the Shipowners or Charterers is allowed in general average the allowance shall be for the net freight lost, to be ascertained by deducting from the gross freight sacrificed the expenses that would have been incurred, subsequent to the sacrifice, to earn it, but which, because of the sacrifice, have not been incurred.

Where the general average is prepared in accordance with York/Antwerp Rules and there be any cargo on board on which the freight is not at risk of the Shipowners or Charterers, the deductions made from the freight at their risk to arrive at the contributory value of freight shall be determined in accordance with the principles set forth above.

XV. CLASSIFICATION SURVEYORS' FEES— PARTICULAR AVERAGE
Adopted April 19, 1923; Amended October 14, 1937

Fees of Classification Societies for surveys of particular average damages shall be allowed (notwithstanding that a survey of such damages would have been required for classification purposes) in addition to a fee paid an independent surveyor.

XVI. COMPENSATION AND EXPENSES OF OWNERS' SUPERINTENDENT
Adopted April 19, 1923

In cases where a superintendent, or other shore employee, in the permanent employ of the owner of a vessel, superintends the repair of average damage, compensation for such service and incidental expenses shall be allowed in average:

First—When an independent surveyor, or outside man, has not been employed for this purpose, and the vessel is repaired at a port other than where the superintendent, or other employee, makes his headquarters; or

Second—When the owner has incurred extra expense by employing, temporarily, another man to do the work of the superintendent, or other shore employee, while either of the latter is engaged in superintending repair of average damage.

XVII. ALLOWANCES FOR CARGO DAMAGED AND SOLD AND CONTRIBUTORY VALUE OF SAME
Adopted June 2, 1927

Where cargo is damaged, as a consequence of a general average act, and sold, and the extent of the loss has not been otherwise determined, the amount, if any, to be made good for same shall be based on the market value at the date of arrival or at the termination of the adventure (dependent on the facts) and shall be determined on the "salvage loss" basis irrespective of the date of sale.

The contributory value of such cargo shall be based on the proceeds of sale to which shall be added any amount made good; deduction being made of charges incurred subsequent to the general average act, except such charges as are allowed in general average.

"The date of arrival" in the case of a vessel herself delivering all cargo saved shall be the last day of discharge; and in complex cases this principle shall be followed as far as possible.

XVIII. WAGES AND PROVISIONS—GENERAL AVERAGE
Adopted October 14, 1937

In making allowance for wages and provisions in General Average either under American law or York/Antwerp Rules a period of less than twelve hours, either alone or in excess of a number of complete days, shall be disregarded and a period of twelve hours or more, either alone or in excess of a number of complete days, shall be treated as a whole day.

XIX. FIRE EXTINGUISHERS
Adopted October 14, 1937

The cost of replacing gas or any commodity used in efforts to extinguish a fire on board a vessel shall be allowed in general average even though the gas or commodity was on board the vessel at the time the fire was discovered.

XX. APPORTIONMENT OF LEGAL COSTS AND/OR OTHER EXPENSES IN COLLISION CASES
Adopted April 13, 1961

In cases involving collisions, the legal costs and/or other expenses incurred to determine liability either by court action, arbitration or determination by consent of the parties shall be apportioned rateably over the full provable damages, excluding interest and costs, of the claim and counter-claim which have been or would have been allowed.

Nothing contained in this rule shall affect those legal costs and/or other expenses incurred specifically for the purpose of defense or recovery which shall be charged accordingly.

XXI. AIR FREIGHT
Adopted April 13, 1961

The cost of air freight on repair parts shall be allowed as part of the reasonable cost of repairs when the shipment of such parts by water and/or land conveyance would result in unreasonable delay.

Nevertheless when shipment by air saves General Average expense the extra cost of shipment by air over the cost of water and/or land conveyance shall be allowed in General Average up to the expense saved.

Rules of Practice for American Lake Adjustment of the Great Lakes Average Adjusting Committee and Great Lakes Protective Association

1. *Docking for Sight and Survey.* When a vessel has an accident for which the Underwriters' representative recommends dry docking for sight and survey and no damage requiring repair is found, Underwriters shall bear the entire dry docking expense provided the owner complies with the Underwriters' representative's recommendation with respect to time and place of dry docking.

2. *Deductions from Cost of Repairs in Adjusting General Average.* In adjusting claims for general average, repairs to be allowed in general average shall not be subject to deductions in respect of "new for old."

3. *Compensation and Expenses of Owner's Surveyor or Representative.* In the event of loss or damage, the Owner may employ an independent surveyor or use his own employee for surveys thereof and to superintend repairs, and compensation and incidental expenses for such service shall be allowed in average.

4. *Towage Expense.* While towage to and from the shipyard is generally allowed as part of the cost of repairs, if, after repairs are completed, the vessel is at a place more advantageous to take on cargo some credit must be given on the towage expense. For example: If a damaged vessel, after discharging her cargo, is taken to a shipyard for repairs enroute, or adjacent to a place where she is to load cargo after being repaired, only the extra towage expense taking her to and from the shipyard is collectible. In other words, the owner of the ship must pay for the ordinary towage which would have been required in any event.

5. Deferment of *Repairs for Convenience of Owner* (See No. 14). Where repairs of known damage are deferred for the convenience of the owner beyond the vessel's navigation season, any increase in the claim against Underwriters resulting from such deferment shall be borne by the owner, except increase in ship repairers' charges occurring during the 15-month period under the Limitation of Date of Repair or Claim clause. Nevertheless, if it can be established that such deferment resulted in a saving to the Underwriters,

such increased costs, up to the amount of the saving effected, may be included in the claim. Notwithstanding the foregoing, repairs to damages resulting from disasters occurring subsequent to November 1 and effected during the following winter season shall not be considered as deferred repairs.

6. *Temporary Repairs.* The cost of temporary repairs shall be allowed as part of the claim when temporary repairs are necessary to enable the vessel to proceed safely to a port of repair. On the other hand, whenever temporary repairs are made solely for the purpose of permitting the vessel to continue in operation and repairs are deferred until later, such increased expense is to be charged to the owner alone. However, under such circumstances, when it can be shown that making temporary repairs resulted in an ultimate saving to the Underwriters (applying the same principles governing Rule 5), the cost of temporary repairs, up to the amount of the saving effected, may be included in the claim. In addition to the above, cases may arise where it may be perfectly proper for an owner to charge for temporary repairs when parts or material cannot be obtained except after an unreasonable delay, so that permanent repairs are postponed on this account and not merely for the convenience of the owner.

7. *Interest and Commissions in General Average.* Interest or commissions on allowances, sacrifices or expenditures are not allowable in General Average in ballast cases or in cases involving the carriage of bulk cargoes unless the bill of lading or contract of affreightment covering the particular shipment expressly refers to the York/Antwerp Rules or some other set of rules providing for interest or commissions.

8. *Valuation of Contributing Interests in General Average.* The contributory values for general average involving the carriage of bulk cargoes, unless the bill of lading or contract of affreightment covering the particular shipment expressly refers to the York/Antwerp Rules or other rules requiring appraisals or other determinations of value, shall be based upon the full agreed insurance valuation of the vessel appearing in the regular hull insurance policies excluding any increased value or excess liabilities insurance on the said vessel, the insured value of cargo or its invoice value if uninsured including guaranteed freight paid or payable, and the gross amount of freight at risk and earned less one-half.

9. *Cargo and Freight—Amount Made Good in General Average.* The amounts to be made good as General Average for damage to or loss of cargo and loss of freight arising therefrom shall be calculated on the same basis as for the contributory values dealt with in Rule 8.

10. *Wages and Provisions in General Average.*
   (A) Where cargo is lightered, wages and provisions are allowable while the cargo is being reloaded.
   (B) In making allowances for wages and provisions in General Average at a port or place of refuge, a period of less than 12 hours, either alone or in excess of a number of complete days, shall be disregarded and a period of 12 hours or more, either alone or in excess of the number of complete days, shall be treated as a complete day.

11. *Apportionment of Common Expense When Repairs Are Made.* Common expenses for making repairs such as moving the vessel to and from a repair yard, towage, docking and undocking, dry dock charges and other expenses which are common and required by both classes of work, shall be apportioned between the owner and the Underwriters when a vessel is dry docked and/or undergoes repairs:

(A) For owner's account and damage previously unknown is discovered chargeable to Underwriters for which repairs are concurrently made; or

(B) For survey and/or repairs chargeable to Underwriters and repairs for owner's account are concurrently made which are immediately necessary for the seaworthiness or the continued operation of the vessel even though the necessity for such owner's repairs was previously unknown.

A classification survey, although it is for the owner's account, shall not be considered as requiring the apportionment of common expenses under this Rule since classification societies defer such surveys for the owner's convenience and the entire amount of the common expense shall be chargeable to the Underwriters unless repairs are concurrently made for owner's account which are immediately necessary for seaworthiness or the continued operation of the vessel.

When as a matter of convenience an owner takes advantage of the vessel being at a repair yard for Underwriters' repairs and makes repairs or has maintenance work performed for owner's account not immediately necessary for seaworthiness or the continued operation of the vessel, the entire amount of the common expense shall be chargeable to the Underwriters.

12. *Maintenance of Class Charges.* Some adjusters have included two Maintenance of Class charges of the American Bureau of Shipping in their adjustments of Particular Average damage, one at the time preliminary survey of the damage was held and one at the time permanent repairs are made at the shipyard. This practice is not justified, the original service relating merely to the determination of whether or not the vessel is seaworthy to continue in operation without making immediate repairs, the postponement being for the convenience of the owner to permit the ship to continue in operation without making permanent repairs until some later date. It would appear as though the services relate more to obtaining a Certificate of Seaworthiness and therefore entirely for the benefit of the owner and an expense which he should bear, except where it can be established that the services resulted in an ultimate saving to the Underwriters, as provided for in the latter part of the following rule:

When a vessel meets with an accident which a survey discloses has not affected her seaworthiness and a certificate to that effect is issued by a Classification Society surveyor, granting permission to postpone permanent repairs until a later date, and a second survey for Maintenance of Class is made when repairs are finally carried out, the Underwriters will recognize only the second Maintenance of Class charge, unless it develops that the services result in an ultimate saving to the Underwriters, in which event the extra expense may be asserted in an amount up to the saving effected.

13. *Division of Legal Expense.*
    1. Legal expenses shall be divided into the following categories:
        (A) Attack relating to the proceedings for the recovery of damages sustained by the insured ship in collision.
        (B) Defense relating to proceedings against the insured ship for damage sustained by another ship in collision.
    2. Owner and Underwriters shall contribute to the legal expense of attack in the proportion that owner's claim for deductible average, demurrage or other expense, and Underwriters' claim for the balance, bears to the entire provable damage claim of the insured ship.
    3. Where the insured ship becomes legally liable for the damage sustained by another ship, the legal expense of defense shall be charged to the Underwriters, but where defense is successfully maintained legal expense shall be divided between owner and Underwriters in the proportion which the owner's deductible average, the payment of which is avoided, bears to the estimated potential liability of the insured ship to the other ship.

    This latter method of apportionment of legal expense shall also be applied to any case where the collision damages, as finally determined, are less than the owner's deductible average, provided the collision liability claim as originally asserted, based upon reasonable and proper estimates, exceeds the deductible average, the owner's participation in the claim and legal expense not to exceed the amount of his deductible average.
    4. In cross actions involving both attack and defense, legal expense shall be apportioned between owner and Underwriters to the extent to which each is interested in accordance with the foregoing principles. That is to say:
        (A) Attack expenses charged to owners and Underwriters in proportion to the extent to which they are interested.
        (B) Defense expenses charged to Underwriters.
    5. The foregoing principles shall govern in respect to compromise settlements and arbitrations.

14. *Repairs Not Made Within 15-Month Period* (See No. 5). When repairs are not made within the fifteen-month period and for the convenience of the owner an extension is granted to defer repairs beyond this period, the Underwriters will only pay their proportion of the reasonable cost of what repairs would have amounted to had repairs been made within the fifteen-month period. For example: In a case where permission is given an owner to defer repairs beyond the fifteen-month period and in the meantime shipyard costs for labor and material have increased and repairs are made, such extra cost will be disallowed. Nevertheless, if it can be established that such deferment resulted in a saving to the Underwriters, such increased costs, up to the amount of the saving effected, may be included in the claim.

15. *Commencement and Termination of a Voyage.* Navigating risk shall attach when a vessel, light or loaded, sails on the first voyage of the season by breaking ground for the voyage in complete readiness for the voyage with the present intention of immediately quitting the port. Conversely, port risk shall attach at the time a vessel reaches its final port of destination at the

close of the navigating season subject to the provision of the Trading Warranty and Season of Navigation clause in the Association's Certificate which provides: "A Vessel may discharge inward cargo, take in outward cargo, retain cargo onboard, and move in port during the period she is in Winter lay-up. For purposes of this provision, such of the following places as are designated by a single numeral shall be deemed one port: (1) Duluth-Superior, (2) Detroit-Dearborn-River Rouge-Ecorse-Wyandotte-Windsor, (3) Kingston-Portsmouth."

Association of Average Adjusters of Canada Rules of Practice for the Great Lakes

(Adopted February 16, 1971; Confirmed March 17, 1971)

(These Rules shall also apply to adjustments governed by Contracts of Affreightment providing for adjustments according to American Lake Practice or American Lake Adjustment.)

1. DOCKING FOR SIGHT AND SURVEY. When a vessel meets with an accident on account of which she is recommended by the underwriters' representative to be placed on drydock specially for sight and survey and no damage requiring repair is found, underwriters shall bear the entire dry-docking expense provided the owner complies with the underwriters' representative's recommendation with respect to time and place of drydocking.

2. DEDUCTIONS FROM COST OF REPAIRS IN ADJUSTING GENERAL AVERAGE. In adjusting claims for General Average, repairs to be allowed in General Average shall not be subject to deductions in respect of "new for old."

3. SUE AND LABOUR. There shall be no deductible average applied to claims arising under the Sue and Labour Clause.

4. CREDIT FOR EXPENSES SAVED BY TOWAGE TO A PLACE OF REPAIR. If a damaged vessel, after discharging her cargo at destination, is taken to a shipyard for repairs en route, or adjacent to a place where she is to load cargo after being repaired, only the extra towage expense taking her to and from the shipyard shall be charged to underwriters.

5. DEFERMENT OF REPAIRS FOR OWNERS' CONVENIENCE. Where repairs of known damage are deferred for the convenience of the owner beyond fifteen (15) months, any increase in the claim upon underwriters resulting from such deferment shall be borne by the owners. Nevertheless, if it can be established that such deferment resulted in a saving to underwriters, the increase in the amount of the claim up to the amount of saving to underwriters effected, shall be charged to underwriters.

6. TEMPORARY REPAIRS.
    (A) The cost of reasonable temporary repairs shall be charged to underwriters:

    When made in order to effect a saving in the cost of permanent repairs;

When complete repairs cannot be made at the port where the vessel is, or cannot be made when parts or material cannot be obtained except after an unreasonable delay.

(B) Where temporary repairs are reasonably effected at a port of loading, call or refuge, for the common safety or for the safe prosecution of the voyage, the cost of such repairs shall be allowed as General Average.

The Adjuster shall insert a note in the Average Statement in explanation of the allowances made.

7. INTEREST AND COMMISSION IN GENERAL AVERAGE.

(A) Bulk Cargo and Vessel in Ballast.

Interest and commission on allowances, sacrifices or expenditures are not allowable in General Average in ballast cases or in cases involving the carriage of bulk cargoes.

(B) General Cargo.

(1) Where allowances, sacrifices or expenditures are charged or made good in General Average, interest shall be allowed thereon at the legal rate prevailing at the last place or port of destination.

(2) A commission of 2½ per cent on General Average disbursements, other than the wages and maintainance of master, officers and crew and fuel and stores not replaced during the voyage, shall be allowed in General Average.

8. VALUATION OF CONTRIBUTING INTERESTS IN GENERAL AVERAGE. The vessel shall contribute to General Average on a value based upon the full agreed insurance valuation appearing in the insurance policy or policies on Hull and Machinery, without taking into consideration any insurance effected on said vessel on increased value or excess liabilities.

The cargo shall contribute in General Average on a value based upon its insured value or if uninsured its invoice value including guaranteed freight paid or payable.

The freight shall contribute to General Average based on the gross amount at risk and earned less one half.

Electronic equipment or other equipment not included in the vessel's insured value shall contribute on a value based upon its insured value or if uninsured upon its actual value.

9. CARGO AND FREIGHT—AMOUNT MADE GOOD IN GENERAL AVERAGE. The amounts to be made good as General Average for damage to or loss of cargo and loss of freight arising therefrom shall be calculated on the same basis as for the contributory values dealt with in Rule No. 8.

10. WAGES AND PROVISIONS IN GENERAL AVERAGE.

(A) Where cargo is lightered, wages and provisions are allowable while the cargo is being reloaded.

(B) In making allowances for wages and provisions in General Average at a port or place of refuge, a period of less than twelve hours either alone or in excess of a number of complete days, shall be disregarded and a period of twelve hours or more, either alone or in excess of a number of complete days, shall be treated as a complete day.

11. APPORTIONMENT OF COMMON EXPENSE WHEN REPAIRS ARE MADE. Common expenses for making repairs such as moving the vessel to

and from a repair yard, towage, docking and undocking, dry dock charges and other expenses which are common and required by both classes of work, shall be divided equally between the owner and the underwriters when a vessel is dry docked and/or undergoes repairs:

(A) For owner's account and damage previously unknown is discovered chargeable to underwriters for which repairs are concurrently made; or

(B) For survey and/or repairs chargeable to underwriters and repairs for owner's account are concurrently made which are immediately necessary for the seaworthiness or the continued operation of the vessel even though the necessity for such owner's repairs was previously unknown.

A classification survey, although it is for the owner's account, shall not be considered as requiring the division of common expenses under this Rule since classification societies defer such surveys for the owner's convenience and the entire amount of the common expense shall be chargeable to the underwriters unless repairs are concurrently made for owner's account which are immediately necessary for seaworthiness or the continued operation of the vessel. When as a matter of convenience an owner takes advantage of the vessel being at a repair yard for underwriters' repairs and makes repairs or has maintenance work performed for owner's account not immediately necessary for seaworthiness or the continued operation of the vessel, the entire amount of the common expense shall be chargeable to the underwriters.

12. MAINTENANCE OF CLASS CHARGES. When a vessel meets with an accident which a survey discloses has not affected her seaworthiness and a certificate or report to that effect is issued by a Classification Society, granting permission to postpone permanent repairs until a later date, and a second certificate or report for maintenance is issued when repairs are finally carried out, only the charge for the second classification certificate or report will be recognized, unless it develops that the services for the first certificate or report result in an ultimate saving to underwriters, in which event the first charge may be allowed in an amount up to the saving effected.

13. DIVISION OF LEGAL EXPENSE.
   1. Legal expenses shall be divided into the following categories:
      (a) Attack relating to the proceedings for the recovery of damages sustained by the insured ship in collision.
      (b) Defense relating to proceedings against the insured ship for damage sustained by another ship in collision.
   2. Owner and underwriters shall contribute to the legal expense of attack in the proportion that owner's claim for deductible average, demurrage or other expense, and underwriters' claim for the balance, bears to the entire provable damage claim of the insured ship.
   3. Where the insured ship becomes legally liable for the damage sustained by another ship, the legal expense of defense shall be charged to the underwriters, but where defense is successfully maintained legal expense shall be divided between owner and underwriters in the proportion which the owner's deductible average, the payment of which is avoided, bears to the estimated potential liability of the insured ship to the other ship.

This latter method of apportionment of legal expense shall also be applied to any case where the collision damages, as finally determined, are less than the owner's deductible average, provided the collision liability claim as originally asserted, based upon reasonable and proper estimates, exceeds the deductible average, the owner's participation in the claim and legal expense not to exceed the amount of his deductible average.

4. In cross actions involving both attack and defense, legal expense shall be apportioned between owner and underwriters to the extent to which each is interested in accordance with the foregoing principles. That is to say:

(a) Attack expenses charged to owners and underwrites in proportion to the extent to which they are interested.

(b) Defense expenses charged to underwriters.

5. The foregoing principles shall govern in respect to compromise settlements and arbitrations.

Marine Insurance Act, 1906

ARRANGEMENT OF SECTIONS

MARINE INSURANCE ACT, 1906

An Act to codify the Law relating to Marine Insurance.

Be it enacted by the King's most Excellent Majesty, by and with the advice and consent of the Lords Spiritual and Temporal, and Commons, in his present Parliament assembled, and by the authority of the same, as follows—

MARINE INSURANCE.

1. MARINE INSURANCE DEFINED. A contract of marine insurance is a contract whereby the insurer undertakes to indemnify the assured, in manner and to the extent thereby agreed, against marine losses, that is to say, the losses incident to marine adventure.

2. MIXED SEA AND LAND RISKS.
   (1) A contract of marine insurance may, by its express terms, or by usage of trade, be extended so as to protect the assured against losses on inland waters or on any land risk which may be incidental to any sea voyage.
   (2) Where a ship in course of building, or the launch of a ship, or any adventure analogous to a marine adventure, is covered by a policy in the form of a marine policy, the provisions of this Act, in so far as applicable, shall apply thereto; but, except as by this section provided, nothing in this Act shall alter or affect any rule of law applicable to any contract of

insurance other than a contract of marine insurance as by this Act defined.

3. MARINE ADVENTURE AND MARITIME PERILS DEFINED

(1) Subject to the provisions of this Act, every lawful marine adventure may be the subject of a contract of marine insurance.

(2) In particular there is a marine adventure where—

(a) Any ship goods or other movables are exposed to maritime perils. Such property is in this Act referred to as "insurable property";

(b) The earning or acquisition of any freight, passage money, commission, profit, or other pecuniary benefit, or the security for any advances, loan, or disbursements, is endangered by the exposure of insurable property to maritime perils;

(c) Any liability to a third party may be incurred by the owner of, or other person interested in or responsible for, insurable property, by reason of maritime perils.

"Maritime perils" means the perils consequent on, or incidental to, the navigation of the seas, fire, war perils, pirates, rovers, thieves, captures, seizures, restraints, and detainments of princes and peoples, jettisons, barratry, and any other perils, either of the like kind or which may be designated by the policy.

INSURABLE INTEREST.

4. AVOIDANCE OF WAGERING OR GAMING CONTRACTS

(1) Every contract of marine insurance by way of gaming or wagering is void.

(2) A contract of marine insurance is deemed to be a gaming or wagering contract-

(a) Where the assured has not an insurable interest as defined by this Act, and the contract is entered into with no expectation of acquiring such an interest; or

(b) Where the policy is made "interest or no interest," or "without further proof of interest than the policy itself," or "without benefit of salvage to the insurer," or subject to any other like term:

Provided that, where there is no possibility of salvage, a policy may be effected without benefit of salvage to the insurer.

5. INSURABLE INTEREST DEFINED

(1) Subject to the provisions of this Act, every person has an insurable interest who is interested in a marine adventure.

(2) In particular a person is interested in a marine adventure where he stands in any legal or equitable relation to the adventure or to any insurable property at risk therein, in consequence of which he may benefit by the safety or due arrival of insurable property, or may be prejudiced by its loss, or by damage thereto, or by the detention thereof, or may incur liability in respect thereof.

6. WHEN INTEREST MUST ATTACH

(1) The assured must be interested in the subject-matter insured at the time of the loss though he need not be interested when the assurance is effected:

Provided that where the subject-matter is insured "lost or not lost," the assured may recover although he may not have acquired his interest until after the loss, unless at the time of effecting the contract of insurance the assured was aware of the loss, and the insurer was not.

(2) Where the assured has no interest at the time of the loss, he cannot acquire interest by any act or election after he is aware of the loss.

7. DEFEASIBLE OR CONTINGENT INTEREST

(1) A defeasible interest is insurable, as also is a contingent interest.

(2) In particular, where the buyer of goods has insured them, he has an insurable interest, notwithstanding that he might, at his election, have rejected the goods, or have treated them as at the seller's risk, by reason of the latter's delay in making delivery or otherwise.

8. PARTIAL INTEREST. A partial interest of any nature is insurable.

9. REINSURANCE

(1) The insurer under a contract of marine insurance has an insurable interest in his risk, and may re-insure in respect of it.

(2) Unless the policy otherwise provides, the original assured has no right or interest in respect of such re-insurance.

10. BOTTOMRY. The lender of money on bottomry or respondentia has an insurable interest, in respect of the loan.

11. MASTER'S AND SEAMEN'S WAGES. The master or any member of the crew of a ship has an insurable interest, in respect of his wages.

12. ADVANCE FREIGHT. In the case of advance freight, the person advancing the freight has an insurable interest, in so far as such freight is not repayable in case of loss.

13. CHARGES OF INSURANCE. The assured has an insurable interest in the charges of any insurance which may he may effect.

14. QUANTUM OF INTEREST

(1) Where the subject-matter insured is mortgaged, the mortgagor has an insurable interest in the full value thereof, and the mortgagee has an insurable interest in respect of any sum due or to become due under the mortgage.

(2) A mortgagee, consignee, or other person having an interest in the subject-matter insured may insure on behalf and for the benefit of other persons interested as well as for his own benefit.

(3) The owner of insurable property has an insurable interest in respect of the full value thereof, notwithstanding that some third person may have agreed, or be liable, to indemnify him in case of loss.

15. ASSIGNMENT OF INTEREST. Where the assured assigns or otherwise parts with his interest in the subject-matter insured, he does not thereby transfer to the assignee his rights under the contract of insurance, unless there be an express or implied agreement with the assignee to that effect.

But the provisions of this section do not affect a transmission of interest by operation of law.

INSURABLE VALUE.

16. MEASURE OF INSURABLE VALUE. Subject to any express provision or valuation in the policy, the insurable value of the subject-matter insured must be ascertained as follows—

(1) In insurance on ship, the insurable value is the value, at the commencement of the risk, of the ship, including her outfit, provisions and stores for the officers and crew, money advanced for seamen's wages, and other disbursements (if any) incurred to make the ship fit for the voyage or adventure contemplated by the policy, plus the charges of insurance upon the whole:

The insurable value, in the case of a steamship, includes also the machinery, boilers, and coals and engine stores if owned by the assured, and, in the case of a ship engaged in special trade, the ordinary fittings requisite for that trade:

(2) In insurance on freight, whether paid in advance or otherwise, the insurable value is the gross amount of the freight at the risk of the assured, plus the charges of insurance:

(3) In insurance on goods or merchandise, the insurable value is the prime cost of the property insured, plus the expenses of and incidental to shipping and the charges of insurance upon the whole:

(4) In insurance on any other subject-matter, the insurable value is the amount at the risk of the assured when the policy attaches, plus the charges of insurance.

DISCLOSURE AND REPRESENTATIONS.

17. INSURANCE IS UBERRIMAE FIDEI. A contract of marine insurance is a contract based upon the utmost good faith, and, if the utmost good faith be not observed by either party, the contract may be avoided by the other party.

18. DISCLOSURE BY ASSURED

(1) Subject to the provisions of this section, the assured must disclose to the insurer, before the contract is concluded, every material circumstance which is known to the assured, and the assured is deemed to know every circumstance which, in the ordinary course of business, ought to be known by him. If the assured fails to make such disclosure, the insurer may avoid the contract.

(2) Every circumstance is material which would influence the judgment of a prudent insurer in fixing the premium, or determining whether he will take the risk.

(3) In the absence of inquiry the following circumstances need not be disclosed, namely—

(a) Any circumstance which diminishes the risk;

(b) Any circumstance which is known or presumed to be known to the insurer. The insurer is presumed to know matters of common notoriety or knowledge, and matters which an insurer in the ordinary course of his business, as such, ought to know;

(c) Any circumstance as to which information is waived by the insurer;

(d) Any circumstance which it is superfluous to disclose by reason of any express or implied warranty.

    (4) Whether any particular circumstance, which is not disclosed, be material or not is, in each case, a question of fact.

    (5) The term "circumstance" includes any communication made to, or information received by, the assured.

19. DISCLOSURE BY AGENT EFFECTING INSURANCE. Subject to the provisions of the preceding section as to circumstances which need not be disclosed, where an insurance is effected for the assured by an agent, the agent must disclose to the insurer—

    (a) Every material circumstance which is known to himself, and an agent to insure is deemed to know every circumstance which in the ordinary course of business ought to be known by, or to have been communicated to, him; and

    (b) Every material circumstance which the assured is bound to disclose, unless it comes to his knowledge too late to communicate it to the agent.

20. REPRESENTATIONS PENDING NEGOTIATION OF CONTRACT

    (1) Every material representation made by the assured or his agent to the insurer during the negotiations for the contract, and before the contract is concluded, must be true. If it be untrue the insurer may avoid the contract.

    (2) A representation is material which would influence the judgment of a prudent insurer in fixing the premium, or determining whether he will take the risk.

    (3) A representation may be either a representation as to a matter of fact, or as to a matter of expectation or belief.

    (4) A representation as to a matter of fact is true, if it be substantially correct, that is to say, if the difference between what is represented and what is actually correct would not be considered material by a prudent insurer.

    (5) A representation as to a matter of expectation or belief is true if it be made in good faith.

    (6) A representation may be withdrawn or corrected before the contract is concluded.

    (7) Whether a particular representation be material or not is, in each case, a question of fact.

21. WHEN CONTRACT IS DEEMED TO BE CONCLUDED. A contract of marine insurance is deemed to be concluded when the proposal of the assured is accepted by the insurer, whether the policy be then issued or not; and for the purpose of showing when the proposal was accepted, reference may be made to the slip or covering note or other customary memorandum of the contract, although it be unstamped.

THE POLICY.

22. CONTRACT MUST BE EMBODIED IN POLICY. Subject to the provisions of any statute, a contract of marine insurance is inadmissible in evidence unless it is embodied in a marine policy in accordance with this Act. The policy may be executed and issued either at the time when the contract is concluded, or afterwards.

23. WHAT POLICY MUST SPECIFY. A marine policy must specify—

    (1) The name of the assured, or of some person who effects the insurance on his behalf:

    (2) The subject-matter insured and the risk insured against:

    (3) The voyage, or period of time, or both, as the case may be, covered by the insurance:

(4) The sum or sums insured:

(5) The name or names of the insurers.

24. SIGNATURE OF INSURER

(1) A marine policy must be signed by or on behalf of the insurer, provided that in the case of a corporation the corporate seal may be sufficient, but nothing in this section shall be construed as requiring the subscription of a corporation to be under seal.

(2) Where a policy is subscribed by or on behalf of two or more insurers, each subscription, unless the contrary be expressed, constitutes a distinct contract with the assured.

25. VOYAGE AND TIME POLICIES

(1) Where the contract is to insure the subject-matter at and from, or from one place to another or others, the policy is called a "voyage policy," and where the contract is to insure the subject-matter for a definite period of time the policy is called a "time policy." A contract for both voyage and time may be included in the same policy.

(2) Subject to the provisions of section eleven of the Finance Act, 1901, a time policy which is made for any time exceeding twelve months is invalid.

26. DESIGNATION OF SUBJECT-MATTER

(1) The subject-matter insured must be designated in a marine policy with reasonable certainty.

(2) The nature and extent of the interest of the assured in the subject-matter insured need not be specified in the policy.

(3) Where the policy designates the subject-matter insured in general terms, it shall be construed to apply to the interest intended by the assured to be covered.

(4) In the application of this section regard shall be had to any usage regulating the designation of the subject-matter insured.

27. VALUED POLICY

(1) A policy may be either valued or unvalued.

(2) A valued policy is a policy which specifies the agreed value of the subject-matter insured.

(3) Subject to the provisions of this Act, and in the absence of fraud, the value fixed by the policy is, as between the insurer and assured, conclusive of the insurable value of the subject intended to be insured whether the loss be total or partial.

(4) Unless the policy otherwise provides, the value fixed by the policy is not conclusive for the purpose of determining whether there has been a constructive total loss.

28. UNVALUED POLICY. An unvalued policy is a policy which does not specify the value of the subject-matter insured, but, subject to the limit of the sum insured, leaves the insurable value to be subsequently ascertained, in the manner herein-before specified.

29. FLOATING POLICY BY SHIP OR SHIPS

(1) A floating policy is a policy which describes the insurance in general terms, and leaves the name of the ship or ships and other particulars to be defined by subsequent declaration.

(2) The subsequent declaration or declarations may be made by indorsement on the policy, or in other customary manner.

(3) Unless the policy otherwise provides, the declarations must be made in the order of dispatch or shipment. They must, in the case of goods, comprise all consignments within the terms of the policy, and the value of the goods or other property must be honestly stated, but an omission or erroneous declaration may be rectified even after loss or arrival, provided the omission or declaration was made in good faith.

(4) Unless the policy otherwise provides, where a declaration of value is not made until after notice of loss or arrival, the policy must be treated as an unvalued policy as regards the subject-matter of that declaration.

30. CONSTRUCTION OF TERMS IN POLICY

(1) A policy may be in the form in the First Schedule to this Act.

(2) Subject to the provisions of this Act, and unless the context of the policy otherwise requires, the terms and expressions mentioned in the First Schedule to this Act shall be construed as having the scope and meaning in that schedule assigned to them.

31. PREMIUM TO BE ARRANGED

(1) Where an insurance is effected at a premium to be arranged, and no arrangement is made, a reasonable premium is payable.

(2) Where an insurance is effected on the terms that an additional premium is to be arranged in a given event, and that event happens but no arrangement is made, then a reasonable additional premium is payable.

DOUBLE INSURANCE.

32. DOUBLE INSURANCE

(1) Where two or more policies are effected by or on behalf of the assured on the same adventure and interest or any part thereof, and the sums insured exceed the indemnity allowed by this Act, the assured is said to be over-insured by double insurance.

(2) Where the assured is over-insured by double insurance—

(a) The assured, unless the policy otherwise provides, may claim payment from the insurers in such order as he may think fit, provided that he is not entitled to receive any sum in excess of the indemnity allowed by this Act;

(b) Where the policy under which the assured claims is a valued policy, the assured must give credit as against the valuation for any sum received by him under any other policy without regard to the actual value of the subject-matter insured;

(c) Where the policy under which the assured claims is an unvalued policy he must give credit, as against the full insurable value, for any sum received by him under any other policy;

(d) Where the assured receives any sum in excess of the indemnity allowed by this Act, he is deemed to hold such sum in trust for the insurers, according to their right of contribution among themselves.

WARRANTIES, ETC.

33. NATURE OF WARRANTY

(1) A warranty, in the following sections relating to warranties, means a promissory warranty, that is to say, a warranty by which the assured undertakes that some particular thing shall or shall not be done, or that some condition shall be fulfilled, or whereby he affirms or negatives the existence of a particular state of facts.

(2) A warranty may be express or implied.

(3) A warranty, as above defined, is a condition which must be exactly complied with, whether it be material to the risk or not. If it be not so complied with, then, subject to any express provision in the policy, the insurer is discharged from liability as from the date of the breach of warranty, but without prejudice to any liability incurred by him before that date.

34. WHEN BREACH OF WARRANTY EXCUSED

(1) Non-compliance with a warranty is excused when, by reason of a change of circumstances, the warranty ceases to be applicable to the circumstances of the contract, or when compliance with the warranty is rendered unlawful by any subsequent law.

(2) Where a warranty is broken, the assured cannot avail himself of the defence that the breach has been remedied, and the warranty complied with, before loss.

(3) A breach of warranty may be waived by the insurer.

35. EXPRESS WARRANTIES

(1) An express warranty may be in any form of words from which the intention to warrant is to be inferred.

(2) An express warranty must be included in, or written upon, the policy, or must be contained in some document incorporated by reference into the policy.

(3) An express warranty does not exclude an implied warranty, unless it be inconsistent therewith.

36. WARRANTY OF NEUTRALITY

(1) Where insurable property, whether ship or goods, is expressly warranted neutral, there is an implied condition that the property shall have a neutral character at the commencement of the risk, and that, so far as the assured can control the matter, its neutral character shall be preserved during the risk.

(2) Where a ship is expressly warranted "neutral" there is also an implied condition that, so far as the assured can control the matter, she shall be properly documented, that is to say, that she shall carry the necessary papers to establish her neutrality, and that she shall not falsify or suppress her papers, or use simulated papers. If any loss occurs through breach of this condition, the insurer may avoid the contract.

37. NO IMPLIED WARRANTY OF NATIONALITY. There is no implied warranty as to the nationality of a ship, or that her nationality shall not be changed during the risk.

38. WARRANTY OF GOOD SAFETY. Where the subject-matter insured is warranted "well" or "in good safety" on a particular day, it is sufficient if it be safe at any time during that day.

39. WARRANTY OF SEAWORTHINESS OF SHIP
  (1) In a voyage policy there is an implied warranty that at the commencement of the voyage the ship shall be seaworthy for the purpose of the particular adventure insured.
  (2) Where the policy attaches while the ship is in port, there is also an implied warranty that she shall, at the commencement of the risk, be reasonably fit to encounter the ordinary perils of the port.
  (3) Where the policy relates to a voyage which is performed in different stages, during which the ship requires different kinds of or further preparation or equipment, there is an implied warranty that at the commencement of each stage the ship is seaworthy in respect of such preparation or equipment for the purposes of that stage.
  (4) A ship is deemed to be seaworthy when she is reasonably fit in all respects to encounter the ordinary perils of the seas of the adventure insured.
  (5) In a time policy there is no implied warranty that the ship shall be seaworthy at any stage of the adventure, but where, with the privity of the assured, the ship is sent to sea in an unseaworthy state, the insurer is not liable for any loss attributable to unseaworthiness.

40. NO IMPLIED WARRANTY THAT GOODS ARE SEAWORTHY
  (1) In a policy on goods or other movables there is no implied warranty that the goods or movables are seaworthy.
  (2) In a voyage policy on goods or other movables there is an implied warranty that at the commencement of the voyage the ship is not only seaworthy as a ship, but also that she is reasonably fit to carry the goods or other movables to the destination contemplated by the policy.

41. WARRANTY OF LEGALITY. There is an implied warranty that the adventure insured is a lawful one, and that, so far as the assured can control the matter, the adventure shall be carried out in a lawful manner.

THE VOYAGE.

42. IMPLIED CONDITION AS TO COMMENCEMENT OF RISK
  (1) Where the subject-matter is insured by a voyage policy "at and from" or "from" a particular place, it is not necessary that the ship should be at that place when the contract is concluded, but there is an implied condition that the adventure shall be commenced within a reasonable time, and that if the adventure be not so commenced the insurer may avoid the contract.
  (2) The implied condition may be negatived by showing that the delay was caused by circumstances known to the insurer before the contract was concluded, or by showing that he waived the condition.

43. ALTERATION OF PORT OF DEPARTURE. Where the place of departure is specified by the policy, and the ship instead of sailing from that place sails from any other place, the risk does not attach.

44. SAILING FOR DIFFERENT DESTINATION. Where the destination is specified in the policy, and the ship, instead of sailing for that destination, sails for any other destination, the risk does not attach.

45. CHANGE OF VOYAGE

(1) Where, after the commencement of the risk, the destination of the ship is voluntarily changed from the destination contemplated by the policy, there is said to be a change of voyage.

(2) Unless the policy otherwise provides, where there is a change of voyage, the insurer is discharged from liability as from the time of change, that is to say, as from the time when the determination to change it is manifested; and it is immaterial that the ship may not in fact have left the course of voyage contemplated by the policy when the loss occurs.

46. DEVIATION

(1) Where a ship, without lawful excuse, deviates from the voyage contemplated by the policy, the insurer is discharged from liability as from the time of deviation, and it is immaterial that the ship may have regained her route before any loss occurs.

(2) There is a deviation from the voyage contemplated by the policy—
   (a) Where the course of the voyage is specifically designated by the policy, and that course is departed from; or
   (b) Where the course of the voyage is not specifically designated by the policy, but the usual and customary course is departed from.

(3) The intention to deviate is immaterial; there must be a deviation in fact to discharge the insurer from his liability under the contract.

47. SEVERAL PORTS OF DISCHARGE

(1) Where several ports of discharge are specified by the policy, the ship may proceed to all or any of them, but, in the absence of any usage or sufficient cause to the contrary, she must proceed to them, or such of them as she goes to, in the order designated by the policy. If she does not there is a deviation.

(2) Where the policy is to "ports of discharge," within a given area, which are not named, the ship must, in the absence of any usage or sufficient cause to the contrary, proceed to them, or such of them as she goes to, in their geographical order. If she does not there is a deviation.

48. DELAY IN VOYAGE.
In the case of a voyage policy, the adventure insured must be prosecuted throughout its course with reasonable dispatch, and, if without lawful excuse it is not so prosecuted, the insurer is discharged from liability as from the time when the delay became unreasonable.

49. EXCUSES FOR DEVIATION OR DELAY

(1) Deviation or delay in prosecuting the voyage contemplated by the policy is excused—
   (a) Where authorised by any special term in the policy; or
   (b) Where caused by circumstances beyond the control of the master and his employer; or
   (c) Where reasonably necessary in order to comply with an express or implied warranty; or
   (d) Where reasonably necessary for the safety of the ship or subject-matter insured; or
   (e) For the purpose of saving human life, or aiding a ship in distress where human life may be in danger; or
   (f) Where reasonably necessary for the purpose of obtaining medical or surgical aid for any person on board the ship; or

    (g) Where caused by the barratrous conduct of the master or crew, if barratry be one of the perils insured against.

    (2) When the cause excusing the deviation or delay ceases to operate, the ship must resume her course, and prosecute her voyage, with reasonable despatch.

ASSIGNMENT OF POLICY.

50. WHEN AND HOW POLICY IS ASSIGNABLE

    (1) A marine policy is assignable unless it contains terms expressly prohibiting assignment. It may be assigned either before or after loss.

    (2) Where a marine policy has been assigned so as to pass the beneficial interest in such policy, the assignee of the policy is entitled to sue thereon in his own name; and the defendant is entitled to make any defence arising out of the contract which he would have been entitled to make if the action had been brought in the name of the person by or on behalf of whom the policy was effected.

    (3) A marine policy may be assigned by indorsement thereon or in other customary manner.

51. ASSURED WHO HAS NO INTEREST CANNOT ASSIGN. Where the assured has parted with or lost his interest in the subject-matter insured, and has not, before or at the time of so doing, expressly or impliedly agreed to assign the policy, any subsequent assignment of the policy is inoperative:

    Provided that nothing in this section affects the assignment of a policy after loss.

THE PREMIUM.

52. WHEN PREMIUM PAYABLE. Unless otherwise agreed, the duty of the assured or his agent to pay the premium, and the duty of the insurer to issue the policy to the assured or his agent, are concurrent conditions, and the insurer is not bound to issue the policy until payment or tender of the premium.

53. POLICY EFFECTED THROUGH BROKER

    (1) Unless otherwise agreed, where a marine policy is effected on behalf of the assured by a broker, the broker is directly responsible to the insurer for the premium, and the insurer is directly responsible to the assured for the amount which may be payable in respect of losses, or in respect of returnable premium.

    (2) Unless otherwise agreed, the broker has, as against the assured, a lien upon the policy for the amount of the premium and his charges in respect of effecting the policy; and, where he has dealt with the person who employs him as a principal, he has also a lien on the policy in respect of any balance on any insurance account which may be due to him from such person, unless when the debt was incurred he had reason to believe that such person was only an agent.

54. EFFECT OF RECEIPT ON POLICY. Where a marine policy effected on behalf of the assured by a broker acknowledges the receipt of the premium, such acknowledgment is, in the absence of fraud, conclusive as between the insurer and the assured, but not as between the insurer and broker.

LOSS AND ABANDONMENT.

55. INCLUDED AND EXCLUDED LOSSES

(1) Subject to the provisions of this Act, and unless the policy otherwise provides, the insurer is liable for any loss proximately caused by a peril insured against, but, subject as aforesaid, he is not liable for any loss which is not proximately caused by a peril insured against.

(2) In particular—

(a) The insurer is not liable for any loss attributable to the wilful misconduct of the assured, but, unless the policy otherwise provides, he is liable for any loss proximately caused by a peril insured against, even though the loss would not have happened but for the misconduct or negligence of the master or crew;

(b) Unless the policy otherwise provides, the insurer on ship or goods is not liable for any loss proximately caused by delay, although the delay be caused by a peril insured against;

(c) Unless the policy otherwise provides, the insurer is not liable for ordinary wear and tear, ordinary leakage and breakage, inherent vice or nature of the subject-matter insured, or for any loss proximately caused by rats or vermin, or for any injury to machinery not proximately caused by maritime perils.

56. PARTIAL AND TOTAL LOSS

(1) A loss may be either total or partial. Any loss other than a total loss, as hereinafter defined, is a partial loss.

(2) A total loss may be either an actual total loss, or a constructive total loss.

(3) Unless a different intention appears from the terms of the policy, an insurance against total loss includes a constructive, as well as an actual, total loss.

(4) Where the assured brings an action for a total loss and the evidence proves only a partial loss, he may, unless the policy otherwise provides, recover for a partial loss.

(5) Where goods reach their destination in specie, but by reason of obliteration of marks, or otherwise, they are incapable of identification, the loss, if any, is partial, and not total.

57. ACTUAL TOTAL LOSS

(1) Where the subject-matter insured is destroyed, or so damaged as to cease to be a thing of the kind insured, or where the assured is irretrievably deprived thereof, there is an actual total loss.

(2) In the case of an actual total loss no notice of abandonment need be given.

58. MISSING SHIP. Where the ship concerned in the adventure is missing, and after the lapse of a reasonable time no news of her has been received, an actual total loss may be presumed.

59. EFFECT OF TRANSHIPMENT, ETC. Where, by a peril insured against, the voyage is interrupted at an intermediate port or place, under such circumstances as, apart from any special stipulation in the contract of affreightment, to justify the master in landing and re-shipping the goods or other movables, or in transhipping them, and sending them on to their

destination, the liability of the insurer continues, notwithstanding the landing or transhipment.

60. CONSTRUCTIVE TOTAL LOSS DEFINED

(1) Subject to any express provision in the policy, there is a constructive total loss where the subject-matter insured is reasonably abandoned on account of its actual total loss appearing to be unavoidable, or because it could not be preserved from actual total loss without an expenditure which would exceed its value when the expenditure had been incurred.

(2) In particular, there is a constructive total loss—

    (i) Where the assured is deprived of the possession of his ship or goods by a peril insured against, and *(a)* it is unlikely that he can recover the ship or goods, as the case may be, or *(b)* the cost of recovering the ship or goods, as the case may be, would exceed their value when recovered; or

    (ii) In the case of damage to a ship, where she is so damaged by a peril insured against that the cost of repairing the damage would exceed the value of the ship when repaired.

In estimating the cost of repairs, no deduction is to be made in respect of general average contributions to those repairs payable by other interests, but account is to be taken of the expense of future salvage operations and of any future general average contributions to which the ship would be liable if repaired; or

    (iii) In the case of damage to goods, where the cost of repairing the damage and forwarding the goods to their destination would exceed their value on arrival.

61. EFFECT OF CONSTRUCTIVE TOTAL LOSS.
Where there is a constructive total loss the assured may either treat the loss as a partial loss, or abandon the subject-matter insured to the insurer and treat the loss as if it were an actual total loss.

62. NOTICE OF ABANDONMENT

(1) Subject to the provisions of this section, where the assured elects to abandon the subject-matter insured to the insurer, he must give notice of abandonment. If he fails to do so the loss can only be treated as a partial loss.

(2) Notice of abandonment may be given in writing, or by word of mouth, or partly in writing and partly by word of mouth, and may be given in any terms which indicate the intention of the assured to abandon his insured interest in the subject-matter insured unconditionally to the insurer.

(3) Notice of abandonment must be given with reasonable diligence after the receipt of reliable information of the loss, but where the information is of a doubtful character the assured is entitled to a reasonable time to make inquiry.

(4) Where notice of abandonment is properly given, the rights of the assured are not prejudiced by the fact that the insurer refuses to accept the abandonment.

(5) The acceptance of an abandonment may be either express or implied from the conduct of the insurer. The mere silence of the insurer after notice is not an acceptance.

(6) Where notice of abandonment is accepted the abandonment is irrevocable. The acceptance of the notice conclusively admits liability for the loss and the sufficiency of the notice.

(7) Notice of abandonment is unnecessary where, at the time when the assured receives information of the loss, there would be no possibility of benefit to the insurer if notice were given to him.

(8) Notice of abandonment may be waived by the insurer.

(9) Where an insurer has re-insured his risk, no notice of abandonment need be given by him.

63. EFFECT OF ABANDONMENT

(1) Where there is a valid abandonment the insurer is entitled to take over the interest of the assured in whatever may remain of the subject-matter insured, and all proprietary rights incidental thereto.

(2) Upon the abandonment of a ship, the insurer thereof is entitled to any freight in course of being earned, and which is earned by her subsequent to the casualty causing the loss, less the expenses of earning it incurred after the casualty; and, where the ship is carrying the owner's goods, the insurer is entitled to a reasonable remuneration for the carriage of them subsequent to the casualty causing the loss.

PARTIAL LOSSES (INCLUDING SALVAGE AND GENERAL
AVERAGE AND PARTICULAR CHARGES).

64. PARTICULAR AVERAGE LOSS

(1) A particular average loss is a partial loss of that subject-matter insured, caused by a peril insured against, and which is not a general average loss.

(2) Expenses incurred by or on behalf of the assured for the safety or preservation of the subject-matter insured, other than general average and salvage charges, are called particular charges. Particular charges are not included in particular average.

65. SALVAGE CHARGES

(1) Subject to any express provision in the policy, salvage charges incurred in preventing a loss by perils insured against may be recovered as a loss by those perils.

(2) "Salvage charges" means the charges recoverable under maritime law by a salvor independently of contract. They do not include the expenses of services in the nature of salvage rendered by the assured or his agents, or any person employed for hire by them, for the purpose of averting a peril insured against. Such expenses, where properly incurred, may be recovered as particular charges or as a general average loss, according to the circumstances under which they were incurred.

66. GENERAL AVERAGE LOSS

(1) A general average loss is a loss caused by or directly consequential on a general average act. It includes a general average expenditure as well as a general average sacrifice.

(2) There is a general average act where any extraordinary sacrifice or expenditure is voluntarily and reasonably made or incurred in time of peril for the purpose of preserving the property imperilled in the common adventure.

(3) Where there is a general average loss, the party on whom it falls is entitled, subject to the conditions imposed by maritime law, to a rateable contribution from the other parties interested, and such contribution is called a general average contribution.

(4) Subject to any express provision in the policy, where the assured has incurred a general average expenditure, he may recover from the insurer in respect of the proportion of the loss which falls upon him; and, in the case of a general average sacrifice, he may recover from the insurer in respect of the whole loss without having enforced his right of contribution from the other parties liable to contribute.

(5) Subject to any express provision in the policy, where the assured has paid, or is liable to pay, a general average contribution in respect of the subject insured, he may recover therefor from the insurer.

(6) In the absence of express stipulation, the insurer is not liable for any general average loss or contribution where the loss was not incurred for the purpose of avoiding, or in connexion with the avoidance of, a peril insured against.

(7) Where ship, freight, and cargo, or any two of those interests, are owned by the same assured, the liability of the insurer in respect of general average losses or contributions is to be determined as if those subjects were owned by different persons.

MEASURE OF INDEMNITY.

67. EXTENT OF LIABILITY OF INSURER FOR LOSS

(1) The sum which the assured can recover in respect of a loss on a policy by which he is insured, in the case of an unvalued policy to the full extent of the insurable value, or, in the case of a valued policy to the full extent of the value fixed by the policy, is called the measure of indemnity.

(2) Where there is a loss recoverable under the policy, the insurer, or each insurer if there be more than one, is liable for such proportion of the measure of indemnity as the amount of his subscription bears to the value fixed by the policy in the case of a valued policy, or to the insurable value in the case of an unvalued policy.

68. TOTAL LOSS. Subject to the provisions of this Act and to any express provision in the policy, where there is a total loss of the subject-matter insured—

(1) If the policy be a valued policy, the measure of indemnity is the sum fixed by the policy:

(2) If the policy be an unvalued policy, the measure of indemnity is the insurable value of the subject-matter insured.

69. PARTIAL LOSS OF SHIP. Where a ship is damaged, but is not totally lost, the measure of indemnity, subject to any express provision in the policy, is as follows—

(1) Where the ship has been repaired, the assured is entitled to the reasonable cost of the repairs, less the customary deductions, but not exceeding the sum insured in respect of any one casualty:

(2) Where the ship has been only partially repaired, the assured is entitled to the reasonable cost of such repairs, computed as above, and also to be

indemnified for the reasonable depreciation, if any, arising from the unrepaired damage, provided that the aggregate amount shall not exceed the cost of repairing the whole damage, computed as above:

(3) Where the ship has not been repaired, and has not been sold in her damaged state during the risk, the assured is entitled to be indemnified for the reasonable depreciation arising from the unrepaired damage, but not exceeding the reasonable cost of repairing such damage, computed as above.

70. PARTIAL LOSS OF FREIGHT. Subject to any express provision in the policy, where there is a partial loss of freight, the measure of indemnity is such proportion of the sum fixed by the policy in the case of a valued policy, or of the insurable value in the case of an unvalued policy, as the proportion of freight lost by the assured bears to the whole freight at the risk of the assured under the policy.

71. PARTIAL LOSS OF GOODS, MERCHANDISE, ETC. Where there is a partial loss of goods, merchandise, or other movables, the measure of indemnity, subject to any express provision in the policy, is as follows—

(1) Where part of the goods, merchandise or other movables insured by a valued policy is totally lost, the measure of indemnity is such proportion of the sum fixed by the policy as the insurable value of the part lost bears to the insurable value of the whole, ascertained as in the case of an unvalued policy:

(2) Where part of the goods, merchandise, or other movables insured by an unvalued policy is totally lost, the measure of indemnity is the insurable value of the part lost, ascertained as in case of total loss:

(3) Where the whole or any part of the goods or merchandise insured has been delivered damaged at its destination, the measure of indemnity is such proportion of the sum fixed by the policy in the case of a valued policy, or of the insurable value in the case of an unvalued policy, as the difference between the gross sound and damaged values at the place of arrival bears to the gross sound value:

(4) "Gross value" means the wholesale price or, if there be no such price, the estimated value, with, in either case, freight, landing charges, and duty paid beforehand; provided that, in the case of goods or merchandise customarily sold in bond, the bonded price is deemed to be the gross value. "Gross proceeds" means the actual price obtained at a sale where all charges on sale are paid by the sellers.

72. APPORTIONMENT OF VALUATION

(1) Where different species of property are insured under a single valuation, the valuation must be apportioned over the different species in proportion to their respective insurable values, as in the case of an unvalued policy. The insured value of any part of a species is such proportion of the total insured value of the same as the insurable value of the part bears to the insurable value of the whole, ascertained in both cases as provided by this Act.

(2) Where a valuation has to be apportioned, and particulars of the prime cost of each separate species, quality, or description of goods cannot be

ascertained, the division of the valuation may be made over the net arrived sound values of the different species, qualities, or descriptions of goods.

73. GENERAL AVERAGE CONTRIBUTIONS AND SALVAGE CHARGES

(1) Subject to any express provision in the policy, where the assured has paid, or is liable for, any general average contribution, the measure of indemnity is the full amount of such contribution, if the subject-matter liable to contribution is insured for its full contributory value; but, if such subject-matter be not insured for its full contributory value, or if only part of it be insured, the indemnity payable by the insurer must be reduced in proportion to the under-insurance, and where there has been a particular average loss which constitutes a deduction from the contributory value, and for which the insurer is liable, that amount must be deducted from the insured value in order to ascertain what the insurer is liable to contribute.

(2) Where the insurer is liable for salvage charges the extent of his liability must be determined on the like principle.

74. LIABILITIES TO THIRD PARTIES. Where the assured has effected an insurance in express terms against any liability to a third party, the measure of indemnity, subject to any express provision in the policy, is the amount paid or payable by him to such third party in respect of such liability.

75. GENERAL PROVISIONS AS TO MEASURE OF INDEMNITY

(1) Where there has been a loss in respect of any subject-matter not expressly provided for in the foregoing provisions of this Act, the measure of indemnity shall be ascertained, as nearly as may be, in accordance with those provisions, in so far as applicable to the particular case.

(2) Nothing in the provisions of this Act relating to the measure of indemnity shall affect the rules relating to double insurance, or prohibit the insurer from disproving interest wholly or in part, or from showing that at the time of the loss the whole or any part of the subject-matter insured was not at risk under the policy.

76. PARTICULAR AVERAGE WARRANTIES

(1) Where the subject-matter insured is warranted free from particular average, the assured cannot recover for a loss of part, other than a loss incurred by a general average sacrifice, unless the contract contained in the policy be apportionable; but, if the contract be apportionable, the assured may recover for a total loss of any apportionable part.

(2) Where the subject-matter insured is warranted free from particular average, either wholly or under a certain percentage, the insurer is nevertheless liable for salvage charges, and for particular charges and other expenses properly incurred pursuant to the provisions of the suing and labouring clause in order to avert a loss insured against.

(3) Unless the policy otherwise provides, where the subject-matter insured is warranted free from particular average under a specified percentage, a general average loss cannot be added to a particular average loss to make up the specified percentage.

(4) For the purpose of ascertaining whether the specified percentage has been reached, regard shall be had only to the actual loss suffered by the

subject-matter insured. Particular charges and the expenses of and incidental to ascertaining and proving the loss must be excluded.

77. SUCCESSIVE LOSSES

(1) Unless the policy otherwise provides, and subject to the provisions of this Act, the insurer is liable for successive losses, even though the total amount of such losses may exceed the sum insured.

(2) Where, under the same policy, a partial loss which has not been repaired or otherwise made good, is followed by a total loss, the assured can only recover in respect of the total loss:

Provided that nothing in this section shall affect the liability of the insurer under the suing and labouring clause.

78. SUING AND LABOURING CLAUSE

(1) Where the policy contains a suing and labouring clause, the engagement thereby entered into is deemed to be supplementary to the contract of insurance, and the assured may recover from the insurer any expenses properly incurred pursuant to the clause, notwithstanding that the insurer may have paid for a total loss, or that the subject-matter may have been warranted free from particular average, either wholly or under a certain percentage.

(2) General average losses and contributions and salvage charges, as defined by this Act, are not recoverable under the suing and labouring clause.

(3) Expenses incurred for the purpose of averting or diminishing any loss not covered by the policy are not recoverable under the suing and labouring clause.

(4) It is the duty of the assured and his agents, in all cases, to take such measures as may be reasonable for the purpose of averting or minimising a loss.

RIGHTS OF INSURER ON PAYMENT.

79. RIGHT OF SUBROGATION

(1) Where the insurer pays for a total loss, either of the whole, or in the case of goods of any apportionable part, of the subject-matter insured, he thereupon becomes entitled to take over the interest of the assured in whatever may remain of the subject-matter so paid for, and he is thereby subrogated to all rights and remedies of the assured in and in respect of that subject-matter as from the time of the casualty causing the loss.

(2) Subject to the foregoing provisions, where the insurer pays for a partial loss, he acquires no title to the subject-matter insured, or such part of it as may remain, but he is thereupon subrogated to all rights and remedies of the assured in and in respect of the subject-matter insured as from the time of the casualty causing the loss, in so far as the assured has been indemnified, according to this Act, by such payment for the loss.

80. RIGHT OF CONTRIBUTION

(1) Where the assured is over-insured by double insurance, each insurer is bound, as between himself and the other insurers, to contribute ratably to the loss in proportion to the amount for which he is liable under his contract.

(2) If any insurer pays more than his proportion of the loss, he is entitled to maintain an action for contribution against the other insurers, and is entitled to the like remedies as a surety who has paid more than his proportion of the debt.

81. EFFECT OF UNDER-INSURANCE. Where the assured is insured for an amount less than the insurable value or, in the case of a valued policy for an amount less than the policy valuation, he is deemed to be his own insurer in respect of the uninsured balance.

RETURN OF PREMIUM.

82. ENFORCEMENT OF RETURN. Where the premium, or a proportionate part thereof is, by this Act, declared to be returnable—
(a) If already paid, it may be recovered by the assured from the insurer; and
(b) If unpaid, it may be retained by the assured or his agent.

83. RETURN BY AGREEMENT. Where the policy contains a stipulation for the return of the premium, or a proportionate part thereof, on the happening of a certain event, and that event happens, the premium, or, as the case may be, the proportionate part thereof, is thereupon returnable to the assured.

84. RETURN FOR FAILURE OF CONSIDERATION
(1) Where the consideration for the payment of the premium totally fails, and there has been no fraud or illegality on the part of the assured or his agents, the premium is thereupon returnable to the assured.
(2) Where the consideration for the payment of the premium is apportionable and there is a total failure of any apportionable part of the consideration, a proportionate part of the premium is, under the like conditions, thereupon returnable to the assured.
(3) In particular—
(a) Where the policy is void, or is avoided by the insurer as from the commencement of the risk, the premium is returnable, provided that there has been no fraud or illegality on the part of the assured; but if the risk is not apportionable, and has once attached, the premium is not returnable;
(b) Where the subject-matter insured, or part thereof, has never been imperilled, the premium, or, as the case may be, a proportionate part thereof, is returnable:
Provided that where the subject-matter has been insured "lost or not lost" and has arrived in safety at the time when the contract is concluded, the premium is not returnable unless, at such time, the insurer knew of the safe arrival;
(c) Where the assured has no insurable interest throughout the currency of the risk, the premium is returnable, provided that this rule does not apply to a policy effected by way of gaming or wagering;
(d) Where the assured has a defeasible interest which is terminated during the currency of the risk, the premium is not returnable;
(e) Where the assured has over-insured under an unvalued policy, a proportionate part of the premium is returnable;

(f) Subject to the foregoing provisions, where the assured has over-insured by double insurance, a proportionate part of the several premiums is returnable:

Provided that, if the policies are effected at different times, and any earlier policy has at any time borne the entire risk, or if a claim has been paid on the policy in respect of the full sum insured thereby, no premium is returnable in respect of that policy, and when the double insurance is effected knowingly by the assured no premium is returnable.

MUTUAL INSURANCE.

85. MODIFICATION OF ACT IN CASE OF MUTUAL INSURANCE

(1) Where two or more persons mutually agree to insure each other against marine losses there is said to be a mutual insurance.

(2) The provisions of this Act relating to the premium do not apply to mutual insurance, but a guarantee, or such other arrangement as may be agreed upon, may be substituted for the premium.

(3) The provisions of this Act, in so far as they may be modified by the agreement of the parties, may in the case of mutual insurance be modified by the terms of the policies issued by the association, or by the rules and regulations of the association.

(4) Subject to the exceptions mentioned in this section the provisions of this Act apply to a mutual insurance.

SUPPLEMENTAL

86. RATIFICATION BY ASSURED. Where a contract of marine insurance is in good faith effected by one person on behalf of another, the person on whose behalf it is effected may ratify the contract even after he is aware of a loss.

87. IMPLIED OBLIGATIONS VARIED BY AGREEMENT OR USAGE

(1) Where any right, duty, or liability would arise under a contract of marine insurance by implication of law, it may be negatived or varied by express agreement, or by usage, if the usage be such as to bind both parties to the contract.

(2) The provisions of this section extend to any right, duty, or liability declared by this Act which may be lawfully modified by agreement.

88. REASONABLE TIME, ETC., A QUESTION OF FACT. Where by this Act any reference is made to reasonable time, reasonable premium, or reasonable diligence, the question what is reasonable is a question of fact.

89. SLIP AS EVIDENCE. Where there is a duly stamped policy, reference may be made, as heretofore, to the slip or covering note, in any legal proceeding.

90. INTERPRETATION OF TERMS. In this Act, unless the context or subject-matter otherwise requires—

"Action" includes counter-claim and set off:

"Freight" includes the profit derivable by a shipowner from the employment of his ship to carry his own goods or movables, as well as freight payable by a third party, but does not include passage money:

"Movables" means any movable tangible property, other than the ship, and includes money, valuable securities, and other documents:

"Policy" means a marine policy.

91. SAVINGS

(1) Nothing in this Act, or in any repeal effected thereby, shall affect—

(a) The provisions of the Stamp Act, 1891, or any enactment for the time being in force relating to the revenue;

(b) The provisions of the Companies Act, 1862, or any enactment amended or substituted for the same;

(c) The provisions of any statute not expressly repealed by this Act.

(2) The rules of the common law including the law merchant, save in so far as they are inconsistent with the express provisions of this Act, shall continue to apply to contracts of marine insurance.

92. REPEALS. The enactments mentioned in the Second Schedule to this Act are hereby repealed to the extent specified in that schedule.

93. COMMENCEMENT. This Act shall come into operation on the first day of January one thousand nine hundred and seven.

94. SHORT TITLE. This act may be cited as the Marine Insurance Act, 1906.

SCHEDULES

First Schedule: Section 30, Form of Policy [Lloyd's S. G. Policy]

Be it known that   as well in
own name as for and in the name and names of all and every other person or persons to whom the same doth, may, or shall appertain, in part or in all doth make assurance and cause

and them, and every of them, to be insured lost or not lost, at and from

Upon any kind of goods and merchandises, and also upon the body, tackle, apparel, ordnance, munition, artillery, boat, and other furniture, of and in the good ship or vessel called the

whereof is master under God, for this present voyage,

or whosoever shall go for master in the said ship, or by whatsoever other name or names the said ship, or the master thereof, is or shall be named or called; beginning the adventure upon the said goods and merchandises from the loading thereof aboard the said ship,

and so shall continue and endure during her abode there.

upon the said ship, etc. And further, until the said ship, with all her ordnance, tackle, apparel, etc., and goods and merchandises whatsoever shall be arrived at

upon the said ship, etc., until she hath moored at anchor twenty-four hours in good safety; and upon the goods and merchandises, until the same be there discharged and safely landed. And it shall be lawful for the said ship, etc., in this voyage, to proceed and sail to and touch and stay at any ports or places whatsoever without prejudice to this insurance. The said ship, etc., goods and merchandises, etc., for so much as concerns the assured by agreement between the assured and assurers in this policy, are and shall be valued at

Touching the adventures and perils which we the assurers are contented to bear and do take upon us in this voyage: they are of the seas, men-of-war, fire, enemies, pirates, rovers, thieves, jettisons, letters of mart and countermart, surprisals, takings at sea, arrests, restraints, and detainments of all kings, princes, and people, of what nation, condition, or quality soever, barratry of the master and mariners, and of all other perils, losses, and misfortunes, that have or shall come to the hurt, detriment, or damage of the said goods and merchandises, and ship, etc., or any part thereof.

SUE AND LABOUR CLAUSE. And in case of any loss or misfortune it shall be lawful to the assured, their factors, servants and assigns, to sue, labour, and travel for, in and about the defence, safeguards, and recovery of the said goods and merchandises, and ship, etc., or any part thereof, without prejudice to this insurance; to the charges whereof we, the assurers, will contribute each one according to the rate and quantity of his sum herein assured.

WAIVER CLAUSE. And it is especially declared and agreed that no acts of the insurer or insured in recovering, saving or preserving the property insured shall be considered as a waiver, or acceptance of abandonment. And it is agreed by us, the insurers, that this writing or policy of assurance shall be of as much force and effect as the surest writing or policy of assurance heretofore made in Lombard Street, or in the Royal Exchange, or elsewhere in London. And so we, the assurers, are contented, and do hereby promise and bind ourselves, each one for his own part, our heirs, executors, and goods to the assured, their executors, administrators, and assigns, for the true performance of the premises, confessing ourselves paid the consideration due unto us for this assurance by the assured, at and after the rate of

IN WITNESS whereof we, the assurers, have subscribed our names and sums assured in London.

MEMORANDUM

N.B.—Corn, fish, salt, fruit, flour, and seed are warranted free from average, less general, or the ship be stranded—sugar, tobacco, hemp, flax, hides and skins are warranted free from average, under five pounds per cent., and all other goods, also the ship and freight, are warranted free from average, under three pounds per cent. unless general, or the ship be stranded.

RULES FOR CONSTRUCTION OF POLICY.

The following are the rules referred to by this Act for the construction of a policy in the above or other life form, where the context does not otherwise require—

1. LOST OR NOT LOST. Where the subject-matter is insured "lost or not lost," and the loss has occurred before the contract is concluded, the risk attaches unless, at such time the assured was aware of the loss, and the insurer was not.

2. FROM. Where the subject-matter is insured "from" a particular place, the risk does not attach until the ship starts on the voyage insured.

3. AT AND FROM SHIP.

    (a) Where a ship is insured "at and from" a particular place, and she is at that place in good safety when the contract is concluded, the risk attaches immediately.

    (b) If she be not at that place when the contract is concluded the risk attaches as soon as she arrives there in good safety, and, unless the policy otherwise provides, it is immaterial that she is covered by another policy for a specified time after arrival.

    FREIGHT

    (c) Where chartered freight is insured "at and from" a particular place, and the ship is at that place in good safety when the contract is concluded the risk attaches immediately. If she be not there when the contract is concluded, the risk attaches as soon as she arrives there in good safety.

    (d) Where freight, other than chartered freight, is payable without special conditions and is insured "at and from" a particular place, the risk attaches *pro rata* as the goods or merchandise are shipped; provided that if there be cargo in readiness which belongs to the shipowner, or which some other person has contracted with him to ship, the risk attaches as soon as the ship is ready to receive such cargo.

4. FROM THE LOADING THEREOF. Where goods or other movables are insured "from the loading thereof," the risk does not attach until such goods or movables are actually on board, and the insurer is not liable for them while in transit from the shore to the ship.

5. SAFELY LANDED. Where the risk on goods or other movables continues until they are "safely landed," they must be landed in the customary manner and within a reasonable time after arrival at the port of discharge, and if they are not so landed the risk ceases.

6. TOUCH AND STAY. In the absence of any further licence or usage, the liberty to touch and stay "at any port or place whatsoever" does not authorise the ship to depart from the course of her voyage from the port of departure to the port of destination.

7. PERILS OF THE SEAS. The term "perils of the seas" refers only to fortuitous accidents or casualties of the seas. It does not include the ordinary action of the winds and waves.

8. PIRATES. The term "pirates" includes passengers who mutiny and rioters who attack the ship from the shore.

9. THIEVES. The term "thieves" does not cover clandestine theft or a theft committed by any one of the ship's company, whether crew or passengers.

10. RESTRAINT OF PRINCES. The term "arrests, etc., of kings, princes, and people" refers to political or executive acts, and does not include a loss caused by riot or by ordinary judicial process.

11. BARRATRY. The term "barratry" includes every wrongful act wilfully committed by the master or crew to the prejudice of the owner, or, as the case may be, the charterer.

12. ALL OTHER PERILS. The term "all other perils" includes only perils similar in kind to the perils specifically mentioned in the policy.

13. AVERAGE UNLESS GENERAL. The term "average unless general" means a partial loss of the subject-matter insured other than a general average loss, and does not include "particular charges."

14. STRANDED. Where the ship has stranded, the insurer is liable for the excepted losses, although the loss is not attributable to the stranding, provided that when the stranding takes place the risk has attached and, if the policy be on goods, that the damaged goods are on board.

15. SHIP. The term "ship" includes the hull, materials and outfit, stores and provisions for the officers and crew, and, in the case of vessels engaged in a special trade, the ordinary fittings requisite for the trade, and also, in the case of a steamship, the machinery, boilers, and coals and engine stores, if owned by the assured.

16. FREIGHT. The term "freight" includes the profit derivable by a shipowner from the employment of his ship to carry his own goods or movables, as well as freight payable by a third party, but does not include passage money.

17. GOODS. The term "goods" means goods in the nature of merchandise, and does not include personal effects or provisions and stores for use on board.

In the absence of any usage to the contrary, deck cargo and living animals must be insured specifically, and not under the general denomination of goods.

The York/Antwerp Rules, 1974

CONTRASTED WITH YORK/ANTWERP RULES, 1950

YORK/ANTWERP RULES, 1974	YORK/ANTWERP RULES, 1950

RULE OF INTERPRETATION. In the adjustment of general average the following lettered and numbered Rules shall apply to the exclusion of any Law and Practice inconsistent therewith.

Except as provided by the numbered Rules, general average shall be adjusted according to the lettered Rules.

RULE A. There is a general average act when, and only when, any extraordinary sacrifice or expenditure is intentionally and reasonably made or incurred for the common safety for the purpose of preserving from peril the property involved in a common maritime adventure.

RULE B. General average sacrifices and expenses shall be borne by the different contributing interests on the basis hereinafter provided.

RULE C. Only such losses, damages or expenses which are the direct consequence of the general average act shall be allowed as general average.

Loss or damage sustained by the ship or cargo through delay, whether on the voyage or subsequently, such as demurrage, and any indirect loss whatsoever, such as loss of market, shall not be admitted as general average.

RULE OF INTERPRETATION. In the adjustment of general average the following lettered and numbered Rules shall apply to the exclusion of any Law and Practice inconsistent therewith.

Except as provided by the numbered Rules, general average shall be adjusted according to the lettered Rules.

RULE A. There is a general average act when, and only when, any extraordinary sacrifice or expenditure is intentionally and reasonably made or incurred for the common safety for the purpose of preserving from peril the property involved in a common maritime adventure.

RULE B. General average sacrifices and expenses shall be borne by the different contributing interests on the basis hereinafter provided.

RULE C. Only such losses, damages or expenses which are the direct consequence of the general average act shall be allowed as general average.

Loss or damage sustained by the ship or cargo through delay, whether on the voyage or subsequently, such as demurrage, and any indirect loss whatsoever, such as loss of market, shall not be admitted as general average.

RULE D. Rights to contribution in general average shall not be affected, though the event which gave rise to the sacrifice or expenditure may have been due to the fault of one of the parties to the adventure, but this shall not prejudice any remedies *or defences* which may be open against *or to* that party *in respect* of such fault.

RULE E. The onus of proof is upon the party claiming in general average to show that the loss or expense claimed is properly allowable as general average.

RULE F. Any extra expense incurred in place of another expense which would have been allowable as general average shall be deemed to be general average and so allowed without regard to the saving, if any, to other interests, but only up to the amount of the general average expense avoided.

RULE G. General average shall be adjusted as regards both loss and contribution upon the basis of values at the time and place when and where the adventure ends.

This rule shall not affect the determination of the place at which the average statement is to be made up.

RULE I. JETTISON OF CARGO. No jettison of cargo shall be made good as general average, unless such cargo is carried in accordance with the recognized custom of the trade.

RULE II. DAMAGE BY JETTISON AND SACRIFICE FOR THE COMMON SAFETY. Damage done to a ship and cargo, or either of them, by or in consequence of a sacrifice made for the common safety, and by water which goes down a ship's hatches opened or other opening made for the purpose of making a jettison for the common safety, shall be made good as general average.

RULE D. Rights to contribution in general average shall not be affected, though the event which gave rise to the sacrifice or expenditure may have been due to the fault of one of the parties to the adventure; but this shall not prejudice any remedies which may be open against that party for such fault.

RULE E. The onus of proof is upon the party claiming in general average to show that the loss or expense claimed is properly allowable as general average.

RULE F. Any extra expense incurred in place of another expense which would have been allowable as general average shall be deemed to be general average and so allowed without regard to the saving, if any, to other interests, but only up to the amount of the general average expense avoided.

RULE G. General Average shall be adjusted as regards both loss and contribution upon the basis of values at the time and place when and where the adventure ends.

This rule shall not affect the determination of the place at which the average statement is to be made up.

RULE I. JETTISON OF CARGO. No jettison of cargo shall be made good as general average, unless such cargo is carried in accordance with the recognized custom of the trade.

RULE II. DAMAGE BY JETTISON AND SACRIFICE FOR THE COMMON SAFETY. Damage done to a ship and cargo, or either of them, by or in consequence of a sacrifice made for the common safety, and by water which goes down a ship's hatches opened or other opening made for the purpose of making a jettison for the common safety, shall be made good as general average.

RULE III. EXTINGUISHING FIRE ON SHIPBOARD. Damage done to a ship and cargo, or either of them, by water or otherwise, including damage by beaching or scuttling a burning ship, in extinguishing a fire on board the ship, shall be made good as general average; except that no compensation shall be made for damage *by smoke or heat however caused.*

RULE IV. CUTTING AWAY WRECK. Loss or damage sustained by cutting away wreck *or parts of the ship* which have been previously carried away *or are effectively lost by accident* shall not be made good as general average.

RULE V. VOLUNTARY STRANDING. When a ship is intentionally run on shore for the common safety, *whether or not she might have been driven on shore,* the consequent loss or damage shall be allowed in general average.

RULE VI. *SALVAGE REMUNERATION. Expenditure incurred by the parties to the adventure on account of salvage, whether under contract or otherwise, shall be allowed in general average to the extent that the salvage operations were undertaken for the purpose of preserving from peril the property involved in the common maritime adventure.*

RULE III. EXTINGUISHING FIRE ON SHIPBOARD. Damage done to a ship and cargo, or either of them, by water or otherwise, including damage by beaching or scuttling a burning ship, in extinguishing a fire on board the ship, shall be made good as general average; except that no compensation shall be made for damage to such portions of the ship and bulk cargo, or to such separate packages of cargo, as have been on fire.

RULE IV. CUTTING AWAY WRECK. Loss or damage caused by cutting away the wreck or remains of spars or of other things which have previously been carried away by sea-peril, shall not be made good as general average.

RULE V. VOLUNTARY STRANDING. When a ship is intentionally run on shore, and the circumstances are such that if that course were not adopted she would inevitably drive on shore or on rocks, no loss or damage caused to the ship, cargo and freight or any of them by such intentional running on shore shall be made good as general average, but loss or damage incurred in refloating such a ship shall be allowed as general average.

In all other cases where a ship is intentionally run on shore for the common safety, the consequent loss or damage shall be allowed as general average.

RULE VI. CARRYING PRESS OF SAIL—DAMAGE TO OR LOSS OF SAILS. Damage to or loss of sails and spars, or either of them, caused by forcing a ship off the ground or by driving her higher up the ground, for the common safety, shall be made good as general average; but where a ship is afloat, no loss or damage caused to the ship, cargo and freight, or any of them, by carrying a press of sail, shall be made good as general average.

RULE VII. DAMAGE TO MACHINERY AND BOILERS. Damage caused to *any* machinery and boilers of a ship which is ashore and in a position of peril, in endeavouring to refloat, shall be allowed in general average when shown to have arisen from an actual intention to float the ship for the common safety at the risk of such damage; but where a ship is afloat no loss or damage caused by working the *propelling* machinery and boilers shall in any circumstances be made good as general average.

RULE VIII. EXPENSES LIGHTENING A SHIP WHEN ASHORE, AND CONSEQUENT DAMAGE. When a ship is ashore and cargo and ship's fuel and stores or any of them are discharged as a general average act, the extra cost of lightening, lighter hire and reshipping (if incurred), and the loss or damage sustained thereby, shall be admitted as general average.

RULE IX. SHIP'S MATERIALS AND STORES BURNT FOR FUEL. Ship's materials and stores, or any of them, necessarily burnt for fuel for the common safety at a time of peril, shall be admitted as general average, when and only when an ample supply of fuel had been provided; but the estimated quantity of fuel that would have been consumed, calculated at the price current at the ship's last port of departure at the date of her leaving, shall be credited to the general average.

RULE X. EXPENSES AT PORT OF REFUGE, ETC.

(a) When a ship shall have entered a port or place of refuge, or shall have returned to her port or place of loading in consequence of accident, sacrifice or other extraordinary circum-

RULE VII. DAMAGE TO MACHINERY AND BOILERS. Damage caused to machinery and boilers of a ship which is ashore and in a position of peril, in endeavouring to refloat, shall be allowed in general average when shown to have arisen from an actual intention to float the ship for the common safety at the risk of such damage; but where a ship is afloat no loss or damage caused by working the machinery and boilers, including loss or damage due to compounding of engines or such measures, shall in any circumstances be made good as general average.

RULE VIII. EXPENSES LIGHTENING A SHIP WHEN ASHORE, AND CONSEQUENT DAMAGE. When a ship is ashore and cargo and ship's fuel and stores or any of them are discharged as a general average act, the extra cost of lightening, lighter hire and reshipping (if incurred), and the loss or damage sustained thereby, shall be admitted as general average.

RULE IX. SHIP'S MATERIALS AND STORES BURNT FOR FUEL. Ship's materials and stores, or any of them, necessarily burnt for fuel for the common safety at a time of peril, shall be admitted as general average, when and only when an amply supply of fuel had been provided; but the estimated quantity of fuel that would have been consumed, calculated at the price current at the ship's last port of departure at the date of her leaving, shall be credited to the general average.

RULE X. EXPENSES AT PORT OF REFUGE, ETC.

(a) When a ship shall have entered a port or place of refuge, or shall have returned to her port or place of loading in consequence of accident, sacrifice or other extraordinary circum-

|

stances, which render that necessary for the common safety, the expenses of entering such port or place shall be admitted as general average; and when she shall have sailed thence with her original cargo, or a part of it, the corresponding expenses of leaving such port or place consequent upon such entry or return shall likewise be admitted as general average.

When a ship is at any port or place of refuge and is necessarily removed to another port or place because repairs cannot be carried out in the first port or place, the provisions of this Rule shall be applied to the second port or place as if it were a port or place of refuge *and the cost of such removal including temporary repairs and towage shall be admitted as general average.* The provisions of Rule XI shall be applied to the prolongation of the voyage occasioned by such removal.

(b) The cost of handling on board or discharging cargo, fuel or stores whether at a port or place of loading, call or refuge shall be admitted as general average, when the handling or discharge was necessary for the common safety or to enable damage to the ship caused by sacrifice or accident to be repaired, if the repairs were necessary for the safe prosecution of the voyage, *except in cases where the damage to the ship is discovered at a port or place of loading or call without any accident or other extraordinary circumstances connected with such damage having taken place during the voyage.*

The cost of handling on board or discharging cargo, fuel or stores shall not be admissible as general average when incurred solely for the purpose of re-stowage due to shifting during the voyage unless such re-stowage is necessary for the common safety.

stances, which render that necessary for the common safety, the expenses of entering such port or place shall be admitted as general average; and when she shall have sailed thence with her original cargo, or a part of it, the corresponding expenses of leaving such port or place consequent upon such entry or return shall likewise be admitted as general average.

When a ship is at any port or place of refuge and is necessarily removed to another port or place because repairs cannot be carried out in the first port or place, the provisions of this Rule shall be applied to the second port or place as if it were a port or place of refuge. The provisions of Rule XI shall be applied to the prolongation of the voyage occasioned by such removal.

(b) The cost of handling on board or discharging cargo, fuel or stores whether at a port or place of loading, call or refuge, shall be admitted as general average when the handling or discharge was necessary for the common safety or to enable damage to the ship caused by sacrifice or accident to be repaired, if the repairs were necessary for the safe prosecution of the voyage.

YORK/ANTWERP RULES, 1974	YORK/ANTWERP RULES, 1950

(c) Whenever the cost of handling or discharging cargo, fuel or stores is admissible as general average, *the costs of storage, including insurance if reasonably incurred, reloading and stowing of such cargo, fuel or stores shall likewise be admitted as general average.*

But when the ship is condemned or does not proceed on her original voyage *storage expenses shall be admitted as general average only up to the date of the ship's condemnation or of the abandonment of the voyage or up to the date of completion of discharge of cargo if the condemnation or abandonment takes place before that date.*

(d) Deleted

(c) Whenever the cost of handling or discharging cargo, fuel or stores is admissible as general average, the cost of reloading and stowing such cargo, fuel or stores on board the ship, together with all storage charges (including insurance, if reasonably incurred) on such cargo, fuel or stores, shall likewise be so admitted. But when the ship is condemned or does not proceed on her original voyage, no storage expenses incurred after the date of the ship's condemnation or of the abandonment of the voyage shall be admitted as general average. In the event of the condemnation of the ship or the abandonment of the voyage before completion of discharge of cargo, storage expenses, as above, shall be admitted as general average up to the date of completion of discharge.

(d) If a ship under average be in a port or place at which it is practicable to repair her, so as to enable her to carry on the whole cargo, and if, in order to save expense, either she is towed thence to some other port or place of repair or to her destination, or the cargo or a portion of it is transshipped by another ship, or otherwise forwarded, then the extra cost of such towage, transshipment and forwarding, or any of them (up to the amount of the extra expense saved) shall be payable by the several parties to the adventure in proportion to the extraordinary expense saved.

RULE XI. WAGES AND MAINTENANCE OF CREW AND OTHER EXPENSES BEARING UP FOR AND IN A PORT OF REFUGE, ETC.

(a) Wages and maintenance of master, officers and crew reasonably incurred and fuel and stores consumed during the prolongation of the

RULE XI. WAGES AND MAINTENANCE OF CREW AND OTHER EXPENSES BEARING UP FOR AND IN A PORT OF REFUGE, ETC.

(a) Wages and maintenance of master, officers and crew reasonably incurred and fuel and stores consumed during the prolongation of the voyage occasioned by a ship entering a voyage occasioned by a ship entering a port or place of refuge or returning to her port or place of loading shall be admitted as general average when the expenses of entering such port or place are allowable in general average in accordance with Rule X (a).

(b) When a ship shall have entered or been detained in any port or place in consequence of accident, sacrifice or other extraordinary circumstances which render that necessary for the common safety, or to enable damage to the ship caused by sacrifice or accident to be repaired, if the repairs were necessary for the safe prosecution of the voyage, the wages and maintenance of the master, officers and crew reasonably incurred during the extra period of detention in such port or place until the ship shall or should have been ready to proceed upon her voyage, shall be admitted in general average.

Provided that when damage to the ship is discovered at a port or place of loading or call without any accident or other extraordinary circumstance connected with such damage having taken place during the voyage, then the wages and maintenance of master, officers and crew and fuel and stores consumed during the extra detention for repairs to damages so discovered shall not be admissible as general average, even if the repairs are necessary for the safe prosecution of the voyage.

When the ship is condemned or does not proceed on her original voyage, *wages and maintenance of the master, officers and crew and fuel and stores consumed shall be admitted as general average only up to* the date of the ship's condemnation or of the abandonment of the voyage *or up to the date of completion of discharge of cargo if the condemnation or abandonment takes place before that date.*

port or place of refuge or returning to her port or place of loading shall be admitted as general average when the expenses of entering such port or place are allowable in general average in accordance with Rule X (a).

(b) When a ship shall have entered or been detained in any port or place in consequence of accident, sacrifice or other extraordinary circumstances which render that necessary for the common safety, or to enable damage to the ship caused by sacrifice or accident to be repaired, if the repairs were necessary for the safe prosecution of the voyage, the wages and maintenance of the master, officers and crew reasonably incurred during the extra period of detention in such port or place until the ship shall or should have been made ready to proceed upon her voyage, shall be admitted in general average. When the ship is condemned or does not proceed on her original voyage, the extra period of detention shall be deemed not to extend beyond the date of the ship's condemnation or of the abandonment of the voyage or, if discharge of cargo is not then completed, beyond the date of completion of discharge.

Fuel and stores consumed during the extra period of detention shall be admitted as general average, except such fuel and stores as are consumed in effecting repairs not allowable in general average.

Port charges incurred during the extra period of detention shall likewise be admitted as general average except such charges as are incurred solely by reason of repairs not allowable in general average.

|

Fuel and stores consumed during the extra period of detention shall be admitted as general average, except such fuel and stores as are consumed in effecting repairs not allowable in general average.

Port charges incurred during the extra period of detention shall likewise be admitted as general average except such charges as are incurred solely by reason of repairs not allowable in general average.

(c) For the purpose of this and the other Rules wages shall include all payments made to or for the benefit of the master, officers and crew, whether such payments be imposed by law upon the shipowners or be made under the terms or articles of employment.

(c) For the purpose of this and the other Rules wages shall include all payments made to or for the benefit of the master, officers and crew, whether such payments be imposed by law upon the shipowners or be made under the terms or articles of employment.

(d) When overtime is paid to the master, officers or crew for maintenance of the ship or repairs, the cost of which is not allowable in general average, such overtime shall be allowed in general average only up to the saving in expense which would have been incurred and admitted as general average, had such overtime not been incurred.

(d) When overtime is paid to the master, officers or crew for maintenance of the ship or repairs, the cost of which is not allowable in general average, such overtime shall be allowed in general average only up to the saving in expense which would have been incurred and admitted as general average, had such overtime not been incurred.

RULE XII. DAMAGE TO CARGO IN DISCHARGING, ETC. Damage to or loss of cargo, fuel or stores caused in the act of handling, discharging, storing, reloading and stowing shall be made good as general average, when and only when the cost of those measures respectively is admitted as general average.

RULE XII. DAMAGE TO CARGO IN DISCHARGING, ETC. Damage to or loss of cargo, fuel or stores caused in the act of handling, discharging, storing, reloading and stowing shall be made good as general average, when and only when the cost of those measures respectively is admitted as general average.

RULE XIII. DEDUCTIONS FROM COST OF REPAIRS. *Repairs to be allowed in general average shall not be subject to deductions in respect of "new for old" where old material or parts are replaced by new unless the ship is over fifteen years old in which case there shall be a deduction of one-third. The deductions shall be regu-*

RULE XIII. DEDUCTIONS FROM COST OF REPAIRS. In adjusting claims for general average, repairs to be allowed in general average shall be subject to deductions in respect of "new for old" according to the following rules, where old material or parts are replaced by new.

YORK/ANTWERP RULES, 1974

lated by the age of the ship from the 31st of December of the year of completion of construction to the date of the general average act, except for insulation, life- and similar boats, communications and navigational apparatus and equipment, machinery and boilers for which the deductions shall be regulated by the age of the particular parts to which they apply. The deductions shall be made only from the cost of the new material or parts when finished and ready to be installed in the ship.

No deduction shall be made in respect of provisions, stores, anchors and chain cables.

Drydock and slipway dues and costs of shifting the ship shall be allowed in full.

The costs of cleaning, painting or coating of bottom shall not be allowed in general average unless the bottom has been painted or coated within the twelve months preceding the date of the general average act in which case one-half of such costs shall be allowed.

YORK/ANTWERP RULES, 1950

The deductions to be regulated by the age of the ship from date of original register to the date of accident, except for provisions and stores, insulation, life- and similar boats, gyrocompass equipment, wireless, direction finding, echo sounding and similar apparatus, machinery and boilers for which the deductions shall be regulated by the age of the particular parts to which they apply.

No deduction to be made in respect of provisions, stores and gear which have not been in use.

The deduction shall be made from the cost of new material or parts, including labour and establishment charges, but excluding cost of opening up.

Drydock and slipway dues and costs of shifting the ship shall be allowed in full.

No cleaning and painting of bottom to be allowed, if the bottom has not been painted within six months previous to the date of the accident.

A. UP TO ONE YEAR OLD. All repairs to be allowed in full, except scaling and cleaning and painting or coating of bottom, from which one-third is to be deducted.

B. BETWEEN 1 AND 3 YEARS OLD. Deduction off scaling, cleaning and painting bottom as above under Clause A.

One-third to be deducted off sails, rigging, ropes, sheets and hawsers (other than wire and chain), awnings, covers, provisions, and stores and painting.

One-sixth to be deducted off woodwork of hull, including hold ceiling, wooden masts, spars and boats, furniture, upholstery, crockery, metal- and glass-ware, wire rigging, wire ropes and wire hawsers, gyrocompass equipment, wireless, direction find-

YORK/ANTWERP RULES, 1950

ing, echo sounding and similar apparatus, chain cables and chains, insulation, auxiliary machinery, steering gear and connections, winches and cranes and connections and electrical machinery and connections other than electric propelling machinery; other repairs to be allowed in full.

Metal sheathing for wooden or composite ships shall be dealt with by allowing in full the cost of a weight equal to the gross weight of metal sheathing stripped off, minus the proceeds of the old metal. Nails, felt and labour metalling are subject to a deduction of one-third.

C. BETWEEN 3 AND 6 YEARS. Deductions as above under Clause B, except that one-third be deducted off woodwork of hull including hold ceiling, wooden masts, spars and boats, furniture, upholstery, and one-sixth be deducted off iron work of masts and spars and all machinery (inclusive of boilers and their mountings).

D. BETWEEN 6 AND 10 YEARS. Deductions as above under Clause C, except that one-third be deducted off all rigging, ropes, sheets, and hawsers, iron work of masts and spars, gyrocompass equipment, wireless, direction finding, echo sounding and similar apparatus, insulation, auxiliary machinery, steering gear, winches, cranes and connections and all other machinery, (inclusive of boilers and their mounting).

E. BETWEEN 10 AND 15 YEARS. One-third to be deducted off all renewals, except iron work of hull and cementing and chain cables, from which one-sixth to be deducted, and anchors, which are allowed in full.

F. OVER 15 YEARS. One-third to be deducted off all renewals, except chain cables, from which one-sixth to be deducted, and anchors, which are allowed in full.

RULE XIV. TEMPORARY RE-PAIRS. Where temporary repairs are effected to a ship at a port of loading, call or refuge, for the common safety, or of damage caused by general average sacrifice, the cost of such repairs shall be admitted as general average.

Where temporary repairs of accidental damage are effected *in order to* enable the adventure to be completed, the cost of such repairs shall be admitted as general average without regard to the saving, if any, to other interests, but only up to the saving in expense which would have been incurred and allowed in general average if such repairs had not been effected there.

No deductions "new for old" shall be made from the cost of temporary repairs allowable as general average.

RULE XV. LOSS OF FREIGHT. Loss of freight arising from damage to or loss of cargo shall be made good as general average, either when caused by a general average act, or when the damage to or loss of cargo is so made good.

Deduction shall be made from the amount of gross freight lost, of the charges which the owner thereof would have incurred to earn such freight, but has, in consequence of the sacrifice, not incurred.

RULE XVI. AMOUNT TO BE MADE GOOD FOR CARGO LOST OR DAMAGED BY SACRIFICE. The amount to be made good as general average for damage to or loss of *cargo* sacrificed shall be the loss which has *been* sustained thereby based on the *value at the time of discharge, ascertained from the commercial invoice rendered to the receiver or if there is no such invoice from the shipped value. The value at the time of discharge shall include the cost of insurance and freight except insofar as such freight is at the risk of interests other than the cargo.*

RULE XIV. TEMPORARY RE-PAIRS. Where temporary repairs are effected to a ship at a port of loading, call or refuge, for the common safety, or of damage caused by general average sacrifice, the cost of such repairs shall be admitted as general average.

Where temporary repairs of accidental damage are effected merely to enable the adventure to be completed, the cost of such repairs shall be admitted as general average without regard to the saving, if any, to other interests, but only up to the saving, in expense which would have been incurred and allowed in general average if such repairs had not been effected there.

No deductions "new for old" shall be made from the cost of temporary repairs allowable as general average.

RULE XV. LOSS OF FREIGHT. Loss of freight arising from damage to or loss of cargo shall be made good as general average, either when caused by a general average act, or when the damage to or loss of cargo is so made good.

Deduction shall be made from the amount of gross freight lost, of the charges which the owner thereof would have incurred to earn such freight, but has, in consequence of the sacrifice, not incurred.

RULE XVI. AMOUNT TO BE MADE GOOD FOR CARGO LOST OR DAMAGED BY SACRIFICE. The amount to be made good as general average for damage to or loss of goods sacrificed shall be the loss which the owner of the goods has sustained thereby, based on the market values at the last day of discharge of the vessel or at the termination of the adventure where this ends at a place other than the original destination.

Where goods so damaged are sold and the amount of the damage has not been otherwise agreed, the loss to be

When cargo so damaged *is* sold and the amount of the damage has not been otherwise agreed, the loss to be made good in general average shall be the difference between the net proceeds of sale and the net sound value *as computed in the first paragraph of this Rule.*

RULE XVII. CONTRIBUTORY VALUES. The contribution to a general average shall be made upon the actual net values of the property at the termination of the adventure *except that the value of cargo shall be the value at the time of discharge ascertained from the commercial invoice rendered to the receiver or if there is no such invoice from the shipped value. The value of the cargo shall include the cost of insurance and freight unless and insofar as such freight is at the risk of interests other than the cargo, deducting therefrom any loss or damage suffered by the cargo prior to or at the time of discharge. The value of the ship shall be assessed without taking into account the beneficial or detrimental effect of any demise or time charter party to which the ship may be committed.*

To *these* values shall be added the amount made good as general average for property sacrificed, if not already included, deduction being made from the freight and passage money at risk, of such charges and crew's wages as would not have been incurred in earning the freight had the ship and cargo been totally lost at the date of the general average act and have not been allowed as general average; deduction being also made from the value of the property of all *extra* charges incurred in respect thereof subsequently to the general average act, except such charges as are allowed in general average.

Where cargo is sold short of destination, however, it shall contribute upon the actual net proceeds of sale, with the addi-

made good in general average shall be the difference between the net proceeds of sale and the net sound value at the last day of discharge of the vessel or at the termination of the adventure where this ends at a place other than the original destination.

RULE XVII. CONTRIBUTORY VALUES. The contribution to a general average shall be made upon the actual net values of the property at the termination of the adventure, to which values shall be added the amount made good as general average for property sacrificed, if not already included, deduction being made from the shipowner's freight and passage money at risk, of such charges and crew's wages as would not have been incurred in earning the freight had the ship and cargo been totally lost at the date of the general average act and have not been allowed as general average; deduction being also made from the value of the property of all charges incurred in respect thereof subsequently to the general average act, except such charges as are allowed in general average.

Passengers' luggage and personal effects not shipped under bill of lading shall not contribute in general average.

tion of any amount made good as general average.

Passengers' luggage and personal effects not shipped under bill of lading shall not contribute in general average.

RULE XVIII. DAMAGE TO SHIP.

The amount to be allowed as general average for damage or loss to the ship, her machinery and/or gear *caused by a general average act shall be as follows:*

(a) When repaired or replaced, the actual reasonable cost of repairing or replacing such damage or loss, subject to deductions in accordance with Rule XIII.

(b) When not repaired or replaced, the reasonable depreciation arising from such damage or loss, but not exceeding the estimated cost of repairs. But where the ship is an actual total loss or when the cost of repairs of the damage would exceed the value of the ship when repaired, the amount to be allowed as general average shall be the difference between the estimated sound value of the ship after deducting therefrom the estimated cost of repairing damage which is not general average and the value of the ship in her damaged state which may be measured by the net proceeds of sale, if any.

RULE XIX. UNDECLARED OR WRONGFULLY DECLARED CARGO.

Damage or loss caused to goods loaded without the knowledge of the shipowner or his agent or to goods wilfully misdescribed at time of shipment shall not be allowed as general average, but such goods shall remain liable to contribute, if saved.

Damage or loss caused to goods which have been wrongfully declared on shipment at a value which is lower than their real value shall be contributed for at the declared value, but such goods shall contribute upon their actual value.

RULE XVIII. DAMAGE TO SHIP.

The amount to be allowed as general average for damage or loss to the ship, her machinery and/or gear when repaired or replaced shall be the actual reasonable cost of repairing or replacing such damage or loss, subject to deductions in accordance with Rule XIII. When not repaired, the reasonable depreciation shall be allowed, not exceeding the estimated cost of repairs.

Where there is an actual or constructive total loss of the ship the amount to be allowed as general average for damage or loss to the ship caused by a general average act shall be the estimated sound value of the ship after deducting therefrom the estimated cost of repairing damage which is not general average and the proceeds of sale, if any.

RULE XIX. UNDECLARED OR WRONGFULLY DECLARED CARGO.

Damage or loss caused to goods loaded without the knowledge of the shipowner or his agent or to goods wilfully misdescribed at time of shipment shall not be allowed as general average, but such goods shall remain liable to contribute, if saved.

Damage or loss caused to goods which have been wrongfully declared on shipment at a value which is lower than their real value shall be contributed for at the declared value, but such goods shall contribute upon their actual value.

YORK/ANTWERP RULES, 1974

RULE XX. PROVISION OF FUNDS. A commission of 2 per cent. on general average disbursements, other than the wages and maintenance of master, officers and crew and fuel and stores not replaced during the voyage, shall be allowed in general average, but when the funds are not provided by any of the contributing interests, the necessary cost of obtaining the funds required by means of a bottomry bond or otherwise, or the loss sustained by owners of goods sold for the purpose, shall be allowed in general average.

The cost of insuring money advanced to pay for general average disbursements shall also be allowed in general average.

RULE XXI. INTEREST ON LOSSES MADE GOOD IN GENERAL AVERAGE. Interest shall be allowed on expenditure, sacrifices and allowances charged to general average at the rate of 7 *per cent. per annum,* until the date of the general average statement, due allowance being made for any interim reimbursement from the contributory interests or from the general average deposit fund.

RULE XXII. TREATMENT OF CASH DEPOSITS. Where cash deposits have been collected in respect of cargo's liability for general average, salvage or special charges, such deposits shall be paid without any delay into a special account in the joint names of a representative nominated on behalf of the shipowner and a representative nominated on behalf of the depositors in a bank to be approved by both. The sum so deposited, together with accrued interest, if any, shall be held as security for payment to the parties entitled thereto of the general average, salvage or special

YORK/ANTWERP RULES, 1950

RULE XX. PROVISION OF FUNDS. A commission of 2 per cent. on general average disbursements, other than the wages and maintenance of master, officers and crew and fuel and stores not replaced during the voyage, shall be allowed in general average, but when the funds are not provided by any of the contributing interests, the necessary cost of obtaining the funds required by means of a bottomry bond or otherwise, or the loss sustained by owners of goods sold for the purpose, shall be allowed in general average.

The cost of insuring money advanced to pay for general average disbursements shall also be allowed in general average.

RULE XXI. INTEREST ON LOSSES MADE GOOD IN GENERAL AVERAGE. Interest shall be allowed on expenditure, sacrifices and allowances charged to general average at the rate of 5 per cent. per annum, until the date of the general average statement, due allowance being made for any interim reimbursement from the contributory interests or from the general average deposit fund.

RULE XXII. TREATMENT OF CASH DEPOSITS. Where cash deposits have been collected in respect of cargo's liability for general average, salvage or special charges, such deposits shall be paid without any delay into a special account in the joint names of a representative nominated on behalf of the shipowner and a representative nominated on behalf of the depositors in a bank to be approved by both. The sum so deposited, together with accrued interest, if any, shall be held as security for payment to the parties entitled thereto of the general average, salvage or special

YORK/ANTWERP RULES, 1974	YORK/ANTWERP RULES, 1950
charges payable by cargo in respect to which the deposits have been collected. Payments on account or refunds of deposits may be made if certified to in writing by the average adjuster. Such deposits and payments or refunds shall be without prejudice to the ultimate liability of the parties.	charges payable by cargo in respect to which the deposits have been collected. Payments on account or refunds of deposits may be made if certified to in writing by the average adjuster. Such deposits and payments or refunds shall be without prejudice to the ultimate liability of the parties.

NOTE: In 1990, arising out of the International Convention on Salvage, 1989 (q.v.) Rule VI of the York/Antwerp Rules, 1974 was revised to make quite clear the extent of the allowances to be made in general average when salvage remuneration or special compensation is assessed in accordance with Art. 13 and Art. 14 of the salvage convention (see Chapter Seven for the new text of Rule VI and a discussion of this minor change). The new text of the York/Antwerp Rules including the amended Rule VI is to be referred to as "York/Antwerp Rules, 1974 as amended 1990."

Lloyd's Standard Form of Salvage Agreement

LOF 1990

LLOYD'S

STANDARD FORM OF

SALVAGE AGREEMENT

(APPROVED AND PUBLISHED BY THE COUNCIL OF LLOYD'S)

NO CURE - NO PAY

NOTES

1. *Insert names of persons signing on behalf of Owner of property to be salved. The Master should sign whenever possible.*

2. *The Contractor's name should always be inserted in line 4 and whenever the agreement is signed by the Master of the Salving vessel or other person on behalf of the Contractor; the name of the Master or other person must also be inserted in line 4 before the words "for and on behalf of." The words "for and on behalf of" should be deleted where a Contractor signs personally.*

3. *Insert place if agreed in clause 1(a)(i) and currency if agreed in clause 1(e).*

On board the..

Dated..

IT IS HEREBY AGREED between the Captain[1] ....for and on behalf of the Owners of the ".." her cargo freight bunkers stores and any other property thereon (hereinafter collectively called "the Owners") and..(hereinafter called "the Contractor"[2]) that:

1. (a) The Contractor shall use his best endeavours:

    (i) to salve the ".." and/or her cargo freight bunkers stores and any other property thereon and take them to[3] ....or to such other place as may hereafter be agreed either place to be deemed a place of safety or if no such place is named or agreed to a place of safety and

    (ii) while performing the salvage services to prevent or minimize damage to the environment

    (b) Subject to clause 2 incorporating Convention Article 14 the services shall be rendered and accepted as salvage services upon the principle of "no cure - no pay."

656

(c) The Contractor's remuneration shall be fixed by Arbitration in London in the manner hereinafter prescribed and any other difference arising out of this Agreement or the operations thereunder shall be referred to Arbitrators in the same way.

(d) In the event of the services referred to in this Agreement or any part of such services having been already rendered at the date of this Agreement by the Contractor to the said vessel and/or her cargo freight bunkers stores and any other property thereon the provisions of this Agreement shall apply to such services.

(e) The security to be provided to the Council of Lloyd's (hereinafter called "the Council") the Salved Value(s) the Award and/or any Interim Award(s) and/or any Award on Appeal shall be in[3] ....currency.

(f) If clause 1(e) is not completed then the security to be provided and the Salved Value(s) the Award and/or interim Award(s) and/or Award on Appeal shall be in Pounds Sterling.

(g) This Agreement and Arbitration thereunder shall except as otherwise expressly provided be governed by the law of England, including the English law of salvage.

PROVISIONS AS TO THE SERVICES

2. Articles 1(a) to (e), 8, 13.1, 13.2 first sentence, 13.3 and 14 of the International Convention on Salvage 1989 ("the Convention Articles") set out hereafter are hereby incorporated into this Agreement. The terms "Contractor" and "services"/"salvage services" in this Agreement shall have the same meanings as the terms "salvor(s)" and "salvage operation(s)" in the Convention Articles.

3. The Owners their Servants and Agents shall co-operate fully with the Contractor in and about the salvage including obtaining entry to the place named or the place of safety as defined in clause 1. The Contractor may make reasonable use of the vessel's machinery gear equipment anchors chains stores and other appurtenances during and for the purpose of the salvage services free of expense but shall not unnecessarily damage abandon or sacrifice the same or any property the subject of this Agreement.

PROVISIONS AS TO SECURITY

4. (a) The Contractor shall immediately after the termination of the services or sooner notify the council and where practicable the Owners of the amount for which he demands security (inclusive of costs expenses and interest) from each of the respective Owners.

    (b) Where the exception to the principle of "no cure - no pay" under Convention Article 14 becomes likely to be applicable the owners of the vessel shall on the demand of the Contractor provide security for the Contractor's special compensation.

(c) The amount of any such security shall be reasonable in the light of the knowledge available to the Contractor at the time when the demand is made. Unless otherwise agreed such security shall be provided (i) to the Council (ii) in a form approved by the Council and (iii) by persons firms or corporations either acceptable to the Contractor or resident in the United Kingdom and acceptable to the Council. The Council shall not be responsible for the sufficiency (whether in amount or otherwise) of any security which shall be provided nor for the default or insolvency of any person firm or corporation providing the same.

(d) The owners of the vessel their Servants and Agents shall use their best endeavours to ensure that the cargo owners provide their proportion of security before the cargo is released.

5. (a) Until security has been provided as aforesaid the Contractor shall have a maritime lien on the property salved for his remuneration. The property salved shall not without the consent in writing of the Contractor (which shall not be unreasonably withheld) be removed from the place to which it has been taken by the Contractor under clause 1(a).

(b) The Contractor shall not arrest or detain the property salved unless:

   (i) security is not provided within 14 days (exclusive of Saturdays and Sundays or other days observed as general holidays at Lloyd's) after the date of the termination of the services or

   (ii) he has reason to believe that the removal of the property salved is contemplated contrary to clause 5(a) or

   (iii) any attempt is made to remove the property salved contrary to clause 5(a).

(c) The Arbitrator appointed under clause 6 or the Appeal Arbitrator(s) appointed under clause 11(d) shall have power in their absolute discretion to include in the amount awarded to the Contractor the whole or part of any expenses reasonably incurred by the Contractor in:

   (i) ascertaining demanding and obtaining the amount of security reasonably required in accordance with clause 4

   (ii) enforcing and/or protecting by insurance or otherwise or taking reasonable steps to enforce and/or protect his lien.

PROVISIONS AS TO ARBITRATION

6. (a) Where security is provided to the Council in whole or in part the Council shall appoint an Arbitrator in respect of the property covered by such security.

(b) Whether security has been provided or not the Council shall appoint an Arbitrator upon receipt of a written request made by letter telex facsimile or in any other permanent form provided that any party requesting such appointment shall if required by the Council undertake to pay the reasonable fees and expenses of the Council and/or any Arbitrator or Appeal Arbitrator(s).

(c) Where an Arbitrator has been appointed and the parties do not proceed to arbitration the Council may recover any fees costs and/or expenses which are outstanding and thereupon terminate the appointment of such Arbitrator.

7. The Contractor's remuneration shall be fixed by the Arbitrator appointed under clause 6. Such remuneration shall not be diminished by reason of the exception to the principle of "no cure - no pay" under Convention Article 14.

REPRESENTATION

8. Any party to this Agreement who wishes to be heard or to adduce evidence shall nominate a person in the United Kingdom to represent him failing which the Arbitrator or Appeal Arbitrator(s) may proceed as if such party had renounced his right to be heard or adduce evidence.

CONDUCT OF THE ARBITRATION

9. (a) The Arbitrator shall have power to:

   (i)   admit such oral or documentary evidence or information as he may think fit
   (ii)   conduct the Arbitration in such manner in all respects as he may think fit subject to such procedural rules as the Council may approve
   (iii) condemn the Contractor in his absolute discretion in the whole or part of the expense of providing excessive security and deduct the amount in which the Contractor is so condemned from the salvage remuneration and/or special compensation
   (iv)   make Interim Award(s) on such terms as may be fair and just
   (v)   make such orders as to costs fees and expenses including those of the Council charged under clauses 9(b) and 12(b) as may be fair and just.

   (b) The Arbitrator and the Council may charge reasonable fees and expenses for their services whether the Arbitration proceeds to a hearing or not and all such fees and expenses shall be treated as part of the costs of the Arbitration.

   (c) Any Award shall (subject to Appeal as provided in this Agreement) be final and binding on all the parties concerned whether they were represented at the arbitration or not.

INTEREST

10. Interest at rates per annum to be fixed by the Arbitrator shall (subject to Appeal as provided in this Agreement) be payable on any sum awarded taking into account any sums already paid:

659

(i) from the date of termination of the services unless the Arbitrator shall in his absolute discretion otherwise decide until the date of publication by the Council of the Award and/or Interim Award(s) and

(ii) from the expiration of 21 days (exclusive of Saturdays and Sundays or other days observed as general holidays at Lloyd's) after the date of the publication by the Council of the Award and/or interim Awards(s) until the day of payment is received by the Contractor or the Council both dates inclusive.

PROVISIONS AS TO APPEAL

11. (a) Notice of Appeal if any shall be given to the Council within 14 days (exclusive of Saturdays and Sundays or other days observed as general holidays at Lloyds) after the date of publication by the Council of the Award and/or Interim Award(s).

(b) Notice of Cross-Appeal if any shall be given to the Council within 14 days (exclusive of Saturdays and Sundays or other days observed as general holidays at Lloyd's) after notification by the Council to the parties of any Notice of Appeal. Such notification if sent by post shall be deemed received on the working day following the day of posting.

(c) Notice of Appeal or Cross-Appeal shall be given to the Council by letter telex facsimile or in any other permanent form.

(d) Upon receipt of Notice of Appeal the Council shall refer the Appeal to the hearing and determination of the Appeal Arbitrator(s) selected by it.

(e) If any Notice of Appeal or Cross-Appeal is withdrawn the Appeal hearing shall nevertheless proceed in respect of such Notice of Appeal or Cross-Appeal as may remain.

(f) Any Award on Appeal shall be final and binding on all the parties to that Appeal Arbitration whether they were represented either at the Arbitration or at the Appeal Arbitration or not.

CONDUCT OF THE APPEAL

12. (a) The Appeal Arbitrator(s) in addition to the powers of the Arbitrator under clauses 9(a) and 10 shall have power to:

(i) admit the evidence which was before the Arbitrator together with the Arbitrator's notes and reasons for his Award and/or Interim Award(s) and any transcript of evidence and such additional evidence as he or they may think fit

(ii) confirm increase or reduce the sum awarded by the Arbitrator and to make such order as to the payment of interest on such sum as he or they may think fit

(iii) confirm revoke or vary any order and/or Declaratory Award made by the Arbitrator.

660

(b)   The Appeal Arbitrator(s) and the Council may charge reasonable fees and expenses for their services in connection with the Appeal Arbitration whether it proceeds to a hearing or not and all such fees and expenses shall be treated as part of the costs of the Appeal Arbitration.

PROVISIONS AS TO PAYMENT

13. (a)   In case of Arbitration if no Notice of Appeal be received by the Council in accordance with clause 11(a) the Council shall call upon the party or parties concerned to pay the amount awarded and in the event of non-payment shall subject to the Contractor first providing to the Council a satisfactory Undertaking to pay all the costs thereof realize or enforce the security and pay therefrom to the Contractor (whose receipt shall be a good discharge to it) the amount awarded to him together with interest if any. The Contractor shall reimburse the parties concerned to such extent as the Award is less then any sums paid on account or in respect of Interim Award(s).

(b)   If Notice of Appeal be received by the Council in accordance with clause 11 it shall as soon as the Award on Appeal has been published by it call upon the party or parties concerned to pay the amount awarded and in the event of non-payment shall subject to the Contractor first providing to the Council a satisfactory Undertaking to pay all the costs thereof realize or enforce the security and pay therefrom to the Contractor (whose receipt shall be a good discharge to it) the amount awarded to him together with interest if any. The Contractor shall reimburse the parties concerned to such extent as the Award on Appeal is less than any sums paid on account or in respect of the Award or Interim Award(s).

(c)   If any sum shall become payable to the Contractor as remuneration for his services and/or interest and/or costs as the result of an agreement made between the Contractor and the Owners or any of them the Council in the event of non-payment shall subject to the Contractor first providing to the Council a satisfactory Undertaking to pay all the costs thereof realize or enforce the security and pay therefrom to the Contractor (whose receipt shall be a good discharge to it) the said sum.

(d)   If the Award and/or Interim Award(s) and/or Award on Appeal provides or provide that the costs of the Arbitration and/or of the Appeal Arbitration or any part of such costs shall be borne by the Contractor such costs may be deducted from the amount awarded or agreed before payment is made to the Contractor unless satisfactory security is provided by the Contractor for the payment of such costs.

(e)   Without prejudice to the provisions of clause 4(c) the liability of Council shall be limited in any event to the amount of security provided to it.

GENERAL PROVISIONS

14.   The Master or other person signing this Agreement on behalf of the property to be salved enters into this Agreement as agent for the vessel

her cargo freight bunkers stores and any other property thereon and the respective Owners thereof and binds each (but not the one for the other or himself personally) to the due performance thereof.

15. In considering what sums of money have been expended by the Contractor in rendering the services and/or in fixing the amount of the Award and/or Interim Award(s) and/or Award on Appeal the Arbitrator or Appeal Arbitrator(s) shall to such an extent and in so far as it may be fair and just in all the circumstances give effect to the consequences of any change or changes in the relevant rates of exchange which may have occurred between the date of termination of the services and the date on which the Award and/or Interim Award(s) and/or Award on Appeal is made.

16. Any Award notice authority order or other document signed by the Chairman of Lloyd's or any person authorised by the Council for the purpose shall be deemed to have been duly made or given by the Council and shall have the same force and effect in all respects as if it had been signed by every member of the Council.

17. The Contractor may claim salvage and enforce any Award or agreement made between the Contractor and the Owners against security provided under clause 4 if any in the name and on behalf of any Sub-Contractors, Servants or Agents including Masters and members of the crews of vessels employed by him or by any Sub-Contractors in the services provided that the first provides a reasonably satisfactory indemnity to the Owners against all claims by or liabilities to the said persons.

18. When there is no longer any reasonable prospect of a useful result leading to a salvage reward in accordance with Convention Article 13 the owners of the vessel shall be entitled to terminate the services of the Contractor by giving notice to the Contractor in writing.

19. No person signing this Agreement or any party on whose behalf it is signed shall at any time or in any manner whatsoever offer provide make give or promise to provide demand or take any form of inducement for entering into this Agreement.

THE CONVENTION ARTICLES

Article 1

Definitions

(a) *Salvage operation* means any act or activity undertaken to assist a vessel or any other property in danger in navigable waters or in any other waters whatsoever.

(b) *Vessel* means any ship or craft, or any structure capable of navigation

(c) *Property* means any property not permanently and intentionally attached to the shoreline and includes freight at risk

(d) *Damage to the environment* means substantial physical damage to human health or to marine life or resources in coastal or inland waters or areas adjacent thereto, caused by pollution, contamination, fire, explosion or similar major incidents

(e) *Payment* means any reward, remuneration or compensation due under this Convention

Article 8

Duties of the Salvor and of the Owner and Master

1. The salvor shall owe a duty to the owner of the vessel or other property in danger:

(a) to carry out the salvage operations with due care;

(b) in performing the duty specified in subparagraph (a). to exercise due care to prevent or minimize damage to the environment;

(c) whenever circumstances reasonably require, to seek assistance from other salvors; and

(d) to accept the intervention of other salvors when reasonably requested to do so by the owner or master of the vessel or other property in danger; provided however that the amount of his reward shall not be prejudiced should it be found that such a request was unreasonable

2. The owner and master of the vessel or the owner of other property in danger shall owe a duty to the salvor:

(a) to co-operate fully with him during the course of the salvage operations;

(b) in so doing, to exercise due care to prevent or minimize damage to the environment; and

(c) when the vessel or other property has been brought to a place of safety, to accept redelivery when reasonably requested by the salvor to do so

Article 13

Criteria for fixing the reward

1. The reward shall be fixed with a view to encouraging salvage operations, taking into account the following criteria without regard to the order in which they are presented below:

663

(a) the salved value of the vessel and other property;

(b) the skill and efforts of the salvors in preventing or minimizing damage to the environment;

(c) the measure of success obtained by the salvor;

(d) the nature and degree of the danger;

(e) the skill and efforts of the salvors in salving the vessel, other property and life;

(f) the time used and expenses and losses incurred by the salvors;

(g) the risk of liability and other risks run by the salvors or their equipment;

(h) the promptness of the services rendered;

(i) the availability and use of vessels or other equipment intended for salvage operations;

(j) the state of readiness and efficiency of the salvor's equipment and the value thereof

2. Payment of a reward fixed according to paragraph 1 shall be made by all of the vessel and other property interests in proportion to their respective salved values

3. The rewards, exclusive of any interest and recoverable legal costs that may be payable thereon, shall not exceed the salved value of the vessel and other property

Article 14

Special Compensation

1. If the salvor has carried out salvage operations in respect of a vessel which by itself or its cargo threatened damage to the environment and has failed to earn a reward under Article 13 at least equivalent to the special compensation assessable in accordance with this Article, he shall be entitled to special compensation from the owner of that vessel equivalent to his expenses as herein defined

2. If, in the circumstances set out in paragraph 1, the salvor by his salvage operations has prevented or minimized damage to the environment, the special compensation payable by the owner to the salvor under paragraph 1 may be increased up to a maximum of 30% of the expenses incurred by the salvor. However, the Tribunal, if it deems it fair and just to do so and bearing in mind the relevant criteria set out in Article

[handwritten margin note: If it's G.A. you will contribute for the your share to pay part of this (wg) cargo owners Policy.]

664

13, paragraph 1, may increase such special compensation further, but in no event shall the total increase be more than 100% of the expenses incurred by the salvor

3. Salvor's expenses for the purpose of paragraphs 1 and 2 means the out-of-pocket expenses reasonably incurred by the salvor in the salvage operation and a fair rate for equipment and personnel actually and reasonably used in the salvage operation, taking into consideration the criteria set out in Article 13, paragraph 1(h), (i) and (j)

4. The total special compensation under this Article shall be paid only if and to the extent that such compensation is greater than any reward recoverable by the salvor under Article 13

5. If the salvor has been negligent and has thereby failed to prevent or minimize damage to the environment, he may be deprived of the whole or part of any special compensation due under this Article

6. Nothing in this Article shall affect any right of recourse on the part of the owner of the vessel

For and on behalf of the Contractor	For and on behalf of the Owners of the property to be salved.
.... (To be signed either by the Contractor personally or by the Master of the salving vessel or other person whose name is inserted in line 4 of this Agreement.)	.... (To be signed by the Master or other person whose name is inserted in line 1 of this Agreement.)

International Convention on Salvage, 1989

THE STATES PARTIES TO THE PRESENT CONVENTION

RECOGNIZING the desirability of determining by agreement uniform international rules regarding salvage operations,

NOTING, that substantial development, in particular the increased concern for the protection of the environment, have demonstrated the need to review the international rules presently contained in the Convention for the Unification of Certain Rules of Law relating to Assistance and Salvage at Sea, done at Brussels, 23 September 1910,

CONSCIOUS of the major contribution which efficient and timely salvage operations can make to the safety of vessels and other property in danger and to the protection of the environment,

CONVINCED of the need to ensure that adequate incentives are available to persons who undertake salvage operations in respect of vessels and other property in danger,

HAVE AGREED *as follows:*

International Convention on Salvage, 1989

CHAPTER I - GENERAL PROVISIONS

1. DEFINITIONS

For the purpose of this Convention:

(a) *Salvage operation* means any act or activity undertaken to assist a vessel or any other property in danger in navigable waters or in any other waters whatsoever.

(b) *Vessel* means any ship or craft, or any structure capable of navigation.

(c) *Property* means any property not permanently and intentionally attached to the shoreline and includes freight at risk.

(d) *Damage to the environment* means substantial physical damage to human health or to marine life or resources in coastal or inland waters or areas adjacent thereto, caused by pollution, contamination, fire, explosion or similar major incidents.

(e) *Payment* means any reward, remuneration or compensation due under this Convention.

(f) *Organization* means the International Maritime Organization.

(g) *Secretary-General* means the Secretary-General of the Organization.

2. APPLICATION OF THE CONVENTION

This Convention shall apply whenever judicial or arbitral proceedings relating to matters dealt with in this Convention are brought in a State Party.

3. PLATFORMS AND DRILLING UNITS

This Convention shall not apply to fixed or floating platforms or to mobile offshore drilling units when such platforms or units are on location engaged in the exploration, exploitation or production of sea-bed mineral resources.

4. STATE-OWNED VESSELS

1. Without prejudice to article 5, this Convention shall not apply to warships or other non-commercial vessels owned or operated by a State and entitled, at the time of salvage operations, to sovereign immunity under generally recognized principles of international law unless that State decides otherwise.

2. Where a State Party decides to apply the Convention to its warships or other vessels described in paragraph 1, it shall notify the Secretary-General thereof specifying the terms and conditions of such application.

5. SALVAGE OPERATIONS CONTROLLED BY PUBLIC AUTHORITIES

1. This Convention shall not affect any provisions of national law or any international convention relating to salvage operations by or under the control of public authorities.

2. Nevertheless, salvors carrying out such salvage operations shall be entitled to avail themselves of the rights and remedies provided for in this Convention in respect of salvage operations.

3. The extent to which a public authority under a duty to perform salvage operations may avail itself of the rights and remedies provided for in this Convention shall be determined by the law of the State where such authority is situated.

6. SALVAGE CONTRACTS

1. This Convention shall apply to any salvage operations save to the extent that a contract otherwise provides expressly or by implication.

2. The master shall have the authority to conclude contracts for salvage operations on behalf of the owner of the vessel. The master or the owner of the vessel shall have the authority to conclude such contracts on behalf of the owner of the property on board the vessel.

3. Nothing in this article shall affect the application of article 7 nor duties to prevent or minimize damage to the environment.

7. ANNULMENT AND MODIFICATION OF CONTRACTS

A contract or any terms thereof may be annulled or modified if:

(a) the contract has been entered into under undue influence or the influence of danger and its terms are inequitable; or

(b) the payment under the contract is in an excessive degree too large or too small for the services actually rendered.

CHAPTER II - PERFORMANCE OF SALVAGE OPERATIONS

8. DUTIES OF THE SALVOR AND OF THE OWNER AND MASTER

1. The salvor shall owe a duty to the owner of the vessel or other property in danger:

(a) to carry out the salvage operations with due care;

(b) in performing the duty specified in subparagraph (a), to exercise due care to prevent or minimize damage to the environment;

(c) whenever circumstances reasonably require, to seek assistance from other salvors; and

(d) to accept the intervention of other salvors when reasonably requested to do so by the owner or master of the vessel or other property in danger; provided however that the amount of his reward shall not be prejudiced should it be found that such a request was unreasonable.

2. The owner and master of the vessel or the owner of other property in danger shall owe a duty to the salvor:

(a) to co-operate fully with him during the course of the salvage operations;

(b) in so doing, to exercise due care to prevent or minimize damage to the environment; and

(c) when the vessel or other property has been brought to a place of safety, to accept redelivery when reasonably requested by the salvor to do so.

9. RIGHTS OF COASTAL STATES

Nothing in this Convention shall effect the right of the coastal State concerned to take measures in accordance with generally recognized principles of international law to protect its coastline or related interests from pollution or the threat of pollution following upon a maritime casualty or acts relating to such a casualty which may reasonably be expected to result in major harmful consequences, including the right of a coastal State to give directions in relation to salvage operations.

10. DUTY TO RENDER ASSISTANCE

1. Every master is bound, so far as he can do so without serious danger to his vessel and persons thereon, to render assistance to any person in danger of being lost at sea.

2. The States Parties shall adopt the measures necessary to enforce the duty set out in paragraph 1

3. The owner of the vessel shall incur no liability for a breach of the duty of the master under paragraph 1.

11. CO-OPERATION

A State Party shall, whenever regulating or deciding upon matters relating to salvage operations such as admittance to ports of vessels in distress or the provision of facilities to salvors, take into account the need for co-operation between salvors, other interested parties and public authorities in order to ensure the efficient and successful performance of salvage operations for the purpose of saving life or property in danger as well as preventing damage to the environment in general.

CHAPTER III - RIGHTS OF SALVORS

12. CONDITIONS FOR REWARD

1. Salvage operations which have had a useful result give right to a reward.

2. Except as otherwise provided, no payment is due under this Convention if the salvage operations have had no useful result.

3. This chapter shall apply, notwithstanding that the salved vessel and the vessel undertaking the salvage operations belong to the same owner.

13. CRITERIA FOR FIXING THE REWARD

1. The reward shall be fixed with a view to encouraging salvage operations, taking into account the following criteria without regard to the order in which they are presented below:

      (a) the salved value of the vessel and other property;

(b) the skill and efforts of the salvors in preventing or minimizing damage to the environment;

(c) the measure of success obtained by the salvor;

(d) the nature and degree of the danger;

(e) the skill and efforts of the salvors in salving the vessel, other property and life;

(f) the time used and expenses and losses incurred by the salvors;

(g) the risk of liability and other risks run by the salvors or their equipment;

(h) the promptness of the services rendered;

(i) the availability and use of vessels or other equipment intended for salvage operations;

(j) the state of readiness and efficiency of the salvor's equipment and the value thereof.

2. Payment of a reward fixed according to paragraph 1 shall be made by all of the vessel and other property interests in proportion to their respective salved values. However, a State Party may in its national law provide that the payment of a reward has to be made by one of these interests, subject to a right of recourse of this interest against the other interests for their respective shares. Nothing in this article shall prevent any right of defence.

3. The rewards, exclusive of any interest and recoverable legal costs that may be payable thereon, shall not exceed the salved value of the vessel and other property.

14. SPECIAL COMPENSATION

1. If the salvor has carried out salvage operations in respect of a vessel which by itself or its cargo threatened damage to the environment and had failed to earn a reward under article 13 at least equivalent to the special compensation assessable in accordance with this article, he shall be entitled to special compensation from the owner of that vessel equivalent to his expenses as herein defined.

2. If, in the circumstances set out in paragraph 1, the salvor by his salvage operations has prevented or minimized damage to the environment, the special compensation payable by the owner to the salvor under paragraph 1 may be increased up to a maximum of 30% of the expenses incurred by the salvor. However, the tribunal, if it deems it fair and just to do so and bearing in mind the relevant criteria set out in article 13, paragraph 1, may increase such special compensation further, but in no event shall the total increase be more than 100% of the expenses incurred by the salvor.

3. Salvor's expenses for the purpose of paragraphs 1 and 2 means the out-of-pocket expenses reasonably incurred by the salvor in the salvage operation and a fair rate for equipment and personnel actually and reasonably used in the salvage operation, taking into consideration the criteria set out in article 13, paragraph 1(h), (i) and (j).

4. The total special compensation under this article shall be paid only if and to the extent that such compensation is greater than any reward recoverable by the salvor under article 13.

5. If the salvor has been negligent and has thereby failed to prevent or minimize damage to the environment, he may be deprived of the whole or part of any special compensation due under this article.

6. Nothing in this article shall affect any right of recourse on the part of the owner of the vessel.

15. APPORTIONMENT BETWEEN SALVORS

1. The apportionment of a reward under article 13 between salvors shall be made on the basis of the criteria contained in that article.

2. The apportionment between the owner, master and other persons in the service of each salving vessel shall be determined by the law of the flag of that vessel. If the salvage has not been carried out from a vessel, the apportionment shall be determined by the law governing the contract between the salvor and his servants.

16. SALVAGE OF PERSONS

1. No remuneration is due from persons whose lives are saved, but nothing in this article shall affect the provisions of national law on this subject.

2. A salvor of human life, who has taken part in the services rendered on the occasion of the accident giving rise to salvage, is entitled to a fair share of the payment awarded to the salvor for salving the vessel or other property or preventing or minimizing damage to the environment.

17. SERVICES RENDERED UNDER EXISTING CONTRACTS

No payment is due under the provisions of this Convention unless the services rendered exceed what can be reasonably considered as due performance of a contract entered into before the danger arose.

18. THE EFFECT OF SALVOR'S MISCONDUCT

A salvor may be deprived of the whole or part of the payment due under the Convention to the extent that the salvage operations have become necessary or more difficult because of fault or neglect on his part or if the salvor has been guilty of fraud or other dishonest conduct.

19. PROHIBITION OF SALVAGE OPERATIONS

Services rendered notwithstanding the express and reasonable prohibition of the owner or master of the vessel or the owner of any other property in danger which is not and has not been on board the vessel shall not give rise to payment under this Convention.

CHAPTER IV - CLAIMS AND ACTIONS

20. MARITIME LIEN

1. Nothing in this Convention shall affect the salvor's maritime lien under any international convention or national law.

2. The salvor may not enforce his maritime lien when satisfactory security for his claim, including interest and costs, has been duly tendered or provided.

21. DUTY TO PROVIDE SECURITY

1. Upon the request of the salvor a person liable for a payment due under this Convention shall provide satisfactory security for the claim, including interest and costs of the salvor.

2. Without prejudice to paragraph 1, the owner of the salved vessel shall use his best endeavors to ensure that the owners of the cargo provide satisfactory security for the claims against them including interest and costs before the cargo is released.

3. The salved vessel and other property shall not, without the consent of the salvor, be removed from the port or place at which they first arrive after the completion of the salvage operations until satisfactory security has been put up for the salvor's claim against the relevant vessel or property.

22. INTERIM PAYMENT

1. The tribunal having jurisdiction over the claim of the salvor may, by interim decision, order that the salvor shall be paid on account such amount as seems fair and just, and on such terms including terms as to the security where appropriate, as may be fair and just according to the circumstances of the case.

2. In the event of an interim payment under this article the security provided under article 21 shall be reduced accordingly.

23. LIMITATION OF ACTIONS

1. Any action relating to payment under this Convention shall be time-barred if judicial or arbitral proceedings have not been instituted within a period of two years. The limitation period commences on the day on which the salvage operations are terminated.

2. The person against whom a claim is made may at any time during the running of the limitation period extend that period by a declaration to the claimant. This period may in the like manner be further extended.

3. An action for indemnity by a person liable may be instituted even after the expiration of the limitation period provided for in the preceding paragraphs, if brought within the time allowed by the law of the State where proceedings are instituted.

24. INTEREST

The right of the salvor to interest on any payment due under this Convention shall be determined according to the law of the State in which the tribunal seized of the case is situated.

25. STATE-OWNED CARGOES

Unless the State owner consents, no provision of this Convention shall be used as a basis for the seizure, arrest or detention by any legal process of, nor for any proceedings *in rem* against, non-commercial cargoes owned by a State and entitled, at the time of the salvage operations, to sovereign immunity under generally recognized principles of international law.

26. HUMANITARIAN CARGOES

No provision of this Convention shall be used as a basis for the seizure, arrest or detention of humanitarian cargoes donated by a State, if such State has agreed to pay for salvage services rendered in respect of such humanitarian cargoes.

27. PUBLICATION OF ARBITRAL AWARDS

States Parties shall encourage, as far as possible and with the consent of the parties, the publication of arbitral awards made in salvage cases.

CHAPTER V - FINAL CLAUSES

28. SIGNATURE, RATIFICATION, ACCEPTANCE, APPROVAL AND ACCESSION

1. This Convention shall be open for signature at the Headquarters of the Organization from 1 July 1989 to 30 June 1990 and shall thereafter remain open for accession.

2. States may express their consent to be bound by this Convention by:
> (a) signature without reservation as to ratification, acceptance or approval; or
> (b) signature subject to ratification, acceptance or approval, followed by ratification, acceptance or approval; or
> (c) accession.

3. Ratification, acceptance, approval or accession shall be effected by the deposit of an instrument to that effect with the Secretary-General.

29. ENTRY INTO FORCE

1. This Convention shall enter into force one year after the date on which 15 States have expressed their consent to be bound by it.

2. For a State which expresses its consent to be bound by this Convention after the conditions for entry into force thereof have been met, such consent shall take effect one year after the date of expression of such consent.

30. RESERVATIONS

1. Any State may, at the time of signature, ratification, acceptance, approval or accession, reserve the right not to apply the provisions of this Convention:

(a) when the salvage operation takes place in inland waters and all vessels involved are of inland navigation;

(b) when the salvage operations take place in inland waters and no vessel is involved;

(c) when all interested parties are nationals of that State;

(d) when the property involved is maritime cultural property of prehistoric, archaeological or historic interest and is situated on the sea-bed.

2. Reservations made at the time of signature are subject to confirmation upon ratification, acceptance or approval.

3. Any State which had made a reservation to this Convention may withdraw it at any time by means of a notification addressed to the Secretary-General. Such withdrawal shall take effect on the date the notification is received. If the notification states that the withdrawal of a reservation is to take effect on a date specified therein, and such date is later than the date the notification is received by the Secretary-General, the withdrawal shall take effect on such later date.

31. DENUNCIATION

1. This Convention may be denounced by any State Party at any time after the expiry of one year from the date on which this Convention enters into force for that State.

2. Denunciation shall be effected by the deposit of an instrument of denunciation with the Secretary-General.

3. A denunciation shall take effect one year, or such longer period as may be specified in the instrument of denunciation, after the receipt of the instrument of denunciation by the Secretary-General.

32. REVISION AND AMENDMENT

1. A conference for the purpose of revising or amending this Convention may be convened by the Organization.

2. The Secretary-General shall convene a conference of the States Parties to this Convention for revising or amending the Convention, at the request of eight States Parties, or one fourth of the States Parties, whichever is the higher figure.

3. Any consent to be bound by this Convention expressed after the date of entry into force of an amendment to this Convention shall be deemed to apply to the Convention as amended.

33. DEPOSITARY

1. This Convention shall be deposited with the Secretary-General.
2. The Secretary-General shall:

(a) inform all States which have signed this Convention or acceded thereto, and all Members of the Organization, of:

(i) each new signature or deposit of an instrument of ratification, acceptance, approval or accession together with the date thereof;

(ii) the date of the entry into force of this Convention;

(iii) the deposit of any instrument of denunciation of this Convention together with the date on which it is received and the date on which the denunciation takes effect;

(iv) any amendment adopted in conformity with article 32;

(v) the receipt of any reservation, declaration or notification made under this Convention;

(b) transmit certified true copies of this Convention to all States which have signed this Convention or acceded thereto.

3. As soon as this Convention enters into force, a certified true copy thereof shall be transmitted by the Depositary to the Secretary-General of the United Nations for registration and publication in accordance with Article 102 of the Charter of the United Nations.

34. LANGUAGES

This Convention is established in a single original in the Arabic, Chinese, English, French, Russian and Spanish languages, each text being equally authentic.

IN WITNESS WHEREOF the undersigned being duly authorized by their respective Governments for that purpose have signed this Convention.

DONE AT LONDON this twenty-eighth day of April one thousand nine hundred and eighty-nine.

ATTACHMENT 1

COMMON UNDERSTANDING CONCERNING ARTICLES 13 AND 14 OF THE INTERNATIONAL CONVENTION ON SALVAGE, 1989

It is the common understanding of the Conference that, in fixing a reward under article 13 and assessing special compensation under article 14 of the International Convention on Salvage, 1989 the tribunal is under no duty to fix a reward under article 13 up to the maximum salved value of the vessel and other property before assessing the special compensation to be paid under article 14.

ATTACHMENT 2

RESOLUTION REQUESTING THE AMENDMENT OF THE YORK-ANTWERP RULES, 1974

THE INTERNATIONAL CONFERENCE ON SALVAGE, 1989,

HAVING ADOPTED the International Convention on Salvage, 1989,

CONSIDERING that payments made pursuant to article 14 are not intended to be allowed in general average,

REQUESTS the Secretary-General of the International Maritime Organization to take the appropriate steps in order to ensure speedy amendment of the York-Antwerp Rules, 1974, to ensure that special compensation paid under article 14 is not subject to general average.

Index